An Introduction to Financial Accounting

Third Edition

Andrew Thomas

JAMES   WRIGHT

The McGraw-Hill Companies

London · Burr Ridge, IL · New York · St Louis · San Francisco · Auckland
Bogotá · Caracas · Lisbon · Madrid · Mexico · Milan · Montreal
New Delhi · Panama · Paris · San Juan · São Paulo · Singapore
Sydney · Tokyo · Toronto

Published by
McGRAW-HILL BOOK COMPANY EUROPE
Shoppenhangers Road, Maidenhead, Berkshire, SL6 2QL, England
Telephone 01628 23432
Facsimile 01628 770224

British Library Cataloguing in Publication Data
A catalogue record for this book is available from the British Library

ISBN 0-07-709480 8

Further information on this title is to be found at
http:///www.mcgraw-hill.co.uk/thomas

Publisher: Alfred Waller
Desk Editor: Alastair Lindsay

Created for McGraw-Hill by the independent production company
Steven Gardiner Ltd TEL +44 (0)1223 364868 FAX +44 (0)1223 364875

McGraw-Hill

A Division of The McGraw-Hill Companies

1 2 3 4 5   CUP 3 2 1 0 9

Printed and bound in the United Kingdom at the University Press, Cambridge

Contents

Preface

This book is primarily intended to be an introductory text for students taking a degree in accounting or business studies with a substantial element of accounting. However, it also covers the financial accounting syllabus for the Foundation stage of the Association of Chartered Certified Accountants, the Chartered Institute of Public Finance and Accountancy, Stage One of the Chartered Institute of Management Accountants, and the Preliminary and Intermediate examinations of the Association of Accounting Technicians. Furthermore, the book provides a more than adequate coverage of the financial accounting content of the accounting syllabuses for the General Certificate of Education at Advanced level of the Associated Examining Board and the Joint Matriculation Board.

The author is a senior lecturer in accounting at the University of Birmingham, a Certified Accountant, and has been a member of the panel of examiners of one of the major professional accountancy bodies for over fifteen years. He is also an assessor on the teaching quality assessment panel of the Higher Education Funding Council for England and Wales.

The main aim of this book is to provide an in-depth detailed introduction to financial accounting with the greatest possible clarity of exposition and academic rigour. Another major aim is the provision of an appropriate balance between theory and the application of accounting methods. Each element in this balance is important. A proper understanding of accounting requires underpinning by an appreciation of its theoretical foundations. Although this may be readily recognized in the case of degree students, it is no less true of other students. Theory is often presented in textbooks in isolation, but this book integrates theory into understanding of accounting methods. The other side of this balance, represented by the application of accounting, depends upon a thorough grasp of the mechanics of financial accounting. The book therefore examines in depth many of what are normally regarded as the basic aspects of accounting, particularly where this involves applications of important points of principle.

The structure of the book follows a proven pattern based on the author's not inconsiderable experience of teaching at this level. Each chapter deals with a specific aspect of accounting, irrespective of how brief or lengthy this might be. This is intended to permit lecturers to choose that combination of chapters which fits their syllabus. However, it is important to appreciate that the order in which the chapters are presented is significant. There are also particular groupings of chapters, for example: Chapters 6 to 8 deal with books of prime entry; Chapters 16 to 18 examine aspects of internal control and accuracy; and Chapters 19 and 20 involve a consideration of incomplete records.

The structure within each chapter also follows a deliberate pattern. These usually start by examining the purpose, theoretical foundation and practical relevance of the topic. This is followed by a description of the accounting methods and then comprehensive examples. A further unique feature of the book is that after most examples there is a series of notes. These are intended to explain the unfamiliar and more difficult aspects of the example in order that the reader is able to follow the example. The notes also provide guidance on further aspects of the topic that may be encountered in examination questions, such as alternative forms of wording.

Each chapter also contains a set of written and numerical exercises designed by the author to test whether the student has fulfilled the learning objectives set out in the chapter, as well as past questions from various examining bodies. ACCA students should note that not all of the latter fall within the current syllabus. The exercises are presented in a coherent progressive sequence. These start with a number of written questions designed to test understanding of terminology, legal requirements, theoretical foundations, etc. They are followed by mainly numerical questions that are presented in order of difficulty. The later examples are therefore often quite demanding. However, students should be able to answer these from reading the chapter. Moreover, the questions are not repetitive but have been selected because each tests some aspect of the topic not covered in a previous question. The student may be assured that the somewhat longer later questions have a deliberate purpose representing the most advanced aspects of the topic which they are likely to encounter. All users, especially lecturers, should also be aware that some questions are extensions of other questions in previous chapters. This is intended to provide a more comprehensive understanding of the relationship between different topics in accounting, such as day books and cash books, provisions for depreciation and bad debts, etc.

Each chapter also includes learning objectives, learning activities, a summary, and a list of key terms and concepts. The learning objectives at the start of each chapter set out the abilities and skills that the student should be able to demonstrate after reading the chapter. Students should also refer back to these after reading each chapter. Similarly students should satisfy themselves that they can explain the meaning of the key terms and concepts listed at the end of each chapter. The summaries provide a comprehensive but concise review of the contents of each chapter that students should find useful for revision purposes. The learning activities differ from those found in most other textbooks which often take the form of mini-questions with model answers similar to the exercises for each chapter. In contrast, the learning activities in this book are mostly real-life activities of a project/case study type which require students to apply their knowledge to practical situations. They frequently necessitate students collecting publicly available data from actual companies, or their own financial affairs.

The third edition of the book incorporates various recent developments in the regulatory framework of accounting such as the ASB *Statement of Principles for Financial Reporting* (1995), FRS1 (revised), FRS3, FRS10, and FRS12. It has also been extended to cover those topics that have become more common in the professional accountancy bodies examinations, namely the dissolution of partnerships, published financial statements, and payroll accounting. Furthermore, the exercises have been updated to include more relevant (and coherent) past examination questions of the professional accountancy bodies. Moreover the answers to most of the numerical questions written by the author, that were previously in the *Students' Solution Manual*, have now been incorporated in an appendix to the textbook, for ease of reference. Answers to the rest of the numerical exercises in the book are contained in a new *Teacher's Solutions Manual*.

Chapter 32 on the use of computers in accounting has been completely rewritten and updated. The aim has been to explain the possibilities that are opened up by the new technology, and to identify some of the changes in working practice which are required. The author is indebted to Dr Andrew J. Hawker for writing this chapter. Dr Hawker, a lecturer in computing in the Department of Accounting at the University of Birmingham, has spent most of his working life in large industrial computer companies dealing with applications of computers to accounting.

The author gratefully acknowledges the permission of the following bodies to reproduce copies of their past examination questions: The Association of Chartered Certified Accountants (ACCA): The Association of Accounting Technicians (AAT): The Associated Examining Board (AEB); and The Joint Matriculation Board (JMB).

Finally, my thanks to Mrs Karen Hanson for her patience and accuracy in the typing of the original manuscript.

1. The nature and objectives of financial accounting

Learning objectives

After reading this chapter the student should be able to:
1. Explain the meaning of the key terms and concepts listed at the end of the chapter.
2. Describe the nature and functions of double entry bookkeeping and financial accounting.
3. Discuss the objectives of company annual accounts.
4. Identify the users of annual reports and describe their information needs.
5. Describe the legislation and other rules governing the contents of company annual reports.
6. Describe the current institutional framework relating to the setting and enforcement of accounting standards.

The nature and functions of financial accounting

Financial accounting may be defined as the process of designing and operating an information system for collecting, measuring and recording an enterprises transactions, and summarizing and communicating the results of these transactions to users to facilitate making financial/economic decisions.

The first part of this definition, relating to collecting and recording transactions, refers to *double entry bookkeeping*, which consists of maintaining a record of the money value of the transactions of an enterprise. In many businesses this may be done using a computer. The second part of the definition, relating to communicating the results, refers to preparing final accounts and statements from the books of account (or any other system of recording) showing the profit earned during a given period and the financial state of affairs of a business at the end of that period.

These two functions of financial accounting may be broken down further as described below.

The recording and control of business transactions

This includes records of:

1. The amount of cash and cheques received, for what and from whom.
2. The amount of cash and cheques paid, for what and to whom. Records of money received and paid are kept so that the business knows how much money it has at any time.

3. Assets, expenses and goods purchased on credit. This is so that the business knows to whom it owes money and how much. These are referred to as *creditors*.
4. Assets and goods sold on credit. This is so that the business knows who owes it money and how much. These are referred to as *debtors*.

The accountant has been traditionally regarded as the 'holder of the purse strings' and responsible for 'safeguarding' the assets of the business. The control aspect of this function includes ensuring that the correct amounts are paid to those entitled to them at the appropriate time, collecting the business's debts, safeguarding against fraud and misappropriation of goods or cash, etc. The latter function is often referred to as *internal control*.

To maintain accuracy in recording

Double entry bookkeeping is generally regarded as the most accurate method of bookkeeping, primarily because each transaction is entered in the books twice. This duplication, referred to as a form of *'internal check'*, highlights any errors.

To meet the requirements of the law

The law, in the form of the Companies Acts, states that companies must keep proper records of their transactions. There is no legislation that specifically requires sole traders or partnerships to keep records of their transactions. However, when the Inland Revenue makes a demand for income tax on self-employed persons, it usually asks for more than business proprietors would pay if they presented accounts showing their profit for the year. There is thus a financial incentive for sole traders and partnerships to maintain proper records. Furthermore, the Inland Revenue expects accounts to be kept. In addition any trader who does not keep proper records and goes bankrupt will find it more difficult to obtain discharge from bankruptcy.

To present final accounts to the owners of the business

These comprise a profit and loss account showing the amount of profit for the period and a balance sheet showing the financial position at the end of that period. The latter will include the following items:

1. The amount of cash and money at the bank.
2. Other assets that the business owns, such as goods for resale, vehicles, machinery, etc.
3. The debtors and creditors.
4. The amount of capital that has been invested in the business by its owner(s).
5. Any money that has been borrowed by the business.

In the case of a sole trader, these final accounts show the owner his or her 'earnings' for the period and may be used to evaluate the profitability of the business. However, they are often primarily used to determine the owner's tax liability. Final accounts perform similar functions in the case of companies. However, company final accounts are also designed to give information to third parties to enable them to evaluate the profitability and financial stability of the company. These include prospective shareholders, trade unions and employees, creditors and those who have lent the company money, government departments, and social pressure groups. This is discussed further later.

This function of financial accounting is often referred to as *stewardship* which may be defined as the accountability of an enterprise's management for the resources entrusted to them. *Accountability* refers to the management's responsibility to provide an account/report on the way in which the resources entrusted to them have been used.

To present other financial reports and analyses

This includes the use of ratios to evaluate the following matters:

1. The profitability of the business.
2. The level of activity and productivity.
3. The solvency and liquidity position (i.e. whether the business will be able to pay its debts).
4. The efficiency of credit control procedures.
5. The efficiency of stock control procedures.
6. The effect of any loans on the business's profitability and financial stability.

To facilitate the efficient allocation of resources

Viewing the function of financial accounting at a more general abstract level, its ultimate raison d'etre is usually described as being to facilitate the efficient and effective allocation of resources. This is generally given a macro-economic interpretation as providing information to investors so that capital is directed towards more efficient firms. A less common but similar interpretation would be to extend this to providing information to prospective employees so that labour is directed towards more efficient firms. The same interpretation could also be extended to other potential users of final accounts and providers of resources in a broad sense that embraces quality of life and environmental considerations, etc. This would include others such as bank lenders, creditors/suppliers, the government, and the public generally.

This function of financial accounting can also be viewed at a micro-economic or individual firm level. One of the main purposes of financial accounting may be said to be to enable an organization's management to operate the enterprise efficiently and effectively. This embraces at least three of the functions referred to above namely, the recording and control of business transactions, accuracy in recording, and the preparation of final accounts (for management use). However, this function of accounting is more commonly attributed to management accounting, particularly in larger organizations.

Management accounting can be defined as the provision of information to an organizations management for the purposes of planning, control and decision-making. The latter includes production, marketing and financing decisions.

Learning activity 1.1

Imagine that you are in business as a small general store or plumber. Prepare a list of the financial information about the business that you would expect to be able to obtain from your records. Compare this with the above and consider any differences.

The objectives of company accounts

As explained above, one of the main functions of financial accounting is the preparation of *final accounts*, also commonly referred to as *financial statements*. These consist of a profit and loss account and a balance sheet. In the case of companies, the final accounts are often referred to as *published accounts*. These are sent to shareholders in the form of a pamphlet known as the *annual* or *corporate report*. It is therefore usual to discuss the objectives of company final accounts in terms of the functions of annual reports.

The function of annual reports is related to beliefs about the role of business organizations in society and their objectives. Up until about the mid-1970s the accountancy profession took the view that the primary objective of a business enterprise was to maximize its profit and the wealth of its shareholders. This was reinforced by disciplines such as economics that gave prominence to the classical theory of the firm. The function of annual reports was thus regarded as being to provide information about the profitability and financial position of a company to those with whom it has a capital contractual relationship, namely shareholders and loan creditors.

However, during the 1960s and early 1970s there was a swing in society's beliefs towards the idea that business enterprises exist for the benefit of the community as a whole. Similarly, developments in disciplines such as economics and modern organization theory cast doubt on whether profit maximization was a meaningful description of business objectives. For example, Herbert Simon argues that business enterprises are 'satisficers', that is, they seek to earn a satisfactory level of profit. Also, a survey of large UK companies undertaken by the accountancy profession found that 'the majority view of those replying to the survey seems to be that their primary objective is to make a profit for the benefit of a number of groups. It is not the majority view that the maximization of shareholder's profit is the primary objective.' Other respondents to this survey described their primary objective as being survival, or in terms of the service they provide.

It follows from this that enterprises are accountable to a number of different groups (e.g. employees, the public, etc.), and that the function of annual reports is to provide each of them with information. This is the view taken by *The Corporate Report*[1] which is the UK accountancy bodies' most detailed statement on the function/objective of annual reports, their users and the information that they need. It is not mandatory, but represents one of the most comprehensive pieces of published work in this area, and has probably led to a number of new developments in accounting practices and more recent UK statements on these matters.

During the 1980s there may have been a swing in society's beliefs back to an emphasis on the profit objective and shareholders as a result of the political philosophy known as 'enterprise culture'. There has been relatively little legislation that gives other groups access to annual reports or provides for the disclosure of more information of a social or environmental nature. However, EU Directives on company law and other matters (e.g. employee participation) are likely to require greater disclosure. Furthermore, the privatization of government-owned enterprises and greater environmental awareness has probably resulted in more exposure of members of the public, such as small investors, to annual reports. This may lead to further developments in corporate reporting in the near future.

The 'basic philosophy' of *The Corporate Report* is reflected in the need for what is called '*public accountability*':

> there is an implicit responsibility to report publicly . . . incumbent on every entity whose size or format renders it significant; . . . we consider the responsibility to report publicly (referred to . . . as public accountability) is separate from and broader than the legal obligation to report and arises from the custodial role played in the community by economic entities; . . . they are involved in the maintenance of standards of life and the creation of wealth for and on behalf of the community.

The 'custodial role' of business enterprises refers to their responsibility to use the assets with which they have been entrusted to create wealth, maintain the standard of living, and other considerations such as the quality of the environment. It follows from this notion of public accountability that the objective or function of annual reports is thus:

> to communicate economic measurements of and information about the resources and performance of the reporting entity useful to those having reasonable rights to such information.

'Reasonable rights' is defined as follows:

> A reasonable right to information exists where the activities of an organisation impinge or may impinge on the interest of a user group.

A similar study of the function of annual reports was undertaken in 1973 by the American Institute of Certified Public Accountants (AICPA); this is known as *The Objectives of Financial Statements*.[2] This document emphasizes the use to which the information is put:

> The basic objective of financial statements is to provide information useful for making economic decisions.

It also regards annual reports as principally intended for those groups who only have access to limited information about the enterprise:

> An objective of financial statements is to serve primarily those users who have limited authority, ability, or resources to obtain information and who rely on financial statements as their principal source of information about an enterprise's economic activities.

The most recent pronouncement by the UK accountancy profession on the objective of financial statements is in the *Statement of Principles for Financial Reporting* prepared by the Accounting Standards Board (ASB) in 1995.[3] It is similar to the material in *The Corporate Report*[1] but contains some significant developments. The main parts of this document are reproduced below:

> The objective of financial statements is to provide information about the financial position, performance and financial adaptability of an enterprise that is useful to a wide range of users for assessing the stewardship of management and for making economic decisions.
>
> Stewardship in this context is the accountability of management for the resources entrusted to it. Those users who wish to assess the stewardship of management do so in order to make economic decisions; for example, whether to hold or sell their investment in the enterprise or whether to re-appoint or replace the management.
>
> Financial statements prepared for this purpose meet the common needs of most users. However, financial statements do not provide all the information that users may need to make economic decisions, since they largely portray the financial effects of past events and do not necessarily provide non-financial information.

The users of annual reports and their information needs

The users of annual reports identified in *The Corporate Report* are as follows:[1]

1. *The equity investor group* including existing and potential shareholders.
2. *The loan creditor group* including existing and potential holders of debentures and loan stock, and providers of short-term secured and unsecured loans and finance.
3. *The employee group* including existing, potential and past employees.
4. *The analyst–adviser group* including financial analysts and journalists, economists, statisticians, researchers, trade unions, stockbrokers and other providers of advisory services such as credit rating agencies.
5. *The business contact group* including customers, trade creditors and suppliers and in a

different sense competitors, business rivals and those interested in mergers, amalgamations and takeovers.

6. *The government* including tax authorities, departments and agencies concerned with the supervision of commerce and industry, and local authorities.

7. *The public* including taxpayers, ratepayers, consumers and other community and special interest groups such as political parties, consumer and environmental protection societies and regional pressure groups.

Each of the above groups is said by *The Corporate Report* to have certain 'information needs'. These are described below in respect of each group of users.

The equity investor group

A basic premiss in *The Corporate Report* is that 'investors require information to assist in reaching share trading decisions . . . and in reaching voting decisions at general meetings. . . . In particular investors will wish to make judgments concerning likely movements in share prices [and] likely levels of future dividend payments.' Similarly, the US *Objectives of Financial Statements* says that 'An objective of financial statements is to provide information useful to investors . . . for predicting potential cash flows to them'. Thus, according to *The Corporate Report* (p. 20) investors require information for the following purposes:

1. To evaluate the performance of the entity and its management, and assess the effectiveness of the entity in achieving its objectives.
2. To assess the economic stability and vulnerability of the reporting entity including its liquidity (i.e. whether it will have enough money to pay its debts), its present or future requirements for additional capital, and its ability to raise long- and short-term finance.
3. To estimate the value of users' own or other users' present or prospective interests in or claims on the entity.
4. To ascertain the ownership and control of the entity.
5. To estimate the future prospects of the entity, including its capacity to pay dividends and to predict future levels of investment.

Accountants have traditionally regarded published accounts as fulfilling two main functions: (1) stewardship, and (2) facilitating share trading and lending decisions. The concept of stewardship roughly corresponds with everyday usage of the word and refers to the directors' responsibility to account for the uses to which they have put the shareholders' investment. This is the one function of published accounts on which most accountants agree. *The Corporate Report* does not discuss this as such but rather emphasizes the share trading and decision making function of annual reports. However, it is debatable whether past data is likely to be useful in predicting future profits, dividends or share prices. The literature on efficient market theory suggests that the content of annual reports has little, if any, predictive value. Published accounts may therefore only perform a stewardship and feedback function.

The loan creditor group

According to *The Corporate Report* 'the information needs of loan creditors are similar in many respects to the needs of equity investors. If their securities are listed on a stock exchange they will have to make trading decisions.' However, certain information will be of particular relevance such as that relating to:

1. The present and likely future cash position since this will determine whether the company will be able to pay the annual interest on loans and repay the moneys borrowed as and when they become due.
2. The economic stability and vulnerability of the company in so far as this reflects the risk of possible default in repayment of moneys borrowed by the company.
3. Prior claims on the company's assets in the event of it going into liquidation.

The employee group

The Corporate Report states that the rights of the employee group to information arises because 'the reporting entity has a responsibility for the future livelihood and prospects of its employees' (p. 21). Employees will require information to enable them to assess the security of employment and the prospects of promotion. They may also require information for the purpose of wage bargaining. Such information may relate to 'the ability of the employer to meet wage demands, management's intentions regarding employment levels, locations and working conditions, the pay, conditions and terms of employment of various groups of employees and the contributions made by employees in different divisions. In addition, employees are likely to be interested in indications of the position, progress and prospects of the employing enterprise as a whole and about individual establishments and bargaining units.' Some companies produce employee reports that usually contain a summary of the year's trading results in a simplified form.

The analyst–adviser group

According to *The Corporate Report* 'the information needs of the analyst–adviser group are likely to be similar to the needs of the users who are being advised. For example, the information needs of stockbrokers are likely to be similar to the needs of investors and those of trade unions are likely to be similar to the needs of employees.' *The Corporate Report* also makes the point that this group, because of their expertise, will tend to demand more elaborate information than other groups.

The business contact group

This consists of the following groups:

1. *Customers*. These may be concerned about the reporting entity's continued existence because of its importance as a source of supply, particularly where long-term contracts for the supply of goods have been entered into. Similarly, if the reporting entity is engaged in construction work, customers will wish to assess the likelihood of its being able to complete long-term contracts. In the case of manufactured goods, such as computers, vehicles, etc., customers will be concerned about the reporting entity's continued existence because of its warranty obligations and the need for spare parts. Annual reports may thus be useful to customers in assessing the likelihood of the reporting entity's continued existence.
2. *Suppliers*. Trade creditors will obviously want information relating to the reporting entity's ability to pay its debts. In addition, they would be concerned about the reporting entity's continued existence if it is a major customer. A supplier may also have to decide whether to increase its production capacity in order to meet the reporting entity's future demands.
3. *Competitors and takeover bidders*. The rationale for competitors having a right to

information is a little vague but seems to rest on the premiss that inter-firm comparisons of performance and costs can facilitate improvements in efficiency. Similarly, given that mergers and takeovers of less efficient firms are in the public interest, a case can be made for the disclosure of information to potential bidders.

The government

The Corporate Report states that 'central and local government departments and agencies have a right to information as representatives of the public and other user groups'. The Inland Revenue and HM Customs & Excise have a statutory right to information about the reporting entity for the purpose of assessing its liability to taxation. Furthermore, the 'government needs information to estimate the effects of existing and proposed levies and other financial and economic measures, to estimate economic trends including balance and payment figures [and] to promote economic efficiency'.[1] In the UK most of this information is collected through special Government returns. However, in many other countries corporate reports perform this function.

The public

According to *The Corporate Report* the public has a right to information because of the custodial role that economic entities play in society and the impact they can have on the community and the environment.

Such organisations, which exist with the general consent of the community, are afforded special legal and operational privileges, they compete for resources of manpower, materials and energy and they make use of community owned assets such as roads and harbours.

Some members of the public may be concerned about the employment policies of the reporting entity and therefore want information relating to local employment levels or discrimination in employment for example. Other members of the public may be interested in any plans that the reporting entity has that affect the environment, including issues relating to conservation and pollution. There are also a number of other matters of a political or moral nature that may be of particular concern to some sections of the community such as contributions to political organizations, pressure groups or charities, and whether the reporting entity is trading with countries having repressive political regimes. Some of this information must be disclosed under the Companies Acts (i.e. donations to political parties and charities) but *The Corporate Report* implies that the reporting entity also has a responsibility to make public any matters that might be regarded by the community as of general concern.

Users and their information needs

The most recent pronouncement by the UK accountancy profession on the users of financial statements and their information needs is in the *Statement of Principles for Financial Reporting* prepared by the Accounting Standards Board (ASB) in 1995.[3] It is similar to the material in *The Corporate Report* but contains some slight differences, and provides a useful summary of the users and their information needs. The main parts of this document are reproduced below.

Investors, as the providers of risk capital to the enterprise (and their advisors), are interested in information that helps them to assess the performance of management. They are also concerned with the risk inherent in, and return provided by, their investments, and need information that helps them to assess the ability of the enterprise to pay dividends, and to determine whether they should buy, hold or sell their investments.

Users of financial statements other than investors include employees, lenders, suppliers and other trade creditors, customers, governments and their agencies and the public. They use financial statements to satisfy some of their different needs for information. These needs include the following:

Employees. Employees and their representative groups are interested in information about the stability and profitability of their employers. They are also interested in information that enables them to assess the ability of the enterprise to provide remuneration, employment opportunities and retirement benefits.

Lenders. Lenders are interested in information that enables them to determine whether their loans will be repaid, and the interest attaching to them, paid when due.

Suppliers and other creditors. Suppliers and other creditors are interested in information that enables them to decide whether to sell to the enterprise and to assess the likelihood that amounts owing to them will be paid when due. Trade creditors are likely to be interested in an enterprise over a shorter period than lenders unless they are dependent upon the continuation of the enterprise as a major customer.

Customers. Customers have an interest in information about the continuance of an enterprise, especially when they have a long-term involvement with, or are dependent on, the enterprise.

Governments and their agencies. Governments and their agencies are interested in the allocation of resources and, therefore, the activities of enterprises. They also require information in order to regulate the activities of enterprises, assess taxation and provide a basis for national statistics.

The public. Enterprises affect members of the public in a variety of ways. For example, enterprises may make a substantial contribution to a local economy by providing employment and using local suppliers. Financial statements may assist the public by providing information about the trends and recent developments in the prosperity of the enterprise and the range of its activities.

Learning activity 1.2

Write to the head office of a large public limited company asking for a copy of their latest annual report and accounts. Read through it and make a note of whatever information you find that is likely to be useful to a potential investor. Then draw up a list of any other information that you think would be useful to a potential investor.

The regulatory framework of accounting

The *regulatory framework of accounting* is a general term used to describe the legislation and other rules that govern the content and format of company final accounts. There is no legislation or other regulations covering the final accounts of sole traders and partnerships. However, it is generally accepted that their accounts should closely follow the rules and regulations relating to companies since these are regarded as 'best practice'. There are three sources of rules and regulations governing the content and format of company final accounts, as follows:

1. The Companies Act with which all companies are required to comply.
2. The International Stock Exchange, London Admission of Securities to Listing regulations (commonly known as the Yellow Book) with which all companies whose shares are listed on the London Stock Exchange are expected to comply.
3. The accounting standards produced by the Accounting Standards Committee and financial reporting standards of the Accounting Standards Board with which most (but not all) companies are expected to comply. These are discussed further later.

The UK accountancy profession comprises six major professional accountancy bodies as follows:

1. The Institute of Chartered Accountants in England and Wales (ICAEW)
2. The Institute of Chartered Accountants in Scotland (ICAS)

3. The Institute of Chartered Accountants in Ireland (ICAI)
4. The Association of Chartered Certified Accountants (ACCA)
5. The Chartered Institute of Management Accountants (CIMA)
6. The Chartered Institute of Public Finance and Accountancy (CIPFA)

In 1970 the ICAEW set up the Accounting Standards Steering Committee (ASSC). Subsequently all the other above professional bodies became members of this committee. Its name was changed in 1975 to the Accounting Standards Committee (ASC). In 1990 the ASC was replaced by the Accounting Standards Board (ASB).

The ASC represented the six major professional accountancy bodies on matters relating to the form and content of company final accounts. It issued accounting standards known as *Statements of Standard Accounting Practice* (SSAP) with which most company final accounts are still expected to comply. Each of these SSAPs specifies how particular items or transactions are to be treated in the final accounts of companies.

The Accounting Standards Board (ASB) is continuing to perform the same function as the ASC, but is more independent of the professional accountancy bodies and has greater power to enforce accounting standards. Before the ASC could issue an SSAP, it required the approval of each of the six professional accountancy bodies. In contrast, the ASB can issue a *Financial Reporting Standard* (FRS) without approval from any other body.

A more detailed description of the UK institutional framework concerned with the setting of accounting standards is shown diagrammatically in Figure 1.1. It comprises the following bodies:

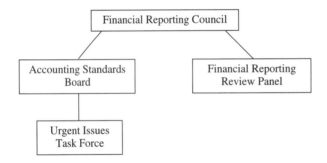

Figure 1.1 The institutional framework for setting accounting standards.

The Financial Reporting Council (FRC)

The FRC is a company limited by guarantee that is financed in approximately equal proportions by its members which comprise the Government, City institutions (such as the London Stock Exchange, the clearing banks, etc.) and the six major professional accountancy bodies. Its Chairperson is appointed jointly by the Secretary of State for Trade and Industry and the Governor of the Bank of England.

The FRC has overall responsibility for standard setting in the UK. Its main roles are to: (1) guide the ASB on work programmes, broad policy matters and issues of public concern: (2) ensure that the work of the standard setting bodies is properly financed and carried out efficiently and effectively; and (3) act as a proactive voice in public debate and to make representations to Government and the accounting profession to improve the quality of relevant legislation and accounting practice.

The Accounting Standards Board (ASB)

The ASB is also a limited company established as a subsidiary of the FRC with a full-time Chairperson and Technical Director. A subsidiary is a company that is owned and/or controlled by another company. In short, its main role is to develop, issue, revise and withdraw accounting standards. These are referred to as *Financial Reporting Standards* (FRS). The published accounts of most companies are expected to comply with Statements of Standard Accounting Practice (SSAP) and Financial Reporting Standards (FRS).

Before the ASB issues a FRS it publishes a *Discussion Draft* (DD) which later becomes a *Financial Reporting Exposure Draft* (FRED). These are essentially proposed standards which are open to public debate and representations to the ASB. After examining public representations on a FRED it is often amended by the ASB before being issued as a FRS.

The ASB has published a *Statement of Aims*[4] which sets out its aims and how it intends to achieve these aims. The more important parts of this are reproduced below:

Aims
The aims of the Accounting Standards Board (the Board) are to establish and improve standards of financial accounting and reporting, for the benefit of users, preparers, and auditors of financial information.
The Board intends to achieve its aims by:
1. Developing principles to guide it in establishing standards and to provide a framework within which others can exercise judgement in resolving accounting issues.
2. Issuing new accounting standards, or amending existing ones, in response to evolving business practices, new economic developments and deficiencies being identified in current practice.
3. Addressing urgent issues promptly.

This may be contrasted with the aims of Statements of Standard Accounting Practices (SSAPs) formulated by the Accounting Standards Committee (ASC) in their *Explanatory Foreword to SSAPs*[5] which states that 'their primary aim is to narrow the areas of difference and variety in the accounting treatment of the matters with which they deal'.

The Financial Reporting Review Panel (FRRP)

The FRRP is a subsidiary of the FRC. Its function is to investigate complaints about any company's published accounts where these contain an apparent material departure from an accounting standard and/or the Companies Act including in particular the requirement to show 'a true and fair view'. If the Review Panel decides that the departure results in failure to give a true and fair view, it will in the first instance request the company to revise its accounts. Where a company's directors decline the FRRP request, it is empowered by the Companies Act to apply to the court for a declaration that the accounts do not comply with the requirements of the Companies Act and an order requiring the directors of the company to prepare revised accounts.

The Urgent Issues Task Force (UITF)

The UITF is a committee of the ASB whose members are people of major standing with expertise in financial reporting. It produces what are referred to as consensus pronouncements under the title of *Abstracts*. The following description of the role of the UITF is taken from the *Foreword to UITF Abstracts*[6]:

The UITF's main role is to assist the ASB with important or significant accounting issues where there exists an accounting standard or a provision of companies legislation (including the requirement to give a true and fair view) and where unsatisfactory or conflicting interpretations have developed or seem likely to develop. In such circumstances it operates by seeking a consensus as to the accounting treatment that should be adopted. Such a consensus is reached against the background of the ASB's declared aim of relying on principles rather than detailed prescription.

The published accounts of companies are expected to comply with the Abstracts issued by the UITF. Abstracts consequently may be taken into consideration by the Financial Reporting Review Panel in deciding whether financial statements call for review.

Summary

Financial accounting is the process of designing and operating an information system for collecting, measuring and recording business transactions, and summarizing and communicating the results of these transactions to users to facilitate the making of financial/economic decisions. The first part of this definition, relating to collecting and recording business transactions, is called double entry bookkeeping. The purposes of financial accounting are to record and control the business transactions, maintain accuracy in recording, meet the requirements of the law, present final accounts and other financial reports to the owners of the enterprise, and to facilitate the efficient allocation of resources.

The final accounts of companies are often referred to as the published accounts or financial statements, and include a profit and loss account and balance sheet. These are contained in a document called the annual report and accounts. The functions of annual reports are related to society's beliefs about the objective(s) of business enterprises. The basic philosophy of the accountancy bodies is that of public accountability. This underlies their view of the objective of financial statements as being to provide information about the financial position, performance and financial adaptability of an enterprise that is useful to a wide range of users for assessing the stewardship of management and for making economic decisions. These users include investors, employees, lenders, suppliers and other trade creditors, customers, government and their agencies, and the public. Each of these will have particular information needs.

The contents of company financial statements are governed by what is called the regulatory framework. This comprises the Companies Acts, London Stock Exchange regulations, and accounting standards. The latter includes Statements of Standard Accounting Practice (SSAP) issued by the now defunct Accounting Standards Committee (ASC), and Financial Reporting Standards (FRS) issued by the Accounting Standards Board (ASB). The standard setting process is currently under the control of the Financial Reporting Council (FRC) and also includes a Financial Reporting Review Panel (FRRP) and the Urgent Issues Task Force (UITF).

Key terms and concepts

Abstracts, accountability, Accounting Standards Board (ASB), Accounting Standards Committee (ASC), annual/corporate reports, creditor, debtor, Discussion Draft (DD), double entry bookkeeping, final accounts, financial accounting, Financial Reporting Council (FRC), Financial Reporting Exposure Draft (FRED), Financial Reporting Review Panel (FRRP), Financial Reporting Standard (FRS), financial statements, internal check, internal control, management accounting, public accountability, published accounts, regulatory framework of accounting, Statement of Standard Accounting Practice (SSAP), stewardship, Urgent Issues Task Force (UITF), Yellow Book.

References

1. Accounting Standards Steering Committee (1975). *The Corporate Report* (ICAEW).
2. American Institute of Certified Public Accountants (1973). *The Objectives of Financial Statements* (AICPA).
3. Accounting Standards Board (1995). *Statement of Principles for Financial Reporting* (ASB).
4. Accounting Standards Board (1991). *Statement of Aims* (ASB).
5. Accounting Standards Committee (1986). *Explanatory Foreword to SSAPs* (ICAEW).
6. Accounting Standards Board (1994). *Foreword to UITF Abstracts* (ASB).

Exercises

An asterisk after the question number indicates that there is a suggested answer in the Appendix.

1.1. Explain the nature of financial accounting.

1.2. Describe the main functions of financial accounting.

1.3. (a) What do you understand by the term 'stewardship' in financial accounting?
(b) Describe the recording and control function of financial accounting.
(c) Explain the role of financial accounting with regard to the presentation of final accounts.

1.4. (a) Explain the 'basic philosophy' of *The Corporate Report* and the notion of 'public accountability'.
(b) What is the objective of corporate annual reports and what is meant by 'a reasonable right to information'?

1.5. (a) Which users of corporate annual reports are identified in *The Corporate Report*?
(b) Describe the information needs of any two substantially different groups of users.

1.6. (a) Outline the objective of financial statements as set out in the ASB *Statement of Principles for Financial Reporting* (1995).
(b) Identify the users of financial statements and briefly describe their information needs as set out in the ASB *Statement of Principles for Financial Reporting* (1995).

1.7.* (a) Describe the sources of the rules and regulations that govern the content and format of company final accounts.
(b) Outline the institutional framework by which the accountancy profession has influenced the content and format of company final accounts during the last two decades.

1.8. Describe the current institutional framework concerned with the setting and enforcement of accounting standards.

1.9. Explain the aims of the Accounting Standards Board and the means by which it intends to achieve these aims.

1.10. The objective of financial statements is to provide information about the financial position, performance and financial adaptability of an enterprise that is useful to a wide range of users for assessing the stewardship of management and for making economic decisions. (Draft *Statement of Principles for Financial Reporting*, issued by the UK Accounting Standards Board in November 1995).

Required:

(a) State five potential users of company published financial statements, briefly explaining for each one their likely information needs from those statements.

(b) Briefly discuss whether you think that UK company published financial statements achieve the objective stated above, giving your reasons. Include in your answer two ways in which you think the quality of the information disclosed in financial statements could be improved.

(ACCA)

1.11. The existing procedures for setting accounting standards in the UK were established in 1990.

Required:

(a) Explain the roles of the following in relation to accounting standards:
  (i)   Financial Reporting Council (FRC)
  (ii) Accounting Standards Board (ASB)
  (iii) Financial Reporting Review Panel (FRRP)
  (iv) Urgent Issues Task Force (UITF)

(b) Explain how the standard setting authority approaches the task of producing a standard, with particular reference to the ways in which comment or feedback from interested parties is obtained.

(c) It is possible that there could be a difference between the requirements of Financial Reporting Standards and those of the Companies Acts in preparing financial statements? How may such a difference be resolved?

(ACCA)

2. The accounting equation and its components

Learning objectives

After reading this chapter the student should be able to:

1. Explain the meaning of the key terms and concepts listed at the end of the chapter.
2. Explain the relevance of the accounting entity concept in financial accounting.
3. Describe the accounting equation including how it is reflected in balance sheets.
4. Explain the nature of assets, liabilities and capital.
5. Explain the nature of profit and capital maintenance including their interrelationship.
6. Prepare simple balance sheets and compute the profit from these.
7. Explain the relevance of the accounting period concept in financial accounting.
8. Distinguish between revenue expenditure and capital expenditure including their effects on a balance sheet.
9. Discuss the relevance and limitations of the historic cost concept in financial accounting.

The accounting entity

The fundamental objective of company final accounts was stated very precisely by the Accounting Standards Committee[1] as 'to communicate economic measurements of, and information about, the resources and performance of the reporting entity useful to those having reasonable rights to such information'. This statement includes a reference to a critically important concept for accounting: 'the reporting entity'. Before we can go any further this entity concept must be clarified. Actually, the idea is really so basic that it might have passed the casual observed unnoticed. However, explicit recognition will help avoid many sources of potential confusion and set the foundation for the subsequent development of a structure for accounting processes.

At its simplest, the reporting or *accounting entity* is just the organizational unit which is the object of focus of the particular accounting process. It might be a particular company, club or business partnership which forms the entity, for example. Of course, we are used to hearing that a financial report relates to a specific organization, but now the organization is being called an entity. The use of the word entity emphasizes the properties of being separate and discrete. Greater precision is demanded by accounting in deciding what is, and is not, part of the entity. Boundaries are being created to separate out the accounting entity. Realizing that these boundaries are necessary, even though they

15

may be artificial, is the key to the entity concept. It becomes possible to accept that a business may be separate from its sole proprietor.

By defining the boundaries of the organizational unit, the accounting entity concept determines the transactions that will be recorded in the accounts. For example, when a local plumber buys tools to carry out his work, that action can be regarded as a purchase by the business, while when the same man buys a cinema ticket this would be seen as a personal purchase. In the same way, the salary paid to a company director is treated not as some internal transfer within a company but as a payment to an officer as a separate individual. In general, accounting sets up 'the business', 'the company' and 'the club' as entities which are artificial constructs, separate from their owners and employees as individuals.

At times this approach is shared with that of the law. In the UK, a company is a legal entity regarded, in law, as a separate body and, correspondingly, the company is an accounting entity. By contrast, there may be no legal demarcation between an unincorporated business and its sole proprietor. The artificial nature of accounting entities has implications of its own, which are most obvious in the case of the single-owner, unincorporated business. The accountant might set up the business as an accounting entity, but this does not and cannot give it a legal existence which enables it, in the eyes of the law, to separately own property or other possessions, make contractual agreements or carry out transactions. What the accountant has created as separate is, in fact, just a part of the proprietor's domain so that anything that can be treated as being owned by the business actually belongs to the proprietor. The 'business' is simply a useful connector.

As will be seen in later chapters, one accounting entity can be a part of another accounting entity. For example, a branch of a retail chain store (such as Marks & Spencer plc) may be treated as a separate accounting entity for internal reporting purposes. However, the branch will also be a part of the business as a whole, which would be treated as another accounting entity for external reporting purposes. Similarly one company may be a subsidiary of (i.e. owned by) another (holding) company. In this case the subsidiary will be one accounting entity, and, its final accounts must also be consolidated with those of the holding (owner) company into group final accounts, representing another accounting entity.

In sum, an accounting entity can be a legal entity, part of a legal entity, a combination of several legal entities, part of another accounting entity, or a combination of accounting entities.

The balance sheet as an accounting equation

An accounting entity may also be viewed as a set of assets and liabilities. Perhaps the most familiar form this takes is the *balance sheet*. As an equation this would appear as follows:

Proprietor's ownership interest in the business = net resources of the business

The ownership interest or claims are called *owner's equity* or *owner's capital*. The net resources are analysed into assets and liabilities.

In relatively simple terms, an *asset* can be defined as a tangible or intangible resource that is owned or controlled by an accounting entity, and which is expected to generate future economic benefits. Examples of assets include land and buildings; motor vehicles; plant and machinery; tools; office furniture, fixtures and fittings; office equipment; goods for resale (known as stock/inventory); amounts owed to the accounting entity by its customers (i.e. debtors); money in a bank cheque account; and cash in hand.

The use of the word 'net' to describe the resources possessed by the business is to recognize that there are some amounts set against or to be deducted from the assets. There are two major types of such deductions: liabilities and provisions. In relatively simple terms, a *liability* can be defined as a legal obligation to transfer assets or provide services to another entity which arises from some past transaction or event. Liabilities represent claims by outsiders (as compared to the owners, whose claims are equity or capital) and may include such items as loans made to the business and amounts owed for goods supplied (ie creditors). As the name suggests, *provisions* are amounts provided to allow for liabilities which may be anticipated but not yet quantified precisely, or for reductions in asset values. However, although there are a number of important matters to consider in relation to provisions, it will be entirely appropriate for present purposes to think of provisions as simply a special category of liability, and to postpone detailed attention until later. Chapters 11 and 12 are both particularly concerned with provisions.

Given that liabilities can be regarded as being negative in sign in relation to assets the *accounting equation* can now be stated in the form:

$$\text{Capital} = \text{Assets} - \text{Liabilities}$$

or alternatively

$$\text{Assets} = \text{Capital} + \text{Liabilities}$$

This is a fundamental equation and is a valuable basis from which to begin understanding the whole process of accounting. It sets out the balance sheet relationship which will hold at any point in time, although in practice a complete and detailed balance sheet may only be produced once in a period of a month or even a year. It is worth pointing out, then, that most accounting activity is concerned with individual transactions; nevertheless the balance sheet equation remains a focus towards which the activity is directed.

However, for now we will examine accounting simply in terms of balance sheets. Let us trace how this approach reflects the setting up of the plumbing business mentioned earlier.

Suppose Adam Bridgewater decided to start his business by opening a bank account for business transactions and depositing £2,000 into it on 1 July 19X1. The balance sheet equation would show owner's capital as being equal to cash at the bank, both being £2,000. There are a number of ways of presenting this: that used by companies usually adopts a so-called vertical approach placing capital vertically below net assets in the form:

Bridgewater (Plumber)
Balance sheet as at 1 July 19X1

Assets	£
Cash at bank	2,000
Capital	2,000

However, a side-by-side or horizontal presentation may illustrate more clearly the equation format. A question arises: on which side should assets be included? In practice there is considerable variation and it becomes a matter of convention. The most useful convention at this stage (and that given support by the 1981 and subsequent Companies Acts) is to show assets on the left-hand side, i.e.

Bridgewater (Plumber)
Balance sheet as at 1 July 19X1

Assets	£			£
Cash at bank	2,000		Capital	2,000

If on 2 July 19X1 he draws out £800 cash and spends it all purchasing tools, then cash at bank will be decreased and a new asset, the tools, is introduced on the balance sheet.

Bridgewater (Plumber)
Balance sheet as at 2 July 19X1

Assets	£			£
Tools	800		Capital	2,000
Cash at bank	1,200			
	2,000			

In this case one asset is increased by exactly the same amount as another is decreased so that the accounting equation, Assets equals Capital plus Liabilities, continues to exist.

On 3 July he buys a range of plumbing accessories for £300 from the local storekeeper, but arranges to pay in the next few days. The arrangement is described as 'on credit'. The storekeeper becomes a creditor since he is now owed a debt of £300. There is no problem in maintaining the balance of the equation when including the effects of this transaction in the business balance sheet, since the new liability of £300 owed to the store exactly complements the £300 increase in assets represented by the accessories:

Bridgewater (Plumber)
Balance sheet as at 3 July 19X1

Assets	£			£
Tools	800		Capital	2,000
Accessories	300		Liability—creditor	300
Cash at bank	1,200			2,300
	2,300			

The manner in which the two components of the change in the balance sheet are complementary, so that the equality of the two sides remains intact, is worthy of note since it underlies the principles of double entry bookkeeping developed in Chapter 4. Another event in the life of this business offers further illustration. If the next day, Bridgewater pays the store the £300 to clear the outstanding debt this will decrease both the cash and the creditor—an asset and a liability—by the same amount giving:

Bridgewater (Plumber)
Balance sheet as at 4 July 19X1

Assets	£			£
Tools	800		Capital	2,000
Accessories	300			
Cash at bank	900			
	2,000			

Learning activity 2.1

Prepare a balance sheet listing your assets and liabilities, or those of your family. Use the original purchase price of the assets.

The accounting equation and profit reporting

Drawing up a balance sheet after each of the enormous number of transactions carried out every week in large corporations would be very time consuming and inefficient, and a business cannot be expected to do so. However, it is normal for even small businesses to produce a balance sheet once a year. Annual reporting has taken on a significance of its own for many reasons. A year's activity encompasses all the seasons, and many statistics of economic and business performance are produced on this basis. Examples include annual inflation rates, annual interest rates, annual salaries, annual tax allowances and, not surprisingly, annual profits.

Bridgewater may be interested to see how his business has progressed in its first year. For him to be able to draw up a balance sheet he needs to know the amounts to include for assets and liabilities at that date. Suppose he has the following amounts relating to the position at the end of the day's trading on 30 June 19X2:

Assets of business: Building £5,000; tools £1,100; stock of accessories £500; debtors £350; cash at bank £200.
Liabilities: Bank loan £3,500; creditors £450.

A number of changes and transactions are likely to have taken place during the year to produce this position, but these have not been tracked from the balance sheet to balance sheet. The absence of a figure for capital will not prevent the balance sheet being drawn up given that it is the only missing figure in the accounting equation. So the balance sheet becomes:

Bridgewater (Plumber)
Balance sheet as at 30 June 19X2

Assets	£	Liabilities	£
Building	5,000	Bank loan	3,500
Tools	1,100	Creditors	450
Accessories	500		3,950
Debtors	350	Capital (to balance)	3,200
Cash	200		7,150
	7,150		

Capital has been made to be the balancing item, and by this means all balance sheets would inevitably balance. This inevitability is consistent with recognizing that the business is an entity which is an artificial creation. It cannot have any net ownership of its own. However, the capital figure at the end of the year is different to that at the beginning, and analysis and explanation of that change is needed to provide a more complete picture. In this case we see that the increase in the year by the difference between opening and closing capital is £3,200 − £2,000 = £1,200. How could this have arisen?

One possible explanation is that Bridgewater paid some more money into the business. In this case let us decide that we know he did pay in a further £1,000. Of course, the opposite to paying would be taking money out, so let us say that he took out £750 for personal use. The net effect will produce an increase of £1,000 − £750 = £250. The rest of the increase (i.e. £1,200 − £250 = £950) would be profit, i.e. increased capital generated by the business itself.

A simple example will illustrate how profit is able to generate increases in capital. A trader is able to start a small venture with £30 in cash, equivalent to £30 capital. She uses the money to buy a bath. When she sells the bath for £40 she now has £40 cash and has increased capital by £10.

To provide a more useful definition of profit as increased capital, accounting has made use of explanations given by the economist Hicks,[2] to define *profit* as the maximum amount that could be withdrawn in a period from the business while leaving the capital intact. In the case of Bridgewater's business, the capital which is kept intact is the £2,000 figure at the start of the period. Measuring profit in relation to capital which is kept intact is commonly described as a *capital maintenance* approach, which forms one of the major pillars of profit measurement theory. It is implicit in all profit measurement approaches that will be drawn upon in this book.

The accounting period and profit reporting

The *accounting period* concept is a means of dividing up the life of an accounting entity into discrete periods for the purpose of reporting performance and showing its financial position (in a balance sheet). This is usually periods of one year, and thus often referred to as the accounting or financial year. Each accounting year of an entity's life normally ends on the anniversary of its formation, and therefore does not necessarily coincide with the calendar year. It could thus end on any day of the calendar year, but for convenience the accounting year is nearly always taken to be the end of a calendar month, and sometimes adjusted to the end of the calendar year (e.g. for tax reasons).

The previous section commenced by recognizing the significance of annual reporting in assessing business performance. Profit is defined in terms of potential consumption 'in a period'. Although the use of a period of a year is no more than a convention—albeit a very useful one—the idea of periodic reporting is fundamental to present-day accounting. In relation to maintenance of capital, the second year of the plumbing business's performance will be measured in profit terms in relation to that year's opening capital, i.e. the £3,200 closing capital from year one. The approach adopted in accounting is an extension of the use of the entity concept. For accounting purposes, each complete period, usually of a year, is treated as a separate entity. It inherits as its opening balance sheet the closing balance sheet of the previous period.

One response which follows from the needs of periodic reporting is to classify items into two types—those that will be included in the closing balance sheet to be properly carried forward as part of the opening position of the new entity commencing next period, and those that are properly attributable to the period just finished. An aspect of this has already been seen in the simple illustration of buying and selling a bath to make a profit. The transactions involved are all treated as being complete by the time the profit figure for the year is calculated. Details of the buying and selling transactions are not part of the next year's position except to the extent that they form an element contained within the total capital figure.

The approach which is being adopted here will be only briefly described now, it is taken up more fully in Chapter 10. It is known as the matching process. Sales associated with a particular period are recognized as the revenue of that period. The expenditures used up in that period in creating those sales are matched against them. The aggregate sales less the aggregate expenditures matched against them gives the profit for the year.

Expenditure of the type which is to be matched against the period's revenue and is used up in the period is identified as *revenue expenditure*, and this is distinguished from *capital expenditure*—that which represents amounts which it is appropriate to carry forward as part of the next year's opening balance sheet. Expenditure on tools, which represent the long-term equipment of the business, is capital expenditure and is carried forward from balance sheet to balance sheet. Rental expenditure on a building used during the year will be revenue expenditure—what it provides is used up in the period; the purchase of the building, however, would be capital expenditure, as it is entirely appropriate to represent ownership being carried forward from period to period.

Static and dynamic approaches to profit determination

The previous two sections have been describing two approaches to measuring profit in the accounts of business. The first can be identified as a comparative static approach. It computes profit through a comparison of the opening and closing capital positions adjusting these for additions and withdrawals of capital made by the owners during the year. Each balance sheet is a static representation of the elements of the accounting equation at a particular point in time.

The alternative is a more dynamic approach attempting to record increases and decreases in capital values throughout the period by recognizing the increases as revenue items and deducting from these the decreases or costs incurred in producing those revenues. By tracking the changes within a period the latter 'transaction based or net production method' indicates the sources of profit.

Elements of the use and limitations of historical cost in accounting measurement

For accounting statements to represent the various values of assets and liabilities and to be able to aggregate these, it is necessary for a *measurement unit* to be established and a *valuation model* to be adopted. We have already been using a measurement unit, the £ sterling. Providing this represents a stable unit for expressing economic values, money measurement will be appropriate to accounting statements intended to reflect the performance and financial position of business entities. Money provides a common denominator for measuring, aggregating and reporting the performance of an accounting entity and the attributes of transactions and items. For the sake of example, other less plausible alternatives might include the amount of energy (eg. electrical) or labour hours consumed in creating an asset.

As regards a valuation model, the price which is agreed in an arm's-length transaction when an asset or liability is originally acquired provides readily available objective valuations expressed in terms of monetary units of measurement. This is the major source of valuation utilized by *historical cost accounting*. Sales are recorded at the contracted sales value and purchases at the agreed purchase price. This approach has many strengths. It permits accounts to be produced by collecting information about the business transactions—clearly a process which is commercially useful in tracking down what amounts have to be paid and collected and what cash balances remain after making payments and collections. Amounts are determined 'automatically' by the transactions themselves rather than being left to the judgement and possible abuse of individuals. For these and other reasons historical cost continues to be the predominant basis for accounting record keeping and reporting.

However, it is not without disadvantages. These arise largely because there is change over time in prices (both of individual items and as a result of inflation). As a result, accounting reports based on historical costs may become unrealistic. Balance sheets will contain values for assets which are out of date, being based on prices when they were originally purchased, which may be several years ago; capital which is being maintained in the profit measurement process represents a value which is also out of date, both in terms of its value to the owners, and in the capacity of the facilities it could provide for the business. The matching process becomes debased to the extent that sales may be made at prices which, although above the original purchase price of the items being sold, are below the current replacement price. This would mean that a business might be reporting a profit on a sale even though this put it in the position where it was no longer able to buy the goods it owned prior to the sale.

These limitations must be borne in mind when, at a later stage, we consider the appraisal of accounts in Chapter 29. Attempts to address these drawbacks produce considerable complexity. As a result these will not be considered in any depth until Chapter 33.

Learning activity 2.2

Repeat Learning activity 2.1 in about one month's time, or better still for about a year ago if possible. Calculate the change in the value of capital over this period and list the main reasons for the change. What do these tell you about the nature of the profit, capital maintenance and the effect of valuing assets at their historic cost?

Summary

The accounting entity concept defines the boundaries of the organizational unit which is the focus of the accounting process, and thus the transactions that will be recorded. An accounting entity may also be viewed as a set of assets and liabilities, the difference between the money values of these being the capital. This is referred to as the accounting equation, and can be presented in the form of a balance sheet in which the assets and liabilities are valued at their historical cost.

The accounting period concept divides up the life of an entity into discrete periods (of usually one year) for the purpose of reporting profit and its financial state of affairs. The profit for an accounting year can be measured either in terms of the change in the value of the capital over this period, or by a process of matching sales revenue with the expenditure incurred in generating that revenue. This involves distinguishing between revenue expenditure and capital expenditure.

Key terms and concepts

Accounting entity, accounting equation, accounting period and year, asset, balance sheet, capital/equity, capital expenditure, capital maintenance, historical cost accounting, liability, measurement unit, profit, provision, revenue expenditure, valuation model.

References

1. Accounting Standards Committee (1975). *The Corporate Report* (ICAEW), p. 28.
2. Hicks, J. R. (1946). *Value and Capital* (2nd edn), Clarendon Press, Oxford.

Exercises

An asterisk after the question number indicates that there is a suggested answer in the Appendix.

2.1. Explain the relevance of the entity concept in accounting.

2.2. Define and distinguish between the following:
   (a) assets and liabilities;
   (b) capital and revenue expenditure.

2.3. (a) State the accounting equation and explain its components.
   (b) The financial position of a business at any time is represented in the balance sheet. Why is it that every business entity's position should 'balance'?

2.4. Explain briefly what is meant by the following terms: profit; capital; capital maintenance.

2.5. Explain the relevance of the accounting period concept in accounting.

2.6. Discuss the relevance and limitations of the historical cost concept in accounting.

2.7.* J. Frank commenced business on 1 January 19X9. His position was:

Assets: land and buildings, £7,500; fixtures, £560; balance at bank, £1,740.
Liabilities: mortgage on land and buildings £4,000.

He traded for a year, withdrawing £500 for his personal use and paying in no additional capital. His position on 31 December 19X9 was:

Assets: land and buildings, £7,500; fixtures, £560; delivery van, £650; sundry debtors, £470; stock, £940; balance at bank, £1,050; cash in hand, £80.
Liabilities: loan on mortgage of land and buildings, £5,000; sundry creditors, £800.

Calculate Frank's profit or loss for 19X9.

3. Basic documentation and books of account

Learning objectives

After reading this chapter the student should be able to:

1. Explain the meaning of the key terms and concepts listed at the end of the chapter.
2. Distinguish between cash transactions and credit transactions.
3. Describe the nature of trade discount and cash discount.
4. List the documents and describe the procedure relating to a credit transaction.
5. Describe the contents of those documents which are entered in the books of account.
6. Explain the purpose of books of prime entry.
7. List the books of prime entry and state what each is used to record.

Basic documentation for cash and credit transactions

In accounting, a *cash transaction* is one where goods or services are paid for in cash or by cheque when they are received or delivered. A *credit transaction* is one where payment is made or received some time after delivery (normally in one instalment). This should not be confused with hire purchase or credit card transactions. Credit transactions are extremely common in many industries. The credit terms of most UK businesses are that goods which are delivered at any time during a given calendar month should be paid for by the end of the following calendar month.

Credit transactions often involve *trade discount*. This is a discount given by one trader to another. It is usually expressed as a percentage reduction of the recommended retail price of the goods, and is deducted in arriving at the amount the buyer is charged for the goods.

A large number of businesses also allow their customers *cash discount*. This is a reduction in the amount that the customer has to pay provided payment is made within a given period stipulated by the seller at the time of sale (e.g. $2\frac{1}{2}$ per cent or 5 per cent if paid in 10 days).

A cash transaction is recorded in the books of account from the receipt received if paid in cash, or from the cheque book stub if paid by cheque. A credit transaction, on the other hand, involves a number of documents, not all of which are recorded in the books of account. Figure 3.1 shows, in chronological order, the documents and procedures relating to a business transaction on credit, including who originates each document. Note that only the invoice, debit note, credit note and cheque are recorded in the books of account.

The main documents involved in a credit transaction are discussed below.

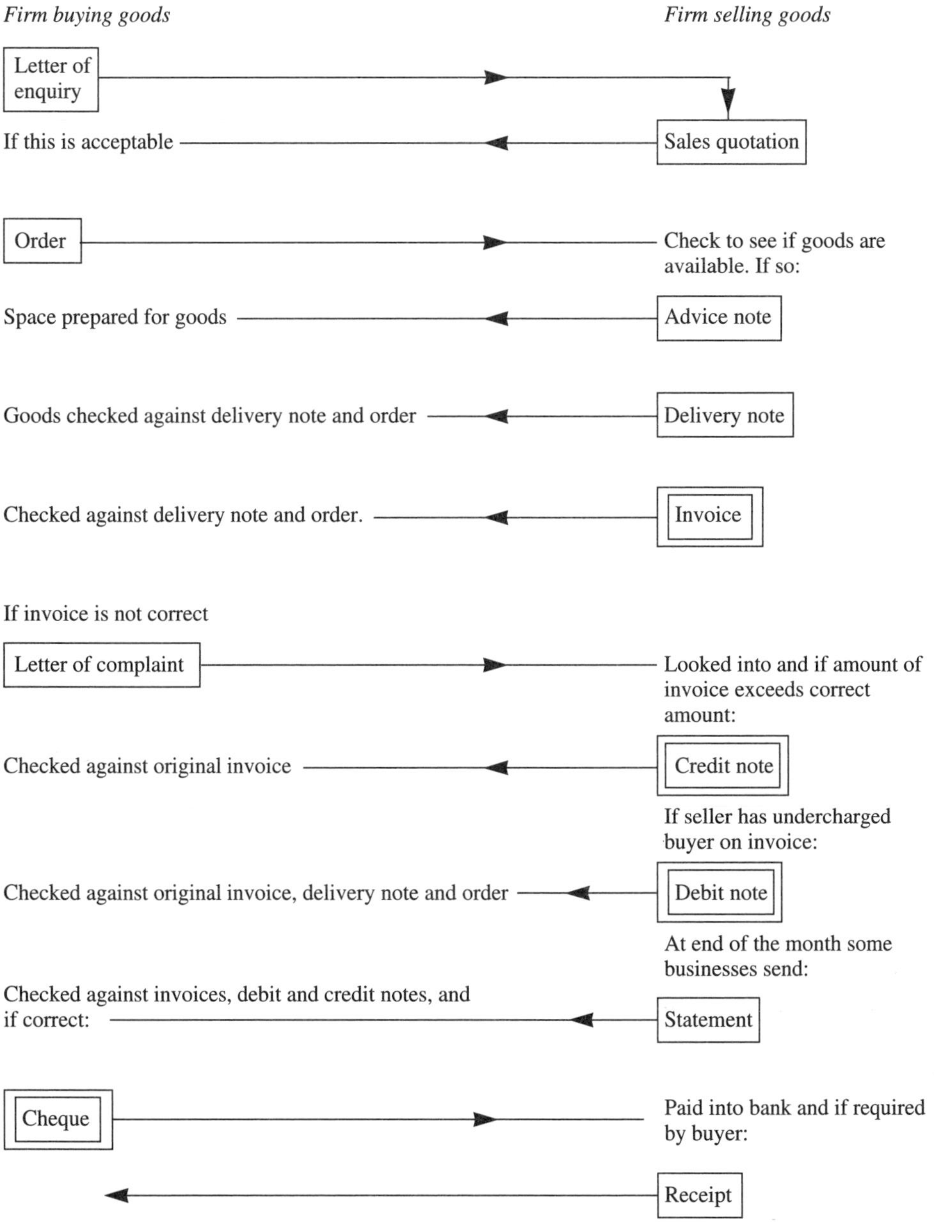

Firm buying goods   *Firm selling goods*

Letter of enquiry ──────────────────────────────────▶

If this is acceptable ──────────────────◀────────── Sales quotation

Order ──────────────────────────────▶──────────── Check to see if goods are available. If so:

Space prepared for goods ──────────────◀────────── Advice note

Goods checked against delivery note and order ──◀──── Delivery note

Checked against delivery note and order. ──◀──────── Invoice

If invoice is not correct

Letter of complaint ────────────────▶──────────── Looked into and if amount of invoice exceeds correct amount:

Checked against original invoice ──────◀────────── Credit note

If seller has undercharged buyer on invoice:

Checked against original invoice, delivery note and order ──◀── Debit note

At end of the month some businesses send:

Checked against invoices, debit and credit notes, and if correct: ──────────────────◀────────── Statement

Cheque ──────────────────────────▶──────────── Paid into bank and if required by buyer:

◀──────────────────────────────────── Receipt

Note that the documents are raised by the firm shown at the head of the column in which the document is shown. All of the documents are usually send by post except where shown otherwise. The documents recorded in the buyer's and seller's books consist of those shown by a double lined box.

Figure 3.1   Inter-firm documentation for a credit transaction.

	FROM: Trendy Gear Ltd High Street London		

TO: Catalogue Times Ltd
      Middlesex Street
      London

INVOICE NO: 38167
DATE: 30 January 19X5

Delivered to: 23 Oxford Road, London

No. of units	Details	Unit price	Total price
100	Dresses size 14, pattern No. 385	£6.50	£650
50	Leather bags, pattern No. 650	£3.00	£150
			£800
	Less: 25 per cent trade discount		£200
			£600
	Add: VAT at 17½ per cent		£105
			£705
	Tights unavailable—to follow later		

Date of Delivery: 30 January 19X5
Mode of Delivery: Our transport
Cash Discount Terms: 5 per cent monthly account
Your Order No: 6382

Figure 3.2   An invoice.

The invoice

The purpose of the invoice, which is sent by the seller, is primarily to inform the buyer how much is owed for the goods supplied. It is *not* a demand for payment. A specimen invoice is shown in Figure 3.2. The information shown on an invoice consists of the following items:

1. The name and address of the seller
2. The name and address of the buyer
3. The invoice and delivery note number of the seller (usually the same)
4. The date of the invoice
5. The address to which the goods were delivered
6. The buyer's order number
7. The quantity of goods sold
8. Details of the goods supplied
9. The price per unit of each of the goods
10. The total value of the invoice before value added tax (VAT)*

*Value added tax affects a large number of sales and purchase transactions which in turn must be incorporated in the recording of those transactions. Including VAT introduces little in the way of principles but some additional detail. In order to concentrate on the subject matter developed in this book, VAT is recognized here but its treatment is then postponed to a later chapter.

11. The trade and cash discount
12. VAT payable and the total value of the invoice including VAT
13. When payment should be made
14. The seller's terms of trade.

The buyer checks the invoice against his or her order and the delivery note (or usually with a goods received note prepared by his or her receiving department). If correct, the invoice is then entered in the buyer's books. Similarly, a copy of the invoice would have been entered in the seller's books.

The debit note

A debit note is sent by the seller if s/he has undercharged the buyer on the invoice. It has basically the same layout and information as the invoice except that instead of details of the goods it shows details of the undercharge. It is recorded in the books of the seller and buyer in the same way as an invoice.

The credit note

A credit note may be sent by the seller for a number of reasons. These include:

1. The buyer has returned goods because they were not ordered, or they were the wrong type, quantity or quality, or are defective.
2. The seller has overcharged the buyer on the invoice. This may be due to an error in the unit price or calculations.

A credit note has basically the same layout and information as an invoice, except that instead of the details of the goods it will show the reason why it has been issued.

A credit note will be recorded in the books of the seller and buyer in a similar way to the invoice, except that the entries are the reverse. It is perhaps worth mentioning here the reason why this document is called a credit note. This is because it informs the buyer that his account in the books of the seller is being credited. Conversely, a debit note informs the buyer that his account in the seller's book is being debited. This is discussed in a later chapter in more depth.

A statement

As explained above, the most common terms of credit in the UK are that a buyer should pay for all the goods invoiced to him or her by the seller during a particular calendar month at the end of the following calendar month. The statement is a list of the invoices, debit notes and credit notes that the seller has sent to the buyer during a given calendar month, and thus shows how much the buyer owes the seller and when it should be paid. The statement is often a copy of the buyer's account in the seller's books. This is illustrated in Figure 3.3. The layout shown is a computerized system of bookkeeping.

The statement may be kept by the buyer for reference purposes or returned to the seller with the buyer's cheque. In either case neither the buyer nor the seller records the statement in the books. Not all businesses use statements.

	Seller's name and address			
Buyer's name and address:				Month: January 19X5
Date of invoice	Invoice/Credit note no.	Debits (amount of invoices and debit	Credits (amount of credit notes and payments)	Balance
2 Jan	426	£23.12		£23.12
9 Jan	489	£16.24		£39.36
16 Jan	563	£52.91		£92.27
22 Jan	Cheque		£25.14	£67.13
25 Jan	1326		£6.00	£61.13
			Amount due on 28 February	£61.13
Cash discount terms: 5 per cent monthly				

Figure 3.3 A statement.

The cheque

This is the most common form of payment in business because of its convenience and safety. Most cheques are crossed and therefore have to be paid into a bank account. This makes it possible to trace the cheque if stolen and fraudulently passed on to someone else. A crossed cheque may be paid into anyone's bank account if the payee endorses (i.e. signs) the back of the cheque. However, if the words 'account payee only' are written between the crossings it must be paid into the account of the person named on the cheque.

The information that must be shown on a cheque consists of the following items:

1. The date
2. The signature of the drawer (i.e. payer)
3. The name of the drawee (i.e. the bank at which the drawer has his or her account)
4. The name of the payee (i.e. who is to receive the money)
5. The words 'Pay . . . or Order the sum of . . .'
6. The amount of money in figures and in words.

The bank account number of the drawer, the cheque and bank number are also shown on preprinted cheques.

Since there is only one copy of a cheque it is essential to write on the cheque stub or counterfoil to whom the cheque was paid (i.e. the payee), the amount and what the payment was for. Without this information the books of account cannot be written up.

The bank paying-in book

The paying-in book provides a record of the cash and cheques received that have been paid into the business's bank account. The information shown on the bank paying-in book stub consists of:

1. The date
2. The amounts paid in, from whom they were received, and to what they relate.

The receipt

The law requires the seller to give the buyer a receipt for goods which have been paid for in cash. However, there is no legal requirement to do so in the case of payments by cheque. A receipt must contain the following information:

1. The name of the payer
2. The signature of the recipient
3. The amount of money in figures and in words
4. The date.

A receipt is only recorded in the books of accounts when it relates to cash receipts and payments.

Books of account

The main book of account in which all transactions are recorded is called the *ledger*. However, before a transaction is recorded in the ledger it must first be entered in a *book of prime entry*. These are designed to show more detail relating to each transaction than appears in the ledger. They also facilitate making entries in the ledger, in that transactions of the same type can be posted periodically in total rather than one at a time. Sometimes there are analysis columns in each book of prime entry in which are collected all those transactions relating to the same type of expenditure or income. A business may use up to nine books of prime entry, which consist of:

1. *The sales day book*, in which is recorded the sale on credit of those goods bought specifically for resale. It is written up from copies of sales invoices and debit notes retained by the seller. The amount entered in the sales day book is after deducting trade discount (but before deducting cash discount).
2. *The sales returns day book*, in which is recorded the goods sold on credit that are returned by customers. It is written up from copies of credit notes retained by the seller.
3. *The purchases day book*, in which is recorded the purchase on credit of goods intended for resale. It is written up from the invoices and debit notes received from suppliers. The amount entered in the purchases day book is after deducting trade discount (but before deducting cash discount).
4. *The purchases returns day book*, in which is recorded the goods purchased on credit that are returned to suppliers. It is written up from the credit notes received from suppliers.
5. *The petty cash book*, in which is recorded cash received and cash paid. This is written up from receipts (or petty cash vouchers where employees are reimbursed expenses).
6. *The cash book*, in which are recorded cheques received and cash paid into the bank and payments made by cheque. This is written up from the bank paying-in book and cheque book stubs.
7. *The bills receivable book*, in which are recorded bills of exchange received by the business from debtors. A bill of exchange can best be described as being similar to a post-dated cheque, except that instead of being written out by the person paying the money, it is prepared by the business to whom the money is owed and then signed by the debtor. When the period of credit given by the bill of exchange has expired, which is usually 30, 60 or 90 days, the creditor then presents the bill to the debtor's bank and receives payment.

8. *The bills payable book*, in which are recorded bills of exchange given to suppliers as payment.

9. *The journal*, in which are recorded any transactions that are not included in any of the other books of prime entry. At one time all entries were passed through the journal, but now it is primarily used to record the purchase and sale of fixed assets on credit, the correction of errors, opening entries in new sets of books and any remaining transfers. Fixed assets are items not brought specifically for resale, such as land and buildings, machinery, vehicles, etc. The journal is written up from copies of the invoice.

Figure 3.4 provides a summary of the different books of prime entry, including the documents from which each is written up. Each of these books of prime entry is discussed in depth in later chapters.

Summary

In accounting a distinction is made between cash and credit transactions. A cash transaction is one where goods or services are paid for in cash or by cheque when they are received or delivered. A credit transaction is one where payment is made or received some time after delivery. Credit transactions often involve trade discount and cash discount. Trade discount is a discount given by one trader to another in arriving at the price of the goods. Cash discount is a reduction in the amount that the customer has to pay provided payment is made within a given period of time stipulated by the seller.

Cash transactions are recorded in the books of account from the receipt if paid or received in cash, or from the cheque book and bank paying-in book if paid or received by cheque. Cash receipts and payments are entered in a book of prime entry known as the petty cash book. Cheque receipts and payments are entered in the cash book.

Credit transactions involve a number of different documents but those which are recorded in the books of account comprise invoices, debit notes and credit notes. These arise in connection with both purchases and sales, and are entered in a set of books of prime entry commonly known as day books. Purchase invoices and debit notes are entered in the purchases day book, and purchases credit notes in the purchases returns day book. Sales invoices and debit notes are entered in the sales day book, and sales credit notes in the sales returns day book.

A further book of prime entry known as the journal is used to record all other transactions, particularly the purchase and sale of fixed assets on credit.

Key terms and concepts

Bank paying-in book, bills payable, bills receivable, books of prime entry, cash book, cash discount, cash transaction, cheque, credit note, credit transactions, debit note, invoice, journal, ledger, petty cash book, purchases day book, purchases returns day book, receipt, sales day book, sales return day book, statement, trade discount.

Basic documents   *Books of prime entry*

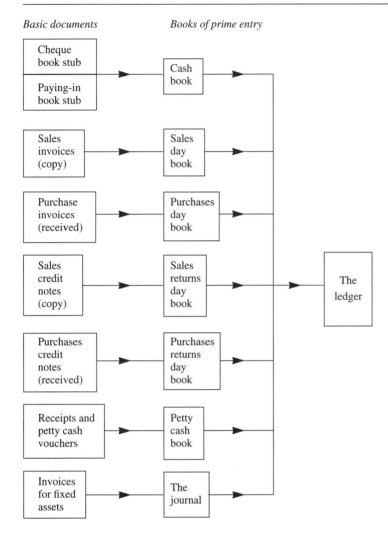

Figure 3.4   Books of account and related documents.

Exercises

An asterisk after the question number indicates that there is a suggested answer in the Appendix.

3.1. Explain the difference between a cash transaction and a credit transaction.

3.2. Explain the difference between trade discount and cash discount.

3.3. Outline the purpose and content of: (a) an invoice; (b) a debit note; and (c) a credit note.

3.4. Explain the difference between an invoice and: (a) a statement; (b) a receipt.

3.5.* List the books of prime entry with which you are familiar and briefly describe what each is intended to record, including the documents used to write them up.

3.6. Briefly describe the nature of a bill of exchange.

3.7. Explain the purpose of books of prime entry.

4. The general ledger

<table>
<tr><td>

Learning objectives

After reading this chapter the student should be able to:

1. Explain the meaning of the key terms and concepts listed at the end of the chapter.
2. Explain the principles of double entry bookkeeping including the purpose of having different ledger accounts.
3. Describe the format and contents of the ledger and ledger accounts.
4. Enter cash (including cheque) transactions and credit transactions in the ledger.
5. Distinguish between asset and expense accounts, and between capital, liability and income accounts.

</td></tr>
</table>

The principles of double entry bookkeeping

Double entry bookkeeping is a systematic method of recording an enterprise's transactions in a book called the *ledger*. Each page of the ledger is split into two halves, *the left half called the DEBIT side and the right half called the CREDIT side*. The ledger is divided into sections called *accounts*. In practice, each of these accounts is on a separate page.

The money value of each transaction is entered once on each side of the ledger in different accounts. For example, if we take one transaction such as the sale of goods for cash of £100 on 6 January this would be recorded as follows:

Debit				Credit			
Date	Details	Folio	Amount	Date	Details	Folio	Amount
			Cash account (page 1)				
6 Jan	Sales	p. 2	100				

			Sales account (page 2)				
				6 Jan	Cash	p. 1	100

The main purposes of this system are to provide a means of ascertaining the total amount of each type of income and expenditure, the value of the assets owned by the business (e.g. cash), and how much is owed to and by the business. For example, the cash account shows how much money the business has at any time. Also, when there are several transactions, the sales account will contain all the sales made during a period and thus it is possible to see at a glance the total sales for that period. Similarly, other accounts, such as wages, postage, etc., will show the total amount spent on each of these types of expenses. These are referred to as *expense or nominal accounts*. The information is used to ascertain the profit or loss for a given period.

When the total amount of money on the debit side of an account is greater than that on the credit side, the account is said to have a *debit balance*. When the reverse is the case, the account is said to have a *credit balance. An account which contains a debit balance represents either an asset (such as cash) or an expense or loss. An account with a credit balance represents capital, a liability, income (such as sales) or a gain.*

Ledger entries for cash transactions

When cash is received it is entered on the debit side of the *cash account* and credited to the account to which the transaction relates. When cash is paid out it is entered on the credit side of the cash account and on the debit side of the account to which the transaction relates. The same occurs with cheques received and paid, except that they are entered in an account called the *bank account* instead of the cash account.

When someone starts a business they usually put money into the business. This is debited to the cash or bank account (depending on whether it is cash or a cheque) and credited to a *capital account*. Money introduced at a later date by the proprietor as additional capital is treated in the same way. Any money withdrawn by the proprietor is credited in the cash or bank account (depending on whether it is cash or a cheque) and debited to a *drawings account*.

Sometimes businesses also borrow money. The amount received is debited to the cash or bank account (depending on whether it is cash or a cheque) and credited to an account in the name of the lender who is referred to as a *loan creditor*.

The ledger entries for various cash transactions are illustrated in Example 4.1.

Example 4.1
S. Baker started business on 1 January 19X0 as a grocer with a capital in cash of £1,000. She also borrowed £500 in cash from London Bank Ltd. Her transactions during January, which are all in cash, were as follows:

1 Jan	Paid one month's rent for the shop: £100
2 Jan	Bought fixtures and fittings for the shop: £300
8 Jan	Purchased goods for resale: £400
9 Jan	Paid £25 carriage inwards
10 Jan	Bought stationery for £50
15 Jan	Paid £200 in wages for shop assistant
20 Jan	Cash taken by S. Baker for her private use: £150
31 Jan	Cash takings for the month: £600

You are required to write up the accounts in the general ledger.

	Debit			Credit	
Date	Details	Amount	Date	Details	Amount

Cash account

	Debit			Credit	
19X0			19X0		
1 Jan	Capital	1,000	1 Jan	Rent	100
1 Jan	Loan—London Bank Ltd	500	2 Jan	Fixtures and fittings	300
31 Jan	Sales	600	8 Jan	Purchases	400
			9 Jan	Carriage inwards	25
			10 Jan	Stationery	50
			15 Jan	Wages	200
			20 Jan	Drawings	150

Capital

			1 Jan	Cash	1,000

Loan—London Bank

			1 Jan	Cash	500

Sales

			31 Jan	Cash	600

Rent

1 Jan	Cash	100			

Fixtures and fittings

2 Jan	Cash	300			

Purchases

8 Jan	Cash	400			

Carriage inwards

9 Jan	Cash	25			

Stationery

10 Jan   Cash   50

Wages

15 Jan   Cash   200

Drawings

20 Jan   Cash   150

Notes

1. The narrative in the details column of an account specifies the name of the account that contains the other entry for each transaction.
2. Carriage inwards refers to haulage costs relating to goods that this business has purchased and is responsible for transporting from the sellers' premises.

Learning activity 4.1

Prepare a cash account for your cash transaction over the forthcoming week or month. Make the necessary double entry in the other ledger accounts.

Ledger entries for credit transactions

The entries in the ledger for credit transactions are more complicated than those for cash transactions. This is because a credit transaction involves at least two (and sometimes three) events, each of which is recorded in double entry form. The first event consists of the purchase or sale of goods on credit as evidenced by an invoice. The invoice is recorded in the ledger as follows:

1 Feb   Sold goods on credit to AB Ltd for £500.

Sales

                                          1 Feb   AB Ltd   500

AB Ltd

1 Feb   Sales   500

2 Feb   Purchased goods on credit from CD Ltd for £250.

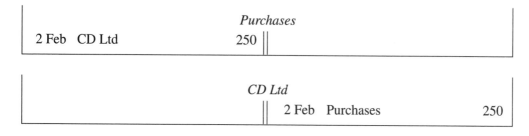

Purchases

2 Feb CD Ltd	250		

CD Ltd

		2 Feb Purchases	250

The business or person to whom goods are sold on credit is referred to as a *trade debtor*. In the above example, AB Ltd is a debtor of the business whose books are being prepared. The term 'debtor' arises from the existence of an account in the seller's books which contains more on the debit side than on the credit side.

The business or person from whom goods are purchased on credit is referred to as a *trade creditor*. In the above example, CD Ltd is a creditor of the business whose books are being prepared. The term 'creditor' arises from the existence of an account in the purchaser's books which contains more on the credit side than on the debit side.

A second event which may occur when goods are bought and sold on credit is the return of goods. This can arise because some of the goods delivered were not ordered, or are defective, etc. When goods are returned the seller sends the buyer a credit note. This is recorded in the ledger as follows:

3 Feb   AB Ltd returned goods invoiced for £100.

*Sales returns
(inwards)*

3 Feb AB Ltd	100		

AB Ltd

1 Feb Sales	500	3 Feb Sales returns	100

4 Feb   Returned goods to CD Ltd invoiced for £50.

*Purchases returns
(outwards)*

		4 Feb CD Ltd	50

CD Ltd

4 Feb Purchases returns	50	2 Feb Purchases	250

The debtor's and creditor's accounts thus show the amounts of money owed at any point in time.

The third event which occurs when goods are bought and sold on credit is the transfer of money in settlement of the debt. This is recorded in the ledger as follows:

5 Feb   Received from AB Ltd cash of £400.

Cash

5 Feb AB Ltd	400	

AB Ltd

1 Feb Sales	500	3 Feb Sales returns	100	
		5 Feb Cash	400	

6 Feb   Paid CD Ltd £200 in cash.

Cash

	6 Feb CD Ltd	200

CD Ltd

4 Feb Purchases returns	50	2 Feb Purchases	250
6 Feb Cash	200		

An illustration of both credit and cheque transactions is shown in Example 4.2.

Example 4.2

E. Blue commenced business in 1 July 19X0 as a wholesale greengrocer with a capital in the bank of £2,000. His transactions during July were as follows:

 1 July   Bought a second-hand van by cheque for £800
 3 July   Paid insurance on the van by cheque for £150
 7 July   Purchased goods costing £250 on credit from A. Brown
11 July   Sold goods on credit to B. Green amounting to £450
14 July   Paid carriage outwards by cheque amounting to £20
16 July   Returned goods to A. Brown of £50
18 July   Repairs to van paid by cheque: £30
20 July   B. Green returned goods of £75
23 July   Sent A. Brown a cheque for £140
26 July   Received a cheque from B. Green for £240
31 July   Paid telephone bill by cheque: £65
31 July   Paid electric bill by cheque: £45

You are required to write up the accounts in the general ledger.

Debit			Credit		
Date	Details	Amount	Date	Details	Amount

Bank account

19X0			19X0		
1 July	Capital	2,000	1 July	Vehicles	800
26 July	B. Green	240	3 July	Motor expenses	150
			14 July	Carriage outwards	20
			18 July	Motor expenses	30
			23 July	A. Brown	140
			31 July	Telephone and postage	65
			31 July	Light and heat	45

Capital

			1 July	Bank	2,000

Vehicles

1 July	Bank	800			

Motor expenses

3 July	Bank	150			
18 July	Bank	30			

Purchases

7 July	A. Brown	250			

A. Brown

16 July	Returns	50	7 July	Purchases	250
23 July	Bank	140			

Sales

			11 July	B. Green	450

B. Green

11 July	Sales	450	20 July	Returns	75
			26 July	Bank	240

Purchases returns (outwards)	
	16 July A. Brown 50

Sales returns (inwards)	
20 July B. Green 75	

Carriage outwards	
14 July Bank 20	

Telephone and Postage	
31 July Bank 65	

Light and heat	
31 July Bank 45	

Notes

1. The narrative in the details column of the expense accounts is 'bank' because the double entry is in the bank account.
2. Where there is more than one transaction relating to the same type of expenditure these are all entered in the same account (e.g. motor expenses). However, the purchase of a vehicle is shown in a different account from the running costs, referred to as an *asset account*.
3. Lighting and heating expenses, such as coal, electricity, gas, heating oil, etc., are usually all entered in an account called light and heat. The same principle is applied in the case of the telephone and postage account, the rent and rates account and the printing and stationery account.
4. Carriage outwards refers to haulage costs relating to goods that this business has sold and is responsible for delivering.
5. Sometimes a business pays cash into its bank account and at other times withdraws cash from its bank account. The ledger entries for these transactions are as follows:

   (a) Paying cash into the bank:
        Debit bank account
        Credit cash account
   (b) Withdrawing cash from a bank account:
        Debit cash account
        Credit bank account

A further related complication occurs where a business pays cash sales into its bank account. This can be treated as two transactions. The first being cash sales which are recorded as a debit in the cash account and a credit in the sales account. The second being the payment of this money into the bank which is recorded as in (a) above. Alternatively, where cash sales are banked on a regular basis, such as daily, the more common method of recording this is simply to debit the bank account and credit the sales account. There are thus no entries in the cash account.

Learning activity 4.2

Prepare a bank account for your cheque transactions over the forthcoming week or month. Make the necessary double entry in the other ledger accounts.

Summary

After being recorded in a book of prime entry all business transactions are entered in another book called the ledger. This is based on the double entry principle and comprises various accounts. Each account is divided into two halves, the left half called the debit side, and the right half called the credit side. The money value of every transaction is recorded once on each side of the ledger in different accounts. The main purposes of this system are to provide a means of ascertaining the total amount of each type of income and expenditure, and the value of the assets and liabilities at any point in time. When the total amount on the debit side of an account is greater than that on the credit side, the account is said to have a debit balance. When the reverse is the case, the account is said to have a credit balance. An account which contains a credit balance represents either an asset, expense or a loss. An account with a credit balance represents capital, a liability, income or a gain.

The ledger entries for cash transactions are made in a cash account (if in cash) or a bank account (if by cheque). These are then posted to the opposite side of another account representing the nature of the transaction. The ledger entries for credit transactions are more complicated because these are treated in accounting as comprising at least two separate transactions—the purchase (or sale) of goods on credit, and the settlement of the debt. The purchase of goods is debited to the purchasers' account and credited to a creditors' account. The sale of goods is credited to the sales account and debited to a debtors' account. When the creditor is paid this is credited to the cash (or bank) account and debited to the creditors' account. When money is received from a debtor this is debited to the cash (or bank) account and credited to the debtors' account.

Key terms and concepts

Account, asset account, bank account, capital account, cash account, credit side, debit side, double entry bookkeeping, drawings account, expense account, ledger, loan creditor, purchases account, sales account, trade creditor, trade debtor.

Exercises

An asterisk after the question number indicates that there is a suggested answer in the Appendix.

4.1.* H. George commenced business as a butcher on 1 October 19X6 with a capital in cash of £5,000. Her transactions during October 19X6, which were all in cash, are as follows:

    1 Oct Rent of shop: £200
    2 Oct Purchases of goods: £970
    4 Oct Bought fixtures and fittings: £1,250
    6 Oct Borrowed £3,500 from S. Ring
    9 Oct Purchased delivery van: £2,650
  12 Oct Sold goods for £1,810
  15 Oct Paid wages of £150
  18 Oct Purchases: £630
  19 Oct Drawings: £350
  21 Oct Petrol for van: £25
  22 Oct Printing costs: £65
  24 Oct Sales: £1,320
  25 Oct Repairs to van: £45
  27 Oct Wages: £250
  28 Oct Purchased stationery costing £35
  30 Oct Rates on shop: £400
  31 Oct Drawings: £175

You are required to record the above transactions in the ledger.

4.2.* L. Johnson started business on 1 March 19X8 with a capital of £10,000 in a bank current/cheque account. During March 19X8 he made the following transactions:

    1 Mar Paid £5,000 by cheque for a 10 year lease on a shop
    2 Mar Bought office equipment by cheque at a cost of £1,400
    4 Mar Bought goods costing £630 from E. Lamb on credit
    6 Mar Paid postage of £35 by cheque
    9 Mar Purchases by cheque: £420
  11 Mar Sold goods on credit to G. Lion for £880
  13 Mar Drawings by cheque: £250
  16 Mar Returned goods costing £180 to E. Lamb
  18 Mar Sold goods and received a cheque for £540 in payment
  20 Mar Paid telephone bill by cheque: £120
  22 Mar G. Lion returned goods invoiced at £310
  24 Mar Paid gas bill by cheque: £65
  26 Mar Sent E. Lamb a cheque for £230
  28 Mar Received a cheque for £280 from G. Lion
  30 Mar Paid electricity bill of £85 by cheque
  31 Mar Paid bank charges of £45

You are required to enter the above transactions in the ledger.

4.3. N. Moss commenced business on 1 May 19X4 with a capital of £5,000 of which £1,000 was in cash and £4,000 in a bank current/cheque account. Her transactions during May were as follows:

1 May   Borrowed £2,000 from Birmingham Bank Ltd in the form of a cheque
2 May   Paid rent of £750 by cheque
5 May   Paid wages of £120 in cash
8 May   Purchased goods for £1,380 by cheque
10 May   Sold goods for £650 cash
12 May   Drawings in cash: £200
15 May   Bought goods on credit for £830 from S. Oak
18 May   Sold goods on credit for £1,250 to K. Heath
20 May   Bought shop fittings of £2,500 by cheque
23 May   Paid water rates of £325 in cash
25 May   Paid gas bill of £230 by cheque
27 May   Returned goods costing £310 to S. Oak
28 May   K. Heath returned goods with an invoice value of £480
29 May   N. Moss introduced further capital of a £3,000 cheque
30 May   Bought stationery of £90 in cash
31 May   Sent S. Oak a cheque for £300
31 May   Received a cheque for £500 from K. Heath.

You are required to show the above transactions in the general ledger.

5. The balancing of accounts and the trial balance

Learning objectives

After reading this chapter the student should be able to:

1. Explain the meaning of the key terms and concepts listed at the end of the chapter.
2. Balance and close ledger accounts.
3. Describe the nature and purposes of a trial balance.
4. Prepare a trial balance from the ledger or a list of ledger account balances.
5. Describe the types of errors that cause a trial balance to disagree.
6. Make the ledger entries necessary to correct errors that cause a trial balance to disagree.

The balancing of accounts

At the end of every accounting period it is necessary to balance each account in the ledger. This would have to be done at least annually, and more likely monthly.

The procedure for balancing an account is as follows:

1. Leave two lines under the last entry in the ledger account and draw parallel lines on the top and bottom lines of the next line in the amounts column on each side.
2. Add up each side of the ledger account and calculate the difference using a separate piece of paper.
3. If the amount of the debit side exceeds that on the credit side, enter the difference on the credit side immediately after the last entry on that side. Where the amount on the credit side exceeds that on the debit side, the difference should be entered on the debit side immediately after the last entry on that side. This should be ascribed as the 'balance carried down' (c/d) and appear above the parallel lines. Enter the same figure on the opposite side below the parallel lines. This should be described as the 'balance brought down' (b/d).
4. Enter the total of each side of the ledger account between the parallel lines. These two figures should now be the same.

This is illustrated below using three accounts from the answer to Example 4.2.

Bank account

19X0			19X0		
1 July	Capital	2,000	1 July	Vehicle	800

44

26 July	B. Green	240	3 July	Motor expenses	150
			14 July	Carriage outwards	20
			18 July	Motor expenses	30
			23 July	A. Brown	140
			31 July	Telephone	65
			31 July	Light and heat	45
			31 July	Balance c/d	990
		2,240			2,240
1 Aug	Balance b/d	990			

A. Brown

16 July	Returns	50	7 July	Purchases	250
23 July	Bank	140			
31 July	Balance c/d	60			
		250			250
			1 Aug	Balance b/d	60

B. Green

11 July	Sales	450	20 July	Returns	75
			26 July	Bank	240
			31 July	Balance c/d	135
		450			450
1 Aug	Balance c/d	135			

If an account contains only one entry it is not necessary to calculate the balance. Where an account contains several entries all on the same side the balance may be entered as described above. However, in practice it is common just to enter a sub-total as follows:

Motor expenses

3 July	Bank	150
18 July	Bank	30
		180

If the total of each side of an account is the same there will be no balance and thus the total amount is simply entered between the parallel lines.

The purposes and preparation of a trial balance

The trial balance is neither a part of the ledger nor a book of prime entry (although it is often prepared on paper with the same ruling as the journal). It is a list of the balances in the ledger at the end of an accounting period, divided between those accounts with debit balances and those with credit balances. Since every transaction recorded in the ledger consists of both a debit and a credit entry, the total of the balances on each side should be the same. This is checked by entering on the trial balance the balance of each account in the ledger, and adding up each side.

The purposes of the trial balance may be summarized as follows:

1. To ascertain whether the total of the accounts with debit balances equals the total of the accounts with credit balances. If so, this proves that the same money value of each transaction has been entered on both sides of the ledger. It also proves the arithmetic accuracy of the ledger accounts. However, a trial balance can agree but there may still be errors in the ledger. For example, an amount may have been entered on the correct side but in the wrong account, or a transaction could have been completely omitted.
2. The trial balance is also used for the preparation of final accounts which show the profit or loss for the period and the assets and liabilities at the end of that period. In practice this is done in the form of an extended trial balance. This is discussed further in Chapter 14.

An illustration of the preparation of a trial balance is given in Example 5.1. The amounts are taken from the ledger in Example 4.2.

Example 5.1
E. Blue
Trial balance as at 31 July 19X0

Name of account	Debit	Credit
Bank	990	
Capital		2,000
Vehicles	800	
Motor expenses	180	
Purchases	250	
A. Brown		60
Sales		450
B. Green	135	
Purchases returns		50
Sales returns	75	
Carriage outwards	20	
Telephone and postage	65	
Light and heat	45	
	2,560	2,560

If a trial balance does not agree, students often fail to take a systematic approach to ascertaining the reason. It is therefore suggested that the following procedure be adopted, which will minimize effort and time spent looking for the errors.

1. Recast the trial balance.
2. Check that no account has been omitted from the trial balance. This sometimes happens with the cash and bank balances as they are usually in separate books.

3. Check that each amount entered in the trial balance is on the correct side. This is quick to do once you become familiar with the nature of different ledger accounts.
4. Check to see that the amounts entered in the trial balance are the same as those shown in the ledger accounts.
5. If the error has still not been found it will then be necessary to check all the entries in the ledger.

It is also worth noting that often in examinations no marks are given for correct trial balance totals. The student will therefore only lose marks for the error that caused it to disagree. Thus do not spend more than a few minutes trying to make a trial balance agree.

A further illustration of the preparation of a trial balance is given in Example 5.2. The data in the question would not be presented in this manner in practice, but the question is a useful way of testing your knowledge of which ledger accounts contain debit balances and which contain credit balances.

Example 5.2

The following is a list of the balances appearing in the general ledger of T. Wall at 30 September 19X0:

	£
Capital	32,890
Drawings	5,200
Loan from M. Head	10,000
Cash	510
Bank overdraft	1,720
Sales	45,600
Purchases	29,300
Returns inwards	3,800
Returns outwards	2,700
Carriage inwards	960
Carriage outwards	820
Trade debtors	7,390
Trade creditors	4,620
Land and buildings	26,000
Plant and machinery	13,500
Listed investments	4,800
Interest paid	1,200
Interest received	450
Rent received	630
Salaries	3,720
Repairs to buildings	810
Plant hire charges	360
Bank charges	240

You are required to prepare a trial balance.

T. Wall
Trial balance as at 30 September 19X0

Name of account	Debit	Credit
Capital		32,890
Drawings	5,200	
Loan from M. Head		10,000
Cash	510	
Bank overdraft		1,720
Sales		45,600
Purchases	29,300	
Returns inwards	3,800	
Returns outwards		2,700
Carriage inwards	960	
Carriage outwards	820	
Trade debtors	7,390	
Trade creditors		4,620
Land and buildings	26,000	
Plant and machinery	13,500	
Listed investments	4,800	
Interest paid	1,200	
Interest received		450
Rent received		630
Salaries	3,720	
Repairs to buildings	810	
Plant hire charges	360	
Bank charges	240	
	98,610	98,610

Notes

1. The cash account can only have a debit balance. However, the bank account may contain either a debit or a credit balance. A credit balance occurs where the business is overdrawn at the bank.
2. The items 'Trade debtors' and 'Trade creditors' are common in trial balances. These are the totals of the individual personal accounts of credit customers and suppliers respectively.
3. The item 'Listed investments' refers to money invested in stocks and shares that are listed/quoted on the International Stock Exchange, London.

Learning activity 5.1

Prepare a trial balance for the ledger relating to Learning activities 4.1 and 4.2.

Type of errors that cause a trial balance to disagree

As explained above, one of the purposes of a trial balance is to ascertain whether the total of the debit balances in the ledger is the same as the total of the credit balances. The reason why this may not be the case is because of the existence of one or more of the following errors:

1. *Arithmetic errors*, such as the incorrect addition of the amounts on one side of an account, and/or in the calculation of a balance.
2. *Posting errors*. These may take three forms: (a) where a transaction has been entered on one side of the ledger but not on the other side; (b) where a transaction has been entered twice on the same side; (c) where the correct amount of a transaction has been entered on one side of the ledger but the wrong amount has been entered on the other side. The most common errors of the latter type are of two forms: (i) where a zero is omitted from the end of an amount (for example, transaction for £33,000 entered on one side of the ledger as £3,300), and (ii) *transposed figures* where the correct amount of a transaction has been entered on one side of the ledger but two or more of the figures have been reversed when the entry was made on the other side. For example, an amount of £323 entered on one side as £332. A difference of 9, 90, or other number divisible by 9 on the trial balance may indicate that there is a transposition error.
3. *Extraction error*, where the correct balance is shown in the ledger account but the wrong amount is entered on the trial balance, or the correct amount is put on the wrong side.

The first two types of error above have to be corrected by a one-sided ledger entry. The correction may be done by changing the figure to the correct amount. However, it is argued that the correction should take the form of another entry so that some record exists of the correction of the error. Furthermore, in practice it is frequently impractical to correct errors by simply changing a figure to the correct amount, since this usually also necessitates numerous other changes to subsequent totals and balances (e.g. an error in the bank account which occurred several months previously). Where an error is corrected by means of another entry it is essential that the details of the correction indicate where the original error is located.

An illustration of the types of error described above and their correction is given in Example 5.3.

Example 5.3
The following examples are shown in the same order as the types of error described above.

Error		*Correction*	
(1)	The debit side of the cash account has been overcast by £1,000 and this is reflected in the balance brought down	(1)	Credit the cash account with £1,000
(2a)	Cash purchases of £200 have been credited in the cash account but not entered in the purchases account.	(2a)	Debit the purchases account with £200

(2b) Rent paid of £50 has been credited in the cash account but also credited in error to the rent account

(2b) Debit the rent account with £100 (i.e. £50 × 2)

(2cii) Bank charges of £23 shown in the bank account have been debited to the bank charges account as £32

(2cii) Credit the bank charges account with £9

(3) The sales account shows a balance of £2,000 which has been entered on the trial balance as £200

(3) Delete the wrong figure on the trial balance and insert the correct amount

Summary

At the end of each accounting year every account in the ledger must be balanced. The balance is the difference between the monetary amounts on the two sides of an account. This is entered in the account as a balance carried down at the end of the year, and as a balance brought down at the start of the following year.

The balances on all the ledger accounts are used to prepare a trial balance on a loose sheet of paper. A trial balance is a list of the balances in a ledger at a specific point in time, divided between those with debit balances and those with credit balances. Since every transaction is recorded in the ledger on both the debit and credit sides, the total of the accounts with debit should equal the total of the accounts with credit balances. The main purpose of the trial balance is to ascertain whether this is the case, and thus to check the accuracy of the ledger. Another function of the trial balance is to facilitate the preparation of final accounts.

If the total of the debit balances in a trial balance does not equal the total of the credit balances, this means that there are certain types of errors. The types of errors that cause a trial balance to disagree comprise arithmetic errors, posting errors, and extraction errors. These will need to be corrected by a one-sided entry in the ledger or trial balance.

Key terms and concepts

Account balance, arithmetic error, credit balance, debit balance, extraction error, posting error, transposed figures, trial balance.

Exercises

An asterisk after the question number indicates that there is a suggested answer in the Appendix.

5.1. Explain the main purposes of a trial balance.

5.2.* Prepare a trial balance for Example 4.1.

5.3.* Prepare a trial balance from your answer to Question 4.1 in Chapter 4.

5.4.* Prepare a trial balance from your answer to Question 4.2 in Chapter 4.

5.5. Prepare a trial balance from your answer to Question 4.3 in Chapter 4.

5.6.* The following is a list of balances in the ledger of C. Rick at 31 May 19X3:

	£
Cash at bank	2,368
Purchases	12,389
Sales	18,922
Wages and salaries	3,862
Rent and rates	504
Insurance	78
Motor expenses	664
Printing and stationery	216
Light and heat	166
General expenses	314
Premises	10,000
Motor vehicles	3,800
Fixtures and fittings	1,350
Debtors	3,896
Creditors	1,731
Cash in hand	482
Drawings	1,200
Capital	12,636
Bank loan	8,000

Prepare a trial balance.

5.7.* The following is a list of balances in the general ledger of R. Keith at 30 June 19X2:

	£
Capital	39,980
Drawings	14,760
Loan—Bromsgrove Bank	20,000
Leasehold premises	52,500
Motor vehicles	13,650
Investment	4,980
Trade debtors	2,630
Trade creditors	1,910
Cash	460
Bank overdraft	3,620
Sales	81,640
Purchases	49,870
Returns outwards	960
Returns inwards	840
Carriage	390
Wages and salaries	5,610
Rent and rates	1,420
Light and heat	710
Telephone and postage	540

Printing and stationery	230
Bank interest	140
Interest received	620

Prepare a trial balance.

5.8. Describe the types of error that cause a trial balance to disagree.

5.9.* A trial balance failed to agree. On investigation the following errors were found:
  (a) Wages of £250 have been credited in the cash account but no other entry has been made.
  (b) The credit side of the sales account has been undercast by £100 and this is reflected in the balance brought down.
  (c) Purchases of £198 shown in the purchases' account have been entered in the creditors' account as £189.
  (d) The drawings account contains a balance of £300, but this has been entered on the trial balance as £3,000.
  (e) Bank interest received of £86 has been credited in the bank account and the interest received account.

Describe the entries needed to correct the above errors.

6.   Day books and the journal

Learning objectives

After reading this chapter the student should be able to:

1. Explain the meaning of the key terms and concepts listed at the end of the chapter.
2. Describe the transactions and documents that are recorded in each of the day books and the journal.
3. Enter credit transactions in the appropriate day books or journal and post these to the relevant ledger accounts.
4. Prepare opening journal entries to record capital introduced other than cash, and the takeover of another sole trader.

The contents of the day books and the journal

Before a transaction is recorded in the ledger, it must first be entered in a book of prime entry. These are intended to facilitate the posting of the ledger, in that transactions of the same type are entered in the same book of prime entry which is periodically posted to the ledger in total (rather than one transaction at a time).

There are several books of prime entry. This chapter examines only those which are used to record credit transactions. These consist of: (1) the sales day book; (2) the purchases day book; (3) the sales returns day book; (4) the purchases returns day book; and (5) the journal. The transactions recorded in these books are as follows:

The sales day book

This is used to record the sale on credit of those goods bought specifically for resale. It is written up from copies of the sales invoices and debit notes retained by the seller. The amount entered in the sales day book is after deducting trade discount. At the end of each calendar month the total of the sales book is credited to the sales account in the ledger and the amount of each invoice and debit note is debited to the individual debtors' accounts.

The purchases day book

This is used to record the purchase on credit of those goods bought specifically for resale. It is written up from the invoices and debit notes received from suppliers. The amount entered in the purchases day book is after deducting trade discount. At the end of each calendar month the total of the purchases day book is debited to the purchases account in the ledger and the amount of each invoice and debit note received is credited to the individual creditors' accounts.

The sales returns day book

This is used to record the credit notes sent to customers relating to goods they have returned or where they have been overcharged on the invoice. Note that the entry is made when a credit note has been issued, and not when the goods are returned or the amount of the invoice is queried. The sales returns day book is written up from copies of the credit notes retained by the seller. The amount shown in the sales returns day book is after deducting trade discount. At the end of each calendar month the total of the sales returns day book is debited to the sales returns account in the ledger and the amount of each credit note credited to the individual debtors' accounts.

The purchases returns day book

This is used to record the credit notes received from suppliers relating to goods returned or where there has been an overcharge on the invoice. Note that the entry is made when a credit note is received and not when the goods are returned or the amount of the invoice is queried. The purchases returns day book is written up from the credit notes received from suppliers. The amount entered in the purchases returns day book is after deducting trade discount. At the end of each calendar month the total of the purchases returns day book is credited to the purchases returns account in the ledger and the amount of each credit note received is debited to the individual creditors' accounts.

The journal

The journal is used to record a variety of things, most of which consist of accounting adjustments, such as the correction of errors, rather than transactions. However, the journal is also used to record transactions which are not appropriate to any other book of prime entry, the most common being the purchase and sale of *fixed assets* on credit. These are items not specifically bought for resale but to be used in the production and distribution of those goods normally sold by the business. Fixed assets are durable goods that usually last for several years and are normally kept by the business for more than one year. Examples include land and buildings, plant and machinery, motor vehicles, furniture, fixtures and fittings, office equipment, etc.

Unlike the sales, purchases and returns day books, the journal has debit and credit columns. These are not a part of the double entry in the ledger. They are used to indicate what entries are going to be made in the ledger in respect to a given transaction or adjustment. Each entry in the journal consists of the name of the account which is to be debited (and the amount) and the name of the account that is to be credited (and the amount). The nature of the entry must also be explained in a narrative which commonly starts with the word 'being'. This is of particular importance because of the variety of entries that are made in the journal.

An illustration of the entries in the above five books of prime entry is given in Example 6.1.

Another use of the journal is referred to as *opening entries*. This is an entry to record the capital introduced into the business by the owner when it consists of assets in addition to cash and, possibly, liabilities. As the name implies, this entry usually occurs when the business is formed and the books are being opened. However, it is also used to record the takeover of another business. This is illustrated in Example 6.2.

Example 6.1

Bright Spark is an electrical goods wholesaler. The transactions during June 19X0, which are all on credit, were as follows:

1 June   Bought on credit from Lights Ltd various bulbs with a retail price of £1,000 and received 20 per cent trade discount

4 June   Sold goods on credit to Electrical Retailers Ltd for £500 and allowed them 10 per cent trade discount on this amount

8 June   Sent Electrical Retailers Ltd a credit note for goods returned that had a retail value of £300

10 June   Sold goods on credit to Smith Retailers Ltd for £600 after deducting 40 per cent trade discount

12 June   Purchased goods with a retail value of £1,000 from Switches Ltd who allowed us 30 per cent trade discount

15 June   Purchases on credit from Cables Ltd goods costing £550

16 June   Sent Smith Retailers Ltd a credit note for goods returned which had a retail value of £100

18 June   Switches Ltd sent us a credit note for £300 in respect of goods returned

19 June   Received a credit note for goods returned to Lights Ltd that had a retail value of £250

25 June   Sold goods to General Builders Ltd on credit for £250

27 June   Sent General Retailers Ltd a credit note for £50 to rectify an overcharge on their invoice

28 June   Sold goods on credit to Electrical Retailers Ltd at a price of £560

29 June   Purchased on credit a motor van from Brown Ltd which costs £800

30 June   Sold on credit to London Trading Co. some fixtures and fittings no longer required in the shop for £350. (Prior to this the business owned fixtures costing £1,000.)

You are required to make the necessary entries in the books of prime entry and general ledger.

Sales day book

Date	Name of debtor	Our invoice number	Folio	Amount £
19X0				
4 June	Electrical Retailers Ltd			450
10 June	Smith Retailers Ltd			600
25 June	General Retailers Ltd			250
28 June	Electrical Retailers Ltd			560
				£1,860

Sales returns day book

Date	Name of debtor	Our credit note number	Folio	Amount £
19X0				
8 June	Electrical Retailers Ltd			270
16 June	Smith Retailers Ltd			60
27 June	General Retailers Ltd			50
				£380

Purchases day book

Date	Name of creditor	Our ref. no. for supplier's invoice	Folio	Amount £
19X0				
1 June	Lights Ltd			800
12 June	Switches Ltd			700
15 June	Cables Ltd			550
				£2,050

Purchases returns day book

Date	Name of creditor	Our ref. no. for supplier's credit note	Folio	Amount £
19X0				
18 June	Switches Ltd			300
19 June	Lights Ltd			200
				£500

The ledger

Debit			Credit		
Date	Details	Amount	Date	Details	Amount

Sales

			30 June	Total per sales day book	1,860

Electrical Retailers Ltd

4 June	Sales	450	8 June	Returns	270
28 June	Sales	560			

Smith Retailers Ltd

10 June	Sales	600	16 June	Returns	60

General Retailers Ltd

25 June	Sales	250	27 June	Returns	50

Sales returns

30 June	Total per sales returns day book	380

Purchases

30 June	Total per purchases day book	2,050

Lights Ltd

19 June	Returns	200	1 June	Purchases	800

Switches Ltd

18 June	Returns	300	12 June	Purchases	700

Cables Ltd

	15 June	Purchases	550

Purchases returns

	30 June	Total per purchases returns day book	500

Notes

1. The amount posted to the sales account is the total credit sales for the month as shown in the sales day book; the amounts entered in the debtors' accounts are the amounts of each invoice as shown in the sales day book.
2. The amount posted to the purchases account is the total credit purchases for the month as shown in the purchases day book; the amounts posted to the creditors' accounts are the amounts of the invoices as shown in the purchases day book.
3. The entries for returns are made in the same way. That is, the totals of the returns day books are entered in the returns accounts and the amount of each credit note is posted to the appropriate debtor's or creditor's account.

The journal

Date	Details (account in which the ledger entry is to be made)	Folio	Debit amount	Credit amount
19X0 29 June	Motor vehicles Dr To Brown Ltd Being purchased on credit of motor van reg. no. ABC123		800	800
30 June	London Trading Co. Dr To fixtures and fittings Being sale on credit of shop fittings		350	350

The ledger

Motor vehicles

29 June	Brown Ltd	800

Brown Ltd

		29 June	Motor vehicles	800

Fixtures and fittings

1 June	Balance b/d	1,000	30 June	London Trading Co.	350
			30 June	Balance c/d	650
		1,000			1,000

1 July	Balance b/d	650

London Trading Co.

30 June	Fixtures and fittings	350

Notes

1. The fixtures and fittings that were sold must obviously have already been owned by the business. Their cost is therefore included in the balance brought down on the debit side of the fixtures and fittings account along with the cost of other fixtures and fittings owned at that date.
2. The London Trading Co. is referred to as a sundry debtor and Brown Ltd as a sundry creditor.

Example 6.2

A. King went into business on 1 March 19X6 by taking over a firm owned by B. Wright. The purchase consideration was £47,500 which had been computed by valuing the assets and liabilities that were taken over as follows:

	£
Shop	30,000
Fixtures and fittings	12,500
Stock	4,600
Trade debtors	3,100
Trade creditors	2,700

You are required to show the opening entries in the journal of A. King.

The journal

Date	Details/account		Debit	Credit
19X6 1 Mar	Land and buildings	Dr	30,000	
	Fixtures and fittings	Dr	12,500	
	Stock	Dr	4,600	
	Trade debtors	Dr	3,100	
	To trade creditors			2,700
	To capital			47,500
			50,200	50,200
	Being assets and liabilities introduced into business by owner from takeover of an existing business			

Notes

1. The ledger entries will consist of debiting and crediting the accounts shown above in the details column. In the case of debtors and creditors the amounts will be entered in the personal accounts of the individuals/firms concerned.
2. The capital of £47,000 is the difference between the total assets and liabilities brought into the business. This will be credited to the capital account.

Summary

Before a transaction is recorded in the ledger, it must first be entered in a book of prime entry. These are intended to facilitate the posting of the ledger, in that transactions of the same type are entered in the same book of prime entry which is periodically posted to the ledger in total rather than one transaction at a time.

Credit transactions are recorded in a set of books of prime entry known as day books. The sales day book is used to record the sale of goods on credit of those goods specifically bought for resale, and is written up from copies of the sales invoices. The purchases day book is used to record the purchase on credit of those goods intended for resale, and is written up from the invoices received from suppliers. The sales returns and purchases returns day books are used to record returns, and are written up from the credit notes.

The posting of day books to the ledger follows a common principle. The total of the day book is entered in the relevant nominal account (i.e. sales, purchases, sales returns or purchases returns), and the individual invoices or credit notes shown in the day book are posted to the debtors' or creditors' personal accounts.

Credit transactions not relating to goods for resale (or services), such as the purchase and sale of fixed assets, are recorded in another book of prime entry known as the journal. This is also used to record transactions which are not appropriate to any other book of prime entry, and various accounting adjustments that are not the subject of a transaction such as the correction of errors. The format of the journal includes a details column and two money columns labelled debit and credit. The narrative in the details column and amounts in the money columns indicates the entries that will be made in the ledger in respect of a given transaction or item.

Key terms and concepts

Fixed assets, journal, opening entries, purchases day book, purchases returns day book, sales day book, sales returns day book, trade discount.

Exercises

An asterisk after the question number indicates that there is a suggested answer in the Appendix.

6.1. (a) Outline the purposes of those books of prime entry referred to as day books.
    (b) Describe the contents, and state which documents are used to write up each of the following:

        (i) The sales day book;
        (ii) The purchases day book;
        (iii) The sales returns day book;
        (iv) The purchases returns day book.

6.2. (a) State two fundamentally different types of transactions/items that are recorded in the journal.
    (b) Describe how these two transactions are recorded in the journal.

6.3. B. Jones is in business as a builders' merchants. The following credit transactions took place during April 19X5:

    1 Apr   Bought goods on credit from Brick Ltd for £725.
    2 Apr   Sold goods on credit to Oak Ltd for £410.
    4 Apr   Bought goods costing £315 from Stone Ltd on credit.
    7 Apr   Sold goods on credit to Pine Ltd for £870.
    11 Apr   Bought goods costing £250 from Slate Ltd on credit.

15 Apr   Sold goods to Lime Ltd for £630 on credit.
17 Apr   Bought goods on credit from Brick Ltd for £290.
19 Apr   Received a credit note for £120 from Brick Ltd.
22 Apr   Sent Oak Ltd a credit note for £220.
24 Apr   Stone Ltd sent us a credit note for £75 in respect of goods returned.
27 Apr   Sent Pine Ltd a credit note for £360.

You are required to make the necessary entries in the books of prime entry and the general ledger.

6.4.* B. Player buys and sells soft furnishings and office equipment. During August 19X7 she had the following credit transactions:

1 Aug   Bought goods on credit from Desks Ltd which had a retail price of £1,000 and trade discount of 25 per cent.
3 Aug   Purchased goods with a retail price of £500 from Chairs Ltd who allowed 30 per cent trade discount.
6 Aug   Sold goods on credit to British Cars Ltd for £700 less 10 per cent trade discount.
10 Aug   Received a credit note from Desks Ltd in respect of goods returned which had a retail price of £300 and trade discount of 25 per cent.
13 Aug   Sold goods to London Beds Ltd on credit. These had a retail value of £800 and trade discount of 15 per cent.
16 Aug   Sent British Cars Ltd a credit note in respect of goods returned that were invoiced at a retail price of £300 less 10 per cent trade discount.
18 Aug   Purchased goods on credit from Cabinets Ltd that had a retail value of £900 and trade discount of 20 per cent.
21 Aug   Received a credit note from Chairs Ltd for goods returned that had a retail price of £200 and 30 per cent trade discount.
23 Aug   Sold goods on credit to English Carpets Ltd for £1,300 less 10 per cent trader discount.
25 Aug   Sent London Beds Ltd a credit note relating to an over charge of £100 in the retail value of those goods delivered on 13 August which carried trade discount of 15 per cent.

You are required to make the necessary entries in the books of prime entry and the ledger.

6.5.* Show the journal and ledger entries in respect of the following:

(a) On 20 April 19X5 purchased on credit a machine not for resale from Black Ltd at a cost of £5,300.
(b) On 23 April 19X5 sold on credit a motor vehicle for £3,600 to White Ltd. This had previously been used to deliver goods sold.
(c) On 26 April 19X5 purchased some shop fittings for £480 on credit from Grey Ltd. These were not for resale.
(d) On 28 April 19X5 sold on credit to Yellow Ltd for £270 a typewriter that had previously been used in the sales office.

6.6.* W. Green decided to go into business on 1 August 19X8 by purchasing a firm owned by L. House. The purchase consideration was £96,000 which had been computed by valuing the assets and liabilities that were taken over as follows:

	£
Premises	55,000
Plant and machinery	23,000
Goods for resale	14,600
Trade debtors	6,300
Trade creditors	2,900

You are required to show the opening entries in the journal and ledger of W. Green.

7. The cash book

Learning objectives

After reading this chapter the student should be able to:

1. Explain the meaning of the key terms and concepts listed at the end of the chapter.
2. Explain the relationship between a cash book and the cash and bank accounts in the ledger including the implications of it being a book of prime entry as well as a part of the double entry system.
3. Describe the format of two-column and three-column cash books.
4. Explain the function of the cash discount columns in cash books.
5. Enter transactions in a two-column or three-column cash book and post these to the appropriate ledger accounts.

Introduction

The pages of the cash book, like the ledger, are divided into two halves, the debit on the left and the credit on the right. A cash book can take one of three forms as follows:

1. A two-column cash book in which are recorded cash received and paid in one column on each side, and cheques received and paid in the other column on each side. This essentially combines and replaces the ledger accounts for cash and bank.
2. A two-column cash book in which are recorded cheques received and paid in one column on each side, and cash discount in the other column on each side (discussed further below).
3. A three-column cash book in which are recorded: (a) cash received and paid in one column on each side; (b) cheques received and paid in one column on each side; and (c) cash discount in the remaining column on each side (discussed further below).

In practice, cash received and paid is usually recorded in a separate petty cash book. Thus the cash book normally consists of a two-column cash book of type 2 above.

The two-column cash book

The two-column cash book is used to record receipts and payments by cheque. It is written up from the bank paying-in book and cheque book stubs. The cash book is used instead of a bank account in the ledger. This is because there are usually a large number of transactions involving the receipt and payment of cheques, and if these were recorded in a bank account in the ledger it would become cumbersome. Moreover it permits a division of labour in that one person can write up the cash book while another is working on the ledger. This also reduces the possibility of errors and provides a check on the work of the person who writes up the cash book where it is posted to the ledger by someone else.

In addition to being a book of prime entry, the cash book is also part of the double entry system. This, debits in this book are credited to an account in the ledger and no further entries are necessary. Similarly, credits in this book are debited to an account in the ledger and no further entries are necessary.

The two-column cash book gets its name from the existence of two money columns on the debit side and two on the credit side. The additional column on the debit side is used to record the *cash discount allowed* to debtors and the extra column on the credit side is used to record the *cash discount received* from creditors. Both of these additional columns are, like the day books, memorandum columns in that each item entered in these columns requires both a debit and credit in the ledger.

Cash discount is a reduction given (in addition to trade discount) by the supplier of goods to a buyer if the latter pays for them within a period stipulated by the seller at the time of sale. Often in practice all goods supplied during a particular calendar month must be paid for by the end of the following calendar month if cash discount is to be obtained. Note that cash discount is not deducted on the invoice but is calculated from the amount shown on the invoice, and deducted at the time of payment.

Apart from the entries in these two additional columns, the cash book is written up in the same way as the bank account. A debit balance on the cash book represents the amount of money the business has in the bank. Unlike the cash account, the cash book may have a credit balance which means the business has an overdraft at the bank.

An illustration of the entries in the two-columns cash book is given in Example 7.1.

Example 7.1
Using the answer to Example 6.1, enter the following transactions in a two-column cash book and write up the accounts in the general ledger.

Capital at 1 July £5,750
Bank balance at 1 July £4,750

Bright Spark has the following cheque receipts and payments during July.

1 July   Cash sales paid into the bank: £625
3 July   Received a cheque for £70 for goods sold
4 July   Paid rent by cheque: £200
6 July   Received a cheque from the London Trading Co. for £350
8 July   Paid an electricity bill by cheque: £50
11 July   Sent Brown Ltd a cheque for £800
13 July   Bought a car which cost £1,000 and paid by cheque
16 July   The owner of Bright Spark paid into the business a cheque for £900 as additional capital
20 July   Paid wages of £150 by cheque
23 July   Purchases paid for by cheque: £670
24 July   The proprietor withdrew a cheque for £100
31 July   Paid Lights Ltd a cheque for their June account of £600 and they allowed us 5 per cent cash discount

31 July   Sent Switches Ltd a cheque for their June account of £400 and deducted 2½ per cent cash discount

31 July   Paid Cables Ltd a cheque for £300 on account

31 July   Received from Smith Retailers Ltd a cheque for £525 after allowing them £15 cash discount

31 July   Received a cheque for £720 from Electrical Retailers Ltd in full settlement of their account, which amounted to £740

31 July   General Retailers Ltd paid £190 by cheque after deducting cash discount of £10 which was not allowed by us

The entries in the cash book are shown on page 66. As explained above, the cheques received and paid shown in the debit and credit amount columns are posted to the relevant ledger amounts in the normal manner. However, the amounts shown in the memorandum columns relating to the discount allowed and received require both a debit and credit entry in the ledger. In simple terms the entry for discount allowed is:

Debit   Discount allowed account
Credit   Debtor's personal account

Similarly the entry for discount received is:

Debit   Creditor's personal account
Credit   Discount received account

This can be illustrated using just two of the personal accounts in the above example as follows:

Smith Retailers Ltd

10 June	Sales	600	16 June	Returns	60
			31 July	Bank	525
			31 July	Discount allowed	15
		600			600

Discount allowed

| 31 July | Smith Retailers | 15 | | | |

Lights Ltd

19 June	Returns	200	1 June	Purchases	800
31 July	Bank	570			
31 July	Discount received	30			
		800			800

Discount received

| | | | 31 July | Lights Ltd | 30 |

The cash book

Debit side

Date	Details	Folio	Memo: Discount allowed	Debit amount
1 July	Balance	b/d		4,750
1 July	Sales			625
3 July	Sales			70
6 July	London Trading Co			350
16 July	Capital			900
31 July	Smith			
31 July	Retailers Ltd		15	525
31 July	Electrical Retailers		20	720
31 July	General Retailers Ltd			190
			35	8,130
1 Aug	Balance	b/d		3,900

Credit side

Date	Details	Folio	Cheque number	Memo: Discount received	Credit amount
4 July	Rent and rates		54301		200
8 July	Light and heat		2		50
11 July	Brown Ltd		3		800
13 July	Motor vehicles		4		1,000
20 July	Wages		5		150
23 July	Purchases		6		670
24 July	Drawings		7		100
31 July	Lights Ltd		8	30	570
24 July	Switches Ltd		9	10	390
31 July	Cables Ltd		10		300
31 July	Balance	c/d			3,900
				40	8,130

However, entering each item of discount in the discount allowed and discount received accounts individually is inefficient, and defeats the main objective of the two-column cash book. The memorandum columns in the two-column cash book are intended to provide a means of ascertaining the total discount allowed and discount received for the period. The total of the memorandum discount allowed column is debited to the discount allowed account and the amount of each item of discount allowed is credited to the individual debtors' accounts. Similarly the total of the memorandum discount received column is credited to the discount received account and the amount of each item of discount received is debited to the individual creditors' accounts.

It can thus be seen that the memorandum discount columns in the cash book operate on the same principle, and perform the same function, as day books. That is, they facilitate the bulk posting of transactions to the ledger by aggregating items of the same type. However, since they are not a part of the double entry system, each item requires both a debit and credit entry in the ledger.

The proper ledger entries for discount allowed and discount received can now be illustrated by completing Example 7.1 using the answer to Example 6.1 as follows:

The ledger

Sales

30 June	Total per sales returns day book	380	30 June	Total per sales day book	1,860
			1 July	Bank	625
			3 July	Bank	70

London Trading Co.

30 June	Fixtures and fittings	350	6 July	Bank	350

Fixtures and fittings

1 June	Balance b/d	1,000	30 June	London Trading Co.	350
			31 July	Balance c/d	650
		1,000			1,000
1 Aug	Balance b/d	650			

Capital

24 July	Bank—drawings	100	1 July	Balance b/d	5,750
31 July	Balance c/d	6,550	16 July	Bank—capital introduced	900
		6,650			6,650
			1 Aug	Balance b/d	6,550

Discount allowed

31 July	Total per cash book	35

Smith Retailers Ltd

10 June	Sales	600	16 June	Returns	60
			31 July	Bank	525
			31 July	Discount allowed	15
		600			600

Electrical Retailers Ltd

4 June	Sales	450	8 June	Returns	270
28 June	Sales	560	31 July	Bank	720
			31 July	Discount allowed	20
		1,010			1,010

General Retailers Ltd

25 June	Sales	250	27 June	Returns	50
			31 July	Bank	190
			31 July	Balance c/d	10
		250			250
1 Aug	Balance c/d	10			

Rent and Rates

4 July	Bank	200

Light and Heat

8 July	Bank	50

Brown Ltd

11 July	Bank	800	29 July	Motor vehicles	800

Motor vehicles

29 June	Brown Ltd	800	31 July	Balance c/d	1,800
13 July	Bank	1,000			
		1,800			1,800
1 Aug	Balance b/d	1,800			

Wages

20 July	Bank	150

Purchases

30 June	Total per purchases day book	2,050	30 June	Total per purchases returns day book	500
23 July	Bank	670			

Discount received

			31 July	Total per cash book	40

Lights Ltd

19 June	Returns	200	1 June	Purchases	800
31 July	Bank	570			
31 July	Discount received	30			
		800			800

Switches Ltd

18 June	Returns	300	12 June	Purchases	700
31 July	Bank	390			
31 July	Discount received	10			
		700			700

Cables Ltd

31 July	Bank	300	15 June	Purchases	550
31 July	Balance c/d	250			
		550			550
			1 Aug	Balance b/d	250

Notes

1. The personal accounts are usually balanced at the end of each month.
2. The entries in the purchases and sales accounts in respect of returns are an inferior alternative to having purchases returns and sales returns accounts.
3. The entry in the capital account in respect of drawings is an inferior alternative to having a drawings account.

The three-column cash book

The three-column cash book is not common in practice, but is sometimes required in examination questions. It can be seen as an extension of the two-column cash book described above. The additional column on each side is used to record cash received (debit side) and cash payments (credit side). These columns are intended to replace the cash account in the ledger. Thus the three-column cash book is used instead of the cash account and bank account in the ledger.

In addition to being a book of prime entry, the three-column cash book is also part of the double entry system. Thus entries in either the cash or bank columns require only one further entry in another ledger account on the opposite side.

The only additional complication that arises in the case of the three-columns cash book concerns cash paid into the bank and cash withdrawn from the bank. At this point the reader may find it useful to refer back to Note 5 of Example 4.2 which explains the double entry for these items. The form which this takes in the three-column cash book is as follows:

(a) Paying cash into the bank:

Debit   Bank account column
Credit   Cash account column

(b) Withdrawing cash from the bank:

Debit   Cash account column
Credit   Bank account column

The three-column cash book is not common in practice because in most businesses cash received and paid is usually recorded in a separate petty cash book instead of a cash account. This is discussed further in the next chapter.

An illustration of the three-column cash book is given in Example 7.2.

Example 7.2

B. Andrews is in business as a motor factor and parts agent. The balances shown in her cash book at 1 December 19X2 were: bank, £1,630 and cash, £820. The following receipts and payments occurred during December 19X2:

2 Dec   Received a cheque for £1,000 from J. Sutcliffe as a loan repayable in five years
3 Dec   Purchased a personal computer for £1,210 and paid by cheque
4 Dec   Purchased in cash goods for resale costing £340
5 Dec   Paid wages of £150 in cash
6 Dec   Cash sales paid into bank: £480
8 Dec   Purchases by cheque: £370
9 Dec   Cash sales of £160
11 Dec Cheque sales: £280
12 Dec Paid telephone bill of £320 by cheque
15 Dec Paid cash of £200 into bank
17 Dec Drawings by cheque: £250
18 Dec Bought stationery of £80 in cash
20 Dec Introduced additional capital in the form of a cheque for £500
21 Dec Paid water rates of £430 by cheque
23 Dec Withdrew cash of £100 from the bank
24 Dec Sent K. Vale a cheque for £530 after deducting cash discount of £40
24 Dec Received a cheque for £640 from A. Green who deducted £35 cash discount
27 Dec Paid M. Fenton £720 by cheque after deducting £25 cash discount
28 Dec J. Evans sent us a cheque for £860 after deducting £45 cash discount
29 Dec Received a cheque from B. Court for £920 who deducted £50 cash discount which we did not allow

You are required to enter the above transactions in a three-column cash book.

Cash book

Debit (left side)

Date	Details	Memo: Discount allowed	Bank	Cash
19X2				
1 Dec	Balance b/d	–	1,630	820
2 Dec	J. Sutcliffe –loan		1,000	
6 Dec	Sales		480	160
9 Dec	Sales			
11 Dec	Sales		280	
15 Dec	Cash		200	
20 Dec	Capital		500	
23 Dec	Bank			100
24 Dec	A. Green	35	640	
28 Dec	J. Evans	45	860	
29 Dec	B. Court		920	
		80	6,510	1,080
19X3				
1 Jan	Balance b/d	–	2,580	310

Credit (right side)

Date	Details	Memo: Discount received	Bank	Cash
3 Dec	Office equipment		1,210	
4 Dec	Purchases			340
5 Dec	Wages			150
8 Dec	Purchases		370	
12 Dec	Telephone		320	
15 Dec	Bank			200
17 Dec	Drawings		250	
18 Dec	Stationery			80
21 Dec	Rates		430	
23 Dec	Cash		100	
24 Dec	K. Vale	40	530	
27 Dec	M. Fenton	25	720	
31 Dec	Balance c/d		2,580	310
		65	6,510	1,080

Learning activity 7.1

Prepare a two-column cash book with cash and bank columns to record your cash and cheque transactions over the forthcoming week or month. Make the necessary double entry in the other ledger accounts.

Summary

The cash book is both a book of prime entry and part of the double entry system in the ledger, and thus has the same format as a ledger account. It usually takes one of two forms—a two-column cash book or a three-column cash book. The two-column cash book has two money columns on each side. One column on each side is used to record cheques received and paid. The other column on each side is used to record cash discount allowed and cash discount received. The two-column cash book replaces the bank account in the ledger, and is written up from the bank paying-in book and cheque book stubs. The three-column cash book has three money columns on each side. Two of these are the same as the two-column cash book. The third is used to record cash receipts and payments, and is written up from copies of the receipts. The three-column cash book replaces the bank and cash accounts in the ledger.

Because the cash book is a part of the double entry system, entries in the cash book in respect of cash and cheque transactions need only to be posted to the opposite side of the relevant ledger account. However, this is not the case with regard to the entries in the cash discount columns. These columns are memorandum, and essentially intended to serve the same purpose as day books, namely to facilitate the periodic bulk posting of items of the same type. Thus the total of the memo discount allowed column is debited to the discount allowed account in the ledger, and the individual amounts credited to the relevant debtors' personal accounts. Similarly the total of the memo discount received column of the cash book is credited to the discount received account, and the individual amounts debited to the relevant creditors' personal accounts.

Key terms and concepts

Cash book, cash discount, discount allowed, discount received, three-column cash book, two-column cash book.

Exercises

An asterisk after the question number indicates that there is a suggested answer in the Appendix.

7.1. Describe the different forms of two- and three-column cash books with which you are familiar.

7.2. Describe the entries in the cash book and ledger in respect of discount allowed and discount received.

7.3. B. Jones is in business as builders' merchants. The following receipts and payments by cheque took place during May 19X5:

   1 May   Bank balance per cash book: £3,680

   3 May   Introduced additional capital: £2,000

   4 May   Sales by cheque: £840

   7 May   Purchases by cheque: £510

10 May   Paid wages by cheque: £200

13 May   Paid rent by cheque: £360

15 May   Cash sales paid into bank: £490

18 May   Purchased shopfittings for £2,450

20 May   Paid gas bill of £180

23 May   Bought stationery by cheque: £70

26 May   Drawings by cheque: £250

31 May   Sent Brick Ltd a cheque for £850 after deducting £45 cash discount

31 May   Received a cheque from Oak Ltd for £160 after deducting £30 cash discount

31 May   Paid Stone Ltd £220 after deducting cash discount of £20

31 May   Pine Ltd sent us a cheque for £485 after deducting £25 cash discount

31 May   Sent Slate Ltd a cheque for £480 after deducting cash discount of £40. However, Slate Ltd did not allow the discount

31 May   Lime Ltd sent us a cheque for £575

Show the entries in respect of the above in a two-column cash book.

7.4. (a) Using your answers to Question 6.3 in Chapter 6 and Question 7.3 above, make the necessary entries in the general ledger given a balance on the capital account at 1 May 19X5 of £3,680; and

(b) Prepare a trial balance at 31 May 19X5.

7.5.* B. Player buys and sells soft furnishings and office equipment. During September 19X7 the following receipts and payments occurred:

   1 Sept   Bank balance per cash book: £1,950

   1 Sept   Cash balance per cash book: £860

   3 Sept   Cash sales paid into bank: £470

   4 Sept   Cash purchases: £230

   6 Sept   Paid electricity bill of £510 by cheque

   9 Sept   Sales by cheque: £380

10 Sept   Drew a cheque for £250 in respect of wages

12 Sept   Cash sales: £290

15 Sept   Paid £40 in cash for travelling expenses

16 Sept   Paid water rates by cheque: £410

19 Sept   Drawings in cash: £150

20 Sept   Purchases by cheque: £320

21 Sept   Paid postage of £30 in cash

22 Sept   Paid cash of £350 into bank

24 Sept   Introduced further capital of £500 by cheque

25 Sept   Purchased a delivery vehicle for £2,500 and paid by cheque

26 Sept   Received a cheque for £1,000 from B. Jones as a three-year loan

27 Sept	Returned goods costing £170 and received a cash refund
28 Sept	Paid tax and insurance on delivery vehicle of £280 in cash
29 Sept	Withdrew cash of £180 from bank
30 Sept	Received a cheque from British Cars Ltd for £350 after deducting £10 cash discount
30 Sept	Received a cheque from London Beds Ltd for £580 after deducting £15 cash discount
30 Sept	Paid Desks Ltd a cheque for £500 after deducting £25 cash discount
30 Sept	Paid Chairs Ltd a cheque for £190 after deducting £20 cash discount
30 Sept	Received a cheque from English Carpets Ltd for £1,100 after deducting £70 cash discount. However, this cash discount was not allowed
30 Sept	Paid Cabinets Ltd a cheque for £500 on account

Enter the above in a three-column cash book.

7.6.* Using your answers to Question 6.4 in Chapter 6 and Question 7.5 above:

(a) make the necessary entries in the ledger given a balance on the capital account at 1 September 19X7 of £2,810; and

(b) prepare a trial balance at 30 September 19X7.

8. The petty cash book

Learning objectives

After reading this chapter the student should be able to:

1. Explain the meaning of the key terms and concepts listed at the end of the chapter.
2. Explain the relationship between a petty cash book and the cash account in the ledger including the implications of the petty cash book being a book of prime entry as well as a part of the double entry system.
3. Describe the format of a columnar petty cash book.
4. Explain the function of the analysis columns in a columnar petty cash book.
5. Describe the petty cash imprest system and its advantages.
6. Enter transactions in a columnar petty cash book using the imprest system, and post these to the appropriate ledger accounts.

Introduction

The petty cash book is used to record the receipt and payment of small amounts of cash. Any large amounts of cash received and cash takings are usually paid into the bank and thus recorded in the cash book. The petty cash book is written up from receipts and petty cash vouchers (where employees are reimbursed expenses).

The petty cash book is used instead of a cash account in the ledger. This is because there are usually a large number of transactions in cash, and if these were recorded in a cash account in the ledger it would become cumbersome. Like the cash book, it also permits a division of labour and facilitates improved control. In addition to being a book of prime entry, the petty cash book is also part of the double entry system. Thus debits in this book are credited to an account in the ledger and no further entries are necessary. Similarly, credits in this book are debited to an account in the ledger and no further entries are necessary.

The columnar petty cash book

It is usual for a petty cash book to have analysis columns on the credit side. Each column relates to a particular type of expenditure, such as postage, stationery, travelling expenses, etc. These are intended to facilitate the posting of entries to the ledger. Every item of expenditure is entered both in the credit column and an appropriate analysis column. At the end of each calendar week or month the total of each analysis column is debited to the relevant account in the ledger. Thus, instead of posting each transaction to the ledger separately, expenditure of the same type is collected together in each analysis column and the total for the period posted to the relevant ledger account.

The imprest system

Many firms also operate their petty cash on an imprest system. At the beginning of each period (week or month) the petty cashier has a fixed amount of cash referred to as a 'float'. At the end of each period (or the start of the next) the petty cashier is reimbursed the exact amount spent during the period, thus making the float up to its original amount. The reimbursement usually takes the form of a cheque drawn for cash. The amount of the petty cash float is determined by reference to the normal level of petty cash expenditure in each period.

The advantages of the imprest system are as follows:

1. It facilitates control of the total petty cash expenditure in each period as the petty cashier cannot spend more than the amount of the float except by applying to the management for an increase.
2. It deters theft of cash by the petty cashier since a large cash balance cannot be accumulated by drawing cash from the bank at irregular intervals.
3. The entries in the petty cash book are kept up to date because the cash expenditure is not reimbursed until the petty cash book is written up and the total amount of expenditure for the period is known.
4. It discourages the practice of loans and subs from petty cash since these would have to be accounted for at the end of the period, and in addition may result in insufficient cash to meet the necessary expenditure.

An illustration of a columnar petty cash book and the imprest system is shown in Example 8.1.

Example 8.1

A. Stone uses a columnar petty cash book to record his cash payments. He also operates an imprest system with a float of £150. During August 19X6 the cash transactions were as follows:

  1 Aug   Postage stamps: £5
  2 Aug   Cleaning materials: £13
  4 Aug   Telegram: £2
  5 Aug   Gratuity to delivery man: £4
  7 Aug   Tea, milk, etc.: £1
  9 Aug   Rail fare: £11
 10 Aug   Paper clips and pens: £6
 13 Aug   Window cleaner: £10
 18 Aug   Travelling expenses: £7
 21 Aug   Envelopes: £3
 22 Aug   Postage stamps: £9
 24 Aug   Stationery: £14
 27 Aug   Taxi fare: £12
 28 Aug   Office cleaning: £8
 31 Aug   Received reimbursement to make float up to £150

You are required to make the necessary entries in the petty cash book using appropriate analysis columns, and show the relevant ledger accounts.

The petty cash book

Debit Amount £	Date	Details	Amount £	Postage £	Cleaning £	Stationery £	Travelling expenses £	Miscellaneous expenses £
b/d 150	19X6							
	1 Aug	Stamps	5	5				
	2 Aug	Materials	13		13			
	4 Aug	Telegram	2	2				
	5 Aug	Gratuity	4					4
	7 Aug	Tea and milk	1					1
	9 Aug	Rail fare	11				11	
	10 Aug	Clips and pens	6			6		
	13 Aug	Windows	10		10			
	18 Aug	Travelling	7				7	
	21 Aug	Envelopes	3			3		
	22 Aug	Stamps	9	9				
	24 Aug	Stationery	14			14		
	27 Aug	Taxi	12				12	
	28 Aug	Office	8		8			
105	31 Aug	Reimbursement	105	16	31	23	30	5
	31 Aug	Balance c/d	150					
255			255					
b/d 150	1 Sept							

In some firms the cash reimbursement is made at the beginning of the next period, in which case the entries are as follows:

Debit	Date	Details	Amount £	Postage £	Cleaning £	Stationery £	Travelling expenses £	Miscellaneous expenses £
	31 Aug	Totals	105	16	31	23	30	5
	31 Aug	Balance c/d	45					
150			150					
b/d 45								
105	1 Sept	Reimbursement						
150								

The ledger

Telephone and postage

31 Aug   Total per PCB   16

Cleaning

31 Aug   Total per PCB   31

Printing and stationery

31 Aug   Total per PCB   23

Travelling and entertaining

31 Aug   Total per PCB   30

Miscellaneous expenses

31 Aug   Total per PCB   5

Cash book

31 Aug   Cash   105

Notes

1. When designing a columnar petty cash book it is necessary first to decide on the appropriate number of analysis columns. This is done by identifying the number of different types of expenditure for which there is more than one transaction. In Example 8.1 there are four different types, namely postage, cleaning, stationery and travelling expenses. These four plus a column for miscellaneous expenses give five columns. The headings for each of these columns should be the same as the name of the ledger account to which the total of the column will be posted.

2. The details column of the petty cash book is used to describe the nature of each transaction rather than the name of the ledger account containing the double entry, since this is given at the head of the analysis column in which the item is entered.

3. The items entered in the miscellaneous expenses column often have to be entered in several different ledger accounts according to the nature of each transaction.

4. When cash is withdrawn from the bank to restore the float to its original amount the ledger entry consists of:

   Debit petty cash book
   Credit cash book (bank account)

5. When answering examination questions which contain cash and cheque items but do not specifically require a petty cash book, it is advisable to use a three-column cash book.

Learning activity 8.1

Prepare a columnar petty cash book for your cash transactions over the forthcoming week or month. Make the necessary double entry in the other ledger accounts.

Summary

The petty cash book is both a book of prime entry and a part of the double entry system in the ledger, and thus has the same format as a ledger account. It is used to record cash receipts and payments, and is written up from copies of the receipts and petty cash vouchers. The petty cash book replaces the cash account in the ledger, and thus entries in this book need only to be posted to the opposite side of the relevant ledger accounts.

The most common form of petty cash book is a columnar petty cash book. This has several analysis columns on the credit side, each relating to a particular type of expenditure. These columns are memorandum, and essentially intended to serve the same purpose as day books, namely to facilitate the periodic bulk posting of transactions of the same type.

Many organizations also operate their petty cash on an imprest system. This essentially comprises a fixed cash float which is replenished at the end of each period by an amount equal to that period's cash expenditure. The imprest system has several very important advantages including facilitating control of the total cash expenditure for a period, deterring the theft of cash, discouraging cash loans/subs, and ensuring that the entries in the petty cash book are kept up to date.

Key terms and concepts

Columnar petty cash book, imprest system, petty cash book.

Exercises

An asterisk after the question number indicates that there is a suggested answer in the Appendix.

8.1. (a) Describe the purpose and format of a columnar petty cash book.
(b) Explain how you would determine the appropriate number of analysis columns.

8.2. (a) Describe how a petty cash imprest system operates.
(b) Explain how such a system facilitates control.

8.3.* C. Harlow has a petty cash book which is used to record his cash receipts and payments. This also incorporates an imprest system which has a float of £400. During February 19X2 the following cash transactions took place:

  1 Feb Purchases: £31
  3 Feb Wages: £28
  6 Feb Petrol for delivery van: £9
  8 Feb Bus fares: £3
11 Feb Pens and pencils: £8
12 Feb Payments for casual labour: £25
14 Feb Repairs to delivery van: £17

16 Feb Typing paper: £15
19 Feb Goods for resale: £22
20 Feb Train fares: £12
21 Feb Repairs to premises: £35
22 Feb Postage stamps: £6
23 Feb Drawings: £20
24 Feb Taxi fares: £7
25 Feb Envelopes: £4
26 Feb Purchases: £18
27 Feb Wages: £30
28 Feb Petrol for delivery van: £14

On 28 February 19X2 the cash float was restored to £400.

Record the above in the petty cash book using appropriate analysis columns and make the necessary entries in the ledger.

8.4. The Oakhill Printing Co. Ltd operates its petty cash account on the imprest system. It is maintained at a figure of £80 on the first day of each month. At 30 April 19X7 the petty cash box held £19.37 in cash. During May 19X7, the following petty cash transactions arose:

19X7		£
1 May	Cash received to restore imprest	to be derived
1 May	Bus fares	0.41
2 May	Stationery	2.35
4 May	Bus fares	0.30
7 May	Postage stamps	1.70
7 May	Trade journal	0.95
8 May	Bus fares	0.64
11 May	Correcting fluid	1.29
12 May	Typewriter ribbons	5.42
14 May	Parcel postage	3.45
15 May	Paper clips	0.42
15 May	Newspapers	2.00
16 May	Photocopier repair	16.80
19 May	Postage stamps	1.50
20 May	Drawing pins	0.38
21 May	Train fare	5.40
22 May	Photocopier paper	5.63
23 May	Display decorations	3.07
23 May	Correcting fluid	1.14
25 May	Wrapping paper	0.78
27 May	String	0.61
27 May	Sellotape	0.75
27 May	Biro pens	0.46
28 May	Typewriter repair	13.66
30 May	Bus fares	2.09
1 June	Cash received to restore imprest	to be derived

Required:

Open and post the company's petty cash account for the period 1 May to 1 June 19X7 inclusive and balance the account at 30 May 19X7

In order to facilitate the subsequent double entry postings, all items of expense appearing in the 'payments' column should then be analysed individually into suitably labelled expense columns. (ACCA)

9. The final accounts of sole traders

Learning objectives

After reading this chapter the student should be able to:

1. Explain the meaning of the key terms and concepts listed at the end of the chapter.
2. Explain the purpose and structure of profit and loss accounts including the subtotals for gross profit and net profit.
3. Explain the purpose and structure of balance sheets including the sub-totals for net current assets, total assets less current liabilities, and net assets.
4. Describe the nature of administrative expenses, selling and distribution expenses, fixed assets, current assets, current liabilities, long-term liabilities, and capital.
5. Explain the relevance of stock and the cost of sales in the determination of the gross profit.
6. Prepare a simple trading and profit and loss account and balance sheet from a trial balance using either an account/horizontal format or vertical format.
7. Make all the necessary ledger account and journal entries relating to the preparation of trading and profit and loss accounts.

Introduction

Final accounts consist of a profit and loss account and balance sheet. These are prepared at the end of the business's accounting year after the trial balance has been completed. Some businesses also produce final accounts half yearly, quarterly or even monthly. The purpose, structure and preparation of the profit and loss account and balance sheet are discussed below.

The purpose and structure of profit and loss accounts

The profit and loss account provides a summary of the results of a business's trading activities during a given accounting year. It shows the profit or loss for the year. The purpose of a profit and loss account is to enable users of accounts, such as the owner, to evaluate the performance of a business for a given accounting year. It may be used to determine the amount of taxation on the profit.

Chapter 2 explained that profit can be defined as the amount which could be taken out of a business as drawings in the case of a sole trader or partnership, or is available for distribution as dividends to shareholders in the case of a company, after maintaining the value of the capital of a business. Profit is not the same as an increase in the amount of money the business possesses. It is the result of applying certain accounting rules known as concepts and bases to the transactions of the business. These will be described in detail in the next chapter.

The basic format of a profit and loss account is as follows:

ABC
Profit and loss account for the year ended . . .

	£	£
Sales		X
Less: cost of sales		X
Gross profit		X
Less: other costs and expenses:		
Selling and distribution costs	X	
Administrative expenses	X	
Interest payable on loans	X	
		X
Net profit		X

In the accounts of sole traders and partnerships the actual composition of each of the above groupings of costs would be shown. Selling and distribution costs might consist of, for example, advertising expenditure, the wages of delivery van drivers, motor expenses including petrol and repairs, etc. Administrative expenses usually comprise the salaries of office staff, rent and rates, light and heat, printing and stationery, telephone and postage, etc. The published final accounts of companies contain a classification of costs similar to that shown above.

The purpose and structure of balance sheets

The balance sheet is a list of the assets and liabilities of a business at the end of a given accounting year. It therefore provides information about the resources and debts of the reporting entity. This enables users of accounts to evaluate its financial position in particular whether the business is likely to be unable to pay its debts. The balance sheet is like a photograph of the financial state of affairs of a business at a specific point in time.

Balance sheets contain five groups of items as follows:

1. *Fixed assets*
   These are items not specifically bought for resale but to be used in the production or distribution of those goods normally sold by the business. Fixed assets are durable goods that usually last for several years, and are normally kept by a business for more than one accounting year. Examples of fixed assets include land and buildings; plant and machinery; motor vehicles; office equipment; furniture, fixtures and fittings.
2. *Current assets*
   These are items that are normally kept by a business for less than one accounting year. Indeed, the composition of each type of current asset is usually continually changing. Examples include stocks, trade debtors, short-term investments, money in a bank cheque account and cash.

3. *Current liabilities*
   These are debts owed by a business that are payable within one year (often considerably less) of the date of the balance sheet. Examples include trade creditors and bank overdrafts.
4. *Long-term liabilities*
   These are debts owed by a business that are not due until after one year (often much longer) from the date of the balance sheet. Examples include loans and mortgages.
5. *Capital*
   This refers to the amount of money invested in the business by the owner(s).

The structure of a balance sheet is shown in the diagram below. Note that the items shown in an italic typeface are sub-totals or totals which should be shown on the balance sheet:

ABC
Balance sheet as at . . .

Fixed assets

+

$\left\{\begin{array}{l} \text{Current assets} \\ -\ \text{Current liabilities} \\ =\ \textit{Net current assets} \end{array}\right\}$

=

Total assets less current liabilities

−

Long-term liabilities

=

Net assets

=

Capital

Learning activity 9.1

Prepare a balance sheet listing your assets and liabilities, or those of your family. Use an appropriate method of classifying the assets and liabilities and show the relevant totals and sub-totals.

The gross profit: stock and the cost of sales

The first stage in the determination of the profit for the year involves calculating the gross profit. It is usually carried out in the profit and loss account. However, this part of the profit and loss account is sometimes presented as a separate account referred to as the *trading account*.

The *gross profit* for a given period is computed by subtracting the cost of goods sold/cost of sales from the sales revenue. It is important to appreciate that the cost of goods sold is not usually the same as the amount of purchases. This is because most businesses will have purchased goods that are unsold at the end of the accounting period. This is referred to as *stock or inventory*.

A manufacturing business will have a number of different types of stocks. However, for simplicity the following exposition is confined to non-manufacturing businesses whose stock consists of goods purchased for resale that have not undergone any further processing by the entity.

The *cost of sales* is determined by taking the cost of goods in stock at the start of the period, adding to this the cost of goods purchased during the period, and subtracting the cost of goods unsold at the end of the period. The cost of sales is then deducted from the sales revenue to give the gross profit. This is illustrated in Example 9.1.

Example 9.1

S. Mann, whose accounting year ends on 30 April, buys and sells one type of aluminium engine head for sports cars. On 1 May 19X8 there were 50 units in stock which had cost £100 each. During the subsequent accounting year he purchased a further 500 units at a cost of £100 each and sold 450 units at a price of £150 each. There were 100 units which cost £100 each that had not been sold at 30 April 19X9. You are required to compute the gross profit for the year.

S. Mann
Trading account for the year ended 30 April 19X9

Units		£	£
450	Sales revenue		67,500
	Less: Cost of goods sold:		
50	Stock of goods at 1 May 19X8	5,000	
500	*Add*: Goods purchased during the year	50,000	
550	Cost of goods available for sale	55,000	
	Less: Stock of goods at		
100	30 April 19X9	10,000	
450	Cost of sales		45,000
	Gross profit for the year		22,500

Notes

1. The numbers of units are not usually shown in the trading account. They have been included in the above to demonstrate that the cost of sales relates to the number of units that were sold.

The preparation of final accounts

The trading account

The trading account is an account in the ledger and is thus a part of the double entry system. It is used to ascertain the gross profit and is prepared by transferring the balances on the sales, purchases and returns accounts to the trading account. In addition certain entries are required in respect of stock. These are as follows:

1. Stock at the end of the previous period:
    Debit trading account
    Credit stock account
2. Stock at the end of the current period:
    Debit stock account
    Credit trading account

Note that the stock at the end of the previous period will be the stock at the start of the current period. The ledger entries in respect of stocks are illustrated below using the data in Example 9.1. Prior to the preparation of the trading account the ledger will appear as follows:

Sales

	19X9		
	30 Apr	balance b/d	67,500

Purchases

19X9			
30 Apr	Balance b/d	50,000	

Stock

19X8			
30 Apr	Balance b/d	5,000	

The trading account will then be prepared as follows:

Sales

19X9			19X9		
30 Apr	Trading a/c	67,500	30 Apr	Balance b/d	67,500

Purchases

19X9			19X9		
30 Apr	Balance b/d	50,000	30 Apr	Trading a/c	50,000

Stock

19X8			19X9		
30 Apr	Balance b/d	5,000	30 Apr	Trading a/c	5,000
19X9					
30 Apr	Trading a/c	10,000			

S. Mann
Trading account for year ending 30 April 19X9

	£		£
Stock at 1 May 19X8	5,000	Sales	67,500
Purchases	50,000	Stock at 30 April 19X9	10,000
Gross profit c/d	22,500		
	77,500		77,500
		Gross profit b/d	22,500

Notes

1. The gross profit is the difference between the two sides of the trading account and must be brought down to the opposite side of the account.
2. No dates are shown in the trading account since they appear as part of the heading of the account.
3. When the trading account is prepared in account form the stock at the end of the year may be shown as either a credit entry or deducted on the debit side as follows:

S. Mann
Trading account for the year ended 30 April 19X9

Opening stock	5,000	Sales	67,500
Add: Purchases	50,000		
	55,000		
Less: Closing stock	10,000		
Cost of sales	45,000		
Gross profit c/d	22,500		
	67,500		67,500
		Gross profit b/d	22,500

This has the advantage of showing the cost of sales.

4. The trading account is an account in the ledger and thus part of the double entry system. However, when it is prepared for submission to the management, the owner(s) of a business or the Inland Revenue, it is often presented vertically as shown at the start of Example 9.1.
5. No entries other than those shown above (and the correction of errors) should be made in a stock account. It is not a continuous record of the value of stock.
6. The debit balance in the stock account on 30 April 19X8 was the result of an entry identical to that on 30 April 19X9.
7. The stock show in a trial balance will always be that at the end of the previous year (and thus the opening stock of the year to which the trial balance relates).

The profit and loss account

The profit and loss account is an account in the ledger and thus a part of the double entry system. It is used to ascertain the net profit (or loss) for the year and is prepared in the same way as the trading account. That is, the balances on the income and expense accounts in the ledger are transferred to the profit and loss account by means of a double entry.

The balance sheet

The balance sheet is a list of the balances remaining in the ledger after the trading and profit and loss accounts have been prepared. In effect it is like a trial balance except that the balance sheet is presented using a different format. Note that the balances are not transferred to the balance sheet by means of a double entry.

In practice, and in examinations, it is usual to prepare final accounts from the information given in the trial balance. However, it is important to appreciate that the ledger entries described above also have to be done, although students are not normally expected to show them in their answer to examination questions.

An illustration of the preparation of final accounts, including the required ledger entries, is shown in Example 9.2.

Example 9.2

The following is the trial balance of A. Dillon at 31 March 19X0.

	Debit	Credit
Capital		42,140
Drawings	13,600	
Loan from S. Rodd		10,000
Bank	5,800	
Cash	460	
Sales		88,400
Purchases	46,300	
Sales return	5,700	
Purchases returns		3,100
Stock at 1 April 19X9	8,500	
Carriage inwards	2,400	
Carriage outwards	1,600	
Trade debtors	15,300	
Trade creditors		7,200
Motor vehicles	23,100	
Fixtures and fittings	12,400	
Wages and salaries	6,800	
Rent	4,100	
Light and heat	3,200	
Telephone and postage	1,700	
Discount allowed	830	
Discount received		950
	151,790	151,790

The stock at 31 March 19X0 was valued at £9,800. The loan from S. Rodd is repayable on 1 January 19X4.

You are required to prepare the trading and profit and loss accounts and a balance sheet.

Sales			
Trading a/c	88,400	Balance b/d	88,400

Sales returns			
Balance b/d	5,700	Trading a/c	5,700

Purchases			
Balance b/d	46,300	Trading a/c	46,300

Purchases returns

Trading a/c	3,100	Balance b/d	3,100

Stock

Balance b/d	8,500	Trading a/c	8,500
Trading a/c	9,800		

Carriage inwards

Balance b/d	2,400	Trading a/c	2,400

Carriage outwards

Balance b/d	1,600	Profit and loss a/c	1,600

Wages and salaries

Balance b/d	6,800	Profit and loss a/c	6,800

Rent

Balance b/d	4,100	Profit and loss a/c	4,100

Light and heat

Balance b/d	3,200	Profit and loss a/c	3,200

Telephone and postage

Balance b/d	1,700	Profit and loss a/c	1,700

Discount allowed

Balance b/d	830	Profit and loss a/c	830

Discount received

Profit and loss a/c	950	Balance b/d	950

Drawings

Balance b/d	13,600	Capital	13,600

Capital

Drawings	13,600	Balance b/d	42,140
Balance c/d	49,660	Profit for year	21,120
	63,260		63,260
		Balance b/d	49,660

All other accounts contain only the balances shown in the trial balance.

A. Dillon
Trading and profit and loss accounts for the year ended 31 March 19X0

	£	£		£
Stock at 1 April 19X9		8,500	Sales	88,400
Purchases	46,300		*Less*: returns	5,700
Less: Returns	3,100			82,700
	43,200			
Add: Carriage inwards	2,400	45,600		
		54,100		
Less: Stock at 31 March 19X0		9,800		
Cost of sales		44,300		
Gross profit c/d		38,400		
		82,700		82,700
Carriage outwards		1,600	Gross profit b/d	38,400
Wages and salaries		6,800	Discount received	950
Rent		4,100		
Light and heat		3,200		
Telephone and postage		1,700		
Discount allowed		830		
Net profit c/d		21,120		
		39,350		39,350
Capital a/c		21,120	Net profit b/d	21,120

A. Dillon
Balance sheet as at 31 March 19X0

Credit	£		*Debit*		£
Capital			*Fixed assets*		
Balance at 1 April 19X9	42,140		Motor vehicles		23,100
Add: Profit for year	21,120		Fixtures and fittings		12,400
	63,260				35,500
Less: Drawings	13,600				
Balance at 31 March 19X0	49,660		*Current assets*		
			Stock	9,800	
Long-term liabilities			Debtors	15,300	
Loan from S. Rodd	10,000		Bank	5,800	
			Cash	460	
Current liabilities					31,360
Creditors	7,200				
	66,860				66,860

Notes

1. The gross profit is the difference between the two sides of the trading account and must be brought down to the opposite side of the profit and loss account.
2. The net profit is the difference between the two sides of the profit and loss account. This is brought down to the credit side of the profit and loss account and then transferred to the capital account by debiting the profit and loss account and crediting the capital account. The reason for this transfer is because the profit belongs to the owner and it increases the amount of capital she has invested in the business.
3. If the debit side of the profit and loss account exceeds the credit side this is shown as a net loss (carried down) on the credit side and debited to the capital account.
4. The balance on the drawings account at the end of the period must be transferred to the capital account.
5. Each of the transfers from the ledger accounts to the trading and profit and loss accounts should also be entered in the journal.
6. Notice that the debit balances remaining in the ledger after the profit and loss account has been prepared are shown on the right-hand side of the balance sheet and the credit balances on the left-hand side. This may seem inconsistent with the debit and credit sides of the ledger being on the left and right respectively. However, it is a common form of presentation in accounting.

   Like the trial balance, the total of each side of the balance sheet should be the same. That is, the total of the ledger accounts with debit balances should equal the total of the ledger accounts with credit balances. If this is not the case it indicates that an error has occurred in the preparation of the trading and profit and loss account (or the balance sheet).
7. The current assets in the balance sheet are shown in what is called their reverse order of liquidity. The latter refers to how easily assets can be turned into cash.
8. The current liabilities are sometimes shown on the balance sheet as a deduction from current assets.
9. The entries on the balance sheet in respect of capital are a summary of the capital account in the ledger.
10. Carriage inwards is added to the cost of purchases because it relates to the haulage costs of goods purchased. Carriage outwards is shown in the profit and loss account because it relates to the haulage costs of goods sold and is thus a selling and distribution expense.

When the trading and profit and loss account and balance sheet are presented to the owner(s) of a business and the Inland Revenue it is common to use a vertical format. This is illustrated below using the data in Example 9.2.

A. Dillon
Trading and profit and loss accounts for the year ending 31 March 19X0

	£	£	£
Sales			88,400
Less: Returns			5,700
			82,700
Less: Cost of sales:			
Stock at 1 April 19X9		8,500	
Add: Purchases	46,300		
Less: Returns	3,100		
		43,200	
Add: Carriage inwards		2,400	
		54,100	
Less: Stock at 31 March 19X0		9,800	
			44,300
Gross profit			38,400
Add: Discount received			950
			39,350
Less: Expenditure:			
Carriage outwards		1,600	
Wages and salaries		6,800	
Rent		4,100	
Light and heat		3,200	
Telephone and postage		1,700	
Discount allowed		830	18,230
Net profit for the year			21,120

Balance sheet as at 31 March 19X0

	£	£
Fixed assets		
Motor vehicles		23,100
Fixtures and fittings		12,400
		35,500
Current assets		
Stock	9,800	
Debtors	15,300	
Bank	5,800	
Cash	460	
	31,360	
Less: Current Liabilities		
Creditors	7,200	
Net current assets		24,160
Total assets less current liabilities		59,660
Less: Long-term liabilities		
Loan from S. Rodd		10,000
Net assets		49,660

Capital

Balance at 1 April 19X9	42,140
Add: Profit for year	21,120
	63,260
Less: Drawings	13,600
Balance at 31 March 19X0	49,660

Summary

Final accounts comprise a trading and profit and loss account, and balance sheet. These are prepared at the end of the accounting year after the trial balance has been completed. The trading and profit and loss accounts provide a summary of the results of a business's trading activities during a given accounting year. They show the gross and net profit or loss for the year, and enable users to evaluate the performance of the enterprise. The balance sheet is a list of the assets and liabilities (and capital) of a business at the end of a given accounting year. It enables users to evaluate the financial position of the enterprise, including whether it is likely to be able to pay its debts. In the balance sheet assets are classified as either fixed or current, and liabilities as either current or long term. The balance sheet also contains several useful sub-totals comprising net current assets, total assets less current liabilities, and net assets.

The gross profit is the difference between the sales revenue and the cost of sales. The cost of sales is the amount of purchases as adjusted for the opening and closing stocks. The stock at the end of an accounting year has to be entered in the ledger by debiting a stock account and crediting the trading account. The trading and profit and loss accounts are then prepared by transferring the balances on the nominal accounts in the ledger to these accounts.

The balance sheet is a list of the balances remaining in the ledger after the trading and profit and loss accounts have been prepared. It is extracted in essentially the same way as a trial balance, but presented using a more formal layout to show the two groups of both assets and liabilities, and pertinent sub-totals.

Key terms and concepts

Balance sheet, capital, cost of sales, current assets, current liabilities, fixed assets, gross profit, inventory, long-term liabilities, loss, net assets, net current assets, net profit, profit, profit and loss account, stock, total assets less current liabilities, trading account.

Exercises

An asterisk after the question number indicates that there is a suggested answer in the Appendix.

9.1. (a) Explain the purposes of a profit and loss account and a balance sheet.

  (b) Describe the structure of each.

9.2. Explain the relevance of stocks of goods for resale in the determination of the gross profit.

9.3. Explain each of the entries in the following stock account:

	Stock		
Trading account	4,600	Trading account	4,600
Trading account	6,300		

9.4.* The following is the trial balance of R. Woods at 30 September 19X6:

	Debit	Credit
	£	£
Stock 1 October 19X5	2,368	
Purchases	12,389	
Sales		18,922
Salaries and wages	3,862	
Rent and rates	504	
Insurance	78	
Motor expenses	664	
Printing and stationery	216	
Light and heat	166	
General expenses	314	
Premises	5,000	
Motor vehicles	1,800	
Fixtures and fittings	350	
Debtors	3,896	
Creditors		1,731
Cash at bank	482	
Drawings	1,200	
Capital		12,636
	33,289	33,289

The stock at 30 September 19X6 is valued at £2,946.

You are required to prepare a trading and profit and loss account for the year ended 30 September 19X6 and a balance sheet at that date.

9.5.* On 31 December 19X3, the trial balance of Joytoys showed the following accounts and balances:

	Debit	Credit
	£	£
Bank	500	
Capital		75,000
Bank loan		22,000
Inventory	12,000	
Purchases	108,000	
Sales		167,000
Rent, rates and insurance	15,000	
Plant and machinery at cost	70,000	

Office furniture and fittings at cost	24,000	
Discount allowed	1,600	
Bank interest	400	
Discount received		3,000
Wages and salaries	13,000	
Light and heat	9,000	
Drawings	10,000	
Returns outwards		4,000
Returns inwards	1,000	
Creditors		16,000
Debtors	22,500	
	287,000	287,000

You are given the following information:

1. The inventory at 31 December 19X3 was valued at £19,500.
2. The bank loan is repayable in 5 years' time.

You are required to prepare a trading and profit and loss account for the year ended 31 December 19X3, and a balance sheet at that date.

9.6.* The following is the trial balance of A. Evans as at 30 June 19X2:

	Debit £	Credit £
Capital		39,980
Drawings	14,760	
Loan—Solihull Bank		20,000
Leasehold premises	52,500	
Motor vehicles	13,650	
Investments	4,980	
Trade debtors	2,630	
Trade creditors		1,910
Cash	460	
Bank overdraft		3,620
Sales		81,640
Purchases	49,870	
Returns outwards		960
Returns inwards	840	
Carriage outwards	390	
Stock	5,610	
Rent and rates	1,420	
Light and heat	710	
Telephone and postage	540	
Printing and stationery	230	
Bank interest	140	
Interest received		620
	148,730	148,730

You are given the following additional information:

1. The stock at 30 June 19X2 has been valued at £4,920.
2. The bank loan is repayable on 1 June 19X5.

You are required to prepare a trading and profit and loss account for the year ended 30 June 19X2 and a balance sheet as at that date.

9.7. The following is the trial balance of J. Peters as at 30 September 19X0:

	Debit £	Credit £
Capital		32,890
Drawings	5,200	
Loan from A. Drew		10,000
Cash	510	
Bank overdraft		1,720
Sales		45,600
Purchases	29,300	
Returns inwards	3,800	
Returns outwards		2,700
Carriage inwards	960	
Carriage outwards	820	
Trade debtors	7,390	
Trade creditors		4,620
Land and buildings	26,000	
Plant and machinery	13,500	
Listed investments	4,800	
Interest paid	1,200	
Interest received		450
Rent received		630
Stock	3,720	
Repairs to buildings	810	
Plant hire charges	360	
Bank charges	240	
	98,610	98,610

Further information:

1. The stock at 30 September 19X0 was valued at £4,580.
2. The loan from A. Drew is repayable on 1 January 19X7.

You are required to prepare a trading and profit and loss account for the year ended 30 September 19X0 and a balance sheet at that date.

10. Accounting concepts, principles and conventions

Learning objectives

After reading this chapter the student should be able to:

1. Explain the meaning of the key terms and concepts listed at the end of the chapter.
2. Explain the nature, difference and interrelationship between accounting concepts, bases and policies.
3. Explain the nature of the accounting concepts of going concern, consistency, accruals, prudence, objectivity and materiality.
4. Apply accounting concepts to specific transactions and items in order to determine the most appropriate treatment in the accounts.
5. Discuss a variety of issues relating to possible inconsistencies between accounting concepts and their application in practice with particular reference to the prudence concept.

Introduction

An appreciation of the conceptual/theoretical foundations of financial accounting is fundamental to the understanding and interpretation of final accounts. This can be described as a set of rules, principles, postulates, conventions and methods. However, to avoid confusion, in 1971 the Accounting Standard Steering Committee (ASSC or ASC) issued *Statement of Standard Accounting Practice No 2—Disclosure of Accounting Policies* (SSAP2) which describes the conceptual foundations of accounting as comprising accounting concepts, accounting bases and accounting policies. These are discussed below.

Accounting concepts, bases and policies

The measurement of profit and the valuation of assets and liabilities involves a number of *accounting concepts*. These are defined in SSAP2 as 'broad basic assumptions which underlie the periodic financial accounts of business enterprises'.[1]

However, accounting concepts do not in themselves provide sufficient guidance as to how they should be applied. This requires the specification of *accounting bases*. These are defined in SSAP2 as 'the methods which have been developed for expressing or applying fundamental accounting concepts to financial transactions and items'.[1]

There are several different accounting bases which could be applied to a particular item or transaction. Each company has to choose that basis which is most appropriate in the circumstances. These are referred to as *accounting policies*, and are defined in SSAP2 as 'the specific accounting bases judged by business enterprises to be most appropriate to their circumstances and adopted by them for the purpose of preparing their financial accounts'.[1]

Various accounting bases and policies will be discussed in depth in subsequent chapters. This chapter examines the nature of certain accounting concepts and their implication for the preparation of final accounts.

Accounting concepts in SSAP2

There are a considerable number of accounting concepts, some of which were referred to earlier (see Chapter 2) such as the accounting entity concept, the accounting period, the money/unit of measurement concept, etc. However, SSAP2 identifies what is described as four fundamental accounting concepts. These are explained below.

The going concern/continuity concept

The going concern concept refers to the assumption that an 'enterprise will continue in operational existence for the foreseeable future'.[1] The implication of this is that assets will be valued at their historical cost and shown in the balance sheet at this value. It is assumed that the business will continue to operate over the remaining useful life of the assets. Similarly, monetary assets and liabilities, such as debtors and creditors, are shown in the balance sheet at the amount that will be received and paid in the ordinary course of business. However, if there is reason to believe that the entity will not be able to continue in business, the assets should be valued on a cessation basis. That is, at their net realizable value.

The consistency/comparability concept

The consistency concept dictates that there should be 'consistency of accounting treatment of like items within each accounting period and from one period to the next'.[1] For example, if the purchase of certain types of tools and equipment is treated as fixed assets, then similar tools and equipment bought in the same period should be treated in the same way. Furthermore, the tools and equipment should also be treated as a fixed asset in subsequent years.

The purpose of this is to limit the possibility of misrepresentation, and to ensure that meaningful comparisons can be made between the results of different accounting periods. Judgments about a firm's performance and financial position depend to a large extent on the validity of comparisons. It is therefore essential that items and transactions of the same type are accounted for in the same way.

The accruals concept and the matching principle

According to SSAP2, under the accruals concept 'revenue and costs are accrued (that is, recognized as they are earned or incurred, not as money is received or paid), matched with one another so far as their relationship can be established or justifiably assumed, and dealt with in the profit & loss account of the period to which they relate'.[1]

The accruals concept is usually taken to include the matching principle. However, it can be argued that these are two separate assumptions. This is probably a useful premiss for the purpose of the following explanation.

The matching principle is fundamental to the determination/identification of the point in time at which profits are deemed to occur. There is no natural or common-sense law about this. It is a convention which is generally accepted in accounting. The *matching principle* refers to the assumption that costs should be set against the revenue which they generate at the point in time when this arises. A classic example of the application of the matching principle is stock. Where goods are bought in one year but sold in the next, their cost is carried forward as goods in stock and set against the proceeds of sale in the year in which it occurs. This is expounded in SSAP9—*Stocks and Long Term Contracts*[2] as follows:

> The determination of profit for an accounting year requires the matching of costs with related revenues. (When costs) have been incurred in the expectation of future revenue, and when this will not arise until a later year it is appropriate to carry forward this cost to be matched with the revenue when it arises; the applicable concept is the matching of cost and revenue in the year in which the revenue arises rather than in the year in which the cost is incurred.

In terms of the calculation of the gross profit in the trading account, this process of carrying forward costs takes the form of the computation of the cost of sales. The cost is carried forward by being deducted from purchases in the form of the stock at the end of the year. It is brought forward to the following year in the form of the opening stock which is matched against the proceeds of sale by virtue of its being included in the cost of sales.

Another example of the application of the matching principle is depreciation. This is discussed in depth in Chapter 11.

A more theoretical view of the matching principle is that it refers to ascertaining profit on the basis of a cause and effect relationship. Costs cause or give rise to certain effects which take the form of revenue. Matching is thus the determination of profit by attributing specific causes to particular effects at the point in time at which the effects occur.

The accruals concept may be further subdivided into the realization concept, accrued costs and prepayments. The *realization or revenue recognition concept* refers to the assumption that a sale is deemed to have taken place at that point in time at which the goods are delivered or services provided and not when the proceeds of sale are received. In practice this is normally also the date on which the invoice is rendered. However, where the invoice is rendered some time after the date of delivery, the sale is deemed to have taken place on the date of delivery and not the date of the invoice. This is referred to in the above SSAP2 definition of the accruals concept as being the point in time at which revenue is 'earned'.

The *accrued costs concept* refers to the assumption that costs should be recognized as arising when they are incurred, and not as money is paid. That is, goods and services are deemed to have been purchased on the date they are received. This is referred to in the above SSAP2 definition of the accruals concept as being the point in time at which costs are 'incurred'. Thus services consumed for which no invoice has been received at the end of an accounting year (e.g. electricity, gas, telephone) are treated as a cost for that year, and the amount due as a liability.

Prepayments relate to services paid for in advance (e.g. rent, local government taxes, insurance, road tax) which have not been received at the end of an accounting year. These are treated as a cost of the following year and thus carried forward as an asset at the end of the current year. Accrued costs and prepayments are dealt with in depth in a later chapter.

The accruals concept and matching principle can be illustrated vividly by a simplified example. Suppose a business only had the following transactions:

15 Jan   purchased goods costing £100 on credit
15 Feb   paid for goods purchased on 15 January
15 Mar   sold on credit for £150 the goods purchased on 15 January
15 Apr   received payment for the goods sold on 15 March

The accruals (and matching) concept dictates that:

1. The cost of the goods was *incurred* in January.
2. The sales revenue was *earned* in March.
3. There is no profit or loss in January, February or April. The profit of £50 arose in March; the cost of the goods being carried forward as stock at the end of January and February.

The prudence/conservatism concept

The prudence concept is said to require that 'revenue and profits are not anticipated, but are recognised by inclusion in the profit and loss account only when realised in the form either of cash or of other assets the ultimate cash realisation of which can be assessed with reasonable certainty; provision is made for all known liabilities (expenses and losses) whether the amount of these is known with certainty or is a best estimate in the light of the information available'.[1]

It should be emphasized that the first part of this definition does not mean that sales revenue should only be recognized when the proceeds of sale are received in cash. The reference to 'other assets the ultimate cash realisation of which can be assessed with reasonable certainty' relates to debtors. Thus the prudence concept dictates that sales revenue should only be recognized in the profit and loss account if debtors are likely to pay their debts. This highlights an example of the application of the prudence concept which takes the form of a provision for bad debts. If it is anticipated that some debtors will default, the amount of this potential loss should be provided for in the profit and loss account and valuation of debtors in the balance sheet. Provisions for bad debts are examined in depth in Chapter 12.

Another example of the application of the prudence concept is the valuation of stock and work in progress at the lower of cost or net realizable value. Where the market or resale value of goods in stock has fallen below its cost, the amount of this reduction is taken into the trading account as a loss even though the goods have not been sold and the loss is as yet unrealized. In contrast, *unrealized holding gains*, such as an increase in the market value of buildings or investments are not recorded in the profit and loss account until the asset is sold.

A somewhat simpler but less valid description of the prudence concept is that it refers to the belief that it is better to report the lowest of the possible values of revenue and assets, and the highest of the possible values of costs and liabilities.

However, neither of the above explanations of the prudence concept makes reference to what is probably its most contentious application, namely the decision whether to treat expenditure (such as advertising, research and development expenditure, etc.) as an expense in the year it is incurred or as a fixed asset. The prudence concept dictates that if the resulting future revenue cannot be assessed with reasonable certainty the expenditure should be treated as an expense in the profit and loss account of the year in which it is incurred (e.g. research expenditure). The criterion used in applying the prudence concept thus concerns whether future revenue can be 'assessed with reasonable certainty'. This refers to whether it is possible to estimate reasonably accurately each of the future years' revenue that will be generated as a result of the expenditure in question (e.g. advertising expenditure).

There are three main arguments which are usually cited as justification for the prudence concept. First, it is necessary to compensate for the frequent over-optimism of managers in financial reporting. Second, overstating profits is potentially disastrous because it can lead to a reduction of capital. Third, it is the only practical way of dealing with uncertainty about potential revenues, expenses, asset values and liabilities.

The prudence concept may be inconsistent with certain other accounting concepts. It is argued that the prudence concept conflicts with the consistency concept and results in a lack of comparability because there can be no uniform standards in its application. Furthermore, the prudence concept may conflict with the going concern concept. Taken to its extreme the prudence concept may be interpreted to mean that all assets ought to be valued at their lowest possible value; that is, at their net realizable value. However, the going concern concept dictates that assets should be shown in final accounts at their historical cost.

The prudence concept is also said to be inconsistent with the matching principle. This requires that certain costs such as development expenditure should be carried forward to future years as a fixed asset and matched with the sales revenue generated by this expenditure. However, the prudence concept dictates that if future revenues are difficult to predict accurately, cost such as development expenditure should be written off to the profit and loss account in the year in which they are incurred. SSAP2 states that where the matching principle/accruals concept is 'inconsistent with the prudence concept, the latter prevails'.[1]

Other accounting concepts and conventions

There are several other accounting concepts which is not contained in SSAP2. The most commonly cited are explained below.

Objectivity

The term objectivity implies that the information contained in final accounts should be objective and not subjective. This is a gross oversimplification in that much of the information in final accounts requires a subjective judgement by the preparer. For example, is advertising or development expenditure to be treated as an expense or a fixed asset; what is the net realizable value of stocks; which debtors may turn out to be bad debts, etc.?

This is probably the reason why pronouncements by professional accountancy bodies and other authors often refer to objectivity using another phrase. For example, the Accounting Standards Board (ASB) and International Accounting Standard Committee (IASC) described this as 'faithful representation' and 'neutrality'. Objectivity is also often commonly taken to include verifiability and freedom from prejudice or bias. One way of defining objectivity is thus as referring to the assumption that final accounts should be verifiable and neutral.

Verifiability has traditionally been interpreted to mean that there should be documentary evidence to support the items in the final accounts. Usually this takes the form of sales and purchases invoices, credit notes, invoices in respect of expenses and the purchase of fixed assets, bank statements, etc. However, not all items in the final accounts are based on documentary evidence. Sometimes estimates (e.g. of bad debts and the net realizable value of stocks) have to be made. In this case the assumptions, available evidence and method of measurement should be open to inspection and capable of duplication.

Neutrality is often linked with the idea that final accounts should be accurate, precise, unbiased and not favour a particular interest group. According to *The Corporate Report*, 'the information presented (in final accounts) should be objective and unbiased in that it should meet all proper user needs and neutral in that the perception of the measurer should not be biased towards the interest of any one user group'.[3] Similarly, the ASB defines neutrality by arguing that 'financial statements are not neutral if they include information that has been selected or presented in such a way as to influence the making of a decision or judgement in order to achieve a predetermined result or outcome'.[4]

It should be noted that objectivity must incorporate both verifiability and neutrality because, while an item in the final accounts may be based on verifiable documentary evidence, selection of the evidence could be biased. For example, it could be deliberately intended to over- or understate profits and/or the value of assets. Conversely, an item which may be regarded as a legitimate asset (i.e. an unbiased selection) should not be included in the final accounts where its measurement/valuation is too subjective and thus unverifiable (e.g. fixed assets created by the business for which there is not a well developed or readily available market).

The objectivity concept is obviously applied throughout the preparation of final accounts. However, there are a few contentious applications, mostly relating to certain types of intangible fixed assets known as non-purchased goodwill and brand names. It is argued by the ASB that these should not be included on the balance sheet since their value cannot be determined objectively.

Finally, it is sometimes argued that there is an inconsistency between the objectivity and prudence concepts. The former demands freedom from bias whereas the latter is said to be a deliberate attempt to introduce bias in the form of understating profits and the value of net assets. However, this may be a misinterpretation of the concept of neutrality, which refers to not selecting measures that favour a particular group of users or give a predetermined outcome.

Materiality

The materiality concept provides guidance as to how a transaction or item of information should be classified in the final accounts and/or whether it should be disclosed separately rather than being aggregated with other similar items. This depends on whether the item is of a significant amount, relative to the size of the business. Whether or not a transaction or item is material or significant is generally taken to be a matter of professional judgement. In practice this is usually regarded as dependent on how large the amount is in relation to a business's total sales, the value of its assets, or other items of the same type. However, sometimes an item is taken as not being material simply because the absolute amount is small.

A common application of the materiality concept concerns whether an item of expenditure is to be regarded as a fixed asset. Where the amount is not material, the item would be treated as an expense even though it is expected to have a useful life of more than one accounting year and thus normally regarded as a fixed asset (e.g. relatively inexpensive tools and items of office equipment, fixtures and fittings, etc.).

Another common application of the materiality concept relates to the separate disclosure of certain items in final accounts. There are numerous references to materiality in the Companies Acts, Statements of Standard Accounting Practice and Financial

Reporting Standards which require the separate disclosure of items such as plant hire charges, rents receivable, etc., where the amounts are material.

A related, but slightly different, way of explaining the materiality concept is in terms of the degree of aggregation of data in final accounts. The users of final accounts are unable to assimilate large amounts of detailed information. This necessitates considerable aggregation of data. The materiality concept provides guidance on what transactions are to be aggregated by virtue of it specifying which items should be disclosed separately.

Finally, another interpretation of the materiality concept concerns whether the disclosure of certain items is likely to influence decisions made by the users of final accounts. One criterion which can be used to decide if an item is material is whether or not it may be expected to influence the judgements, decisions or actions of users of final accounts. If this is expected to occur, then the item is said to be material and should be disclosed separately from other similar items. This interpretation of the materiality concept is found in the ASB definition of materiality as follows:

> Information is material if it could influence users' decisions taken on the basis of the financial statements. If that information is misstated or if certain information is omitted the materiality of the misstatement or omission depends on the size and nature of the item in question judged in the particular circumstances of the case.[4]

Summary

The preparation of final accounts is based on a theoretical/conceptual framework of accounting. This is articulated in SSAP2 as including accounting concepts, bases and policies. Accounting concepts are the broad basic assumptions which underlie periodic financial accounts. Accounting bases are the methods which have been developed for expressing or applying accounting concepts to financial transactions and items. Accounting policies are the specific accounting bases adopted by an enterprise for the purpose of preparing its financial accounts.

SSAP2 identifies four fundamental accounting concepts—going concern, consistency, accruals and prudence. The going concern concept refers to the assumption that an enterprise will continue in operational existence for the foreseeable future. The consistency concept dictates that there should be consistency of accounting treatment of like items within each accounting period and from one period to the next. Under the accruals concept revenue and costs are accrued (that is, recognized as they are earned or incurred, not as money received or paid), matched with one another so far as their relationship can be established or justifiably assumed, and dealt with in the profit and loss account of the period to which they relate. The prudence concept requires that revenue and profits are not anticipated, but are recognized by inclusion in the profit and loss account only when realized in the form either of cash or of other assets the ultimate cash realization of which can be assessed with reasonable certainty; provision is made for all known liabilities (expenses and losses) whether the amount of these is known with certainty or is a best estimate in the light of the information available.

Two other accounting concepts/conventions are objectivity and materiality. Objectivity refers to the assumption that the items in financial statements should be verifiable and neutral. An item is said to be verifiable if there is documentary evidence of its value (e.g. an invoice), or the method used in its measurement is open to inspection and capable of duplication. Financial statements are not neutral if they include information that has been selected or presented in such a way as to influence the making of a decision or judgement in order to achieve a predetermined result or outcome. Information is material if it could influence users' decisions taken on the basis of the financial statements. Materiality depends on the size and nature of the item in question judged in the particular circumstances of the case.

Key terms and concepts

Accounting bases, accounting concepts, accounting policies, accruals concept, consistency concept, going concern concept, matching principle, materiality, neutrality, objectivity, prepayments, prudence concept, realization concept, revenue recognition concept, unrealized holding gains, verifiability.

References

1. Accounting Standards Steering Committee (1971). *Statement of Standard Accounting Practice 2—Disclosure of Accounting Policies* (ICAEW).
2. Accounting Standards Committee (1988). *Statement of Accounting Practice 9—Stocks and Long Term Contracts* (ICAEW).
3. Accounting Standards Steering Committee (1975). *The Corporate Report* (ICAEW).
4. Accounting Standards Board (1995). *Statement of Principles for Financial Reporting* (ASB).

Exercises

An asterisk after the question number indicates that there is a suggested answer in the Appendix.

10.1.   Explain the difference and interrelationship between accounting concepts, accounting bases and accounting policies.

10.2.   Explain each of the following accounting concepts including their implications for the preparation of final accounts:

(a) going concern
(b) consistency
(c) realization/revenue recognition.

10.3.   Explain fully the accruals concept and the matching principle. Give an example of the application of the matching principle in final accounts.

10.4.   Explain fully the prudence concept. Give examples of its application in final accounts.

10.5.   Discuss the assertion that the prudence concept is inconsistent with other accounting concepts and the matching principle.

10.6.   Explain each of the following accounting concepts including their implications for the preparation of final accounts:

(a) objectivity
(b) materiality.

10.7. An acquaintance of yours, H. Gee, has recently set up in business for the first time as a general dealer. The majority of his sales will be on credit to trade buyers but he will sell some goods to the public for cash. He is not sure at which point of the business cycle he can regard his cash and credit sales to have taken place.

After seeking guidance on this matter from his friends, he is thoroughly confused by the conflicting advice he has received. Samples of the advice he has been given include:

The sale takes place when:
1. You have bought goods which you know you should be able to sell easily.
2. The customer places the order.
3. You deliver the goods to the customer.
4. You invoice the goods to the customer.
5. The customer pays for the goods.
6. The customer's cheque has been cleared by the bank.

He now asks you to clarify the position for him.

Required:
(a) Write notes for Gee, setting out, in as easily understood a manner as possible, the accounting conventions and principles which should generally be followed when recognizing sales revenue.
(b) Examine each of the statements 1–6 above and advise Gee (stating your reasons) whether the method advocated is appropriate to the particular circumstances of his business. (ACCA)

10.8. 'If a business invests in shares, and the market value of the shares increases above cost then, until and unless the business sells them, no profit is made. If the business invests in stock for resale, and the market value of the stock falls below cost then the loss is recognized even though no sale has taken place.'

'If a business undertakes an intensive advertising campaign which will probably result in increased sales (and profit) in succeeding years it will nevertheless usually write off the cost of the campaign in the year in which it is incurred.'

Required:
Explain the reasoning behind the application of accounting principles in situations such as these and discuss the effect on the usefulness of accounting information in relation to users' needs. (ACCA)

10.9. On 20 December 19X7 your client paid £10,000 for an advertising campaign. The advertisements will be heard on local radio stations between 1 January and 31 January 19X8. Your client believes that as a result sales will increase by 60 per cent in 19X8 (over 19X7 levels) and by 40 per cent in 19X9 (over 19X7 levels). There will be no further benefits.

Required:
Write a memorandum to your client explaining your views on how this item should be treated in the accounts for the three years 19X7 to 19X9. Your answer should include explicit reference to at least *three* relevant traditional accounting conventions, and to the requirements of *two* classes of user of published financial accounts. (ACCA)

10.10.* One of your clients is a beef farmer. She informs you that the price of beef has fallen dramatically over the last few months and that she expects it to fall even further over the next three months. She therefore argues that the prudence concept should be applied to the valuation of her beef herd at the lower of cost or net realizable value; in this case at the latter value. She further asserts that this treatment is reasonable on the grounds that it will reduce her profit for tax purposes by the loss in value of her herd.

One of your colleagues has advised you that this may be a misinterpretation of the prudence concept and could contravene the objectivity concept. Discuss.

10.11.* One of your clients owns a garage and car sales business. He intends to bring into the business a veteran car which he inherited from his father. This will be kept in the car showroom and used in marketing and promotion. It will not be offered for sale.

There is no well-developed or readily available market for this car but your client wants to bring it into the books as a fixed asset valued at £50,000 along with the other motor vehicles. You suspect that part of the motive for this is to boost the value of assets on the balance sheet in order to obtain a loan from the bank.

You are required to discuss whether including this in the final accounts is a contravention of the objectivity concept.

10.12.* One of your clients has observed that in the final accounts you treat items of office equipment with a useful life of more than one year as expenses where they are relatively inexpensive whereas when they cost considerably more these are shown as fixed assets. She claims that this is a breach of the consistency concept and the matching principle.

You are required to explain the justification for this apparent inconsistency in the treatment of office equipment and briefly discuss the assertion that it contradicts the consistency concept and the matching principle.

10.13.* One of your clients is a building contractor who has asked you to prepare a set of final accounts which he intends to submit to his bank in support of an application for a loan to purchase some plant and machinery. He has noticed that you included in the profit and loss account an amount of £15,000 in respect of plant hire charges as a separate item from the costs of operating plant and machinery which amount to £20,000. Your client has suggested to you that these two items should be aggregated on the grounds of consistency.

You are required to explain the justification for showing these two items separately.

11. Depreciation and fixed assets

Learning objectives

After reading this chapter the student should be able to:

1. Explain the meaning of the key terms and concepts listed at the end of this chapter.
2. Distinguish between capital expenditure and revenue expenditure.
3. Describe the nature and valuation of fixed assets including intangible fixed assets such as goodwill and development expenditure.
4. Apply the criteria relating to the nature of fixed assets to specific transactions and items to determine the most appropriate accounting treatment.
5. Discuss the nature of depreciation.
6. Describe the straight line and reducing balance methods of depreciation including the resulting pattern of charges to the profit and loss account over an asset's useful life, and the circumstances in which each might be the most appropriate.
7. Compute the amount of depreciation using either of the methods in item 6, and show the relevant entries in the journal, ledger, profit and loss account and balance sheet.
8. Compute the depreciation on an asset in the years if acquisition and disposal, and the profit or loss on disposal; and show the relevant entries in the journal, ledger, profit and loss account, and balance sheet.

The nature and types of fixed assets

Fixed assets are items not specifically bought for resale but to be used in the production or distribution of those goods normally sold by the business. They are durable goods that usually last for several years, and are normally kept by a business for more than one accounting year. However, as discussed in the previous chapter, expenditure on such items is only regarded as a fixed asset if it is of a material amount, as defined by the materiality concept. The Accounting Standards Committee (ASC) defines a *fixed asset* as 'an asset that: (a) is held by an enterprise for use in the production or supply of goods and services, for rental to others, or for administrative purposes and may include items held for the maintenance or repair of such assets; (b) has been acquired or constructed with the intention of being used on a continuing basis; and (c) is not intended for sale in the ordinary course of a business'. A slightly different way of expressing the criterion for what constitutes a fixed asset is that the expenditure must be expected to generate revenue over a number of future years. This is arguably the most important criterion in determining whether expenditure is to be classified as a fixed asset.

Money spent on fixed assets is referred to as *capital expenditure*. All other costs and expenses are referred to as *revenue expenditure*. The latter are entered in the profit and loss account of the year in which the costs are incurred.

Examples of tangible fixed assets include land and buildings; plant and machinery; motor vehicles; furniture, fixtures and fittings; office equipment (such as computers); and loose tools. Tools that are only expected to last for less than one year are referred to as consumable tools, and treated as revenue expenditure.

Fixed assets are classified as either tangible or intangible. *Intangible assets* are defined by the ASB as 'non-financial fixed assets that do not have physical substance but are identifiable and are controlled by the entity through custody or legal rights'. Examples include goodwill, patents, trade marks and development expenditure. Non-financial, also called non-monetary, assets are assets other than cash, money in a bank cheque or deposit account, investments, and amounts receivable such as debtors.

Goodwill usually arises in the balance sheet because at some time in the past the business has taken over, or been formed from, another business. The figure shown in the balance sheet for goodwill is the difference between the amount paid for that business and the value of its net assets. Goodwill is sometimes said to represent the potential future profits or sales arising from a business's reputation and the continuing patronage of existing customers. However, it is much more than this, in that it represents the advantages which are gained from taking over an existing business rather than building up a new business from scratch (e.g. not having to recruit staff, find premises, identify suppliers, etc.). Goodwill is discussed in depth in Chapter 25.

Investments are also frequently included under the heading of fixed assets. These may consist of shares and/or debentures that are listed (quoted) on a stock exchange and unlisted securities. Investments should only by classified as a fixed asset where they are held on a long-term basis for the purpose of generating income. If this is not the case, investments should be treated as a current asset.

The valuation of fixed assets

The term 'valuation' refers to the amount at which assets are shown in the balance sheet. In historical cost accounting fixed assets are valued at their historical cost less the *aggregate/accumulated depreciation* from the date of acquisition to the date of the balance sheet. The resulting figure is known as the *written down value* (WDV) or net *book value*. Depreciation is discussed below. Historical cost refers to the purchase price excluding value added tax. The historical cost of a fixed asset may also include a number of additional costs. The cost of land and buildings, for example, may include legal expenses, and the cost of any subsequent extensions and improvements (but not repairs and renewals). Similarly, the cost of machinery is taken to include delivery charges, installation expenses and any costs associated with testing the machine prior to its use in normal production such as experimental/trial/dummy production runs, defective output etc. However, the costs of any extended warranty, maintenance agreement and replacement/spare parts (for future use) that have been included in the purchase price must be removed. Similarly, the cost of vehicles must exclude the first year's road tax and fuel where these have been included in the purchase price.

The nature of depreciation

The purchase of a fixed asset occurs in one year but the revenue generated from its use normally arises over a number of years. This is referred to as its *useful economic life*. If the cost of fixed assets were treated as an expense in the profit and loss account in the year of purchase this would probably result in an excessive loss in that year, and excessive profits in the years in which the revenue arose. This gives a misleading view of the profits and losses of each year and distorts comparisons over time. Thus the cost of a fixed asset is not treated as an expense in the year of purchase but rather carried forward and written off to the profit and loss account over the useful economic life of the asset in the form of depreciation. This is an application of the matching principle. According to the matching principle, that part of the cost of an asset which is 'used up' or 'consumed' in each year of the asset's useful economic life must be set against the revenue that this generates (in conjunction with other factors of production). That part of the cost of a fixed asset which is 'used up' or 'consumed' during an accounting period is referred to as depreciation. Thus depreciation may be defined as the allocation of the cost of a fixed asset over the accounting periods that comprise its useful economic life to the business according to some criterion regarding the amount which is 'used up' or 'consumed' in each of these periods.

SSAP12 *Accounting for Depreciation* (ASC, 1987) defines *depreciation* as 'the measure of the wearing out, consumption or other reduction in the useful economic life of a fixed asset whether arising from use, effluxion of time or obsolescence through technological or market changes.'[1] *Obsolescence* through technological change refers to where a new model of the asset which is significantly more efficient or performs additional functions comes onto the market. Obsolescence through market changes occurs when there is a substantial reduction in demand for the firm's product because of, for example, technological advances in competitors' products. Both of these causes of obsolescence usually result in a sudden relatively large decrease in value of the asset, particularly where it cannot be used for any other purpose.

Another common way of defining depreciation is that it refers to the permanent decrease in value of a fixed asset during a given accounting period. The Companies Act states that 'provisions for diminution in value shall be made in respect to any fixed asset which has diminished in value if the reduction in its value is expected to be permanent'. This conceptualization of depreciation leaves unanswered the question of what is meant by 'value'. Furthermore, many accountants would probably deny that the amount of depreciation shown in final accounts is a reflection of the loss in value of a fixed asset. They argue that accountants are not valuers, and that depreciation is simply the allocation of the cost of a fixed asset over its useful economic life to the business. There is no simple reconciliation of this schizophrenia which is said to arise from the dual purpose of depreciation as a means of measuring profit and valuing assets.

Depreciation can also be viewed as a provision for the replacement of fixed assets. The annual charge for depreciation in the profit and loss account represents a setting aside of some of the income so that over the useful life of the asset sufficient 'funds' are retained in the business to replace the asset. However, it must be emphasized that no money is usually specifically set aside. Thus, when the time comes to replace the asset, the money needed to do so will not automatically be available. Furthermore, where depreciation is based on the historical cost of the asset the amount of funds set aside will be insufficient to provide for any increase in the replacement cost of the asset. This is discussed further in Chapter 33.

Depreciation can therefore be said to be also an application of the prudence concept in that it is a provision for the loss in value of a fixed asset.

Finally, it should be noted that SSAP12 requires all tangible fixed assets except land and investments to be depreciated. This includes depreciating buildings. The reason is that although the market value of buildings at any point in time may exceed their historical cost, they nevertheless have a finite life and thus should be depreciated over their useful economic life. However, some businesses do not depreciate their buildings on the grounds that the market value at the end of the year, and/or the estimated residual value at the end of their expected useful life, is not less than the original cost. It is also sometimes argued that since repairs and maintenance costs on buildings are charged to the profit and loss account, to also charge depreciation on an asset, the useful life of which is being effectively maintained into perpetuity, would amount to a double charge and the creation of secret reserves. However, these arguments ignore that depreciation is not a method of valuation of assets but rather a process of allocation of the cost over the asset's useful life which, however long, must still be finite. Buildings can, for example, be entered in the balance sheet at a revalued amount in excess of their cost but this revalued amount should still be depreciated. Revaluations are discussed further in Chapter 27.

Methods/bases of depreciation

A number of different methods have been developed for measuring depreciation each of which will give a different annual charge to the profit and loss account. There is no one method of depreciation that is superior to all others in all circumstances. The most appropriate method will depend on the type of asset and the extent to which it is used in each period:

> There is a range of acceptable depreciation methods. Management should select the method regarded as most appropriate to the type of asset and its use in the business so as to allocate depreciation as fairly as possible to the periods expected to benefit from the asset's use.[1]

The method/basis of depreciation that is chosen is referred to as one of the business's accounting policies, and should be applied consistently each year.

Whichever method is used to calculate depreciation, at least three pieces of data relating to the asset in question are needed: (1) the historical cost; (2) the length of the asset's expected useful economic life to the business; and (3) the estimated residual value of the asset at the end of its useful economic life. The *useful life* of an asset refers to the period which the business regards as being the most economical length of time to keep the particular asset. This will depend on a number of factors, such as the pattern of repair costs, etc. The useful life of an asset may well be considerably shorter than its total life. *Residual value* refers to the estimated proceeds of sale at the end of the asset's useful life to the business. This is usually considerably more than its scrap value. It should be noted that both the useful life and the residual value have to be estimated when the asset is purchased.

The two most common methods of depreciation are the straight line and reducing balance methods. These are described below:

The straight line/fixed instalment method

Under this method the annual of depreciation which will be charged to the profit and loss account is computed as follows:

$$\frac{\text{Cost} - \text{Estimated residual value}}{\text{Estimated useful life in years}}$$

However, in practice, and in examination questions, the rate of depreciation is usually expressed as a percentage. The annual amount of depreciation is then calculated by applying the percentage to the cost of the asset.

This method gives the same charge for depreciation in each year of the asset's useful life. It is therefore most appropriate for assets which are depleted as a result of the passage of time (e.g. buildings, leases, pipelines, storage tanks, patents and trade marks). The method may also be suitable where the utilization of an asset is the same in each year.

The main advantages of the straight line method are that it is easy to understand and the computations are simple. The main disadvantage is that it may not give an accurate measure of the loss in value or reduction in the useful life of an asset.

The diminishing/reducing balance method

Under this method it is necessary first to compute the rate of depreciation as a percentage as follows:

$$100 - \left[\left(\frac{\text{Residual value}}{\text{Cost}} \right)^{\frac{1}{el}} \times 100 \right]$$

where el refers to the estimated useful life.

The annual amount of depreciation which will be charged to the profit and loss account is then computed thus:

$$\text{Rate of depreciation} \times \text{Written down value of asset}$$
$$\text{(at start of year)}$$

The written down value (WDV) of the asset refers to its cost less the aggregate depreciation of the asset since the date of acquisition. This method thus gives a decreasing annual charge for depreciation over the useful life of the asset. It is therefore most appropriate for fixed assets that deteriorate primarily as a result of usage where this is greater in the earlier years of their life (e.g. plant and machinery, motor vehicles, furniture and fittings, office equipment). However, this method may also be suitable even if the utilization is the same in each year. The logic behind this apparently contradictory assertion involves taking into consideration the pattern of repair costs. These will be low in the earlier years of the asset's life and high in later years. Thus the decreasing annual amount of depreciation combined with the increasing repair costs will give a relatively constant combined annual charge in each year of the asset's useful life which is said to reflect the constant annual usage.

The reducing balance method is also said to be a more realistic measure of the reduction in the market value of fixed assets, since this is likely to be greater in the earlier years of the asset's life than later years. However, it is highly questionable whether the written down value of a fixed asset is intended to be a reflection of its market value.

The main criticisms of this method relate to its complexity, and there is an arbitrary assumption about the rate of decline built into the formula.

A numerical example of the above methods of depreciation is given in Example 11.1.

Accounting for depreciation

The accounting entries in respect of the annual charge for depreciation are made after the trial balance has been extracted when the profit and loss account is being prepared. These consist of the following:

Debit   Depreciation expense account
Credit   Provision for depreciation account

The depreciation expense account is transferred to the profit and loss account thus:

Debit   Profit and loss account
Credit   Depreciation expense account

The effect is to accumulate the provision while making a charge in the profit and loss account each year.

Example 11.1

D. McDonald has an accounting year ending on 31 December. On 1 January 19X1 he purchased a machine for £1,000 which has an expected useful life of three years and an estimated residual value of £343.
    You are required to:

(a) Calculate the amount of depreciation in each year of the asset's useful life using: (i) the straight line method; and (ii) the reducing balance method.
(b) Show the journal and ledger entries relating to the purchase and the provision for depreciation in each year (using the amounts calculated from the straight line method).
(c) Show the relevant entries on the balance sheet for 19X2 (using the amounts calculated from the straight line method).

(a) *The calculation of depreciation*
    (i)   *The straight line method*:

$$\text{Annual depreciation} = \frac{£1,000 - £343}{3} = £219 \text{ per annum}$$

    (ii) *The reducing balance method*:

$$\text{Rate} = 100 - \left[\left(\frac{343}{1,000}\right)^{1/3} \times 100\right] = 100 - (7/10 \times 100) = 30 \text{ per cent}$$

The annual amount of depreciation is calculated by applying this rate to the cost of the asset minus the aggregate depreciation of previous years (i.e. the written down value at the start of each year) as follows:

For 19X1:   30 per cent of £1,000 = £300
For 19X2:   30 per cent of (£1,000 − 300) = £210
For 19X3:   30 per cent of [£1,000 − (£300 + £210)] = £147

(b) *The ledger entries*

Plant and machinery

19X1
1 Jan   Bank   1,000

*Provision for depreciation on
plant and machinery*

19X1   19X1
31 Dec   Balance c/d   219   31 Dec   Depreciation expense
                                                       account   219

19X2			19X2		
31 Dec	Balance c/d	438	1 Jan	Balance b/d	219
			31 Dec	Depreciation expense	
				account	219
		438			438
19X3			19X3		
31 Dec	Balance c/d	657	1 Jan	Balance b/d	438
			31 Dec	Depreciation expense	
				account	219
		657			657
			19X4		
			1 Jan	Balance b/d	657

Depreciation expense account

19X1	Depreciation on		19X1	Profit and loss	
31 Dec	plant	219	31 Dec	account	219
19X2	Depreciation on		19X2	Profit and loss	
31 Dec	plant	219	31 Dec	account	219
19X3	Depreciation on		19X3	Profit and loss	
31 Dec	plant	219	31 Dec	account	219

The journal entries

19X1				
31 Dec	Depreciation expense	Dr	219	
	To provision of depreciation			219
	Being the charge for depreciation on plant for 19X1			
31 Dec	Profit and loss account	Dr	219	
	To depreciation expense			219
	Being the entry to close the depreciation expense account at the year end			

The entries for 19X2 and 19X3 would be exactly the same.

(c) *The balance sheet* at 31 December 19X2 would appear as follows:

Fixed assets	Cost	Aggregate depreciation	WDV
Plant and machinery	1,000	438	562

Notes

1. The entries on the balance sheet comprise the balance on the fixed asset account at the end of the year and the balance on the provision for depreciation account at the end of the year. The latter is referred to as the *aggregate or accumulated depreciation* and is deducted from the historical cost to give the WDV, which is the only one of these three figures that enter into the computation of the total of the balance sheet.
2. Because the entries in the depreciation expense account only ever consist of a single debit and credit of the same amount, most people do not use this account. Instead the annual charge is credited to the provision for depreciation account and debited directly to the profit and loss account. This practice will be adopted in future examples and answers to exercises.

Profits and losses on the disposal of fixed assets

Almost with exception, when an asset is sold at the end of (or during) its useful life the proceeds of sale differ from the estimated residual value (or written down book value if sold during its useful life). Where the proceeds are less than the written down value, this is referred to as a *loss on sale*. Where the proceeds are greater than the written down value this is referred to as a *profit on sale*. This can be illustrated using Example 11.1. Suppose the asset was sold on 31 December 19X3 for £400. The written down value is the difference between the cost of the asset and the aggregate depreciation up to the date of disposal. That is, £1,000 − £657 = £343. The profit (or loss) on sale is the difference between the proceeds of sale and the written down value of the asset. There is thus a profit on sale of £400 − £343 = £57.

The disposal of fixed assets and the resulting profit or loss on sale must be recorded in the ledger. The procedure is as follows:

1. Credit the proceeds of sale to the fixed asset account.
2. Transfer the aggregate depreciation up to the date of disposal from the provision for depreciation account to the fixed asset account.
3. A loss on sale should then be credited to the fixed asset account and debited to the profit and loss account. A profit on sale would be debited to the asset account and credited to the profit and loss account.

The effect of these entries is to eliminate the original cost of the asset from the fixed asset account. This is illustrated below using Example 11.1 and the additional data above.

The ledger entries

Provision for depreciation

19X3			19X3		
31 Dec	Plant and machinery	657	31 Dec	Balance b/d	657

Plant and machinery

19X1			19X3		
1 Jan	Bank—purchase	1,000	31 Dec	Bank—proceeds of sale	400
19X3			31 Dec	Provision for depreciation	657
31 Dec	Profit and loss a/c		31 Dec	Profit and loss a/c	
	—profit on sale	57		(any loss on sale)	—
		1,057			1,057

Profit and loss account

| Loss of sale of fixed assets | — | Profit on sale of plant and machinery | 57 |

Before the above entries are made in the ledger the following journal entries are necessary:

The journal entries

19X3 31 Dec	Provision for depreciation	Dr	657	
	To plant and machinery			657
	Being the aggregate depreciation at the date of sale of the asset			
19X3 31 Dec	Plant and machinery	Dr	57	
	To profit and loss account			
	Being the profit on sale of plant			57

The depreciation charge on an asset in the years of acquisition and disposal

The previous example dealt with the highly unlikely situation of an asset being purchased and sold on the first day and last day of an accounting year respectively. In practice, these transactions could occur on any day of the year. The way in which depreciation would then be computed depends on the usual practice of the business, or in examinations on what you are explicitly or implicitly instructed to do. Unless the question states otherwise, the depreciation must be calculated on a strict time basis for the period the asset is owned. In examination questions, assets tend to be purchased and sold on the first or last day of a calendar month for simplicity of calculation. It can be argued in practice one should also calculate depreciation on a strict time basis. The charge for depreciation in the year of purchase would be as follows:

$$\frac{\text{Rate of}}{\text{depreciation}} \times \frac{\text{Cost of}}{\text{asset}} \times \frac{\text{Number of months (or days) between the date of purchase and the end of the accounting year in which the asset is purchased}}{12 \text{ (or 365)}}$$

The charge for depreciation in the year of sale would be as follows:

$$\frac{\text{Rate of}}{\text{depreciation}} \times \frac{\text{Cost of asset}}{\text{(or WDV)}} \times \frac{\text{Number of months (or days) between the start of the accounting year in which the asset is sold and the date of sale}}{12 \text{ (or 365)}}$$

In practice, to avoid these tedious calculations, some firms have a policy of charging a full year's depreciation in the year of purchase and none in the year of sale. There is little theoretical justification for this. Also, in examination questions, where the date of purchase or sale is not given, this is usually an indication to adopt this policy.

The accounting entries in respect of depreciation on acquisitions and disposals are illustrated in Example 11.2.

Example 11.2

P. Smith has an accounting year ending on 31 December. On 31 December 1990 her ledger contained the following accounts:

	£
Motor vehicles	50,000
Provision for depreciation on vehicles	23,000

Vehicles are depreciated using the straight line method at a rate of 20 per cent per annum on a strict time basis.

The following transactions occurred during 1991:

Apr 1   Purchase a van for £5,000
Aug 31   Sold a vehicle for £4,700. This cost £7,500 when it was bought on 31 July 1989.
Sept 30 Put one car in part exchange for another. The part exchange allowance on the old car was £4,100 and the balance of £3,900 was paid by cheque. The old car cost £10,000 when it was bought on 1 January 1989.

You are required to show the entries in the motor vehicles and provision for depreciation accounts in respect of the above from 1991.

Date of acquisitions and disposals	*Details*	*Total depreciation on disposals*	*Depreciation charge for year ending 31 Dec 1991*
		£	£
	Depreciation on disposals		
31 July 1989	For year ending 31/12/89:		
	20 per cent × 7,500 × 5/12	625	
	For year ending 31/12/90:		
	20 per cent × 7,500	1,500	
31 August 1991	For year ending 31/12/91:		
	20 per cent × 7,500 × 8/12	1,000	1,000
		3,135	

Book value at 31/8/91:
   7,500 − 3,125 = 4,375

Profits on sale
   4,700 − 4,375 = 325

1 Jan 1989	For year ending 31/12/89: 20 per cent $\times$ 10,000	2,000	
	For year ending 31/12/90: 20 per cent $\times$ 10,000	2,000	
30 Sept 1991	For year ending 31/12/91: 20 per cent $\times$ 10,000 $\times$ 9/12	1,500	1,500
		5,500	

Balance value at 30/9/91:
10,000 − 5,500 = 4,500

Loss on sale
4,500 − 4,100 = 400

Depreciation on acquisitions

| 1 Apr 1991 | 20 per cent $\times$ 5,000 $\times$ 9/12 | 750 |
| 30 Sept 1991 | 20 per cent $\times$ (3,900 + 4,100) $\times$ 4/12 | 400 |

Depreciation on remainder

| 20 per cent $\times$ (50,000 − 7,500 − 10,000) | 6,500 |
| | 10,150 |

Note

1. The 'depreciation on the remainder' of the plant is calculated on the plant owned at the end of the previous year that was not disposed of during the current year. Those items that were bought and sold during the year having already been depreciated in the previous calculations.

The ledger entries

Motor vehicles

1991			1991		
1 Jan	Balance b/d	50,000	31 Aug	Bank	4,700
1 Apr	Bank	5,000	31 Aug	Provision for depn.	3,125
31 Aug	Profit and loss a/c		30 Sept	Part exchange contra	4,100
	—profit on sale	325	30 Sept	Provision for depn.	5,500
30 Sept	Bank	3,900	30 Sept	Profit and loss a/c	
30 Sept	Part exchange			—loss on sale	400
	contra	4,100	31 Dec	Balance c/d	45,500
		63,325			63,325

1992		
1 Jan	Balance b/d	45,500

Provision for depreciation

1991			1991		
31 Aug	Vehicles	3,125	1 Jan	Balance b/d	23,000
30 Sept	Vehicles	5,500	31 Dec	Profit and loss a/c	10,150
31 Dec	Balance c/d	24,525			
		33,150			33,150
			1992		
			1 Jan	Balance b/d	24,525

Notes

1. When one asset is put in part exchange for another, the part exchange allowance is both debited and credited to the asset account and referred to as a contra. The credit entry represents the proceeds of sale of the old asset, and the debit entry represents a part payment for the new asset. The balance which has to be paid for the new asset in cash is debited to the asset account in the normal way. This together with the debit contra represents the total cost of the new asset.

2. The transfer from the provision for depreciation account to the fixed asset account relating to the aggregate depreciation on disposals must include the depreciation on disposals in respect of the current year. This therefore cannot be done until the total depreciation for the current year has been ascertained. Thus all the entries in the provision for depreciation account are usually made at the end of the year after the trial balance has been prepared. It is important to note that this also means that any balance on a provision for depreciation account shown in a trial balance must relate to the balance at the end of the previous year.

3. There is another method of accounting for disposals which involves the use of a disposals account. Some examination questions explicitly require the use of a disposals account. Under this method, when a fixed asset is sold the cost of the asset is transferred from the fixed asset account to a fixed asset disposals account. The aggregate depreciation on the asset that has been sold, the proceeds of sale, and the profit or loss on sale are all entered in the disposals account instead of the fixed asset account. The provision for depreciation account contains the same entries whether a disposals account is used or not. The use of a disposals account is illustrated below, taking the information from Example 11.2.

Motor vehicles

1991			1991		
1 Jan	Balance b/d	50,000	31 Aug	Disposals account	7,500
1 Apr	Bank	5,000	30 Sept	Disposals account	10,000
30 Sept	Bank	3,900	31 Dec	Balance c/d	45,500
30 Sept	Disposals account				
	—part exchange	4,100			
		63,000			63,000
1992					
1 Jan	Balance b/d	45,500			

Motor vehicles disposals

1991			1991		
31 Aug	Motor vehicles	7,500	31 Aug	Bank	4,700
31 Aug	Profit and loss a/c		31 Aug	Provision for depn.	3,125
	—profit on sale	325	30 Sept	Motor vehicles	
30 Sept	Motor vehicles	10,000		—part exchange	4,100
			30 Sept	Provision for depn.	5,500
			30 Sept	Profit and loss a/c	
				—loss on sale	400
		17,825			17,825

There should never be a balance on the disposals account at the end of the year after the profit and loss account has been prepared.

Accounting for research and development expenditure

SSAP13—Accounting for Research and Development[2] divides research and development expenditure into three categories: (1) pure (or basic) research; (2) applied research, and (3) development. These are defined as follows:

1. *Pure (or basic) research*: experimental or theoretical work undertaken primarily to acquire new scientific or technical knowledge for its own sake rather than directed towards any specific aim or application.
2. *Applied research*: original or critical investigation undertaken in order to gain new scientific or technical knowledge and directed towards a specific practical aim or objective.
3. *Development*: use of scientific or technical knowledge in order to produce new or substantially improved materials, devices, products or services, to install new processes or systems prior to the commencement of commercial production or commercial applications, or to improving substantially those already produced or installed.

The accounting treatment of expenditure on pure and applied research may differ from that for development expenditure. SSAP13, like the Companies Act, dictates that expenditure on pure and applied research must be treated as an expense in the year incurred. However, SSAP13 and the Companies Act allow development expenditure to be either expensed in the year incurred or alternatively treated as an intangible fixed asset (and depreciated/amortized). The reason for allowing either the expressing or capitalization of development expenditure is said to be because of the conflicting requirements of the matching principle and prudence concept (as discussed in Chapter 10). If development expenditure is expected to generate revenue in future years (which is often the case), the matching principle dictates that this expenditure be capitalized. However, if the resulting future revenue cannot be assessed with reasonable certainty (which is also often the case), the prudence concept dictates that development expenditure should be expensed. The most appropriate accounting treatment for development expenditure thus hinges on whether the resulting future revenue can be assessed with reasonable certainty, which is why SSAP13 contains the following set of detailed requirements relating to the accounting treatment of development costs:

Development expenditure should be written off in the year of expenditure except in the following circumstances when it may be deferred to future periods:
(a) there is a clearly defined project, and
(b) the related expenditure is separately identifiable, and
(c) the outcome of such a project has been assessed with reasonable certainty as to:

>   (i)   its technical feasibility, and
>   (ii) its ultimate commercial viability considered in the light of factors such as likely market conditions (including competing products), public opinion, consumer and environmental legislation, and

(d) the aggregate of the deferred development costs, any further development costs, and related production, selling and administration costs is reasonably expected to be exceeded by related future sales or other revenues, and
(e) adequate resources exist, or are reasonably expected to be available, to enable the project to be completed and to provide any consequential increases in working capital.

There is also certain information relating to research and development expenditure that should be disclosed in the notes to published company accounts. The requirements of SSAP13 are reproduced below. Notice that the reference to 'deferred expenditure' relates to development expenditure that has been treated as an intangible fixed asset.

(a) The accounting policy on research and development expenditure should be stated and explained.
(b) The total amount of research and development expenditure charged in the profit and loss account should be disclosed, analysed between the current year's expenditure and amounts amortised from deferred expenditure.
(c) Movements on deferred expenditure and the amount carried forward at the beginning and the end of the period should be disclosed. Deferred development expenditure should be disclosed under intangible fixed assets in the balance sheet.

Summary

A fixed asset is an asset that is held by an enterprise for use in the production or supply of goods and services, has been acquired with the intention of being used on a continuing basis, and is not intended for sale in the ordinary course of business. It is also usually expected to generate revenue over more than one accounting year. Fixed assets are classified as either tangible or intangible (such as goodwill). Money spent on fixed assets is referred to as capital expenditure. All other costs are referred to as revenue expenditure. Fixed assets are normally valued in the balance sheet as historical cost which refers to their purchase price.

All fixed assets except land and investments must be depreciated in the final accounts. Depreciation is the measure of the wearing out, consumption or other reduction in the useful economic life of a fixed asset whether arising from use, effluxion of time or obsolescence.

There is a range of acceptable depreciation methods. Management should select the method regarded as most appropriate to the type of asset and its use in the business so as to allocate depreciation as fairly as possible to the periods expected to benefit from the asset's use. The two most common methods are the straight line/fixed instalment method and diminishing/reducing balance method. The former gives the same charge for depreciation in each year of the asset's useful life. The latter results in a decreasing annual charge over the useful life of the asset.

Where an asset is acquired or disposed of during the accounting year, it is normal to compute the depreciation for that year according to the period over which the asset was owned. When an asset is disposed of during the accounting year this usually also gives rise to profit or loss on sale. This is the difference between the proceeds of sale and the written down or book value of the asset. The WDV is the difference between the historic cost and the accumulated/aggregate depreciation from the date of acquisition to the date of disposal.

The ledger entries for depreciation are to credit a provision for depreciation account and debit a depreciation expense account with the annual amount of depreciation. The balance on the depreciation expense account is transferred to the profit and loss account representing the charge for the year. The balance on the provision for depreciation account is shown on the balance sheet as a deduction from the cost of the fixed asset to give the written down value which enters into the total of the balance sheet. However, the aggregate depreciation on fixed assets disposed of during the year must first be transferred from the provision for depreciation account to the fixed asset account. Any profit or loss on disposal is also entered in the fixed asset account and transferred to the profit and loss account.

Intangible fixed assets include development expenditure. SSAP13 dictates that research expenditure must be treated as an expense in the year incurred. However, development expenditure can be capitalized as a fixed asset (and depreciated) provided that the resulting future revenue can be assessed with reasonable certainty. If not, it should be expensed in the year incurred.

Key terms and concepts

Aggregate/accumulated depreciation, book value, capital expenditure, depreciation, depreciation expense, diminishing balance method, fixed asset, fixed instalment method, intangible fixed asset, loss on sale, obsolescence, profit on sale, reducing balance method, residual value, revenue expenditure, straight line method, useful (economic) life, written down value.

References

1. Accounting Standards Committee (1987). *Statement of Standard Accounting Practice 12—Accounting for Depreciation* (ICAEW).
2. Accounting Standards Committee (1989). *Statement of Standard Accounting Practice 13—Accounting for Research and Development* (ICAEW).

Exercises

An asterisk after the question number indicates that there is a suggested answer in the Appendix.

11.1. Examine the nature of fixed assets.

11.2. (a) Explain the difference between capital expenditure and revenue expenditure.
   (b) What criteria would you use to decide whether expenditure should be classified as relating to a fixed asset?

11.3. Briefly explain the circumstances in which each of the following would be regarded as a fixed asset: (a) tools; (b) investments; and (c) advertising expenditure.

11.4. (a) Define each of the following: (i) pure (or basic) research; (ii) applied research; and (iii) development.
  (b) Describe fully the permissible accounting treatments for research and development expenditure including the circumstances in which each may be acceptable.
  (c) Describe the information that should be disclosed in the notes to the accounts of companies in respect of research and development expenditure.

11.5. What is goodwill and how does it usually arise in a balance sheet?

11.6. Describe how fixed assets are valued in historical cost accounting.

11.7. Explain fully the nature of depreciation.

11.8. 'Depreciation is the loss in value of a fixed asset.' Discuss.

11.9. Describe the data needed in order to compute depreciation.

11.10. Describe two methods of depreciation including the resulting pattern of charges to the profit and loss account for depreciation expense over an asset's useful economic life. In what circumstances might each of these be the most appropriate method and why?

11.11. 'Although the straight line method is the simplest to apply, it may not always be the most appropriate' (ASC, SSAP12, 1987). Explain and discuss.

11.12. In the year to 31 December 19X9, Amy bought a new fixed asset and made the following payments in relation to it:

	£	£
Cost as per supplier's list	12,000	
Less: agreed discount	1,000	11,000
Delivery charge		100
Erection charge		200
Maintenance charge		300
Additional component to increase capacity		400
Replacement parts		250

Required:
  (a) State and justify the cost figure which should be used as the basis for depreciation.
  (b) What does depreciation do, and why is it necessary?
  (c) Briefly explain, without numerical illustration, how the straight line and reducing balance methods of depreciation work. What different assumptions does each method make?
  (d) Explain the term objectivity as used by accountants. To what extent is depreciation objective?
  (e) It is common practice in published accounts in Germany to use the reducing balance method for a fixed asset in the early years of its life, and then to change to the straight line method as soon as this would give a higher annual charge. What do you think of this practice? Refer to relevant accounting conventions in your answer.   (ACCA)

11.13. Pusher commenced business on 1 January 19X9 with two lorries—A and B. A cost £1,000 and B cost £1,600. On 3 March 19X0, A was written off in an accident and Pusher received £750 from the Insurance Company. This vehicle was replaced on 10 March 19X0 by C which cost £2,000.

A full year's depreciation is charged in the year of acquisition and no depreciation charged in the year of disposal.

(a) You are required to show the appropriate extracts from Pusher's balance sheet and profit and loss account for the three years to 31/12/X9, 31/12/X0 and 31/12/X1 assuming that
   (i) the vehicles are depreciated at 20 per cent on the straight line method, and
   (ii) the vehicles are depreciated at 25 per cent on the reducing balance method.
(b) Comment briefly on the pros and cons of using the straight line and reducing balance methods of depreciation.   (ACCA)

11.14.* A. Black & Company Limited owned two machines which had been purchased on 1 October 1990, at a combined cost of £3,100 ex works. They were identical as regards size and capacity and had been erected and brought into use on 1 April 1991. The cost of transporting the two machines to the factory of A. Black & Company Limited was £130 and further expenditure for the installation of the two machines had been incurred totalling £590 for the foundations, and £180 for erection.

Provision for depreciation using the straight line method has been calculated from the date on which the machines started work, assuming a life of ten years for the machines. The first charge against profits was made at the end of the financial year, 30 September 1991.

One of the machines was sold on 31 March 1999 for £800 ex factory to H. Johnson. The work of dismantling the machine was undertaken by the staff of Black & Company Limited at a labour cost of £100. This machine was replaced on 1 May 1999, by one exactly similar in every way, which was purchased from R. Adams at a cost of £2,800, which covered delivery, erection on the site of the old machine, and the provision of adequate foundations. This new machine was brought into general operation on 1 July 1999.

You are required to show:

(a) the journal entries which should be made on 31 March and 1 May 1999, and
(b) how you would arrive at the amount of the provision for depreciation as regards the three machines for the year ended 30 September 1999.

NB. It is the practice of the company to charge depreciation on a *pro rata* time basis each year, and to operate a machinery disposal account where necessary.

                   (ACCA)

11.15. Makers and Co. are a partnership with a small factory on the outskirts of London. They decide to erect an extension to their factory.

The following items appear in the trial balance of the firm, as at 31 December 19X9:

	Debit £	Credit £
Purchases	12,800	
Wages	16,400	
Hire of machinery	520	
Plant and machinery at cost to 31 December 19X8	5,900	
Plant and machinery purchased during the year	2,540	
Plant and machinery sold during the year (cost in 19X0 £900; depreciation to 31 December 19X8 £540)		160
Freehold premises at cost to 31 December 19X8 (Land £3,000; Buildings £4,000)	7,000	
Freehold land purchased during the year for a factory extension	2,800	
Provision for depreciation of plant and machinery at 31 December 19X8		2,400
Legal charges	280	

In the course of your examination of the books you ascertain that:

1. Building materials used in building the extension and costing £1,800 had been charged to the purchases account.
2. Wages paid to men engaged in building the extension amounted to £1,500 and had been charged to the wages account.
3. The hire charge was in respect of machinery used exclusively in the construction of the extension.
4. The legal charges, apart from £50 relating to debt collecting, were incurred in the purchase of the land.

It is decided that depreciation on plant and machinery is to be provided at $12\frac{1}{2}$ per cent on the closing book value.

You are required to:

(a) write up the following ledger accounts.
   Factory extensions, Freehold premises, Plant and machinery, and Provision for depreciation of plant and machinery, and
(b) show therefrom the particulars that should appear on the firm's balance sheet at 31 December 19X9. (ACCA)

11.16.* Wexford Ltd, who prepare their accounts on 31 December each year, provide for depreciation of their vehicles by a reducing balance method, calculated as 25 per cent on the balance at the end of the year. Depreciation of plant is calculated on a straight line basis at 10 per cent per annum on cost; a full year's depreciation is charged in the year in which plant is acquired and none in the year of sale.

The balance sheet for 31 December 1992 showed:

	Vehicles £	Plant £
Original cost	25,060	96,920
Accumulated depreciation	14,560	50,120
Net book value	10,500	46,800

During the year ended 31 December 1993 the following transactions took place:

Purchase of vehicles   £4,750
Purchases of plant   £33,080

	Year of purchase £	Original cost £	Proceeds of sale £
Sale of vehicle 1	1990	3,200	1,300
Sale of vehicle 2	1991	4,800	2,960
Sale of plant	1987	40,000	15,000

You are required to:

(a) present the ledger accounts relating to the purchases and sales of vehicles and plant for the year ended 31 December 1993; and
(b) show the journal entries for depreciation for the year.

11.17. The balance sheet of Beta Ltd as at 30 June 19X9 shows motor vehicles as follows:

	£
Motor vehicles at cost	61,850
Less: Depreciation	32,426
Net Book Value	29,424

Vehicles are depreciated on the straight line basis over a five year life. Depreciation is charged *pro rata* to time in the year of acquisition but no charge is made in the year of disposal. The disposal account is written up on the last day of each year.

During 19X9–X0 the following vehicle transactions took place:

30 Sept Purchased delivery van: £8,600
31 Oct   Purchased sales manager's car: £10,700
28 Feb   Purchased lorry: £4,000

The lorry was second-hand and originally cost £9,600.

Sales of vehicles:

31 Oct   Car   £300 originally cost £2,800
31 Dec   Tractor £540 originally cost £2,400
31 Mar   Van   £420 originally cost £1,900

The car was originally purchased 1 July 19X5, the tractor 30 November 19X6 and the van 1 April 19X7.

   You are required to write up the accounts for vehicles, vehicle depreciation and vehicle disposals.   (ACCA adapted)

12. Bad debts and provisions for bad debts

Learning objectives

After reading this chapter the student should be able to:

1. Explain the meaning of the key terms and concepts listed at the end of the chapter.
2. Explain the conceptual foundation of provisions generally, and the purpose of a provision for doubtful debts in particular.
3. Describe the nature of bad debts, provisions, and provisions for doubtful debts.
4. Distinguish between specific and general provisions for doubtful debts.
5. Show the entries for bad debts and provisions for doubtful debts in the journal, ledger, profit and loss account and balance sheet.

The nature of and ledger entries for bad debts

When goods are sold on credit it sometimes transpires that the debtor is unwilling or unable to pay the amount owed. This is referred to as a *bad or irrecoverable debt*. The decision to treat a debt as bad is a matter of judgement. A debt may be regarded as irrecoverable for a number of reasons, such as being unable to trace the debtor, not worth taking the debtor to court, or the debtor is bankrupt. However, if a debtor is bankrupt this does not necessarily mean that the debt is irrecoverable. When a person is bankrupt his or her possessions are seized and sold in order to pay the creditors. Such payments are often made in instalments known as dividends. Frequently the dividends do not consist of the repayment of the whole of the debt. Thus when the 'final dividend' is received the remainder of the debt is irrecoverable.

When a debt is regarded as irrecoverable the entries in the ledger are as follows:

Debit: Bad debts account
Credit: Debtor's account

Occasionally debts previously written off as bad are subsequently paid. When this happens the ledger entries are the reverse of the above, and the debtors' account is credited with the money received in the normal way.

At the end of the accounting year the balance on the bad debts account is transferred to the profit and loss account.

The nature of and ledger entries for provisions for bad debts

Provisions are an application of the prudence concept (note the definition in Chapter 10). *A provision is the setting aside of income to meet a known or highly probable future liability or loss, the amount and/or timing of which cannot be ascertained exactly*, and is thus an estimate. An example would be a provision for damages payable resulting from a legal action where the verdict had gone against the business but the amount of the damages had not been fixed by the court at the end of the accounting year. If the damages had been fixed these would not be treated as a provision but as a liability. Another example of a provision is depreciation.

It should be noted that when accountants talk of setting aside income what they mean is that 'funds' are being retained in the business but not put into a separate bank account. The funds are automatically retained in the business by designating part of the income as a provision, since this reduces the profit which is available for withdrawal by the owner(s) of the business.

The need for a *provision for bad/doubtful* debts essentially arises because goods sold and recognized as sales revenue in one accounting year may not become known to be a bad debt until the following accounting year. Thus the profit of the year in which the goods are sold would be overstated by the amount of the bad debt. In order to adjust for this, a provision in respect of possible bad debts is created in the year of sale.

A provision for bad debts may consist of either a *specific provision* and/or a *general provision*. A specific provision involves ascertaining which particular debtors at the year end are unlikely to pay their debts. A general provision is an estimate of the total amount of bad debts computed using a percentage (based on previous years' figures) of the debtors at the end of the current year. Where both specific and general provisions are made, the two amounts are added together and the total is entered in the ledger.

The accounting entries in respect of a provision for bad debts are made after the trial balance has been extracted when the profit and loss account is being prepared. A charge (or credit) is made to the profit and loss account in each year which consists of an amount necessary to increase (or decrease) the provision at the end of the previous year to the amount required at the end of the current year.

An increase in a provision always consists of:

Debit: Profit and loss account
Credit: Provision for bad debts account

A decrease in a provision is entered:

Debit: Provision for bad debts account
Credit: Profit and loss account

It is important to appreciate that any balance on a provision for bad debts account shown in a trial balance must therefore relate to the balance at the end of the previous year. The treatment of bad debts and provisions for bad debts is illustrated in Examples 12.1 and 12.2.

Example 12.1
A. Jones has an accounting year ending on 30 November. At 30 November 19X7 his ledger contained the following accounts:

	£
Trade debtors	20,000
Provision for bad debts	1,000

The trade debtors at 30 November 19X8 were £18,900. This includes an amount of £300 owed by F. Simons which was thought to be irrecoverable. It also includes amounts of £240 owed by C. Steven, £150, owed by M. Evans and £210 owed by A. Mitchell all of which are regarded as doubtful debts.

You have been instructed to make a provision for bad debts at 30 November 19X8. This should include a specific provision for debts regarded as doubtful and a general provision of 5 per cent of trade debtors.

Show the ledger entries in respect of the above and the relevant balance sheet extract.

Provision for bad debts at 30 November 19X8	£
Specific provision—C. Steven	240
M. Evans	150
A. Mitchell	210
	600
General provision—	900
5 per cent × (£18,900 − £300 − £600)	
	1,500

F. Simons

19X8			19X8		
30 Nov	Balance b/d	300	30 Nov	Bad debts	300

Bad debts

19X8			19X8		
30 Nov	F. Simons	300	30 Nov	Profit and loss a/c	300

Provision for bad debts

19X8			19X7		
30 Nov	Balance c/d	1,500	30 Nov	Balance b/d	1,000
			19X8		
			30 Nov	Profit and loss a/c	500
		1,500			1,500
			19X8		
			30 Nov	Balance b/d	1,500

Profit and loss account

Bad debts	300
Provision for bad debts	500

Balance sheet
Current assets

Debtors (18,900 − 300)	18,600
Less: Provision for bad debts	1,500
	17,100

Notes

1. No entries are made in the accounts of those debtors which comprise the specific provision since these are only doubtful debts and thus not yet regarded as irrecoverable.
2. The balance carried down on the provision for bad debts account at the end of the year is always the amount of the new provision. The amount charged to the profit and loss account is the difference between the provision at the end of the current year and that at the end of the previous year. In this example the provision is increased from £1,000 to £1,500 by a means of credit to the provision for bad debts account of £500 and a corresponding debit to the profit and loss account.
3. In computing the amount of the general provision any bad debts and specific provisions must be deducted from the debtors. Otherwise the specific provision would be duplicated and a provision would be made for debts already written off as bad, which is clearly nonsense.
4. The bad debts written off must also be removed from debtors in preparing the balance sheet.
5. There is another method of accounting for bad debts and provisions for bad debts which essentially involves combining these two accounts. This is shown below.

(Provision for) bad debts

19X8			19X7		
30 Nov	F. Simons	300	30 Nov	Balance b/d	1,000
30 Nov	Balance c/d	1,500	19X8		
			30 Nov	Profit and loss a/c	800
		1,800			1,800
			19X8		
			30 Nov	Balance b/d	1,500

Profit and loss account

Bad debts	800	

The combined charge to the profit and loss account for the year in respect of bad debts and the provision for bad debts is the difference between the two sides of the (provision for) bad debts account after inserting the amount of the provision at 30 November 19X8 as a balance carried down. The charge to the profit and loss account under both methods is always the same in total.

Example 12.2 (continuation of Example 12.1)
During the year ended 30 November 19X9 C. Steven was declared bankrupt and a first dividend of £140 was received from the trustee. M. Evans was also declared bankrupt and a first and final dividend of £30 was received from the trustee. A. Mitchell paid his debt in full. A further debt of £350 owed by R. Jackson that is included in the debtors at 30 November 19X8 proved to be bad.

The trade debtors at 30 November 19X9 were £24,570. This figure is after recording all money received but does not take into account bad debts.

You have been instructed to make a provision for bad debts at 30 November 19X9. This should include a specific provision for doubtful debts and a general provision of 5 per cent of trade debtors.

Show the ledger entries in respect of the above and the relevant balance sheet extract.

Provision for bad debts at 30 November 19X9

	£
Specific provision—C. Steven (£240 − £140)	100
General provision—	1,200
5 per cent × (£24,570 − £120 − £350 − £100)	1,300

C. Steven

19X8			19X9		
30 Nov	Balance b/d	240	30 Nov	Bank	140
			30 Nov	Balance c/d	100
		240			240
19X9					
30 Nov	Balance b/d	100			

M. Evans

19X8			19X9		
30 Nov	Balance b/d	150	30 Nov	Bank	30
			30 Nov	Bad debts	120
		150			150

R. Jackson

19X8			19X9		
30 Nov	Balance b/d	350	30 Nov	Bad debts	350

Bad debts

19X9			19X9		
30 Nov	M. Evans	120	30 Nov	Profit and loss a/c	470
30 Nov	R. Jackson	350			
		470			470

Provision for bad debts

19X9			19X8		
30 Nov	Profit and loss a/c	200	30 Nov	Balance b/d	1,500
30 Nov	Balance c/d	1,300			
		1,500			1,500
			19X9		
			30 Nov	Balance b/d	1,300

Profit and loss account

| Bad debts | 470 | Provision for bad debts | 200 |

Balance sheet

Current assets

		£	£
Debtors (£24,570 − £120 − £350)		24,100	
Less: Provision for bad debts		1,300	22,800

Alternative method

(Provision for) bad debts

19X9			19X8		
30 Nov	M. Evans	120	30 Nov	Balance b/d	1,500
30 Nov	R. Jackson	350	19X9		
30 Nov	Balance c/d	1,300	30 Nov	Profit and loss a/c	270
		1,700			1,700
			19X9		
			30 Nov	Balance b/d	1,300

Notes

1. The amount due from M. Evans is written off as a bad debt because the final dividend in bankruptcy was declared, which means that no more money will be received in respect of this debt. However, the amount due from C. Steven is not written off as a bad debt, despite the fact that he was declared bankrupt, because further dividends are expected. Thus this debt is the subject of a specific provision in respect of the amount still outstanding.
2. No entries are required where a debt that was previously treated as specific provision is subsequently paid as in the case of A. Mitchell.
3. The main method shown above which has separate bad debts and provision for bad debts accounts is the most common in practice. However this tends to obscure the logic behind provisions for bad debts, because it accounts for the provision separately from the bad debts. The 'alternative method' shown above allows the logic to be demonstrated as follows. The bad debt for the year (£120 + £350 = £470) are set against the provision at the end of the previous year (£1,500). Any under- or over-provision (£1,500 − £470 = over-provision of £1,030) is written back to the profit and loss account. The amount of the provision required at the end of the current year (£1,300) is then created in full by debiting the profit and loss account with this amount. This can be illustrated as follows:

(Provision for) bad debts

19X9			19X8		
30 Nov	M. Evans	120	30 Nov	Balance b/d	1,500
30 Nov	R. Jackson	350	19X9		
30 Nov	Profit and loss a/c		30 Nov	Profit and loss a/c	1,300
	over-provision	1,030			
30 Nov	Balance c/d	1,300			
		2,800			2,800
			19X9		
			30 Nov	Balance b/d	1,300

The debit entry of £1,030 is the reversal of the over-provision. The credit entry of £1,300 is the creation of the new provision. The net effect is the same as in the previous answer—a debit to the profit and loss account of £270 and a balance on the (provision for) bad debts account of £1,300. However, it should be observed that the over-provision of £1,030 as calculated above is an oversimplification. This is not usually readily identifiable since the bad debts normally comprise not only those relating to sales in the previous year for which a provision was created, but also bad debts arising from sales in the current year. The charge to the profit and loss account shown in the 'alternative method' therefore usually comprises: (a) a reversal of the under- or over-provision; (b) the bad debts arising from sales in the current year; and (c) the amount of the new provision at the end of the current year. Further-more, it should be stressed that nobody would prepare a (provision) for bad debts account in the manner shown immediately above since it involves the unnecessary calculation of the under- or over-provision. However, the illustration serves to demonstrate that: (a) the underlying logic behind the provision for bad debts is essentially to shift the bad debts back into the year in which the goods were sold; (b) this requires an estimate of the provision; and (c) the estimate usually gives rise to an under- or over-provision that has to be reversed. However, this can be done without identifying the under- or over-provision separately by means of a single charge to the profit and loss account when the new provision for bad debts at the end of the current year has been created.

Summary

A debt is treated as irrecoverable if a debtor is unwilling or unable to pay, and the enterprise decides it is uneconomical to pursue the matter further. The ledger entry for irrecoverable debts is to credit the debtors' personal account and debit a bad debts account. The balance on the bad debts account is transferred to the profit and loss account at the end of the accounting year.

Provisions are an application of the prudence concept. A provision is the setting aside of income to meet a known future liability or loss, the amount of which cannot be ascertained exactly, and is thus an estimate. The most common examples are provisions for depreciation and doubtful/bad debts.

A provision for bad debts may consist of either a specific provision and/or a general provision. The accounting entries in respect of a provision for bad debts are made after the trial balance has been extracted when the profit and loss account and balance sheet are being prepared. A charge (or credit) is made to the profit and loss account which consists of an amount necessary to increase (or decrease) the provision at the end of the previous year to the amount required at the end of the current year. The ledger entries are to debit (or credit) the profit and loss account and credit (or debit) a provision for bad debts account. The latter is shown on the balance sheet as a deduction from trade debtors to give a net figure representing the amount the enterprise expects to receive from debtors during the forthcoming accounting year.

Key terms and concepts

Bad debt, general provision for bad debts, irrecoverable debt, provision, provision for bad/doubtful debts, specific provision for bad debts.

Exercises

An asterisk after the question number indicates that there is a suggested answer in the Appendix

12.1. What do you understand by the term 'bad debts'? In what circumstances might a debt be treated as irrecoverable?

12.2. (a) Explain the nature of a provision, including how this differs from a liability.
(b) Give one example of a provision other than provisions for bad debts and depreciation.

12.3. (a) Explain the nature of a provision for bad debts.
(b) Explain the difference between a specific and general provision for bad debts.

12.4. Examine the purpose and logic behind a provision for bad debts, with particular reference to the timing of profits and losses arising from credit sales.

12.5.* A business has an accounting year ending on 31 July. It sells goods on credit and on 31 July 19X1 had trade debtors of £15,680. This includes debts of £410 due from A. Wall and £270 from B. Wood both of which were regarded as irrecoverable.

The business has decided to create a provision for bad debts at 31 July 19X1 of 4 per cent of trade debtors. Previously there was no provision for bad debts.

You are required to show the ledger entries in respect of the above bad debts and provision for bad debts.

12.6.* B. Summers has an accounting year ending on 30 April. At 30 April 19X4 his ledger contained the following accounts.

	£
Trade debtors	25,000
Provision for doubtful debts	750

The trade debtors at 30 April 19X5 were £19,500. This includes £620 due from A. Winters and £880 from D. Spring both of which are thought to be irrecoverable.

You have been instructed to make a provision for bad debts at 30 April 19X5 of 3 per cent of trade debtors.

Show the ledger entries in respect of the bad debts and provision for bad debts.

12.7. The accounts for the year ended 30 November 19X7 of Springboard Limited included a provision for doubtful debts at that date of £900.

During the year ended 30 November 19X8, the company received £500 from Peter Lyon towards the settlement of a debt of £700 which had been written off as irrecoverable by the company in 19X5. There is no evidence that Peter Lyon will be able to make any further payments to the company.

Trade debtors at 30 November 19X8 amounted to £22,000, which includes the following debts it has now been decided to write off as bad:

	£
Mary Leaf	800
Angus Way	300

In its accounts for the year ended 30 November 19X8, the company is to continue its policy of maintaining a provision for doubtful debts of 5 per cent of debtors at the year end.

Note: Bad debts written off or recovered are not to be recorded in the provision for doubtful debts account.

Required:

(a) Prepare the journal entry (or entries) in the books of the company necessitated by the receipt from Peter Lyon.

Notes: 1. Journal entries should include narratives.

2. For the purposes of this question, assume cash receipts are journalized.

(b) Prepare the provision for doubtful debts account in the books of the company for the year ended 30 November 19X8.

(c) The entry for debtors which will be included in the balance sheet as at 30 November 19X8 of the company. (AAT)

12.8. The following transactions are to be recorded. At the beginning of year 1 a provision for doubtful debts account is to be opened. It should show a provision of 2 per cent against debtors of £50,000. During the year bad debts of £2,345 are to be charged to the provision account. At the end of year 1 the bad debts provision is required to be 2 per cent against debtors of £60,000.

In year 2 bad debts of £37 are to be charged against the account. At the end of year 2 a provision of 1 per cent against debtors of £70,000 is required.

Required:

Prepare provision for doubtful debts account for the two years. Show in the account the double entry for each item, and carry down the balance at the end of each year. (ACCA adapted)

12.9. The balance sheet as at 31 December 19X5 of Zoom Products Limited included:

Trade debtors £85,360

The accounts for the year ended 31 December 19X5 included a provision for doubtful debts at 31 December 19X5 of 3 per cent of the balance outstanding from debtors. During 19X6, the company's sales totalled £568,000, of which 90 per cent, in value, was on credit and £510,150 was received from credit customers in settlement of debts totalling £515,000. In addition, £3,000 was received from J. Dodds in a settlement of a debt which had been written off as bad in 19X5; this receipt has been credited to J. Dodds account in the debtors' ledger.

On 30 December 19X6, the following outstanding debts were written off as bad:

J. White £ 600
K. Black £2,000

Entries relating to bad debts are passed through the provision for doubtful debts account whose balance at 31 December 19X6 is to be 3 per cent of the amount due to the company from debtors at that date.

Required:

(a) Write up the provision for doubtful debts account for the year ended 31 December 19X6, bringing down the balance at 1 January 19X7.

(b) Prepare a computation of the amount to be shown as trade debtors in the company's balance sheet at 31 December 19X6.   (AAT)

12.10. Because of their doubtful nature, P. Rudent instructed his accountants to make a specific provision in the accounts for the year ended 30 June 19X5 against the following debts:

	£
J. Black	28
C. Green	6
B. Grey	24
Fawn Ltd	204

He also instructed that a general provision of 5 per cent for doubtful debts should be created on the other debtors, which at 30 June amounted to £8,000.

No further business transactions were entered into with any of these debtors during the year ended 30 June 19X6, but an amount of £9 was received from J. Black's trustee in bankruptcy by way of a first dividend; a first and final dividend of £70 was received from the liquidator of Fawn Ltd and B. Grey paid his debt in full. A further debt of £95 due from S. White proved to be bad.

On 30 June 19X6 P. Rudent instructed his accountants to maintain the provision existing against C. Green's debt and to provide for the balance owing by J. Black, and to make further provision for debts owing by J. Blue £19 and R. Brown £15. The other debtors amounted to £7,500 and the accountants were instructed to make the provision for doubtful debts equal to 5 per cent of these debts.

Show what entries should be made in P. Rudent's nominal ledger to record these facts.   (ACCA)

12.11* M. Shaft has an accounting year ending on 31 December. At 31 December 19X6 the ledger contained the following balances:

	£
Plant and machinery	30,000
Provision for depreciation on plant and machinery	12,500
Trade debtors	10,000
Provision for bad debts	1,260

The provision for bad debts consist of a general provision of £500 and specific provisions comprising: A. Bee £320; C. Dee £180; and F. Gee £260.

The following transactions occurred during 19X7:

31 Mar Part exchanged one piece of plant for another. The part exchange allowance on the old plant was £4,000 and the balance of £1,000 was paid by cheque. The old plant cost £8,000 when it was purchased on 1 July 19X5.

30 Apr A. Bee was declared bankrupt and a first dividend of £70 was received from the trustee.

15 June A debt of £210 owed by J. Kay that is included in the debtors at 31 December 19X6 was found to be bad.

3 Aug C. Dee paid his debt in full.

7 Oct F. Gee was declared bankrupt and a first and final dividend at £110 was received from the trustee.

Plant and machinery is depreciated using the reducing balance method at a rate of 25 per cent per annum on a strict time basis. The trade debtors at 31 December 19X7 were £12,610. This figure is after recording all money received but does not take into account any of the above bad debts. The relevant specific provisions and a general provision for bad debts of 5 per cent should be maintained at 31 December 19X7.

You are required to:

(a) Show the ledger entries in respect of the above, including the charges to the profit and loss account and the balances at 31 December 19X7. Show your workings clearly and take all calculations to the nearest £.

(b) Briefly discuss the similarities between provisions for bad debts and depreciation with particular reference to the accounting concept(s) of which they are applications.

13. Accruals and prepayments

Learning objectives

After reading this chapter the student should be able to:

1. Explain the meaning of the key terms and concepts at the end of the chapter.
2. Explain the conceptual foundation of accruals and prepayments including the nature of the resulting charge to the profit and loss account.
3. Describe the nature of accruals and prepayments and how the amounts can be ascertained in practice.
4. Show the entries for accruals and prepayments in the journal, ledger, profit and loss account and balance sheet.
5. Prepare simple final accounts from a trial balance making the required adjustments for accruals and prepayments.

The nature of and ledger entries for accrued expenses

As discussed in Chapter 10, the accruals concept dictates that costs are recognized as they are incurred, not when money is paid. That is, goods and services are deemed to have been purchased on the date they are received. This gives rise to *accrued expenses/accruals*. These are *'creditors' in respect of services received which have not been paid for at the end of the accounting year*. Accrued expenses can obviously only occur where services are paid for in arrear, such as electricity, gas, etc.

An accrual may comprise either or both of the following:

1. Invoices received (for expenses) that have not been paid at the end of the accounting year.
2. The value of services received for which an invoice has not been rendered at the end of the accounting year.

In the case of the latter, this requires an estimate to be made of the amount of the services consumed during the period between the date of the last invoice and the end of the accounting year. This may be based on any one of the following:

1. A meter reading taken at the end of the accounting year.
2. The amount consumed over a corresponding period of time during the current year.
3. The amount consumed during the same period of the previous year as adjusted for any increase in the unit price.

However, in practice final accounts are often not prepared until some time after the end of the accounting year. By that time the invoice covering the period in question is likely to have been received and can thus be used to ascertain the value of the services consumed during the relevant period.

Although accrued expenses are essentially creditors, rather than have a separate creditors' account it is usual to enter accruals in the relevant expense account. This consists of debiting the amount owing at the end of the year to the expense account as a balance *carried down* and crediting the same account as a balance *brought down*. Thus the amount that will be transferred to the profit and loss account consists of the amount paid during the year plus the accrual at the end of the year (less the accrual at the start of the year). This will reflect the total value of the services that have been received during the current accounting year. The balance brought down is entered on the balance sheet as a current liability. This is illustrated in Example 13.1.

Example 13.1

D. Spring has an accounting year ending on 31 December. The following amounts have been paid for electricity:

Date paid	Quarter ended	£
29 March 19X6	28 February 19X6	96
7 July 19X6	31 May 19X6	68
2 October 19X6	31 August 19X6	73
5 January 19X7	30 November 19X6	82
3 April 19X7	28 February 19X7	105

You are required to show the entries in the light and heat account for the year ended 31 December 19X6 and the relevant balance sheet extract.

Workings
Accrual at 1 Jan 19X6 = $\frac{1}{3} \times$ £96 = £32
Accrual at 31 Dec 19X6 = £82 + ($\frac{1}{3} \times$ £105 = £35) = £117

Light and heat

19X6			19X6		
29 Mar	Bank	96	1 Jan	Accrual b/d	32
7 July	Bank	68	31 Dec	Profit and loss a/c	322
2 Oct	Bank	73			
31 Dec	Accrual c/d	117			
		354			354
			19X7		
			1 Jan	Accrual b/d	117

Balance sheet as at 31 December 19X6

£

Current liabilities
Creditors and accrued expenses   117

Note

1. The amount transferred to the profit and loss account is the difference between the two sides of the light and heat account after entering the accrual at the end of the year.

The nature of and ledger entries for prepaid expenses

The accruals concept also gives rise to *prepaid expenses/prepayments*. These can be described as *debtors in respect of services that have been paid for but not received at the end of the accounting year*. Prepayments can obviously only occur where services are paid for in advance, such as rent, local government taxes, road tax, insurance, etc.

The amount of the prepayment is ascertained by determining on a time basis how much of the last payment made during the accounting year relates to the services that will be received in the following accounting year.

Although prepaid expenses are essentially debtors, rather than have a separate debtors' account it is usual to enter the prepayment in the relevant expense account. This consists of crediting the amount of the prepayment to the expense account as a balance *carried down* and debiting the same account as a balance *brought down*. Thus the amount that will be transferred to the profit and loss account consists of the amount paid during the year minus the prepayment at the end of the year (plus the prepayment at the start of the year). This will reflect the total value of the services that have been received during the current accounting year. The balance brought down is entered on the balance sheet as a current asset. This is illustrated in Example 13.2.

Example 13.2
M. Waters has an accounting year ending on 30 June. The following amounts have been paid as rent:

Date paid	Quarter ended	£
2 June 19X5	31 August 19X5	600
1 September 19X5	30 November 19X5	600
3 December 19X5	28 February 19X6	660
5 March 19X6	31 May 19X6	660
4 June 19X6	31 August 19X6	720

You are required to show the entries in the rent account for the year ended 30 June 19X6 and the relevance balance sheet extract.

Workings
Prepaid at 1 July 19X5 = $^2/_3$ × £600 = £400
Prepaid at 30 June 19X6 = $^2/_3$ × £720 = £480

Rent

19X5			19X6		
1 July	Prepayment b/d	400	30 June	Profit and loss	2,560
1 Sept	Bank	600	30 June	Prepayment c/d	480
3 Dec	Bank	660			
19X6					
5 Mar	Bank	660			
4 June	Bank	720			
		3,040			3,040
19X6					
1 July	Prepayments b/d	480			

Balance sheet as at 30 June 19X6

Current assets	£
Debtors and prepayments	480

Note

1. The amount transferred to the profit and loss account is the difference between the two sides of the rent account after entering the prepayment at the end of the year.

Accruals and prepayments and the preparation of final accounts from the trial balance

The profit and loss account is usually prepared from the trial balance. This involves adjusting the amounts shown in the latter for any accruals and prepayments at the end of the accounting year. It is important to appreciate that because the trial balance is taken out at the end of the accounting year, the amounts shown in it include any accruals and prepayments at the start of the year. Thus, when preparing a profit and loss account from the trial balance, it is only necessary to add to the amount shown in the trial balance any accruals at the end of the accounting year and to subtract any prepayments.

Learning activity 13.1

Get copies of the electricity bills for the house in which you live. From these prepare a light and heat account relating to the last complete calendar year. Repeat this exercise for your car road tax and insurance.

Summary

The accruals concept dictates that costs are recognized as they are incurred, not as money is paid. That is, goods and services are deemed to have been purchased on the date they are received. This gives rise to accrued and prepaid expenses. Accrued expenses are creditors in respect of services received which have not been paid for at the end of an accounting year. Prepaid expenses are debtors in respect of services that have been paid for but not received at the end of an accounting year.

After a trial balance has been extracted, the final accounts are prepared which necessitates adjustments relating to accrued and prepaid expenses. These adjustments are made in the relevant expense accounts in the form of a balance at the end of the year. The remaining difference between the two sides of the expense account is transferred to the profit and loss account, and represents the cost of services received during the year. The balance on the expense account is shown on the balance sheet as a current liability in the case of accruals, or as a current asset in the case of prepayments.

Key terms and concepts

Accruals, accrued expenses, prepaid expenses, prepayments.

Exercises

An asterisk after the question number indicates that there is a suggested answer in the Appendix.

13.1. (a) Explain the nature of accrued and prepaid expenses.
     (b) Describe how the amount of each may be ascertained.

13.2.* K. Wills has an accounting year ending on 31 December. The following amounts were paid in respect of rent and gas:

Expense	Date paid	Quarter ended	£
Rent	1 Nov 19X1	31 Jan 19X2	900
Rent	29 Jan 19X2	30 April 19X2	930
Gas	6 Mar 19X2	28 Feb 19X2	420
Rent	2 May 19X2	31 July 19X2	930
Gas	4 June 19X2	31 May 19X2	360
Rent	30 July 19X2	31 Oct 19X2	930
Gas	3 Sept 19X2	31 Aug 19X2	270
Rent	5 Nov 19X2	31 Jan 19X3	960
Gas	7 Dec 19X2	30 Nov 19X2	390
Gas	8 Mar 19X3	28 Feb 19X3	450

You are required to show the ledger entries in the rent and light and heat accounts for the year ended 31 December 19X2.

13.3. Oriel Ltd, whose financial year runs from 1 June to the following 31 May, maintains a combined rent and rates account in its ledger.

Rent is fixed on a calendar year basis and is payable quarterly in advance. Rent was £2,400 for the year ended 31 December 19X8 and is £3,00 for the year ending 31 December 19X9.

Oriel Ltd has made the following payments of rent by cheque:

Date	Amount	Details
19X8	£	
3 Jan	600	Quarter to 31 Mar 19X8
1 Apr	600	Quarter to 30 June 19X8
1 July	600	Quarter to 30 Sept 19X8
1 Oct	600	Quarter to 31 Dec 19X8
19X9		
3 Jan	750	Quarter to 31 Mar 19X9
1 Apr	750	Quarter to 30 June 19X9

Rates are assessed annually for the year from 1 April to the following 31 March and are payable in one lump sum by 30 September. The rates assessment was £2,040 for the year ended 31 March 19X9 and £2,280 for the year ending 31 March 19X0.

Oriel Ltd paid the rates for the year ended 31 March 19X9 by cheque on 30 September 19X8 and intends to pay the rates for the year ended 31 March 19X0 on 30 September 19X9.

Required:
(a) Prepare the rent and rates account for the year ended 31 May 19X9 only as it would appear in the ledger of Oriel Ltd.
(b) Explain with particular reference to your answer to (a) the meaning of the term 'matching'.   (AAT)

13.4. Munch Catering Ltd whose financial year runs from 1 December to the following 30 November maintains a 'Building occupancy costs' account in its general ledger. This account is used to record all payments in respect of rent, insurance and property taxes on the company's business premises.

Rent is fixed on a calendar year basis and is payable quarterly in advance. Rent was £1,800 for the year ended 31 December 19X9 and is £2,100 for the year ended 31 December 19X0.

Munch Catering Ltd has made the following payments of rent by cheque:

Date	Amount	Details
19X9	£	
29 Sept	450	Quarter to 31 Dec 19X9
29 Dec	525	Quarter to 31 Mar 19X0
19X0		
30 Mar	525	Quarter to 30 June 19X0
29 June	525	Quarter to 30 Sept 19X0
28 Sept	525	Quarter to 31 Dec 19X0

Munch Catering Ltd paid its building contents insurance premium of £547 for the year to 30 November 19X0 on 17 November 19X9. This policy was cancelled as from 31 May 19X0 and Munch Catering Ltd received a cheque for £150 as a rebate of premium on 21 June 19X0. A new buildings contents insurance policy was taken out with a different insurance company with effect from 1 June 19X0. The premium on this policy was £400 and this was paid in full by cheque by Munch Catering Ltd on 18 May 19X0.

Property taxes are assessed annually for the year from 1 April to the following 31 March and are payable in one lump sum by 30 September. Munch Catering Ltd's assessment was £840 for the year to 31 March 19X0 and £1,680 for the year to 31 March 19X1. Munch Catering Ltd paid the assessment for the year ended 31 March 19X0 by cheque on 2 October 19X9 and the assessment for the year ended 31 March 19X1 by cheque on 26 September 19X0.

Required:
Prepare the 'Building occupancy costs' account for the year ended 30 November 19X0 only as it would appear in the general ledger of Munch Catering Ltd. (AAT)

13.5.* The ledger of RBD & Co included the following account balances:

	At 1 June 19X4	At 31 May 19X5
	£	£
Rents receivable: prepayments	463	517
Rent and rates payable		
prepayments	1,246	1,509
accruals	315	382
Creditors	5,258	4,720

During the year ended 31 May 19X5, the following transactions had arisen:

	£
Rents received by cheque	4,058
Rent paid by cheque	7,491
Rates paid by cheque	2,805
Creditors paid by cheque	75,181
Discounts received from creditors	1,043
Purchases on credit	to be derived

Required:
Post and balance the appropriate accounts for the year ended 31 May 19X5, deriving the transfer entries to profit and loss account, where applicable.

(ACCA adapted)

13.6. The balances on certain accounts of Foster Hardware Co. as at 1 April 19X1 were:

	£
Rent and rates payable—accruals	2,200
—prepayments	1,940
Rent receivable—prepayments	625
Vehicles (at cost)	10,540
Provision for depreciation of vehicles	4,720
During the financial year the business	
paid rent by cheque	5,200
paid rates by cheque	3,050
received cheque for rent of sub-let premises	960
traded in vehicle—original cost	4,710
—accumulated depreciation	3,080
—part exchange allowance	1,100
paid balance of price of new vehicle by cheque	5,280
Closing balances as at 31 March 19X2 were:	
Rent and rates payable—accruals	2,370
—prepayments	1,880
Rent receivable—prepayments	680
Vehicles (at cost)	to be derived
Provision for depreciation of vehicles	3,890

Required:
Post and balance the appropriate accounts for the year ended 31 March 19X2, deriving the transfer entries to profit and loss account where applicable.   (ACCA)

13.7. The trial balance of Snodgrass, a sole trader, at 1 January 19X8 is as follows:

	Debit £000	Credit £000
Capital		600
Fixed assets (net)	350	
Trade debtors	200	
Prepayments—rent	8	
—insurance	12	

Trade creditors		180
Accruals—electricity		9
—telephone		1
Stock	200	
Bank	20	
	790	790

The following information is given for the year:

	£000
Receipts from customers	1,000
Payments to suppliers	700
Payments for: rent	30
insurance	20
electricity	25
telephone	10
wages	100
Proprietor's personal expenses	50
Discounts allowed	8
Bad debts written off	3
Depreciation	50

At 31 December 19X8 the following balances are given:

	£000
Trade debtors	250
Prepayments—rent	10
—telephone	2
Trade creditors	160
Accruals—electricity	7
—insurance	6
Stock	230

Required:
Prepare a trading and profit and loss account for the year, and a balance sheet as at 31 December 19X8.   (ACCA)

14. The preparation of final accounts from the trial balance

Learning objectives

After reading this chapter the student should be able to:

1. Explain the meaning of the key terms and concepts listed at the end of the chapter.
2. Show the journal and ledger entries relating to the treatment of stocks of tools, stationery, fuel, containers, packing materials, livestock, growing crops, etc.
3. Show the journal and ledger entries relating to drawings other than in the form of cash or cheques.
4. Describe the accounting treatment of goods on sale or return and show the ledger entries needed to reverse any incorrect treatment.
5. Prepare an extended trial balance taking into account adjustments for stocks, depreciation, provisions for bad debts, accruals, prepayments, etc.
6. Prepare trading and profit and loss accounts and a balance sheet from an extended trial balance.

Introduction

As explained in Chapter 9, final accounts are prepared after the trial balance has been produced and involves transferring the balances on varies income and expense accounts to the profit and loss account. In addition, the process of preparing final accounts involves a number of *adjustments*, some of which have been described in the last three chapters. These may be summarized as follows:

1. Accounting for stocks and work in progress
2. Provisions for depreciation
3. Provision for bad debts
4. Accruals and prepayments
5. The correction of omissions and errors such as bad debts not written off during the year.

Some further adjustments not addressed in the previous chapters are discussed below.

Stocks of tools, stationery and fuels

As explained in Chapter 11, *loose tools* are regarded as fixed assets, whereas *consumable tools* are designated as revenue expenditure. Thus any stocks of consumable tools, like stocks of stationery and fuel, are treated as current assets. However, irrespective of their classification, the accounting adjustments in respect of these items are essentially the same. That is, the value of the items in stock at the end of the accounting year is entered in the relevant ledger account as a balance carried down on the credit side and as a balance brought down on the debit side (in exactly the same way as with prepaid expenses). The difference between the two sides of the ledger account is then transferred to the profit and loss account. In the case of loose tools this is described as depreciation, which is referred to as having been computed using the revaluation method.

The principle which is applied to each of these items is as follows:

Stock at end of previous year at valuation
Add: Purchases during the year
Less: Stock at end of current year at valuation
= Charge to profit and loss account

The charge to the profit and loss account represents the value of stationery, fuel or tools that has been consumed during the year. The same principle is also applied in the accounts of farming businesses with respect to livestock and growing crops, and in the retailing businesses in accounting for containers and packing materials.

Adjustments for drawings and capital introduced

Drawings may take a number of forms in addition to cash. For example, it is common for the owner to take goods out of the business for his or her personal consumption. This requires an adjustment which may be done by either of two methods: (1) debit drawings and credit purchases with the *cost* of the goods to the business; or (2) debit drawings and credit sales where the goods are deemed to be taken at some other value such as the normal selling price.

Another form of drawings occurs where the business pays the owner's personal debts. A common example of this is taxation on the business profits. Sole traders and partnerships are not liable to taxation as such. It is the owner's personal liability and not that of the business. Therefore if taxation is paid by the business it must be treated as drawings. The ledger entry being to debit drawings and credit the cash book.

A similar form of drawings occurs when the business has paid expenses, some of which relate to the owners private activities. The most common example is where the business has paid motor expenses, some of which relate to the owners private vehicle or the use of a business asset for domestic or social purposes. The ledger entry in this case is to debit drawings and credit the relevant expense account. The principle is exactly the same where the owner takes a fixed asset out of the business for his or her permanent private use.

Some other examples of drawings occasionally found in examination questions include where the owner buys a private asset (e.g. a car, holiday, groceries) for him or herself, or a friend or relative (e.g. spouse), and pays for it from the business cash or bank account. Again the ledger entry is to debit drawings and credit the cash book. A similar but more complicated example is where a debtor of the business either pays the debt to the owner (who pays the money into his or her private bank account), or alternatively the owner accepts some private service (e.g. repairs to his or her private assets, a holiday, etc.) in lieu of payment. In this case the ledger entry is to debit drawings and credit the debtors account.

After all the drawings for the accounting year have been entered in the drawings account, this account must be closed by transferring the balance to the capital account. The entry is to credit the drawings account and debit the capital account.

Capital introduced after the start of a business usually either takes the form of cash/cheques or other assets (e.g. a vehicle). The ledger entry is to credit the capital account and debit the appropriate asset account (e.g. cash book, motor vehicles, etc.). A slight variation of this occurs when the owner buys a business asset (e.g. vehicle or goods for resale) or pays a business expense or liability from his or her private cash/bank account. In this case the ledger entry is to credit the capital account and debit the relevant asset (e.g. motor vehicles), liability, expense or purchases account. A more complicated version of the same principle is where the owner privately provides some service to a creditor of the business in lieu of payment. The ledger entry for this will be to credit the capital account and debit the creditors account.

Some of these examples of drawings and capital introduced are quite common in small businesses, and particularly important in the context of partnerships as will be seen in Chapter 24.

Goods on sale or return

Goods which have been sent to potential customers on sale or return or on approval must not be recorded as sales until actually sold. In the ledger, goods on sale or return at the end of an accounting year are included in stock at cost.

Sometimes, in examination questions, goods on sale or return are recorded as sales. This is an error and must be reversed by means of the following entries:

Debit sales account ⎤   with the selling
Credit trade debtors ⎦   price of the goods

Debit stock account ⎤   with the cost
Credit trading account ⎦   price of the goods

Note that the entries in the stock account and trading account take the form of increasing the amount of the closing stock.

The extended trial balance

As explained above, the preparation of final accounts involves various adjustments. In the preceding three chapters these were described mainly in terms of the necessary ledger entries. However, in practice and in examinations final accounts are usually prepared from the trial balance, the ledger entries being done at some later date when the final accounts are completed.

Because the preparation of final accounts from the trial balance involves a large number of adjustments, in practice it is usual to make these adjustments using an extended trial balance. This may take a number of forms, but a useful approach is to set it up to comprise eight columns made up of four pairs as follows:

1. The trial balance debit side
2. The trial balance credit side
3. Adjustments to the debit side
4. Adjustments to the credit side
5. The profit and loss account debit side

6. The profit and loss account credit side
7. The balance sheet debit side
8. The balance sheet credit side

The first two columns are the normal trial balance. Columns 3 and 4 are used to make adjustments to the figures in the trial balance in respect of provisions for depreciation and bad debts, accruals and prepayments, etc. Columns 5 and 6 are used to compute the amounts that will be entered in the profit and loss account. Columns 7 and 8 are used to ascertain the amounts that will be shown in the balance sheet.

Columns 3 and 4 relating to the adjustments are used like the journal in that items entered in these columns are intended to represent entries that will be made in the ledger. For example, one simple adjustment is the transfer of drawings to the capital account. This takes the form of an entry in the credit adjustment column on the line containing the balance on the drawings account with a corresponding entry in the debit adjustment column on the line containing the balance on the capital account in the trial balance.

Furthermore, adjustments may take the form of an entry in one of the adjustments columns and one of the profit and loss account columns. This is because the adjustment columns and the profit and loss account columns relate to entries that will be made in the ledger. However, no adjustments must be entered in the balance sheet columns because the balance sheet does not involve entries in the ledger.

The most common adjustments found in the extended trial balance are as follows:

1. *Provisions for depreciation*   Debit the profit and loss account column and credit the adjustment column on the line containing the balance on the provision for depreciation account in the trial balance.
2. *Provision for bad debts*   Debit the profit and loss account column and credit the adjustment column on the line containing the balance on the provision for bad debts account with any increase in the provision (opposite for any decrease).
3. *Accruals and prepayments*   Debit and credit the adjustment columns on the line relating to the expense in question.
4. *Stock at the end of the year*   Debit the adjustment column and credit the profit and loss account column. To avoid confusion this may be done on a new line separate from the stock at the start of the year as in Example 14.1 which follows.

After all the necessary adjustments have been made in the adjustment and profit and loss account columns, the amounts that will be entered in the profit and loss account and balance sheet columns can be ascertained. These are found by cross casting the amounts relating to each ledger account shown in the original trial balance. For example, if the original trial balance contained a rent account with a debit balance, any prepayment shown in the credit adjustment column would be deducted from this and the difference entered in the debit profit and loss account column. The prepayment shown in the debit adjustment column would also be extended across and entered in the debit balance sheet column. Expenses with accrued charges are treated in a similar way.

When all the amounts have been entered in the profit and loss account and balance sheet column, the profit (or loss) can be computed in the normal manner as the difference between the two profit and loss account columns. The profit is entered in the profit and loss account debit column and the credit adjustment column. The latter is then extended into the balance sheet credit column and eventually added to the capital account balance.

When all the items in the trial balance have been extended across into the profit and loss account and balance sheet columns and the profit has been ascertained, the amounts in these columns are entered in the final version of the profit and loss account and balance sheet. An illustration of the use of the extended trial balance is given in Example 14.1.

Finally, it should be observed that although the extended trial balance is very common in practice, the time allocated to answering examination questions is unlikely to allow for full presentation of the extended trial balance, and this is rarely a requirement. Without the extended trial balance it becomes difficult to answer final accounts questions in a logical and accurate manner. Some students therefore find it helpful to make use of the trial balance printed on the question paper. Adjustment columns can be drawn on the right-hand side of the trial balance on the question paper, and the necessary adjustments made in rough form to permit the final accounts to be prepared in the examination answer book.

Example 14.1

T. King has an accounting year ending on 30 April. The following trial balance was prepared for the year ended 30 April 19X6:

	Debit £	Credit £
Capital		59,640
Drawings	7,600	
Bank overdraft		1,540
Cash	1,170	
Plant and machinery	87,000	
Provision for depreciation on plant		27,000
Sales		68,200
Purchases	42,160	
Debtors	15,200	
Creditors		12,700
Provision for bad debts		890
Bad debts	610	
Rent	4,200	
Light and heat	3,700	
Stationery	2,430	
Stock	5,900	
	169,970	169,970

You have been given the following additional information:

1. Plant and machinery is depreciated using the reducing balance method at a rate of 10 per cent per annum.
2. The provision for bad debts at 30 April 19X6 should be 5 per cent of debtors.
3. There is an accrual at 30 April 19X6 in respect of gas amounting to £580, and rent prepaid of £600.
4. Stock at 30 April 19X6 was £7,220.

You are required to prepare an extended trial balance at 30 April 19X6 and final accounts in vertical form.

Workings

1. Depreciation = 10 per cent × (£87,000 − £27,000) = £6,000
2. Provision for bad debts = (5 per cent × £15,200) − £890 = £130 decrease

T. King   Extended trial balance as at 30 April 19X6

	Trial balance DR	Trial balance CR	Adjustments DR	Adjustments CR	Profit and loss a/c DR	Profit and loss a/c CR	Balance sheet DR	Balance sheet CR
Capital		59,640						52,040
Drawings	7,600		7,600					
Bank overdraft		1,540		7,600				1,540
Cash	1,170						1,170	
Plant and machinery	87,000						87,000	
Provision for depreciation on plant		27,000		6,000	6,000			33,000
Sales		68,200				68,200		
Purchases	42,160				42,160			
Debtors	15,200						15,200	
Creditors		12,700						12,700
Provision for bad debts		890	130			130		760
Bad debts	610				610			
Rent	4,200		600	600	3,600		600	
Light and heat	3,700		580	580	4,280			580
Stationery	2,430				2,430			
Stock at 1 May 19X5	5,900				5,900			
Stock at 30 April 19X6			7,220			7,220	7,220	
Profit				10,570	10,570			10,570
	169,970	169,970			75,550	75,550	111,190	111,190

T. King
Trading and profit and loss account for the year ended 30 April 19X6

	£	£
Sales		68,200
Less: Cost of sales:		
Stock at 1 May 19X5	5,900	
Add: Purchases	42,160	
	48,060	
Less: Stock at 30 April 19X6	7,220	40,840
Gross profit		27,360
Add: Provision for bad debts		130
		27,490
Less: Expenditure		
Rent	3,600	
Light and heat	4,280	
Stationery	2,430	
Bad debts	610	
Depreciation on plant	6,000	16,920
Net profit		10,570

Balance sheet as at 30 April 19X6

	£	£	£
Fixed assets	*Cost*	*Acc. Depn.*	*WDV*
Plant and machinery	87,000	33,000	54,000
Current assets			
Prepayments		600	
Stock of goods		7,220	
Debtors	15,200		
Less: Provision for bad debts	760	14,440	
Cash		1,170	
		23,430	
Less: Current liabilities			
Accruals	580		
Creditors	12,700		
Bank overdraft	1,540	14,820	
Net current assets			8,610
Net assets			62,610
Capital			
Balance at 1 May 19X5			59,640
Add: net profit			10,570
			70,210
Less: Drawings			7,600
Balance at 30 April 19X6			62,610

Summary

The process of preparing final accounts from a trial balance involves a number of adjustments relating to accounting for stocks, provisions for depreciation, provisions for bad debts, and accruals and prepayments. In addition it will be necessary to make further adjustments in respect of any stocks of tools, stationery, fuel, etc. These are treated as a debit balance on the relevant expense account, and shown on the balance sheet as a current asset. The remaining difference between the two sides of the expense account is transferred to the profit and loss account, and represents the value of goods consumed during the year.

In practice it is common to prepare final accounts using an extended trial balance. This comprises the usual trial balance money columns but with additional money columns to the right. The first pair of these are adjustment columns which are used to make the adjustments referred to above. The second pair represent the entries in the profit and loss account; and the third pair represent the amounts shown in the balance sheet. The amounts which are entered in the profit and loss account and balance sheet columns are ascertained by cross casting the figures relating to each ledger account shown in the original trial balance and the adjustment columns.

Key terms and concepts

Adjustments, consumable tools, drawings, extended trial balance, goods on sale or return, loose tools.

Exercises

An asterisk after the question number indicates that there is a suggested answer in the Appendix.

14.1.* The following is the trial balance of C. Jones as at 31 December 19X9:

	Debit £	Credit £
Capital		45,214
Drawings	9,502	
Purchases	389,072	
Sales		527,350
Wages and salaries	33,440	
Rent and rates	9,860	
Light and heat	4,142	
Bad debts	1,884	
Provision for doubtful debts		3,702
Debtors	72,300	
Creditors		34,308
Cash at bank	2,816	
Cash in hand	334	
Stock	82,124	
Motor car—cost	7,200	
—depreciation		2,100
	£612,674	£612,674

You are provided with the following additional information:

1. Stock at 31 December 19X9 has been valued at £99,356.
2. The rent of the premises is £6,400 p.a., payable half-yearly in advance on 31 March and 30 September.
3. Rates for the year ending 31 March 19X0 amounting to £1,488 were paid on 10 April 19X9.
4. Wages and salaries to be accrued amount to £3,012.
5. Depreciation on the car is to be provided using the straight-line method at a rate of 20 per cent per annum.
6. It has been agreed that further debts amounting to £1,420 are to be written off against specific customers, and the closing provision is to be adjusted to 5 per cent of the revised debtors' figure.

You are required to prepare the trading profit and loss account for the year ended 31 December 19X9, and a balance sheet at that date. This should be done using an extended trial balance.

14.2.* The following is the trial balance of J. Clark at 31 March 19X6:

	Debit £	Credit £
Capital		60,000
Drawings	5,600	
Purchases/sales	34,260	58,640
Returns inwards/outwards	3,260	2,140
Carriage inwards	730	
Carriage outwards	420	
Discount allowed/ received	1,480	1,970
Plant and machinery at cost	11,350	
Provision for depreciation on plant		4,150
Motor vehicles	13,290	
Provision for depreciation on vehicles		2,790
Goodwill	5,000	
Quoted investments	6,470	
Freehold premises at cost	32,000	
Mortgage on premises		10,000
Interest paid/received	1,000	460
Stock	4,670	
Bank and cash	2,850	
Wages	7,180	
Rent and rates	4,300	
Provision for bad debts		530
Debtors/creditors	8,070	4,340
Light and heat	2,640	
Stationery	450	
	145,020	145,020

You are given the following additional information:

1. Goods on sale or return have been treated as sales. These cost £300 and were invoiced to the customer for £400.
2. The provision for bad debts is to be adjusted to 10 per cent of debtors.
3. At 31 March 19X6 there is electricity accrued of £130 and rates prepaid amounting to £210.
4. Stock at 31 March 19X6 was valued at £3,690.
5. During the year the proprietor has taken goods costing £350 from the business for his own use.
6. Depreciation on plant is 25 per cent on the reducing balance method and on vehicles 20 per cent by the same method.
7. Unrecorded in the ledger is the sale on credit on 1 July 19X5 for £458 of a motor vehicle bought on 1 January 19X4 for £1,000.
8. There are bad debts of £370 that have not been entered in the ledger.
9. There was a stock of stationery at 31 March 19X6 which cost £230.

You are required to prepare a trading and profit and loss account for the year and a balance sheet at the end of the year.

14.3. The following trial balance has been extracted from the ledger of Andrea Howell, a sole trader, as at 31 May 19X9, the end of her most recent financial year.

Andrea Howell

Trial balance as at 31 May 19X9	*Debit* £	*Credit* £
Property, at cost	90,000	
Equipment, at cost	57,500	
Provision for depreciation (as at 1 June 19X8)		
—property		12,500
—equipment		32,500
Stock, as at 1 June 19X8	27,400	
Purchases	259,600	
Sales		405,000
Discounts allowed	3,370	
Discounts received		4,420
Wages and salaries	52,360	
Bad debts	1,720	
Loan interest	1,560	
Carriage out	5,310	
Other operating expenses	38,800	
Trade debtors	46,200	
Trade creditors		33,600
Provision for bad debts		280
Cash on hand	151	
Bank overdraft		14,500
Drawings	28,930	
13 per cent loan		12,000
Capital, as at 1 June 19X8		98,101
	612,901	612,901

The following additional information as at 31 May 19X9 is available:

1. Stock as at the close of business was valued at £25,900.
2. Depreciation for the year ended 31 May 19X9 has yet to be provided as follows:
   Property: 1 per cent using the straight line method.
   Equipment: 15 per cent using the straight line method.
3. Wages and salaries are accrued by £140.
4. 'Other operating expenses' include certain expenses prepaid by £500. Other expenses included under this heading are accrued by £200.
5. The provision for bad debts is to be adjusted so that it is 0.5 per cent of trade debtors as at 31 May 19X9.
6. 'Purchases' include goods valued at £1,040 which were withdrawn by Mrs Howell for her own personal use.

Required:
Prepare Mrs Howell's trading and profit and loss account for the year ended 31 May 19X9 and her balance sheet as at 31 May 19X9.   (AAT)

14.4. S. Trader carries on a merchanting business. The following balances have been extracted from his books on 30 September 19X1:

	£
Capital—S. Trader, at 1 October 19X0	24,239
Office furniture and equipment	1,440
Cash drawings—S. Trader	4,888
Stock on hand—1 October 19X0	14,972
Purchases	167,760
Sales	203,845
Rent	1,350
Light and heat	475
Insurance	304
Salaries	6,352
Stationery and printing	737
Telephone and postage	517
General expenses	2,044
Travellers' commission and expenses	9,925
Discounts allowed	517
Discounts received	955
Bad debts written off	331
Debtors	19,100
Creditors	8,162
Balance at bank to S. Trader's credit	6,603
Petty cash in hand	29
Provision for doubtful debts	143

The following further information is to be taken into account:

1. Stock on hand on 30 September 19X1 was valued at £12,972.
2. Provision is to be made for the following liabilities and accrued expenses as at 30 September 19X1: rent £450; lighting and heating £136; travellers' commission and expenses £806; accountancy charges £252.

3. Provision for doubtful debts is to be raised to 3 per cent of the closing debtor balances.
4. Office furniture and equipment is to be depreciated by 10 per cent on book value.
5. Mr Trader had removed stock costing £112 for his own use during the year.

You are required to prepare:

(a) Trading and profit and loss accounts for the year ended 30 September 19X1 grouping the various expenses under suitable headings, and
(b) a balance sheet as at that date   (ACCA)

14.5. F. Harrison is in business as a trader. A trial balance taken out as at 31 January 19X6 was as follows:

	Debit £	Credit £
Purchases	42,400	
Sales		50,240
Returns inwards and outwards	136	348
Salaries and wages	4,100	
Rent, rates and insurance	860	
Sundry expenses	750	
Bad debts	134	
Provision for doubtful debts at 1 February 19X5		280
Stock on hand at 1 February 19X5	13,630	
Fixture and fittings:		
At 1 February 19X5	1,400	
Additions on 30 September 19X5	240	
Motor vehicles:		
At 1 February 19X5	920	
Sale of vehicle (book value at 1 February 19X5 £80)		120
Sundry debtors and creditors	4,610	3,852
Cash at bank and in hand	3,820	
F. Harrison Capital a/c—Balance at 1 February 19X5		20,760
F. Harrison Drawings a/c	2,600	
	£75,600	£75,600

You are required to prepare trading and profit and loss accounts for the year ended 31 January 19X6, and draw up a balance sheet as on that date.
The following information is to be taken into account:

1. Included in sales are goods on sale or return which cost £240 and which have been charged out with profit added at 20 per cent of sale price.
2. Outstanding amounts not entered in the books were: rent £36, sundry expenses £90.
3. Prepayments were: rates £60, insurance £10.
4. Stock on hand on 31 January 19X6 was valued at £15,450.
5. Provision for doubtful debts is to be £340.
6. Depreciation is to be provided for as follows: fixtures and fittings 10 per cent per annum, motor vehicles 25 per cent per annum   (ACCA)

15. Manufacturing accounts and the valuation of stocks

Learning objectives

After reading this chapter the student should be able to:

1. Explain the meaning of the key terms and concepts listed at the end of the chapter.
2. Describe the main difference between the final accounts of a commercial enterprise and those of a manufacturing business.
3. Explain the classification of costs into direct and indirect costs.
4. Describe the different categories of stocks found in a manufacturing business and show how these are treated in the ledger and final accounts.
5. Explain the purpose of a manufacturing account and the various sub-totals normally found in this account.
6. Prepare a manufacturing account, trading and profit and loss account and balance sheet for a manufacturing business in account form or vertical format.
7. Explain the nature of manufacturing profits and show the entries in the final accounts.
8. Describe the methods of valuation of work in progress (WIP) and explain the relationship between these and the treatment of WIP in the manufacturing account.
9. Discuss the method of valuation of finished goods stock including its conceptual foundations and impact on the gross profit.
10. Describe the perpetual inventory system.
11. Describe the main methods of identifying the cost of fungible stocks and demonstrate their application in the valuation of stocks and the cost of sales.
12. Discuss the circumstances in which each of the main methods of identifying the cost of fungible stocks may be justifiable, and describe their impact on the gross profit.

Introduction

The main differences between the accounts of commercial and manufacturing businesses stem from the former buying goods for resale without further processing whereas the latter buy raw materials and components which are processed into finished goods to be sold. This makes it necessary for a manufacturing business to calculate the total factory cost of goods produced. The amount is computed in what is termed a manufacturing account and the result shown in place of 'purchases' in the trading account of a non-manufacturing business. Furthermore, the stocks in the trading account are the stock of finished goods unsold at the start and end of the accounting year. Apart from these differences the profit and loss account of a manufacturing business is the same as that of a commercial business, in that they both contain selling and distribution costs, administrative costs and financial charges (such as interest). The balance sheet is also the same, except that of a manufacturing business will also include a number of different categories of stock, which will be described later.

The classification of costs

One of the major differences between the accounts of a commercial and manufacturing business concerns the classification of costs. In a manufacturing business, costs are usually classified as either direct costs or indirect costs/overheads. *Direct costs* are those which can be traced to or identified with a particular product, and comprise direct materials, direct labour/wages and direct expenses. Overheads are costs which cannot be traced or attributed to a specific product.

Direct materials consist of any goods that form a part of the final product. These are composed of the raw materials and components which a manufacturing business turns into its finished product. In the case of, for example, a car manufacturer, one of its raw materials may be iron ore used to produce engines. However the material inputs do not just consist of raw materials. For example, some of the materials purchased by a car manufacturer may include steel, which is the finished product of another industry. Similarly, many companies find it cheaper to buy rather than manufacture parts of their finished product. For example, car manufacturers buy components such as tyres, lighting equipment, etc., from outside suppliers. Thus direct materials consist of raw materials and various types of components that make up the final product.

Direct labour typically comprises the wages of those employees who physically work on the products or operate the machines that are used to produce the finished products. Wages paid to foremen, supervisors, cleaners, maintenance staff, etc., are not direct wages.

Direct expenses are any expenses that are directly attributable to a specific product. The most common direct expenses are royalties paid for the right to produce the finished product, the cost of any special drawings and sub-contracted work.

Indirect costs/overheads are those costs that cannot be traced, attributed to or identified with a particular product, and comprise factory/production/manufacturing overheads, selling and distribution overheads, and administrative overheads. Examples of factory overheads include the wages of supervisors, foremen, maintenance and cleaning staff, rent and rates, power, light and heat, consumable tools, repairs to plant, depreciation of plant, etc.

Categories of stocks

A manufacturing business also differs from a commercial business in that it has a number of different categories of stocks as follows.

Direct materials

This composed of raw materials and components that have been purchased but not put into production at the end of the accounting year.

Work in progress

This refers to goods that are not complete at the end of the accounting year.

Finished goods

This consists of goods that have been produced but which are unsold at the end of the accounting year.

Purposes and preparation of a manufacturing account

As has already been mentioned, the main purpose of a manufacturing account is to calculate the factory cost of the products that have been completed during the accounting year. This replaces the purchases item in the trading account and thus must be done before the trading account can be prepared (after the trial balance has been completed). In calculating the cost of completed production it is usual to show the following in the manufacturing account in the order shown below.

1. *The direct material cost* of goods that have been put into production during the year. To calculate this it will be necessary to adjust the cost of purchases of direct materials for the opening and closing stocks thus:

   Direct materials in stock at start of year
   add: Purchases of direct materials during year
   less: Direct materials in stock at end of year
   = Cost of direct materials put into production during year

   It is also common to add any carriage inwards to the cost of purchases.

2. *The direct labour costs*
3. *The direct expenses*
4. *The prime cost of production*
   This is the sum of the direct materials, direct labour and direct expenses.
5. *The factory overheads*
6. *The total factory costs*
   This is the sum of the prime costs and the factory overheads.
7. *The factory cost of completed production*
   The total factory costs relate both to those products that have been completed during the year and those which are only partially completed at the end of the year. To arrive at the factory cost of completed production it is therefore necessary to make an adjustment for the opening and closing work in progress thus:

   Work in progress at start of year
   add: Total factory costs
   less: Work in progress at end of year
   = Factory costs of completed production

The factory cost of completed production is transferred to the trading account in place of 'purchases' in a non-manufacturing business. The cost of sales is computed by adjusting the cost of completed production for the opening and closing stocks of finished goods thus:

Stock of finished goods at start of year
add: Factory costs of completed production
less: Stock of finished goods at end of year
= Cost of goods sold

Note that all the above adjustments in respect of direct materials stocks, WIP and finished goods are applications of the matching principle. An illustration of the preparation of a manufacturing account is shown in Example 15.1.

Example 15.1

The following information relating to the year ended 30 April 19X7 has been extracted from the books of A. Bush, a motor vehicle component manufacturer.

	£
Sales	298,000
Stocks of direct materials at 1 May 19X6	7,900
Stocks of direct materials at 30 April 19X7	6,200
Work in progress at 1 May 19X6	8,400
Work in progress at 30 April 19X7	9,600
Stocks of finished goods at 1 May 19X6	5,400
Stocks of finished goods at 30 April 19X7	6,800
Purchase of direct materials	68,400
Direct wages	52,600
Production supervisors' salaries	34,800
Sales staff salaries	41,700
Accounting staff salaries	38,200
Royalties paid for products produced under licence	17,500
Cost of power for machinery	9,200
Repairs to plant	6,700
Bad debts	5,100
Interest on bank loan	7,400
Depreciation on plant	18,600
Depreciation on delivery vehicles	13,200
Depreciation on accounting office equipment	11,500

Prepare manufacturing, trading and profit and loss accounts for the year ended 30 April 19X7, showing clearly the total direct/prime costs, manufacturing/factory costs, cost of completed production and cost of sales.

A Bush
Manufacturing, trading and profit and loss accounts for the year ended 30 April 19X7

Direct materials:	£		£
Stock at 1/5/X6	7,900	*Cost of completed*	
Add: Purchases	68,400	*production c/d*	208,300
	76,300		
Less: Stock at 30/4/X7	6,200		
	70,100		
Direct wages	52,600		
Royalties	17,500		
Prime costs	140,200		

Factory overheads:				
Supervisors' salaries	34,800			
Power	9,200			
Repairs to plant	6,700			
Depreciation on plant	18,600			
Manufacturing costs	209,500			
Add: WIP at 1/5/X6	8,400			
	217,900			
Less: WIP at 30/4/X7	9,600			
	208,300			208,300
Finished goods:		Sales		298,000
Stock at 1/5/X6	5,400			
Add: Cost of completed				
production b/d	208,300			
	213,700			
Less: Stock at 30/4/X7	6,800			
Cost of sales	206,900			
Gross profit c/d	91,100			
	298,000			298,000
Selling and distribution				
costs		*Gross profit b/d*		91,100
Sales staff salaries	41,700			
Depreciation on				
vehicles	13,200			
Bad debts	5,100			
Administrative costs:				
Staff salaries	38,200			
Depreciation on				
equipment	11,500			
Interest on loan	7,400	*Net loss c/d*		26,000
	117,100			117,100
Net loss b/d	26,000			

Notes

1. The above has been shown in account form to emphasize the double entry. However, a vertical presentation is usually preferable.
2. Any proceeds from the sale of scrap direct materials is normally credited to the manufacturing account thus reducing the cost of completed production.

Manufacturing profits

In some businesses, manufactured goods are transferred from the factory to the warehouse at market prices, or an approximation thereof in the form of cost plus a given percentage for profit. This is intended to represent the price that the warehouse would have to pay if it bought the goods from an external supplier, or the price the factory would receive if it sold the goods to an external customer. This is commonly referred to as the *transfer price*. The purpose of having internal transfer prices is said to be to make the managers in the factory and warehouse more aware of the impact of market forces, increase motivation and facilitate the evaluation of their performance.

The accounting entries are relatively straightforward. The figure for completed production carried down from the manufacturing account to the trading account will simply be at some transfer price or valuation other than cost. This gives rise to a manufacturing profit (or loss) which will be the difference between the two sides of the manufacturing account. The double entry for this profit (or loss) is to credit (or debit) the profit and loss account.

The valuation of finished goods and work in progress

The work in progress shown in the manufacturing account is usually valued at production/factory cost; that is, prime costs plus factory overheads. This is why the adjustment for the opening and closing work in progress is made after the total factory costs have been computed. Similarly, the finished goods stock shown in the trading account is normally valued at factory costs. This is consistent with the valuation of the completed production, which is also included in the trading account at factory cost. Thus neither the work in progress nor finished goods stock includes other overheads such as selling and distribution costs, administrative costs and interest. Sometimes work in progress is valued at prime cost: that is, excluding factory overheads. In this case the adjustment for work in progress must be made before the factory overheads in the manufacturing account.

The above assertions relating to the valuation of work in progress (WIP) and finished goods stock can be explained further by reference to *Statement of Standard Accounting Practice 9—Stocks and Long Term Contracts*.[1] This states that 'in order to match costs and revenue, costs of stocks should comprise that expenditure which has been incurred in the normal course of business in bringing the product or service to its present location and condition. This expenditure should include, in addition to cost of purchase (of direct materials), such costs of conversion as are appropriate to the location and condition. Costs of conversion comprises: (a) costs which are specifically attributable to units of production, i.e. direct labour, expenses and sub-contracted work; (b) production overheads.' Note that this specifically excludes selling, distribution and administrative overheads.

Finally, it is important to consider that sometimes goods in stock may have to be sold at a price which is below their cost. If there are goods in stock at the end of a given accounting year which are expected to result in a loss, those goods should be valued and entered in the accounts at their expected proceeds of sale and not their cost. This is an application of the prudence concept in that a potential loss is being recognized in the accounts before it is realized. SSAP9 therefore dictates that 'stocks normally need to be stated at cost, or, if lower, at net realisable value. The comparison of cost and net realisable value needs to be made in respect of each item of stock separately. *Net realisable value* [NRV] is the estimated proceeds from the sale of items of stock (and WIP) less all further costs to completion and less all costs to be incurred in marketing, selling and distributing directly related to the items in question.'[1]

The identification of the cost of stock

In the case of both manufacturing and non-manufacturing businesses the determination of the cost/purchase price of goods in stock often presents a major problem. It is frequently not possible to identify the particular batch(es) of goods that were purchased which are in stock at the end of the year. This is referred to as *fungible stock*, which means substantially indistinguishable goods. In these circumstances it is necessary to make an *assumption* about the cost of goods in stock. There are a number of possible assumptions, but the most reasonable assumption will depend on the type of goods involved, the procedure for handling the receipt and sale of stocks, prices, etc. According to SSAP9, the most appropriate assumption is one which 'provides a fair approximation to the expenditure actually incurred'.[1] This is discussed further below.

Most large businesses operate what is called a *perpetual inventory system*, which is a continuous record of the quantity and value of stock. It includes a stores ledger containing an account for each type of good that is purchased. The *stores ledger* accounts are used to record the quantities and prices of goods purchased, the quantities and cost of goods sold (or issued to production in the case of direct materials), and thus the balance and cost of goods in stock after each receipt and sale. However, this system also requires an assumption or decision about the cost of goods in stock, and thus the cost of goods that were sold.

As explained above, there are a number of possible assumptions, or what are referred to as bases/methods of identifying/pricing the cost of stock. The bases make assumptions about the flow of items in stock. These flow assumptions are not selected as a result of the actual way in which stock is used but in order to reflect a particular view of the economic effects of stock usage in accounts. Three common approaches are: (1) 'first in, first out' (FIFO); (2) 'last in, first out' (LIFO); and (3) weighted average. These assume, respectively, that: (1) the oldest stock is sold first; (2) the most recently purchased stock is sold first; and (3) the cost of sales comprises the average cost of all the purchases in stock. Each of these methods is described below using Example 15.2.

Example 15.2

P. Easton commenced business on 1 January 19X1 as a dealer in scrap iron. The following purchases and sales were made during the first six months of 19X1:

> Jan   Purchased 40 tonnes at £5 per tonne
> Feb   Purchased 50 tonnes at £6 per tonne
> Mar   Sold 30 tonnes at £10 per tonne
> Apr   Purchased 70 tonnes at £7 per tonne
> May   Sold 80 tonnes at £15 per tonne

You are required to prepare:

(a)   a perpetual inventory record of the quantities and values of goods purchased, sold and stock; and

(b)   a trading account showing the gross profit for the six months to 30 June 19X1 given that the above are the only purchases and sales.

State any assumptions that you make.

Learning activity 15.1

Attempt part (b) of the above example before proceeding further. Note that an answer which claims it cannot be done is not acceptable. It must be done!

---

1.   First in, first out (FIFO)

The FIFO assumption is that the goods sold are those which have been in stock for the longest time. The stock is therefore composed of the most recent purchases that make up the quantity in stock, and the cost of stock is the price paid for these. Given the FIFO assumption, the answer to Example 15.2 will be as follows:

Stores ledger account

Date	Purchases			Cost of sales			Stock		
	Units	Price	Value	Units	Price	Value	Units	Price	Value
Jan	40	5	200				40	5	200
Feb	50	6	300				40	5	200
							50	6	300
							90		500
Mar				30	5	150	10	5	50
							50	6	300
							60		350
Apr	70	7	490				10	5	50
							50	6	300
							70	7	490
							130		840
May				10	5	50			
				50	6	300			
				20	7	140	50	7	350
				80		490			
Totals	160		990	110		640	50		350

P. Easton
Trading account for the six months ended 30 June 19X1

		£	£
Sales:	30 tonnes @ £10	300	
	80 tonnes @ £15	1,200	1,500
Less:	Cost of sales—		
	Purchases	990	
	Less: Stock at 30 June 19X1	350	640
Gross profit			860

The FIFO method is based on the premiss that the physical movement of goods over time will have this sequence of events, particularly where the goods are perishable. The use of the first in, first out method is favoured by SSAP9, and the Inland Revenue.

2.   Last in, first out (LIFO)

The LIFO assumption is that the goods sold are those which have been in stock for the shortest time. The stock is therefore composed of those goods which have been held for the longest time, and the cost of stock is the price paid for these. Given the LIFO assumptions, the answer to Example 15.2 will be as follows:

Stores ledger account

Date	Purchases			Cost of sales			Stock		
	Units	Price	Value	Units	Price	Value	Units	Price	Value
Jan	40	5	200				40	5	200
Feb	50	6	300				50	6	300
							40	5	200
							90		500
Mar				30	6	180	20	6	120
							40	5	200
							60		320
Apr	70	7	490				70	7	490
							20	6	120
							40	5	200
							130		810
May				70	7	490			
				10	6	60	10	6	60
				80		550	40	5	200
							50		260
Totals	160		990	110		730	50		260

P. Easton
Trading account for the six months ended 30 June 19X1

		£	£
Sales			1,500
Less: Cost of sales—			
Purchases		990	
Less: Stock at 30 June 19X1		260	730
Gross profit			770

The LIFO method may be in accordance with the physical movement of goods in some circumstances. For example, purchases of coal, iron ore, sand and gravel are likely to be piled one on top of the other, and thus goods taken from the top of the heap will probably consist of the most recent purchases. In most other instances it is an unrealistic assumption. However, even where this is the case the LIFO method may be justified in times of rising prices on the grounds that the cost of sales will reflect the most recent prices. This is said to give a more realistic figure of profit since the most recent price is an approximation of the current cost of the goods sold (i.e. their replacement cost). Thus one argument for the LIFO method is that where historical cost accounting is used it gives a 'true and fair view' of the profit in times of changing prices.

Paradoxically the LIFO method is permitted under the Companies Act, but is discouraged by SSAP9 and the Inland Revenue. It is common practice in the USA. The arguments put forward against its use in the UK are that LIFO 'results in stocks being stated in the balance sheet at amounts that bear little relationship to recent cost levels',[1] and it is a poor substitute for a proper system of accounting for changing prices.

3. Weighted average method

The weighted average method is based on the assumption that the goods sold and the stock, comprise a mixture of each batch of purchases. The cost of sales and stock is therefore taken to be a weighted average of the cost of purchases. Given the weighted average assumption, the answer to Example 15.2 will be as follows. Notice that a new weighted average is computed after each purchase.

Stores ledger account

Date	Purchases			Cost of sales			Stock	Weighted	
	Units	Price	Value	Units	Price	Value	Units	average	Value
Jan	40	5	200				40	5	200
Feb	50	6	300				90	5.556	500
Mar				30	5.556	167	60	5.556	333
Apr	70	7	490				130	6.331	823
May				80	6.331	506	50	6.331	317
Totals	160		990	110		673	50		317

Workings for weighted average cost:
February = £500 ÷ 90 units = £5.556
April = £823 ÷ 130 units = £6.331
All calculations to 3 decimal places.

P. Easton
Trading account for the six months ended 30 June 19X1

	£	£
Sales		1,500
Less: Cost of sales—		
Purchases	990	
Less: Stock at 30 June 19X1	317	673
Gross profit		827

Where purchases are mixed together the weighted average method can be justified on the grounds that it is in accordance with the physical events. This often occurs when goods are stored in a single container that is rarely completely emptied, such as in the case of nuts and bolts, liquids and granular substances, etc. Another justification is that when prices are fluctuating it gives a more representative normal price and thus more comparable cost of sales figures.

The weighted average method is approved by SSAP9 and acceptable to the Inland Revenue.

FIFO and LIFO compared

Clearly each of these methods of calculating the cost of stock results in different values for stock and profit. In times of constantly rising prices, FIFO will give a higher figure of profits and value of stock than LIFO to the extent that it matches older, lower costs against revenues. A business should choose whichever method is appropriate to its particular circumstances and apply this consistently in order that meaningful comparisons can be made.

FIFO is by far the most common method used in practice in the UK because it is favoured by SSAP9 and the Inland Revenue. However, some businesses and accountants still advocate the use of LIFO on the grounds that this gives a more realistic figure of profit in times of rising prices. The valuation of stocks is a controversial issue in accounting, and is one of the areas most open to deliberate manipulation. The debate is further accentuated by the fact that the Companies Act and the International Accounting Standards Committee (IASC) permit the use of either FIFO or LIFO. It remains to be seen whether the courts in the UK will insist on the use of those methods favoured by SSAP9, such as FIFO.

Summary

Manufacturing businesses usually classify all their costs as either direct or indirect/overheads. Direct costs comprise direct materials, direct labour and direct expenses. Overheads are classified as either factory overheads, selling and distribution costs, or administrative expenses. Manufacturing businesses also normally have a number of different types of stocks which comprise stocks of direct materials, work in progress (WIP) and finished goods.

The main difference between the final accounts of manufacturing businesses and those of commercial undertakings is that the former includes a manufacturing account. This is used to ascertain the cost of completed production which is entered in the trading account in place of the purchases of a non-manufacturing business. The computation of the cost of completed production necessitates certain adjustments in respect of stocks of direct materials and WIP which are similar to those relating to the calculation of the cost of sales.

WIP and finished goods stocks are usually valued at their factory cost. Direct materials stocks are normally valued at cost. However, SSAP9 dictates that if the net realizable value (NRV) of any of these stocks is lower than their cost, they must be included in the final accounts at their NRV. This is an application of the prudence concept. Furthermore, it is frequently not possible to identify the cost of goods in stock. This is referred to as fungible stock which means that the goods are substantially indistinguishable from each other. In these circumstances it is necessary to make an assumption about the cost of goods in stock and thus the cost of goods sold (or issued to production in the case of direct materials). The most common assumptions are first in, first out (FIFO), last in, first out (LIFO), and a weighted average cost. In times of changing prices each will give a different value of stocks, the cost of sales and thus the profit.

Key terms and concepts

Administrative overheads, cost of completed production, direct cost, direct expense, direct labour, direct material, factory/manufacturing/production cost, factory/production overheads, finished goods, first in first out, fungible stock, indirect cost, last in first out, manufacturing account, manufacturing profits, net realizable value, overheads, perpetual inventory system, prime cost, selling and distribution overheads, stores ledger, transfer price, weighted average cost, work in progress.

Reference

1. Accounting Standards Committee (1988). *Statement of Standard Accounting Practice 9—Stocks and Long Term Contracts* (ICAEW).

Exercises

An asterisk after the question number indicates that there is a suggested answer in the Appendix.

15.1. (a) Explain the difference between direct costs and overheads.
  (b) Describe the different types of direct costs and overheads found in a manufacturing business.

15.2. Describe the different categories of stocks normally held by a manufacturing business.

15.3. (a) Explain the main purpose of a manufacturing account.
  (b) Describe the structure and main groups of costs found in a manufacturing account.

15.4. (a) Explain the difference between the total factory cost of production and the factory cost of completed production.
  (b) What is the justification for adjusting the total factory cost for work in progress rather than, say, the total prime/direct cost?

15.5. Work in progress and finished goods stocks should be valued at the cost of purchase and conversion. Explain.

15.6. Explain the circumstances in which stocks might be shown in the accounts at a value different from their historical cost.

15.7. Explain fully the basis on which finished goods stock and work in progress should be valued in final accounts.

15.8. Explain how the matching principle and the accruals concept are applied to the valuation of stocks.

15.9. (a) What is a perpetual inventory system?
  (b) Describe three methods of calculating the cost of fungible stocks.
  (c) Explain the circumstances in which each of these methods may be justifiable.

15.10.   'In selecting a method of calculating the cost of stock, management should ensure that the method chosen bears a reasonable relationship to actual costs. Methods such as . . . LIFO do not usually bear such a relationship' (ASC, SSAP9). Discuss.

15.11.* The trial balance extracted at 30 April 19X4 from the books of Upton Upholstery, a furniture manufacturer, is given below.

	Debit £	Credit £
Factory machinery at cost	28,000	
Factory machinery depreciation 1/5/X3		5,000
Office equipment	2,000	
Office equipment depreciation 1/5/X3		800
Trade debtors and creditors	15,000	16,000
Cash and bank	2,300	
Bank loan		11,000
Stocks 1/5/X3—Raw materials	4,000	
Incomplete production	16,400	
Finished goods	9,000	
Carriage inwards	1,200	
Carriage outwards	700	
Purchases—raw material	84,000	
Light and heat	3,000	
Rent and rates	6,600	
Direct factory wages	19,900	
Office wages	5,200	
Sales commission to selling agents	1,400	
Sales of finished goods		140,000
Capital account		35,000
Drawings	9,100	
	£207,800	£207,800

Notes

1. At 30 April 19X4, accrued direct factory wages amounted to £600 and office wages £100; rent paid included £600 paid on 20 January 19X4, for the period 1 January to 30 June 19X4.
2. Records showed that, at the year end, stock values were as follows; raw materials £5,400; incomplete production £17,000; finished goods £8,000.
3. Depreciation should be allowed for factory machinery on the straight line method over seven years, and office equipment on the reducing balance method at 25 per cent p.a.
4. A provision of £1,000 should be made for doubtful debts.
5. Light and heat should be apportioned between the factory and office in the ratio 4 : 1 respectively; rent and rates in the ratio 3 : 1 respectively.

You are required to prepare manufacturing, trading and profit and loss accounts for the year ended 30 April 19X4 and a balance sheet at that date.

15.12.* From the following information prepare manufacturing, trading and profit and loss accounts for the year ended 31 December 19X9. Show clearly the prime cost, factory cost of completed production, cost of sales, gross profit, administrative overheads, selling and distribution overheads and net profit.

	£
Stock of raw materials at 1 Jan 19X9	2,453
Work in progress valued at factory cost at 1 Jan 19X9	1,617
Stock of finished goods at 1 Jan 19X9	3,968
Purchases of raw materials	47,693
Purchases of finished goods	367
Raw materials returned to suppliers	4,921
Carriage outwards	487
Carriage inwards	683
Direct wages	23,649
Administrative salaries	10,889
Supervisors' wages	5,617
Royalties payable	7,500
Electricity used in factory	2,334
Light and heat for administrative offices	998
Sales staff salaries and commission	8,600
Bad debts	726
Discount received	2,310
Discount allowed	1,515
Depreciation—plant	13,400
—delivery vehicles	3,700
—office fixtures and furniture	1,900
Rent and rates (factory $^3/_4$, office $^1/_4$)	4,800
Delivery expenses	593
Postage and telephone	714
Printing and stationery	363
Proceeds from the sale of scrap metal	199
Interest payable on loan	3,000
Bank charges	100
Insurance on plant	1,750
Advertising	625
Repairs to plant	917
Sales	145,433

Purchases of raw materials include £2,093, and direct wages £549, for materials and work done in constructing an extension to the factory.

Stock of raw materials at 31 Dec 19X9	3,987
Work in progress valued at factory cost at 31 Dec 19X9	2,700
Stock of finished goods at 31 Dec 19X9	5,666

15.13. W. Wagner, a manufacturer, provided the following information for the year ended 31 August 19X0:

	£
Stocks at 1 September 19X9	
Raw materials	25,000
Work in progress	15,900
Finished goods	26,600
Raw materials purchased	176,600
Factory general expenses	14,800
Direct wages	86,900
Repairs to plant and machinery	9,900
Factory lighting and heating	20,010
Carriage inwards	1,910
Carriage outwards	2,500
Sales	320,000
Raw materials returned	7,800
Factory maintenance wages	19,000
Administrative expenses	30,000
Selling and distribution expenses	15,100
Plant and machinery at cost	178,000
Freehold land and buildings at cost	160,000
Provision for depreciation on plant and machinery	
(at 1 September 19X9)	80,000

Additional information:

1. Amounts owing at 31 August 19X0:

	£
Direct wages	4,800
Factory heating and lighting	1,500

2. Depreciation on plant and machinery is to be provided at 10 per cent per annum on cost. There were no sales or purchases of plant and machinery during the year.

3. Stocks at 31 August 19X0:

	£
Raw materials	30,000
Work in progress	17,800
Finished goods	35,090

The raw materials are valued at cost, the work in progress at factory cost, while the stock of finished goods is valued at the factory transfer price.

4. All manufactured goods are transferred to the warehouse at factory cost plus 10 per cent.

5. Other balances at 31 August 19X0:

	£
Trade debtors	26,000
Trade creditors	38,000

Required:
(a)   A manufacturing account for the year ended 31 August 19X0.
(b)   A trading and profit and loss account for the year ended 31 August 19X0.

(AEB adapted)

15.14. Zacotex Ltd, a manufacturer, produced the following financial information for the year ended 31 March 19X9.

	£
Raw material purchases	250,000
Direct labour	100,000
Direct expenses	80,900
Indirect factory labour	16,000
Factory maintenance costs	9,700
Machine repairs	11,500
Sales of finished goods during the year	788,100
Stocks at 1 April 19X8:	
Raw materials	65,000
Finished goods	48,000
Work in progress	52,500
Other factory overhead	14,500
Factory heating and lighting	19,000
Factory rates	11,500
Administration expenses	22,000
Selling and distribution expenses	36,800

Additional information:

1. The stocks held at 31 March 19X9 were:

Raw materials	£51,400
Finished goods	£53,800
Work in progress	£41,000

NB: Raw materials are valued at cost; finished goods at factory cost; work in progress at factory cost.

Of the raw materials held in stock at 31 March 19X9, £15,000 had suffered flood damage and it was estimated that they could only be sold for £2,500. The remaining raw material stock could only be sold on the open market at cost less 10 per cent.

2. One quarter of the administration expenses are to be allocated to the factory.

3. The raw materials purchases figure for the year includes a charge for carriage inwards. On 31 March 19X9 a credit note for £1,550 was received in respect of a carriage inwards overcharge. No adjustment had been made for this amount.

4. Expenses in arrear at 31 March 19X9 were:

	£
Direct labour	6,600
Machine repairs	1,700
Selling and distribution expenses	4,900

5. Plant and machinery at 1 April 19X8:

	£
At cost	250,000
Aggregate depreciation	75,000

During the year an obsolete machine (cost £30,000, depreciation to date £8,000) was sold as scrap for £5,000. On 1 October 19X8 new machinery was purchased for £70,000 with an installation charge of £8,000.

The company depreciates its plant and machinery at 10 per cent per annum on cost on all items in company ownership at the end of the accounting year.

6. An analysis of the sales of finished goods revealed the following:

	£
Goods sold for cash	105,000
Goods sold on credit	623,100
Goods sold on sale or return: returned	25,000
Goods sold on sale or return: retained and invoice confirmed	35,000
	788,100

7. On 1 April 19X8 the company arranged a long-term loan of £250,000 at a fixed rate of interest of 11 per cent per annum. No provision had been made for the payment of the interest.

Required:

For the year ended 31 March 19X9:

(a) A manufacturing account showing prime cost and factory cost of goods produced.

(b) A trading and profit and loss account.   (AEB adapted)

15.15. On 1 April 19X5, Modern Dwellings Ltd commenced business as builders and contractors. It expended $14,000 on the purchase of six acres of land with the intention of dividing the land into plots and building 72 houses thereon.

During the year ended 31 March 19X6 roads and drains were constructed for the project at a total cost of £8,320. Building was commenced, and on 31 March 19X6, 30 houses had been completed and eight were in course of construction. During the year the outlay on houses was as follows:

	£
Materials, etc.	36,000
Labour and sub-contracting	45,000

The value of the work in progress on the uncompleted houses at 31 March 19X6 amounted to £8,500, being calculated on the actual cost of materials, labour and sub-contracting to date.

During the year, 24 houses had been sold, realizing £80,000.

Prepare a trading account for the year ended 31 March 19X6. It can be assumed that the plots on which the 72 houses are to be built are all of equal size and value.

(ACCA)

15.16. After stocktaking for the year ended 31 May 19X5 had taken place, the closing stock of Cobden Ltd was aggregated to a figure of £87,612.

During the course of the audit which followed, the undernoted facts were discovered:

1. Some goods stored outside had been included at their normal cost price of £570. They had, however, deteriorated and would require an estimated £120 to be spent to restore them to their original condition, after which they could be sold for £800.

2. Some goods had been damaged and were now unsaleable. They could, however, be sold for £110 as spares after repairs estimated at £40 had been carried out. They had originally cost £200.

3. One stock sheet had been over-added by £126 and another under-added by £72.

4. Cobden Ltd had received goods costing £2,010 during the last week of May 19X5 but because the invoices did not arrive until June 19X5, they have not been included in stock.

5. A stock sheet total of £1,234 had been transferred to the summary sheet as £1,243.

6. Invoices totalling £638 arrived during the last week of May 19X5 (and were included in purchases and in creditors) but, because of transport delays, the goods did not arrive until late June 19X5 and were not included in closing stock.

7. Portable generators on hire from another company at a charge of £347 were included, at this figure, in stock.

8. Free sample sent to Cobden Ltd by various suppliers had been included in stock at the catalogue price of £63.

9. Goods costing £418 sent to customers on a sale or return basis had been included in stock by Cobden Ltd at their selling price, £602.

10. Goods sent on a sale or return basis to Cobden Ltd had been included in stock at the amount payable (£267) if retained. No decision to retain had been made.

Required:
Using such of the above information as is relevant, prepare a schedule amending the stock figure as at 31 May 19X5. State your reason for each amendment or for not making an amendment. (ACCA)

15.17. Your company sells, for £275 each unit, a product which it purchases from several different manufacturers, all charging different prices. The manufacturers deliver at the beginning of each week throughout each month. The following details relate to the month of February.

	Quantity	Cost each £	Sales (units)
Opening stock	10	145	
Deliveries: Week 1	20	150	15
Week 2	34	165	33
Week 3	50	145	35
Week 4	30	175	39

From the above data you are required to:

(a) prepare stock records detailing quantities and values using the following pricing techniques:

    (i)   last in, first out (LIFO);

    (ii)   first in, first out (FIFO);

    (iii) weighted average cost (calculated monthly to the nearest £).

(b) prepare trading accounts using each of the stock pricing methods in (a) above and showing the gross profit for each method.

(c) compare the results of your calculations and state the advantages and disadvantages of FIFO and LIFO pricing methods in times of inflation.   (JMB)

15.18.* A businessman started trading with a capital in cash of £6,000 which he placed in the business bank account at the outset.

His transactions, none of which were on credit, were as follows (in date sequence) for the first accounting period. All takings were banked immediately and all suppliers were paid by cheque. He traded in only one line of merchandise.

Purchases		Sales	
Quantity	Price per unit	Quantity	Price per unit
No.	£	No.	£
1,200	1.00		
1,000	1.05	800	1.70
600	1.10	600	1.90
900	1.20	1,100	2.00
800	1.25	1,300	2.00
700	1.30	400	2.05

In addition he incurred expenses amounting to £1,740, of which he still owed £570 at the end of the period.

Required:

Prepare separately using the FIFO (first in, first out), the LIFO (last in, first out) and weighted average (calculated for the period to the nearest penny) methods of stock valuation:

(a) a statement of cost of sales for the period; and

(b) a balance sheet at the end of the period.

Note: Workings are an integral part of the answer and must be shown.

(ACCA adapted)

15.19 S. Bullock, a farmer, makes up his accounts to 31 March each year. The trial balance extracted from his books as at 31 March 19X6 was as follows:

	Debit £	Credit £
Purchases—livestock, seeds, fertilizers, fodder, etc.	19,016	
Wages and National Insurance	2,883	
Rent, rates, telephone and insurance	1,018	
Farrier and veterinary charges	34	

Carriage	1,011	
Motor and tractor running expenses	490	
Repairs—Farm buildings	673	
Implements	427	
Contracting for ploughing, spraying and combine work	308	
General expenses	527	
Bank charges	191	
Professional charges	44	
Sales		29,162
Motor vehicles and tractors—as at 1 April 19X5	1,383	
additions	605	
Implements—as at 1 April 19X5	2,518	
additions	514	
Valuation as at 1 April 19X5:		
Livestock, seeds, fertilizers, fodder, etc.	14,232	
Tillages and growing crops	952	
Loan from wife		1,922
Minister Bank		4,072
S. Bullock—Capital at 1 April 19X5		6,440
Current Account at 1 April 19X5		6,510
Drawings during the year	1,280	
	£48,106	£48,106

	£	£
On 31 March 19X6:		
Debtors and prepayments were:		
Livestock sales	1,365	
Motor licences	68	
Liabilities were: Seeds and fertilizers		180
Rent, rates and telephone		50
Motor and tractor running expenses		40
Professional charges		127
Contracting		179
General expenses		54

Included in the above-mentioned figure of £50 is £15 for rent and this is payable for the March 19X6 quarter. In arriving at this figure the landlord has allowed a deduction of £235 for materials purchased for repairs to the farm buildings, which were carried out by S. Bullock, and is included in the 'Repairs to farm buildings' shown in the trial balance. In executing these repairs it was estimated that £125 labour costs were incurred and these were included in 'Wages and National Insurance'. This cost was to be borne by S. Bullock.

The valuation as at 31 March 19X6 was:

	£
Livestock, seeds, fertilizers, fodder, etc.	12,336
Tillages and growing crops	898

Depreciation, calculated on the book value as at 31 March 19X6, is to be written off as follows:

Motor vehicles and tractors   25 per cent per annum
Implements   12½ per cent annum

You are requested to prepare:

(a) the profit and loss account for the year ended 31 March 19X6, and
(b) the balance sheet as at that date   (ACCA)

16. The bank reconciliation statement

Learning objectives

After reading this chapter the student should be able to:

1. Explain the meaning of the key terms and concepts listed at the end of the chapter.
2. Explain the purpose and nature of bank reconciliations.
3. Identify and correct errors and omissions in a cash book.
4. Prepare a bank reconciliation statement.

The purpose and preparation of bank reconciliations

The purpose of preparing a bank reconciliation statement is to ascertain whether or not the balance shown in the cash book at the end of a given accounting period is correct by comparing it with that shown on the bank statement/passbook supplied by the bank. In practice, these two figures are rarely the same because of errors, omissions and the timing of bank deposits and cheque payments.

The bank reconciliation is not done in a book of account and thus is not a part of the double entry system. It must be prepared at least yearly before the final accounts are compiled. Because most businesses usually have a large number of cheque transactions they often prepare a bank reconciliation statement either monthly or at least quarterly.

The first step in the preparation of a bank reconciliation involves identifying payments, and sometimes receipts, that are on the bank statement but which have not been entered in the cash book. Such payments may include cheques dishonoured, bank charges and interest, standing orders for hire purchase instalments, insurance premiums, loan interest, etc. Occasionally, receipts such as interest and dividends received by credit transfer are also found to be on the bank statement but not in the cash book. When these omissions of receipts and payments occur the remedy is obviously to enter them in the cash book and compute a new balance. However, in examination questions the student is sometimes required to build them into the bank reconciliation statement instead.

In addition to the above omissions there are nearly always also receipts and payments in the cash book which at the date of the reconciliation have not yet been entered by the bank on the bank statement. These consist of:

1. Cheques and cash received that have been paid into the bank and entered in the cash book but which have not *yet* been credited on the bank statement at the end of the accounting period when the bank reconciliation statement is being prepared.

2. Cheques drawn that have been sent to the payee and entered in the cash book but which have not *yet* been presented to our bank for payment or which have not *yet* passed through the bank clearing system and thus do not appear on the bank statement at the end of the accounting period when the bank reconciliation statement is being prepared.

Example 16.1 shows the procedure involved in preparing a bank reconciliation statement.

Example 16.1
The following is the cash book of J. Alton for the month of June 19X5.

Cash book

19X5			19X5		
1 June	Balance b/d	1,000	2 June	D. Cat	240✓
11 June	A. Hand	370✓	13 June	E. Dog	490✓
16 June	B. Leg	510✓	22 June	F. Bird	750
24 June	C. Arm	620	30 June	Balance c/d	1,200
30 June	Cash	180			
		2,680			2,680

The following is the statement of J. Alton received from his bank:

Bank statement

Date	Details	Debit	Credit	Balance
19X5				
1 June	Balance			1,000
5 June	D. Cat	240✓		760
15 June	A. Hand		370✓	1,130
18 June	E. Dog	490✓		640
20 June	Dividend received		160	800
21 June	B. Leg		510✓	1,310
30 June	Bank charges	75		1,235

In practice bank statements do not usually show the names of the people from whom cheques were received and paid. It is therefore necessary to identify the payments by means of the cheque number. However, the use of names simplifies the example for ease of understanding. The procedure is essentially the same.

The first step is to tick all those items which appear in both the cash book and on the bank statement during the month of June. A note is made of the items which are unticked:

1. Cheques and cash paid into the bank and entered in the cash book but not credited on the bank statement by 30 June 19X5 = C. Arm £620 + Cash £180 = £800.
2. Cheques drawn and entered in the cash book not presented for payment by 30 June 19X5 = F. Bird £750.
3. Amounts received by credit transfer shown on the bank statement not entered in the cash book = Dividends £160.
4. Standing orders and other payments shown on the bank statement not entered in the cash book = Bank charges £75.

Clearly items 1 and 2 above will eventually appear on the bank statement in a later month. Items 3 and 4 must be entered in the cash book. However, the purpose of the bank reconciliation statement is to ascertain whether the difference between the balance in the cash book at 30 June 19X5 of £1,200 and that shown on the bank statement at the same date of £1,235 is explained by the above list of unticked items. Alternatively, are there other errors or omissions that need to be investigated?

The bank reconciliation statement will appear as follows:

J. Alton
Bank reconciliation statement as at 30 June 19X5

	£	£
Balance per cash book		1,200
Add: Dividends received not entered in cash book	160	
Cheques not yet presented	750	910
		2,110
Less: Bank charges not entered in cash book	75	
Amounts not yet credited	800	875
Balance per bank statement		1,235

It can thus be seen that since the above statement reconciles the difference between the balances in the cash book and on the bank statement, there are unlikely to be any further errors or omissions.

Notes

1. The dividends received are added to the cash book balance because it is lower than the bank statement balance as a result of this omission. Also it will increase by this amount when the dividends are entered in the cash book.
2. The bank charges are deducted from the cash book balance because the bank statement balance has been reduced by this amount but the cash book balance has not. Also, the cash book balance will decrease by this amount when the bank charges are entered in the cash book.
3. The cheques not yet presented are added to the cash book balance because it has been reduced by this amount whereas the bank statement balance has not.
4. The amounts not yet credited are deducted from the cash book balance because it has been increased by this amount whereas the bank statement balance has not.

Sometimes in examination questions the student is not given the cash book balance. In this case the bank reconciliation statement is prepared in reverse order as follows:

	£	£
Balance per bank statement		1,235
Add: Amounts not yet credited	800	
Payments on bank statement not in the cash book	75	875
		2,110
Less: Cheques not yet presented	750	
Receipts on bank statement not in the cash book	160	910
= Balance per cash book		1,200

An alternative method of dealing with bank reconciliations is to amend the cash book for any errors and omissions, and only include in the bank reconciliation statement those items which constitute timing differences. This is illustrated in Example 16.2, along with some other items frequently found in examination questions.

Example 16.2
The following is a summary from the cash book of Shopping Ltd for March 19X8;

Cash book

Opening balance b/d	5,610	Payments	41,890
Receipts	37,480	Closing balance c/d	1,200
	43,090		43,090

When checking the cash book against the bank statement the following discrepancies were found:

1. Bank charges of £80 shown in the bank statement have not been entered in the cash book.
2. The bank has debited a cheque for £370 in error to the company's account.
3. Cheques totalling £960 have not yet been presented to the bank for payment.
4. Dividends received of £420 have been credited on the bank statement but not recorded in the cash book.
5. There are cheques received of £4,840 which are entered in the cash book but not yet credited to the company's account by the bank.
5. A cheque for £170 has been returned by the bank marked 'refer to drawer' but no entry relating to this has been made in the books.
7. The opening balance in the cash book should have been £6,510 and not £5,610.
8. The bank statement shows that there is an overdraft at 31 March 19X8 of £1,980.

You are required to:

(a) make the entries necessary to correct the cash book; and
(b) prepare a bank reconciliation statement as at 31 March 19X8.

Cash book

Balance b/d	1,200	Bank charges	80
Dividends	420	Refer to drawer	170
Error in balance	900	Balance c/d	2,270
	2,520		2,520
Balance b/d	2,270		

Shopping Ltd
Bank reconciliation statement as at 31 March 19X8

	£	£
Balance per cash book		2,270
Add: Cheques not yet presented		960
		3,230

Less: Amounts not yet credited	4,840	
Cheque debited in error	370	5,210
Balance per bank statement (overdrawn)		1,980

Notes

1. The cheque debited in error is shown in the bank reconciliation statement rather than the cash book because it will presumably be corrected on the bank statement in due course and thus not affect the cash book.
2. Sometimes in examination questions the cash book contains a credit (i.e. overdrawn) balance. In this case, the bank reconciliation statement is prepared by reversing the additions and subtractions which are made when there is a favourable cash book balance. The bank reconciliation statement will thus appear as follows:

Balance per cash book (credit/overdrawn)
Add: Amounts not yet credited
Less: Cheques not yet presented
= Balance per bank statement

   Alternatively if the cash book balance is not given in the question and the bank statement contains an overdrawn balance, the bank reconciliation statement would be prepared as follows:

Balance per bank statement (debit/overdrawn)
Add: Cheques not yet presented
Less: Amounts not yet credited
 = Balance per cash book

Learning activity 16.1

Get out your most recent bank statement and your cheque book. Prepare a reconciliation of the balance shown on your bank statement with that shown on your record of cheques received and drawn. If you do not keep a continuous record of your cheque receipts and payments, and thus the current balance, do so in future and repeat the exercise when you receive your next bank statement.

Summary

After extracting a trial balance but before preparing final accounts at the end of each accounting year, the first thing that needs to be done is to check the accuracy of the cash book (or bank account in the ledger). This takes the form of a bank reconciliation, which involves reconciling the balance in the cash book at the end of the year with that shown on the statement received from the bank. These will probably be different for two main reasons. First there may be errors or omissions where amounts shown on the bank statement have not been entered properly in the cash book. These should be corrected in the cash book. Second there are likely to be timing differences. These consist of cheques paid into the bank and cheques drawn entered in the cash book, but not shown on the bank statement at the end of the year. These timing differences are entered on the bank reconciliation statement as explanations for the difference between the balance in the cash book and that on the bank statement. If the timing differences provide a reconciliation of the two balances, the cash book balance is deemed to be correct. Otherwise the reasons for any remaining difference will need to be investigated.

Key terms and concepts

Amounts not yet credited, bank reconciliation statement, cheques not yet presented.

Exercises

An asterisk after the question number indicates that there is a suggested answer in the Appendix.

16.1. Explain the purpose of a bank reconciliation statement.

16.2. Describe the procedures involved in the collection of the data needed to prepare a bank reconciliation statement.

16.3. The following is a summary from the cash book of the Hozy Company Limited for October 19X7.

	£		£
Opening balance b/d	1,407	Payments	15,520
Receipts	15,073	Closing balance c/f	960
	£16,480		£16,480

On investigation you discover that:

1. Bank charges of £35 shown on the bank statement have not been entered in the cash book.
2. A cheque drawn for £47 has been entered in error as a receipt.
3. A cheque for £18 has been returned by the bank marked 'refer to drawer', but it has not been written back in the cash book.
4. An error of transposition has occurred in that the opening balance in the cash book should have been carried down as £1,470.
5. Three cheques paid to suppliers for £214, £370 and £30 have not yet been presented to the bank.
6. The last page of the paying-in book shows a deposit of £1,542 which has not yet been credited to the account by the bank.
7. The bank has debited a cheque for £72 in error to the company's account.
8. The bank statement shows an overdrawn balance of £124.

   You are required to:

   (a) show what adjustments you would make in the cash book; and
   (b) prepare a bank reconciliation statement as at 31 October 19X7.   (ACCA)

16.4.* The following is a summary of the cash book of Grow Ltd for March 19X9:

Opening balance b/d	4,120	Payments	46,560
Receipts	45,320	Closing balance c/d	2,880
	49,440		49,440

On investigation you discover that at 31 March 19X9:

1. The last page of the paying-in book shows a deposit of £1,904 which has not yet been credited by the bank.
2. Two cheques paid to suppliers for £642 and £1,200 have not yet been presented to the bank.
3. Dividends received of £189 are shown on the bank statement but not entered in the cash book.
4. Bank charges of £105 shown on the bank statement have not been entered in the cash book.
5. A cheque for £54 has been returned by the bank marked 'refer to drawer', but it has not been written back in the cash book.
6. A cheque drawn for £141 has been entered in error as a receipt in the cash book.
7. The bank has debited a cheque for £216 in error to the company's account.

You are required to:

(a) show the adjustments that should be made in the cash book; and
(b) prepare a bank reconciliation statement at 31 March 19X9.

16.5.* On 15 May 19X8, Mrs Lake received her monthly bank statement for the month ended 30 April 19X8. The bank statement contained the following details:

Date	Particulars	Payments	Receipts	Balance
		£	£	£
1 Apr	Balance			1,053.29
2 Apr	236127	210.70		842.59
3 Apr	Bank Giro Credit		192.35	1,034.94
6 Apr	236126	15.21		1,019.73
6 Apr	Charges	12.80		1,006.93
9 Apr	236129	43.82		963.11
10 Apr	427519	19.47		943.64
12 Apr	236128	111.70		831.94
17 Apr	Standing Order	32.52		799.42
20 Apr	Sundry Credit		249.50	1,048.92
23 Apr	236130	77.87		971.05
23 Apr	236132	59.09		911.96
25 Apr	Bank Giro Credit		21.47	933.43
27 Apr	Sundry Credit		304.20	1,237.63
30 Apr	236133	71.18		1,166.45

For the corresponding period, Mrs Lake's own records contained the following bank account:

Date	Details	£	Date	Detail	Cheque No.	£
1 Apr	Balance	827.38	5 Apr	Purchases	128	111.70
2 Apr	Sales	192.35	10 Apr	Electricity	129	43.82
18 Apr	Sales	249.50	16 Apr	Purchases	130	87.77
24 Apr	Sales	304.20	18 Apr	Rent	131	30.00
30 Apr	Sales	192.80	20 Apr	Purchases	132	59.09
			25 Apr	Purchases	133	71.18
			30 Apr	Wages	134	52.27
			30 Apr	Balance		1,310.40
		£1,766.23				£1,766.23

Required:
(a) Prepare a statement reconciling the balance at 30 April as given by the bank statement to the balance at 30 April as stated in the bank account.
(b) Explain briefly which items in your bank reconciliation statement would require further investigation.   (ACCA)

16.6. A young and inexperienced bookkeeper is having great difficulty in producing a bank reconciliation statement at 31 December. He gives you his attempt to produce a summarized cash book, and also the bank statement received for the month of December. These are shown below. You may assume that the bank statement is correct. You may also assume that the trial balance at 1 January did indeed show a bank overdraft of £7,000.12.

Cash book summary—draft

	£	£	£	
1 Jan				
Opening overdraft		7,000.12	35,000.34	Payments Jan–Nov
Jan–Nov receipts	39,500.54			
Add: Discounts	500.02			
		40,000.56	12,000.34	Balance 30 Nov
		47,000.68	47,000.68	
1 Dec		12,000.34		Payments Dec Cheque No.
Dec receipts	178.19		37.14	7654
	121.27		192.79	7655
	14.92		5,000.00	7656
	16.88		123.45	7657

		329.26	678.90	7658
			1.47	7659
Dec Receipts	3,100.00		19.84	7660
	171.23		10.66	7661
	1,198.17	4,469.40	10,734.75	Balance c/d
		16,799.00	16,799.00	
31 Dec Balance		10,734.75		

Bank statement—31 December

Withdrawals		Deposits	Balance		
	£	£			£
			1 Dec	O/D	800.00
7650	300.00	178.19			
7653	191.91	121.27			
7654	37.14	14.92			
7651	1,111.11	16.88			
7656	5,000.00	3,100.00			
7655	129.79	171.23			
7658	678.90	1,198.17			
Standing order	50.00	117.98			
7659	1.47				
7661	10.66				
Bank charges	80.00		31 Dec	O/D	3,472.34

Required:
(a) A corrected cash book summary and a reconciliation of the balance on this revised summary with the bank statement balance as at 31 December, as far as you are able.
(b) A brief note as to the likely cause of any remaining difference. (ACCA)

16.7. The balance sheet and profit and loss account of Faults Ltd show the following two items:

Bank balance—Overdrawn £3,620
Profit and loss account—Trading profit for year £23,175

However, the balance as a shown on the bank statement does not agree with the balance as shown in the cash book. Your investigation of this matter reveals the following differences, and additional information:

1. Cheque payments entered in the cash book but not presented to the bank until after the year end—£3,138.
2. Bankings entered in the cash book but not credited by the bank until after the year end—£425.
3. Cheques for £35 and £140 received from customers were returned by the bank as dishonoured, but no entries concerning these events have been made in the cash book.
4. Items shown on bank statements but not entered in the cash book;

Bank charges, £425.
Standing order—Hire purchase repayments on purchase of motor car 12 @ £36.

Standing order—Being quarterly rent of warehouse, £125, due on each quarter day.

Dividend received on investment, £90.

5. The cheques were returned by the bank for the following reasons: the £35 cheque requires an additional signature and should be honoured in due course; the £140 cheque was unpaid due to the bankruptcy of the drawer and should be treated as a bad debt.

6. The hire purchase repayments of £36 represent £30 capital and £6 interest.

7. A cheque for £45 received from a customer in settlement of his account had been entered in the cash book as £450 on the payments side, analysed to the purchases ledger column and later posted.

You are required to prepare:

(a) a statement reconciling the cash book balance with the bank statement, and

(b) a statement showing the effect of the alterations on the trading profit.

(ACCA adapted)

17. Control accounts

Learning objectives

After reading this chapter the student should be able to:

1. Explain the meaning of the key terms and concepts listed at the end of the chapter.
2. Describe the division of the general ledger into several different ledgers.
3. Explain the nature of control accounts including the sources of the entries.
4. Prepare sales/debtors' ledger control and purchases/creditors' ledger control accounts.
5. Explain the purposes of control accounts.
6. Identify and correct errors and omissions relating to the different personal ledgers and control accounts.

The nature and preparation of control accounts

Up until this point it has been assumed that the books of account include a single general ledger. However, in practice it is usual for this to be split into at least three different ledgers, consisting of the following:

1. *A sales/debtors' ledger* which contains all the personal accounts of debtors.
2. *A purchases/creditors' ledger* which contains all the personal accounts of creditors.
3. *An impersonal ledger* which contains all the other accounts. These comprise the nominal (i.e. sales, purchases, wages and expense) accounts, and assets and liabilities other than debtors and creditors.

The main reasons for dividing the general ledger into three ledgers in a manual accounting system are:

1. Where there are a large number of transactions a single ledger becomes physically too heavy to handle;
2. It allows more than one person to work on the ledgers at the same time;
3. It provides a means of *internal control* for checking the accuracy of the ledgers, facilitates the location of errors, and can deter fraud and the misappropriation of cash. This is achieved through the use of control accounts which are described below.

The above also serves to highlight that the advantages of dividing the general ledger, and having control accounts, are minimal where the accounting system is computerized.

In a manual accounting system with the above three ledgers, it is usual for the impersonal ledger to contain a *sales/debtors' ledger control account* and a *purchases/creditors' ledger control account* (sometimes also referred to as *total accounts*). These control accounts contain *in total* the entries that are made in the personal ledgers, and are normally written up monthly from the total of the relevant books of prime entry. For example, in the case of credit sales, the individual invoices shown in the sales day book are entered in each of the debtor's personal accounts in the sales ledger, and the total sales for the month as per the sales day book is debited to the debtors' control account in the impersonal ledger and credited to the sales account.

Where an impersonal ledger contains debtors' and creditors' control accounts these constitute part of the double entry and therefore enter into the trial balance which would be prepared for the impersonal ledger alone. In these circumstances the sales and purchases ledgers are outside the double entry system and are thus not entered in the trial balance.

A simple illustration of the preparation of control accounts is shown in Example 17.1.

Example 17.1

The books of Copper Tree Ltd include three ledgers comprising an impersonal ledger, debtors' ledger and creditors' ledger. The impersonal ledger contains debtors' ledger and creditors' ledger control accounts as part of the double entry.

The following information relates to the accounting year ended 30 June 19X8:

	£
Debtors' ledger control account	
balance on 1 July 19X7 (debit)	5,740
Creditors' ledger control account	
balance on 1 July 19X7 (credit)	6,830
Sales	42,910
Purchases	38,620
Cheques received from debtors	21,760
Cheques paid to creditors	19,340
Returns outwards	8,670
Returns inwards	7,840
Carriage outwards	1,920
Carriage inwards	2,130
Discount received	4,560
Discount allowed	3,980
Bills of exchange payable	5,130
Bills of exchange receivable	9,720
Bad debts	1,640
Provision for bad debts	2,380
Amounts due from customers as shown by debtors' ledger,	
transferred to creditors' ledger	950
Cash received in respect of a debit balance on	
a creditors' ledger account	810

You are required to prepare the debtors' ledger and creditors' ledger control accounts.

Debtors' ledger control

Balance b/d	5,740	Bank	21,760
Sales	42,910	Returns inwards	7,840
		Discount allowed	3,980
		Bills receivable	9,720
		Bad debts	1,640
		Transfer to creditors	950
		Balance c/d	2,760
	48,650		48,650
Balance b/d	2,760		

Creditors' ledger control

Bank	19,340	Balance b/d	6,830
Returns outwards	8,670	Purchases	38,620
Discount received	4,560	Cash	810
Bills payable	5,130		
Transfer from debtors	950		
Balance c/d	7,610		
	46,260		46,260
		Balance b/d	7,610

Notes

1. Carriage inwards, carriage outwards and provisions for bad debts are not entered in the control accounts since they do not appear in the individual debtors' or creditors' accounts in the personal ledgers.
2. The transfer of £950 between the debtors' and creditors' control accounts is intended to reflect the total of the transfers between the debtors' and creditors' ledgers during the year. These usually occur where the business buys and sells goods to the same firm. Thus instead of exchanging cheques, the amount due as shown in the debtors' ledger is set against the amount owed as shown in the creditors' ledger (or vice versa depending on which is the smaller).
3. The cash received of £810 in respect of a debit balance on a creditors' ledger account is credited to the creditors' account and the creditors' control account. A debit balance in the creditors' ledger usually arises because a supplier has been overpaid as a result of either duplicating a payment or paying for goods that are the subject of a credit note. The cash received is a refund to correct the previous overpayment.
4. Bills of exchange were explained briefly at the end of Chapter 3. The most relevant characteristics are that bills of exchange are a method of payment where the business which owes the money signs a document undertaking to make payment after the expiry of a specified period of time (usually 30, 60 or 90 days). This document is referred to as a *bill of exchange receivable* in the case of a debtor and a *bill of exchange payable* in the case of a creditor. The essential point is that in the debtors' and creditors' personal accounts the debt is treated as paid on the date the bill of exchange is signed (and not when the money is actually received or paid which is at a later date). The same therefore applies in the control accounts.

5. The balances carried down on the control accounts at the end of the period are the difference between the two sides of the accounts.
6. Some examination questions contain amounts described as a *credit* balance on the debtors' control account and/or a *debit* balance on the creditors' control account (at the beginning and/or end of the period). Although individual debtors' and creditors' personal accounts can have credit or debit balances respectively (for the reasons outlined in note 3 above), it is unclear how the control accounts can have such balances. Each control account can only throw up one balance which is the difference between the two sides of the account. However, if these perverse balances are encountered in an examination question, the following procedure should be adopted: a credit balance on the debtors' control account should be entered as a credit balance brought down (and debit balance carried down), and the closing debit balance calculated as the difference between the two sides of the control account in the normal way. Similarly a debit balance on the creditors' control account should be entered as a debit balance brought down (and credit balance carried down), and the closing credit balance calculated as the difference between the two sides of the control account in the normal way.
7. The entries for any bad debts recovered are the reverse of those for bad debts. Allowances given and allowances received should be treated in the same way as returns inwards and outwards respectively. Any interest charged on overdue (debtors') accounts should be debited to the debtors' control account and credited to an interest receivable account.

Purposes of control accounts

The main purpose of a control account is to provide a check on the accuracy of the ledger to which it relates. Since the entries in the control account are the same (in total) as those in the ledger to which it relates, the balance on the control account should equal the total of a list of balances of the individual personal accounts contained in the ledger. If the balance on the control account is the same as the list of balances, this proves that the ledger is arithmetically accurate and that all the items in the books of prime entry have been entered in the ledger on the correct side.

The main function of control accounts is therefore to facilitate the location of errors highlighted in the trial balance by pinpointing the personal ledger in which these errors are likely to be found. Furthermore, the existence of control accounts is likely to deter fraud and the misappropriation of funds since it is usually prepared by the accountant as a check on the clerk who is responsible for the personal ledger. Finally, control accounts facilitate the preparation of (monthly or quarterly) final accounts since the total values of debtors and creditors are immediately available.

The use of control accounts in the location of errors is illustrated in Example 17.2.

Example 17.2
The books of C. Hand, Ltd include three ledgers comprising an impersonal ledger, debtors' ledger and creditors' ledger. The impersonal ledger contains debtors' ledger and creditors' ledger control accounts as part of the double entry.

The following information relates to the accounting year ended 30 April 19X8:

	£
Debtors' ledger control account	
balance on 1 May 19X7 (debit)	8,460
Cheques received from debtors	27,690
Sales	47,320
Returns outwards	12,860
Returns inwards	7,170
Carriage inwards	3,940
Bills receivable	8,650
Bills payable	4,560
Discount received	5,710
Discount allowed	2,830
Provision for bad debts	1,420
Bad debts	970
Proceeds of bills receivable	6,150
Amounts due from customers as shown by	
debtors' ledger transferred to creditors' ledger	830
Total of balances in debtor's ledger on 30 April 19X8	9,460

(a) You are required to prepare the debtors' ledger control account for the year ended 30 April 19X8.

(b) After the preparation of the control account the following errors were identified:

   (i)   The total of the sales returns day book has been over-cast by £360.

  (ii)   Cheques received of £225 has been entered on the wrong side of a debtors' personal account.

 (iii)   The total of the discount allowed column in the cash book is shown as £2,830 when it should be £3,820.

 (iv)   A sales invoice for £2,000 has been entered in the sales day book as £200 in error.

Prepare a statement showing the amended balances on the debtors' ledger and the debtors' ledger control account. Compute the amount of any remaining undetected error.

(a)   *Debtors' ledger control*

	£		£
Balance b/d	8,460	Bank	27,690
Sales	47,320	Returns inwards	7,170
		Bills receivable	8,650
		Discount allowed	2,830
		Bad debts	970
		Transfer to creditors	830
		Balance c/d	7,640
	55,780		55,780
Balance b/d	7,640		

(b)   *Debtors' ledger*

	£
Original balances	9,460
Add: Sales day book error (£2,000 − £200)	1,800
	11,260
Less: Cheque received posted to wrong side of debtors' account (£225 × 2)	450
Amended balance	10,810

Debtors' ledger control account

		£
Original balance		7,640
Add: Sales returns day book over-cast	360	
Sales day book error (£2,000 − £200)	1,800	2,160
		9,800
Less: Discount allowed under-cast		990
Amended balance		8,810

Undetected error = £10,810 − £8,810 = £2,000

Notes

1. The returns outwards, carriage inward, bills payable, discount received and provision for bad debts are not entered in the debtors' ledger control account. The proceeds of bills of exchange receivable should also not be entered in the debtors' ledger control account. As explained above, the entry in the control account in respect of bills receivable of £8,650 is made when the bills were signed as accepted by the debtor and not when the proceeds are received. This is dealt with in a separate account shown below.

Bills receivable

Debtors' control	8,650	Bank	6,150
		Balance c/d	2,500
	8,650		8,650
Balance b/d	2,500		

2. The difference of £2,000 between the amended balances on the debtors' ledger and the debtors' ledger control account indicates that there are still one or more errors in the debtors' ledger and /or the debtors' ledger control account.

3. Instead of computing the amended balance on the debtors ledger control account in vertical/statement form above, some examination questions require this to be done in the debtors ledger control account. It can take two forms. One way is to prepare a control account containing the correct amounts for all the items. The other method is to prepare a control account with the original (uncorrected) amounts and after computing the closing balance, show the entries necessary to correct the errors. Notice that this is essentially the same procedure as that shown in Example 16.2 relating to bank reconciliations. The first method is usually expected where an examination question describes the errors before stating the requirement to prepare a control account. The

second method is usually expected where an examination question states the requirement to prepare a control account before describing the errors, such as in Example 17.2 above, but unlike the example above, doesn't explicitly require a statement showing the amended balance on the control account. In this case the items shown in the answer to Example 17.2 that have been added to the "original" debtors ledger control account balance would be simply debited to the control account, and those that have been deducted would be credited to the control account. In practice errors are not normally identified until after the control accounts have been prepared and thus these would usually be corrected as separate entries in the control accounts.

Alternative systems

Sometimes, in practice, control accounts are not part of the double entry in the impersonal ledger. Instead they are prepared on a loose sheet of paper and are thus purely memoranda. The entries still consist of totals from the relevant day books and other books of prime entry. However, in this case the impersonal and personal ledgers must be taken together to produce a trial balance. The values of debtors and creditors in such a trial balance are therefore a list of the balances in the personal ledgers.

Summary

It is common for medium and large enterprises to divide their general ledger into three ledgers—an impersonal ledger, a sales/debtors' ledger, and a purchases/creditors' ledger. The impersonal ledger usually contains a control account for each of the other two personal ledgers. These constitute a part of the double entry and are thus included in the trial balance that would be prepared for the impersonal ledger alone. Thus sales and purchases ledgers are maintained on a single entry memorandum basis and are not included in the trial balance.

The purchases and sales ledger control accounts are written up from the totals of the relevant books of prime entry. The main purpose of a control account is to provide a check on the accuracy of the ledger to which it relates, and facilitate the location of errors. The balance on a control account should equal the total of a list of balances in the ledger to which it relates. If this is not the case the reasons for the difference will need to be investigated.

Key terms and concepts

Bills (of exchange) payable, bills (of exchange) receivable, control account, creditors'/purchase ledger control account, debtors'/sales ledger control account, impersonal ledger, purchases/creditors' ledger, sales/debtors' ledger, total account.

Exercises

An asterisk after the question number indicates that there is a suggested answer in the Appendix.

17.1. Explain the main purposes of control accounts.

17.2.* The following information has been extracted from the books of a trader at 1 July 19X6:

	£
Amount owing by debtors	40,000
Amount owing by creditors	31,200

The transactions during the year ended 30 June 19X7 were as follows:

	£
Returns inwards	15,750
Returns outwards	8,660
Discounts received	3,187
Discount allowed	5,443
Sales	386,829
Purchases	222,954
Bad debts written off	3,400
Cheques received from customers	230,040
Cheques paid to suppliers	108,999

You are required to write up the sales ledger control account and the purchase ledger control account for the year ended 30 June 19X7.

17.3. The following particulars relating to the year ended 31 March 19X9 have been extracted from the books of a trader.

	£
Debtors' ledger control account balance on 1 April 19X8 (debit)	7,182
Sales	69,104
Cash received from debtors	59,129
Discounts allowed	1,846
Discounts received	1,461
Returns inwards	983
Returns outwards	627
Bills receivable accepted by debtors	3,243
Bad debts written off	593
Cash paid in respect of a credit balance on a debtors' ledger account	66
Amounts due from customers as shown by debtors's ledger transferred to creditors' ledger	303
Interest charged on debtors' overdue account	10
Credit balance on debtors' ledger control account on 31 March 19X9	42

Prepare the debtors' ledger control account for the year ended 31 March 19X9, using relevant figures selected from the data shown above. (ACCA)

17.4.* The books of Trader Ltd include three ledgers comprising an impersonal ledger, debtors' ledger and creditors' ledger. The impersonal ledger contains debtors' ledger and creditors' ledger control accounts as part of the double entry.
The following information relates to the month of January 19X1:

	£
Debtors' control account balance on 1 January 19X1	4,200 debit
Debtors' control account balance on 1 January 19X1	300 credit

Creditors' control account balance on 1 January 19X1	250 debit
Creditors' control account balance on 1 January 19X1	6,150 credit
Credit sales for the month	23,000
Credit purchases for the month	21,500
Returns inward	750
Returns outward	450
Carriage inwards	25
Carriage outwards	15
Cheques received from debtors	16,250
Cheques paid to creditors	19,800
Discount allowed	525
Discount received	325
Irrecoverable debts	670
Provision for bad debts	400
Cheques received from debtors, dishonoured	1,850
Bills of exchange payable, accepted by us	4,500
Bills of exchange receivable, accepted by debtors	5,300
Bad debts recovered	230
Cash received from bills receivable	4,850
Debtors' balances set against accounts in the creditors' ledger	930
Cash paid on bills payable	3,700
Interest charged on debtors' overdue accounts	120
Allowances received	280
Allowances given	340
Debtors' control account balance on 31 January 19X1	240 credit
Creditors' control account balance on 31 January 19X1	420 debit

You are required to prepare the debtors' ledger and creditors' ledger control accounts for January 19X1.

17.5.* The following particulars relating to the year ended 31 March 19X7, have been extracted from the books of Ball and Chain Ltd. All sales have been recorded in personal accounts in the debtors' ledger, and the debtors' ledger control account is part of the double entry in the impersonal ledger.

	£
Debtors' ledger control account balance on 1 April 19X6 (debit)	14,364
Sales	138,208
Cheques received from debtors including bad debts recovered of £84	118,258
Discounts allowed	3,692
Discounts received	2,922
Returns inwards	1,966
Returns outwards	1,254
Bills receivable	6,486
Bad debts written off	1,186
Provision for bad debts	1,800
Cash paid in respect of a credit balance on a debtors' ledger account	132

Amounts due from customers as shown by debtors' ledger transferred to creditors' ledger	606
Interest charged on debtors' overdue account	20
Total of balances in debtors' ledger on 31 March 19X7 (debit)	20,914

(a) Prepare the debtors' ledger control account for the year ended 31 March 19X7 using relevant figures selected from the data shown above.

(b) Subsequently the following errors have been discovered:

(i) The total of the sales day book has been under-cut by £1,000.

(ii) An entry of £125 in the returns inward book has been entered on the wrong side of the debtor's personal account.

(iii) Discount allowed of £50 had been entered correctly in a debtor's personal account but no other entries have been made in the books.

(iv) A cheque for £3,400 from a debtor has been entered correctly in the cash book but has been posted to the debtor's personal account as £4,300.

Prepare a statement showing the amended balances on the debtors' ledger and the debtors' ledger control account.

17.6.* The books of K. Wills include three ledgers comprising the impersonal ledger, debtors' ledger and creditors' ledger. The impersonal ledger contains debtors' ledger and creditors' ledger control accounts as part of the double entry.

The following information relates to the accounting year ended 30 June 19X9:

	£
Debtors' ledger control account balance on 1 July 19X8 (debit)	17,220
Creditors' ledger control account balance on 1 July 19X8 (credit)	20,490
Cheques received from debtors	45,280
Cheques paid to creditors	38,020
Sales	98,730
Purchases	85,860
Returns outwards	16,010
Returns inwards	18,520
Bills of exchange payable	21,390
Bills of exchange receivable	29,160
Discount received	7,680
Discount allowed	6,940
Bad debts	4,920
Cash received in respect of a debit balance on a creditor's ledger account	2,430
Amount due from customers as shown by debtors' ledger, transferred to creditors' ledger	2,850
Total balances in creditors' ledger on 30 June 19X9 (credit)	20,700

(a) You are required to prepare the debtors' ledger and creditors' ledger control accounts.

(b) After the preparation of the above control accounts the following errors were discovered:

(i) The total of the purchases day book has been over-cast by £500.

(ii) Returns outwards of £180 have been entered on the wrong side of the personal account concerned.

(iii) Discount received of £120 has been entered correctly in the appropriate personal account but is shown in the cash book as £210.

(iv) A cheque paid for £340 has been entered correctly in the cash book but has been posted to the creditors' personal account as £3,400.

You are required to prepare a statement showing the amended balances on the creditors' ledger and the creditors' ledger control account. Compute the amount of any remaining undetected error.

17.7. The following figures relating to the year ended 31 March 19X8 have been extracted from the books of a manufacturer:

	£
Total of sales ledger balances as per list	8,300
Total of bought ledger balances as per list	1,270
Balance on sales ledger control account	8,160
Balance on bought ledger control account	1,302

The balances on the control accounts, as shown above, have been included in the trial balance and in this trial balance the total of the credit balances exceeded the total of the debit balances by £58.

Subsequently, the following errors have been discovered:

1. Goods returned by a customer to the value of £10 have been entered on the wrong side of his personal account.
2. The total of the sales day book for the month of March has been under-cast by £80.
3. The total of the purchases for the month of March had been correctly shown as £653 in the bought day book and control account, but incorrectly posted to the purchases account as £635.
4. An allowance of £10 made by a supplier because of a slight defect in the goods supplied had been correctly entered in the personal account concerned, but no other entries had been made in the books.
5. A credit balance of £22 on a supplier's personal account had been overlooked and therefore did not appear in the list of bought ledger balances.

An undetected error still remained in the books after the discovery of the above-mentioned errors.

You are required to:
(a) prepare a statement showing the amended totals of the balances on the sales and bought ledgers and the amended balances on each of the control accounts assuming that the errors discovered have been corrected;
(b) calculate the amount of undetected error and to state where in the books you consider such error is to be found. (ACCA)

17.8. Fox and Company maintain control accounts, in respect of both the sales ledger and purchase ledger, within their nominal ledger. On 31 December 19X1 the net total of the balances extracted from the sales ledger amounted to £9,870, which figure did not agree with the balance shown on the sales ledger control account. An examination of the books disclosed the following errors and omissions, which when rectified resulted in the corrected net total of the sales ledger balances agreeing with the amended balance of the control account.

1. £240 standing to the credit of Rice's account in the purchase ledger had been transferred to his account in the sales ledger, but no entries had been made in the control accounts in respect of this transfer.
2. Debit balances of £42 in the sales ledger had been extracted as credit balances when the balances were listed at 31 December 19X1.
3. £8,675, a month's total in the sales day book, had been posted to the control account as £8,765 although posted correctly to the sales account.
4. A balance of £428 owing by Stone had been written off to bad debts as irrecoverable, but no entry had been made in the control account.
5. Entries on the debit side of Hay's account in the sales ledger had been undercast by £100.
6. The following sales ledger balances had been omitted from the list of balances at 31 December 19X1—debits £536, credits £37.
7. The sale of goods to Croft amounting to £60 had been dealt with correctly and debited to his account. Croft had returned such goods as not being up to standard and the only treatment accorded thereto was the crossing out of the original entry in Croft's account.
8. £22 allowed to Field as discount had been correctly recorded and posted. Subsequently this discount had been disallowed and a like amount had been entered in the discounts received column in the cash book and posted to Field's account in the purchase ledger and included in the total of discounts received.

You are required to:

(a) give the journal entries, where necessary, to rectify these errors and omissions, and, if no journal entry is necessary, to state how they should be rectified; and
(b) prepare the sales ledger control account showing the balance before and after rectification has been made, and reconcile the balance carried forward on this account with the total of balances extracted from the sales ledger.   (ACCA)

18. Errors and suspense accounts

Learning objectives

After reading this chapter the student should be able to:

1. Explain the meaning of the key terms and concepts listed at the end of the chapter.
2. Describe the types of errors which do not cause a trial balance to disagree.
3. Explain the purposes of a suspense account.
4. Show journal and ledger entries for the correction of both errors which do and do not cause a trial balance to disagree including those relating to suspense accounts.
5. Prepare a revised profit and loss account and balance sheet after the correction of errors.

Introduction

As explained in Chapter 5, one of the main purposes of the trial balance is to check the accuracy of a ledger. If a trial balance agrees this indicates the following:

1. There are no arithmetic errors in the ledger accounts.
2. Every transaction recorded in the ledger has been entered once on each side.

However, there can still be errors in the ledger that do not cause a trial balance to disagree. These are explained below.

Types of error which do not cause a trial balance to disagree

Error of principle

This refers to when a transaction has been entered on both sides of the ledger but one of the entries is in the wrong *class/type* of account. For example, an expense that has been debited to an asset account in error (or vice versa), or income being credited to a liability account in error (or vice versa). Another common example is where the proceeds of sale of a fixed asset have been credited to the sales account in error.

Error of commission

This refers to when a transaction has been entered on both sides of the ledger and in the correct *class/type* of account but one of the entries is in the wrong account. For example, stationery entered in the purchases account in error, or cheques posted to the wrong personal account.

Error of omission

This refers to where a transaction has not been recorded anywhere in the books of account. The classic example is bank charges omitted from the cash book.

Error of original/prime entry

This refers to when a wrong amount has been entered in a book of prime entry. That is, the amount entered in the book of prime entry is different from that shown on the original document. This will mean that the wrong amount has been entered on both sides of the ledger. For example, a sales invoice for £980 entered in the sales day book as £890 will result in both the sales and debtors' (control) accounts containing a figure of £890 instead of £980.

Compensating errors

A compensating error is two separate errors which are totally unrelated to each other except that they are both of the same amount. Neither of these two errors is of the four types above but rather would individually cause a trial balance to disagree.

Double posting error

This refers to where the correct amount has been entered in a day book (of prime entry) but the wrong amount is shown on both sides of the ledger. Another type of double posting error can be said to have occurred when the correct amount of a transaction has been entered on the wrong side of both of the accounts to which it has been posted. A slightly different example is rent received recorded as rent paid.

Illustrations of these errors and their correction are shown in Example 18.1. The errors are presented in the same order as the above list.

Example 18.1
State the title of each of the following errors and show the journal entries needed for their correction.

1. Plant that was acquired at a cost of £5,000 has been credited in the cash book but debited to the purchases account in error.
2. The purchase of consumable tools for £80 has been debited to the repairs account in error.
3. Bank charges of £27 shown on the bank statement have not been entered in the cash book.
4. A purchase invoice received from A. Creditor for £1,000 has been entered in the purchases day book as £100.
5. Wages paid of £40 have not been posted to the wages account, and the debit side of the purchases account has been over-cast by £40.
6. Rent received of $400 has been entered in both the cash book and the ledger as rent paid.

The journal			*Debit*	*Credit*
			£	£
1.	Plant and machinery	Dr	5,000	
	To purchases account			5,000
	Being correction of error of principle			
2.	Consumable tools	Dr	80	
	To repairs account			80
	Being correction of error of commission			
3.	Bank charges	Dr	27	
	To cash book			27
	Being correction of error of omission			
4.	Purchases account	Dr	900	
	To A. Creditor/creditors control			900
	Being correction of error of prime entry (no correction of purchases day book is necessary)			
5.	Wages account	Dr	40	
	To purchases account			40
	Being correction of compensating error —wages not posted and purchases account over-cast			
6.	Cash book	Dr	800	
	To rent payable account			400
	To rent receivable account			400
	Being correction of rent receivable of £400 entered as rent payable			

Suspense accounts

Suspense accounts are used for two purposes as follows:

1. Recording undefined transactions. That is, where money is received or paid but there is no record of what it relates to, the amount would be entered in the cash book and posted to a suspense account. When the nature of the transaction is known, the amount is transferred from the suspense account to the appropriate account.
2. To record in the ledger any difference on a trial balance and thus make it agree. If a trial balance fails to agree by a relatively small amount and the error(s) cannot be found quickly, the difference is inserted in the trial balance (to make it agree) and in a suspense account. The entry in the suspense account must be on the same side of the ledger as the entry in the trial balance. At a later date when the error(s) are located they are corrected by means of an entry in the suspense account and the other in the account containing the error. This correction through the suspense account is necessary because the original entry in the suspense account (which made the trial

balance agree) in effect corrected all the errors in total. Thus the correction must effectively be moved from the suspense account to the account that contains the error.

An illustration of the use of suspense accounts is given in Example 18.2.

Example 18.2
A trial balance failed to agree because the debit side exceeds the credit side by £2,509. A suspense account has been opened into which the difference is entered. Subsequently the following errors were identified:

1. The debit side of the cash book has been over-cast by £1,000.
2. Goods bought by cheque for £200 have been credited in the cash book but not entered in the purchases account.
3. Rent paid of £50 has been credited in the cash book but also credited in error to the rent account.
4. Car repairs of £23 shown in the cash book have been debited to the motor expenses account as £32 in error.
5. The sales account contains a balance of £2,000 but this has been entered in the trial balance as £200.

You are required to prepare the journal entries needed to correct the above errors and show the entries in the suspense account.

Suspense account

Cash book	1,000	Difference on trial balance	2,509
Motor expenses	9	Purchases	200
Extraction error on sales	1,800	Rent	100
	2,809		2,809

The journal

			Debit £	Credit £
1.	Suspense account	Dr	1,000	
	Cash book			1,000
	Being correction of arithmetic error			
2.	Purchases account	Dr	200	
	Suspense account			200
	Being correction of posting error			
3.	Rent account	Dr	100	
	Suspense account			100
	Being correction of posting error (£50 × 2)			
4.	Suspense account	Dr	9	
	Motor expenses			9
	Being correction of transposed figures			
5.	Suspense account	Dr	1,800	
	Trial balance (no ledger entry)			1,800
	Being correction of extraction error			

Notes

1. It should be noted that only errors of the type which cause a trial balance to disagree are corrected by means of an entry in the suspense account; that is, arithmetic and posting errors described in Chapter 5. This is clearly because errors which cause a trial balance to disagree give rise to the original entry in the suspense account.

2. The correction of errors via a suspense account always involves a double entry, with one exception. This relates to the correction of extraction errors, such as item 5 above, where the only entry is in the suspense account. A useful way of working out whether the entry in the suspense account is a debit or credit is to imagine what entry is needed to correct the trial balance; the entry in the suspense account will be on the opposite side of the ledger.

3. Sometimes in examination questions and in practice the errors which have been identified are not the only errors. Obviously in this case there will still be a balance on the suspense account after the known errors have been corrected. This shows the amount of the remaining errors.

Summary

There are two main types of errors that will cause a trial balance to disagree. These consist of arithmetic and posting errors. There are six types of errors that do not cause a trial balance to disagree. These consist of errors of principle, errors of commission, errors of omission, errors of original/prime entry, compensating errors, and double posting errors. Errors that cause a trial balance to disagree are normally corrected by means of a one-sided ledger (and journal) entry. Errors that do not cause a trial balance to disagree are always corrected by means of a two-sided ledger (and journal) entry.

Suspense accounts are used for two purposes. One is to record transactions, the nature of which is unknown. The other is to record in the ledger any difference on a trial balance, and thus make it agree. When the error(s) which gave rise to the difference are located, these are corrected by means of one entry in the suspense account and a corresponding entry in the account containing the error. Only errors that cause a trial balance to disagree are corrected by means of an entry in the suspense account.

Errors giving rise to the creation of a suspense account should be located and corrected before final accounts are prepared. However, if errors are discovered after the preparation of the final accounts, the effect of their correction on the profit and loss account and balance sheet should be taken into consideration. This may involve preparing revised final accounts.

Key terms and concepts

Compensating errors, double posting error, error of commission, error of omission, error of original/prime entry, error of principle, suspense account.

Exercises

An asterisk after the question number indicates that there is a suggested answer in the Appendix.

18.1. Describe the types of errors that:

(a) cause a trial balance to disagree;

(b) do not cause a trial balance to disagree.

18.2. Describe the two main uses of a suspense account.

18.3. The draft trial balance of Regent Ltd as at 31 May 19X8 agreed. The business proceeded with the preparation of the draft final accounts and these showed a profit of £305,660. However, a subsequent audit revealed the following errors:

1. Bank charges of £56 had been omitted from the cash book.
2. The purchases journal had been over-cast by £400.
3. The sales journal had been under-cast by £100.
4. An invoice for £127 received from Alpha Ltd had been entered into the purchases journal as £217. (This is quite independent of the error made in the purchases journal referred to above.)
5. It is now considered prudent to write off the balance of £88 on P. Shadey's account as bad.
6. An invoice from Caring Garages Ltd for £550 in respect of servicing Regent Ltd's motor vehicles had been posted to the debit of motor vehicles account.
7. Depreciation of 10 per cent per annum has been provided for on motor vehicles inclusive of the £550 invoice referred to in point 6 above.

Regent Ltd maintains control accounts for debtors and creditors in its general ledger. Individual accounts for debtors and creditors are maintained on a memorandum basis only.

Required

(a) Prepare journal entries to show how the above errors would be corrected. (Note: dates and narratives not required.)

(b) What is the profit for the year after correcting the above errors?   (AAT)

18.4.* When preparing a trial balance the bookkeeper found it disagreed by £600, the credit side being that much greater than the debit side. The difference was entered in a suspense account. The following errors were subsequently found:

1. A cheque for £32 for electricity was entered in the cash book but not posted to the ledger.
2. The debit side of the wages account is over-cast by £28.
3. There is a debit in the rent account of £198 which should be £918.
4. The purchase of a van for £300 has been posted to the debit side of the purchases account in error.
5. A cheque received from A. Watt for £80 has been credited to A. Watson's account in error.
6. The sale of some old loose tools for £100 had been credited to sales account in error.
7. An amount of £17 paid for postage stamps has been entered in the carriage outwards account in error.
8. Bank charges of £41 shown on the bank statement have not been entered in the books.
9. An amount of £9 for stationery has been entered in the cash book but not

posted to the stationery account. Cash sales of £43 are entered correctly in the cash book but posted to the sales account as £34.

10. A credit sale to J. Bloggs of £120 was entered in the sales day book as £12.

11. A credit balance of £62 shown in the discount received account has been entered on the debit side of the trial balance.

You are required to prepare the journal entries necessary to correct the above errors and show the suspense account.

18.5. At the end of January 19X0 a trial balance extracted from the ledger of Gerald Ltd did not balance and a suspense account was opened for the amount of the difference. Subsequently the following matters came to light:

1. £234 had been received during January from a debtor who owed £240. No entry has been made for the £6 outstanding but it is now decided to treat it as a cash discount.

2. Returns to suppliers during January were correctly posted individually to personal accounts but were incorrectly totalled. The total, overstated by £100, was posted to the returns account.

3. A bank statement drawn up to 31 January 19X0 showed a credit balance of £120 while the balance of the bank account in the trial balance was an overdraft of £87. The difference was found on reconciliation to comprise:

   (i)   a direct debit for the annual subscription to a trade association, £70, for which no entry had been made in the books of account.

   (ii)   entry in the bank account for payment to a supplier shown as £230 instead of £320.

   (iii) unpresented cheques on 31 January totalled £327.

   (iv)   the remainder of the difference was due to an addition error in the bank account.

4. A cheque for £163 was received during January in full settlement of a debt which was written off in the previous financial year. It was correctly entered in the bank account but not posted elsewhere, pending instructions.

5. A debtor's account with a balance of £180 had been taken out of the loose-leaf ledger when a query was investigated and not replaced at the time the trial balance was extracted.

6. A credit note for £5 sent to a customer in respect of an allowance had been posted to the wrong side of the customer's personal account.

Required:

Show what correcting entries need to be made in the ledger accounts in respect of these matters. Set out your answer as follows:

Item	Account(s) to be debited £	Account(s) to be credited £

(ACCA adapted)

18.6. Chi Knitwear Ltd is an old-fashioned firm with a handwritten set of books. A trial balance is extracted at the end of each month, and a profit and loss account and balance sheet are computed. This month however the trial balance will not balance, the credits exceeding debits by £1,536.

You are asked to help and after inspection of the ledgers discover the following errors.

1. A balance of £87 on a debtor's account has been omitted from the schedule of debtors, the total of which was entered as debtors in the trial balance.
2. A small piece of machinery purchased for £1,200 had been written off to repairs.
3. The receipts side of the cash book had been under-cast by £720.
4. The total of one page of the sales day book had been carried forward as £8,154, whereas the correct amount was £8,514.
5. A credit note for £179 received from a supplier had been posted to the wrong side of his account.
6. An electricity bill in the sum of £152, not yet accrued for, is discovered in a filing tray.
7. Mr Smith, whose past debts to the company had been the subject of a provision, at last paid £731 to clear his account. His personal account has been credited but the cheque has not yet passed through the cash book.

You are required to:

(a) write up the suspense account to clear the difference; and
(b) state the effect on the accounts of correcting each error.   (ACCA)

18.7. The draft final accounts of RST Ltd for the year ended 30 April 19X5 showed a net profit for the final year of £78,263.

During the subsequent audit, the following errors and omissions were discovered. At the draft stage a suspense account had been opened to record the net difference.

1. Trade debtors were shown as £55,210. However:

   (i)   bad debts of £610 had not been written off;
   (ii) the existing provision for doubtful debtors, £1,300, should have been adjusted to 2 per cent of debtors;
   (iii) a provision of 2 per cent for discounts on debtors should have been raised.

2. Rates of £491 which had been prepaid at 30 April 19X4 had not been brought down on the rates account as an opening balance.
3. A vehicle held as a fixed asset, which had originally cost £8,100 and for which £5,280 had been provided as depreciation, had been sold for £1,350. The proceeds had been correctly debited to bank but had been credited to sales. No transfers had been made to disposals account.
4. Credit purchases of £1,762 had been correctly debited to purchases account but had been credited to the supplier's account as £1,672.
5. A piece of equipment costing £9,800 and acquired on 1 May 19X4 for use in the business had been debited to purchases account. (The company depreciates equipment at 20 per cent per annum on cost).

6. Items valued at £2,171 had been completely omitted from the closing stock figure.
7. At 30 April 19X5 an accrual of £543 for electricity charges and an insurance prepayment of £162 had been omitted.
8. The credit side of the wages account had been under-added by £100 before the balance on the account had been determined.

Required:
Using relevant information from that given above:
(a) prepare a statement correcting the draft net profit;
(b) post and balance the suspense account. (Note: The opening balance of this account has not been given and must be derived.)   (ACCA)

18.8. * Miscup showed a difference on their trial balance of £14,650. This was posted to a suspense account so that the accounts for the year ended 31 March 19X9 could be prepared. The following balance sheet was produced:

Miscup
Balance sheet as at 31 March 19X9

	£	£		Cost	Depreciation	Net
			Fixed assets	£	£	£
Capital		125,000	Freehold premises	60,000	—	60,000
Profit for the year		33,500	Motor vehicles	25,000	11,935	13,065
		158,500	Fixtures and	1,500	750	750
			fittings			
				86,500	12,685	73,815
Current liabilities			*Current assets*			
Trade creditors and			Stocks		75,410	
accrued charges	41,360		Debtors		37,140	
Bank overdraft	1,230		Cash in hand		75	
		42,590				112,625
						186,440
			Suspense account			14,650
		£201,090				£201,090

On checking the books to eliminate the suspense account you find the following errors:

1. The debit side of the cash book is under-cast by £10,000.
2. A credit item of £5,000 in the cash book on account of a new building has not been posted to the nominal ledger.
3. The purchase day book has been summarized for posting to the nominal ledger but an item of purchases of £100 has been entered in the summary as £1,000 and a further transport charge of £450 has been entered as £45.
4. An item of rent received, £45, was posted twice to the nominal ledger from the cash book.
5. The debit side of the debtors' control account was under-cast by £100.
6. On reconciling the bank statement with the cash book it was discovered that bank charges of £3,250 had not been entered in the cash book.

7. Depreciation of motor vehicles was undercharged by £500.
8. Stocks were undervalued by £1,250.
9. Suppliers' invoices totalling £2,110 for goods included in stock, had been omitted from the books.

You are required to show:

(a) the journal entries necessary to eliminate the balance on the suspense account; and
(b) the balance sheet of Miscup as at 31 March 19X9, after correcting all the above errors. (ACCA)

19. Single entry and incomplete records

Learning objectives

After reading this chapter the student should be able to:

1. Explain the meaning of the key terms and concepts listed at the end of the chapter.
2. Describe the different forms of incomplete records.
3. Prepare final accounts from incomplete records and single entry.

Introduction

Incomplete records is a general term given to a situation where the transactions of an organization have not been recorded in double entry form (or using a computer system), and thus there is not a full set of records of the organizations transactions. There is no legislation which requires bodies sole (i.e. sole traders or partnerships) to keep records in double entry form. Furthermore, it is often too expensive for small businesses to maintain a complete system of double entry bookkeeping. In addition, many small businesses claim to have little practical use for any records other than how much money they have, and the amounts of debtors and creditors. Many sole traders are usually able to remember, without records, what fixed assets they own, and any long-term liabilities they owe. In the case of small businesses the accountant is therefore usually engaged not to write up the books, but to ascertain the profit of the business for tax purposes. Often, but not always, a balance sheet is also prepared.

In practice there are three different forms of incomplete records:

1. *Incomplete records of revenue income and expenditure.* That is, there are no basic documents or records of revenue income and expenditure, or the records are inadequate. This situation usually arises where the books and documents have been accidentally destroyed (e.g. in a fire) or the owner failed to keep proper records. In these circumstances it is not possible to construct a trading and profit and loss account. However, it may still be possible to ascertain the profit for the period provided there is information available relating to the assets and liabilities of the business at the start and end of the relevant period.

2. *Single entry*   This term is used to describe a situation where the business transactions have only been entered in a book of prime entry, usually a cash book, and not in the ledger. However, one would also expect to be able to obtain documents or information relating to the value of fixed assets, stocks, debtors, creditors, accruals, prepayments and any long-term liabilities. Given that this is available, it would be possible to prepare a trading and profit and loss account and balance sheet.

3. *Incomplete single entry* This term may be used to describe a variation on point 2 above where there are no books of account (or these are incomplete) but the receipts and payments can be ascertained from the bank statements and/or supporting documents. In this case it would be necessary to produce a cash book summary from the information given on the bank statements, paying in book and cheque book stubs. The final accounts will then be prepared from cash book summary together with the supporting documents and information referred to in point 2 above.

The procedure for preparing final accounts from the above three different forms of incomplete records is described below.

Incomplete records of revenue income and expenditure

As explained above, in these circumstances it is not possible to construct a trading and profit and loss account. However, it may still be possible to ascertain the profit for the relevant period provided that the information to prepare a balance sheet at the start and end of the period is available.

The profit (or loss) is found by calculating the difference between the net asset value of the business at the start and end of the period as shown by the two balance sheets. The logic behind this computation is that an increase in net assets can only come from two sources, either additional capital introduced by the owner or profits generated from the sale of goods and/or other assets. This is illustrated below.

Balance sheet as at 1 January 19X1

Capital	20,000	Assets	25,000
		Less: Liabilities	5,000
	20,000	Net assets	20,000

Balance sheet as at 31 December 19X1

Capital	30,000	Assets	38,000
		Less: Liabilities	8,000
	30,000	Net assets	30,000

Ignoring the possibility of additional capital introduced during the year, this business has a profit for the year of £30,000 − £20,000 = £10,000. This is computed by ascertaining the increase in either the net assets or the capital. Both must give the same answer. Any decrease in net assets or capital will mean there has been a loss for the year.

However, part of the increase in net assets and capital may be due to additional capital being introduced during the year of, say, £3,000. In this case the profit for the year is that part of the increase in net assets and capital which is not the result of additional capital introduced during the year thus:

	£
Net assets/capital at end of year	30,000
Less: Net assets/capital at start of year	20,000
Increase in capital	10,000
Less: Capital introduced	3,000
Profit for the year	7,000

In addition the owner of the business may have made drawings during the year of, say, £4,000. These will reduce the capital and net assets at the end of the year. In this case the profit for the year is the increase in net assets/capital less the capital introduced, plus the drawings for the year (i.e. £10,000 − £3,000 + £4,000 = £11,000).

In sum, profits (or losses) are reflected in an increase (or decrease) in the net asset value of a business over a given period. The net asset value corresponds to the capital. The profit or loss can thus be ascertained by computing the change in capital over the year and adjusting this for any capital introduced and/or drawings during the year. This is presented in the form of a statement, as shown below. Notice that this statement is simply a reordering of the entries normally shown in the capital account of a sole trader as presented in the balance sheet. Note also the similarity with the discussion in Chapter 2 relating to the nature of profit and its computation using a comparative static approach.

Statement of profit or loss for the year ended . . .

	£
Capital at end of current year	30,000
Less: Capital at end of previous year	20,000
Increase in capital	10,000
Add: Drawings during the year including any goods taken by the proprietor for his or her own use	4,000
	14,000
Less: Capital introduced during the year either in the form of cash or any other asset	3,000
Profit for the year	11,000

Before this statement can be prepared it is necessary to calculate the capital at the end of the current year and at the end of the previous year. This is done by preparing a balance sheet at each of these dates. These are referred to as a *statement of affairs*. This is illustrated in Example 19.1.

Example 19.1

A. Ferry has been in business for the last 10 years as an electrical retailer, and has asked you to compute her profit for the year ended 31 December 19X8.

She has no business bank account and kept no records of her income and expenditure apart from the purchase and sale of fixed assets, stock, debtors and creditors, and a running cash balance. She has been able to give you the following information relating to her affairs:

1. At 31 December 19X8 the business owns freehold land and buildings used as a shop and workshop. This cost £10,000 on 1 July 19X2.
2. During the year ended 31 December 19X8 the business owned the following vehicles:

Date of purchase	Cost	Date of sale	Proceeds
31 Mar 19X5	£1,000	31 Oct 19X8	£625
1 May 19X6	£1,200	unsold at 31 Dec 19X8	
1 July 19X8	£2,000	unsold at 31 Dec 19X8	

You estimate that the above vehicles have a useful working life of five years and no residual value. In previous years these have been depreciated using the straight line method.

3. During the year ended 31 December 19X8 the owner has put £5,280 in cash into the business and taken out £15,900 as drawings.

4. Amounts outstanding at:

	31 December 19X7	31 Dec 19X8
	£	£
Debtors	865	645
Creditors	390	480
Accruals	35	20
Prepayments	40	25

Included in debtors at 31 December 19X8 are doubtful debts of £85.

5. Stocks have been valued at £565 on 31 December 19X7, and £760 on 31 December 19X8. The latter amount includes a television which cost £60 and was worthless at that date due to it having been accidentally damaged beyond repair.

6. The cash balances at 31 December 19X7 and 19X8 were £285 and £165, respectively.

You are required to calculate the profit for the year ended 31 December 19X8, showing clearly your workings.

Workings

	£	£
Motor vehicles owned at 31 December 19X7		
Purchased 31/3/X5		1,000
Purchased 1/5/X6		1,200
Total cost		2,200
Depreciation using the fixed instalment method		
20 per cent × £1,000 × 2 years 9 months	550	
20 per cent × £1,200 × 1 year 8 months	400	
		950
Written down value at 31 Dec 19X7		1,250

	£	£
Motor vehicles owned at 31 December 19X8		
Purchased 1/5/X6		1,200
Purchased 1/7/X8		2,000
Total cost		3,200
Depreciation using the fixed instalment method		
20 per cent × £1,200 × 2 years 8 months	640	
20 per cent × £2,000 × 6 months	200	
		840
Written down value at 31 Dec 19X8		2,360

A. Ferry
Statement of affairs as at 31 December 19X7

	£		£
Capital	12,580	Freehold land and buildings	10,000
Accruals	35	Motor vehicles	1,250
Creditors	390	Stock	565
		Debtors	865
		Prepayments	40
		Cash	285
	13,005		13,005

A. Ferry
Statement of affairs as at 31 December 19X8

	£	£		£	£
Capital		13,310	*Fixed assets*		
			Freehold land & buildings at cost		10,000
Current liabilities			Motor vehicles at cost	3,200	
Accruals	20		*Less*: Aggregate		
Creditors	480	500	depreciation	840	2,360
					12,360
			Current assets		
			Prepayments		25
			Stock (760 − 60)		700
			Debtors	645	
			Less: Provision		
			for doubtful		
			debts	85	560
			Cash		165
					1,450
		13,810			13,810

A. Ferry
Statement of profit for the year ended 31 December 19X8

	£
Capital at 31 December 19X8	13,310
Less: Capital at 31 December 19X7	12,580
	730
Add: Drawings	15,900
	16,630
Less: Capital introduced	5,280
Net profit for the year	11,350

Notes

1. There is no need to compute the profit or loss on disposals of fixed assets since this will automatically be reflected in the increase in net assets/capital. However, it is necessary to compute the written down value (or possible market value) of fixed assets at the end of each year as shown in the workings in order to prepare the statement of affairs.
2. The stock at 31 December 19X8 excludes the cost of the television that was damaged beyond repair of £60.
3. Doubtful debts have been provided for by reducing the amount of debtors at 31 December 19X8.
4. The amounts for capital in the statement of affairs are the difference between the two sides of these balance sheets.
5. It is usual to treat the statement of affairs at the end of the previous year as workings not requiring any formal presentation. However, the statement of affairs at the end of the current year should contain the usual headings and sub-totals and be in a form presentable to the owner and other interested parties such as the Inland Revenue. A vertical presentation may therefore be preferable.

Single entry

As explained previously single entry refers to the situation where a business has some record of its receipts and payments, fixed assets, stocks, debtors, creditors, accruals, prepayments and long-term liabilities. However, these records are not in double entry forms and usually consist of just a cash book.

One possibility is for the accountant to complete the records by posting the receipts and payments to the appropriate accounts in the ledger either in full or summarized form. The final accounts are then prepared from the trial balance in the normal way. This is common in practice. However, in very small businesses this may be too expensive and/or impractical. In this case the final accounts are prepared directly from the cash book or a summary thereof, and the appropriate adjustments made for debtors, creditors, provisions, accruals, prepayments, etc. Examination questions on this topic also usually take the same form. An illustration of this treatment of single entry records is given in Example 19.2. Because of the importance and length of the workings, the procedure for answering the question is presented as a series of steps. These are well worth memorizing as a model for answering such questions.

Example 19.2
The following is the balance sheet of L. Cook at 31 December 19X5.

	£		£
		Freehold land and buildings	
Capital	19,240	at cost	12,500
Trade creditors	2,610	Motor vehicles (cost £5,000)	2,900
Electricity accrued	30	Rates prepaid	60
		Stock of goods for resale	1,650
		Trade debtors	3,270
		Bank	1,500
	21,880		21,880

The only book kept by Cook is a cash book, a summary of which for the year ended 31 December 19X6 has been prepared as follows:

	£		£
Balance b/d	1,500	Rates	140
Cash takings banked	4,460	Salaries	2,820
Cheques from debtors	15,930	Electricity	185
Additional capital	500	Bank charges	10
		Motor expenses	655
		Payments to creditors	16,680
		Stationery	230
		Sundry expenses	40
		Balance c/d	1,630
	22,390		22,390

From the supporting documents it has been ascertained that:

1. The following amounts have been paid from the cash takings before they were banked:

Drawings	£22,000
Purchases	£560
Petrol	£85
Repairs to buildings	£490

2. Cook has taken goods out of the business for his own use that cost £265.
3. Motor vehicles have been depreciated in past years at 20 per cent per annum by the reducing balance method.
4. Stock at 31 December 19X6 was valued at £1,960.
5. The trade debtors and trade creditors outstanding at the end of the year are £2,920 and £2,860 respectively.
6. At 31 December 19X6 there are rates prepaid of £70 and electricity accrued of £45. You expect to charge cook £100 for your services.

Prepare a trading and profit and loss account for the year ended 31 December 19X6 and a balance sheet at that date. Present your answer in vertical form and show all your workings clearly.

Workings/procedure

1. If necessary prepare a statement of affairs as at the end of the previous year to ascertain the capital at that date.
2. If necessary prepare a summarized cash book from the bank statements, etc. to ascertain the balance at the end of the year and the total amounts received and spent on each type of income and expenditure, and assets.
3. (a) Compute the net credit purchases by preparing a creditors' control account as follows:

Creditors' control

19X6			19X6		
31 Dec	Bank	16,680	1 Jan	Balance b/d	2,610
31 Dec	Balance c/d	2,860	31 Dec	Net Purchases	16,930
		19,540			19,540

The net purchases figure is the difference between the two sides.
(b) Compute the cash and cheque purchases and then the total purchases:

$$\text{Total purchases} = £560 + £16,930 = £17,490$$

4. (a) Compute the net credit sales by preparing a debtors' control account as follows:

Debtors' control

19X6			19X6		
1 Jan	Balance b/d	3,270	31 Dec	Bank	15,930
31 Dec	Net sales	15,580	31 Dec	Balance c/d	2,920
		18,850			18,850

The net sales figure is the difference between the two sides.
(b) Compute the cash and cheque sales and then the total sales:

$$\text{Cash sales} = £4,460 + £22,000 + £560 + £85 + £490 = £27,595$$

$$\text{Total sales} = £27,595 + £15,580 = £43,175$$

Note that sometimes the computations in (a) and (b) have to be combined. This is necessary when the cash and/or cheque sales are not given separately from the cheques received from debtors. In this case the total cash and cheques received in respect of sales are credited to the control account. The same principle would also have to be used in the case of purchases when cash and/or cheque purchases are not given separately from cheques paid to creditors.

5. Compute the charges to the profit and loss account for those expenses with accruals or prepayments by preparing the relevant ledger accounts. Alternatively, in examinations this may be shown as workings in the profit and loss account.

Light and heat

19X6			19X6		
31 Dec	Bank	185	1 Jan	Accrual b/d	30
31 Dec	Accrual c/d	45	31 Dec	Profit and loss a/c	200
		230			230

Rates

19X6			19X6		
1 Jan	Prepayment b/d	60	31 Dec	Profit and loss a/c	130
31 Dec	Bank	140	31 Dec	Prepayment c/d	70
		200			200

6. Compute the charges and/or credits to the profit and loss account in respect of any provisions for bad debts, depreciation, sales of fixed assets, etc. Alternatively if these are relatively simple, in examinations, they may be shown as workings in the profit and loss account.

Motor vehicles

$$\text{Depreciation expense} = 20\% \times £2,900 = £580$$

$$\text{Aggregate depreciation} = (£5,000 - £2,900) + £580 = £2,680$$

7. Prepare the final accounts, remembering to add together any cheque and cash expenditure of the same type (e.g. motor expenses in this example), and include any fixed assets acquired, drawings (e.g. goods taken by the proprietor), capital introduced, etc.

L. Cook
Trading and profit and loss account for the year ended 31 December 19X6

	£	£
Sales		43,175
Less: Cost of sales—		
Stock at 1 Jan 19X6	1,650	
Add: Purchases (17,490 − 265)	17,225	
	18,875	
Less: Stock at 31 Dec 19X6	1,960	16,915
Gross profit		26,260
Less: Expenditure—		
Rates (60 + 140 − 70)	130	
Salaries	2,820	
Light and heat (185 + 45 − 30)	200	
Bank charges	10	
Motor expenses (655 + 85)	740	
Stationery	230	
Sundry expenses	40	
Repairs to buildings	490	
Depreciation on vehicles (20 per cent × 2,900)	580	
Accountancy fees	100	5,340
Net profit		20,920

Balance sheet as at 31 December 19X6

Fixed assets	Cost	Agg. Depn.	WDV
	£	£	£
Freehold land and buildings	12,500	—	12,500
Motor vehicles	5,000	2,680	2,320
	17,500	2,680	14,820
Current assets			
Stock		1,960	
Trade debtors		2,920	
Prepayments		70	
Bank		1,630	
		6,580	
Current liabilities			
Trade creditors	2,860		
Accruals (45 + 100)	145	3,005	
Net current assets			3,575
Net assets			18,395

Capital

Balance at 1 Jan 19X6	19,240
Add: Capital introduced	500
Net profit	20,920
	40,660
Less: Drawings (22,000 + 265)	22,265
Balance at 31 Dec 19X6	18,395

Notes

1. The goods taken by the proprietor for his own use of £265 have been added to drawings and deducted from purchases (rather than added to sales) because the question gives their cost.

2. In the workings for the debtors' control account, the term net sales is used to emphasize that this is after deducting returns, the amount of which is unknown and cannot be ascertained. However, if the returns were known, these would be entered in the debtors' control account and the profit and loss account in the normal manner. More importantly if the value of any bad debts, discount allowed, etc., was known, these would have to be entered in the debtors control account and profit and loss account in the normal way. The same principles apply to the creditors' control account where there are returns, discount received, etc.

3. In some single entry questions there are petty cash balances at the start and end of the accounting year. Where the balance in cash at the end of the year is greater than at the start, the increase must be added to the cash takings that were banked in order to ascertain the cash sales (in Workings 4(b) above). The reason is simply because the increase in the cash float must have come from cash sales. Put another way, the cash takings banked are after deducting/excluding the increase in the cash balance. To ascertain the cash sales therefore necessitates adding back any increase in the cash float, or deducting any decrease from the cash takings that were banked. Where there are cash balances/floats at the start and end of the year, an alternative to the one line computation of cash sales shown in Workings 4(b) above is to prepare a petty cash account. The cash sales will be the difference between the two sides of the account after entering the opening and closing cash balances, the amounts paid from the cash takings, and the takings that were banked. This may have the added advantage of reminding students to include the various items of petty cash expenditure in the final accounts.

4. Many businesses accept *credit cards* such as Visa, Mastercard, etc., in payment for goods that they sell to the public. This gives rise to special problems where there are incomplete records in the form of single entry. Most credit card companies charge a commission of up to 5 per cent of the value of goods sold. Thus if a business sells goods with a selling price of, say, £200 the amount it receives will be £190 (i.e. 95 per cent of £200). The normal ledger entries for this sale will be to credit the sales account with £200 and debit a credit card debtors' account with the amount it expects to receive of £190. The difference of £10 commission should be debited to a commission account that will be transferred to the profit and loss account at the end of the year.

Where there is only single entry, the accounting records in respect of credit card sales will consist of a debit in the cash book of the amounts received from the credit card company during the year. It is therefore necessary to compute the value of sales before deducting the commission. This is done in two stages. The first stage is to calculate the total credit card sales for the year after deducting commission by means of a credit card debtors' account in which the amount received is adjusted to take into account the opening and closing amounts owing. The second stage is to gross up the total credit card sales after deducting commission to as certain the total credit card sales before deducting commission. Using the example above this would be $100/95 \times £190 = £200$. The £200 is then included in sales in the trading account, and the difference of $£200 - £190 = £10$ commission is shown as a separate item of expense in the profit and loss account.

Summary

There are three different forms of incomplete records. The first is incomplete records of revenue income and expenditure. This refers to where there are no documents or records of revenue income and expenditure. It is therefore not possible to prepare a profit and loss account. However, the profit may be ascertained by calculating the difference between the capital/net asset value of the business at the start and end of the year by preparing balance sheets at each of these dates. The profit is found by adjusting the change in capital over the year for any capital introduced and/or drawings.

The second form of incomplete records is known as single entry. This refers to where the business transactions have been entered in a cash book but not posted to a ledger. The third form of incomplete records is incomplete single entry. This refers to where there are no books of account but a cash book summary can be prepared from the bank statements and/or supporting documents.

In this case of incomplete single entry and single entry it is therefore possible to prepare a profit and loss account and balance sheet. This can be done by posting the amounts shown in the summarized cash book to the ledger, extracting a trial balance, and preparing final accounts in the normal way. Alternatively students are normally required in examinations to prepare final accounts from the summarized cash book by means of workings. These usually take the form of creditors' and debtors' control accounts, in order to ascertain the purchases and sales respectively, together with those expense accounts which have accruals and/or prepayments at the start and end of the year.

Key terms and concepts

Credit card sales, incomplete records, single entry, statement of affairs.

Exercises

An asterisk after the question number indicates that there is a suggested answer in the Appendix.

19.1.   Describe the different forms of incomplete records with which you are familiar.

19.2.* The following is the balance sheet of Round Music as at 30 June 19X4:

	£		£
Capital	42,770	Plant	31,000
Creditors	5,640	Stock	9,720
Accruals	90	Debtors	6,810
		Prepayments	150
		Bank	820
	48,500		48,500

During the year ended 30 June 19X5 there was a fire which destroyed the books of account and supporting documents. However, from questioning the proprietor you have been able to obtain the following information:

1. The plant at 30 June 19X4 cost £50,000 and has been depreciated at 10 per cent per annum by the fixed instalment method on a strict time basis. Additional plant was purchased on the 1 April 19X5 at a cost of £20,000. Plant costing £10,000 on 1 January 19X2 was sold on 1 October 19X4 for £4,450.
2. Stock at 30 June 19X5 was valued at £8,630. This includes goods costing £1,120 that are worthless because of fire damage.
3. Debtors and creditors at 30 June 19X5 were £6,120 and £3,480 respectively. Debtors include doubtful debts of £310.
4. Accruals and prepayments at 30 June 19X5 were £130 and £80 respectively.
5. There was a bank overdraft at 30 June 19X5 of £1,430.
6. During the year the business had borrowed £7,000 from Lickey Bank which was repayable on 1 January 19X8.
7. During the year the owner introduced additional capital of £5,000 and made drawings of £18,500 by cheque. The proprietor also took goods costing £750 from the business for his own use.

You are required to compute the profit for the year ended 30 June 19X5 and prepare a balance sheet at that date. Present your answer in vertical form showing clearly the cost of fixed assets and the aggregate depreciation.

19.3. Jane Grimes, retail fruit and vegetable merchant, does not keep a full set of accounting records. However, the following information has been produced from the business's records:

1. Summary of the bank account for the year ended 31 August 19X8:

	£		£
1 Sept 19X7 balance		Payments to suppliers	72,000
brought forward	1,970	Purchase of motor van (E471 KBR)	13,000
Receipts from		Rent and rates	2,600
trade debtors	96,000	Wages	15,100
Sale of private yacht	20,000	Motor vehicle expenses	3,350
Sale of motor van		Postage and stationery	1,360
(A123 BWA)	2,100	Drawings	9,200
		Repairs and renewals	650
		Insurances	800
		31 Aug 19X8 balance carried forward	2,010
	£120,070		£120,070

2. Assets and liabilities, other than balance at bank:

As at		1 Sept 19X7	31 Aug 19X8
		£	£
Trade creditors		4,700	2,590
Trade debtors		7,320	9,500
Rent and rates accruals		200	260
Motor vans: A123 BWA— At cost		10,000	—
	Provision for depn.	8,000	—
E471 KBR— At cost		—	13,000
	Provision for depn.	—	To be determined
Stock in trade		4,900	5,900
Insurances prepaid		160	200

3. All receipts are banked and all payments are made from the business bank account.
4. A trade debt of £300 owing by Peter Blunt and included in the trade debtors at 31 August 19X8 (see point 2 above), is to be written off as a bad debt.
5. It is Jane Grime's policy to provide depreciation at the rate of 20 per cent on the cost of motor vans held at the end of each financial year; no depreciation is provided in the year of sale or disposal of a motor van.
6. Discounts received during the year ended 31 August 19X8 from trade creditors amounted to £1,000.

Required:

(a) Prepare Jane Grime's trading and profit and loss account for the year ended 31 August 19X8.
(b) Prepare Jane Grime's balance sheet as at 31 August 19X8.   (AAT)

19.4.* The following is the balance sheet of A. Fox at 31 July 19X8.

	£		£
Capital	48,480	Freehold land and buildings (at cost)	35,000
Creditors	5,220	Fixtures and fittings (cost £10,000)	5,800
Electricity accrued	60	Stock	3,300
		Debtors	6,540
		Bank	3,000
		Telephone prepaid	120
	53,760		53,760

The only book kept by A. Fox is a cash book in which all transactions passed through the bank account are recorded. A summary of the cash book for the year ended 31 July 19X9 has been prepared as follows:

	£		£
Balance b/d	3,000	Wages	5,640
Cash takings banked	18,920	Telephone	280
Cheques from debtors	31,860	Electricity	370
Additional capital	1,000	Motor expenses	1,810
		Payments to creditors	33,360

Printing	560
Purchases	4,500
Balance c/d	8,260

54,780	54,780

From the supporting documents it has been ascertained that:

(i)   The following amounts have been paid from the cash takings before they were banked:

	£
Drawings	4,000
Purchases	1,120
Car repairs	980
Window cleaning	170

(ii)   Stock at 31 July 19X9 was valued at £3,920.

(iii)   At 31 July 19X9 there are telephone charges prepaid of £140 and electricity accrued of £290.

(iv)   The trade debtors and trade creditors outstanding at the end of the year are £5,840 and £5,720 respectively.

(v)   Fox has taken goods out of the business for his own use that cost £530.

(vi)   Fixtures and fittings have been depreciated in past years at 20 per cent per annum by the reducing balance method.

You are required to prepare a trading and profit and loss account for the year ended 31 July 19X9 and a balance sheet at that date. Present your answer in vertical form.

19.5.   Miss Fitt owns a retail shop. The trading and profit and loss account and balance sheet are prepared annually by you from records consisting of a bank statement and a file of unpaid suppliers and outstanding debtors.

The following balances were shown on her balance sheet at 1 January 19X8:

	£
Shop creditors	245
Shop fittings (cost £250) at written down value	200
Stock in hand	475
Debtors	50
Cash at bank	110
Cash float in till	10

The following is a summary of her bank statement for the year ended 31 December 19X8:

	£
Takings banked	6,983
Payments to suppliers	6,290
Rent of premises to 31 December 19X8	400
A. Smith—shopfitters	85
Advertising in local newspaper	50
Sundry expenses	38

You obtain the following additional information:

1. Takings are banked daily and all suppliers are paid by cheque, but Miss Fitt keeps £15 per week for herself, and pays her assistant £11 per week out of the takings.
2. The work done by A. Smith was for new shelving and repairs to existing fittings. The cost of new shelves was estimated at £50.
3. The cash float in the till was considered insufficient and raised to £15.
4. Miss Fitt took £75 worth of goods for her own use without payment.
5. Your charges will be £25 for preparing the accounts.
6. The outstanding accounts file shows £230 due to suppliers, £10 due in respect of sundry expenses, and £85 outstanding debtors.
7. Depreciation on shop fittings is provided at 10 per cent on cost, a full year's charge being made in year of purchase.
8. Stock in hand at 31 December 19X8 was £710.

You are required to prepare Miss Fitt's trading and profit and loss account for the year ended 31 December 19X8, and her balance sheet as at that date.   (ACCA)

19.6. A year ago, you prepared accounts for A. Wilson, a retailer. His closing position was then:

Balance sheet at 31 March 19X0

	£	£
Delivery van (cost £4,800 in May 19X8)		2,880
Stock		6,410
Debtors (£1,196 *less* provision £72)		1,124
Owing from Askard Ltd		196
		10,610
Bank balance	70	
Trade creditors	2,094	
Accountant's fee	120	
Provision for legal claim	600	2,884
Wilson's capital		£7,726

Mr Wilson does not keep full records (despite your advice) and once again you have to use what information is available to prepare his accounts to 31 March 19X1. The most reliable evidence is a summary of the bank statements for the year. It shows:

	£	£
Balance at 1 April 19X0 (overdraft)		(70)
Cash and cheques from customers		33,100
Cheques from Askard Ltd		7,840
		40,870
Less cheques drawn for:		
Wilson's personal expenses	7,400	
Van—tax, insurance, repairs	440	
Rent, rates and general expenses	2,940	
Cash register	400	

Accountant's fee	120	
Trade creditors	28,284	
Legal claim settled	460	40,044
Balance at 31 March 19X1		826

For some of the sales Askard credit cards are accepted. Askard Ltd charges 2 per cent commission. At the end of the year the amount outstanding from Askard Ltd was £294.

Some other sales are on credit terms. Wilson keeps copies of the sales invoices in a box until they are settled. Those still in the 'unpaid' box at 31 March 19X1 totalled £1,652 which included one for £136 outstanding for four months—otherwise they were all less than two months old. Wilson thinks he allowed cash discounts of about £150 during the year. The debt of £72 outstanding at the beginning of the year for which a provision was made was never paid.

The amount of cash and cheques received from credit customers and from cash sales was all paid into the bank except that some cash payments were made first. These were estimated as:

	£
Part-time assistance	840
Petrol for van	800
Miscellaneous expenses	200
Wilson's drawings	2,000

Invoices from suppliers of goods outstanding at the year end totalled £2,420. Closing stock was estimated at £7,090 (cost price) and your fee has been agreed at £200. It has been agreed with the Inspector of Taxes that £440 of the van expenses should be treated as Wilson's private expenses.

Required:
Prepare the profit and loss account for Wilson's business for the year to 31 March 19X1 and a balance sheet at that date.   (ACCA)

19.7. David Denton set up in business as a plumber a year ago, and he has asked you to act as his accountant. His instructions to you are in the form of the following letter.

Dear Henry
I was pleased when you agreed to act as my accountant and look forward to your first visit to check my records. The proposed fee of £250 p.a. is acceptable. I regret that the paperwork for the work done during the year is incomplete. I started my business on 1 January last, and put £6,500 into a business bank account on that date. I brought my van into the firm at that time, and reckon that it was worth £3,600 then. I think it will last another three years after the end of the first year of my business use.

I have drawn £90 per week from the business bank account during the year. In my trade it is difficult to take a holiday, but my wife managed to get away for a while. The travel agent's bill for £280 was paid out of the business account. I bought the lease of the yard and office for £6,500. The lease has ten years to run, and the rent is only £300 a year payable in advance on the anniversary of the date of purchase, which was 1 April. I borrowed £4,000 on that day from Aunt Jane to help pay for the lease. I have agreed to pay her 10 per cent interest per annum, but have been too busy to do anything about this yet.

I was lucky enough to meet Miss Prism shortly before I set up on my own, and she has worked for me as an office organizer right from the start. She is paid a salary of £3,000 per annum. All the bills for the year have been carefully preserved in a tool box, and we analysed them last week. The materials I have bought cost me £9,600, but I reckon there was £580-worth left in the yard on 31 December. I have not paid for them all yet; I think we owed £714 to the suppliers on 31 December. I was surprised to see that I had spent £4,800 on plumbing equipment, but it should last me five years or so. Electricity bills received up to 30 September came to £1,122; but motor expenses were £912, and general expenses £1,349 for the year. The insurance premium for the year to 31 March next was £800. All these have been paid by cheque but Miss Prism has lost the rate demand. I expect the Local Authority will send a reminder soon since I have not yet paid. I seem to remember that the rates came to £180 for the year to 31 March next.

Miss Prism sent out bills to my customers for work done, but some of them are very slow to pay. Altogether the charges made were £29,863, but only £25,613 had been received by 31 December. Miss Prism thinks that 10 per cent of the remaining bills are not likely to be paid. Other customers for jobs too small to bill have paid £3,418 in cash for work done, but I only managed to bank £2,600 of this money. I used £400 of the difference to pay the family's grocery bills, and Miss Prism used the rest for general expenses, except for £123 which was left over in a drawer in the office on 31 December.

Kind regards,
Yours sincerely,
David.

You are required to draw up a profit and loss account for the year ended 31 December, and a balance sheet as at that date: (ACCA)

For further questions on incomplete records see Chapter 24 on the final accounts of partnerships.

20. The final accounts of clubs

Learning objectives

After reading this chapter the student should be able to:

1. Explain the meaning of the key terms and concepts listed at the end of the chapter.
2. Describe the main differences between the final accounts of a business enterprise and those of a club with particular reference to its capital.
3. Show the accounting entries in respect of annual subscriptions and explain their conceptual foundation.
4. Prepare the final accounts of clubs, including from incomplete records, comprising a receipts and payments account, bar trading account, income and expenditure account, and statement of affairs.
5. Show the accounting entries in respect of various items usually only arising in the accounts of clubs, and explain their conceptual foundation.
6. Apply the principles in point 5 above to other transactions, items and organizations such as charities.

Introduction

A club is an organization whose primary aim is to provide a service to its members (e.g. sports and social clubs) and/or some section of the community (e.g. senior citizens). One of its main financial objectives is therefore not to earn a profit but often simply to break even. Thus in the final accounts of clubs the profit and loss account is replaced with an *income and expenditure account*. Any difference between the income and expenditure for the year is referred to as an excess of income over expenditure or vice versa (i.e. not a profit or loss). The income and expenditure account is prepared using the same principles as the profit and loss account, namely the matching and accrual of revenue income and expenditure. However, the contents differ in that income will take the form of subscriptions, entrance fees from sports activities, surpluses on a bar, dances, raffles, gaming machines, annual dinners, etc.

Another major difference between clubs and business enterprises is that clubs are usually managed by voluntary officers. Members of the club therefore frequently expect them to provide an account of the money that has been received and the way in which it has been spent. Thus final accounts of clubs often include a *receipts and payments account*. This is simply a summary of the cash book showing the opening and closing cash and bank balances and the total amounts received and spent on each type of income and expenditure, assets, etc.

Many clubs are quite small and may have few, if any, assets and liabilities other than cash. It therefore serves little purpose to prepare a balance sheet, particularly if a receipts and payments account has been produced. However, some clubs are relatively large. In this case the final accounts should include a balance sheet which is also sometimes called a *statement of affairs*. It will take the same form as for business enterprises with one major difference which is that the capital account is replaced by an *accumulated/general fund*. This is an accumulation of previous years' surpluses (less deficits) of income over expenditure, and represents the net worth of the club. Unlike the capital account of business enterprises, there cannot be capital introduced or drawings against the accumulated fund. The only other significant difference between the balance sheet of a business enterprise and that of a club is that the latter also contains subscriptions in arrears and subscriptions in advance. These are examined further later.

Although clubs are not primarily trading organizations they frequently engage in certain activities that are intended to make a profit/ surplus as a way of raising additional funds or subsidizing other functions, for example, the sale of drinks and snacks, gaming machines, raffles, dances, etc. Where these involve material amounts of money it is usual to compute the profit or loss on the activity in a separate account such as a *bar trading account*. Similarly, where the amounts are less significant it is usual also to compute the surplus or deficit (e.g. on a dance) and show this as a separate item in the income and expenditure account.

Annual subscriptions

Many clubs require their members to pay an annual subscription. These are usually accounted for on an accruals basis, that is, applying the accruals concept. This means that the amount which is credited to the income and expenditure account in respect of subscriptions is the amount due for the year, irrespective of whether this has all been received.

The application of the accruals concept gives rise to subscriptions in arrear and subscriptions in advance in the final accounts. Where some members have not paid their subscriptions at the end of a given accounting year these are referred to as *subscriptions in arrear*, and treated as debtors. Where some members have paid their subscriptions for the following accounting year these are referred to as *subscriptions in advance*, and treated as creditors.

However, as in the case of accrued and prepaid expenses, debtors and creditors in respect of subscriptions are not entered in separate personal accounts. Instead, these are recorded in the subscriptions account. Subscriptions in arrear are entered in the subscriptions account as a balance carried down on the credit side and a balance brought down on the debit side. Subscriptions in advance are entered in the subscriptions account as a balance carried down on the debit side and a balance brought down on the credit side. Thus subscriptions in arrear are shown on the balance sheet as a current asset and subscriptions in advance are shown as a current liability.

Sometimes subscriptions are recorded in the income and expenditure account on a strict cash received basis and not an accruals basis. In this case there will not be any subscriptions in arrear or advance in the final accounts. This is said to be an application of the prudence concept. It is sometimes justified on the grounds that members, unlike other debtors, are more likely to fail to pay subscriptions in arrear, and clubs are unlikely to take legal or other action to force payment. However, the use of the cash received basis is not common in examination questions and should only be applied where specifically required.

The preparation of final accounts of clubs

It is common to find that the books of accounts of a club have been kept on a *single entry* basis. This means that the procedure to be followed in the preparation of the final accounts will be as described in the previous chapter. This is illustrated in Example 20.1 below.

Example 20.1

City Football Club has the following assets and liabilities at 1 July 19X7: freehold land and buildings at cost £50,000; equipment at WDV £12,200; grass mower at cost £135; bar creditors £1,380; subscriptions in advance £190; subscriptions in arrear £105; bar stocks £2,340; rates in advance £240; electricity accrued £85.

A summary of the receipts and payments during the year ended 30 June 19X8 is as follows:

	£		£
Bank balance at 1 July 19X7	695	Rates	490
Bar takings banked	5,430	Electricity	255
Subscriptions received	3,610	Purchase of new	
Sale of dance tickets	685	grass mower	520
Gate money received	8,490	Bar steward's wages	2,200
		Bar creditors	4,980
		Band for dance	490
		Postage and telephone	310
		Printing and stationery	175
		Bank balance at	
		30 June 19X8	9,490
	18,910		18,910

You are given the following additional information:

1. Bar stocks at 30 June 19X8 £2,560.
2. Bar creditors at 30 June 19X8 £980.
3. Rates paid include £400 for the six months to 30 September 19X8.
4. Electricity in arrear at 30 June 19X8 £70.
5. Subscriptions in arrear at 30 June 19X8 £95.
6. Subscriptions in advance at 30 June 19X8 £115.
7. The following amounts have been paid from bar takings before they were banked: sundry expenses £25, bar purchases £235, office salaries £1,200, stationery £45, and travelling expenses £140.
8. The new grass mower was purchased by putting in part exchange the old one, for which the trade in value was £180.
9. Depreciation on the equipment is 20 per cent p.a. using the reducing balance method. No depreciation is charged on the grass mower.

You are required to prepare:

(a) a bar trading account for the year ended 30 June 19X8.
(b) an income and expenditure account for the year ended 30 June 19X8.
(c) a balance sheet as at 30 June 19X8.

Show clearly all your workings.

Workings/procedure

1. If necessary prepare a statement of affairs as at the end of the previous year in order to ascertain the accumulated/general fund.

City Football Club
Statement of affairs as at 30 June 19X7

	£	£	£
Fixed assets			
Freehold land and buildings at cost			50,000
Equipment at WDV			12,200
Grass mower at cost			135
			62,335
Current assets			
Payments in advance		240	
Stock		2,340	
Subscriptions in arrear		105	
Bank		695	
		3,380	
Less: Current liabilities			
Accrued expenses	85		
Creditors	1,380		
Subscriptions in advance	190	1,655	
			1,725
Accumulated fund at 30 June 19X7			64,060

2. If necessary prepare a receipts and payments account for the year in order to ascertain the bank and cash balance at the end of the year and the total amounts received and spent on each type of income and expenditure, and on assets.
3. (a) Compute the net credit bar purchases by preparing a creditors' control account:

Creditor's control

19X8			19X7		
30 June	Bank	4,980	1 July	Balance b/d	1,380
30 June	Balance c/d	980	19X8		
			30 June	Net purchases	4,580
		5,960			5,960

The figure for net credit purchases is the difference between the two sides.
   (b) Compute the cash and cheque bar purchases and then the total bar purchases:

$$\text{Total purchases} = £235 + £4,580 = £4,815$$

4. (a) Compute the net credit bar sales if any by preparing a debtors' control account.
   (b) Compute the cash and cheque bar sales and then the total bar sales:

$$\text{Cash and total sales} = £5,430 + £25 + £235 + £1,200 + £45 + £140$$

$$= £7,075$$

5. Ascertain the income for the year in respect of subscriptions by preparing the ledger account. Alternatively, in examinations this may be shown as workings in the income and expenditure account.

Subscriptions

19X7				19X7		
1 July	Subs in arrear b/d	105		1 July	Subs in advance b/d	190
19X8				19X8		
30 June	Subs for year	3,675		30 June	Bank	3,610
30 June	Subs in advance c/d	115		30 June	Subs in arrear c/d	95
		3,895				3,895

The figure for subs for the year of £3,675 is the difference between the two sides. It is credited to the income and expenditure account.

6. Compute the expenditure for the year in respect to those expenses with accruals and prepayments by preparing the relevant ledger accounts. Alternatively, in examinations this may be shown as workings in the income and expenditure account:

Rates

19X7				19X8		
1 July	Prepayment b/d	240		30 June	Income and expenditure a/c	530
19X8				30 June	Prepayment c/d	200
30 June	Bank	490				
		730				730

Light and heat

19X8				19X7		
30 June	Bank	255		1 July	Accrual b/d	85
30 June	Accrual c/d	70		19X8		
				30 June	Income and expenditure a/c	240
		325				325

7. Ascertain the depreciation charges for the year and any profit or loss on the sale of fixed assets:

$$\text{Depreciation on equipment} = 20 \text{ per cent} \times £12,200 = £2,440$$

$$\text{Profit on sale of grass mower} = £180 - £135 = £45$$

8. Prepare the bar trading account, income and expenditure account and balance sheet remembering to add together any cheque and cash expenditure of the same type (e.g. stationery) and make any other necessary adjustments, such as the purchase of fixed assets.

City Football Club
Bar trading account for the year ended 30 June 19X8

	£	£
Sales		7,075
Less: Cost of sales—		
Stock at 1 July 19X7	2,340	
Add: Purchases	4,815	
	7,155	
Less: Stock at 30 June 19X8	2,560	
	4,595	
Other bar costs—		
Steward's wages	2,200	6,795
Profit on bar		280

City Football Club
Income and expenditure account for the year ended 30 June 19X8

	£	£
Income		
Gate receipts		8,490
Subscriptions		3,675
Profit on bar		280
Income from dance	685	
Cost of dance	(490)	
Surplus on dance		195
Profit on sale of fixed assets		45
		12,685
Less: Expenditure		
Rates (490 + 240 − 200)	530	
Light and heat (255 + 70 − 85)	240	
Postage and telephone	310	
Printing and stationery (175 + 45)	220	
Sundry expenses	25	
Office salaries	1,200	
Travelling expenses	140	
Depreciation on equipment	2,440	5,105
Excess of income over expenditure		7,580

City Football Club
Balance sheet as at 30 June 19X8

	£	£	£
Fixed assets			
Freehold land and buildings at cost			50,000
Equipment at WDV		12,200	
Less: Depreciation		2,440	9,760
Grass mower (520 + 180)			700
			60,460

Current assets			
Prepayments		200	
Stock		2,560	
Subscriptions in arrear		95	
Bank		9,490	
		12,345	
Less: Current liabilities			
Accruals	70		
Subscriptions in advance	115		
Creditors	980	1,165	
Net current assets			11,180
Net assets			71,640
Accumulated fund			
Balance at 30 June 19X7			64,060
Add: Excess of income over			
expenditure for the year			7,580
Balance at 30 June 19X8			71,640

Special items

As seen above, clubs have a variety of different forms of income, many of which are not found in business enterprises. Some of these are not common in practice but provide examples that examiners can use to test important principles. Those most frequently encountered in examinations are discussed below.

Donations, bequests and gifts

Small donations, bequest and gifts in the form of money are credited to the income and expenditure account. Donations and gifts in the form of domestic goods (such as furniture for the clubhouse or old clothes for resale) with a relatively small value are not usually recorded in the income and expenditure account (until they are sold, when just the sale proceeds are recorded).

However, where donations of money or other assets are of a material amount (i.e. large in relation to the size of the club's normal income), the generally accepted best practice is to credit such items direct to the accumulated fund instead of the income and expenditure account. This is because it would probably be misleading to credit the income and expenditure account with large amounts of income which is of a non-recurring nature. Members might be misled into thinking that the resulting surplus for the year was likely to be repeated in future years and thus could be used to cover additional recurring expenditure or reduced bar prices! The corresponding debit entry would be in the receipts and payments account in the case of money, or to the relevant asset account where the donation or bequest takes some other form, such as land, buildings, paintings, etc. In the latter case the amount entered in the accounts would be a valuation.

Membership/entrance fees

Clubs which have valuable assets that are in great demand, such as golf and other sports facilities, often require new members to pay an entry or joining fee (in addition to the annual subscription). To treat this as income for the year in which it was received by crediting the income and expenditure account would be a breach of the matching principle, the reason being that this fee is in the nature of a prepayment by the member for services which the club is obliged to provide over his or her period of membership, which is usually several years.

Such fees are referred to as *deferred income*, and the matching principle dictates that these should be credited to the income and expenditure account over the number of years which the club expects to have to provide the member with its services. Clearly the decision relating to the length of this period is highly subjective. One possibility is the average number of years that people remain a member of the club. However, in practice a more arbitrary period may be selected depending on the nature of the club's services and the size of the membership fee.

The accounting entries in respect of joining fees are thus to credit these to a deferred income account, and each year to transfer a given proportion (e.g. 10 per cent if to be spread over 10 years) to the income and expenditure account. The balance on the deferred income account is shown on the balance sheet after (and separate from) the accumulated fund.

Life membership subscriptions

Instead of paying an annual subscription some clubs permit their members to make a once-only payment which entitles them to membership for life. These are referred to as life membership subscriptions and, like entrance fees above, are in the nature of a prepayment by the member for services that the club is obliged to provide over the remainder of his or her life. They must therefore not be credited to the income and expenditure account as income of the year they are received.

Life membership subscriptions are a form of *deferred income*, and the matching principle dictates that they be spread over the number of years which the club expects to have to provide the life member with its services. Clearly the decision relating to the length of this period is highly subjective. One possibility is the average number of years between people becoming life members and their death. However, in practice a more arbitrary period may be selected depending on the nature of the club's services. For example, the period may be considerably longer for a golf club or social club than an athletics club or senior citizens club, since the period of life membership of the latter is restricted by physical and age constraints.

The accounting entries in respect of life membership subscriptions are thus to credit these to a deferred income account, and each year to transfer a given proportion (e.g. 5 per cent if to be spread over 20 years) to the income and expenditure account. The balance on the deferred income account is shown on the balance sheet after (and separate from) the accumulated fund.

There is, however, an alternative treatment of life membership subscriptions which is an application of the prudence concept rather than the matching principle. This dictates that because the period of membership cannot be predicted with reasonable certainty, the income should not be recognized until the member dies. Thus all the life membership subscriptions are credited to a fund account, and when a member dies his or her subscription is transferred to the accumulated fund (or possibly the income and expenditure account). The life membership subscription fund account is shown in the balance sheet just below the accumulated fund and separate from any items that have been treated as deferred income, such as membership/entrance fees. This method of treating life membership subscriptions would be adopted in examination questions that do not give any indication of the length of time over which these should be credited to income, and which give details of how many life members died during the accounting year.

Prize funds

Some clubs give prizes or other monetary awards to their members and/or other people that they wish to honour or assist for educational reasons. These are frequently financed from a separate fund, which may have been created by the club or from money that was donated for the express purpose of making the award. When the fund is set up the money donated for this purpose is invested in securities which provide some sort of income. This often takes the form of government stocks carrying a fixed rate of interest. The prizes or awards are usually paid out of the interest received and not the original donation, which remains invested.

The accounting entries for prize funds can be confusing partly because they involve two related accounts. The first is a prize fund account which appears on the balance sheet along with other funds such as the accumulated fund and any life membership subscription fund. The other is a prize fund investment account which is usually treated as a fixed asset. When the fund is set up, the money set aside or donated for this purpose is debited to the prize fund investment account and credited to the prize fund account.

When income is received from the prize fund investments this is debited in the receipts and payments account and credited to the prize fund account. When the prizes are awarded the amounts are credited in the receipts and payments account and debited to the prize fund account. This is illustrated in Example 20.2 below.

Example 20.2
Parkview plc donated £10,000 to the City Club on 31 December 19X0. It was agreed that the annual income from this is to be used to make a grant to members' children for educational purposes. The donation was invested in 10 per cent Government Stock on 1 January 19X1. The annual income of £1,000 was received on 31 December 19X1 and this was given to J. Smith as a grant on 1 January 19X2.

Show how this would be recorded in the ledger of City Club.

Receipts and payments

19X0			19X1		
31 Dec	Grant fund—		1 Jan	Grant fund	
	Parkview donation	10,000		investments	10,000
19X1			19X2		
31 Dec	Grant fund—		1 Jan	Grant fund—	
	interest	1,000		J. Smith	1,000

Grant fund investments

19X1		
1 Jan	R & P	10,000

Parkview grant fund

19X2			19X0		
1 Jan	R & P—J Smith	1,000	31 Dec	R & P	10,000
			19X1		
			31 Dec	R & P—interest	1,000

Note

1. The balance on the grant fund at the end of each accounting year is normally the same as that on the grant fund investment account. However, as in the above example, these may differ because of time lags between the receipt of investment income and the payment of the grant.

Learning activity 20.1

Write to the head office of a large charity asking for a copy of their latest annual report and accounts. Prepare a list of the main differences between this document and the annual report of the public limited company you obtained for Learning activity 1.2. Alternatively perform the same task using the annual report of a football club. However, this is likely to be less relevant since professional football clubs are not clubs as such, but rather, like some charities, limited companies a few of whom such as Tottenham and Manchester United, have their shares listed/quoted on the London Stock Exchange.

Summary

The final accounts of clubs differ from those of business enterprises in a number of ways. Because clubs are non-profit-seeking organizations the profit and loss account is replaced by an income and expenditure account. However, this is prepared using the same principles, such as the accruals concept. Clubs are also usually managed by voluntary officers whom the members expect to provide a summarized cash book known as a receipts and payments account. The balance sheet of clubs is much the same as that of a business except that the capital is replaced by a general/accumulated fund which is an accumulation of previous years' excesses of income over expenditure. Some clubs engage in trading activities such as a bar, in which case it is necessary to include in the final accounts a bar trading account.

Another major difference between clubs and businesses is that the former often have a variety of different forms of income not normally associated with the latter—in particular annual subscriptions. These are usually accounted for in the income and expenditure account on an accrual basis. This gives rise to subscriptions in advance and arrear which are shown on the balance sheet as a current liability or current asset respectively. However, sometimes subscriptions are accounted for on a strict cash received basis in accordance with the prudence concept.

The books of account of clubs are often kept on a single entry basis. In which case the final accounts will be prepared using the same procedure as described in the previous chapter, with the addition of workings relating to the subscriptions account.

The final accounts of clubs also sometimes contain a number of special items not normally found in the accounts of businesses, but which involve the application of certain common principles. Two of these are entrance/joining fees and life membership subscriptions. The matching principle dictates that these be treated as deferred income. Furthermore, donations, bequests and gifts of a material amount should be credited direct to the club's accumulated fund rather than the income and expenditure account where it is of a non-recurring nature. Finally a club may operate a prize or grant fund. This must be accounted for by means of a fund separate from the general/accumulated fund, and a separate prize fund investment account.

Key terms and concepts

Accumulated/general fund, bar trading account, deferred income, donations, income and expenditure account, life membership subscriptions, membership fees, prize funds, receipts and payments account, single entry, statement of affairs, subscriptions in advance, subscriptions in arrear.

Exercises

An asterisk after the question number indicates that there is a suggested answer in the Appendix.

20.1.   Explain the difference between a receipts and payments account and an income and expenditure account.

20.2.   Explain the nature of an accumulated fund in the balance sheet of a club.

20.3.   Describe the entries in the accounts of a club for each of the following and explain the justification for each treatment:

(a)   Donation of second-hand clothing for resale.
(b)   A gift of a large amount of cash.
(c)   A bequest of premises to be used as a clubhouse.

20.4.   Describe two possible methods of accounting for each of the following in the accounts of clubs and explain the theoretical/conceptual justification for each method:

(a)   Membership/entrance fees.
(b)   Life membership subscriptions.

20.5.   Explain the nature and accounting entries in respect of prize funds in the accounts of clubs.

20.6.   The secretary of the Woodland Hockey Club gives you the following summary of his cash book for the year ended 31 May 19X9:

	£		£
Balances at commencement			
of year:		Rent	234
At bank	63	Printing and stationery	18
In hand	10	Affilliation fees	12
Subscriptions:		Captain's and secretary's	
Supporters	150	expenses	37
Supporters 19X9–19X0 season	20	Refreshments for	
Fees per game	170	visiting teams	61
Annual social	134	Annual social	102
		Equipment purchased	26
		Balance at close of	
		year: At bank	49
		In hand	8
	£547		£547

The secretary also gives you the following information:

	31 May 19X8	31 May 19X9
	£	£
Amounts due to the club:		
Supporters' subscriptions	14	12
Fees per game	78	53
Re annual social	6	—
Amounts owing by the club:		
Rent	72	54
Printing	—	3
Secretary's expenses	4	8
Refreshments	13	12

On the 31 May 19X8 the club's equipment appeared in the books at £150. It is desired that 12½ per cent be written off the book value of the equipment as it appears on 31 May 19X9.

You are required to:

(a) Show your computation of the club's accumulated fund as on 31 May 19X8.
(b) Prepare the income and expenditure account showing the result for the year ended 31 May 19X9, and the balance sheet as on that date. (ACCA)

20.7. The treasurer of the Senior Social Club has prepared the following summary of the club's receipts and payments for the year ended 30 November 19X0.

Senior Social Club
Receipts and payments account for the year ended 30 November 19X0

	£		£
Cash and bank balances b/f	810	Secretarial expenses	685
Members' subscriptions	4,250	Rent	2,500
Donations	1,480	Visiting speakers' expenses	1,466
Sales of competition tickets	1,126	Donations to charities	380
		Prizes for competitions	550
		Purchase of equipment	1,220
		Stationery and printing	469
		Balance c/f	396
	7,666		7,666

On 1 December 19X9 the club equipment which had cost £3,650 and which was valued at £2,190. The club's equipment as at 30 November 19X0 (inclusive of any purchases during the year) was valued at £1,947.

The following information is available:

As at . . .	1 December 19X9	30 November 19X0
	£	£
Stocks of prizes	86	108
Owing to suppliers of prizes	314	507
Subscriptions in arrears	240	580
Subscriptions in advance	65	105

Required:

(a) Calculate the value of the accumulated fund of the club as at 1 December 19X9.

(b) Prepare a subscriptions account for the year ended 30 November 19X0 showing clearly the amount to be transferred to the club's income and expenditure account for the year.

(c) Prepare a statement showing the surplus or deficit made by the club on competitions for the year ended 30 November 19X0.

(d) Prepare an income and expenditure account for the year ended 30 November 19X0.

(e) Prepare the club's balance sheet as at 30 November 19X0.   (AAT)

20.8.* The Elite Bowling and Social Club prepares its annual accounts to 31 October. The following receipts and payments account has been prepared by the treasurer:

	£		£
Cash in hand, 31 Oct 19X7	10	Bar purchases	1,885
Balances at bank, 31 Oct 19X7		Wages	306
Current account	263	Rent and rates	184
Deposit account	585	Lighting and heating	143
Spectators' entrance fees	54	New mower (less allowance	
Subscriptions: to 31/10/X7	30	for old one £40)	120
to 31/10/X8	574	General expenses	132
to 31/10/X9	44	Catering purchases	80
Bar takings	2,285	Additional furniture	460
Deposit account interest	26	Cash in hand at 31/10/X8	8
Catering receipts	120	Balances at bank 31/10/X8	
		Current account	176
		Deposit account	497
	£3,991		£3,991

The following information is also supplied:

1. The book values of the fixed assets on 31 October 19X7 were: furniture, fixtures and fittings £396 (cost £440) and mower £20 (cost £120).

2. The current assets and liabilities were as follows:

	31 Oct 19X7	31 Oct 19X8
	£	£
Bar stock at cost	209	178
Amount owed to the brewery for		
bar purchases	186	248
Due for rent and rates	12	26
Due for lighting and heating	9	11
Subscriptions in arrear	30	50

3. During the year the steward commenced to provide light refreshments at the bar and it has been agreed that in the annual accounts provision should be made for the payment to him of a bonus of 40 per cent of the gross profit arising from this catering venture.

4. Depreciation to furniture, fixtures and fittings is to be provided at a rate of 10 per cent on cost. No depreciation is to be provided on the new mower, but a full year on the new furniture.

You are required to prepare:

(a) a statement showing the general fund of the club as on 31 October 19X7;
(b) an income and expenditure account for the year ended 31 October 19X8 (showing separately gross profit on bar sales and catering); and
(c) a balance sheet as at 31 October 19X8.   (ACCA)

20.9.* The treasurer of a club has given you the following account of its activities during the year ended 30 June 19X8.

Receipts	£	Payments	£
Bank balance at 1/7/X7 (including £75 received during the year ended 30/6/X7 on the prize fund investments)	390	Additional billiard table with accessories bought 1/7/X7	300
Annual subscriptions (including £20 relating to previous year)	340	Repairs to billiard tables	50
		Purchases for bar	3,680
Life membership subscriptions (5 @ £16)	80	Stewards wages and expenses	400
Sundry lettings	180	Rates	140
Bar receipts	4,590	Lighting and heating	72
Receipts for billiards	275	Cleaning and laundry	138
Gifts from members	3,500	Sundry expenses	80
Income from £1,500 5 per cent defence bonds allocated specifically for a prize fund	75	Prizes awarded for previous year from income available at 1/7/X7	75
		Repayment of 5 per cent mortgage on 30/6/X8 with interest for two years	4,400
		Bank balance at 30/6/X8	95
	£9,430		£9,430

You are also given the following information:

1. The freehold building, owned and occupied by the club, was purchased for £6,000 many years ago.
2. On 1 July 19X2, the club acquired six billiard tables for which they paid £1,200, and it is considered that the tables have a life of 12 years.
3. The bar stock at 1 July 19X7 was £150 and at 30 June 19X8 £180.
4. Annual subscriptions outstanding from members at 30 June 19X8 amounted to £10.
5. On 1 July 19X7 there were 25 life members who had paid subscriptions of £16 each. During the year ended 30 June 19X8 three of these members had died.

You are required to prepare an income and expenditure account and balance sheet showing clearly how you have treated the subscriptions of life members and the prize fund.   (ACCA)

20.10 You have agreed to take over the role of bookkeeper for the AB sports and social club. The summarised balance sheet on 31.12.X4 as prepared by the previous bookkeeper contained the following items. All figures are in £s.

Assets	£	£
Heating oil for clubhouse		1,000
Bar and cafe stocks		7,000
New sportsware, for sale, at cost		3,000
Used sportsware, for hire, at valuation		750
Equipment for groundsperson—cost	5,000	
—depr.	3,500	1,500
Subscriptions due		200
Bank—current account		1,000
—deposit account		10,000
Claims		
Accumulated fund		23,150
Creditors—bar and cafe stocks		1,000
—sportsware		300

The bank account summary for the year to 31.12.X5 contained the following items.

Receipts	£
Subscriptions	11,000
Bankings—bar and cafe	20,000
—sale of sportsware	5,000
—hire of sportsware	3,000
Interest on deposit account	800

Payments	
Rent and repairs of clubhouse	6,000
Heating oil	4,000
Sportsware	4,500
Groundsperson	10,000
Bar and cafe purchases	9,000
Transfer to deposit account	6,000

You discover that the subscriptions due figure as at 31.12.X4 was arrived at as follows.

	£
Subscriptions unpaid for 19X3	10
Subscriptions unpaid for 19X4	230
Subscriptions paid for 19X5	40
Corresponding figures at 31.12.X5 are:	
Subscriptions unpaid for 19X3	10
Subscriptions unpaid for 19X4	20
Subscriptions unpaid for 19X5	90
Subscriptions paid for 19X6	200

Subscriptions due for more than 12 months should be written off with effect from 1.1.X5.

	£
Asset balances at 31.12.X5 include:	
Heating oil for club house	700
Bar and cafe stocks	5,000
New sportsware, for sale, at cost	4,000
Used sportsware, for hire, at valuation	1,000
Closing creditors at 31.12.X5 are:	£
For bar and cafe stocks	800
For sportsware	450
For heating oil for clubhouse	200

$2/3$rds of the sportsware purchases made in 19X5 had been added to stock of new sportsware in the figures given in the list of assets above, and $1/3$ had been added directly to the stock of used sportsware for hire.

Half of the resulting 'new sportsware for sale at cost' at 31.12.X5 is actually over two years old. You decide, with effect from 31.12.X5, to transfer these older items into the stock of used sportsware, at a valuation of 25% of their original cost.

No cash balances are held at 31.12.X4 or 31.12.X5. The equipment for the groundsperson is to be depreciated at 10% per annum, on cost.

Required

Prepare income and expenditure account and balance sheet for the AB sports club for 19X5, in a form suitable for circulation to members. The information given should be as complete and informative as possible within limits of the information given to you. All workings must be submitted.   (ACCA)

21. Accounting for hire purchase transactions

Learning objectives

After reading this chapter the student should be able to:

1. Explain the meaning of the key terms and concepts listed at the end of the chapter.
2. Describe the nature of the hire purchase and instalment credit sale transactions.
3. Explain the conceptual foundations of accounting for hire purchase transactions.
4. Compute the annual interest charge to the profit and loss account using the annuity method and Rule of 78 method.
5. Show the entries in the buyer's/hirer's journal, ledger, profit and loss account and balance sheet in respect of hire purchase transactions including the treatment of interest.

The nature of hire purchase transactions

Hire purchase agreements and instalments sale provide the buyer with the opportunity of making payments over an extended period. This effectively provides some of the finance to make the payment for the purchase, repaying this over time. The legal position relating to these transactions varies. This book is not concerned with the detailed legal considerations necessary to classify specific arrangements. The general features can be set out as follows.

Under a *hire purchase* contract an asset is supplied to the purchaser under an agreement for the purchaser to make a given number of periodic payments, the last of which results in transfer of ownership from the supplier to the purchaser. Although legal title remains with the supplier until this last payment the hirer is granted uninterrupted use of the asset.

In an *instalment credit sale* a series of periodic payments are again to be made. However, legal titles passes when the asset is delivered, although the supplier may have rights to repossession in cases of default.

The conceptual foundations of accounting for hire purchase transactions

The economic effects of both hire purchase and instalment credit sales are very similar and this is reflected in the accounting treatment. Even though hire purchase assets are not owned in strict legal form the *substance* of the agreement gives the purchaser comparable rights to ownership, so the transaction is treated as if a purchase has taken place and the hirer is regarded as a buyer including the asset in the balance sheet. This chapter will consider the entries made to record these types of transactions in the buyer's books. The transactions are more complex than outright purchase for two related reasons.

First, it is recognized that the payments made comprise amounts both for the supply of the asset and for the financing costs. One would expect to pay more when deferring payment over an extended period, equivalent to the interest that would be paid had the sum deferred been borrowed. It would be inconsistent if two businesses buying the same asset, one as a cash purchase and one on hire purchase, recorded the purchase at differing amounts, given that the difference related to financing rather than properties of the asset. The cash price represents a capital expenditure; interest is a revenue expenditure and needs to be separated.

The second matter to be addressed is that where the contract extends over more than one accounting period, interest must be spread over the periods on an appropriate basis for periodic reporting. The accruals concept and matching principle set out in Chapter 10 arise again.

Dividing up the hire purchase payments

Splitting the total payments into the capital and revenue expenditure elements is relatively straightforward given the disclosure of the cash purchase price. The difference between the sum of any initial down payment plus the agreed instalments and the cash purchase price represents the interest element.

For example, an asset, say a computer, which has a cash price of £6,000, is purchased for a down payment of £1,900 plus five annual instalments of £1,000 paid at the end of each year. Total interest is £1,900 + (5 × £1,000) − £6,000 = £900. Spreading the interest payments over the five years is less simple. Supplying businesses might be liable to quote *simple/nominal interest rates* but these do not represent the *effective interest rate* that is being charged. A nominal rate may be quoted as 3 per cent, calculated as:

$$\frac{\text{interest}}{\text{capital}} \div \text{number of years, i.e.} \ \frac{900}{6,000} \div 5 = 3 \text{ per cent}$$

The effective interest rate will be much higher because the amount of finance will be reducing due to the repayments being made. Even if the average of the initial £6,000 and final zero amount is taken, the resulting rate of 6 per cent understates the effective rate.

Identifying the effective rate requires the use of *annuity* calculations, possibly using tables. This is not considered in this book. However, the supplier may provide the result of this calculation. In this case the rate is very close to 7 per cent. Given this information, it is possible to analyse the payments over the period of the agreement as follows:

	Year 1 £	Year 2 £	Year 3 £	Year 4 £	Year 5 £	Sum
Outstanding finance—initial	6,000	4,100	3,387	2,624	1,808	
Capital repayment	1,900	713	763	816	873	
Finance at start of year	4,100	3,387	2,624	1,808	935	
Interest at 7 per cent for year	287	237	184	127	65	900
Capital repayment at year end	713	763	816	873	935	4,100
Instalments	1,000	1,000	1,000	1,000	1,000	5,000

As a method for approximating the annuity calculations, the *Rule of 78 (sum of the years' digits) method* may be used. This is a relatively simple method of apportioning the interest over the period in declining amounts. In this case it is a five year agreement and the sum of the years' digits is $5 + 4 + 3 + 2 + 1 = 15$. The interest is allocated over the five years in the proportions $5:4:3:2:1$, so the first year allocation will be $[5 \div (5 + 4 + 3 + 2 + 1)] \times £900 = £300$. Over the five years, we get:

	Year 1 £	Year 2 £	Year 3 £	Year 4 £	Year 5 £	Sum
Interest	300	240	180	120	60	900
Capital repayment	700	760	820	880	940	4,100

The similarity of the results can be seen.

Learning activity 21.1

Obtain details of the cost of purchasing a car or electrical good on hire purchase. Compute the effective rate of interest if possible. If this is given, analyse the payments over the period of the agreement separating the interest from the capital repayments.

Alternatively if you have a mortgage, ascertain the effective rate of interest from the bank/building society, and analyse your repayments over a given period of time.

Accounting entries in the buyer's books

Two basic approaches can be used to make the entries. The two are not fundamentally different, but differ in the information retained within the double entry system.

The first method which follows is, perhaps, the simplest:

	Debit	Credit
Initial entries		
Cash price of the asset	Asset	Supplier
Initial down payment	Supplier	Cash
On payment of instalment		
Payment made	Supplier	Cash
At the end of each account period		
Interest (as calculated by annuity or Rule of 78)	Hire purchase interest expense (closed to profit and loss)	Supplier

Using the example of the computer, and employing the annuity method of interest apportionment, the ledger entries for the first year will be as follows:

Computer

1 Jan	HP creditor	6,000				

HP creditor

1 Jan	Cash	1,900	1 Jan	Computer	6,000
31 Dec	Cash	1,000	31 Dec	HP interest expense	287
	Balance c/d	3,387			
		6,287			6,287
				Balance b/d	3,387

HP interest expense

31 Dec	HP creditor	287	31 Dec	Profit and loss	287

The computer is shown on the balance sheet as a fixed asset, and the HP creditor as a liability. At the end of Year 1 the latter will comprise a current liability of £763 and a long term liability of £816 + £873 + £935 = £2,624.

The second method presents the position of the supplier more clearly. Here the total liability to make payments to the supplier is recognized at the start rather than being added in as amounts accrue, like the £287 in the first year. However, recognition that the interest element is not yet due is given by creating a *deferred interest account* (also known as an HP interest suspense account) and transferring amounts to the HP interest expense account each year.

	Debit	*Credit*
Initial entries		
Total due to the supplier:		
cash price of the asset	Asset	Supplier
balance being total interest	Deferred interest	Supplier
Initial down payment	Supplier	Cash
On payment of instalment		
Payment made	Supplier	Cash
At the end of each accounting period		
Interest (as calculated)	HP interest expense	Deferred interest

Continuing with the example of the computer, and employing the annuity method of interest apportionment the ledger entries using the deferred interest method for the first year will be as follows:

Computer

1 Jan	HP creditor	6,000	

HP creditor

1 Jan	Cash	1,900	1 Jan	Computer	6,000
31 Dec	Cash	1,000	1 Jan	Deferred interest	900
	Balance c/d	4,000			
		6,900			6,900
				Balance b/d	4,000

Deferred interest

1 Jan	HP creditor	900	31 Dec	HP interest expense		287
				Balance b/d		613
		900				900
	Balance b/d	613				

HP interest expense

31 Dec	Deferred interest	287	31 Dec	Profit and loss	287

The balance on the deferred interest account is set against that on the HP creditor account to give the amount shown on the balance sheet as a liability (i.e. £4,000 − £613 = £3,387).

Summary

The substance concept states that transactions should be accounted for in accordance with their economic reality and not merely their legal form. In the case of assets acquired under a hire purchase agreement, this means that they should be accounted for as the purchase of a fixed asset on credit (and not as the hire of an asset). Thus the cash price of the asset is debited to a fixed asset account and credited to an HP creditor's account.

The instalments paid are debited to the HP creditor's account. However, these contain two elements. One is essentially the repayment of the principal amount borrowed (i.e. the cash price). The other is a financing charge which constitutes revenue expenditure. Given the effective rate of interest, the annual amount of this financing charge can be computed using the annuity method. Alternatively the Rule of 78/sum of the years' digits method can be applied to the total interest. Another simpler, more expedient, but less accurate method is to spread the interest evenly over the period of the agreement on a time basis.

The annual financing charge is credited to the HP creditor's account and debited to an HP interest expense account which is transferred to the profit and loss account. Alternatively the total financing charge can be credited to the HP creditor's account at the start of the agreement period and debited to a deferred interest account. The annual financing charge is then credited to the deferred interest account and debited to the HP interest expense account which is transferred to the profit and loss account.

Key terms and concepts

Annuity, deferred interest, effective interest rate, hire purchase, instalment credit sale, Rule of 78, simple/nominal interest rate, substance, sum of the years' digits.

Exercises

An asterisk after the question number indicates that there is a suggested answer in the Appendix.

21.1. Briefly describe the accounting treatment of assets acquired on hire purchase and explain its theoretical justification.

21.2. Describe two methods of apportioning hire purchase interest over the accounting periods covered by the agreement where it extends over more than one accounting year.

21.3.* On 3 January 19X1, Pulsford (Machinists) acquired machinery from Lawrence Ltd, under a hire purchase agreement extending over three years. The agreement required them to make an initial deposit of £1,600, followed by three annual payments of £1,000 to be made by 31 December each year, commencing 19X1.

The cash price of the machinery is £4,000 and Lawrence Ltd inform Pulsford that the terms represent an effective rate of interest of 12 per cent.

Required:
Show the journal entries that will record the transactions resulting from the hire purchase agreement, assuming that Pulsford make all payments when due, using:
(a)   the annuity method; and
(b)   the Rule of 78 to allocate interest.

21.4. On 1 January 19X7, Carver bought a machine costing £20,000 on hire purchase. He paid a deposit of £6,000 on 1 January 19X7 and he also agreed to pay two annual instalments of £5,828 on 31 December in each year, and a final instalment of £5,831 on 31 December 19X9. The implied rate of interest in the agreement was 12 per cent. This rate of interest is to be applied to the amount outstanding in the hire purchase loan account as at the beginning of the year. The machine is to be depreciated on a straight line basis over five years on the assumption that the machine will have no residual value at the end of that time.

Required:
(a)   Write up the following accounts for each of the three years to 31 December 19X7, 19X8, and 19X9 respectively:

(i)   machine account;
(ii)   accumulated depreciation on machine account; and
(iii)   hire purchase loan account.

(b)   Show the balance sheet extracts for the year as at 31 December 19X7, 19X8 and 19X9 respectively for the following items:

(i)   machine cost;
(ii)   accumulated depreciation on the machine;
(iii)   long-term liabilities—obligations under hire purchase contract; and
(iv)   current liabilities—obligations under hire purchase contract.   (AAT)

21.5. Morris, a general dealer making his accounts up annually on 31 December, purchased two vehicles on hire purchase. The details are as follows:

	Vehicle A	*Vehicle B*
Date of purchase	1.7.X6	1.4.X7
Cost	£750	£1,000
Deposit paid at date of purchase	£350	£400
Hire purchase monthly repayments 24 @	£20	£30

Vehicle A was sold for £400 cash on 1 October 19X8.

Depreciation is provided by means of the straight line method based on a five year life, a full year's depreciation being provided in the year of purchase but none in the year of sale. The charge for interest is to be spread evenly over the period of the loan pro rata to time, and the first monthly repayment is due on the last day of the month of purchase.

You are required to show for each of the years ended 31 December 19X6, 19X7, 19X8, 19X9:

(a) the relevant entries as regards hire purchase and motor vehicles in the profit and loss account of Morris;

(b) the suggested drafting of the item motor vehicles as it might appear in the balance sheet. (ACCA)

21.6. A. Carrier & Co. are acquiring two motor vehicles under hire purchase agreements, details of which are as follows:

	Vehicle A	Vehicle B
Date of purchase	30 April 19X0	30 September 19X0
Cash price	£2,280	£1,560
Deposit	£432	£264
Interest	£216	£168

In accordance with its customary practice, A. Carrier & Co. brings the vehicles into its books at their cash price and spreads the interest evenly over the period of the agreement. In both agreements it is provided for payment to be made by 24 equal monthly instalments, the first payment to be due on the last day of the month after the date of purchase and following payments on the last day of the month thereafter.

Following an accident, on 1 May 19X1, Vehicle B became a total loss. Full settlement as regards the loss of this vehicle was made on 15 May 19X1, as follows:

1. £1,220 was received from an insurance company under a comprehensive policy.
2. £950 was accepted by the hire purchase company for termination of the agreement.

A Carrier & Co's accounts are prepared annually to 31 March. Depreciation for motor vehicles is provided on a straight line basis at a rate of 25 per cent, a full year's provision being made in the year of purchase but no provision in the year of disposal.

All instalments were paid on the due dates.

As regards Vehicle B, the balance on the hire purchase company account relating to same is to be written off.

From the information given, you are required to prepare the following accounts, bringing down the balances as on 31 March 19X2:

(a) Motor vehicles on hire purchase.
(b) Provision for depreciation of motor vehicles.
(c) Motor vehicles disposals.
(d) Hire purchase company. (ACCA)

21.7. I.R. Plant commenced business on 1 October 19X0 to hire out machines to civil engineering contractors. The trial balance extracted from his books as on 30 September 19X1 was as follows:

	Dr. £	Cr. £
Capital introduced		17,700
Plant and machinery:		
Machine No. 1 purchased on 1.10.X0	4,100	
Machine No. 2 purchased on 1.12.X0	4,800	
Transporter lorry purchased on 1.10.X0	3,600	
Machine No. 3 (under hire purchase):		
Deposit paid on 1 April 19X1	2,600	
Hire purchase instalments paid	1,620	
Hire of machines		12,267
Wages and national insurance	3,062	
General expenses	197	
Transporter lorry running expenses	204	
Insurance	130	
Office rent and rates	280	
Machine repairs	298	
Bank balance	5,393	
Debtors	1,722	
I.R. Plant—Drawings	1,961	
	£29,967	£29,967

The following information is given to you:

1. As regards machine No. 3, the balance remaining, after the payment of the deposit, is to be discharged by 24 equal monthly instalments of £270, the first being payable on 30 April 19X1. The machine is to be brought into the books at its cash price which was £8,120 and the hire purchase interest is to be spread evenly over the 24-month period.

2. Depreciation is to be written off on the straight line method as follows:
   (i)   on the machines at a rate based on the assumption that they will have a residual value of 10 per cent of cost after six years; and
   (ii) on the transporter lorry at 25 per cent per annum with no residual value.

   Depreciation in the first accounting year after purchase is calculated pro rata to time.

   You are required to:

   (a) write up the ledger accounts for the year relating to:
        Plant and machinery
        Transporter lorry
        Hire purchase interest in suspense
        Hire purchase vendor;
   (b) show your calculation of depreciation on the machines;
   (c) prepare a profit and loss account for the year ended 30 September 19X1, and balance sheet as on that date.   (ACCA)

22. Investment accounts

Learning objectives
After reading this chapter the student should be able to: 1. Explain the meaning of key terms and concepts listed at the end of the chapter. 2. Describe the format of investment accounts and explain the reasons for this, including its conceptual origins. 3. Show the entries in the ledger relating to the purchase and sale of investments. 4. Show the year-end entries in the ledger and final accounts relating to accrued interest receivable and profits/losses on the sale of investments.

The format of investment accounts

The activities of businesses extend not only to manufacturing and the supply of goods and services but also to external *investment* in the share of companies and various forms of loan stock, including debentures and government stock. The accounts which record these investments may have the appearance of being different and complex. However, the accounting involved is just an application of the accruals and prepayments approach introduced in Chapter 10 and applied in detail in Chapter 13. A particular layout is used which is intended to achieve two aims: clarify the accruals approach by separating the revenue (income) and capital element of entries; keep a record of the number of units of shares or stock owned. As a result, investment accounts are presented with three columns on each side comprising the following:

1. The first column records the *nominal value* of the security held—the nominal values of securities are fixed when they are issued so, even if the market prices fluctuate, nominal values will remain constant unless the investing business disposes of some or acquires additional units of the security. Although not part of the double entry, this column provides a useful running total indicating the quantity of units held.
2. The second column records the *income* elements—typically interest is paid on debentures and government stock at particular dates. Interest represents income and payment does not produce any change in the nominal value of the security held.
3. The third column records the *capital value* of the security and, with the income column, is part of the double entry accounting. This column will contain entries to record the cost of acquiring securities and the proceeds of the sale.

Purchase and sale of fixed interest securities

Interest is usually fixed on the issue of a security as a given percentage of the nominal value, payable at predetermined dates, often half yearly or quarterly. Consider the example of 8 per cent government stock, interest payable on 30 June and 31 December. Government stocks prices are usually quoted at the price for £100 nominal value of the stock. These prices will vary in the market but, say, on 29 June 19X1 the 8 per cent stock is priced at 84 (i.e. to buy £100 nominal, a purchaser would pay £84). The interest payable on £100 nominal at the end of every June and December would be £4 (i.e. half of 8 per cent of the *nominal value*). A business buying £25,000 of the stock on 29 June 19X1 would pay $84 \times £25,000 \div 100 = £21,000$. The next day, interest would be payable of $4 \times £25,000 \div 100 = £1,000$. The company would know this when it bought the stock, so it was effectively paying £20,000 for the capital element of the stock plus £1,000 for interest it was about to receive. Provided no other factors in the market changed, the market price of the stock would be expected to fall, as soon as the interest is paid, by £1,000 to £20,000. One can see that recognizing the £1,000 in this way is an application of the accruals principle.

A security purchased to include interest due at the next payment date is described as *cum. interest* (cum. int) and similarly shares purchased which include the right to a dividend that has been declared are known as *cum. div.* In fact, a time must be set when the lists of owners entitled to interest (or dividends) are finalized, so that those making the payment can identify who to pay. This point in time will normally be at the close of trading on a particular day before the payment is due. It is very important if you are buying to be sure about entitlement to interest (or dividend) so, to make this clear, the description changes. Loan stock becomes *ex interest* and shares *ex div.* when they are traded without entitlement to a forthcoming payment. Thus when a share goes ex div. a fall in price is to be expected. The sudden change in price when stock goes ex interest gives a clear indication of the income element. In the absence of either the cum.- or ex-description, it is assumed that a security would be cum. int. (or cum. div.).

Of course, understanding of accruals procedures would indicate that transactions at intermediate dates also include income components. Using the same 8 per cent stock, a purchase on 31 March at 78 includes an accrual of three months' interest which, on £25,000 nominal, would be $£25,000 \times 8$ per cent $\div 4 = £500$. The total amount paid is $78 \times £25,000 \div 100 = £19,500$ which would be split £500 to income, £19,000 to capital. Sales follow similar principles. If £9,000 nominal were sold on 30 April (one month later) at 88, this would include four months' interest, amounting to $^4/_{12} \times 8$ per cent $\times £9,000 = £240$. The total amount realized would be £7,920, split £240 income, £7,680 capital. On 30 June, half year's interest of £640 would be received (i.e. 4 per cent $\times £16,000$). These transactions would be recorded in the investment account as follows:

8 per cent government stock

		Nominal £	Income £	Capital £			Nominal £	Income £	Capital £
19X1	Cash—				19X1	Cash—sale			
31 Mar	purchase				30 Apr	at 88	9,000	240	7,680
	at 78	25,000	500	19,000	30 Jun	Cash—			
						interest		640	

Year-end entries

At the end of the accounting year, say 30 September 19X1, it will be necessary to make a number of closing entries as follows:

1. Carry down the balance on the memorandum nominal value columns which is simply the difference between the two sides.
2. Make an accrual in the income columns in respect of interest from the date of the last amount received to the end of the accounting year. That is, $3/12 \times 8$ per cent $\times £16,000 = £320$. Notice that this is the accrued income and thus the entry is a balance carried down on the credit side and a balance brought down on the debit side. The difference between the income columns on each side is transferred to the credit side of the profit and loss account (and added to the gross profit where the profit and loss account is prepared using a vertical presentation). The accrued interest is shown on the balance sheet as a current asset.
3. Transfer the profit or loss on the sale of investments to the profit and loss account and carry down the remaining balance on the capital columns. The profit/loss on sale is computed as follows: the cost of the investments sold is $£9,000/£25,000 \times £19,000 = £6,840$. The capital content of the proceeds of sale is £7,680. There is thus a profit on sale of $£7,680 - £6,840 = £840$. The remaining balance on the capital columns of the investment account should be $£16,000/£25,000 \times £19,000 = £12,160$. This is shown on the balance sheet as either a fixed or current asset, depending on how long the enterprise intends to keep the investments.

The entries in the investment account in respect of the above are shown below together with those for the following year to illustrate the effect of accrued income.

8 per cent government stock

		Nominal £	Income £	Capital £			Nominal £	Income £	Capital £
19X1	Cash—								
31 Mar	purchase at				19X1	Cash—			
	78	25,000	500	19,000	30 Apr	sale at 88	9,000	240	7,680
30 Sep	Profit and				30 Jun	Cash—			
	loss—profit					interest		640	
	on sale			840	30 Sep	c/d	16,000	320	12,160
30 Sep	Profit and								
	loss—								
	investment								
	income		700						
		25,000	1,200	19,840			25,000	1,200	19,840
1 Oct	b/d	16,000	320	12,160	31 Dec	Cash—			
19X2						interest		640	
30 Sep	Profit and				19X2				
	loss—				30 Jun	Cash—			
	investment					interest		640	
	income		1,280		30 Sep	c/d	16,000	320	12,160
		16,000	1,600	12,160			16,000	1,600	12,160
	b/d	16,000	320	12,160					

Investment in shares

The accounting entries for investments in shares involve the same principles as those relating to fixed interest securities described above. However, in the case of shares, dividend levels are not fixed until they are declared. As a result it is not appropriate to accrue dividends until the declaration is made, and when this is recognized, the full amount is recorded with no apportionment on a time basis. Discussion of the nature of shares and their issue is presented in Chapters 26 and 28.

Summary

Investment accounts are designed to separate out the revenue income and capital elements of transactions relating to the purchase and sale of fixed interest securities and investments in shares. Securities are bought and sold either ex interest/div. or cum. interest/div. Where securities are bought or sold cum. interest/div. the interest/dividend element must be treated as revenue income. The difference between the purchase or sale price and the interest/dividend element is regarded as the capital element. In the case of a purchase, the capital element represents the cost of the security; in the case of a sale the capital element represents the proceeds of sale. The difference between these two amounts constitutes a profit or loss on sale which is taken to the profit and loss account.

At the end of each accounting year an accrual is made in respect of interest from the date of the last amount received to the end of the accounting year. This is shown on the balance sheet as a current asset. The difference between the income columns on each side of the investment account after entering the accrued interest is transferred to the profit and loss account. Accruals are not made in respect of dividends unless the dividend has been declared, in which case the full amount is accrued with no time apportionment.

> ## Key terms and concepts
>
> Capital value, cum.div., cum.int., ex div., ex int., income, interest, investment, nominal value.

Exercises

An asterisk after the question number indicates that there is a suggested answer in the Appendix.

22.1.* Lane Ltd, which has a year end at 30 September, bought £34,000 of 6 per cent government stock at 78 cum. interest on 1 May 19X0. Interest is paid half yearly on 1 January and 1 July.

The company sold £33,000 of the stock on 1 December 19X0 at 77 ex interest.

Required:
Show the ledger account for the stock for the two years to 30 September, 19X1.

22.2. Savers Ltd held the following investments on 1 May 19X9:

AB Ltd 1,000 ordinary shares of £1 each cost £1,250.
CD Ltd 10,000 5 per cent preference shares of 10 pence each cost £1,200.

During the year ended 30 April 19X0, the following transactions took place:

19X9

31 May	Half year's dividend received from CD Ltd.
30 June	AB Ltd made a rights issue of one share for every two held at a price of £1.20 per share. These shares would not rank for dividend for the year ended 30 June 19X9. Savers Ltd took up their rights.
31 July	Purchase £750 ordinary stock in EF at par.
31 Aug	Received a final dividend from AB Ltd in respect of the year ended 30 June 19X9 of 10 pence per share.
31 Oct	Sold 750 shares in AB Ltd for £1,000
30 Nov	Half year's dividend receive from CD Ltd.
31 Dec	10 per cent interim dividend received from EF Ltd.

19X0

28 Feb	Received an interim dividend from AB Ltd in respect of the year ended 30 June 19X0, of 3.33 pence per share.
31 Mar	Sold all the preference shares in CD Ltd for £1,150.
30 Apr	EF Ltd made a bonus issue of £1 stock for every £3 held.

You are required to show the investment accounts of AB Ltd, CD Ltd and EF Ltd in the books of Savers Ltd for the year ended 30 April 19X0.

Ignore tax.   (ACCA)

23. Departmental and branch accounts

Learning objectives

After reading this chapter the student should be able to:

1. Explain the meaning of key terms and concepts listed at the end of the chapter.
2. Explain how departmental and branch accounting can contribute to the management of such organizations.
3. Prepare departmental trading and profit and loss accounts.
4. Show the journal and ledger entries relating to both integrated and autonomous branches, including the treatment of goods in transit, cash in transit and profit mark-ups.
5. Prepare branch, head office and combined profit and loss accounts in the case of both integrated and autonomous branches.
6. Prepare branch, head office and combined balance sheet in the case of autonomous branches.

Introduction

As organizations become larger they usually decentralize their activities into either separate selling departments, branches, divisions, franchises, etc. They also often form groups of companies.

One of the main purposes of financial accounting is to provide information on the performance and financial position of an accounting entity in the form of final accounts. This not only refers to the entity as a whole, but also information about each of its sub-units such as departments and branches. In addition accounting is intended to provide information for the management and control of a business including its sub-units, such as to facilitate the control of cash and stocks in particular.

As some organizations grow it becomes useful to divide up their operations into separate selling *departments*. You are probably familiar with department stores such as Harrods. Here, a range of different activities are each run as sub-businesses within the whole organization. The store's management will be concerned to know how well the store is performing as a whole, but will also find it useful to have information about the performance of the individual departments. Its significance may be increased by delegation of responsibilities to department heads, and performance related bonuses.

Other organizations grow by becoming geographically more spread, as in the case of retail chain stores such as Asda, B & Q, etc. With each separate *branch* of the business operating from separate and possibly distant locations, considerable responsibility must be delegated to the local manager. Accounting can contribute to the management of such organizations by providing information which not only gives indications of the separate performances but also provides some degree of control over assets such as stock and cash.

We have already seen in Chapter 20 that it is useful to separate some of the activities of an organization in reporting its results. Here, bar trading operations were separately identified within the accounts of a club. These ideas are extended in this chapter, which examines how accounting can be adapted to increasing levels of delegation, starting with simple departments, moving to branches, where, although the head office maintains the accounts, the branch is responsible for its stocks, and concluding with branches which maintain their own self-contained accounting systems. Understanding the accounting methods which are used is valuable in a number of more advanced topics. Large public companies typically consist of many separately identified companies each with their own accounting ledgers but owned by a common parent. The principles developed in branch accounts are applied in extended form to deal with the complexity of such groups of companies, particularly in the combining of individual company statements to form consolidated accounts.

Departmental accounts

Where it is decided to produce separate profit and loss results for each trading department within a business, in addition to identifying the sales for each unit and tracking costs which are specifically identifiable to the departments, it is necessary to *apportion* (i.e. divide up on the basis of ratios) the untraceable overhead costs. No matter how carefully the apportionment ratios are selected, they will depend on the exercise of judgement, and to that extent are arbitrary. The basis should be chosen to attempt to reflect the extra cost likely to be caused by the particular department or, failing that, the benefits the department receives. A simple example making use of the context of the departmental store will be used to illustrate the preparation of departmental accounts.

Example 23.1
Status Stores run three departments, clothing, footwear and stationery. For accounting purposes departmental accounts are to be prepared, apportioning building costs (rent, etc.) on the basis of floor space occupied and office administration in proportion to gross profit. The following information has been extracted from the store's accounts for the year ended 31 December 19X1:

	Clothing £	Footwear £	Stationery £
Sales	47,000	27,000	26,000
Purchases	23,000	16,000	10,500
Wages	2,500	2,100	1,800
Stocks at 1 Jan 19X1	6,000	1,000	500
at 31 Dec 19X1	4,000	2,000	1,000
Floor space (in sq. metres)	3,000	2,000	1,000

Rent, rates, lighting, heating and building maintenance (all departments)	£13,800
Administration and office salaries, etc.	£20,000

Status Stores
Departmental trading and profit and loss accounts for the year ended 31 December 19X1

	Clothing		Footwear		Stationery	
	£	£	£	£	£	£
Sales		47,000		27,000		26,000
Less: Cost of sales:						
opening stock	6,000		1,000		500	
Add: Purchases	23,000		16,000		10,500	
	29,000		17,000		11,000	
Less: Closing stock	4,000	25,000	2,000	15,000	1,000	10,000
Gross profit		22,000		12,000		16,000
Less: Wages	2,500		2,100		1,800	
Building costs (3 : 2 : 1)	6,900		4,600		2,300	
Administration						
(22 : 12 : 16)	8,800	18,200	4,800	11,500	6,400	10,500
Departmental net profit		3,800		500		5,500

It is not usual to have separate balance sheets for each department.

Branch accounts

A branch is a division of a larger organization which has a different geographical location but is not a separate legal entity. It is usually also engaged in the same type of trade or industry as the rest of the organization, is often primarily concerned with selling rather than production, and frequently provides the same range of products or services. Each branch also normally has separately identifiable costs, sales revenues, and thus profit. A common example is retail chain stores such as Marks and Spencer, Sainsbury's etc. It can therefore be seen that there is a widespread need for branch accounting, which is quite common in practice.

A further pertinent feature of branches is that the amount of autonomy granted by the head office to the branch manager varies between organizations. In some business enterprises the branch has considerable freedom of choice concerning what selling price to charge, the recruitment and selection of employees, whether to purchase goods from outside the organization and which suppliers to buy from. However, in other organizations the head office buys in bulk for all its branches and thus directs goods to the branches leaving them little freedom of choice over suppliers, selling prices, recruitment policy, etc. The former are sometimes referred to as *autonomous branches*, and the latter as *non-autonomous* or *integrated branches*.

This gives rise to two different forms of branch accounts. In the case of non-autonomous branches all of the transactions of the branch are recorded in the books of the head office. In the case of autonomous branches the transactions of the branch are recorded in a separate set of books that are kept by the branch. Both of these two forms of branch accounts are explained separately below.

Non-autonomous/integrated branches

The most common examples of businesses with non-autonomous branches are retail chain stores like BHS, Tesco, etc. In these organizations all of the selling activities are carried out by the branches and the remaining functions such as purchasing are undertaken by a central administration or head office. The head office also usually exercises a considerable degree of control over things like employees' conditions of service, branch selling prices, and assets such as stock and cash. The control of selling prices by head office is aimed at ensuring that the selling price of a particular type of good is the same at all the branches and/or that branches do not engage in price competition among themselves. The control of stock and cash is intended to ensure that these assets are used efficiently and that none is misappropriated.

One way of controlling branch selling prices is for goods supplied by the head office to the branch to be charged to the branch at cost and for head office to specify a recommended selling price. However, a more common method which also permits the control of stocks is for goods supplied by the head office to the branch to be charged to the branch at selling price. This is often computed in the form of cost plus a percentage mark-up representing the anticipated gross profit.

The control of cash is achieved in two ways. First, branches are frequently required to pay their cash takings into the head office bank account, usually on a daily basis, or remit the money directly to the head office. Any credit sales would be notified to the head office which will deal with the collection of such debts. Second, cash expenditure by the branch should be controlled using a petty cash imprest system. Alternatively branches are sometimes permitted to make cash payments from cash takings before they are banked. Other costs of operating the branch requiring cheque payments such as salaries, rent, telephone, etc., are often paid by the head office.

The control of stocks is achieved by means of a perpetual inventory system with periodic physical stock counts.

Non-autonomous branches do not usually maintain a separate set of books of account. All the transactions of the branch are recorded in the books of the head office, and thus the branch manager is deliberately kept unaware of the cost and profit mark-up of goods, etc. However, the branch is usually required to supply weekly or monthly returns showing details of credit sales, cash sales, cash banked or remitted to the head office, goods received from head office, goods returned to head office, petty cash expenditure, stock levels, etc. The transactions relating to the branch are entered in the head office books from these returns and other information which the head office already possesses, such as relating to goods sent by the head office to the branch and cash received by the head office from the branch. Periodically the head office will send internal auditors to the branch, without prior notice, to test the accuracy of the branch returns with regard to, for example, stock levels and cash in hand. Test checks by the internal auditors may reveal stock and cash losses. These can be unavoidable such as evaporation of liquids, damaged goods, giving customers too much change, etc. Alternatively they may be the result of pilferage, misappropriation, etc.

To account for the transactions of a non-autonomous branch, the books of the head office must include at least the following additional accounts:

1. A *goods sent to branches day book* kept on the same principle as a sales day book, and a *goods sent to branch account* in the ledger which is in the nature of a combined sales and sales returns account for a particular branch. This represents the goods 'sold' to the branch by the head office, and thus the balance of 'net sales' is transferred to the head office trading account as sales to branch.

2. A *branch expenses account* in which is recorded the expenses relating to the branch whether paid by the head office or the branch. This may be subdivided into a number of accounts relating to different types of expenses.

3. A *branch debtors' (control) account* in which is recorded the credit sales made by the branch, returns from customers, money received from branch debtors, bad debts, etc.
4. A *branch profit and loss account* showing the gross profit (calculated in the branch stock account explained below), the branch expenses referred to above, and thus the branch net profit or loss for the period.
5. A *branch stock account* which is the most confusing aspect of branch accounts and may take two different forms. The most common is in the nature of a combined perpetual inventory/stock account and trading account. The branch stock account has two amounts columns on each side. One of the columns on each side represents the perpetual inventory account and is not a part of the double entry in the ledger. These columns are referred to as memorandum columns. The other column on each side represents the trading account and is part of the double entry.

The entries in the memorandum perpetual inventory columns are *always* shown at selling price (i.e. cost plus the profit mark-up). In essence the debit entries comprise the opening stock and the goods sent to the branch by the head office, and the credit entries consist of the returns to head office, sales by the branch, and the closing stock. The two sides of this account should therefore agree. However, often there is a difference between them which is normally taken to represent stock that has been lost. Part of the purpose of this memorandum perpetual inventory account is to identify any such loss.

The entries in the trading account columns of the branch stock account are slightly more complicated. In essence the debit entries comprise the opening stock and the goods sent to the branch by the head office both of which are shown at cost (to the head office), sales by the branch at selling prices, and the closing stock at cost (to the head office). The difference between the two sides is the branch gross profit (or loss).

It can therefore be seen that items in the memorandum perpetual inventory columns and the trading account columns are identical. However, the amounts relating to each item may differ in that the former will always be at selling price whereas the latter is sometimes at cost (to the head office).

A complication arises where *branch expenses have been paid from cash sales before they are banked or remitted to head office*. These must be entered in both columns on the credit side of the branch stock account as sales, with a corresponding debit to the branch expenses account. The credit entries are intended to ensure that the branch stock account includes all sales (before deducting expenses), and that the trading account columns facilitate the computation of an accurate figure of gross profit (before deducting expenses). The principle is the same as in incomplete records. When calculating the cash sales any expenses that have been paid from the takings before they were banked must be added back.

A further complication concerns any *goods which have been sold by the branch at a price less than that charged to the branch by the head office*. This will cause the memorandum perpetual inventory columns to disagree thus inflating the amount of any apparent stock loss. It is therefore necessary to enter the reduction in the selling price in the credit memorandum perpetual inventory column to prevent this occurring. Note however that it is not entered in the trading account column since the intention is to leave sales at their reduced price in order to reflect this in the gross profit.

Finally there are the problems of goods in transit and cash in transit. As explained above, the branch stock account contains the goods sent to the branch by the head office and not the amount of goods received by the branch from the head office, the difference being *good in transit*. This is essentially stock and is treated in the same way, namely as a balance carried down on the branch stock account. The amount shown in the memorandum perpetual inventory column will be the selling price, and the amount entered in the trading account column will be the cost (to the head office).

The branch stock account also contains the cash received by the head office from the branch in respect of cash sales, and not the amount remitted by the branch to the head office (or collected from customers—some of this cash may still be in the cash till), the difference being referred to as *cash in transit*. This is also treated as a balance carried down on the branch stock account. However, whereas goods in transit are shown in the trading account columns at cost (to the head office), cash in transit is shown at selling price. This is because the balance carried down is intended to represent additional cash sales of the current period, and the balance brought down will be offset by the cash received by the head office in the subsequent period.

The above accounting entries relating to non-autonomous branches are illustrated in Example 23.2.

Example 23.2

Exquisite Retailers whose head office is in Manchester has a branch in Bristol. The transactions of the branch are recorded in the books at head office. All goods are purchased by head office and supplied to, and sold by, the branch at cost plus 25 per cent. Amounts owing in respect of branch credit sales are collected by the head office.

The following items relate to the branch during the year ended 31 December 19X8:

	£
Stock at branch 1 January 19X8 at selling price	6,000
Branch debtors at 1 January 19X8	4,700
Goods supplied by head office	27,500
Goods received by branch	26,500
Returns to head office at selling price	1,500
Credit sales	22,400
Cash received by head office from branch	2,000
Cash remitted to head office by the branch	2,500
Expenses paid by branch from cash sales	300
Authorized reductions in branch selling prices	400
Cheques received from debtors	23,500
Discount allowed to debtors	350
Bad debts written off	250
Stock at branch at 31 December 19X8 at selling price	5,125
Branch debtors at 31 December 19X8	3,000

You are required to show all the ledger entries relating to the branch for the year ended 31 December 19X8. The branch stock account is prepared using memorandum columns for recording the relevant transactions at selling price.

Branch stock account

	Memo			Memo	
Stock b/d	6,000	4,800	Returns from branch	1,500	1,200
Goods to branch	27,500	22,000	Debtors—credit sales	22,400	22,400
P&L—gross profit	—	4,500	Cash—sales	2,000	2,000
			Branch expenses	300	300
			Reduction in selling prices	400	—

			Balances c/d		
			stock	5,125	4,100
			goods in transit	1,000	800
			cash in transit	500	500
			Stock loss	275	—
	33,500	31,300		33,500	31,300
Balances b/d:					
stock	5,125	4,100			
goods in transit	1,000	800			
cash in transit	500	500			

Branch debtors

Balance b/d		4,700	Bank		23,500
Branch stock		22,400	Discount allowed		350
			Bad debts		250
			Balance c/d		3,000
		27,100			27,100
Balance b/d		3,000			

Goods sent to branch

Branch stock—returns	1,200	Branch stock—goods sent	22,000
HO trading a/c (or purchases)	20,800		
	22,000		22,000

Branch expenses

Branch stock	300	Branch P & L	300

Branch discount allowed

Branch debtors	350	Branch P & L	350

Branch bad debts

Branch debtors	250	Branch P & L	250

Cash book

Branch stock	2,000
Branch debtors	23,500

Branch profit and loss account

Branch expenses	300	Branch stock—gross profit	4,500
Discount allowed	350		
Bad debts	250		
Net profit c/d	3,600		
	4,500		4,500
Capital account	3,600	Net profit b/d	3,600

Notes

1. Goods in transit = £27,500 − £26,500 = £1,000
2. Cash in transit = £2,500 − £2,000 = £500.
3. Given that the mark-up on cost is 25 per cent, this means that the selling price is 100 + 25 = 125 per cent of cost, and thus the cost is 100/125 as a percentage of selling price which is 80 per cent. The profit as a percentage of selling price is therefore 100 − 80 = 20 per cent. This is referred to as the sales margin.
4. The stock loss is the difference between the two sides of the memorandum columns of the branch stock account. By not entering the cost of the stock loss in the double entry (trading account) column the gross profit is automatically reduced by the cost of the stock lost. An alternative treatment is to enter the cost of the stock loss in the double entry (trading account) column and debit the branch profit and loss account. This highlights to management the cost of the stock lost in the profit and loss account.
5. It is very important to note that the stock at the end of the year which is entered in the branch stock account is the result of a physical stock count. Otherwise it would not be possible to identify a stock loss from the branch stock account.
6. Some examination questions give rise to a 'stock again', It is unlikely to have a stock gain in practice, and thus this is best referred to as an apparent gain. It can arise from goods being sold at a price in excess of the normal selling price (not given in the question).
7. It is not usual to prepare a separate balance sheet for the branch; only for the business as a whole.

Alternative method

There is another form of branch stock account sometimes referred to as an integrated system. All the other accounts relating to the branch remain the same. However, in the branch stock account *all* the items are recorded at selling price. In other words, the branch stock account comprises only the amounts in the memorandum columns of the branch stock account shown in the previous method but they are no longer memorandum, they are a part of the double entry in the ledger. There are no trading account columns. Instead there is an account called a branch stock mark-up account, which is also a part of the double entry, that is used to ascertain the gross profit.

The branch stock mark-up account records the mark-up on the goods sent to the branch, returns from the branch, and the opening and closing stocks. In essence this account recognizes the profit/mark-up when the goods are sent to the branch rather than when they are sold. However, since the profit is unrealized at this stage it is entered in the branch stock mark-up account (rather than the P & L) which is in the nature of a deferred income account (see Chapter 20). At the end of the accounting year that part of the profit/mark-up on the goods sent to the branch which is realized is transferred to the branch profit and loss account. This is identified as the difference between the two sides of the branch stock mark-up account, and represents the gross profit for the year.

The entries for Example 23.2 using this alternative method are shown below.

Branch stock account

	£		£
Stock b/d	6,000	Returns from branch	1,500
Goods to branch	27,500	Debtors—credit sales	22,400
		Cash—sales	2,000

		Branch expenses	300
		Stock mark-up account—	
		reductions in selling prices	400
		Balances c/d:	
		stock	5,125
		goods in transit	1,000
		cash in transit	500
		Stock mark-up account—	
		stock loss	275
	33,500		33,500

Branch stock mark-up

Returns from branch	300	Stock—unrealized profit b/d	1,200
Reduction in selling price	400	Goods to branch	5,500
Stock loss	275		
Unrealized profit c/d:			
stock	1,025		
goods in transit	200		
P & L—gross profit	4,500		
	6,700		6,700

Notes

1. Computation of mark-ups: opening stock = 20 per cent × £6,000 = £1,200; goods to branch = 20 per cent × £27,500 = £5,500; returns from branch = 20 per cent × £1,500 = £300; closing stock = 20 per cent × £5,125 = £1,025; goods in transit = 20 per cent × £1,000 = £200.
2. The mark-up on the goods in transit is included in the branch stock mark-up account because they are effectively stock. The reductions in selling price and stock loss are included to reduce the gross profit by these amounts.
3. The observant reader may have noticed that the amounts shown in the branch stock mark-up account are also the difference between the amounts in the memorandum column and double entry (trading account) column of the branch stock account prepared using the previous method. This is no coincidence. The mark-up on the goods to branch shown in the branch stock mark-up account is set against the goods to branch shown at selling price in the branch stock account to give the cost of goods to branch which is entered on the credit side of the goods sent to branch account. The same principle is applied to returns from the branch. Also the mark-up on the stock (and goods in transit) shown in the branch stock mark-up account is set against the stock (and goods in transit) shown at selling price in the branch stock account to give the cost of stocks that are entered on the balance sheet.
4. The mark-up on the (opening and closing) stocks (and goods in transit) is an unrealized profit which is why these are entered in the branch stock mark-up account before the gross profit (i.e. the realized profit) can be ascertained.
5. Notice that the branch stock mark-up account contains the mark-up on those items which are normally shown in a trading account except that the purchases are represented by the goods sent to the branch, and the sales are represented by the gross

profit. This is illustrated below:

	£	£
Sales 20 per cent × (22,400 + 2,000 + 300 + 400 + 500 + 275)		5,175
Less: Cost of sales		
Opening stock 20 per cent × 6,000	1,200	
Purchases 20 per cent × (27,000 − 1,500) = 5,500 − 300	5,200	
	6,400	
Less: Closing stock 20 per cent × (5,125 + 1,000) = 1,025 + 200	1,225	5,175

Deducting the reductions in selling price and stock loss will give the gross profit thus: £5,175 − £400 − £275 = £4,500. This is also a useful way of checking whether your answer shown in account form is correct, whichever method is used.

Autonomous branches

As explained earlier, branches differ in the amount of autonomy given by the head office to the branch manager. As a generalization, autonomous branches have more freedom over their choice of suppliers, the recruitment and salaries of staff, selling prices, etc. However, the amount of freedom varies even between so-called autonomous branches in different organizations. An autonomous branch may be allowed to purchase goods from external suppliers, but it is more common for the head office to specify which suppliers must be used, or to buy in bulk and direct goods to the branch. Furthermore, the head office may supply goods to the branch at cost (and allow the branch to fix its own selling price), but it is more common for the head office to charge the branch at cost plus a mark-up (or transfer price).

Given these variations, the reader may be left wondering what precisely distinguishes an autonomous branch from a non-autonomous branch. The answer is three main characteristics as follows:

1. The manager of an autonomous branch is only accountable to the head office for the branch profit. Unlike in the case of non-autonomous branches, the head office has no direct control over stocks, cash, etc. The branch manager is expected to exercise proper control over the branch assets and ensure these are used in an efficient and effective manner.
2. Although an autonomous branch cannot own any assets itself, since it is not a separate legal entity, it usually controls its own assets. That is, the branch is responsible for its own fixed assets, has a separate bank account, collects its own debtors, and pays it own creditors. However, it is frequently required to remit excess cash at the bank to the head office.
3. An autonomous branch maintains a separate set of books, including a branch ledger, and has its own profit and loss account and balance sheet.

It is critical to always remember that the head office and the branch are two separate accounting entities each with their own ledger. No item or transaction can have a debit entry in one ledger and a credit entry in the other, or vice versa. Each must have a debit and credit entry in the same ledger.

The branch ledger will contain a head office current account in place of a capital account, which is in the nature of a combined capital and head office creditor account. It is credited with the goods received by the branch from head office, and the annual branch profit; and debited with goods return to the head office and cash remittances to the head office.

In the head office ledger there will be a branch current account which is in the nature of a combined investment and branch debtor account. It is debited with the goods sent to the branch, and the annual branch profit; and credited with goods returned by the branch and cash received from the branch.

It can thus be seen that the head office current account and the branch current account contain the same items but on opposite sides. These two accounts therefore normally have the same balance. However, the amount relating to goods sent to the branch may differ from that received by the branch because of *goods in transit*. Similarly the amount relating to cash remittances received by the head office may differ from that sent by the branch because of *cash in transit*. Both of these cause the balances on the branch and head office current accounts to differ, and require an adjustment at the end of the accounting year before preparing the final accounts. These adjustments may be made in the branch books but it is more common to do them in the head office books as follows:

Goods in transit
Debit   Goods to branch account
Credit   Branch current account

The debit in the goods to branch account reduces the amount of the goods sent to branch transferred to the head office trading account. This entry will have to be reversed in the next period when the branch receives the goods.

Debit   Goods in transit account
Credit   Head office trading account

The debit to the goods in transit account is added to the head office closing stock in the preparation of its balance sheet, and the credit to the head office trading account is added to its closing stock figure. Next year the balance on the goods in transit account at the end of this year will be transferred to the head office trading account as part of its opening stock.

Cash in transit
Debit   Cash in transit account
Credit   Branch current account

The balance on the cash in transit account is added to the head office cash and bank balance in the preparation of its balance sheet. When the cash in transit is received in the next period it will be credited to the cash in transit account and not the branch current account.

Separate trading and profit and loss accounts are prepared for the branch and head office, in addition to a combined profit and loss account for the business as a whole. It is also common to prepare separate balance sheets for the branch and head office, as well as a combined balance sheet for the business as a whole. The preparation of the combined profit and loss account and balance sheet in branch accounting is relatively straightforward but includes some very important principles that students going on to advanced accounting courses will encounter in group/consolidated accounts. Most of the amounts relating to income and expenses in the combined profit and loss account, and the assets and liabilities in the combined balance sheet, are found by simply adding together the same items in the branch and head office final accounts. The exceptions are as follows:

1. The goods sent to the branch by the head office shown in its profit and loss account as sales (or deducted from purchases) must cancel out the goods received by the branch from the head office shown in its profit and loss account as purchases. These internal transfers cannot appear in the combined profit and loss account.
2. The balances on the branch current account and the head office current account must cancel each other out and thus cannot appear on the combined balance sheet. Only the capital and profit for the business as a whole is entered in the capital section of the combined balance sheet.

Notice, however, that the branch current account appears in the head office balance sheet as an asset which is in the nature of an investment. Similarly the head office current account appears in the branch balance sheet in place of its capital.

A simple illustration of the preparation of the final accounts of autonomous branches is given in Example 23.3.

Example 23.3
Exotic Retailers has a head office in London and a branch in Birmingham. The Birmingham branch maintains its own set of books. All goods are purchased by head office, and those sent to the branch are charged at cost.

The trial balance as at 30 June 19X6 was as follows:

	Head office		Branch	
	Dr	Cr	Dr	Cr
	£000	£000	£000	£000
Branch/head office current account	70			55
Goods to branch		50	40	
Sales		100		90
Purchases	80			
Expenses	35		25	
Fixed assets	150		63	
Debtors	8		2	
Stock	16		12	
Bank	4		3	
Capital		213		
	363	363	145	145

Further information:

1. The stocks at 30 June 19X6 were: head office £13,000, branch £11,000.
2. The branch had sent the head office a cheque for £5,000 on 29 June 19X6 but this was not received until 2 July 19X6.

You are required to prepare separate profit and loss accounts and balance sheets for the head office, the branch and the combined business.

There is obviously cash in transit of £5,000. There are also goods in transit of £10,000 which is the difference between the goods sent to branch shown in the head office trial balance of £50,000 and the goods received by the branch shown in its trial balance of £40,000. The following adjustments must therefore be made in the head office ledger before the final accounts can be prepared.

Cash in transit

Branch current account	5,000

Branch current account

Balance b/d	70,000	Cash in transit	5,000
		Goods to branch	10,000
		Balance c/d	55,000
	70,000		70,000
Balance b/d	55,000		

Goods to branch

Branch current account	10,000	Balance b/d	50,000
Profit and loss account	40,000		
	50,000		50,000

Goods in transit

Profit and loss account	10,000

Exotic Retailers
Profit and loss account for the year ended 30 June 19X6

	Head office		Branch		Combined	
	£000	£000	£000	£000	£000	£000
Sales—external		100		90		190
internal		40		—		—
		140		90		190
Less: Cost of sales						
Stock at 1 July 19X5	16		12		28	
Add: Purchases/transfers	80		40		80	
	96		52		108	
Less: Stock at 30 June 19X6 (13 + 10)	23		11		34	
		73		41		74
Gross profit		67		49		116
Less: Expenses		35		25		60
Net profit		32		24		56

Exotic Retailers
Balance sheet as at 30 June 19X6

	£000	£000	£000	£000	£000	£000
Fixed assets		150		63		213
Current assets						
Stock (13 + 10)	23		11		34	
Debtors	8		2		10	
Bank (4 + 5)	9		3		12	
		40		16		56
		190		79		269
Branch current account		79		—		—
(55 + 24)						
Net assets		269		79		269
Capital/HO current account b/fwd		213		55		213
Add: Profit for year		56		24		56
Capital/HO current account c/fwd		269		79		269

Notes

1. The goods sent to the branch shown in the head office profit & loss account as internal sales could have been deducted from its purchases instead. Whichever treatment is adopted the £40,000 goods to branch in the head office profit & loss account must cancel out the £40,000 goods from the head office in the branch profit & loss account with the result that neither items appear in the combined profit and loss account.
2. Before preparing the balance sheets the branch profit has to be entered in the current accounts as shown below. The branch profit & loss account is obviously an account in the branch ledger. The profit for the year is a credit balance on this account which is transferred to the head office current account as follows:

Profit & loss account

HO current account	24,000	Net profit b/d	24,000

HO current account

Balance c/d	79,000	Balance b/d	55,000
		Profit for year	24,000
	79,000		79,000
		Balance b/d	79,000

Similarly the branch profit is entered in the head office ledger as follows:

Branch current account

Balance b/d	55,000	Balance c/d	79,000
Capital—			
net profit	24,000		
	79,000		79,000
Balance b/d	79,000		

Capital

Balance c/d	269,000	Balance b/d	213,000
		HO P & L—profit	32,000
		Branch current	
		account—profit	24,000
	269,000		269,000
		Balance b/d	269,000

The balances on the head office and branch current accounts cancel each other out and thus do not appear on the combined balance sheet.

3.   Notice that each double entry is within one ledger. That is, there is *never* a debit in the head office ledger with a corresponding credit in the branch ledger (or vice versa). These are two separate accounting entities even though they are the same legal entity. Some textbooks and examination model answers give the impression that a double entry (such as for the branch profit) spans the two ledgers but this is because their workings short-cut the real double entries.

As mentioned previously, sometimes the head office may charge the branch for goods supplied at cost plus a mark-up. This may be the expected selling price, or alternatively the branch may sell the goods at an even higher price. Whichever is the case, some additional accounting complications arise because of the unrealized profit contained in the value of the branch stock (and goods in transit) as follows. Where goods sent to the branch have been charged out at cost plus a mark-up, this mark-up will be included in sales in the head office profit and loss account and thus the profit. However, some of these goods will not have been sold at the end of the accounting year (i.e. the value of branch stock), and to take profit in respect of these is a contravention of the realization and prudence concepts. It is therefore necessary to make a provision for unrealized profit in the head office books in respect of the mark-up contained in the value of the branch stock. This takes the form of a charge (or credit) to the head office profit and loss account to increase (or decrease) the existing provision for unrealized profit in respect of the opening branch stock. The amount of the new provision is then shown on the head office balance sheet, normally as a deduction from the branch current account. Notice that none of the entries relating to a provision for unrealized profit occurs in the branch or combined final accounts.

Furthermore, the mark-up included in any goods in transit must be eliminated before making the entry in the goods in transit account because this profit is also unrealized. However, the mark-up is not eliminated from the entries in the branch current account and goods to branch account in respect of goods in transit because these entries are intended to reverse the original entry relating to the goods sent to the branch which are in transit at the end of the accounting year.

Some further complications where goods are sent to branch at cost plus a mark-up arise in connection with the combined profit and loss account and balance sheet as follows:

1. The opening and closing stocks shown in the combined profit and loss account must exclude the mark-up/unrealized profit which will have been included in the value of the branch closing stock shown in its profit and loss account.
2. Similarly the closing stock shown in the combined balance sheet must exclude the mark-up/unrealized profit which will have been included in the value of the branch closing stock shown in its balance sheet.

An illustration of the preparation of the final accounts of autonomous branches with goods charged to the branch at cost plus a mark-up is shown in Example 23.4.

Example 23.4

Bell, who runs a shop in Bradford selling high quality knitwear, has appointed Wheeler to operate a branch in Hull. All goods are purchased by the head office at Bradford and those sent to Hull are invoiced at cost plus 25 per cent. Wheeler is to receive a commission of 20 per cent of the net profits of the Hull branch before charging salaries.

The trial balances at 31 December 19X4 were as follows:

	Head office		*Branch*	
	£	£	£	£
Capital account		34,000		
Salaries	8,000		9,000	
Fixtures at written down value	15,000		10,000	
Stock at cost 31/12/X3	7,000			
Stock at invoiced value 31/12/X3			7,500	
Sales		50,000		35,000
Purchases	42,000			
Goods to branch at invoiced prices		20,500	17,500	
Branch and head office current account	20,000			17,000
Expenses	12,000		6,500	
Provision for unrealized profit		1,500		
Cash in hand and at bank	2,000		1,500	
	£106,000	£106,000	£52,000	£52,000

Account is to be taken of the following:

1. Stock at the shop at 31/12/X4 amounted to £8,100 at cost at Bradford and £10,000 at invoiced prices at Hull.
2. Goods with an invoice value of £3,000 were sent from the head office but still in transit at 31/12/X4.
3. Depreciation is to be charged at 20 per cent of the written down value of fixtures.

Prepare trading profit and loss accounts and balance sheet for the head office, branch and the business as a whole. Show the branch current account.

Note the following: first, the provision for unrealized profit in the head office trial balance which represents profit in the branch opening stock, i.e. £7,500 includes £1,500 mark-up. Combined stocks are then £7,000 (Bradford) plus £7,500 (Hull) less £1,500 (provision) equals £13,000. Second, the current accounts do not agree. They must be adjusted before balance sheets can be combined. Adjustments for goods in transit are made in the head office books thus:

Branch current account

Balance b/d	20,000	Goods to branch	3,000
		Balance c/d	17,000
	20,000		20,000
Balance c/d	17,000		

The goods in transit will be regarded as part of head office stocks. Although they have an invoiced value of £3,000, eliminating the unrealized profit gives a cost of £2,400. Total closing stocks at Bradford will be £8,100 plus £2,400 goods in transit, i.e. £10,500. The provision for unrealized profit will need to be adjusted to a fifth of the £10,000 stock at Hull, i.e. £2,000, an increase of £500. Combined stocks are then: £10,500 (Bradford) plus £10,000 (Hull) less £2,000 (provision) equals £18,500. The profit and loss accounts for head office, branch and combined business can then be calculated showing transfers as internal sales of the head office on the one hand, and purchases of the branch on the other, but eliminated in the combined accounts.

Profit and loss account for the year ended 31 December 19X4

	Head office £	£	Branch £	£	Combined £	£
Sales—external		50,000		35,000		85,000
internal		17,500		—		—
		67,500				
Opening stock	7,000		7,500		13,000	
Purchases/transfers	42,000		17,500		42,000	
	49,000		25,000		55,000	
Closing stock	10,500		10,000		18,500	
		38,500		15,000		36,500
Gross profit		29,000		20,000		48,500
Expenses	12,000		6,500		18,500	
Depreciation	3,000		2,000		5,000	
		15,000		8,500		23,500
Profit before						
commission and salaries		14,000		11,500		25,000
Salaries	8,000		9,000		17,000	
Commission	—		2,300	11,300	2,300	19,300
		6,000				
Less: Addition to provision						
for unrealized profit		500		—		—
Net profit		5,500		200		5,700

The branch profit of £200 must be transferred to head office. This will be effected by debiting the branch current account and crediting the capital account in the head office books and crediting the head office current account and debiting the profit and loss account in the branch books. This gives a balance in both current accounts of £17,200 and total profits of £5,500 + £200 = £5,700 credited to the capital account.

Balance sheet as at 31 December 19X4

		Head office £	Branch £	Combined £
Fixed assets				
Fixtures		15,000	10,000	25,000
Less: Depreciation		3,000	2,000	5,000
		12,000	8,000	20,000
Current assets				
Stocks		10,500	10,000	18,500
Cash and bank		2,000	1,500	3,500
		24,500	19,500	42,000
Less: Current liabilities				
Commission		—	2,300	2,300
		24,500	17,200	39,700
Branch current account	17,200			
Less: Provision for				
unrealized profit	2,000	15,200	—	—
Net assets		39,700	17,200	39,700
Capital/HO current account b/fwd		34,000	17,000	34,000
Add: Profit for year		5,700	200	5,700
Capital/HO current account c/fwd		39,700	17,200	39,700

Summary

As organizations expand they often divide their operations into departments or branches. This involves the delegation of responsibilities and varying amounts of autonomy to local managers. The senior management will want to evaluate and control the performance of these departments and branches, as well as their managers. Accounting can contribute to the management of such organizations by providing information that not only reports on sub-unit performance but also facilitates control (e.g. of cash and stock).

In some organizations such as department stores it is usually possible to prepare departmental trading accounts (in columnar form). It may also be possible to prepare departmental profit and loss accounts but this often requires the arbitrary apportionment of common costs.

In other organizations such as chain stores the branches do not usually maintain a separate set of books. These are referred to as non-autonomous or integrated branches. The branch is required to supply periodic returns of its activities which are recorded in the books of the head office. The main account relating to the branch is a branch stock account which is used to ascertain the branch gross profit and facilitate the control of stocks. Goods are frequently charged to the branch at cost plus a profit mark-up. The geographic separation of branches from the head office also often gives rise to goods in transit and cash in transit at the end of the accounting period.

In some large decentralized organizations each branch maintains a separate set of books. These are referred to as autonomous branches. Separate trading and profit and loss accounts and balance sheets are prepared for the branch and head office, in addition to a combined set of final accounts for the business as a whole. A particular feature of accounting for autonomous branches is that both the head office and branch ledger contain a current account. In the branch books this is in the nature of a combined capital and head office creditor account. In the head office books this is in the nature of a combined investment and branch debtor account. Goods in transit and cash in transit also often arise with autonomous branches.

Key terms and concepts

Apportion, autonomous branch, branch, branch current account, branch stock account, branch stock mark-up account, cash in transit, department, goods in transit, head office current account, non-autonomous/integrated branch.

Exercises

An asterisk after the question number indicates that there is a suggested answer in the Appendix.

23.1. John Dell commenced trading on 1 April 19X8 as Highway Stores, retail stationers and confectioners, with an initial capital of £3,000 which was utilized in the opening of a business bank account. All receipts and payments are passed through the bank account. The following is a summary of the items credited in the business cash book during the year ended 31 March 19X9:

	£
Purchase of fixtures and fittings:	
Stationery department	2,600
Confectionery department	1,500
Staff wages	
Stationery department	2,200
Confectionery department	1,540
Rent for the period 1 April 19X8 to 30 April 19X9	1,300
Rates for the year ended 31 March 19X9	570
Electricity	370
Advertising	1,100
Payments to suppliers	53,550
Drawings	5,000

The purchases during the year under review were:

	£
Stationery department	26,000
Confectionery department	29,250

The above purchases do not include goods costing £500 bought by the business and then taken by Mr Dell for his own domestic use. The figure of £500 is included in payments to suppliers.

The gross profit in the stationery department is at the rate of 20 per cent of sales while in the confectionery department it is 25 per cent of sales. In both departments, sales each month are always at a uniform level. The policy of Mr Dell is to have the month end stocks in each department just sufficient for the following month's sales. The prices of all goods bought by Highway Stores have not changed since the business began.

Total trade debtors at 31 March 19X9 amounted to £9,000.

In August 19X8 Mr Dell and his sister, Mrs Beck, benefited from legacies from their late mother's estate of £5,000 and £4,000 respectively. Both legacies were paid into the bank account of Highway Stores; Mrs Beck has agreed that her legacy should be an interest free loan to the business.

At 31 March 19X9 electricity charges accrued due, amounting to £110.

Mr Dell has decided that expenses not incurred by a specific department should be apportioned to departments as follows:

1. Rent and rates—according to floor area occupied.
2. Electricity—according to consumption.
3. Advertising—according to turnover.

Two-thirds of the business floor space is occupied by the stationery department while three-quarters of the electricity is consumed by that department. All the floor space of the business is allocated to a department.

It has been decided that depreciation on fixtures and fittings should be provided at the rate of 10 per cent of the cost of assets held at the year end.

Required:

(a) A trading and profit and loss account for the year ended 31 march 19X9 for:
  (i) the stationery department; and
  (ii) the confectionery department.
(b) A balance sheet at 31 March 19X9. (ACCA)

23.2. All-in Stores Ltd with head office in Leeds has a branch in Bradford. All goods are purchased by head office and supplied to and sold by the branch at 25 per cent over cost. Apart from a sales ledger kept at the branch, the whole of the transactions are recorded in the books at head office.

The following are the particulars relating to the transactions at the branch during the year ended 31 December 19X7:

	£
Stock on hand at 1 January 19X7 at price supplied	5,000
Sundry debtors at 1 January 19X7	4,800
Goods supplied by head office	28,500
Returns to head office at price supplied	1,500

Sales on credit	24,000
Sales for cash	2,800
Bad debts written off	200
Cash received from debtors	25,500
Discount allowed to debtors	500
Stock on hand at 31 December 19X7 at price supplied	5,125

From the foregoing particulars compile the branch stock account, branch total debtors' account and branch profit and loss account for the year ended 31 December 19X7 as they would appear in the head office books.   (ACCA)

23.3. Answer Question 23.2 using a branch stock mark-up account.

24.4.* The Shirt Shop is a retailer with a main shop in London and a branch in Birmingham. The accounting year ends on 31 March. The branch has no separate books of account, all its transactions being recorded in the books of the head office in London. All goods are purchased by London and those sent to Birmingham are invoiced at selling price, being cost price plus a mark-up at $12\frac{1}{2}$ per cent. The branch pays local expenses out of cash sales and remits the balance of cash takings to London together with details of the expenses. It also makes credit sales but these are collected by the head office.

On 1 April 19X8 the branch had stocks, at selling price, of £9,360 and there were branch debtors of £10,000.

The following is a summary of the transactions of the branch during the year ended 31 March 19X9:

	£
Goods sent to branch at selling price	100,080
Goods returned by branch at selling price	1,008
Credit sales	54,000
Cash remitted to London	43,200
Local expenses paid from cash sales	1,944
Reductions in selling prices authorized by London	1,098
Cheques received from branch debtors	48,000

On 31 March 19X9 the branch had stocks, at selling price, of £7,380 and there were branch debtors of £16,000. Goods with an invoice value of £540 had been sent to the branch on 29 March 19X9 but not received until 3 April 19X9. There was also cash of £36 from sales at the branch on 31 March 19X9 that had not been remitted to London.

You are required to show all the ledger entries relating to the branch for the year ended 31 March 19X9. The branch stock account is prepared using memorandum columns for recording the relevant transactions at selling price.

23.5.* Answer Question 23.4 using a branch stock mark-up account.

23.6.* The Hat Shop which had operated in the retail trade from a head office in the city centre, opened a branch renting premises in a major suburb on 1 May 19X6. All purchases continue to be made by the head office, goods sent to the branch being charged out at selling price, which is cost plus 50 per cent. The head office only sells to cash customers but the branch sells to some customers on account. Certain expenses are met directly by the branch out of cash receipts and the branch holds a small cash float remitting any remaining cash to the head office regularly.

The branch keeps a sales ledger and collects the amounts owing from its credit customers in cash. The head office operates an integrated system of accounting but has not yet dealt with matters relating to the branch given below:

1. Goods sent by the head office to the branch at selling price: £120,000.
2. Branch expenses of £5,000 were paid out of branch takings before remitting cash to head office.
3. Depreciation is to be provided on branch fixtures and fittings at 25 per cent on cost.
4. Cash in hand at the branch on 30 April 19X7: £2,000.
5. Branch debtors outstanding at 30 April 19X7: £12,000

Before dealing with the above the following trial balance as at 30 April 19X7 was prepared:

	Debit £	Credit £
Proprietor's capital		46,000
Head office premises at cost	25,000	
—depreciation at 1 May 19X6		9,000
Head office—sales		114,000
Purchases	147,000	
Head office stock at cost on 1 May 19X6	13,000	
Head office expenses	16,000	
Branch rent, salaries and expenses	10,000	
Branch fixtures and fittings	8,000	
Cash received from branch		56,000
Balance at bank	6,000	
	225,000	225,000

The head office stock at 30 April 19X7 was £4,000 at cost price. The head office depreciates its premises at 4 per cent per annum using the straight line method.

Stocktaking at the close of trading on 30 April 19X7 had shown that the stock at the branch amounted to £18,000 at selling prices. On 5 May 19X7 the head office received cash of £9,000, which the branch had sent on 30 April 19X7, and on 7 May 19X7 the branch received goods with a selling price of £15,000 that had been dispatched by the head office on 29 April 19X7.
You are required to:

(a) write up the branch stock account using the memorandum column method.
(b) prepare separate head office and branch profit and loss accounts, and a combined profit and loss account, for the year ended 30 April 19X7; and
(c) present a balance sheet for the business at that date.

23.7.* Answer Question 23.6 using a branch stock mark-up account.

23.8. Star Stores has its head office and main store in Crewe, and a branch store in Leek. All goods are purchased by the head office. Goods are invoiced to the branch at cost price plus a profit loading of 20 per cent. The following trial balances have been extracted from the books of account of both the head office and the branch as at 31 December 19X9:

| | Head office | | Branch | |
| | Dr | Cr | Dr | Cr |
	£000	£000	£000	£000
Administrative expenses	380		30	
Distribution costs	157		172	
Capital (at 1 January 19X9)		550		
Cash and bank	25		2	
Creditors and accruals		176		20
Current accounts	255			180
Debtors and prepayments	130		76	
Motor vehicles:				
at cost	470		230	
accumulated depreciation				
at 31 December 19X9		280		120
Plant and equipment:				
at cost	250		80	
accumulated depreciation				
at 31 December 19X9		120		30
Proprietor's drawings during				
the year	64			
Provision for unrealized				
profit on branch stocks				
at 1 January 19X9		5		
Purchases	880			
Sales		1,200		570
Stocks at cost/invoiced amount				
at 1 January 19X9	80		30	
Transfer of goods to the				
branch/from the head office		360	300	
	2,691	2,691	920	920

Additional information:

1. The stocks in hand at 31 December 19X9 were estimated to be as follows:

	£000
At head office (at cost)	100
At the branch (at invoiced cost)	48

In addition, £60,000 of stocks at invoiced price had been dispatched to the branch on 28 December 19X9. These goods had not been received by the branch until 5 January 19X0 and so they had not been included in the branch books of account.

2. On 31 December 19X9, the branch had transferred £15,000 of cash to the head office bank, but this was not received in Crewe until 2 January 19X0.

Required:
(a) Prepare in adjacent columns and using the vertical format: (i) the head office, and (ii) the branch trading, and profit and loss accounts for the year to 31 December 19X9. *Note*: a combined profit and loss account is *not* required.
(b) Prepare in the vertical format, Star Stores' balance sheet as at 31 December 19X9. *Note*: separate balance sheets for the head office and the branch are *not* required.   (AAT)

23.9.* Mapp's head office is in London, and it has a branch in Brighton. The following trial balances have been extracted from the respective books of account of both the head office and the branch as at 30 June 19X8:

	Head office		*Branch*	
	Dr	Cr	Dr	Cr
	£	£	£	£
Administrative expenses	135,000		9,000	
Branch current account	46,000			
Capital		328,000		
Cash at bank and in hand	19,000		2,000	
Creditors		22,500		5,000
Debtors	15,000		20,000	
Distribution costs	30,000		12,000	
Goods sent to branch		166,000		
Head office current account				24,000
Plant and machinery				
(net book value)	383,000		38,000	
Provision for unrealized				
profit on stock				
held by the branch		1,500		
Purchases	225,000		154,000	
Sales		350,000		215,000
Stock at cost or cost to				
branch at 1 July 19X7	15,000		9,000	
	868,000	868,000	244,000	244,000

Additional information:

1. Stock at 30 June 19X8 was valued as follows:

	£
Head office at cost	20,000
Branch at cost to branch	24,000
Goods in transit to branch at cost to branch	12,000

2. Goods purchased by the head office and sold to the branch are transferred at cost plus 20 per cent.

3. At 30 June 19X8 the branch had transferred £10,000 to the head office's bank account but as at that date, no record had been made in the head office's books of account.

Required:

Prepare in adjacent columns the following:

(a) the head office, the branch, and the combined trading, and profit and loss accounts for the year to 30 June 19X8; and

(b) the head office, the branch, and the combined balance sheets as at that date.

(AAT)

For further questions on departmental and branch accounts, see the exercises in Chapter 24 on the final accounts of partnerships.

24. The final accounts of partnerships

Learning objectives

After reading this chapter the student should be able to:

1. Explain the meaning of the key terms and concepts listed at the end of the chapter.
2. Describe the main characteristics of partnerships.
3. Explain how profits may be shared between the partners including the nature and purpose of partners' salaries, interest on capital, and interest on drawings.
4. Explain the difference between partners' capital, current and drawings accounts.
5. Show the journal and ledger entries relating to those items normally found in partners' capital, current and drawing accounts.
6. Prepare partnership final accounts including a profit and loss appropriation account.
7. Show the entries in the ledger and final accounts relating to partners' commission and a guaranteed share of profit.

The law and characteristics of partnerships

For a number of commercial reasons, it may be mutually advantageous for two or more people to form a partnership. The Partnership Act 1890 defines a *partnership* as 'the relation which subsists between persons carrying on business in common with a view of profit'. It cannot have fewer than two partners and, at one time, the Act set a limit of 20 partners. However, with the introduction of the Companies Act 1967 this maximum has been relaxed in the case of a number of professional firms, such as accountants, solicitors, etc.

Since partnerships are not able to limit their liability to creditors and other members of the public, there is no need for any special legislation to protect these groups. Thus partners are largely free to make whatever agreements between themselves that they wish to cover their mutual relationships. The powers and rights of the partners between themselves are governed by any written agreement they may make. This is referred to as the *articles or deed of partnership*. It is important for partners to reach an agreement on matters such as the following:

1. The capital to be introduced by each partner
2. The sharing of profits and losses
3. Partners' drawings
4. The preparation and audit of accounts

5. The dissolution of the partnership
6. The resolution of disputes.

In the absence of any partnership agreement, or if the agreement is silent on any of the items 1–6 above or the following matters, a partnership is subject to the provisions of the Partnership Act 1890, which includes the following:

1. Each partner has *unlimited liability*. That is, if the debts of the partnership cannot be paid because the business has insufficient assets to do so, the creditors have recourse to the private property of the individual partners. The partners are said to be jointly and severally liable for the debts of the firm and therefore a creditor may sue the partnership or any individual partner.
2. Voting powers. In the ordinary day-to-day running of a partnership individual partners often make routine business decisions without consulting the other partners. At the other extreme, certain fundamental decisions, such as to change the type of business the partnership is engaged in, or the admission of a new partner, require the consent of all the partners. Other major decisions are supposed to be determined by a majority vote. Each partner has one vote. However, a partnership deed may specify some other distribution of voting power.
3. Every partner is entitled to take part in the management of the business. However, some partnership agreements provide for certain partners to be sleeping or limited partners. Neither of these normally takes part in the management of the business.
4. Every partner is entitled to access to the books and papers of the partnership. This includes sleeping and limited partners.
5. Each partner is an agent of the partnership and can thus sign contracts on behalf of the partnership, which will then be legally bound to honour them.
6. A new partner can only be admitted to the partnership if all the existing partners give their consent. However, a partnership deed may specify otherwise.
7. A partnership will be dissolved by:
   (a) any partner giving notice to the other partner(s) of his or her intention to leave the partnership;
   (b) the death, insanity or bankruptcy of a partner.

The sharing of profits between the partners

Consider the following situation. A and B enter into partnerships; A is to work full-time in the business while B will only spend a few hours each week on partnership business; B is to put into the business £100,000 as capital whereas A is to contribute capital of only £10,000. You are asked by A and B to suggest how the profits might be shared so as to recompense A for working more hours than B in the business, and to compensate B for having put into the business (and therefore at risk) substantially more capital than A.

The way this is normally done is to give each partner a prior share of the profits as: (1) *a salary* related to the amount of time each devotes to the business; and (2) *interest on the capital* each invests. The remaining profit, which is often referred to as the *residual profit*, can then be divided between the partners according to whatever they agree is fair. This might be equally, since both have already been compensated for the unequal time and capital they contribute.

Another aspect of sharing partnership profits concerns *interest on drawings*. This is intended to compensate the partners which have annual drawings that are less than those of the other partner(s). Each partner is charged interest on drawings for the period from the date of the drawings to the end of the accounting year in which the drawings took place.

It is important to appreciate that partners' 'salaries', 'interest on capital' and 'interest on drawings' are not actual payments of money; they are only part of a profit sharing formula. If any such payments are made to a partner these should be treated as drawings. Indeed as a general rule *all* payments to partners must be treated as drawings. It should also be observed that salaries, interest on capital and interest on drawings will still arise even if the business makes a loss. In these circumstances they effectively become part of a loss sharing formula.

If there is no agreement between the partners concerning how profits and losses should be shared, section 24 of the Partnership Act 1890 would be applied as follows:

1. Profits and losses are to be shared equally between the partners.
2. No partner will receive a salary or interest on capital, or be charged interest on drawings.
3. Any loans made by a partner to the business (as distinct from capital introduced) will be entitled to interest at the rate of 5 per cent per annum.

Capital and current accounts

In the accounts of sole traders there would be a capital account and usually a drawing account. In the books of a partnership there will be:

1. A *capital account* for each partner. Unlike the capital account of a sole trader, this will only contain the original capital put into the business plus any further capital introduced at a later date.
2. A *current account* for each partner, in which is entered:
   (a) drawings of money or goods taken by the partner for his or her own use (debit);
   (b) interest charged on drawings (debit);
   (c) interest on loans to the partnership (credit);
   (d) salary (credit);
   (e) interest on capital (credit);
   (f) the partner's share of the residual profit or loss.

There may also be a *drawings account* for each partner in which all goods or money taken by the partners during the year are entered instead of putting them in the partners' current accounts. However, at the end of the year these are transferred to the partners' current accounts. Note also that current accounts are sometimes labelled drawings accounts.

The partners' capital account are shown on the balance sheet in the same place as that of a sole trader. Underneath these are entered the balances on the partners' current accounts at the end of the year. If a current account has a debit balance it may be entered after the net current assets but it is more common to deduct (in brackets) this from the other partners' current accounts.

The profit and loss appropriation account

In partnership final accounts the profit and loss account contains exactly the same entries as that of a sole trader.

After the profit and loss account has been prepared, the profit for the year is carried down to a profit and loss appropriation accounting in which is shown the sharing of profits between the partners. The basis for sharing may include partners' salaries, interest on capital and interest on drawings, as well as the division of any remaining amount in some agreed portion. The latter is often referred to as the *residual profit*. The appropriation account is a part of the double entry in the ledger and as a general rule it is worth remembering that the double entry for each item in the appropriation account is on the opposite side of the relevant partner's current account. The contents of the profit and loss appropriation account are illustrated in Example 24.1.

Example 24.1

Bonnie and Clyde are in partnership sharing profits in the ratio 2 : 1. From the following you are required to prepare the profit and loss appropriation account for the year ended 31 December 19X8 and show the relevant items in the balance sheet at that date.

	Bonnie £	Clyde £
Capital at 31 December 19X7	100,000	80,000
Current account balances at 31 December 19X7	16,340	28,290
Drawings–1 April 19X8	4,000	8,000
31 August 19X8	6,000	9,000
30 September 19X8	8,000	—
Salaries	20,000 p.a.	25,000 p.a.
Interest on capital	10 per cent p.a.	10 per cent p.a.
Interest on drawings	5 per cent p.a.	5 per cent p.a.

Clyde introduced additional capital of £10,000 in cash on 1 January 19X8 and Bonnie lent the business £20,000 on 30 June 19X8. The profit of the year ended 31 December 19X8 was £78,700.

Before dividing the profit between the partners, the partners' capital accounts need to be adjusted. These ledger account are often prepared in columnar form as follows:

Capital account

Bonnie £	Clyde £			Bonnie £	Clyde £
		19X8			
		1 Jan	Balance b/d	100,000	80,000
		1 Jan	Bank		10,000
					90,000

The loan from Bonnie is not entered in his capital account but rather in a separate loan account, which constitutes a long-term liability.

Next it may be useful to prepare a schedule which shows the division of the profits as follows:

	Bonnie £	Clyde £	Total £
Profit for 19X8			78,700
Loan interest ($^6/_{12}$ × 5 per cent × £20,000)	500	—	(500)
Partners' salaries	20,000	25,000	(45,000)

Interest on capital:

10 per cent × £100,000	10,000	—	—
10 per cent × £90,000	—	9,000	(19,000)
	30,500	34,000	14,200
Interest on drawings (see note 3.)	(350)	(450)	800
	30,150	33,550	15,000
Shares of residual profit (2 : 1)	10,000	5,000	(15,000)
Totals	40,150	38,550	—

Notes

1. The interest on partners' loans is computed using the rate of 5 per cent per annum specified in the Partnership Act 1890, unless you are told that some other rate has been agreed by the partners.
2. The interest on capital is computed using the balances on the partners' capital accounts and not the current accounts, unless you are told the contrary. Note also that in this example the balance on the capital account at the end of the year can be used because the additional capital was introduced at the start of the year. Where additional capital is introduced at some other date it will be necessary to compute the interest on a strict time basis.
3. The interest on drawings is calculated on a monthly basis as follows:

$$£$$

$$\textit{Bonnie} \quad \frac{9}{12} \times 5 \text{ per cent} \times £4,000 = 150$$

$$\frac{4}{12} \times 5 \text{ per cent} \times £6,000 = 100$$

$$\frac{3}{12} \times 5 \text{ per cent} \times £8,000 = \underline{100}$$
$$\overline{\underline{350}}$$

$$\textit{Clyde} \quad \frac{9}{12} \times 5 \text{ per cent} \times £8,000 = 300$$

$$\frac{4}{12} \times 5 \text{ per cent} \times £9,000 = \underline{150}$$
$$\overline{\underline{450}}$$

4. The sum of the total of each column in the above schedule should always equal the profit for the year (i.e. £40,150 + £38,550 = £78,700; £30,150 + £33,550 + £15,000 = £78,700, etc.)

The entries in the appropriation account can now be made. Although the total for each partner could be entered from the schedule, for a fuller presentation and to emphasize the double entry, the separate elements are all shown below:

Bonnie and Clyde
Profit and loss appropriation account for the year ended 31 December 19X8

	£	£		£	£
Loan interest—Bonnie			Net profit for year b/d		78,700
(6/12 × 5 per cent × £20,000)		500	Interest on drawings—		
Salaries—Bonnie	20,000		Bonnie	350	
Clyde	25,000	45,000	Clyde	450	800
Interest on capital—					
Bonnie					
(10 per cent × £100,000)	10,000				
Clyde					
(10 per cent × £90,000)	9,000	19,000			
Shares of residual profit—					
Bonnie	10,000				
Clyde	5,000	15,000			
		79,500			79,500

The double entry for the items in the appropriation account is in the partners' current accounts, which are usually prepared in columnar form as follows:

Current accounts

	Bonnie	Clyde		Bonnie	Clyde
	£	£		£	£
Drawings	18,000	17,000	Balance b/d	16,340	28,290
Interest on drawings	350	450	Loan interest	500	–
Balance c/d	38,490	49,840	Salaries	20,000	25,000
			Interest on capital	10,000	9,000
			Shares of profit	10,000	5,000
	56,840	67,290		56,840	67,290
			Balance b/d	38,490	49,840

The relevant balances will then be included in the balance sheet thus:

Bonnie and Clyde
Balance sheet as at 31 December 19X8

	£	£
Capital		
Bonnie		100,000
Clyde		90,000
		190,000
Current accounts		
Bonnie	38,490	
Clyde	49,840	88,330
Loan—Bonnie		20,000
		298,330

Frequently these are shown on the balance sheet in columnar form as follows:

	£	£	£
	Bonnie	*Clyde*	*Total*
Capital	100,000	90,000	190,000
Current accounts	38,490	49,840	88,330
	138,490	139,840	278,330
Loan—Bonnie			20,000
			298,330

Notes

1. It is usual to prepare the profit and loss appropriation account in vertical form by placing the entries on the debit side underneath those on the credit side. This may also contain an analysis column for each partner which are used in a similar manner to that shown in the schedule of division of profits.
2. Interest on partners loans is commonly entered in the appropriation account, particularly in examination questions that do not require the preparation of a profit and loss account. However, this is not strictly an appropriation of profit but rather an expense that should be entered in the profit and loss account as a charge/deduction in arriving at the profit (or loss) for the year.
3. Where money, which is described as salaries, has actually been paid to the partners this must be treated as drawings and not included in the profit and loss account as wages and salaries. However, this may be interpreted as indicating that the partners wish to give themselves a prior share of profits in the form of a salary. In this case the amounts paid must still be treated as drawings but an equivalent amount is also entered in the appropriation account as salaries, as described above.
4. Additional capital introduced during the year may include assets other than cash. This would usually be entitled to interest on capital from the date the assets were introduced until the end of the year in question (and subsequent years).
5. Interest is usually only charged on cash and cheque drawings and not on goods taken by the partners for their own use.
6. Losses would be shared in the same ratio as profit. If, in the case of Example 24.1, the profit for the year had been only £55,000 the schedule of division of profits would be as follows:

	Bonnie	*Clyde*	*Total*
	£	£	£
Profit for year			55,000
Loan interest	500	—	(500)
Salaries	20,000	25,000	(45,000)
Interest on capital	10,000	9,000	(19,000)
	30,500	34,000	(9,500)
Interest on drawings	(350)	(450)	800
	30,150	33,550	(8,700)
Shares of residual loss (2 : 1)	(5,800)	(2,900)	8,700
	24,350	30,650	—

Note that loan interest, salaries, interest on capital and interest on drawings are included even if there is a net loss for the year (i.e. before the appropriation). Salaries, etc., simply increase the amount of the residual loss.

Partners' commission

Some partnership businesses are departmentalized, with each of the departments being managed by a different partner. In such circumstances it is common for partners' salaries to take the form of an agreed commission expressed as a percentage of the profit of their department. This necessitates the preparation of a trading account for each department which normally takes the form of a columnar trading account containing columns on both the debit and credit sides for each department. Computing the profits of each partner's department is done in the same way as departmental accounts, discussed in Chapter 23. Having ascertained the profit of each department the partner's commission can be calculated and accounted for in exactly the same way as partners' salaries.

A guaranteed share of profit

Some partnership agreements include a clause guaranteeing that if a particular partner's share of profit in any year is below some agreed figure, then all or certain other partners will make it up to the guaranteed amount from their shares of profit. The amount by which the actual share of profit falls short of the guaranteed amount is usually shared (i.e. made up) by the other partners in their profit sharing ratio. Such a guarantee is fairly common in professional firms as an enticement to an employee to become a partner while at the same time being guaranteed an amount equal to the employee's existing remuneration. The guaranteed amount may include or exclude the partner's interest on capital and/or salary, but in the absence of information to the contrary it is usually taken to be the residual profit share that is guaranteed.

If, in the amended Example 24.1, when profits are only £55,000, Bonnie was guaranteed a share of residual profit of at least £2,000, the profit sharing schedule would appear as follows:

	Bonnie £	Clyde £	Total £
Profit for year	—	—	55,000
Salaries, interest on loans and capital	30,150	33,550	(8,700)
Shares of residual loss	2,000	(10,700)	8,700
	32,150	22,850	—

Summary

A partnership exists when between two and twenty (or more in the case of professional firms) carry on business with a view of profit. One of the main characteristics of partnerships is that the partners have unlimited liability. They are thus jointly and severally liable for the partnership debts. Each partner is also an agent of the partnership, entitled to take part in the management, and has equal voting power.

However, the articles or deed of partnership may contain any form of agreement relating to the rights of partners between themselves. This is particularly important with regard to the sharing of profits and losses. Where partners contribute unequal amounts of capital and/or time, it is common to find a profit sharing formula that includes giving each partner a prior share of profits as interest on capital and/or a salary. Similarly where partners have unequal amounts of drawings, they may decide to charge each other interest on drawings as a part of the profit sharing formula.

The profit and loss accounts of partnerships are the same as those of sole traders. However, the net profit (or loss) is carried down into a profit and loss appropriation account in which is shown the shares of profit appropriated to each partner. The balance sheets of partnerships are also the same as those of sole traders except that instead of having a single capital account there is a capital and current account for each partner.

Sometimes partners' salaries take the form of a commission which is expressed as a percentage of the gross (or net) profit of a department or branch that is managed by each partner. Some partnership agreements also contain a clause guaranteeing a particular partner a minimum amount as his or her share of the annual profit. In this case, the amount by which the actual share of the annual profit falls short of the minimum is made up from the other partners' share(s) of profit (in their profit sharing ratio).

Key terms and concepts

Articles/deed of partnership, guaranteed share of profit, interest on capital, interest on drawings, partnership, partners' capital accounts, partners' commission, partners' current accounts, partners' drawings accounts, partners' salaries, profit and loss appropriation account, residual profit/loss, unlimited liability.

Exercises

An asterisk after the question number indicates that there is a suggested answer in the Appendix.

24.1. (a)   Define a partnership.
   (b)   What are the legal limits on the number of partners?
   (c)   Outline the principal matters normally found in the articles or deed of partnership.

24.2. Describe the main characteristics of a partnership.

24.3. If there is no partnership agreement the provisions of the Partnership Act 1890 apply. List the main provisions of this Act with regard to the rights of partners between themselves, including the sharing of profits or losses.

24.4. Explain each of the following in the context of partnership profit sharing:
   (a)   partners' salaries,
   (b)   interest on capital,
   (c)   interest on drawings,
   (d)   residual profit.

24.5. Lane and Hill have decided to form a partnership. Lane is to contribute £150,000 as capital and Hill £20,000. Hill is to work full-time in the business and Lane one day a week. Because Hill has no other income, she anticipates making drawings of £1,000 per month from the partnership. Lane expects to make drawings of about £1,000 per quarter.

You have been asked to advise the partners on how to share profits in such a way as to compensate each of them for their unequal contributions of capital and labour and withdrawals.

24.6. Explain the difference between each of the following ledger accounts in the books of a partnership:
(a)   capital account,
(b)   current account,
(c)   drawings account.

24.7.* Clayton and Hammond are in partnership sharing profits and losses equally. The partnership agreement provides for annual salaries of Clayton: £17,000 and Hammond: £13,000. It also provides for interest on capital of 8 per cent per annum and interest on drawings of 4 per cent per annum.

You are given the following additional information relating to the accounting year ending 30 June 19X6.

	Clayton	Hammond
	£	£
Capital at 1 July 19X5	90,000	60,000
Current account at 1 July 19X5	16,850	9,470
Drawings—1 Oct 19X5	3,000	2,000
1 Mar 19X6	5,000	1,000
Capital introduced—1 Nov 19X5	10,000	—
Loan by Hammond—1 Apr 19X6	—	20,000

The profit shown in the profit and loss account for the year ended 30 June 19X6 was £67,500. You are required to prepare the profit and loss appropriation account, capital and current accounts.

24.8. Light and Dark are in partnership sharing profits and losses in the ratio 7 : 3 respectively. The following information has been taken from the partnership records for the financial year ended 31 May 19X9:

Partners' capital accounts, balances as at 1 June 19X8:

Light   £200,000
Dark   £140,000

Partners' current accounts, balances as at 1 June 19X8:

Light   £15,000 Cr
Dark   £13,000 Cr

During the year ended 31 May 19X9 the partners made the following drawings from the partnership bank account:

Light   £10,000 on 31 August 19X8
          £10,000 on 30 November 19X8
          £10,000 on 28 February 19X9
          £10,000 on 31 May 19X9
Dark   £7,000 on 31 August 19X8

£7,000 on 30 November 19X8
£7,000 on 28 February 19X9
£7,000 on 31 May 19X9

Interest is to be charged on drawings at the rate of 12 per cent per annum. Interest is allowed on capital accounts and credit balances on current accounts at the rate of 12 per cent per annum. Dark is to be allowed a salary of £15,000 per annum.

The net profit of the partnership for the year ended 31 May 19X9 is £102,940.

Required:

(a) A computation of the amount of interest chargeable on each partner's drawings for the year ended 31 May 19X9.

(b) The partnership appropriation account for the year ended 31 May 19X9.

(c) A computation of the balance on each partner''s current account as at 31 May 19X9. (AAT)

24.9. The partnership of Sewell, Grange and Jones has just completed its first year in business. The partnership agreement stipulates that profits should be apportioned in the ratio of Sewell 3, Grange 2 and Jones 1 after allowing interest on capital at 12 per cent per annum and crediting Sewell with a salary of £15,000.

The following information relates to their first financial year which ended on 31 October 19X0.

1. The partners introduced the following amounts as capital on 1 November 19X9:

	£
Sewell	50,000
Grange	40,000
Jones	20,000

2. Cash drawings during the year were:

	£
Sewell	3,900
Grange	4,500
Jones	2,400

3. The draft profit and loss account for the year showed a net trading profit of £61,720.

4. Included in the motor expenses account for the year was a bill for £300 which related to Grange's private motoring expenses.

5. No entries had been made in the accounts to record the following:

(a) As a result of a cash flow problem during April, Grange invested a further £10,000 as capital with effect from 1 May 19X0, and on the same date Jones brought into the business additional items of equipment at an agreed valuation of £6,000. In addition, in order to settle a debt Jones had privately undertaken some work for Foster, a creditor of the partnership. Foster accepted the work as full settlement of the £12,000 the partnership owed her for materials.

(b) Sewell had accepted a holiday provided by Miller, a debtor of the partnership. The holiday which was valued at £1,000 was accepted in full settlement of a debt of £2,500 that Miller owed to be partnership and that he was unable to pay.

(c) Each partner had taken goods for his own use during the year at cost as follows:

	£
Sewell	1,400
Grange	2,100
Jones	2,100

Note: It is the policy of the firm to depreciate equipment at the rate of 10 per cent per annum based on the cost of equipment held at the end of each financial year.

Required:

(a) The profit and loss appropriation account for the year ended 31 October 19X0 showing clearly the corrected net trading profit of the first year's trading.

(b) The capital and current accounts of Sewell, Grange and Jones for the year ended 31 October 19X0. (AEB)

24.10.* The following is the trial balance of Peace and Quiet, grocers, as at 31 December 19X8.

	Debit £	Credit £
Capital: Peace		10,000
Capital: Quiet		5,000
Current account: Peace		1,280
Current account: Quiet		3,640
Purchases/sales	45,620	69,830
Debtors/creditors	1,210	4,360
Leasehold shop at cost	18,000	
Equipment at cost	8,500	
Depreciation on equipment		1,200
Shop assistants' salaries	5,320	
Light and heat	1,850	
Stationery	320	
Bank interest and charges	45	
Stock	6,630	
Bank	3,815	
Drawings—Peace 1 May 19X8	2,200	
—Quiet 1 Sept 19X8	1,800	
	95,310	95,310

Additional information:

1. The stock at 31 December 19X8 was valued at £5,970.
2. There is electricity accrued at the end of the year of £60.
3. Stationery unused at 31 December 19X8 was valued at £50.
4. The equipment is depreciated at 10 per cent p.a. on the reducing balance method.

5. There is a partnership deed which says that each partner is to be credited with interest on capital at 10 per cent per annum; salaries of £6,200 per annum for Peace and £4,800 per annum for Quiet; interest on drawings of 8 per cent p.a. The remainder of the profit is to be divided equally between the partners.

6. Included in the capital of Peace is capital introduced of £1,000 on 1 April 19X8 and a loan to the partnership of £2,000 on 1 October 19X8.

You are required to prepare the profit and loss account and appropriation account for the year and a balance sheet at the 31 December 19X8.

24.11.* Peter and Paul, whose year end is the 30 June, are in business as food wholesalers. Their partnership deed states that:

(a)   profits and losses are to be shared equally;
(b)   salaries are Peter £20,000 per annum and Paul £18,000 per annum;
(c)   interest on capital of 10 per cent is allowed;
(d)   interest on drawings of 5 per cent is charged;
(e)   interest on loans from partners is given at the rate shown in the Partnership Act 1890.

The trial balance as at 30 June 19X8 is as follows:

	Debit £	Credit £
Capital—Peter		100,000
Paul		80,000
Current accounts—Peter	804	
Paul		21,080
Loan at 1 July 19X7—Peter		12,000
Freehold premises at cost	115,000	
Plant and machinery at cost	77,000	
Provision for depreciation on plant		22,800
Motor vehicles at cost	36,500	
Provision for depreciation on vehicles		12,480
Loose tools at 1 July 19X7	1,253	
Stock	6,734	
Debtors	4,478	
Creditors		3,954
Bank	7,697	
Electricity accrued at 1 July 19X7		58
Paid for electricity	3,428	
Purchases	19,868	
Sales		56,332
Warehouse wages	23,500	
Rates	5,169	
Postage and telephone	4,257	
Printing and stationery	2,134	
Provision for bad debts		216
Selling expenses	1,098	
	308,920	308,920

You also ascertain the following:

1. Stock at 30 June 19X8 is £8,264.
2. Depreciation by the straight line method is 10 per cent per annum on plant and machinery and 20 per cent per annum on motor vehicles. The latter are used by the administrative staff. The revaluation method of depreciation is used for loose tools. These have a value at 30 June 19X8 of £927.
3. Included in wages are drawings of £6,000 by Peter on 1 March 19X8 and £8,000 by Paul on 1 October 19X7.
4. The provision for bad debts at 30 June 19X8 is to be £180.
5. Debtors include bad debts of £240.
6. Sales include goods costing £160 which are on sale or return. The selling price of these is £200.
7. Electricity accrued at 30 June 19X8 amounts to £82.
8. Rates prepaid at 30 June 19X8 are £34.

You are required to prepare a profit and loss account and appropriation account for the year ended 30 June 19X8 and a balance sheet at that date. Present your answer in vertical form.

24.12.* Simon, Wilson and Dillon are in partnership. The following trial balance has been prepared on 31 December 19X9:

	Debit £	Credit £
Capital accounts—Simon		35,000
—Wilson		25,000
—Dillon		10,000
Current accounts—Simon		5,600
—Wilson		4,800
—Dillon	1,800	
Freehold land and buildings	65,000	
Stock	34,900	
Bank	10,100	
Delivery vehicles at cost	30,000	
Provision for depreciation on vehicles		18,000
Goodwill at cost	11,000	
8 per cent mortgage on premises		40,000
Salesmen's salaries	19,480	
Debtors' control account	28,000	
Creditors' control account		25,000
Unquoted investments	6,720	
Loose tools at valuation	1,200	
Sales		130,000
Investment income		800
Returns	400	600
Purchases	64,000	
Rates	12,100	

Motor expenses	2,800	
Provision for bad debts		400
Mortgage interest paid	1,600	
Printing and stationery	1,100	
Extension to premises	5,000	
	295,200	295,200

You are also given the following additional information:

1. The stock at 31 December 19X9 was valued at £31,000.
2. There is investment income accrued at 31 December 19X9 of £320.
3. The stock of stationery at 31 December 19X9 was £170.
4. At the same data there were motor expenses accrued of £240 and rates paid in advance of £160.
5. The provision for bad debts at 31 December 19X9 is to be adjusted to 2 per cent of the trade debtors.
6. Mortgage interest accrued should be provided for at the end of the year.
7. Depreciation on vehicles, on a strict time basis, is 10 per cent per annum using the straight line method.
8. The loose tools in stock at 31 December 19X9 were valued at £960.
9. The following errors have been found:

    (a) unrecorded in the ledger is the sale of a delivery vehicle on credit on 1 November 19X9 for £1,900—this vehicle cost £2,400 when it was purchased on 1 April 19X7;
    (b) bad debts for this year of £2,000 have not been written off;
    (c) bank charges of £130 have been omitted from the books.

Simon and Dillon are to be allocated salaries of £15,000 and £10,000 per annum respectively. All partners will be entitled to interest on capital of 10 per cent per annum. The remaining profit or loss is shared between Simon, Wilson and Dillon in the ratio of 2 : 2 : 1 respectively.

You are required to prepare in vertical form a profit and loss account and appropriation account for the year ended 31 December 19X9 and a balance sheet at that date.

24.13. A, B, C and D were partners in a garage business comprising (i) petrol sales, (ii) repairs and servicing and (iii) second-hand car dealing. A was responsible for petrol sales, B for repairs and servicing and C for second-hand car deals, while D acted purely in an advisory capacity.

The partnership agreement provided the following:

(i) Interest on fixed capital at 10 per cent per annum.
(ii) Each working partner to receive commission of 10 per cent of the gross profit of that partner's own department.
(iii) Profits were shared as follows: A: 2/10, B: 3/10, C: 3/10, D: 2/10.
(iv) Accounts to be made up annually to 30 September.

A trial balance extracted from the books at 30 September 19X8 showed the following balances:

		Dr £	Cr £
A	Capital account		3,500
	Current account		1,350
	Drawings account	6,000	
B	Capital account		7,500
	Current account		7,500
	Drawings account	13,250	
C	Capital account		6,500
	Current account		5,500
	Drawings account	10,500	
D	Capital account		12,500
	Current account		2,150
	Drawings account	3,500	
Freehold premises at cost		25,000	
Goodwill at cost		10,000	
Servicing tools and equipment at cost		9,000	
Servicing tools and equipment—accumulated depreciation to 1 October 19X7			1,350
Bank balance			10,105
Stocks at 1 October 19X7—Petrol		950	
	Spares	525	
	Second-hand cars	6,350	
Debtors		4,350	
Cash in hand		125	
Creditors			2,350
Sales—Petrol			68,650
	Servicing and repairs		86,750
	Cars		156,000
Purchases—Petrol		58,500	
	Spares	51,650	
	Second-hand cars	118,530	
Wages—Forecourt attendants		5,750	
	Mechanics	31,350	
	Car sales staff	8,550	
	Office personnel	1,850	
Rates		2,500	
Office expenses		1,800	
Heating and lighting		550	
Advertising		775	
Bank interest		350	
		371,705	371,705

The following additional information is obtained:

1. Stock at 30 September 19X8

	£
Petrol	1,050
Spares	475
Second-hand cars	9,680

2. Depreciation on tools and equipment is to be provided at 5 per cent per annum by the straight line method.
3. Your fees for preparation of the accounts will be £175.
4. The service department did work valued at £11,300 on the second-hand cars.
5. The service department used old cars valued at £550 for spare parts in services and repairs.

You are required to prepare:

(a) Trading and profit and loss account for the year ended 30 September 19X8.
(b) Balance sheet at 30 September 19X8.
(c) Partners' current accounts in columnar form for the year.   (ACCA)

24.14. (a) When accounting for the relationship of partners *inter se*, the partnership agreement provides the rules which in the first instance are to be applied.

What information would you expect to find in a partnership agreement to provide such rules, and what should you do if the agreement fails to deal with any aspect of the partnership relationship which affects the accounts?

(b) A, B, and C are in partnership, agreeing to share profits in the ratio 4 : 2 : 1. They have also agreed to allow interest on capital at 8 per cent per annum; a salary to C of £5,000 per annum; and to charge interest on drawings made in advance of the year end at a rate of 10 per cent per annum.

A has guaranteed B a minimum annual income of £6,500, gross of interest on drawings. The balance sheet as at 30 June 19X9 disclosed the following:

		£	£
Capitals	A	50,000	
	B	30,000	
	C	10,000	90,000
Current accounts	A	2,630	
	B	521	
	C	(418)	
			2,733
Loan account	A		15,000
Net capital employed			107,733

Drawings during the year were: A £6,400; B £3,100; C £2,000.
Net trading profit for the year to 30 June 19X0 was £24,750.
You are required to prepare the current accounts for the partners as at 30 June 19X0.   (ACCA)

24.15. Brick, Stone and Breeze carry on a manufacturing business in partnership, sharing profits and losses: Brick one half, Stone one third and Breeze one sixth. It is agreed that the minimum annual share of profit to be credited to Breeze is to be

£2,200, and any deficiency between this figure and her true share of the profits is to be borne by the other two partners in the ratio that they share profits. No interest is to be allowed or charged on partners' capital or current accounts.

The trial balance of the firm as on 30 June 19X0, was as follows:

	Dr £	Cr £
Stock on 1 July 19X9	7,400	
Purchases	39,100	
Manufacturing wages	8,600	
Salaries	5,670	
Rates, telephone and insurance	1,744	
Incidental trade expenses	710	
Repairs and renewals	1,250	
Cash discounts allowed	280	
Cash discounts received		500
Office expenses	3,586	
Carriage inwards	660	
Carriage outwards	850	
Professional charges	500	
Sales		69,770
Provision for doubtful debts as at 1 July 19X9		400
Provision for depreciation as at 1 July 19X9:		
Machinery and plant		2,500
Motor vehicles		1,300
Capital accounts:		
Brick		9,000
Stone		5,000
Breeze		4,000
Current accounts as at 1 July 19X9:		
Brick		1,900
Stone	500	
Breeze		400
Freehold buildings, at cost	9,800	
Machinery and plant, at cost	8,200	
Motor vehicles, at cost	2,500	
Bank balance	750	
Sales ledger balances	7,000	
Bought ledger balances		4,330
	99,100	99,100

The following information is given to you:

1. An amount of £3,000, for goods sent out on sale or return, has been included in sales. These goods were charged out to customers at cost plus 25 per cent and they were still in the customers' hands on 30 June 19X0, unsold.

2. Included in the item, repairs and renewals, is an amount of £820 for an extension to the factory.

3. Telephone and insurance paid in advance amounted to £424 and £42 was owing in respect of a trade expense.

4. A debt of £80 has turned out to be bad and is to be written off and the provision for doubtful debts is to be increased to £520.

5. Provision for depreciation on machinery and plant and on motor vehicles is to be made at the rate of 10 per cent and 20 per cent per annum respectively on the cost.

6. The value of the stock on hand on 30 June 19X0 was £7,238.

7. Each month Brick has drawn £55, Stone £45 and Breeze £20, and the amounts have been included in salaries.

You are required:

(a) to prepare the trading and profit and loss account for the year ended 30 June 19X0;

(b) to write up the partners' current accounts, in columnar form, for the year; and

(c) to draw up the balance sheet as on 30 June 19X0.   (ACCA)

24.16. A. Cherry owned a farmhouse and land, the latter being used by him and his sons, Tom and Leo, in carrying on a fruit and poultry business in partnership. The partnership agreement stipulated that the father should take one sixth of the profits, such to be not less than £1,200 per annum, the sons sharing the remainder equally.

The following are extracts from the trial balance of the business as on 31 December 19X1:

	Dr £	Cr £
Purchases: Poultry	216	
Feeding stuffs	3,072	
Sprays and fertilizers	1,451	
Spraying machine	460	
Wages	2,908	
General expenses (not apportionable)	842	
Sales: Fruit		6,022
Poultry		558
Eggs		5,843
Motor mower (cost £90 written down to £50)		46
Capital accounts: A. Cherry		6,450
Tom		3,340
Leo	840	
Drawings—A. Cherry	930	
Equipment at 1 January 19X1 at cost	3,420	
Equipment at 1 January provision for depreciation		1,510

Stocks on hand were as follows:

	31 Dec 19X0 £	31 Dec 19X1 £
Sprays and fertilizers	310	289
Poultry	320	154
Feeding stuffs	363	412

The following additional information is given to you:

1. Drawings by Tom and Leo have been £15 and £14 per week respectively, which amounts have been included in the wages account. Of the wages, one quarter is to be charged to the fruit department and three quarters to the poultry department.
2. The father and son Tom live in the farmhouse and are to be charged jointly per annum £30 for fruit, and £68 for eggs and poultry, such charges being shared equally. Leo is to be charged £38 for fruit and £62 for eggs and poultry.
3. Independent of the partnership, Leo kept some pigs on the farm and in respect of this private venture he is to be charged £140 for feeding stuffs and £40 for wages.
4. A. Cherry is to be credited with £360 for rent of the land (to be charged as to two thirds to the fruit and one third to the poultry departments), and Tom is to be credited with £84 by way of salary for packing eggs and dressing poultry.
5. Eggs sold in December 19X1 and paid for in January 19X2 amounted to £243 and this sum was not included in the trial balance.
6. An account to 31 December 19X1 for £24 was received from a veterinary surgeon after the trial balance had been prepared. This account included a sum of £14 in respect of professional work as regards Leo's pigs, which he himself paid.
7. Annual provision was to be made for depreciation on equipment at 10 per cent on cost at the end of the year.

You are required to prepare:

(a) a trading account (showing separately the trading profit on the fruit and poultry departments) and profit and loss and appropriation accounts for the year ended 31 December 19X1, and
(b) the partners' capital accounts in columnar form showing the balances as on 31 December 19X1.   (ACCA)

24.17. Field, Green and Lane are in partnership making up accounts annually to 31 March. Due to staff difficulties proper records were not maintained for the year ended 31 March 19X9, and the partners request your assistance in preparing the accounts for that year.

The balance sheet on 1 April 19X8 was as follows:

	£	£		£	£	£
Capital accounts			*Fixed assets*	*Cost*	*Depn.*	*Net*
Field	10,000		Fixed plant	15,000	6,000	9,000
Green	10,000		Motor vehicles	4,000	1,000	3,000
Lane	2,500		Fixtures and fittings	500	250	250
		22,500		19,500	7,250	12,250
Current accounts			*Current assets*			
Field	5,000		Stock in trade		19,450	
Green	2,000		Debtors		10,820	
Lane	500		Prepayments		250	
		7,500	Cash in till		75	30,595
		30,000				

	£	£		£
Current liabilities				
Trade creditors	5,350			
Accruals	1,125			
Bank overdraft	6,370			
		12,845		
		42,845		42,845

The accruals in the balance sheet comprised: audit fee £600, heat and light £400, and advertising £125. The prepayment of £250 was in respect of rates.

A summary of the bank statement provides the following information for the year to 31 March 19X9.

	£
Takings banked	141,105
Purchases	111,805
Wages	6,875
Rates and water	6,850
Heat and light	1,720
Delivery and travelling	3,380
Repairs and renewals	1,475
Advertising	375
Printing and stationery	915
Sundry office expenses	215
Bank charges	1,100
Audit fee	600

The following items were paid from the takings before they were banked:

Wages: cleaner £5 per week; van driver's mate £10 per week
Casual labour for the year: £555
Paraffin for shop heating: £445
Advertising: £75
Sundry office expenses: £515
Purchases for resale: £12,635
Hire of delivery vehicle: £20 per week
Partners' drawings per week: Field £40, Green £30, Lane £30.

You ascertain the following additional information:

1. The partners are allowed interest of 5 per cent per annum on their capital accounts.
2. Profits and losses are shared in the ratio Field 5, Green 3, Lane 2; with the proviso that Lane is guaranteed by Field an income of £3,000 per annum, excluding his interest on capital.
3. Certain goods had been appropriated by the partners during the year. The selling price of these goods was £460, allocated as follows: Field £235, Green £110, Lane £115.
4. Depreciation on fixed assets is to be provided at the following rates; fixed

plant 5 per cent, motor vehicles 25 per cent and fixtures and fittings 10 per cent, using the straight line method.

5. Accrued charges for heat and light at 31 March 19X9 were £450.
6. Rates of £750 were prepaid at 31 March 19X9.
7. Your charges for the 19X8/X9 audit were estimated at £650.
8. At 31 March 19X9, stocks were £22,345, debtors £11,415, trade creditors £5,920 and cash in till £100.

You are required to prepare:

(a) the partnership's trading and profit and loss account and profit and loss appropriation account for the year ended 31 March 19X9, and
(b) the balance sheet as at 31 March 19X9. (Movements in the partners' current accounts should be shown on the face of the balance sheet.)   (ACCA)

24.18. Scott and Gray are in partnership carrying on a business as retailers sharing profits and losses: Scott two thirds, Gray one third. The partners are entitled to interest on their fixed capitals at the rate of 8 per cent per annum. No interest is to be charged on drawings.

There is a head office with a shop attached, and a branch shop. All goods are purchased by head office, and goods sent to the branch are charged out at cost. Scott acts as buyer for the business, while Gray manages the head office shop. Byron is employed to manage the branch shop. Gray and Byron are entitled to a commission based on the profits of the shop under their control. The commission is to be 10 per cent of the profits after charging such commission.

The trial balance as on 31 March 19X2 was as follows:

	Head office Dr £	Head office Cr £	Branch Dr £	Branch Cr £
Furniture, fixtures and fittings at cost	1,900		1,400	
Bank balances	930			1,920
Stock, 31 March 19X1	16,000		5,600	
Sundry debtors	8,500		3,700	
Sundry creditors		7,100		500
Purchases	45,000			
Sales		46,900		31,520
Goods sent to branch		21,860	21,560	
Trade expenses	4,000		2,200	
Wages and salaries	5,500		3,980	
Postage, carriage and travelling expenses	2,700		1,210	
Drawings and fixed capital accounts:				
Scott	3,300	15,000		
Gray	2,000	6,000		
Branch and head office current accounts	8,400			5,000
Provision for depn. of furniture, fixtures and fittings		640		460
Provision for doubtful debts		730		250
	98,230	98,230	39,650	39,650

The following additional information is given to you:

1. Stocks valued at cost on 31March 19X2, were: head office £18,163, branch £7,840.
2. Depreciation on furniture, fixtures and fittings is to be provided at 10 per cent of cost.
3. Goods charged out at £300 on 31 March 19X2 had been recorded in the head office books but were not received at the branch until after that date. These goods did not appear in the books at the branch, and had not been included in the stock-take. On the same date the branch had sent cash of £3,100 to head office. This payment had been entered in the branch books, but had not been recorded in the head office books. Any adjustments required are to be made in the head office books.
4. The provision for doubtful debts as regards head office debtors is to be decreased to £700, and increased to £300 as regards those of the branch.

You are required to:

(a) prepare trading and profit and loss accounts showing the net profit of the head office and branch respectively, also the appropriation account for the year ended 31 March 19X2;
(b) draw up the balance sheet as on that date; and
(c) show the closing entries in the branch current account and an analysis of the closing balance on that account.   (ACCA)

25. Changes in partnerships

Learning objectives

After reading this chapter the student should be able to:

1. Explain the meaning of the key terms and concepts listed at the end of the chapter.
2. Discuss the nature, valuation and accounting treatment of goodwill.
3. Compute the value of goodwill.
4. Show the journal and ledger entries for the admission of a new partner and/or an outgoing partner including those relating to goodwill and the effects of a revaluation of assets.
5. Show the journal and ledger entries relating to a change in partners' profit sharing ratio including the appropriation of profits in the year of the change.
6. Prepare the balance sheet of a partnership immediately after a change in partners or profit sharing ratio.
7. Show the journal and ledger entries to close the books on a dissolution of partnership.

Introduction

When a partner leaves a partnership due to, for example, retirement or death, or whenever a new partner is admitted, it has the effect of bringing the old partnership to an end and transferring the business to a new partnership. The retiring partner(s) will want to take out their share of the business assets and any new partner(s) may be expected to introduce capital. Furthermore, a new profit sharing agreement must be made. The situation would be relatively simple, in accounting terms, if three conditions could be met:

1. The separate assets and liabilities of the business are all included in the accounts at values the partners agree to be current.
2. No account is taken of 'goodwill'.
3. The change occurs at the end of the year.

The difficulties which arise when these conditions do not apply (which is nearly always) will be discussed later in this chapter. The term goodwill has special significance in accounting and explanation of this is also introduced later.

As explained above, when a partner leaves and/or a new partner is admitted, the law states that the old partnership is dissolved and a new partnership is created. The new partnership frequently takes over the assets and liabilities of the old partnership, normally retains the name of the old partnership (with perhaps a minor amendment to reflect the change of partners), and thus from the perspective of third parties often has the appearance of being a continuing business. For these reasons the partnership usually continues to use the same set of books of account with various adjustments to the capital and current accounts to reflect the change of partners. These are described below.

Retirement of a partner

This can be considered initially using the simplifying assumptions 1, 2 and 3 set out above. The first step in dealing with the retirement of a partner is to ensure that the accounts are complete at the date of retirement, including crediting the partner's current account with the partner's share of profit and debiting the current account with the partner's drawings to this date. The retiring partner's share of the partnership assets is then represented by the sum of the balances on his or her current and capital accounts. As soon as the individual ceases to be a partner, that person no longer has capital invested in the partnership and must thus be treated as a loan creditor. The balances on the former partner's current and capital accounts are, therefore, transferred to a loan account in the individual's name. This loan is eliminated either by one payment, or alternatively there may be a clause in the partnership agreement to make repayment by instalments over time. Since the person is no longer a partner, any interest payable on this loan is an expense of the partnership to be charged in the profit and loss account and not an appropriation of profits as in the case of interest on loans made by partners.

The accounting entries relating to the retirement of a partner are illustrated in Example 25.1.

Example 25.1
Britten, Edwards and Howe are partners sharing profits equally after interest on partners' loans of 5 per cent per annum. Edwards retires on 1 Jan 19X9 and is to be repaid one year later. Interest on money due to her is to be at 8 per cent per annum.

The balance sheet at 31 December 19X8 was summarized as below, before the appropriation of profit:

	£	£
Capital accounts		
Britten		10,000
Edwards		6,000
Howe		5,000
		21,000
Current accounts		
Britten	1,000	
Edwards	1,500	
Howe	1,100	3,600
Profit and loss account—profit for year		1,000
		25,600
Partners' loan from Edwards		2,000
		27,600
Total assets less current liabilities		27,600

First the appropriation of profits should be carried out as follows:

	B £	E £	H £	Total £
Profit for year				1,000
Interest on loan @ 5 per cent		100		(100)
				900
Balance shared equally	300	300	300	(900)
	300	400	300	—

The journal and ledger entries in respect of Edwards' share of profits will be as follows:

		£	£
Profit and loss appropriation account	Dr	400	
Current account—Edwards			400

This produces a balance on Edwards' current account of £1,500 + £400 = £1,900. The balances on the retiring partner's capital, current and loan accounts are then transferred to a new loan account as shown by the following journal entries:

		£	£
Capital account—Edwards	Dr	6,000	
Current account—Edwards	Dr	1,900	
Partners' loan account—Edwards	Dr	2,000	
Loan account—Edwards			9,900
		9,900	9,900

After crediting the other partners' current accounts with their share of profits the balance sheet on 1 January 19X9 after Edwards' retirement will be as follows:

	£	£
Capital accounts		
Britten		10,000
Howe		5,000
		15,000
Current accounts		
Britten	1,300	
Howe	1,400	
		2,700
		17,700
Total assets less current liabilities		27,600
Less: Loan—Edwards		9,900
Net assets		17,700

The revaluation of assets on changes in partners

Learning activity 25:1

Imagine you are in business with assets and capital of £100,000. You decide to admit me to your business as a partner. I will bring in capital of £100,000 in cash, and we will share profits and losses equally. The assets of your old business have a market value of £150,000, but we have agreed that they will remain in the books at their historic cost of £100,000 on the grounds of prudence. The day after my admission I give you notice to dissolve our partnership, and the assets of your old business are sold for £150,000. The profit of £150,000 − £100,000 = £50,000 must be shared equally, and thus our capital is now £100,000 + £25,000 = £125,000 each. This is repaid in cash and I therefore walk away with a gain of £25,000 after only having been a partner for two days.

Describe your feelings about the way in which the profit on realization of the assets has been shared, and whether in retrospect you would have done anything differently. The answer is given later in the text.

The values of assets and liabilities shown in the ledger and the balance sheet (i.e. the book values) are not normally the current market values. Therefore, when a new partner is admitted to a business or an existing partner dies or retires it is usually necessary to revalue all the assets and liabilities. The reason for this revaluation is that since assets are normally shown in the accounts at their historic cost there will be *unrealized holding gains and losses* which have not been recorded in the books (e.g. arising from an increase in the market value of property since the date of purchase). These must be taken into account by means of a *revaluation*, and each partner's capital account credited with their share of the unrealized gains (or debited with their share of any unrealized losses).

Thus when an existing partner dies or retires, the revaluation ensures that the former partner receives his or her share of any unrealized holding gains. Similarly when a new partner is admitted the revaluation is necessary to ensure that the old partners receive recognition of their shares of the unrealized holding gains. If this was not done the new partner would be entitled to a share of these gains when they were eventually realized despite the fact they arose prior to the partner's admission to the partnership.

Learning activity 25.1—answer

You should not have agreed to the assets remaining in the books at their historic cost. The whole of the difference between their market value and historic cost belongs to you. The prudence concept does not apply because the assets of your old business were sold to the new partnership, and thus the gain was realized. You should have brought the revaluation of the assets into the books before admitting me as a partner. That way the whole of the gain would have been credited to your capital account.

An illustration of the ledger entries relating to the revaluation of assets on changes in partners is given in Example 25.2.

Example 25.2

Bill and Harry are in partnership sharing profits equally. On the 1 July 19X1 Harry retired and Jane was admitted as a partner who is to contribute cash of £9,000 as capital. Future profits are to be shared, Bill three fifths and Jane two fifths.

The balance sheet at the 30 June 19X1 was as follows:

	£	£		£	£	£
Capital accounts			*Fixed assets*	*Cost*	*Dep.*	*WDV*
Bill		17,000	Plant	13,500	3,300	10,200
Harry		17,500	Fixtures	10,500	2,700	7,800
		34,500		24,000	6,000	18,000
Current accounts			*Current assets*			
Bill	4,800		Stock		13,800	
Harry	2,100	6,900	Debtors		9,450	
			Cash		3,900	27,150
Current liabilities						
Creditors		3,750				
		45,150				45,150

It was decided that stock is to be valued at £12,000 and fixtures at £13,050 (before deducting depreciation). Of the trade debtors, £1,350 are considered doubtful debts.

The ledger entries relating to the above revaluation and change of partners are required.

It is necessary first to set up a revaluation account in the ledger and enter the increases and decreases in value of all the assets. The resulting profit or loss on revaluation must then be shared between the old partners in their old profit sharing ratio and entered in their capital accounts. The cash introduced by the new partner is simply credited to her capital account. This is shown below.

Fixtures

Balance b/d	10,500		
Revaluation a/c	2,550		
	13,050		

Stock

Balance b/d	13,800	Revaluation a/c	1,800
		Balance c/d	12,000
	13,800		13,800
Balance b/d	12,000		

Provision for bad debts

		Revaluation account	1,350

Revaluation account

Write down of stock	1,800	Write up of fixtures		2,550
Provision for bad debts	1,350	Loss on revaluation—		
		Capital Bill	300	
		Capital Harry	300	600
	3,150			3,150

Capital

	Bill	Harry	Jane		Bill	Harry	Jane
Revaluation a/c	300	300	—	Balance b/d	17,000	17,500	—
Balance c/d	16,700	17,200	9,000	Bank	—	—	9,000
	17,000	17,500	9,000		17,000	17,500	9,000
				Balance b/d	16,700	17,200	9,000

Finally, the transfers in respect of Harry's capital and current accounts must be made, which would involve the following journal entry:

Capital account—Harry	Dr	17,200	
Current account—Harry	Dr	2,100	
Loan account—Harry			19,300
		19,300	19,300

So far, consideration has been given to situations where any deceased or retiring partners' capital accounts have credit balances and the remaining partners are required to make payments to them. If there is a debit balance on a capital account, a retiring partner will be due to pay this to the partnership. However, if the retiring partner is unable to make this payment, there will be a deficiency to be shared among the remaining partners. The partnership agreement may specify how this sharing is to take place. In the absence of such an agreement, then the precedence of a court ruling in the case of Garner v. Murray will apply under English law. Under this rule, the deficiency is shared in proportion to the partners' credit balances on their capital accounts at the last balance sheet date before the retirement. Subsequent revaluations are not taken into account in calculating these proportions nor are profit sharing ratios.

The nature of goodwill

The precise nature of goodwill is difficult to define in a theoretically sound manner. However, it is generally recognized that goodwill exists, since a value is normally attached to it when a business is purchased. Goodwill usually arises in the accounts where another business has been purchased at some time in the past. Its value frequently takes the form of the excess of the purchase price of the other business over the market value of its net assets. The existence of this excess shows that the purchaser of a business is prepared to pay for something in addition to the net assets. Goodwill is the label given to that something. Thus in *Statement of Standard Accounting Practice 22—Accounting for Goodwill*,[1] goodwill is defined as 'the difference between the value of a business as a whole and the aggregate of the fair values of its separable net assets'. Goodwill is therefore by definition incapable of realization separately from the business as a whole. Separable/identifiable net assets are the assets and liabilities of an entity that are capable of being disposed of or settled separately, without necessarily disposing of the business as a whole. Fair value is the amount at which an asset or liability could be exchanged in an arm's length transaction.

Where the value of a business as a whole exceeds the total value of its separable net assets this is sometimes described as *positive goodwill*. Where the value of a business as a whole is less than the total value of its separable net assets this is referred to as *negative goodwill*. This usually arises where a business is expected to make future losses because of a poor reputation, etc.

Most ongoing businesses are normally worth more as a going concern than is shown by the value of their net tangible assets. Otherwise it would probably be better to shut the business down and sell the separate assets. From this standpoint, goodwill may be said to represent the present value of the future profits accruing from an existing business. Thus goodwill arises from a number of attributes that an ongoing business possesses such as the following:

1. The prestige and reputation attaching to the name of a business or its products and thus the likelihood that present customers will continue to buy from the business in future (e.g. Rolls-Royce cars, Levi jeans, Marks & Spencer quality).
2. Existing contracts for the supply of goods in the future (e.g. construction, aerospace, defence equipment, etc.).
3. The location of the business premises (e.g. a newsagent next to a railway station) and other forms of captive customers (e.g. a milk distributor's clientele).
4. The possession of patents, trademarks, brand names and special technical knowledge arising from previous expenditure on advertising and research and development. However, some of these may be accounted for as separate assets.
5. The existence of known sources of supply of goods and services including the availability of trade credit.
6. The existing staff including particular management skills. The costs of recruiting and training present employees give rise to an asset that is not recorded in the balance sheet but nevertheless represents a valuable resource to the business. Furthermore, these costs would have to be incurred if a business was started from scratch.
7. Other set-up factors. An existing business has the advantage of having collected together the various items of equipment and other assets necessary for its operations. Obtaining and bringing together these assets usually involves delay and expense, and avoiding this is an advantage of an ongoing business.

Goodwill is classified as either purchased or non-purchased. *Purchased goodwill* is defined in *Financial Reporting Standard 10—Goodwill and Intangible Assets*[2] as 'the difference between the cost of an acquired entity and the aggregate of the fair values of that entity's identifiable assets and liabilities'. It thus essentially refers to the amount paid for goodwill when one business takes over another business. *Non-purchased goodwill* is defined in SSAP22 as 'any goodwill other than purchased goodwill'. It thus essentially refers to what is sometimes described as the inherent or internally generated goodwill of a business that has not been the subject of a takeover.

The recognition of goodwill in accounts

As explained above, all businesses possess either positive or negative goodwill. However, this may or may not be recorded in the books and thus appear on the balance sheet as an intangible fixed asset. FRS10, which superseded SSAP22, states that 'positive purchased goodwill should be capitalized and classified as an asset on the balance sheet'.[2] It specifically prohibits internally generated, i.e. non-purchased goodwill, being recognized as an asset. The main reason for this is that the valuation of non-purchased goodwill is regarded as highly subjective and thus contravenes the objectivity concept.

Although the accounts of sole traders and partnerships do not have to be prepared in accordance with accounting standards, it is nevertheless highly unlikely that these will include goodwill except possibly when another business has been purchased. In the case of a partnership this includes where a new partner is admitted or an existing partner retires or dies. The law states that in each instance the old partnership is dissolved, and thus effectively taken over by the new partnership. The accounts of the new partnership may therefore include goodwill acquired from the purchase of the old partnership. This is examined in detail later in the chapter.

The current established thinking is that the value of goodwill declines with the passage of time and therefore has a finite life. Thus, like most other fixed assets, when purchased goodwill is recorded in the accounts it should be amortized (i.e. depreciated) over its useful economic life. An alternative approach is to write it off immediately against the partners' capital (or reserves in the case of companies) at the time of purchase. This procedure will be described later. However, there is a school of thought that the value of goodwill can be perpetuated by, for example, expenditure on advertising, training, etc., and thus has an infinite life. It is therefore sometimes argued that it is not necessary to amortize goodwill.

SSAP22 allowed companies to write off positive purchased goodwill against reserves. However, this is now prohibited by FRS10, which requires companies to amortize positive purchased goodwill over its useful economic life. FRS10 further states that 'there is a rebuttable presumption that the useful economic lives of purchased goodwill and intangible assets are limited to periods of 20 years or less. This presumption may be rebutted and a useful economic life regarded as a longer period or indefinite only if: (a) the durability of the acquired business or intangible asset can be demonstrated and justifies estimating the useful economic life to exceed 20 years; and (b) the goodwill or intangible asset is capable of continued measurement (so that annual impairment reviews will be feasible)'. In these circumstances positive purchased goodwill may be amortized over a useful economic life greater than 20 years, or if this is indefinite, should not be amortized. However, where this is the case an annual impairment review must be undertaken. In simple terms, this is essentially a revaluation to ensure that the value of goodwill has not fallen below its book/carrying value.

Finally, FRS10 states that 'no residual value may be assigned to goodwill', and 'a straight-line method should be chosen unless another method can be demonstrated to be more appropriate'.

The valuation of goodwill

As explained previously, the cost of purchased goodwill is deemed to be the excess of the purchase price of a business over the market/fair value of its net assets. In the case of company accounts the value of goodwill is usually computed in precisely this manner. However, in the case of sole traders and partnerships the purchase price of a business is frequently arrived at by valuing the net tangible assets (often at market prices) and, as a separate item, goodwill. This is particularly common where a new partner is admitted or an existing partner leaves.

There are a number of methods of valuing goodwill. These reflect the customs/conventions of businesses generally and certain trades and professions in particular. It should be emphasized that in practice the amount arrived at using one of these methods is frequently regarded as a starting point in negotiating a final value for goodwill. The most common methods are as follows:

1. A given multiple of the annual turnover. The multiple is intended to represent the number of years' future sales that are likely to result from the goodwill presently attaching to the business. The turnover may be an estimate of future sales, or more likely an average of a given number of past periods. This method is common in the case of retail businesses and professional firms such as accountants, solicitors, etc.
2. A given multiple of the annual profit. Again the multiple is intended to represent the number of years' future profits that are likely to be generated from the existing goodwill. The annual profit may be either an estimate of the future profit or more likely an average of a given number of past years. The profits used in the computation may be those shown in the audited accounts or alternatively what is termed the *abnormal or super profit*. This refers to the profit shown in the accounts minus a notional charge for interest on capital and proprietors' salaries. The super profit is intended to represent the return from risking money in a business over and above what could be earned by depositing that money elsewhere at a fixed rate of interest and taking employment with a guaranteed salary. This method of valuing goodwill may be particularly appropriate in riskier industries with fluctuating profits such as engineering and building construction.
3. The excess of the capitalized value of the (past or forecasted) annual (average) profit (or super profit) over the current (market) value of the net tangible assets of the business. The capitalized value is normally computed by multiplying the annual profit by the average price–earnings (P–E) ratio of similar size companies in the same industry whose shares are listed on the stock exchange. The capitalized value is intended to reflect the total value of the business as a going concern. This method may be most appropriate in the case of a large business that is not a company or whose shares are not quoted on a stock exchange. It is a common method of valuing unquoted companies such as for inheritance tax purposes.

The admission of a new partner and the treatment of goodwill

When a new partner is admitted to a partnership the value of the assets introduced into the business will be debited to the relevant asset accounts and credited to the new partner's capital account. Furthermore, an adjustment to the old partners' capital accounts is necessary to recognize the value of goodwill which they have created and therefore belongs to them. The principle is exactly the same as with the revaluation of assets except that the goodwill has not previously been recorded in the books. There are three main ways of dealing with this, each of which is described below and illustrated using Example 25.3.

Example 25.3
A and B are in partnership sharing profits in the ratio 3 : 2. The balances on their capital accounts are: A £15,000 and B £20,000.

On 31 December 19X8 they decide to admit C as a partner who is to bring in £42,000 as her capital and receive half of all future profits. The old partners' profit sharing ratio will continue to be 3 : 2.

Goodwill is to be calculated at twice the average super profits of the last three years. The super profits are after charging interest on capital of 5 per cent per annum and partners' salaries of £12,500 per annum each.

The profits transferred to the profit and loss appropriation account are as follows:

	£
Year ended 31/12/X6	28,560
Year ended 31/12/X7	29,980
Year ended 31/12/X8	32,210

The value to be ascribed to goodwill would first be calculated as follows:

Year ended	Net profits	Salaries	Interest on capital	Super profits
31/12/X6	28,560	25,000	1,750	1,810
X7	29,980	25,000	1,750	3,230
X8	32,210	25,000	1,750	5,460
				10,500

$$\text{Goodwill} = 2 \times \frac{£10,500}{3} = £7,000$$

Note that the new profit sharing ratio will be A3:B2:C5. This can be explained thus: since C is to receive one half of all future profits, A's share will be 3 divided by 3 + 2 multiplied by the remaining one half (i.e. $3/5 \times 1/2 = 3/10$). Similarly B's share will be $2/5 \times 1/2 = 2/10$. Thus the new profit sharing ratio is A 3/10, B 2/10 and C 5/10; or A3:B2:C5.

The different methods of treating goodwill on the admission of a new partner can now be shown as follows:

Method 1

The value of goodwill is debited to a goodwill account and credited to the old partners' capital accounts in their old profit sharing ratio. This method recognizes the existence of the previously unrecorded asset of goodwill by bringing it into the books. The goodwill is shared between the old partners in their old profit sharing ratio because it is an asset created by the old partnership which thus belongs to the old partners.

Goodwill

19X8		
31 Dec	Capital A	4,200
31 Dec	Capital B	2,800
		7,000

Capital

		A	B	C
19X8				
31 Dec	Balance b/d	15,000	20,000	—
31 Dec	Bank	—	—	42,000
31 Dec	Goodwill	4,200	2,800	—

Method 2

Earlier in this chapter it was pointed out that goodwill should be amortized over its useful economic life, or alternatively written off against the partners' capital accounts. In Method 1 above the goodwill would be amortized. Method 2 is the alternative treatment. The value of goodwill is first debited to a goodwill account and credited to the old partners' capital accounts in their old profit sharing ratio (as in Method 1). Then the goodwill is written off by crediting the goodwill account and debiting all the partners in the new partnership in their new profit sharing ratio. The debit to the partners' capital accounts is in their new profit sharing ratio because the writing off of goodwill effectively amounts to recognizing a (paper) loss that would otherwise have been charged to future years' profit and loss accounts (as the amortization of goodwill) and thus shared between the new partners in their new profit sharing ratio.

Goodwill

19X8			19X8		
31 Dec	Capital A	4,200	31 Dec	Capital A	2,100
31 Dec	Capital B	2,800	31 Dec	Capital B	1,400
			31 Dec	Capital C	3,500
		7,000			7,000

Capital

	A	B	C			A	B	C
19X8				19X8				
31 Dec Goodwill	2,100	1,400	3,500	31 Dec Balance b/d	15,000	20,000	—
				31 Dec Bank	—	—	42,000
				31 Dec Goodwill	4,200	2,800	—

The entries in the goodwill account are a waste of time and paper, and thus Method 2 normally involves only the two sets of entries for goodwill on each side of the partners' capital accounts. Note that this method should be used when you are told that no account for goodwill is to be kept/maintained in the books or that goodwill is not to be recorded in the books.

It should also be observed that this method has the effect of charging the new partner with what is referred to as a premium of £3,500 in that her capital introduced has been reduced by £3,500. This premium represents the purchase by the new partner of her share of goodwill, i.e. 1/2 of £7,000 = £3,500. She will get this back when the goodwill is eventually realized (if the business is sold) or she leaves.

Method 3

This method is essentially a further shortcutting of Method 2. The net effects of the entries for goodwill in the partners' capital accounts in Method 2 are: C is debited with £3,500; A is credited with £4,200 − £2,100 = £2,100; and B is credited with £2,800 − £1,400 = £1,400. Method 3 consists of simply entering in the partners' capital accounts these net effects, which are referred to as a premium contra. The amount of the premium is debited to the new partners capital account and credited to the old partners capital accounts in their old profit sharing ratio: A 3/5 × £3,500 = £2,100 and B 2/5 × £3,500 = £1,400.

Capital

	A	B	C			A	B	C
19X8				19X8				
31 Dec Premium	—	—	3,500	31 Dec Balance b/d		15,000	20,000	—
				31 Dec Bank		—	—	42,000
				31 Dec Premium		2,100	1,400	—

This method should normally only be used where you are told that the new partner is to pay a premium representing the purchase of his or her share of goodwill. The premium is usually given but can be calculated from the goodwill. In this example the premium can be calculated as $1/2 \times £7,000 = £3,500$. The ledger entries would be as shown immediately above. It must be emphasized that this method only gives a correct answer where the old partners share profits (and losses) in the new partnership in the same ratio as the old partnership. If this is not the case, Method 2 must be used instead.

Sometimes it is not possible to compute the premium from the figure of goodwill because the partners have not agreed a method of valuation for goodwill. Instead you would be told something along the lines that the new partner receives an interest in the new partnership equity/assets which is less than the amount he or she is to invest/pay into the firm. Using the data in Example 25.3 this can be illustrated as follows. C is to be admitted as a partner with a one half interest in both capital and profits in exchange for £42,000. C's interest in the capital/assets is computed as follows:

	£
Capital/assets/equity of old partnership (£15,000 + £20,000)	35,000
Investment by C	42,000
Capital/assets/equity of new partnership	77,000
C's share of equity of new partnership	
(1/2 × £77,000)	38,500

The premium which C is being charged is therefore $£42,000 - £38,500 = £3,500$. The ledger entries will be similar to those in Method 3. However, these can be shortened to the following:

Journal

		£	£
Bank	Dr	42,000	
Capital—C			38,500
Capital—A			2,100
Capital—B			1,400
		42,000	42,000

Remember that this method only gives the correct answer where the old partners continue to share profits in the same ratio. If this is not the case Method 2 must be used which will require a notional figure for goodwill to be computed by multiplying the premium by the inverse of the new partner profit sharing ratio (i.e. $£3,500 \times 2/1 = £7,000$).

Finally, it should be mentioned that it is possible for the new partner to receive an interest greater than the amount he or she is to invest. This results in a negative premium, sometimes referred to as a bonus, and negative goodwill.

An outgoing partner and the treatment of goodwill

When a partner leaves, the balances on his or her capital and current accounts are repaid. However, it is necessary first to make an adjustment to the partners' capital accounts in recognition of the value of goodwill that has been created, some of which belongs to the outgoing partner. There are three main ways of dealing with this which correspond to Methods 1 to 3, respectively, of treating goodwill on the admission of a new partner.

1. The value of goodwill is debited to a goodwill account and credited to the old partners' capital accounts in their old profit sharing ratio.
2. The value of goodwill is credited to the old partners' capital accounts in their old profit sharing ratio and debited to the remaining partners' capital accounts in their new profit sharing ratio. This effectively results in the remaining partners purchasing the outgoing partners' share of goodwill. No goodwill account is maintained in the books.
3. The outgoing partner's share of goodwill is credited to his or her capital account and debited to the remaining partners' capital accounts in their new profit sharing ratio. Again no goodwill account is maintained in the books. This method only gives a correct answer where the remaining partners share profits in the new partnership in the same ratio as the old partnership. If this is not the case, Method 2 must be used instead.

Sometimes it is not possible to compute the outgoing partner's share of goodwill from the figure of goodwill, because the partners have not agreed a method of valuation for goodwill. Instead you would be told something along the lines that the outgoing partner is to receive more than the balance of his or her capital account. This excess is the outgoing partner's share of goodwill. If necessary, a notional figure for goodwill can be computed by multiplying this excess by the inverse of the outgoing partner's profit sharing ratio.

Incoming and outgoing partners and goodwill

We have thus far dealt with the revaluation of assets on changes in partners and the treatment of goodwill where there is either an incoming or outgoing partner. The final step is to combine all of these and examine the situation where there is both an incoming and outgoing partner. This is a fairly simple step since the treatment of goodwill involves exactly the same principles whether there is an incoming or outgoing partner. An illustration is given in the following example.

Example 25.4

Beech and Oak are in partnership, sharing profits and losses in the ratio 3 : 5 respectively. The balance sheet drawn up on 31 December 19X9 showed the following position:

	£			£	£
Capital accounts:			*Fixed assets:*		
Beech	11,000		Premises	16,000	
Oak	14,000		Fixtures	6,000	22,000
	25,000		*Current assets*		
Creditors	9,000		Stock	4,000	
			Debtors	3,000	
			Cash	5,000	12,000
	34,000				34,000

Beech retired as from 1 January 19X0 and at the same date Maple was admitted to the partnership. For the purpose of these changes, the premises were revalued at £19,500, fixtures at £4,500, stock at £5,800 and goodwill was agreed at £10,000. A provision for bad debts of £200 is also to be created. The new valuations are to be included in the business books but no account for goodwill is to be maintained. In the new partnership, profits and losses will be divided in the proportions 3 : 2 between Oak and Maple respectively. Maple will introduce cash of £15,000 and Beech is to receive payment for his capital in cash, but no other cash is to change hands between partners in implementing the change.

You are required to show the above changes in the revaluation account and the partners' capital accounts.

Revaluation account

Fixtures		1,500	Premises	3,500
Provision for bad debts		200	Stock	1,800
Profit on revaluation—				
Beech	1,350			
Oak	2,250	3,600		
		5,300		5,300

Capital accounts

	Beech	Oak	Maple		Beech	Oak	Maple
Goodwill contra	—	6,000	4,000	Balance b/d	11,000	14,000	—
Cash	16,100	—	—	Profit on			
Balance c/d	—	16,500	11,000	revaluation	1,350	2,250	—
				Goodwill contra	3,750	6,250	—
				Cash	—	—	15,000
	16,100	22,500	15,000		16,100	22,500	15,000

Notes

1. The double entry for the items in the revaluation account will be in the respective asset accounts and the provision for bad debts account.
2. The goodwill is credited to the old partners' capital accounts in their old profit sharing ratio (Beech ³/₈ × £10,000 = £3,750; Oak ⁵/₈ × £10,000 = £6,250) and debited to the new partners' capital accounts in their new profit sharing ratio (Oak ³/₅ × £10,000 = £6,000; Maple ²/₅ × £10,000 = £4,000).
3. The cash paid to Beech of £16,100 is the balance on his capital account after the revaluation of assets and adjustments for goodwill.

Changes in partners' profit sharing ratio

Sometimes partners decide to change the proportions in which they share profits and losses. This may occur when the partners agree that one partner is to spend more (or less) time on partnership business, or alternatively one partner's skills have become more (or less) valuable to the partnership.

If a change in the profit sharing ratio occurs at some time during the accounting year, it will be necessary to divide the profit before appropriations into the periods prior to and after the change. This is usually done on a time basis. The interest on capital and drawings, salaries and shares of residual profit are then computed for each period separately. It should be noted that this procedure also has to be followed when a new partner is admitted and/or a partner leaves during the accounting year.

When there is a change in the profit sharing ratio it is also necessary to revalue the assets including goodwill. As in the case of changes in partners, the profit or loss on revaluation is computed in a revaluation account and transferred to the partners' capital accounts. An adjustment must also be made in respect of goodwill, using the principles already described. A simple illustration is given in Example 25.5.

Example 25.5

X and Y are in partnership sharing profits and losses equally. They have decided that as from 1 October 19X5 the profit sharing ratio is to become X three fifths and Y two fifths.

The accounts are made up to 31 December each year. The profit for the year ended 31 December 19X5 was £60,000. The balance sheet at 31 December 19X5 prior to sharing profits is as follows:

	£
Net assets	210,000
Capital X	80,000
Capital Y	70,000
Profit for the year	60,000
	210,000

It was decided that the impact of the change in profit sharing ratio on each partner's share of the assets would be effected at 31 December 19X5 when the net assets were valued at £250,000. The goodwill was valued at £25,000 but no goodwill account is to be maintained in the books.

You are required to show the entries in the partners' capital accounts and a balance sheet at 31 December 19X5.

Distribution of profit 19X5

	£ Total	£ 1 Jan– 30 Sept	£ 1 Oct– 31 Dec
Profit for the year apportioned on a time basis	60,000	45,000	15,000
Shares of profit—X	31,500	22,500	9,000
—Y	28,500	22,500	6,000
	60,000	45,000	15,000

Revaluation account

Profit on revaluation—			Net assets	40,000
Capital X	20,000		(250,000−210,000)	
Capital Y	20,000	40,000		
		40,000		40,000

Capital accounts

	X	Y		X	Y
Goodwill contra	15,000	10,000	Balance b/d	80,000	70,000
Balance c/d	129,000	121,000	Shares of profit	31,500	28,500
			Profit on		
			revaluation	20,000	20,000
			Goodwill contra	12,500	12,500
	144,000	131,000		144,000	131,000
			Balance b/d	129,000	121,000

X and Y
Balance sheet as at 31 December 19X5

	£
Net assets	250,000
Capital X	129,000
Capital Y	121,000
	250,000

Dissolution of partnerships

As explained at the start of this chapter, when a partner leaves and/or a new partner is admitted the law states that the old partnership is dissolved and a new partnership is created. However, the phrase '*dissolution* of partnerships' refers to the circumstances where all the partners wish to leave, and thus the activities of the partnership are wound up without a new partnership being created. Partnerships are usually dissolved either because it is unprofitable to carry on trading or the partners no longer wish to be associated with each other for personal reasons.

Accounting for the dissolution of partnerships can be quite complicated when the assets are disposed of over a prolonged period of time, known as the piecemeal realization of assets, and/or one or more of the partners is insolvent, which may involve the application of the *Garner v. Murray* rule described in the previous section on the revaluation of assets. However, these circumstances are usually not examined at the foundation level, and are thus beyond the scope of this book. The basic model of accounting for the dissolution of partnerships is relatively simple, at least after grasping the previous contents of this chapter.

The chronological sequence of events on the dissolution of partnerships is as follows:

1. Prepare a set of final accounts from the end of the previous accounting year to the date of dissolution, including the usual entries in the partners current accounts. These will be no different from the usual final accounts apart from relating to a period of less than one year.
2. The assets will be disposed of usually by sale (although some may be taken over by the partners) and the money collected from debtors.
3. The liabilities are repaid in the order trade creditors, loans, and then any partners' loans.
4. The balances on the partners' capital (and current) accounts are paid to them.

At the foundation stage examinations the simplifying assumption is usually made that all of the above occurs on the date of dissolution or within a short period thereafter.

The simplest and a perfectly acceptable way of accounting for a dissolution is to transfer *all* of the balances on the asset (except bank/cash), liability, and provision accounts to a realization account. Then enter in it all the money received from the sale of assets (including that collected from debtors) and paid to trade and loan creditors. If any assets (or liabilities) are taken over by the partners, the value placed on these will be entered in the realization account with a double entry to the relevant partners capital accounts.

However, since liabilities such as trade creditors and loans are technically not realized, some accountants don't enter these in the realization account. Instead the amounts paid are entered in the relevant liability accounts, and any difference between the book values and amounts paid, such as discount received, are transferred to the realization account.

This highlights an important feature of the realization account concerning its purpose, and brings us to the next stage in the accounting procedure. The realization account performs a similar function to the revaluation account except that instead of being used to determine the profit or loss on revaluation, it is used to ascertain the profit or loss on dissolution. This is then transferred to the partners capital accounts in their profit sharing ratio.

Finally the balances on the partners current accounts are transferred to their capital accounts, and the resulting balances on the capital accounts are paid to the partners. This will eliminate the balance on the bank and cash accounts, leaving all the ledger accounts now closed. One last complication arises if the resulting balance on any of the partners capital accounts, before repaying the partners, is a debit balance. At the foundation level students are usually expected to assume that the partner is solvent and thus will pay to the partnership any debit balance on his/her capital account. This should then provide enough money with which to repay the other partners the credit balances on their capital accounts.

An illustration of accounting for the dissolution of partnerships is given in Example 25.6 below.

Example 25.6

Tom and Jerry, whose accounting year end is the 31 December, have been in partnership for several years sharing profits equally. Tom recently seduced Jerry's spouse and thus the partners are unable to work together. They have therefore decided to dissolve the partnership as on the 14 February 19X9. You have already prepared a profit & loss account for the period 1 January 19X9 to 14 February 19X9 and a balance sheet as at the latter date as follows:

	£	£	£
Motor vehicles			20,000
Less: provision for depreciation			6,600
			13,400
Stock		6,700	
Trade debtors	5,900		
Less: provision for bad debts	600	5,300	
Prepaid expenses		500	12,500
			25,900

Less: liabilities			
Trade creditors		3,200	
Bank overdraft		1,600	
Bank loan		2,000	
Loan—Tom		4,000	10,800
			15,100
Capital—Tom			8,000
—Jerry			4,200
			12,200
Current accounts—Tom		4,800	
—Jerry		(1,900)	
			2,900
			15,100

One of the motor vehicles was taken over by Jerry at an agreed valuation of £5,700. The remainder were sold for £6,200. The stock realized £7,100, and £4,900 was received from trade debtors. A refund of the full amount of prepaid expenses was also received.

There were selling expenses in respect of advertising the vehicles and stock for sale of £800. Trade creditors were paid £2,900 in full settlement. The bank loan was repaid including an interest penalty for early settlement of £400.

The partnership also sold its business name and a list of its customers to a competitor for £1,000.

You are required to show all the ledger entries necessary to close the partnership books.

Motor vehicles

Balance b/d	20,000	Realization	20,000

Provision for depreciation

Realization	6,600	Balance b/d	6,600

Stock

Balance b/d	6,700	Realization	6,700

Trade debtors

Balance b/d	5,900	Realization	5,900

Provision for bad debts

Realization	600	Balance b/d	600

Prepaid expenses

Balance b/d	500	Realization	500

Trade creditors

Bank	2,900	Balance b/d	3,200
Realization	300		
	3,200		3,200

Bank loan

Bank	2,400	Balance b/d	2,000
		Realization	400
	2,400		2,400

Loan—Tom

Bank	4,000	Balance b/d	4,000

Realization account

Vehicles	20,000	Prov. for depn.	6,600
Stock	6,700	Prov. for bad debts	600
Trade debtors	5,900	Bank—vehicles	6,200
Prepaid expenses	500	Bank—stock	7,100
Loan interest	400	Bank—debtors	4,900
Bank—expenses	800	Bank—prepayments	500
		Bank—goodwill	1,000
		Trade creditors	300
		Capital—Jerry	5,700
		Loss on realization—	
		Capital Tom	700
		Capital Jerry	700
	34,300		34,300

Current accounts

	Tom	Jerry		Tom	Jerry
Balance b/d	—	1,900	Balance b/d	4,800	—
Capital	4,800	—	Capital	—	1,900
	4,800	1,900		4,800	1,900

Capital accounts

	Tom	Jerry		Tom	Jerry
Current a/c	—	1,900	Balance b/d	8,000	4,200
Loss on			Current a/c	4,800	—
realization	700	700	Bank	—	4,100
Realization—					
vehicle	—	5,700			
Bank	12,100				
	12,800	8,300		12,800	8,300

Bank

Realization—		Balance b/d	1,600
vehicles	6,200	Trade creditors	2,900
stock	7,100	Bank loan	2,400
debtors	4,900	Realization—	
prepayments	500	expenses	800
goodwill	1,000	Loan—Tom	4,000
Capital—Jerry	4,100	Capital—Tom	12,100
	23,800		23,800

Summary

When a new partner is admitted to a partnership, an existing partner leaves, or there is a change in the profit sharing ratio, it is usually necessary to revalue all the assets and liabilities. This ensures that the existing/old partners receive their share of the unrealized holding gains (and losses) which arose prior to the change.

When the assets are revalued it is also usually necessary to make certain adjustments to the partners' capital accounts in respect of goodwill. This is defined in SSAP22 as 'the difference between the value of a business as a whole and the aggregate of the fair values of its separable net assets'. In the case of partnerships, goodwill is normally valued as a given multiple of the annual sales or profits. When there is a change of partners, goodwill is brought into the books by debiting a goodwill account and crediting the capital accounts of the existing/old partners in their old profit sharing ratio. The goodwill must either be amortized over its useful economic life, or alternatively, written off against the new partners' capital accounts in their profit sharing ratio. This latter treatment can be short-cut by means of adjusting entries on both sides of the partners' capital accounts.

Subsequent to the revaluation of assets and goodwill adjustments, when a new partner is admitted, the capital introduced is credited to his or her capital account. When a partner leaves, the balance on this partner's capital, current and any loan account is transferred to a new loan account, which is repaid in due course.

When a partnership activities cease there is a dissolution of the partnership. All the assets are realized and the liabilities paid. Any profit or loss on realization is ascertained via a realization account and transferred to the partners capital accounts. The balances on the partners capital and current accounts are then repaid.

Key terms and concepts

Abnormal/super profit, *Garner v. Murray*, goodwill, negative goodwill, non-purchased goodwill, positive goodwill, purchased goodwill, revaluation, unrealized holding gains/losses.

References

1. Accounting Standards Committee (1989). *Statement of Standard Accounting Practice 22–Accounting for Goodwill* (ICAEW).
2. Accounting Standards Board (1998). *Financial Reporting Standard 10–Goodwill and Intangible Assets* (ASB).

Exercises

An asterisk after the question number indicates that there is a suggested answer in the Appendix.

25.1. (a) Explain the nature of goodwill.
    (b) Describe the business attributes that are thought to give rise to goodwill.

25.2. (a) What is the difference between positive and negative goodwill?
    (b) What is the difference between purchased goodwill and non-purchased goodwill?

25.3. (a) Explain the circumstances in which goodwill might appear in the books of a partnership.
    (b) Describe how it would be treated in the balance sheet.

25.4. A member of the board of Shoprite Enterprises plc has suggested two accounting policies for consideration by the financial director in preparing the latest set of accounts. These have been summarized as follows:

  (i)   The incorporation of goodwill in the accounts as a permanent fixed asset in recognition of the favourable trading situations of several of the business's outlets and also to reflect the quality of management experience in the business.
  (ii) No depreciation to be provided in future on the buildings owned by the company, because their market value is constantly appreciating and, in addition, this will result in an increase of the profit of the company.

  Required:
  (a) Briefly explain you understanding of each of the following:
     (i)   goodwill;
     (ii) depreciation.
  (b) Discuss the acceptability of each of the above suggested accounting policies, highlighting any conflict with accounting concepts and standards.   (AEB)

25.5. Describe three different methods of valuing goodwill where the purchase price is unknown.

25.6. Al and Bert are in partnership, sharing profits equally. At 30 June, they have balances on their capital accounts of £12,000 (Al) and £15,000 (Bert). On that day they agree to bring in their friend Hall as a third partner. All three partners are to share profits equally from now on. Hall is to introduce £20,000 as capital into the business. Goodwill on 30 June is agreed at £18,000.

  Required:
  (a) Show the partners' capital accounts for 30 June and 1 July on the assumption that the goodwill, previously unrecorded, is to be included in the accounts.
  (b) Show the additional entries necessary to eliminate goodwill again from the accounts.
  (c) Explain briefly what goodwill is. Why are adjustments necessary when a new partner joins a partnership?   (ACCA)

25.7.* Brown and Jones are in partnership, sharing profits and losses equally. The balance sheet drawn up on 31 March 19X5 showed the following position:

	£		£	£
Capital accounts		*Fixed assets*		
Brown	110,000	Premises	80,000	
Jones	87,000	Fixtures	60,000	140,000
	197,000	*Current assets*		
Sundry creditors	98,000	Stock	40,000	
		Debtors	30,000	
		Cash	85,000	155,000
	295,000			295,000

Brown retired as from 1 April 19X5 and at the same date Smith was admitted to the partnership. For the purpose of these changes, the premises were revalued at £115,000, fixtures at £68,000, stock at £36,000 and goodwill was agreed at £90,000. A provision for bad debts of £3,000 is also to be created. The new valuations are to be included in the business accounts, but no account for goodwill is to be maintained. In the new partnership, profits and losses will be divided in the proportions 3 : 2 between Jones and Smith respectively. Smith will introduce cash of £100,000 and Brown is to receive payment for his capital in cash but no other cash is to change hands between partners in implementing the change.

You are required to show the above changes in the revaluation account and partners' capital accounts.

25.8.* Blackburn, Percy and Nelson are in partnership sharing profits equally. On 1 January 19X9 Nelson retired and Logan was admitted as a partner. Nelson has agreed to leave the amounts owing to her in the business as a loan until 31 December 19X9. Logan is to contribute £6,000 as capital. Future profits are to be shared, Blackburn one half and Percy and Logan one quarter each.

A goodwill account is to be opened and kept in the books. The goodwill should be valued at the difference between the capitalized value of the estimated super profits for the forthcoming year and the net asset value of the partnership at 31 December 19X8 after revaluing the assets. The capitalized value of the expected super profits is to be computed using the price–earnings ratio, which for this type of business is estimated as 8. The super profits are after deducting notional partners' salaries but not interest on capital. The net profit for 19X9 is estimated as £48,750 and it is thought that the partners could each earn £15,000 a year if they were employed elsewhere.

The balance sheet at 31 December 19X8 was as follows:

	£	£		£	£	£
Capital			*Fixed assets*	*Cost*	*Depn.*	*WDV*
Blackburn		10,000	Plant	9,000	2,200	6,800
Percy		8,000	Vehicles	7,000	1,800	5,200
Nelson		5,000				
		23,000		16,000	4,000	12,000

Current accounts			*Current assets*		
Blackburn	1,300		Stock	9,200	
Percy	1,900		Debtors	6,300	
Nelson	1,400	4,600	Cash	2,600	18,100
Current liabilities					
Creditors		2,500			
		30,100			30,100

It was decided that stock is to be valued at £8,000 and vehicles at £8,500 (before deducting depreciation). Of the trade debtors £900 are considered doubtful debts.

You are required to show the ledger entries relating to the above revaluation and change of partners.

25.9. Gupta, Richards and Jones are in partnership sharing profits and losses in the ratio 5:4:3. On 1 January 19X0 Richards retired from the partnership and it was agreed that Singh should join the partnership, paying a sum of £30,000. From this date, profits are to be shared equally between the three partners and, in view of this, Jones agrees to pay a further £10,000 into the partnership as capital.

The balance sheet at 31 December 19X9 showed:

	£	£
Fixed assets		
Property		60,000
Fixtures		30,000
		90,000
Current assets		
Stock	30,000	
Debtors	15,000	
Bank	5,000	
	50,000	
Creditors	10,000	40,000
		130,000
Capital accounts		
Gupta	60,000	
Richards	40,000	
Jones	25,000	
		125,000
Current accounts		
Gupta	1,000	
Richards	2,500	
Jones	1,500	5,000
		130,000

It was agreed that in preparing a revised opening balance sheet of the partnership on 1 January 19X0 the following adjustments should be made:

1. Property is to be revalued at £70,000 and fixtures are to be revalued at £32,000.
2. Stock is considered to be shown at a fair value in the accounts. A provision for doubtful debts of £1,200 is required.
3. Professional fees of £600 relating to the change in partnership structure are to be regarded as an expense of the year to 31 December 19X9, but were not included in the profit and loss account of that year. They are expected to be paid in March 19X0.
4. Goodwill of the partnership as at 31 December 19X9 is estimated at £30,000. No account for goodwill is to be entered in the books, but appropriate adjustments are to be made in the partners' capital accounts.
5. On retirement, Richards is to be paid a sum of £40,000. The balance owing to her will be recorded in a loan account carrying interest of 12 per cent, to be repaid in full after two years.
6. All balances on current accounts are to be transferred to capital accounts. All balances on capital accounts in excess of £20,000 after this transfer are to be transferred to loan accounts carrying interest at 12 per cent.

You are required to:

(a) compute the balances on the loan accounts of Richards and the new partners on 1 January 19X0, following completion of these arrangements;
(b) prepare an opening balance sheet for the partnership on 1 January 19X0, following completion of these arrangements;
(c) explain briefly *three* factors to be taken into account when establishing profit sharing arrangements between partners.   (JMB adapted)

25.10. Street, Rhode and Close carried on business in partnership sharing profits and losses, Street 5/12, Rhode 4/12 and Close 3/12.

Their draft balance sheet as on 31 March 19X9 was as follows:

	£	£		£	£
Capital accounts			Leasehold premises	8,000	
Street	8,500		*Less*: Amount written off	800	7,200
Rhode	6,000		Plant and machinery		
Close	4,500		at cost	9,200	
		19,000	*Less*: Provision for depn.	2,700	6,500
Current accounts					
Street	850		Stock on hand		5,400
Rhode	1,300		Sundry debtors	4,200	
Close	1,150		*Less*: Provision for		
		3,300	doubtful debts	750	3,450
Loan: Street		4,000	Cash at bank		8,000
Sundry creditors		4,250			
		£30,550			£30,550

Street retired from the partnership on 31 March 19X9 and Rhode and Close decided to carry on the business and to admit Lane as a partner who is to bring in capital of £10,000. Future profits are to be shared equally between Rhode, Close and Lane.

By agreement, the following adjustments were to be incorporated in the books of account as at 31 March 19X9:

1. Plant and machinery to be increased to £6,900, in accordance with a valuer's certificate.
2. Stock to be reduced to £4,860, since some items included therein were regarded as unsaleable.
3. The provision for doubtful debts to be increased to £830.
4. Provision to be made for the valuer's charges, £140.

The partnership deed provided that on the retirement of a partner the value of goodwill was to be taken to be the amount equal to the average annual profit of the three years ending on the date of retirement. The profits of such three years were:

Year ended 31 March 19X7 £7,800
Year ended 31 March 19X8 £9,400
Year ended 31 March 19X9 £11,600

The partners agreed that, in respect of the valuing of goodwill, the profits should be regarded as not being affected by the revaluation. It was decided that an account for goodwill should not be opened in the books, but that the transactions between the partners should be made through their capital accounts.

£3,000 was repaid to Street on 1 April 19X9 and she agreed to leave £12,000 as a loan to the new partnership. Rhode, Close and Lane promised to repay the balance remaining due to Street within six months.

You are required to prepare:

(a) the revaluation account;
(b) the partners' capital accounts (in columnar form);
(c) Street's account showing the balance due to her; and
(d) the balance sheet of Rhode, Close and Lane as on 1 April 19X9.

(ACCA adapted)

25.11. Matthew, Mark and Luke were in partnership sharing profits and losses in the ratio 5 : 3 : 2, accounts being made up annually to 30 June. Fixed capitals were to bear interest at the rate of 5 per cent per annum, but no interest was to be allowed or received on current accounts or drawings. Any balance on current accounts was to be paid at each year end.

Luke left the partnership on 30 September 19X6, but agreed to leave his money in the business until a new partner was admitted, provided interest at 5 per cent was paid on all amounts due to him.

John was admitted to the partnership on 1 January 19X7, providing capital of £2,000. It was agreed that the new profit sharing ratio be Matthew 5, Mark 4, John 1, but Mark was to guarantee John an income of £3,000 per annum in addition to his interest on capital.

At 1 July 19X6 each partner had a fixed capital of £4,000.

Drawings during the year 19X6/19X7 were as follows:

Matthew	£750
Mark	£600
Luke	£220 (to 30 September 19X6)
John	£80

The profit for the year to 30 June 19X7 was £20,000 which may be assumed to have accrued evenly over that period.

You are required to show:

(a) the profit and loss appropriation account, and
(b) the partners' current accounts for the year ended 30 June 19X7.   (ACCA)

25.12. Hawthorn and Privet have carried on business in partnership for a number of years, sharing profits in the ratio of 4 : 3 after charging interest on capital at 4 per cent per annum. Holly was admitted into the partnership on 1 October 19X4, and the terms of the partnership from then were agreed as follows:

1. Partners' annual salaries to be: Hawthorn £1,800, Privet £1,200, Holly £1,100.
2. Interest on capital to be charged at 4 per cent per annum.
3. Profits to be shared: Hawthorn four ninths, Privet three ninths, Holly two ninths.

On 1 October 19X4, Holly paid £7,000 into the partnership bank and of this amount £2,100 was in respect of the share of goodwill acquired by her. Since the partnership has never created, and does not intend to create, a goodwill account, the full amount of £7,000 was credited for the time being to Holly's capital account at 1 October 19X4.

The trial balance of the partnership at 30 June 19X5, was as follows:

	Dr	Cr
	£	£
Cash at bank	3,500	
Stock at 1 July 19X4	11,320	
Purchases	102,630	
Sales		123,300
Wages and salaries	6,200	
Rates, telephone, lighting and heating	2,100	
Printing, stationery and postage	530	
General expenses	1,600	
Bad debts written off	294	
Capital accounts: Hawthorn		22,000
Privet		11,000
Holly		7,000
Current accounts: Hawthorn	2,200	
Privet	1,100	
Holly	740	
Debtors and creditors	27,480	13,744
Freehold premises	12,000	
Furniture, fixtures and fittings at 1 July 19X4	5,800	
Bad debts reserve		450
	£177,494	£177,494

After taking into account the following information and the adjustment required for goodwill, prepare trading and profit and loss accounts for the year ended 30 June 19X5, and a balance sheet as on that date. On 30 June 19X5:

1. Stock was £15,000.
2. Rates (£110) and wages and salaries (£300) were outstanding.
3. Telephone rental paid in advance was £9.
4. Provision for bad debts is to be adjusted to 2½ per cent of debtors.
   Depreciation to be provided on furniture, fixtures and fittings at 10 per cent.
   Apportionments required are to be made on a time basis.   (ACCA)

25.13. Alpha, Beta and Gamma were in partnership for many years sharing profits and losses in the ratio 5 : 3 : 2 and making up their accounts to 31 December each year. Alpha died on 31 December 19X7, and the partnership was dissolved as from that date.

The partnership balance sheet at 31 December 19X7 was as follows:

Alpha, Beta and Gamma
Balance sheet as at 31 December 19X7

	Cost	Aggregate depreciation	Net book Value
	£	£	£
Fixed assets			
Freehold land and buildings	350,000	50,000	300,000
Plant and machinery	220,000	104,100	115,900
Motor vehicles	98,500	39,900	58,600
	668,500	194,000	474,500
Current assets			
Stock		110,600	
Trade and sundry debtors		89,400	
Cash at bank		12,600	
		212,600	
Less:			
Current liabilities—trade and sundry creditors		118,400	94,200
			568,700
Less:			
Long-term liability			
Loan—Delta (carrying interest at 10 per cent per annum)			40,000
			528,700
Capital accounts			
Alpha		233,600	
Beta		188,900	
Gamma		106,200	528,700
			528,700

In the period January to March 19X8 the following transactions took place and were dealt with in the partnership records:

		£
(1)	Fixed assets	
	Freehold land and buildings—sold for	380,000
	Plant and machinery—sold for	88,000
	Motor vehicles: Beta and Gamma took over the	
	cars they had been using at the following agreed values:	
	Beta	9,000
	Gamma	14,000
	The remaining vehicles were sold for	38,000
(2)	Current assets	
	Stock—taken over by Gamma at agreed value	120,000
	Trade and sundry debtors:	
	Cash received	68,400
	Remainder taken over by Gamma at agreed value	20,000
(3)	Current liabilities	
	The trade and sundry creditors were all settled for a total of	115,000
(4)	Long-term liabilities	
	Delta's loan was repaid on 31 March 19X8 with	
	interest accrued since 31 December 19X7	
(5)	Expenses of dissolution £2,400 were paid	
(6)	Capital accounts	
	The final amounts due to or from the estate of Alpha, Beta	
	and Gamma were paid/received on 31 March 19X8	

Required:

Prepare the following accounts as at 31 March 19X8 showing the dissolution of the partnership:

(a)   Realisation account
(b)   Partner's capital accounts
(c)   Cash book (cash account)

Ignore taxation and assume that all partners have substantial resources outside the partnership.   (ACCA)

26. The nature of limited companies and their capital

Learning objectives

After reading this chapter the student should be able to:

1. Explain the meaning of the key terms and concepts listed at the end of the chapter.
2. Describe the main characteristics of limited companies with particular reference to how these differ from partnerships.
3. Describe the different classes of companies limited by shares.
4. Outline the legal powers and duties of limited companies with reference to their Memorandum and Articles of Association.
5. Explain the nature and types of shares and loan capital issued by limited companies.
6. Outline the procedure relating to the issue of shares and debentures.
7. Explain the nature of a share premium, debenture discount, preliminary expenses, interim and final dividends.
8. Discuss the contents and purpose of the auditors' report.
9. Describe the contents of a company's statutory books.
10. Describe the purpose and proceedings of a company's annual general meeting.

Introduction

There are a large number of different legal forms of organization. However, these can be all grouped into two categories, known as bodies sole and bodies corporate. *Bodies sole* consist of sole traders and partnerships. All other forms of organization are bodies corporate. A key feature of *bodies corporate* is that they are recognized by law as being a legal entity separate from their members.

A body corporate is one which is created either by Royal Charter, such as The Institute of Chartered Accountants in England and Wales, or by Act of Parliament. The Act of Parliament may relate to either the creation of a specific organization, such as the British Broadcasting Corporation, or alternatively permit the creation of a particular form of legal entity by any group of individuals. The most common forms of legal entity which can be created under such Acts of Parliament include building societies, charities, clubs and companies.

A *company* can thus be defined as a legal entity which is formed by registration under the Companies Acts, the main one being the Companies Act 1985 as modified by the Companies Act 1989. There are four types of companies, which consist of companies whose liability is limited by shares, companies with unlimited liability, companies whose liability is limited by guarantee and companies limited by shares and guarantee. Companies limited by guarantee include organizations such as some professional bodies where the liability of its members is limited to the amount of their annual subscription. The remainder of this chapter deals with companies whose liability is limited by shares. These are commonly known as limited companies.

The characteristics of companies limited by shares

1. A company is a legal entity separate from its shareholders (owners). This means that companies enter into contracts as legal entities in their own right. Thus creditors and others cannot sue the shareholders of the company but must take legal proceedings against the company. This is referred to as not being able to lift the veil of incorporation.
2. A company has perpetual existence in that the death of one of its shareholders does not result in its dissolution. This may be contrasted with a partnership where the death of a partner constitutes a dissolution.
3. The liability of a company's shareholders is limited to the nominal value of their shares. *Limited liability* means that if a company's assets are insufficient to pay its debts the shareholders cannot be called upon to contribute more than the nominal value of their shares towards paying those debts.
4. The shareholders of a company do not have the right to take part in its management as such. They appoint directors to manage the company. However, a shareholder may also be a director (or other employee).
5. Each voting share carries one vote at general meetings of the company's shareholders (e.g. in the appointment of directors). There may be different classes of shares, each class having different rights and, possibly, some being non-voting.
6. A limited company must have at least two shareholders but there is no maximum number.

The classes of companies limited by shares

There are two classes of companies limited by shares, namely public and private. Under the Companies Act a *public limited company* must be registered as such and is required to have a minimum authorized share capital of £50,000. The principal reason for forming a public limited company is to gain access to greater amounts of capital from investment institutions and members of the public. The shares of many, but not all, public companies in the UK are therefore quoted on the International Stock Exchange, London.

All other limited companies are *private companies*. These are not allowed to offer their shares for sale to the general public and thus do not have a stock exchange quotation. One of the main reasons for forming a private rather than a public company is that it enables its owners to keep control of the business, for example, within the family.

The name of a public company must end with the words 'public limited company' or the abbreviation 'PLC'. The name of a private company must end with the word 'limited' or the abbreviation 'Ltd'. A business which does not have either of these descriptions after its name is not a limited company even if its name contains the word company (the only exception being certain companies which have private company status, such as charities, who are permitted under licence to omit the word limited from their name).

The legal powers and duties of limited companies

A company is formed by sending to the Registrar of Companies certain documents and the appropriate fee. The most relevant of these documents are the Memorandum and Articles of Association. These define a company's powers and duties. The *Memorandum of Association* contains:

1. The name of the company, which must end with the words 'public limited company' or 'limited'.
2. The address of the company's registered office.
3. A statement that the ordinary shareholders' liability is limited to the nominal value of their shares.
4. The objects of the company. These refer to the type of trade or industry in which the company will operate and are usually stated in very broad terms. A company must not engage in any trade or business that is not specific in its Memorandum of Association. If it does so the company is said to be trading *ultra vires*, that is beyond its powers, and any such contrast is void.
5. The authorized/nominal capital of the company. That is, the types, nominal value and maximum number of shares the company can offer for sale. This differs from the issued/allotted share capital, which refers to the actual number of shares that have been sold.
6. A statement that the company is either a public limited company or a private limited company.

Any of the above can be subsequently changed by a special resolution passed at a general meeting of the company's shareholders. Such a resolution requires at least 75 per cent of the votes cast.

The *Articles of Association* can best be described as a rule book which sets out the rights of a company's shareholders between themselves. It contains regulations relating to the issue of shares, conduct of meetings, borrowing powers, the appointment of directors, etc. The Companies Acts have provided a model set of articles known as Table A. A company may either make up its own articles or alternatively adopt those in Table A. Furthermore, where there is nothing in a company's articles relating to a particular matter, Table A will apply.

When a company is registered it is issued with what might be described as a birth certificate by the Register of Companies. This is called a *Certificate of Incorporation*. However, before a public limited company can commence trading it must satisfy the Registrar that certain regulations relating to its capital structure have been complied with. When this is done the Registrar issues a *Trading Certificate* on receipt of which the company can commence trading.

The costs of forming a company, including the above documents, are referred to as *preliminary, promotion or formation expenses*.

The nature and types of shares and loan capital

Companies are financed predominantly by the issue (sale) of shares, loan stock and debentures, and by retaining part of each year's profit. In the UK all shares, loan stock and debentures have a fixed *face/par or nominal value*. This is often £1 or 25 pence in the case of shares and £100 for debentures and loan stock. There are a number of different types of shares and loan capital, each of which is described below.

Ordinary shares

Possession of an ordinary voting share represents part ownership of a company and it entitles the holder to one vote in general meetings of the company's ordinary shareholders. This gives shareholders the power to appoint and dismiss a company's directors. The holder of an ordinary share is also entitled to a share of the company's annual profit in the form of a *dividend*. The amount of the dividend per share is decided each year by the company's directors and varies according to the amount of profit. In years when the company earns high profits the ordinary shareholders normally receive a large dividend. However, ordinary shareholders run two risks. Firstly, when profits are low they may receive little or no dividend. Secondly, should the company go bankrupt (into liquidation is the correct legal term) the ordinary shareholders are not entitled to be repaid the value of their shares until after *all* the other debts have been paid. Often, where a company has made substantial losses, there is little or nothing left for ordinary shareholders after the company has paid its other debts.

It should also be noted that a company does not normally repay its ordinary shareholders the money they have invested except in the event of liquidation (or by court order). If an ordinary shareholder wishes to sell his or her shares a buyer must be found. In the case of public companies whose shares are quoted on the International Stock Exchange, London, the seller may use this as a means of disposing of shares. Similarly, a prospective buyer may acquire 'second-hand' shares through the stock exchange.

Preference shares

Unlike ordinary shares, preference shares carry no voting rights. Preference shareholders are entitled to a fixed rate of dividend each year based on the nominal value of the shares. For example, 8 per cent preference shares with a nominal value of £1 each carry an annual dividend of eight pence per share. A company may make several issues of preference shares each of which can carry a different rate of dividend. Preference shareholders have priority over the ordinary shareholders in that their dividends are a prior claim against profit. The preference dividends are thus deducted before calculating the profit available for distribution to ordinary shareholders as dividends. Like ordinary dividends, the dividend on preference shares is classified as an *appropriation of profit*. The annual dividend on preference shares can be waived (but not varied) but the directors of companies usually try to avoid such drastic action, since it would be an indication of financial weakness.

In the event of a company going into liquidation, the preference shareholders are normally entitled to be repaid the nominal value of their shares before the ordinary shareholders. However, if no money is left after paying the other debts they would get nothing.

As in the case of ordinary shares, companies do not normally repay preference shareholders the money they have invested except in the event of liquidation. Should a preference shareholder wish to dispose of shares he or she must find a buyer or sell them through the International Stock Exchange, London, if the company has a quotation for the preference shares.

There are two advantages of preference shares from the point of view of a company. One is that, since the rate of dividend is fixed, the company knows in advance what its future annual commitment is in respect of preference dividends. The second advantage is that preference shares are a permanent source of long-term capital which does not have to be repaid. However, since the introduction of the corporation tax system in 1965 it has become unpopular to issue preference shares because the dividend is not an allowable charge against income for tax purposes, while interest on debt is allowable. This makes debt a relatively more attractive source of fixed return finance for most companies. Small companies may be able to take advantage of the tax rules applicable to them to offset this difference.

There are a number of different types of preference shares with rights which vary from those described above. These include:

1. *Cumulative preference shares*

   As explained above, if there is insufficient profit in any year a preference shareholder may receive no dividend. However, in the case of cumulative preference shares the holders will receive any such arrears of dividends (before any other shareholder gets a dividend) in the first subsequent year that there is sufficient profit to cover the dividend. Most of the preference shares quoted on the International Stock Exchange, London, are cumulative.

2. *Participating preference shares*

   In addition to receiving a fixed rate of dividend, holders of participating preference shares are entitled, along with the ordinary shareholders, to a share of the profit remaining after deducting preference dividends.

3. *Redeemable preference shares*

   These differ from other preference shares in that they are repayable by the company on a date fixed when the shares are issued. Because such a reduction in capital may endanger the creditor's interests, the Companies Act states that when a redemption takes place the company must either make a new issue of shares with the same total nominal value, or capitalize an equivalent amount of profits. Capitalization refers to a transfer of retained profits to a capital reserve. This means that the amount transferred cannot be distributed as dividends.

Debentures/loan stock

Debentures and loan stock are not shares and have no voting rights. They represent a loan to the company and carry a fixed rate of *interest* per annum based on the nominal value. For example, 10 per cent debentures with a nominal value of £100 each carry annual interest of £10 per debenture. A company may make several issues of debentures or loan stock, each of which can have a different rate of interest. Debenture holders are entitled to their interest before the preference and ordinary shareholders get their dividends, and it must be paid even if there is a loss. The interest on debentures is thus referred to as a charge against profit whereas dividends constitute an appropriation of profit.

In the event of a company going into liquidation the debenture holders are entitled to be repaid the nominal value of their debentures before the preference and ordinary shareholders. Such debentures are usually referred to as *unsecured* in that although they rank before the shareholders they are not entitled to be repaid until after all the other creditors. However, some issues of debentures are *secured* on certain of the company's assets by either a *fixed charge* or *floating charge*. A fixed charge is usually on specified assets such as property, plant or vehicles, and means that the company cannot dispose of those assets. A floating charge is usually on assets such as stock. In this case the company can sell the assets but must replace them with similar assets of an equivalent value.

When debentures are secured, an accountant or solicitor may be appointed by the company to act as a trustee for the debenture holders. It is the trustee's responsibility to ensure that the value of the assets is always sufficient to repay the debenture holders. If this is not the case, or that the company may not be able to pay the annual interest on the debentures, the trustee may take legal possession of the assets, sell them and repay the debenture holders. Such drastic action usually results in the company going into liquidation.

Debentures and loan stock are usually repayable at some future date, which is specified when they are issued. This date is often several decades after they are issued. Should debenture holders wish to dispose of their debentures they must find a buyer or sell them through the International Stock Exchange, London, if the company has a quotation for the debentures.

The main advantages of debentures to a company is that the annual interest on debentures is an allowable charge against income for tax purposes.

A comparatively recent variation on debentures that have proved popular is convertible *loan stock*. These are debentures with a fixed annual rate of interest that also carry the right, at the holder's option, to convert them into a specified number of ordinary shares within a given time period, which is fixed when they are issued. The attraction of convertible loan stock is that the holder hopes to make a capital gain on conversion at some time in the future by virtue of the conversion rate being such that the ordinary shares can be acquired at an effective cost which is lower than the market price at the date of conversion. Suppose, for example, a company issues £100 convertible loan stock at a price of £108, the rate of conversion being 90 ordinary shares for every £100 loan stock. At the date of the issue the ordinary shares are quoted on the stock exchange at a price of £1 each. If at some future date the market price of the shares rises to, say, £1.50 it is beneficial to convert, since the shares would effectively cost £1.20 each (i.e. £108 ÷ 90 shares) compared with a market price of £1.50. These could then be sold for 90 @ £1.50 = £135 to give a capital gain of £135 − £108 = £27. Where the effective cost is more than the current market price it would not be beneficial to convert and so the debentures should be retained.

A summary of the characteristics of shares and loan stock is given in Figure 26.1. A more detailed summary of the different types of preference shares and loan stock is shown in Figure 26.2.

The issue of shares and debentures

Shares can be, and usually are, issued (sold) by the company at a price in excess of their nominal value. The amount by which the issue price exceeds the nominal value is referred to as a *share premium*. In the case of a public limited company whose shares are listed on the stock exchange, the price at which the shares are quoted is usually different from both the nominal value and the issue price. The market price may be either above or below the issue price and the nominal value.

Debentures can be issued by the company at a price that is either greater or less than their nominal value. The latter is referred to as a *debenture discount*.

When shares and debentures are issued the price may be payable by instalments. These consist of amounts payable: (a) on application; (b) on allotment/allocation of the shares by the company; and (c) any number of further instalments, referred to as calls.

Public limited companies offer shares, loan stock and debentures for sale to members of the public by means of a document known as a *prospectus*. This usually takes the form of a booklet sent by the company to anyone who expresses an interest in the issue.

Ordinary/equity shares	*Preference shares*	*Loan stock/debentures*
1. Owners of the company who are normally entitled to vote at general meetings of the company's shareholders (e.g. to elect directors)	1. No voting rights	1. No voting rights
2. Receive a dividend the rate of which is decided annually by the company's directors. It varies each year depending on the profit and is an appropriation of profit.	2. Receive a fixed rate of dividend each year which constitutes an appropriation of profit. Have priority over ordinary dividends	2. Receive a fixed rate of interest which constitutes a charge against income in computing the profit. Have priority over preference dividends
3. Last to be repaid the value of their shares in the event of the company going into liquidation	3. Repaid before the ordinary shareholders in the event of liquidation	3. Repaid before the ordinary and preference shareholders in the event of liquidation
4. Non-repayable except on the liquidation of the company	4. All but one particular type are non-repayable except on liquidation	4. Normally repayable after a fixed period of time
5. Rights specified in Articles of Association	5. Rights specified in Articles of Association	5. Rights specified in the terms of issue
6. Dividends non-deductible for tax purposes	6. Dividends non-deductible for tax purposes	6. Interest deductible for tax purposes

Figure 26.1   A summary of the characteristics of shares and loan stock

Types of preference shares
(1)   Non-cumulative—do not receive arrears of dividends.
(2)   Cumulative—if the dividend on these shares is not paid in any year the holders are entitled to it in the next year that there is sufficient profit before any other shareholder receives a dividend.
(3)   Redeemable—the only type of preference share that is repaid by the company after the expiration of a period specified when they were issued
(4)   Participating—in addition to receiving a fixed annual rate of dividend they are also entitled to a further dividend which is in the nature of a dividend on ordinary shares.

Advantages: (a) non-repayable (except (3) above); (b) the annual cost/dividend is known thus facilitating planning; (c) in extreme circumstances the annual dividend can be waived.

Disadvantages: the dividends are not deductible for tax purposes.

Types of loan stock/debentures
(1)   Unsecured/naked—in the event of the company going into liquidation these are repaid before the shareholders, but after other creditors.
(2)   With a fixed charge—secured on assets that the company cannot dispose of without the trustee for the debenture holders' permission. In the event of the security being in jeopardy, or the company not paying the annual interest, the trustee can take legal possession of the asset(s), sell them and repay the debenture holders.
(3)   With a floating charge—the same as debentures with a fixed charge except that the asset(s) on which the debentures are second can be sold by the company but must be replaced with asset(s) of an equivalent value.
(4)   Convertible loan stock—carry the right, at the holder's option, to convert them into ordinary shares within a given time period fixed when they are issued. The rate of conversion is usually such that the holder obtains ordinary shares at a price which is lower than the market price of the shares at the date of conversion.

Advantages: (a) the annual cost/interest is known; (b) the interest is deductible for tax purposes.

Disadvantages: (a) they have to be repaid after the expiration of the period specified when they were issued; (b) the interest must be paid before the shareholders receive any dividend. This can be a burden when the proceeds of the issue have been used to finance expansion that may not result in revenue during the early years, or where there is a reduction in the annual profit or high interest rates.

Figure 26.2.   A summary of the types of preference shares and loan stock.

It may also consist of a full page advertisement in a national newspaper, such as The Financial Times. The contents of a prospectus include: (a) the total number of shares the company wishes to issue and the minimum subscription (i.e. the smallest number for which the applicant can apply); (b) the price of each share, stating the amounts payable on application, allotment and any calls; (c) details of the rights attaching to all classes of shares; and (d) a report by the company's auditors on the profits and dividends of the last five years, and the assets and liabilities at the end of the previous accounting year.

Interim and final dividends

Most large companies pay both interim and final dividends on their ordinary shares. An *interim dividend* is paid halfway through the accounting year, when the profit for the first six months is known. The amount is decided by the directors. The *final dividend* is additional to the interim dividend and, although it relates to the same accounting year, is paid just after the end of the year. This is because the final dividend has to be approved by the ordinary shareholders at the annual general meeting (AGM), and this is always held after the end of the accounting year when the profit for the year is known. Thus the final dividend is always outstanding at the end of the year, and referred to as a *proposed* final ordinary dividend.

Dividends on preference shares and interest on loan stock and debentures are also often paid in two instalments, one halfway through the accounting year and the other at the end of the year. However, the amount relating to the last half of the year may be outstanding at the end of the accounting year.

The books of account and published accounts

Companies are required by law to keep proper books of account, and each year to prepare a set of published accounts (i.e. a profit and loss account and balance sheet) which conform with the books of account. The 'books' of account need not necessarily actually be in the form of books, but there must be some set of records of the business transactions (e.g. a computerized system). A copy of the published accounts must be sent to each ordinary shareholder and the Registrar of Companies. The latter are available for inspection by the general public at Companies House.

The auditors' report

Most limited companies are required by law to have their books and annual final accounts audited by an independent qualified accountant. The accounts covered by the audit consist of the profit and loss account and balance sheet.

Although paid by the company, the auditors act on behalf of the ordinary shareholders and are appointed by them at the annual general meeting (AGM). The auditors' function is to ascertain, or rather form an opinion of, whether or not the *accounts give a true and fair view of the state of affairs and the profit of the company and have been properly prepared in accordance with the Companies Act*. Their opinion is given in the auditors' report, which is attached to the final accounts, and uses wording similar to that in italics in the last sentence. If the accounts are considered not to give a true and fair view or do not comply with the Companies Acts in some other way, the nature of the departure is usually stated in the auditors' report. This is referred to as a 'qualified' audit report.

It is important to appreciate that the auditor does not guarantee that no fraud or errors have taken place. In the UK, shareholders and loan creditors would be unlikely to receive damages from the auditors if a company subsequently went into liquidation or discrepancies were discovered, unless the auditors are shown to have been negligent. Furthermore, the auditors' report is not intended to be interpreted as passing an opinion on how efficiently and effectively the directors have used the company's assets.

Statutory books

Companies are obliged by law to maintain certain records relating to their capital and directors. These are known as statutory books and consist of the following:

1. Register of Members, containing the name, address and number of shares held by each shareholder.
2. Register of Debenture Holders, containing the name, address and number of debentures/loan stock held by each debenture holder.
3. Register of Directors and Company Secretary, stating the name, address and occupation of each.
4. Register of Directors' Shareholdings, showing the number of shares held by each director.
5. Register of Mortgages and Other Charges secured on the company's assets, showing the name and address of the lender and the amount of each loan.
6. Minute Book of General Meetings of the company's ordinary shareholders, containing details of the proceedings and resolutions.
7. Minute Book of Directors' Meetings, containing details of the resolutions.

Companies are also required by law to submit to the Registrar of Companies each year an annual return, showing changes in the entries in the statutory books during that year. This information is available for inspection by the general public at Companies House. The statutory books (except the Minutes of Directors' Meetings) are also required by law to be available for inspection by members of the public at the company's registered office.

The annual general meeting

The law demands that companies hold an annual general meeting (AGM). This is a meeting of the ordinary/equity shareholders at which they are entitled to vote on a number of matters. These include the following:

1. To receive and adopt the report of the directors and the published accounts for the year. This provides shareholders with an opportunity to question the directors on the contents of the accounts. The accounts are usually adopted, but if shareholders think that the accounts are inaccurate or misleading they may vote not to accept the accounts. If the shareholders vote not to adopt the accounts this does not mean that

another set has to be prepared.

2. To declare and adopt a proposed final dividend for the year on the ordinary shares. The amount of the final dividend is proposed by the directors. The shareholders cannot propose some other figure. Thus if the shareholders vote not to adopt the proposed dividend they will get no final dividend for that year.

3. To elect directors. This is a source of the shareholders' power, in that if they are dissatisfied with the accounts, the dividend, or the company's performance they may vote not to re-elect the existing directors. Shareholders also have the right to nominate other people as directors.

4. To appoint auditors and fix their remuneration. The directors normally suggest a specific firm of auditors, and the power to fix their remuneration is often delegated to the directors by the shareholders at the AGM. Large companies usually appoint a reputable national or international firm of accountants to act as auditors.

Summary

A limited company is a separate legal entity that has perpetual existence, and is managed by directors appointed by the members. The liability of its shareholders is limited to the nominal value of their shares. There are two classes of companies limited by shares—known as private limited companies and public limited companies (PLC). A company's powers and the rights of the shareholders are contained in its Memorandum and Articles of Association.

Limited companies are financed predominantly by the issue of ordinary and preference shares, debentures and loan stock. These have a fixed face or nominal value but may be issued at a premium. Ordinary shares usually carry voting rights which give their holders the power to elect directors. They are also entitled to a share of the annual profits as a dividend which can vary each year. Ordinary shares are the last to be repaid in the event of the company going into liquidation. Preference shares are also entitled to a dividend but this is at a rate fixed at the time of issue. They may be cumulative, participating or redeemable. Preference shares are repaid before the ordinary shares in the event of liquidation. Most shares are non-repayable except on liquidation. All dividends are an appropriation of profits, and may include both an interim and final dividend. Debentures and loan stock represent a loan to the company. These carry a fixed rate of interest which is a charge against income. Debentures and loan stock are repaid before the shares in the event of liquidation, and may be secured by either a fixed or floating charge on the company's assets.

Companies are required by law to keep proper records of their transactions and prepare annual accounts. In most cases these must be audited by independent qualified accountants who prepare a report expressing an opinion on whether the accounts give a true and fair view of the profit and financial state of affairs. A copy of the published accounts and auditors' report must be sent to all the shareholders. Companies are also required by law to maintain statutory books, and hold an annual general meeting (AGM), At the AGM the ordinary shareholders vote on whether to adopt the published accounts, the dividend proposed by the directors, and the election of directors and auditors.

Key terms and concepts

Annual general meeting, appropriation of profit, Articles of Association, auditors' report, body corporate, body sole, certificate of incorporation, company, convertible loan stock, cumulative preference share, debenture, dividend, final dividend, fixed charge, floating charge, interest, interim dividend, limited liability, loan stock, Memorandum of Association, nominal/par/face value, ordinary share, participating preference share, preference share, preliminary/promotion/formation expenses, private limited company, prospectus, public limited company, redeemable preference share, secured loan stock, share premium, statutory books, trading certificate, unsecured loan stock.

Exercises

An asterisk after the question number indicates that there is a suggested answer in the Appendix.

26.1.   Describe the characteristics of companies limited by shares.

26.2.   How does a public limited company differ from a private limited company?

26.3.   Describe the contents of the Memorandum and Articles of Association. What are the purposes of these documents?

26.4.   What are preliminary expenses?

26.5.*   Explain the main similarities and differences between ordinary shares, preference shares and debentures/loan stock.

26.6.   Explain how each of the following arises:
(a)   a share premium;
(b)   a debenture discount.

26.7.   Outline the main contents of a prospectus.

26.8.   What is the difference between an interim dividend and a final dividend?

26.9.   What is the auditors' report? How useful do you think this is in its present form and with its current legal standing in the UK?

26.10.   Describe the contents of the statutory books of companies. What is the purpose of each of these books?

26.11.   What is the annual general meeting of a company? Describe the proceedings at such a meeting.

27. The final accounts of limited companies

Learning objectives

After reading this chapter the student should be able to:

1. Explain the meaning of the key terms and concepts listed at the end of the chapter.
2. Describe the main differences between the final accounts of sole traders and companies with particular reference to those arising from the latter being a separate legal entity.
3. Describe the share capital structure of a company as presented in the balance sheet.
4. Explain the nature and types of reserves.
5. Show the journal and ledger entries relating to the treatment of preliminary expenses, debenture interest, corporation tax, dividends, and transfers to reserves.
6. Prepare the final accounts of limited companies prior to putting them in a form suitable for publication.
7. Demonstrate a basic understanding of the legal format of published company final accounts and the main provisions of FRS3.
8. Prepare a simple set of final accounts in a form suitable for publication and which complies with the Companies Acts, Financial Reporting Standards, and Statements of Standard Accounting Practice.
9. Explain the nature and accounting treatment of discontinued operations, exceptional items, extraordinary items, prior period adjustments, post balance sheet events, and contingencies.

Introduction

The Companies Act requires companies to send their ordinary shareholders a copy of the annual final accounts. These are referred to as the annual report (or published accounts) and include a profit and loss account and balance sheet. There are detailed legal requirements relating to the content and format of annual final accounts. The first two sections of this chapter deal with the preparation of company final accounts prior to putting them in a form suitable for publication. The remaining sections describe some of the legal requirements relating to their presentation.

As in the case of sole traders and partnerships, it is now common practice for companies to prepare final accounts in vertical form. Furthermore, it is usual to combine the trading and profit and loss accounts into a single profit and loss account. The entries are the same as where there are two accounts.

The differences between the final accounts of companies and those of sole traders are explained below.

The profit and loss account

The contents of the profit and loss account of companies are the same as that for sole traders and partnerships, with the following exceptions:

1. In arriving at the net profit, certain items not found in the accounts of sole traders and partnerships must be included. These consist of share transfer fees received, directors' emoluments/remuneration (e.g. fees, salaries, pensions, compensation for loss of office, etc.), auditors' fees and expenses, interest on debentures, and preliminary/formation/promotion expenses. The latter refers to the costs incurred in forming a company, such as registration fees, preparation of the Memorandum and Articles of Association, etc. They must not be retained in the accounts as an asset.
2. After the net profit has been computed, various appropriations are made in a section of the profit and loss account, sometimes referred to as the profit and loss appropriation account. These occur in the following order:

    (a) *Corporation tax.* Since a company is a separate legal entity, it is liable for the taxation on its annual profit, which is referred to as corporation tax. Where the profit and loss appropriation account is prepared in vertical form the corporation tax is deducted from the net profit to give the net profit after tax. The double-entry for the corporation tax *charge* on the annual profit is to debit the profit & loss appropriation account and credit an account in the name of the Inland Revenue, or more likely, corporation tax. Up until 1998 this amount also appeared on the balance sheet as a current liability because it was payable nine months after the end of the accounting year. All the examples and exercises in this book are pre 1999. However, post 1998 most companies are required to make payments on account in respect of the corporation tax on their profits during the year to which they relate. Thus post 1998 examination questions may include corporation tax payments in the trial balance. In this situation it will be necessary to create an accrual/creditor on the corporation tax account in respect of the difference between the amount paid during the year and the estimated *charge* on the profits for that year. The accrual will then be shown on the balance sheet as a current liability. In theory the difference between the tax paid and the charge for the year could give rise to a prepayment although this is not likely to be common in practice.

    No doubt students will find this transition confusing. The essential point to grasp is that pre 1999 the amount of the *charge* for corporation tax shown in the profit & loss account also appears as a current liability on the balance sheet. In contrast, after 1998 the *charge* for corporation tax in the profit & loss account, which will continue to be given as further information in examination questions, needs to be reduced by any corporation tax paid shown in the trial balance to arrive at the resulting accrual (or prepayment) that will appear as a current liability (or asset) on the balance sheet.

    (b) *Preference share dividends.* Where the profit and loss appropriation account is prepared in vertical form, these are deducted from the net profit after tax. This is because they are an appropriation of the profit after tax and not a charge against income (like debenture interest). The preference dividends comprise any interim dividend paid plus the final dividend. The interim dividend paid will have been debited to the preference share dividends account in the ledger and thus shown in the trial balance. The final dividend may be outstanding at the end of the accounting year, in which case it is necessary to create an accrual in the preference dividends account and to show the amount owing on the balance sheet as a current liability. The total of the interim and final dividends is then debited to the profit and loss appropriation account with a corresponding credit in the preference share dividends account.

(c) *Ordinary share dividends.* These are entered in the profit and loss appropriation account after the preference dividends because the latter have a prior claim against profits. The ordinary dividends comprise any interim dividend paid plus the proposed final dividend. The interim dividend paid will have been debited to the ordinary share dividends account and thus shown in the trial balance. The proposed final dividend will always be outstanding at the end of the accounting year and thus it is necessary to create an accrual in the ordinary share dividends account and show the amount owing on the balance sheet as a current liability. The total of the interim and proposed final dividends is then debited to the profit and loss appropriation account and credited to the ordinary share dividends account.

(d) *Transfer to reserves.* The profit remaining after deducting dividends is the undistributed or retained profit for the year and is brought down as a credit balance on the profit and loss appropriation account. Note that it is not transferred to the capital account, as in the case of sole traders and partnerships. However, sometimes companies transfer a part of their retained profit to a reserve account. The reason for this is to indicate to shareholders that the directors do not intend to distribute it as dividends but rather to earmark it for some other use, such as expansion of the business by purchasing additional fixed assets. The entry for a transfer to a reserve is to debit the profit and loss appropriation account and credit the reserve account. There is a difference of opinion in the literature regarding whether the debit entry in the profit and loss appropriation account should appear before or after the preference and ordinary dividends. However, since transfers to reserves are no longer common, the issue is really only academic. Reserves are discussed further below.

The balance sheet

The content of the balance sheet of companies is the same as that of sole traders and partnerships with the following exceptions:

1. The current liabilities of companies also usually include corporation tax on the annual profit, accrued debenture interest, and the outstanding final dividends on preference and ordinary shares.

2. The long-term liabilities of companies also often include the nominal value of loan stock and debentures.

3. The capital and retained profits of a company are shown separately under two headings comprising the nominal value of the share capital and the reserves. The share capital may take a number of forms. As explained in the previous chapter, when shares are issued the price may be payable by instalments. Thus at the end of any given accounting year the proceeds of sale may be at a number of possible stages of collection. Each of these is given a particular label in the balance sheet of companies as follows:

(a) *Authorized/nominal share capital*. This refers to the types, nominal value and maximum number of shares that the company is permitted by its Memorandum of Association to issue.

(b) *Allotted share capital*. This refers to the total nominal value of the number of shares that have actually been issued at the date of the balance sheet. It is sometimes referred to as the issued share capital.

(c) *Called-up share capital*. This refers to that part of the allotted share capital which the company has required the shareholders to pay. It will consist of the amounts payable on application and allotment plus any calls that have been made by the company up to the date of the balance sheet.

The figure for share capital that enters into the total of the balance sheet is the called-up ordinary and preference share capital. This is frequently the same as the allotted share capital. However, if these are different, the allotted capital must be shown as a memorandum figure (i.e. not entering into the total of the balance sheet). The authorized capital must always be disclosed as a memorandum amount.

Reserves are difficult to define because they take a variety of forms. However, they usually represent some sort of gain or profit, and constitute part of a company's capital. Reserves may be of two types, either distributable or non-distributable. These are also frequently referred to as revenue and capital reserves respectively. *Distributable/revenue reserves* are those which can be distributed to shareholders as dividends. These include any *general reserve* and the balance on the *profit and loss account*, both of which consist of retained profits of the current and previous accounting years.

Non-distributable/capital reserves cannot be distributed as dividends. These may take a number of forms. The most common is the balance on a *share premium* account. This arises from shares having been issued at a price in excess of their nominal value. The excess is credited to a share premium account. Another non-distributable reserve is a *revaluation reserve*. This arises if a fixed asset (usually land and buildings) is revalued and shown in the balance sheet at an amount which exceeds its historical cost. The excess is credited to a revaluation reserve account. A third form of non-distributable reserve is a *capital redemption reserve* (CRR). This is a statutory reserve, being identified in the Companies Acts. It arises when shares are redeemed or purchased back from shareholders. Attention is given to the CRR and share repurchase in the next chapter.

The total amount of reserves is added to the called-up share capital and shown on the balance sheet as the *'shareholders' interests'*.

An illustration of the preparation of the final accounts of limited companies is given in Example 27.1.

Example 27.1
The following is the trial balance of XYZ Ltd at 31 March 19X9:

	£	£
Ordinary shares of £1 each, fully paid		100,000
5 per cent preference shares of £1 each, fully paid		20,000
8 per cent debentures		30,000
Share premium		9,500

Revaluation reserve		10,000
General reserve		2,000
Retained profit from previous years		976
Motor vehicles at revaluation	210,000	
Depreciation on vehicles		19,000
Stock	14,167	
Debtors/creditors	11,000	8,012
Provision for doubtful debts		324
Bank balance	9,731	
Purchases/sales	186,000	271,000
Wages and salaries	16,362	
General expenses	3,912	
Directors' remuneration	15,500	
Preliminary expenses	1,640	
Debenture interest	1,200	
Ordinary dividend (interim)	2,000	
	471,512	471,512

You are given the following information:

1. Stock at 31 March 19X9 is valued at £23,487.
2. Depreciation of motor vehicles is to be provided at the rate of 10 per cent per annum on the fixed instalment method.
3. The provision for doubtful debts is to be made equal to 5 per cent of the debtors at 31 March 19X9.
4. Debenture interest of £1,200 and preference share dividends of £1,000 are outstanding at 31 March 19X9.
5. Provision is to be made for taxation on the year's profit amounting to £9,700.
6. There is a proposed final ordinary dividend of 5 pence per share.
7. The directors have decided to increase the general reserve by a further £3,000.
8. The authorized share capital consists of: (a) 200,000 ordinary shares of £1 each; and (b) 50,000 5 per cent preference shares of £1 each. The value of the shares shown in the trial balance is the allotted and called-up capital.

You are required to prepare in vertical form the profit and loss account for the year ended 31 March 19X9 and a balance sheet at that date.

Workings
These could be done arithmetically but are shown below in the form of ledger accounts to help students understand the double entry.

Provision for doubtful debts

Balance c/d	550	Balance b/d	324
(5 per cent × 11,000)		Profit and loss a/c	226
	550		550
		Balance b/d	550

Balance for depreciation

Balance c/d	40,000	Balance b/d	19,000
		Profit and loss a/c	21,000
	40,000		40,000
		Balance b/d	40,000

Debenture interest

Bank	1,200	Profit and loss a/c	2,400
Accrual c/d	1,200		
	2,400		2,400
		Accrual b/d	1,200

Preference dividend

Balance c/d	1,000	Profit and loss a/c	1,000
	1,000		1,000
		Balance b/d	1,000

Ordinary dividends

Bank	2,000	Profit and loss a/c	7,000
Balance c/d	5,000		
(100,000 × 5p)			
	7,000		7,000
		Balance b/d	5,000

Corporation tax

		Profit and loss a/c	9,700

General reserve

Balance c/d	5,000	Balance b/d	2,000
		Profit and loss a/c	3,000
	5,000		5,000
		Balance b/d	5,000

XYZ Ltd
Profit and loss account for the year ended 31 March 19X9

	£	£
Sales		271,700
Less: Cost of sales		
Stock at 1 April 19X8	14,167	
Add: Purchases	186,000	
	200,167	
Less: Stock at 31 March 19X9	23,487	

Cost of sales		176,680
Gross profit		95,020
Less: Expenditure		
Wages and salaries	16,362	
General expenses	3,912	
Provision for depreciation	21,000	
Provision for doubtful debts	226	
Directors' remuneration	15,500	
Preliminary expenses	1,640	
Debenture interest	2,400	
		61,040
Profit on ordinary activities before taxation		33,980
Less: Tax on profit on ordinary activities		9,700
Profit on ordinary activities after taxation		24,280
Less: Dividends—		
preference	1,000	
ordinary	7,000	
		8,000
Retained profit for the financial year		16,280
Less: Transfer to general reserve		3,000
		13,280

XYZ Ltd
Balance sheet as at 31 March 19X9

	£	£	£
Fixed assets			
Motor vehicles at revaluation			210,000
Less: Aggregate depreciation			40,000
			170,000
Current assets			
Stock		23,487	
Debtors	11,000		
Less: Provision for doubtful debts	550	10,450	
Bank		9,731	
		43,668	
Less: creditors: amounts falling due within one year			
Creditors	8,012		
Dividends (1000 + 5000)	6,000		
Corporation tax	9,700		
Debenture interest	1,200	24,912	
Net current assets			18,756
Total assets less current liabilities			188,756

Less: creditors: amounts falling due after *more than one year*	
8 per cent debentures	30,000
Net assets	158,756

Authorized share capital	
200,000 ordinary shares of £1 each	200,000
50,000 5 per cent preference shares of £1 each	50,000
	250,000

Allotted and called-up share capital	
100,000 ordinary shares of £1 each	100,000
20,000 5 per cent preference shares of £1 each	20,000
	120,000

Reserves		
Share premium account	9,500	
Revaluation reserve	10,000	
General reserve	5,000	
Profit and loss account (976 + 13,280)	14,256	
		38,756
Shareholders' interests		158,756

Notes

1. The workings for this example are shown in the form of ledger accounts to help students understand the double entry. In examinations it is usually sufficient to state the necessary additions and subtractions.
2. The amount of the proposed final dividend on ordinary shares is computed by multiplying the dividend per share by the number of shares that have been issued/allotted as shown in the trial balance, (including any issued during the year) i.e. 5p × 100,000 = £5,000. Sometimes the dividend per share is expressed as a percentage. In this case the percentage is applied to the nominal value of the issued/alloted ordinary share capital (e.g. 5 per cent × £100,000 = £5,000).
3. It is important to ensure that the amounts entered in the profit and loss account in respect of debenture interest and preference share dividends are the amounts paid plus any which is outstanding at the end of the year. Sometimes in examination questions students are not told how much is outstanding or even that anything is outstanding. In these circumstances the total amount to be entered in the profit and loss account is ascertained using the information given in the question relating to the rates of debenture interest and preference dividends as follows:

    8 per cent debentures £30,000
    ∴ Annual interest = 8 per cent × £30,000 = £2,400.
    5 per cent preference shares £20,000
    ∴ Annual dividend = 5 per cent × £20,000 = £1,000.

The amounts to be entered as current liabilities in the balance sheet can then be found by subtracting the amounts paid as shown in the trial balance as follows:

Debenture interest outstanding = £2,400 − £1,200 = £1,200
Preference dividends outstanding = £1,000 − £0 = £1,000

The reason for adopting this procedure in the case of debenture interest is that the debentures could have been issued at any time during a previous accounting year and thus the interest may be payable on dates other than the end of the accounting year and half way through the year. This means that the amount of interest outstanding at the end of the accounting year will not necessarily be the total for the year or the last six months. Thus one cannot assume that the accrual should be 6/12 of the total interest for the year even though it often is in examination questions. Where debentures or preference shares have been issued during the year, the amount of interest/dividends that is entered in the profit and loss account needs to be calculated on a strict time basis.

4. It is generally accepted practice to prepare the final accounts of companies in vertical form. However, the profit and loss account (and appropriation account) must also be prepared in the ledger by transferring all the balances on the income and expense accounts to this account in the normal manner. Unlike the profit and loss accounts of sole traders and partnerships, the profit and loss account of companies will always contain a balance brought down from the previous year. The retained profit of the current year (after deducting any transfers to reserves) is added to this balance and the resulting figure is carried forward to the next year. This is shown on the above balance sheet under reserves in computational form as £976 + £13,280 = £14,256. It should also be remembered that journal entries are supposed to be made for all the above entries in the ledger.

5. As explained earlier in this chapter, the law allows revenue reserves such as the general reserve and the balance on the profit and loss account at the end of the previous year to be distributed to shareholders as dividends. This is not common in practice or in examination questions because it is undesirable for economic/commercial reasons. However, a description of the accounting entries may help students to appreciate the nature of reserves. When a dividend is to be distributed from revenue reserves, this will be apparent from the profit and loss appropriation account because the profit after tax will be lower than the amount of the dividends for that year. In this case the retained profit of the previous year (i.e. the balance on the profit and loss account at the end of the previous year shown in the trial balance) should be added to the profit after tax and before dividends. If the profit after tax plus retained profit of the previous year is still less than the dividends, a transfer back from the general reserve must be made of an amount necessary to cover the dividend. The double entry for this transfer is to debit the general reserve and credit the profit and loss appropriation account. In the vertical format this will be an addition to the profit after tax and before dividends.

6. As explained earlier in this chapter, preliminary expenses must not be retained in the accounts as an asset. There are two possible ways of dealing with these. One is to charge them to the profit and loss account as in the above example. However, this reduces the profit, which many companies wish to avoid if possible. The alternative, and preferred treatment, is to charge preliminary expenses against the balance on the share premium account, the double entry being to credit the preliminary expenses

account and debit the share premium account. The amount entered on the balance sheet in respect of the share premium account will then be the difference between the balance shown in the trial balance and the preliminary expenses, that is, the balance on the share premium account after entering the preliminary expenses.

7. In the published accounts of companies current liabilities are referred to as *creditors: amounts falling due within one year*, and long-term liabilities as *creditors: amounts falling due after more than one year.*

8. In the published accounts of companies the net profit (before and after tax) is referred to as the *profit on ordinary activities*. Where a question has no corporation tax the net profit is referred to as the *profit for the financial year.*

Published financial statements

The final accounts of companies that are published and sent to ordinary shareholders in the annual report must be presented in a form that complies with the Companies Acts. The fourth schedule to the Companies Act 1985 contains four permissible formats for the profit and loss account and two permissible formats for the balance sheet. Most companies use what is known as Format 1 for both the profit and loss account and the balance sheet. These are reproduced below in full. They include certain items with which the student will be unfamiliar and go beyond what is required by most of the A level and professional bodies' examinations at this level. In particular students may need to ignore items that include the phrases 'group undertakings, participating interests, or minority interests'. These only apply to companies that own other companies. With the exception of extra-ordinary items and deferred taxation the remainder should be understandable at this level. Extraordinary items are explained in the next section of this chapter, and deferred taxation is not usually examined at this level. The formats are reproduced in full for reference purposes. It is not intended that they should be memorized. A precise explanation of what students are expected to know at this level follows immediately afterwards.

Profit and loss account: Format 1
1. Turnover
2. Cost of sales
3. *Gross profit or loss*
4. Distribution costs
5. Administrative expenses
6. Other operating income
7. Income from shares in group undertakings
8. Income from participating interests (excluding group undertakings)
9. Income from other fixed asset investments
10. Other interest receivable and similar income
11. Amounts written off investments
12. Interest payable and similar charges
13. Tax on profit or loss on ordinary activities
14. *Profit or loss on ordinary activities after taxation*
     Minority interests
15. Extraordinary income
16. Extraordinary charges

17. Extraordinary profit or loss
18. Tax on extraordinary profit or loss
     Minority interests
19. Other taxes not shown under the above items
20. *Profit or loss for the financial year*

Balance sheet: Format 1

A   *Called-up share capital not paid*

B   *Fixed assets*
   I   Intangible assets
       1. Development costs
       2. Concessions, patents, licences, trade marks and similar rights and assets
       3. Goodwill
       4. Payments on account

   II   Tangible assets
       1. Land and buildings
       2. Plant and machinery
       3. Fixtures, fittings, tools and equipment
       4. Payments on account and assets in course of construction

   III   Investments
       1. Shares in group undertakings
       2. Loans to group undertakings
       3. Participating interests (excluding group undertakings)
       4. Loans to undertakings in which the company has a participating interest
       5. Other investments other than loans
       6. Other loans
       7. Own shares

C   *Current assets*
   I   Stocks
       1. Raw materials and consumables
       2. Work in progress
       3. Finished goods and goods for resale
       4. Payments on account

   II   Debtors
       1. Trade debtors
       2. Amounts owed by group undertakings
       3. Amounts owed by undertakings in which the company has a participating interest
       4. Other debtors
       5. Called-up share capital not paid
       6. Prepayments and accrued income

   III   Investments
       1. Shares in group undertakings
       2. Own shares
       3. Other investments

   IV   Cash at bank and in hand

D   *Prepayments and accrued income*

E   *Creditors: amounts falling due within one year*
1. Debenture loans
2. Bank loans and overdrafts
3. Payments received on account
4. Trade creditors
5. Bills of exchange payable
6. Amounts owed to group undertakings
7. Amounts owed to undertakings in which the company has a participating interest
8. Other creditors including taxation and social security
9. Accruals and deferred income

F   *Net current assets (liabilities)*

G   *Total assets less current liabilities*

H   *Creditors: amounts falling due after more than one year*
1. Debenture loans
2. Bank loans and overdrafts
3. Payments received on account
4. Trade creditors
5. Bills of exchange payable
6. Amounts owed to group undertakings
7. Amounts owed to undertakings in which the company has a participating interest
8. Other creditors including taxation and social security
9. Accruals and deferred income

I   *Provisions for liabilities and charges*
1. Pensions and similar obligations
2. Taxation, including deferred taxation
3. Other provisions

J   *Accruals and deferred income*

   Minority interests

K   Capital and reserves

   I   Called-up share capital

   II   Share premium account

   III Revaluation reserve

   IV Other reserves
1. Capital redemption reserve
2. Reserve for own shares
3. Reserves provided for by the articles of association
4. Other reserves

   V   Profit and loss account

   Minority interests

The profit & loss account

The format of published accounts, or what have recently become known as financial statements, must also comply with accounting standards. In particular, *FRS3 – Reporting Financial Performance* requires that the profit & loss account includes certain further items, such as dividends, and some additional sub-totals. Combining the demands of the Companies Acts and FRS3, the following is a relatively definitive specimen published profit & loss account that students are usually expected to comply with at the introductory level:

Profit & loss account

	£'000
Turnover	X
Cost of sales	(X)
Gross profit	X
Distribution costs	(X)
Administrative expenses	(X)
Profit (or loss) on ordinary activities before interest	X
Interest receivable	X
Interest payable	(X)
Profit (or loss) on ordinary activities before taxation	X
Tax on profit on ordinary activities	(X)
Profit (or loss) on ordinary activities after taxation	X
Dividends	(X)
Retained profit (or loss) for the financial year	X

The profit on ordinary activities before and after taxation is referred to as the *profit for the financial year*, where an examination question contains no corporation tax. The precise distinction between these sub-totals is explained later in this chapter.

The key point at this stage is that the separate items which make up the cost of sales, distribution costs, administrative expenses, interest receivable and payable, and dividends should not be shown on the face of the profit & loss account. It is therefore necessary to first ascertain the total of each of these as workings. Note that distribution costs includes selling expenses.

Some of the items that are to be classified as either distribution costs or administrative expenses may be obvious from their descriptions (e.g. salespersons commission, administrative salaries). Others are either less obvious or based on generally accepted conventions. In particular, selling and distribution costs are usually taken to include advertising, carriage outwards, bad debts, changes in the provision for bad debts, discount allowed, motor expenses (including depreciation, profit/losses on disposal) of delivery vehicles, and any costs associated with a warehouse such as wages, repairs to and depreciation of fork-lift trucks and similar 'plant and machinery'. There are few generally accepted conventions regarding the composition of administrative expenses. Examination questions normally need to specify which costs are regarded as administrative expenses, failing which as a last resort these may be taken to include auditors fees and expenses, discount received, directors remuneration, office salaries, rent and rates, light and heat, telephone and postage, carriage inwards, etc. Frequently examination questions also require some items (such as those in the previous sentence) to be apportioned between distribution costs and administrative expenses. This is a relatively simple arithmetic exercise in which the amounts are divided between distribution costs and administrative expenses using the basis of apportionment (i.e. percentages for each) given in the question.

The balance sheet

Turning to the format of balance sheets as shown above, the Companies Act requires those items preceded by a letter or roman numerals to be disclosed on the face of the balance sheet (e.g. B. Fixed assets, K III. Revaluation reserve), whereas those preceded by arabic numerals may be combined where they are not material (e.g. stocks of raw materials, work in progress and finished goods). The following is thus a specimen published balance sheet containing the minimum requirements that students will need to follow at the introductory level. Further detail is unlikely to be penalized.

Balance sheet

	£'000	£'000
Fixed assets		
Intangible assets		X
Tangible assets		X
Investments		X
		X
Current assets		
Stock	X	
Debtors	X	
Investments	X	
Cash at bank and in hand	X	
	X	
Creditors: amounts falling due within one year	(X)	
Net current assets (liabilities)		X
Total assets less current liabilities		X
Creditors: amounts falling due after more than one year		(X)
		X
Capital and reserves		
Called-up share capital		X
Share premium account		X
Revaluation reserve		X
Other reserves		X
Profit & loss account		X
		X

The debtors includes prepayments, and the creditors: amounts falling due within one year includes trade creditors and accruals.

Where this format is followed exactly in answering examination questions, it will be necessary to prepare workings that clearly show how the amounts of, in particular, tangible fixed assets and creditors (both current and long term) have been computed.

Alternatively it is probably advisable, and quicker, to include the items preceded by arabic numerals on the face of the balance sheet where relevant (e.g. trade creditors and accruals).

Notes to the accounts

The Companies Act and accounting standards also require several 'notes' to be attached to the published profit & loss account and balance sheet. Those most commonly examined at the foundation level comprise the following

1. Changes in fixed assets (and accumulated depreciation)
2. Movements on reserves
3. Statement of total recognized gains and losses.

A note on the composition of fixed assets and accumulated depreciation is clearly necessary where only the net written down/book value at the end of the accounting year has been shown on the face of the balance sheet in respect of intangible and tangible fixed assets. In addition, this note must include the cost of acquisitions and disposals, any revaluation, the depreciation charges for the year, and the accumulated depreciation on disposals. An illustration is given later in the text.

The note relating to movements on reserves usually includes the share premium account, any revaluation reserve, and the profit & loss account (i.e. retained profits). Movements on these reserves will arise from the issue of shares at a premium, a surplus on the revaluation of fixed assets, and the retained profit for the financial year, respectively.

The statement of total recognized gains and losses is relatively simple at least at the foundation level. It will contain the profit for the financial year plus any unrealized surplus on the revaluation of fixed assets. The purpose of this statement is to show all the gains (and losses) accruing to the company's shareholders be they either realized, such as the profit for the year, or unrealized as in the case of revaluation surpluses. The statement of total recognized gains and losses is prescribed by FRS3, whereas the other two notes described above are a requirement of the Companies Acts..

An illustration of the preparation of published financial statements including the above three notes is given in Example 27.2 below.

Example 27.2
The following is the trial balance of Oasis Ltd as at 30 September 19X8.

	£'000	£'000
Called-up share capital		1,000
Share premium		500
Profit & loss account 1 Oct 19X7		700
10% Debentures (repayable 20X5)		600
Land & buildings at cost	2,500	
Buildings—accumulated depreciation		90
Motor vehicles—at cost	1,400	
—accumulated depreciation		470
Stock	880	
Trade debtors/creditors	420	360
Purchases/sales	3,650	6,540

Warehouse wages	310	
Administrative salaries	190	
Sales staff salaries	70	
Bad debts	20	
Directors remuneration	280	
Advertising expenditure	60	
Motor expenses	230	
Light & heat	180	
Telephone & postage	80	
Bank overdraft		19
Discount allowed	9	
	10,279	10,279

Further information:

1. The called-up share capital consists of 1 million ordinary shares of £1 each, fully paid.
2. Stock at 30 September 19X8 was £740,000.
3. The auditors fees and expenses for the year are expected to be £71,000.
4. The estimated corporation tax charge on the profit for the year is £250,000.
5. The directors have proposed a final dividend on the ordinary shares in issue at 30 September 19X8 of 10 pence per share.
6. Depreciation is provided on a straight line basis at 2% per annum for buildings and 20% per annum on vehicles. A full years charge is made in the year of acquisition and none in the year of disposal.
7. The following items are to be apportioned between distribution costs and administrative expenses as below:

	Distribution	Administrative
Directors remuneration	25%	75%
Light & heat, telephone & postage, buildings depreciation	40%	60%
Motor expenses, vehicle depreciation	50%	50%

8. The following items were unrecorded in the ledger on 30 September 19X8:

    (i)   The issue of 500,000 ordinary shares at £1.50 each fully paid on 31 August 19X8.
    (ii) The acquisition on credit of a motor vehicle costing £100,000 on 31 August 19X8.
    (iii) The sale on credit of a motor vehicle for £40,000 on 31 August 19X8. This cost £50,000 when purchased on 1 February 19X6.

9. The land included in the above trial balance cost £1m. The directors have decided to revalue this on 30 September 19X8 at £1.3m.

You are required to prepare the company's profit & loss account for the year and a balance sheet as at 30 September 19X8. This should be in a form suitable for publication, comply with the Companies Acts and accounting standards, and include notes relating to changes in fixed assets, movements on reserves, and a statement of total recognized gains and losses.

Workings

1. *Cost of sales*

	£'000
Stock at 1 Oct 19X7	880
Purchases	3,650
	4,530
Stock at 30 Sept 19X8	(740)
Cost of sales	3,790

2. *Depreciation*

	£'000
(a) Buildings at cost (2,500 − 1,000)	1,500
Depreciation expense (2% × 1,500)	30
Accumulated depreciation at 30 Sept 19X8 (90 + 30)	120
(b) Motor vehicles at 1 Oct 19X7 at cost	1,400
Acquisition	100
	1,500
Disposal	(50)
Motor vehicles at 30 Sept 19X8 at cost	1,450
Disposal –	
accumulated depreciation (2 × 20% × 50)	20
book value (50 − 20)	30
profit on sale (40 − 30)	10
Depreciation expense (20% × 1,450)	290
Accumulated depreciation at 30 Sept 19X8 (470 − 20 + 290)	740

3. *Distribution costs and administrative expenses*

	Distribution £'000	Administration £'000
Warehouse wages	310	—
Administrative salaries	—	190
Sales staff salaries	70	—
Bad debts	20	—
Directors remuneration	70	210
Advertising	60	—
Motor expenses	115	115
Vehicle depreciation	145	145
Profit on sale vehicle	(5)	(5)
Light & heat	72	108
Telephone & postage	32	48
Buildings depreciation	12	18
Discount allowed	9	—
Auditors fees & expenses	—	71
	910	900

Oasis Ltd
Profit & loss account for the year ended 30 September 19X8

	£'000
Turnover	6,540
Cost of sales	(3,790)
Gross profit	2,750
Distribution costs	(910)
Administrative expenses	(900)
Profit on ordinary activities before interest	940
Interest payable (10% × 600)	(60)
Profit on ordinary activities before taxation	880
Tax on profit on ordinary activities	(250)
Profit on ordinary activities after taxation	630
Dividends (1.5m @ 10p)	(150)
Retained profit for the financial year	480

Oasis Ltd
Balance sheet as at 30 September 19X8

	£'000	£'000	£'000
Fixed assets			
Tangible assets (Note 1)			3,390
Current assets			
Stock		740	
Trade debtors		420	
Other debtors		40	
Cash at bank (750 – 19)		731	
		1,931	
Creditors: amounts falling due within one year			
Trade creditors	(360)		
Other creditors (100 + 71)	(171)		
Corporation tax	(250)		
Debenture interest	(60)		
Dividends	(150)	(991)	
Net current assets			940
Total assets less current liabilities			4,330
Creditors: amounts falling due after more than one year			
Debenture loans			(600)
			3,730
Capital and reserves			
Called-up share capital			
1.5m ordinary shares of £1 each			1,500
Share premium account (500 + 250)			750
Revaluation reserve			300
Profit & loss account (700 + 480)			1,180
			3,730

Notes to the accounts

1. *Tangible fixed assets*

	Land £'000	Buildings £'000	Vehicles £'000	Total £'000
Cost or valuation				
At 1 Oct 19X7	1,000	1,500	1,400	3,900
Additions	—	—	100	100
Disposals	—	—	(50)	(50)
Revaluation	300	—	—	300
At 30 Sept 19X8	1,300	1,500	1,450	4,250
Accumulated depreciation				
At 1 Oct 19X7	—	90	470	560
Charge for year	—	30	290	320
Disposals	—	—	(20)	(20)
At 30 Sept 19X8	—	120	740	860
Net book value				
At 30 Sept 19X8	1,300	1,380	710	3,390
At 1 Oct 19X7	1,000	1,410	930	3,340

2. *Reserves*

	Share premium £'000	Revaluation reserve £'000	Profit & loss £'000	Total £'000
At beginning of year as previously stated	500	—	700	1,200
Premium on issue of shares	250	—	—	250
Transfer from profit & loss account of the year	—	—	480	480
Surplus on land revaluation	—	300	—	300
At end of year	750	300	1,180	2,230

3. *Statement of total recognized gains and losses*

	£'000
Profit for the financial year	630
Unrealized surplus on revaluation of land	300
Total recognized gains and losses relating to the year	930

Reporting financial performance

The Companies Acts, various SSAP's and FRSs require that certain items be shown separately in published accounts or as notes to the accounts. The most significant of these, which have not been discussed thus far, are explained below. However, it is first necessary to appreciate why these items are required to be shown separately.

As explained in Chapter 1 one of the main objectives of published company accounts is to provide information that is useful in the evaluation of the performance of the reporting entity. One of the principle means of evaluating performance involves making comparisons over time, with other companies and/or forecasts. It may also involve making predictions of future profits, cash flows, etc. Comparisons and predictions of profits are likely to be misleading where the profit includes gains and losses of a non-recurring nature such as relating to operations that have been discontinued or assets destroyed by fire (where uninsured). In order to facilitate comparisons and predictions it is therefore desirable that the following items be disclosed separately in published company accounts.

Acquisitions and discontinued operations

Financial Reporting Standard 3—Reporting Financial Performance (ASB, 1992) defines acquisitions and discontinued operations as follows:

> *Acquisitions.* Operations of the reporting entity that are acquired in the period.
> *Discontinued operations.* Operations of the reporting entity that are sold or terminated and that satisfy all of the following conditions:
>
> (a)   The sale or termination is completed either in the period or before the earlier of three months after the commencement of the subsequent period and the date on which the financial statements are approved.
> (b)   If a termination, the former activities have ceased permanently.
> (c)   The sale or termination has a material effect on the nature and focus of the reporting entity's operations and represents a material reduction in its operating facilities resulting either from its withdrawal from a particular market (whether class of business or geographical) or from a material reduction in turnover in the reporting entity's continuing markets.
> (d)   The assets, liabilities, results of operations and activities are clearly distinguishable, physically, operationally and for financial reporting purposes.
>
> Operations not satisfying all these conditions are classified as continuing.[1]

FRS3 requires an analysis of turnover and operating profit between continuing operations, acquisitions and discontinued operations. These must be shown separately on the face of the published profit and loss account or by way of a note to the accounts. In the former case the profit and loss account will appear as follows:

	£million	£million
Turnover:		
Continuing operations		1,000
Acquisitions		500
		1,500
Discontinued operations		400
		1,900
Cost of sales		(800)
Gross profit		1,100
Net operating expenses		(200)
Operating profit:		
Continuing operations	700	
Acquisitions	50	
Discontinued operations	150	900

FRS3 also requires an analysis of the cost of sales and net operating expenses (i.e. distribution costs and administrative expenses) between continuing operations, acquisitions and discontinued operations, to be shown as a note to the accounts or included on the face of the profit and loss account.

Exceptional items

Exceptional items used to be accounted for in accordance with *Statement of Standard Accounting Practice 6–Extraordinary Items and Prior Year Adjustments.*[2] However, this has been superseded by FRS3 which defines exceptional items as follows:

> Material items which derive from events or transactions that fall within the ordinary activities of the reporting entity and which individually or, if of a similar type, in aggregate, need to be disclosed by virtue of their size or incidence if the financial statements are to give a true and fair view.[1]

Take particular note of the word material and that exceptional items fall within the ordinary activities (i.e. the normal trading activities).

Examples of exceptional items given in FRS3 include: profits or losses on the sale or termination of an operation; costs of a fundamental reorganization or restructuring having a material effect on the nature and focus of the reporting entity's operations; and profits or losses on the disposal of fixed assets. Notice that exceptional items include profits and losses on the termination or disposal of discontinued operations. That is, arising from the sale of fixed assets, as distinct from the operating profit on discontinued operations discussed in the previous section above.

Other examples of exceptional items not given in FRS3 include amounts written off intangible fixed assets (other than amortization); abnormal provisions for bad debts and losses on stock, work in progress and long-term contracts; profits or losses arising on the settlement of insurance claims or the destruction of assets not covered by insurance; and assets that have been nationalized/confiscated by a government.

The treatment of exceptional items in published company accounts depends on the legal requirements relating to the item in question. Where the law requires the item to be shown separately on the face of the profit and loss account in a specific position, then this should be the treatment adopted. Alternatively, where the law requires the item in question to be disclosed as a note to the accounts, then this would be the most appropriate treatment. Similarly, FRS3 requires other exceptional items such as those in the immediately proceeding paragraph (e.g. a material abnormal bad debt) to be disclosed as a note to the accounts distinguishing between those arising from continuing operations and those arising from discontinued operations. However, FRS3 requires the examples given in FRS3, listed above, to be shown on the face of the profit and loss account after the operating profit and before the deduction of interest payable. In each case it is also necessary to distinguish between those exceptional items arising from continuing operations and those arising from discontinued operations. The profit and loss account will thus appear as follows: This should be read as a continuation of the previous numerical example.

	£million
Operating profit	900
Profit on sale of properties in continuing operations	300
Loss on disposal of discontinued operations	(100)
Profit on ordinary activities before interest	1,100
Interest payable	(350)
Profit on ordinary activities before taxation	750

Extraordinary items

Extraordinary items also used to be accounted for in accordance with SSAP6 but this has been superseded by FRS3. In order to understand fully the nature of extraordinary items it is necessary to consider also the nature of ordinary items/activities. These are defined in FRS3 as follows:

> *Ordinary activities.* Any activities which are undertaken by a reporting entity as part of its business and such related activities in which the reporting entity engages in furtherance of, incidental to, or arising from, these activities. Ordinary activities include the effects on the reporting entity of any event in the various environments in which it operates, including the political, regulatory, economic and geographical environments, irrespective of the frequency or unusual nature of the events.
>
> *Extraordinary items.* Material items possessing a high degree of abnormality which arise from events or transactions that fall outside the ordinary activities of the reporting entity and which are not expected to recur. They do not include exceptional items nor do they include prior period items merely because they relate to a prior period.[1]

Take particular note of the word material and that extraordinary items 'are not expected to recur'.

FRS3 deliberately provides no examples of extraordinary items because they 'are extremely rare as they relate to highly abnormal events'.

FRS3 requires any extraordinary profit or loss to be shown separately on the face of the profit and loss account (and the associated corporation tax on such items) after the profit on ordinary activities after tax but before dividends. A breakdown of the amount of each extraordinary item must also either be shown on the face of the profit and loss account or in the notes of the accounts together with a description of the nature of each item. The profit and loss account will therefore appear as follows. This should be read as a continuation of the previous numerical example.

	£million	£million
Profit on ordinary activities before taxation		750
Tax on profit on ordinary activities		(250)
Profit on ordinary activities after taxation		500
Extraordinary profit	50	
Tax on extraordinary profit	(20)	
Extraordinary profit after tax		30
Profit for the financial year		530
Dividends		(370)
Retained profit for the financial year		160

Learning activity 27.1

Students should find it useful at this point to combine the three numerical examples given above in respect of acquisitions, discontinued operations, exceptional items and extraordinary items since these provide a fairly comprehensive model of a published profit and loss account. In addition students may wish to attempt Exercise 27.25 or use the solution as an example of how to answer examination questions on this topic.

Prior period adjustments

These are also defined in FRS3 as 'material adjustments applicable to prior periods arising from changes in accounting policies or from the correction of fundamental errors.

They do not include normal recurring adjustments or corrections of accounting estimates made in prior periods.' Take particular note of the word material, and the exclusion of the correction of accounting estimates relating to, for example, the estimated residual value and useful life of fixed assets, provisions for bad debts, etc.

Examples of prior period adjustments are rare but include a change in the method of depreciation or stock valuation, and an item previously recorded as a fixed asset that should have been treated as an expense (or vice versa). The most common prior period adjustment arises from the issue of a FRS that would necessitate a company to change one of its accounting policies.

Since prior period adjustments do not relate to the current accounting year they are not entered in the current year's profit and loss account. However, FRS3 requires that the comparative figures for the preceding period should all be restated to take into account the prior period adjustment. Furthermore, FRS3 requires prior period adjustments to be shown in the notes to the accounts relating to movements on reserves and the statement of total recognized gains and losses as follows:

Reserves

	Profit and loss account £million
At beginning of year as previously stated	2,450
Prior year adjustment	280
At beginning of year as restated	2,730
Transfer from profit and loss account of the year	160
At end of year	2,890

Statement of total recognized gains and losses

	£million
Profit for the financial year	530
Unrealized surplus on revaluation of properties	40
Total recognized gains and losses relating to the year	570
Prior period adjustment	280
Total gains and losses recognized since last annual report	850

The note to the accounts must also include details of the nature of the prior period adjustment and its associated effect on taxation.

Post balance sheet events

These are defined in *SSAP17—Accounting for Post Balance Sheet Events*[3] as 'those events, both favourable and unfavourable, which occur between the balance sheet date and the date on which the financial statements are approved by the board of directors'. The balance sheet date is of course the end of an accounting year. The date on which the financial statements are approved by the board of directors is usually a month or two after the end of the accounting year since it takes this amount of time to prepare the financial statements. The statements must then be approved at a meeting of the board of directors.

Post balance sheet events are classified as falling into one of two categories as follows:

1. *Adjusting events* are defined as 'events which provide additional evidence of conditions existing at the balance sheet date. They include events which because of statutory or conventional requirements are reflected in financial statements.'

   Examples of adjusting events include any evidence of a permanent diminution in value of fixed assets, investments, stocks and work in progress, the insolvency of a debtor, changes in the rates of taxation, amounts received or receivable in respect of an insurance claim outstanding at the balance sheet date, and errors or frauds which show that the financial statements were incorrect.

   SSAP17 requires that a material adjusting event should be included in the financial statements. For example, stocks would be reduced to their net realizable value, a provision created for an insolvent debtor, errors corrected, etc.

2. *Non-adjusting events* are defined as 'post balance sheet events which concern conditions which did not exist at the balance sheet date'. Examples include mergers and acquisitions, reconstructions, issues of shares and debentures, purchases and sales of fixed assets and investments, losses of fixed assets and stocks resulting from a fire or flood, new trading activities and closing existing trading activities, government action (e.g. nationalization), strikes and other labour disputes.

   SSAP17 requires that details of material non-adjusting events be disclosed as a note to the financial statements. It is not appropriate to include non-adjusting events in the financial statements since they do not relate to conditions which existed at the balance sheet date. However, it is appropriate to disclose non-adjusting events as a note to ensure that financial statements are not misleading where there is some subsequent material event which affects a company's financial position.

Provisions and contingencies

These are the subject of *Financial Reporting Standard 12—Provisions, Contingent Liabilities and Contingent Assets*.[4] This defines a *provision* as 'a liability of uncertain timing or amount'. It further defines *liabilities* as 'obligations of an entity to transfer economic benefits as a result of past transactions or events.'

A *contingency* was defined in *SSAP18–Accounting for Contingencies*[5] as 'a condition which exists at the balance sheet date, where the outcome will be confirmed only on the occurrence or non-occurrence of one or more uncertain future events. A contingent gain or loss is a gain or loss dependent on a contingency.' Note that although the definition does not include the word material, all of the following discussion applies only to contingencies which are material in amount.

Examples of contingent losses include possible liabilities arising from bills of exchange received that have been discounted, corporation tax disputes, failure by another party to pay a debt which the reporting entity has guaranteed, and a substantial legal claim against the company. The latter is the most common example and refers to where a legal action has been brought against the company but the court has not yet pronounced judgment regarding the company's innocence or guilt. This is often simply referred to as a pending legal action. It is regarded as a contingency because whether or not a loss/liability will arise depends on the 'outcome' of the court case (i.e. an 'uncertain future event').

Contingencies comprise contingent asets (or gains) and contingent liabilities (or losses). A *contingent asset* is defined in FRS12 as 'a possible asset that arises from past events and whose existence will be confirmed only by the occurrence of one or more uncertain future events not wholly within the entity's control'. A *contingent liability* is defined in FRS12 as: '(a) a possible obligation that arises from past events and whose existence will be confirmed only by the occurrence of one or more uncertain future events not wholly within the entity's control; or (b) a present obligation that arises from past events but is not recognised because: (i) it is not probable that a transfer of economic benefits will be required to settle the obligation; or (ii) the amount of the obligation cannot be measured with sufficient reliability'.

The accounting treatment of items that may be regarded as either provisions or contingent liabilities hinges on whether the potential obligation has a high or low probability of resulting in a liability. If there is a high probability, or is very likely, then a provision must be created. If there is a low probability, or is only a possibility, then it is treated as a contingent liability. In this case details must be given as a note to the financial statements, but no entries are made in the ledger or final accounts (ie. a provision or liability is not created).

The precise rules about what constitutes a provision are set out in FRS12 as follows:

'A provision should be recognised when: (a) an entity has a present obligation as a result of a past event; (b) it is *probable* that a transfer of economic benefits will be required to settle the obligation; and (c) a reliable estimate can be made of the amount of the obligation'.

The notes to the financial statements should disclose for each class of provision: (1) the carrying amount at the start and end of the period; (2) increases and decreases in the provision; (3) amounts charged against the provision; (4) a brief description of the nature of the obligation, and the expected timing of any resulting transfers of economic benefits; and (5) an indication of the uncertainties about the amount or timing of those transfers of economic benefits.

FRS12 states that 'an entity should not recognise a contingent liability'. That is, it should not be recognised as a provision or liability within the ledger or final accounts. A contingent liability is 'a *possible* obligation' that '*probably will not* require a transfer of economic benefits'. This must be shown as a note to the accounts. According to FRS12, 'unless the possibility of any transfer in settlement is remote, an entity should disclose for each class of contingent liability at the balance sheet date a brief description of the nature of the contingent liability and, where practicable: (1) an estimate of its financial effect; (2) an indication of the uncertainties relating to the amount or timing of any outflow; and (3) the possibility of any reimbursement'.

FRS12 also states that 'an entity should not recognise a contingent asset'. That is, it should not be included in the ledger or final accounts. A contingent asset is 'a possible asset' where the 'inflow of economic benefits is *probable* but not virtually certain'. This must be shown as a note to the accounts. According to FRS12, 'where an inflow of economic benefits is probable, an entity should disclose a brief description of the nature of the contingent assets at the balance sheet date and, where practicable, an estimate of their financial effect'.

A possible asset where the inflow of economic benefits is not probable is not recognised in the accounts and no disclosure in the form of a note is required.

Students may be confused by the apparent inconsistency in the definitions and accounting treatment of contingent assets and contingent liabilities which arises from the application of the prudence concept, whereby probable liabilities are recognised (as provisions) but probable assets are not. Similarly possible (ie. contingent) liabilities must be disclosed as a note but possible assets are not. Furthermore, the standard starts by defining contingent assets and contingent liabilities as *possible* assets and obligations, and then later implies that a contingent asset is a *probable* (not possible) asset.

It should also be noted that although contingencies are conditions which exist at the balance sheet date, their accounting treatment depends on information available up to the date on which the financial statements are approved by the board of directors.

A useful exercise at this point is to consider the similarities and differences between liabilities, provisions and contingent liabilities. A liability is a debt owed to a known party of a known certain amount. A provision is a known or highly probable future liability or loss, the amount and/or timing of which is uncertain (and thus has to be estimated). A contingent liability is uncertain with regard to its existence, timing and amount, and is thus only a possible liability.

Learning activity 27.2

Write to the head office of a large public limited company asking for a copy of their latest annual report and accounts. Examine the contents of the profit and loss account, balance sheet and notes to the accounts paying particular attention to the items discussed in this chapter.

Summary

The profit and loss accounts of companies contain the same items as those of sole traders but in addition include things like directors' remuneration, auditors' fees and interest on debentures/loan stock. As in the case of partnerships, the net profit is carried down into another section of the profit and loss account sometimes referred to as the appropriation account. In this is shown the corporation tax, dividends, and any transfers to reserves.

The balance sheets of companies are also similar to those of sole traders except that the capital account is replaced by the nominal value of the authorized, allotted and called-up share capital, and various reserves. These may be of two sorts, either revenue or capital reserves. Revenue reserves such as the retained profits can be distributed as dividends. Capital reserves such as the share premium, revaluation reserve, and capital redemption reserve, cannot be distributed as dividends. Loan stock and debentures are normally shown on the balance sheet as long-term liabilities at their nominal value.

The final accounts that are published and sent to ordinary shareholders must be presented in a form that complies with the fourth schedule to the Companies Act 1985, and various SSAPs and FRSs. One of the main purposes of many accounting standards, particularly FRS3, is to facilitate comparisons and predictions of performance by showing separately in the profit and loss account any items of a non-recurring nature. Thus FRS3 requires an analysis of turnover and operating profit between continuing operations, acquisitions and discontinued operations. Similarly FRS3 also states that exceptional and extraordinary items should be shown separately in published profit and loss accounts. These both relate to material non-recurring items; the difference being that exceptional items are a part of the ordinary activities whereas extraordinary items fall outside the ordinary activities. Comparisons and predictions may also be distorted where there are material adjustments applicable to prior periods arising from changes in accounting policies or the correction of fundamental errors. These are referred to as prior period adjustments; and FRS3 requires that the comparative figures for the preceeding year be restated, and the effect on the retained profits of the previous year shown as a movement on reserves.

In addition to showing certain items separately in final accounts, the Companies Act and various accounting standards require notes to be attached to the profit and loss account and balance sheet. These provide a more detailed breakdown, and in some cases, additional information about conditions prevailing at the balance sheet date, or events that have occurred since. Two examples are contingencies and post balance sheet events respectively. SSAP17 states that material adjusting events should be provided for in financial statements, and material non-adjusting events be disclosed as a note. Similarly FRS12 requires that probable material contingent losses be recognised in financial statements, and possible but not probable material contingent losses be disclosed as a note.

Key terms and concepts

Acquisitions, adjusting events, allotted/issued share capital, authorized/nominal share capital, called-up share capital, capital/non-distributable reserves, capital redemption reserve, contingencies, contingent assets, contingent liabilities, corporation tax, discontinued operations, exceptional items, extraordinary items, general reserve, non-adjusting events, operating profit, ordinary activities, post balance sheet events, prior period adjustments, profit on ordinary activities, provisions, reserves, retained profits, revaluation reserve, revenue/distributable reserves, shareholders' interests, share premium.

References

1. Accounting Standards Board (1992). *Financial Reporting Standard 3—Reporting Financial Performance* (ASB).
2. Accounting Standards Committee (1986). *Statement of Standard Accounting Practice 6—Extraordinary Items and Prior Year Adjustments* (ICAEW).
3. Accounting Standards Committee (1980). *Statement of Standard Accounting Practice 17—Accounting for Post Balance Sheet Events* (ICAEW).
4. Accounting Standards Board (1998). *Financial Reporting Standard 12—Provisions, Contingent Liabilities and Contingent Assets* (ASB).
5. Accounting Standards Committee (1980). *Statement of Standard Accounting Practice 18—Accounting for Contingencies* (ICAEW).

Exercises

An asterisk after the question number indicates that there is a suggested answer in the Appendix.

27.1. Explain the difference between the authorized share capital, allotted share capital and called-up share capital of companies.

27.2. Explain the difference between distributable reserves and non-distributable reserves, giving three examples of the latter.

27.3. Explain the difference between a reserve and a provision.

27.4. Briefly explain the reason(s) for the separate disclosure of components of financial performance such as discontinued operations, exceptional and extraordinary items in published company accounts.

27.5. (a) Explain with examples the nature of acquisitions and discontinued operations.
(b) Briefly describe the treatment of each of these items in published company accounts.

27.6. (a) Explain with examples the nature of exceptional items and extraordinary items.
(b) Briefly describe the treatment of each of these items in published company accounts.

27.7. (a) Explain with examples the nature of prior period adjustments.
(b) Briefly describe the treatment of prior period adjustments in published company accounts.

27.8. (a) Explain with examples the nature of post balance sheet events.
(b) Describe the treatment of post balance sheet events in published company accounts.

27.9. (a) Explain with examples the nature of contingent assets and contingent liabilities.
(b) Describe the treatment of contingent assets and liabilities in published company accounts.

27.10. Explain with an example the difference between current liabilities, provisions and contingent liabilities.

27.11. Set out below is the capital section of a company's balance sheet.

	31 March 19X8	31 March 19X7
	£'000	£'000
Ordinary share capital	140,000	140,000
Preference share capital	—	30,000
Share premium	20,000	20,000
Capital redemption reserve	30,000	—
Revaluation reserve	9,700	7,200
General reserve	27,000	20,000
Profit and loss account	84,900	70,300
	311,600	287,500

You are required to explain the five different reserves that are shown on this company's balance sheet, including in your answer the possible reasons for their existence. (JMB)

27.12. (a) The following terms usually appear in the final accounts of a limited company:

(i)   interim dividend,
(ii) authorized capital,
(iii) general reserve,
(iv) share premium account.

Required:
An explanation of the meaning of each of the above terms.

(b)   The following information has been obtained from the books of Drayfuss Ltd:

Authorized capital	100,000 8 per cent £1 preference shares
	400,000 50p ordinary shares
Profit and loss account balance	
1 April 19X8	£355,000
General reserve	£105,000
Issued capital	80,000 8 per cent £1 preference shares
	(fully paid)
	250,000 50p ordinary shares
	(fully paid)
Net trading profit for the year	
to 31 March 19X9	£95,000

The preference share interim dividend of 4 per cent had been paid and the final dividend of 4 per cent had been proposed by the directors. No ordinary share interim dividend had been declared, but the directors proposed a final dividend of 15p per share. The directors agreed to transfer to general reserve £150,000.

Required:
The profit and loss appropriation account for the year ended 31 March 19X9. Ignore taxation.   (AEB)

27.13. The following information has been extracted from the balance sheet of Aston Products Ltd as at 30 April 19X5.

	£'000
Authorized share capital	
Ordinary shares of 50 pence each	4,000
6% Preference shares of £1 each	1,500
	5,500
Allotted and called-up share capital	
Ordinary shares of 50 pence each	2,000
6% Preference shares of £1 each	1,000
	3,000
Retained profits	950

There were no other reserves in the balance sheet at the 30 April 19X5.
You are given the following additional information relating to the year ended 30 April 19X6.

1.   The company issued one million ordinary shares at a price of 75 pence each on 1 January 19X6.

2. The management have decided to revalue the land and buildings which cost £400,000 at a value of £600,000.
3. The profit before tax for the year ended 30 April 19X6 was £475,000.
4. The corporation tax on the profit for the year ended 30 April 19X6 was estimated to be £325,000.
5. There was no interim dividend during the year ended 30 April 19X6 but the directors have proposed a final dividend on the preference shares, and a final dividend of 10 pence each on the ordinary shares.
6. The directors have agreed to transfer £350,000 to a general reserve at the 30 April 19X6.

You are required to prepare in vertical form the profit and loss appropriation account for the year ended 30 April 19X6, and a balance sheet extract at that date showing the composition of the shareholders' interests.

27.14. Cold Heart plc which has a turnover of £100 million and pre-tax profit of £10 million has its accounts drawn up on 30 June each year and at 30 June 19X5 the company's accountant is considering the items specified below.

1. The directors have decided that the change in trading prospects evident during the year means that the goodwill shown at 30 June 19X4 at £200,000 has no value at 30 June 19X5.
2. Research and development expenditure of £7 million has been incurred in the year, and has been written off due to the project being abandoned.
3. Unrealized revaluation surplus of £10 million which arose on the revaluation of the company's buildings during the year.
4. A provision for bad debts of £15 million on the collapse of the company's main customer during the year.
5. A loss of £1 million arising from the closure of the company's retailing activities.

You are required to classify each of the above items into one of the following categories explaining the reasons for the classification:

(a) Extraordinary item
(b) Exceptional (abnormal) item
(c) Transfer direct to reserves
(d) Discontinued operations.   (JMB adapted)

27.15. SSAP17 Accounting for post balance sheet events defines the treatment to be given to events arising after the balance sheet date but before the financial statements are approved by the Board of Directors.
Required:

(a) Define the terms 'adjusting events' and 'non-adjustment events' as they are used in SSAP17.
(b) Consider each of the following four post balance sheet events.

If you think the event is an adjusting one, show exactly how items in the accounts should be changed to allow for the event.

If you think the event is non-adjusting, write a suitable disclosure note, including such details as you think fit.

You may assume that all the amounts are material but that none is large enough to jeopardise the going concern status of the company.

(i) The company makes an issue of 100,000 shares which raises £180,000 shortly after the balance sheet date.

(ii) A legal action brought against the company for breach of contract is decided, shortly after the balance sheet date, and as a result the company will have to pay costs and damages totalling £50,000. No provision has currently been made for this event. The breach of contract concerned occurred before the balance sheet date.

(iii) Stock included in the accounts at cost £28,000 was subsequently sold for £18,000.

(iv) A factory in use at the balance sheet date and valued at £250,000 was completely destroyed by fire. Only half of the value was covered by insurance. The insurance company has agreed to pay £125,000 under the company's policy.   (ACCA)

27.16. Your managing director is having a polite disagreement with the auditors on the subject of accounting for contingencies. Since the finance director is absent on sick leave he has come to you for advice.

It appears that your firm is involved in four unrelated legal cases, P, Q, R and S. In case P the firm is suing for £10,000, in case Q the firm is suing for £20,000, in case R the firm is being sued for £30,000 and in case S the firm is being sued for £40,000. The firm has been advised by its expert and expensive lawyers that the chances of the firm winning each case are as follows:

Case	Percentage likelihood of winning
P	8
Q	92
R	8
S	92

Required:
Write a memorandum to the managing director which

(i) explains why FRS12 is relevant to these situations,

(ii) states the required accounting treatment for each of the four cases in the published accounts,

(iii) gives journal entries for any necessary adjustments in the double-entry records,

(iv) suggests the contents of any Notes to the Accounts that are required by the FRS,

(v) briefly discusses whether FRS12 leads to a satisfactory representation of the position.   (ACCA)

27.17. The trial balance of Norr Ltd at 31 December 19X9 appeared as follows:

	Dr	Cr
	£	£
Ordinary shares of £1—fully paid		50,000
Purchases	220,000	
Retained profit		30,000
Freehold property—cost	80,000	
Fixtures—cost	15,000	

Fixtures—accumulated depreciation		9,000
Rates	3,000	
Motor vehicles—cost	28,000	
Motor vehicles—accumulated depreciation		14,000
Insurance	2,000	
Stock	40,000	
Debtors	30,000	
Trade creditors		24,000
Sales		310,000
Bank	12,100	
12 per cent debentures		40,000
Debenture interest	2,400	
Wages and salaries	34,000	
Heat and light	4,100	
Professional fees	3,900	
General expenses	1,200	
Motor expenses	2,000	
Provision for bad debts		1,000
Bad debts	300	
	478,000	478,000

Additional information

1. During the year a motor vehicle purchased on 31 March 19X6 for £8,000 was sold for £3,000. The sale proceeds were debited to the bank account and credited to the sales account, and no other entries have been made in the accounts relating to this transaction.
2. Depreciation has not yet been provided for the year. The following rates are applied on the straight line basis, with the assumption of no residual value:

   Fixtures and fittings   10 per cent
   Motor vehicles   20 per cent

   The company's policy is to provide a full year's depreciation in the year of acquisition and no depreciation in the year of disposal.
3. Stock at 31 December 19X9 amounted to £45,000.
4. Rates paid in advance amount to £400. Insurance includes £200 paid in advance. An electricity bill covering the quarter to 31 December 19X9 and amounting to £320 was not received until February 19X0. It is estimated that the audit fee for 19X9 will be £1,500. An accrual also needs to be made in relation to debenture interest.
5. A general provision for bad debt of 4 per cent of debtors is to be carried forward.
6. The directors propose a dividend of £10,000.

You are required to:

(a) prepare a profit and loss account and balance sheet on the basis of the above information;
(b) explain the meaning of the terms 'provision' and 'reserve', giving one example of each from the balance sheet you have prepared.   (JMB adapted)

27.18. The Cirrus Company Ltd has the following balances on its books at 31 December 19X0.

	Dr £	Cr £
50p ordinary shares		20,000
£1 6 per cent preference shares		14,000
Purchases	240,000	
Sales		310,000
Stock at 1 January 19X0	20,000	
Directors' fees	6,000	
Undistributed profit at 1 January 19X0		35,700
10 per cent debentures		20,000
Debenture interest paid	1,000	
Discounts allowed	500	
Administrative expenses	18,400	
Sales staff salaries	18,500	
Selling and distribution expenses	4,000	
Heating and lighting	2,500	
Rent and rates	1,700	
Debtors	14,000	
Provision for doubtful debts at 1 January		300
Creditors		9,700
Land and buildings at cost	65,000	
Vans at cost less depreciation	19,800	
Cash in hand	400	
Bank balance		2,100
	411,800	411,800

The following information is also given:

1. The stock at 31 December 19X0 has been valued at £32,000. Further investigation reveals that this includes some items originally purchased for £3,000 which have been in stock for a long time. They need modification, probably costing about £600, after which it is hoped they will be saleable for between £3,200 and £3,500. Other items, included in the total at their cost price of £5,000, have been sent to an agent and are still at his premises awaiting sale. It cost £200 for transport and insurance to get them to the agent's premises and this amount is included in the selling and distribution expenses.

2. The balance on the vans account (£19,800) is made up as follows:

	£
Vans at cost (as at 1 January 19X0)	30,000
Less: Provision for depreciation to 1 January 19X0	13,800
	16,200
Additions during 19X0 at cost	3,600
	19,800

Depreciation is provided at 25 per cent per annum on the diminishing balance method. The addition during the year was invoiced as follows:

	£
Recommended retail price	3,000
Signwriting on van	450
Undersealing	62
Petrol	16
Number plates	12
Licence (to 31 December 19X0)	60
	3,600

3. The directors, having sought the advice of an independent valuer, wish to revalue the land and buildings at £80,000.
4. The directors wish to make a provision for doubtful debts of 2½ per cent of the balance of debtors at 31 December 19X0.
5. Rates prepaid at 31 December 19X0 amount to £400, and sales staff's salaries owing at that date were £443.
6. The directors have proposed an ordinary dividend of 5p per share and the 6 per cent preference dividend.
7. Ignore VAT.

Required:
(a) Explain carefully the reason for the adjustments you have made in respect of items 1, 2 and 3 above.
(b) Prepare a trading and profit and loss account for the year ended 31 December 19X0, and a balance sheet as at that date.
(c) Briefly distinguish between your treatment of debenture interest and proposed dividends. (ACCA)

27.19.* The following is the trial balance of D. Cooper Ltd as at 30 September 19X9:

	Debit £	Credit £
Authorized and allotted share capital:		
100,000 ordinary shares of £1 each		100,000
50,000 7 per cent preference shares of 50p each		25,000
Leasehold premises at valuation	140,000	
Goodwill	20,000	
Plant and machinery (cost £80,000)	66,900	
Loose tools (cost £13,000)	9,100	
Stock	9,400	
Debtors/creditors	11,200	8,300
Bank overdraft		7,800
Purchases/sales	49,700	135,250
Directors' salaries	22,000	
Rates	4,650	
Light and heat	3,830	
Plant hire	6,600	

Interest on debentures	1,200	
Preliminary expenses	1,270	
10 per cent debentures		24,000
Provision for bad debts		910
Share premium		35,000
Profit and loss account		2,580
Revenue reserve		10,200
Interim dividend on ordinary shares	3,250	
Audit fees	1,750	
Revaluation reserve		9,860
Bad debts	700	
Listed investments	8,000	
Investment income		650
	359,550	359,550

The following additional information is available:

1. Stock at 30 September 19X9 is valued at £13,480.
2. Rates include a payment of £2,300 for the six months from 1 July 19X9.
3. Depreciation on plant is 15 per cent per annum of cost and the loose tools were valued at £7,800 on 30 September 19X9. The company does not amortize goodwill or premises.
4. The provision for bad debts is to be adjusted to 10 per cent of the debtors at the end of the year.
5. The preference share dividends are outstanding at the end of the year and the last half year's interest on the debentures has not been paid.
6. The corporation tax on this year's profit is £6,370.
7. The directors propose to declare a final dividend on the ordinary shares of 13 pence per share and transfer £2,500 to the revenue reserve.

You are required to prepare in vertical form a profit and loss account for the year ended 30 September 19X9 and a balance sheet at that date.

27.20.* The following is the trial balance of L. Johnson Ltd at 31 December 19X8:

	Debit £	Credit £
Authorized capital:		
200,000 ordinary shares of £1 each		200,000
90,000 5 per cent preference shares of £1 each		90,000
Issued capital:		
80,000 ordinary shares		80,000
50,000 5 per cent preference shares		50,000
Freehold buildings (at valuation)	137,000	
Motor vehicle (cost £35,000)	29,400	
Plant and machinery (cost £40,000)	32,950	
Development costs (cost £10,000)	6,600	
Interim dividend on preference shares	1,250	
Provision for bad debts		860

Wages and salaries	5,948	
Bad debts	656	
Discount allowed/received	492	270
Goodwill	10,000	
Listed investments	4,873	
Purchases/sales	78,493	130,846
Capital redemption reserve fund		9,000
Revaluation reserve		13,500
Formation expenses	250	
Directors' emoluments	13,000	
Returns inwards/outwards	1,629	1,834
Rates	596	
Dividends received		310
Profit and loss account		3,126
Share transfer fees received		126
Light and heat	1,028	
Audit fee	764	
Revenue reserve		8,400
Share premium		5,600
10 per cent debentures		30,000
Stock	9,436	
Debtors/creditors	11,600	8,450
Bank overdraft		3,643
	345,965	345,965

You are given the following additional information:

1. Corporation tax of £2,544 will be payable on the profit of 19X8.
2. Rates include £200 for the half year ended on 31 March 19X9.
3. Electricity for the quarter to 31 January 19X9 of £330 is not included in the trial balance.
4. The provision for bad debts is to be adjusted to 5 per cent of the debtors at the end of the year.
5. Annual depreciation on the reducing balance method is 25 per cent of vehicles, 20 per cent of plant and 10 per cent of development costs. The company does not amortize goodwill or buildings.
6. Formation expenses are to be written off against the share premium account.
7. Stock at 31 December 19X8 was £12,456.
8. It is proposed to pay a final dividend on the ordinary shares of 6.25 pence per share.
9. The directors have decided to transfer £4,000 to the revenue reserve this year.
10. The debenture interest for the year and the final dividend on the preference shares are outstanding at the end of the year.

You are required to prepare in vertical form a profit and loss account for the year ended 31 December 19X8 and a balance sheet at that date.

27.21.* The following is the trial balance of Oakwood Limited as at 30 June 19X5:

	Debit £	Credit £
Authorized capital:		
150,000 ordinary shares of £1 each		150,000
70,000 5 per cent preference shares of £1 each		70,000
Allotted capital:		
125,000 ordinary shares		125,000
60,000 5 per cent preference shares		60,000
Freehold buildings at cost	165,000	
Development costs (cost £12,000)	5,400	
Goodwill	8,000	
Delivery vehicles (cost £28,000)	18,700	
Plant and machinery (cost £34,000)	31,900	
Listed investments	3,250	
10 per cent debentures		20,000
Share premium		9,000
Revenue reserve		6,100
Interim dividend on ordinary shares	2,000	
Interim dividend on preference shares	1,500	
Provision for bad debts		730
Administrative salaries	6,370	
Bad debts	740	
Discount allowed/received	290	300
Purchases/sales	81,230	120,640
Audit fee	390	
Preliminary expenses	200	
Directors' remuneration	14,100	
Returns inwards/outwards	230	640
Carriage inwards	310	
Rates	600	
Interest received		410
Profit and loss account		7,700
Share transfer fees received		140
Light and heat	940	
Postage and telephone	870	
Stock	8,760	
Debtors/creditors	10,400	7,890
Bank overdraft		2,630
	361,180	361,180

Additional information:

1. Corporation tax of £1,080 will be payable on the profit of this year.
2. Rates include a prepayment of £150.
3. Gas used in May and June 19X5 of £270 is not included in the trial balance.
4. Stock at 30 June 19X5 was £11,680.

5. The provision for bad debts is to be adjusted to 5 per cent of debtors at 30 June 19X5.

6. Annual depreciation on the reducing balance method is 20 per cent of plant, 10 per cent of vehicles, 25 per cent of development costs. The company does not amortize buildings or goodwill.

7. Sales includes goods on sale or return at 30 June 19X5 which cost £500 and were invoiced to debtors at a price of £1,000.

8. Included in plant and machinery are consumable tools purchased during the year at a cost of £300.

9. The preliminary expenses are to be written off against the share premium account balance.

10. It is proposed to pay a final dividend on the ordinary shares of 3.2 pence per share.

11. The directors have decided to transfer £3,000 to the revenue reserve.

You are required to prepare in vertical form a profit and loss account for the year ended 30 June 19X5 and a balance sheet at that date.

27.22. The trial balance of Harmonica Limited at 31 December 19X5 is given below.

	Dr	Cr
	£000	£000
Purchases and sales	18,000	28,600
Stock at 1 January 19X5	4,500	
Warehouse wages	850	
Salespersons' salaries and commission	1,850	
Administrative salaries	3,070	
General administrative expenses	580	
General distribution expenses	490	
Directors' remuneration	870	
Debenture interest paid	100	
Dividends – interim dividend paid	40	
Fixed assets – cost	18,000	
– aggregate depreciation, 1 January 19X5		3,900
Trade debtors and creditors	6,900	3,800
Provision for doubtful debts at 1 January 19X5		200
Balance at bank		2,080
10% Debentures (repayable 20X0)		1,000
Called up share capital (£1 ordinary shares)		4,000
Share premium account		1,300
Profit and loss account, 1 January 19X5		8,720
Suspense account (see Note 3 below)		1,650
	55,250	55,250

The following further information should be allowed for:

(1) Closing stock amounted to £5m.

(2) A review of the trade debtors total of £6.9m showed that it was necessary to write off debts totalling £0.4m, and that the provision for doubtful debts should be adjusted to 2% of the remaining trade debtors.

(3) Two transactions have been entered in the company's cash record and transferred to the suspense account shown in the trial balance. They are:

    (a) The receipt of £1.5m from the issue of 500,000 £1 ordinary shares at a premium of £2 per share.

    (b) The sale of some surplus plant. The plant had cost £1m and had a written down value of £100,000. The sale proceeds of £150,000 have been credited to the suspense account but no other entries have been made.

(4) Depreciation should be charged at 10% per annum on cost at the end of the year and allocated 70% to distribution costs and 30% to administration.

(5) The directors propose a final dividend of 4 pence per share on the shares in issue at the end of the year.

(6) Accruals and prepayments still to be accounted for are:

	Prepayments £000	Accruals £000
General administrative expenses	70	140
General distribution expenses	40	90
	110	230

(7) Directors' remuneration is to be analysed between distribution costs and administrative expenses as follows:

	£000
—distribution	300
—administration	570
	870

(8) Ignore taxation.

Required:

Prepare the company's trading and profit and loss account for the year ended 31 December 19X5 and balance sheet as at 31 December 19X5 in a form suitable for publication. Notes to the accounts are not required. (ACCA)

27.23. Before attempting this question students will need to read the sections of the next chapter relating to rights issues and bonus issues.

The summarized balance sheet of Arbalest Limited at 30 September 19X6 was as follows:

	Cost £000	Aggregate depreciation £000	Net book value £000
Fixed assets			
Land	2,000	nil	2,000
Buildings	1,500	450	1,050
Plant and machinery	2,800	1,000	1,800
	6,300	1,450	4,850

Current assets	3180	
Less: Current liabilities	<u>2,070</u>	1,110
		<u>5,960</u>
Capital and reserves		
Called-up share capital		
3,000,000 ordinary shares of 50p each		1,500
Share premium account		400
Profit and loss account		<u>4,060</u>
		<u>5,960</u>

During the year ended 30 September 19X7 the company had the following transactions:

1 November 19X6: A rights issue of one share for every three held at a price of £1.50 per share. All the rights issue shares were taken up.

1 December 19X6: Sale for £70,000 of plant and machinery which had cost £1,000,000 and had a book value of £200,000.

1 March 19X7: A bonus (capitalisation) issue of one share for every one held at that date using the share premium account as far as possible for the purpose.

1 June 19X7: Purchased a new factory block for £3,000,000 (including land £600,000).

1 July 19X7: Purchased plant and machinery for £1,600,000.

30 September 19X7: The company decided to revalue the freehold land held at 30 September 19X6 from £2,000,000 to £2,500,000.

The company depreciation policies are:

Land	no depreciation
Buildings	2% per annum on cost straight-line basis
Plant and machinery	10% per annum on cost, straight-line basis

Proportionate depreciation is provided in the year of purchase of an asset, with none in the year of disposal.

The retained profit for the year was £370,000, and the profit for the year was £840,000.

Prepare the following notes required for the company's balance sheet for publication at 30 September 19X7:

(a)   Movements on fixed assets
(b)   Movements on reserves
(c)   A statement of total recognised gains and losses

Ledger accounts for the transactions are not required.   (ACCA adapted)

27.24. The following balances existed in the accounting records of Koppa Limited at 31 December 19X7:

	£000
Development costs capitalised, 1 January 19X7	180
Freehold land as revalued 31 December 19X7	2,200
Buildings —cost	900
—aggregate depreciation at 1 January 19X7	100
Office equipment —cost	260
—aggregate depreciation at 1 January 19X7	60
Motor vehicles —cost	200
—aggregate depreciation at 1 January 19X7	90
Trade debtors	1,360
Cash at bank	90
Trade creditors	820
12% debentures (issued 19X0 and redeemable 20X7)	1,000
Called up share capital—ordinary shares of 50p each	1,000
Share premium account	500
Revaluation reserve	200
Profit and loss account 1 January 19X7	1,272
Sales	8,650
Purchases	5,010
Research and development expenditure for the year	162
Stock 1 January 19X7	990
Distribution costs	460
Administrative expenses	1,560
Debenture interest	120
Interim dividend paid	200

In preparing the company's profit and loss account and balance sheet at 31 December 19X7 the following further information is relevant:

(1) Stock at 31 December 19X7 was £880,000.

(2) Depreciation is to be provided for as follows:

Land	nil
Buildings	2% per annum on cost
Office equipment	20% per annum, reducing balance basis
Motor vehicles	25% per annum on cost

Depreciation on buildings and office equipment is all charged to administrative expenses. Depreciation on motor vehicles is to be split equally between distribution costs and administrative expenses.

(3) The £180,000 total for development costs as at 1 January 19X7 relates to two projects:

	£000
Project 836: completed project:	82
(balance being amortised over the period expected to benefit from it. Amount to be amortised in 19X7: £20,000)	
Project 910: in progress:	98
	180

(4)   The research and development expenditure for the year is made up of:

	£000
Research expenditure	103
Development costs on Project 910 which continues to satisfy the requirements in SSAP13 for capitalisation	59
	162

(5)   The freehold land had originally cost £2,000,000 and was revalued on 31 December 19X7.

(6)   Prepayments and accruals at 31 December 19X7 were:

	Prepayments £000	Accruals £000
Administrative expenses	40	11
Sundry distribution costs		4

(7)   The share premium account balance arose as a result of the issue during 19X7 of 1,000,000 50p ordinary shares at £1.00 each. All shares qualify for the proposed final dividend to be provided for (see note below).

(8)   A final dividend of 20p per share is proposed.

Required:

Prepare the company's profit and loss account for the year ended 31 December 19X7 and balance sheet as at that date, in a form suitable for publication as far as the information provided permits. The note detailing reserve movements for the year should be given, but no other notes are required. Ignore taxation.   (ACCA)

27.25*   Topaz Limited makes up its accounts regularly to 31 December each year. The company has operated for some years with four divisions A, B, C and D, but on 30 June 19X6 Division B was sold for £8m, realising a profit of £2.5m. During 19X6 there was a fundamental reorganisation of Division C, the costs of which were £1.8m.

The trial balance of the company at 31 December 19X6 included the following balances:

	Division B		Divisions A, C and D Combined	
	Dr £m	Cr £m	Dr £m	Cr £m
Sales		13		68
Costs of sales	8		41	
Distribution costs (including a bad debt of £1.9m – Division D)	1		6	
Administrative expenses	2		4	
Profit on sale of Division B		2.5		

Reorganisation costs,
Division C   1.8
Interest on £10m 10% debenture
stock issued in 19X0   1
Taxation   4.8
Interim dividend paid   2
Revaluation reserve   10

A final dividend of £4m is proposed.

The balance on the revaluation reserve relates to the company's freehold property and arose as follows:

	£m
Balance at 1.1.X6	6
Revaluation during 19X6	4
Balance at 31.12.X6 per trial balance	10

Required:

(a) (i) Prepare the profit and loss account of Topaz Limited for the year ended 31 December 19X6 complying as far as possible with the provisions of the Companies Act 1985 and *FRS3 Reporting Financial Performance.*

   (ii) Prepare the statement of total recognised gains and losses for the year as required by FRS3

(b) Explain why the changes to the profit and loss account introduced by FRS3 improve the quality of information available to users of the financial statements. (ACCA)

28.   Changes in share capital

Learning objectives

After reading this chapter the student should be able to:

1.   Explain the meaning of the key terms and concepts listed at the end of the chapter.
2.   Describe the procedures relating to the issue of shares to the public, forfeited shares, reissued shares, rights issues, bonus issues, and the purchase and redemption of shares.
3.   Explain the nature and purpose of rights issues and bonus issues.
4.   Describe the legal restrictions on the purchase and redemption of shares including the reasons for these restrictions.
5.   Show the journal and ledger entries relating to public issues, forfeited shares, reissued shares, rights issues, bonus issues, and the purchase and redemption of shares.
6.   Prepare the balance sheet of a limited company immediately after a change in share capital.

Introduction

A feature distinguishing companies from other forms of business organization is the use of equity finance through the issue of shares. Chapter 26 drew attention to the characteristics of company capital. This chapter focuses on the special accounting procedures which are used to record expansion in the number of shares through issues, and reductions through redemptions.

Share issues to the public

Other share issues involve very large sums of money and, given that a series of actions needs to be taken, are complex matters. Since, in addition, this money is being paid in by members of the public, great care must be taken in the procedures which record the various actions.

It may be useful, before considering the accounting procedures themselves, to review the whole process. A number of methods may be used to issue shares to the public, but the accounting procedures are similar and these can be presented most appropriately by considering an *Offer for Sale*.

First an offer is made to the public to apply for shares. At this time the price to be paid for the share is set. This price may be the same as, or above, the par/nominal value of the share. However, under the Companies Acts shares may not be issued at below their par value. Thus a £1 share may be issued at £1 or any price above £1, say £3. The additional amount included in the price is the share premium, which must be recorded as one of the capital reserves considered in the previous chapter.

On *application* it is usual for applicants to be required to send money representing part but not all of the price of the shares for which they apply (known as application money). Once the closing date for applications is reached the number of shares applied for must be compared with the number on offer. If applications are lower than the number on offer, the issue is undersubscribed and the company will either be required to cancel the offer and refund the application money or to call upon the underwriters to take up the remaining shares. If the issue is oversubscribed, then a basis for allotting shares must be established. Some applications may be rejected and the application money must be refunded; some may get a reduced allocation and their application money used as further payment towards the price of the shares.

Having established the basis for allocation, shares can then be issued to those who are to get them—an action known as *allotment*. The balance of the price is, typically, payable in instalments, perhaps some on allotment (known as 'allotment money') and some *calls* at a later date (known as 'call money'). There may be more than one instalment, so there would be a first call, second call, etc. Anyone failing to pay a call is liable to *forfeit* their partly paid shares and once forfeited, these may be *reissued* to others on terms agreed for this purpose.

Learning activity 28.1

Watch the financial press for an issue of shares to the public, such as a government privatization. Obtain a copy of the prospectus and read carefully the terms of the issue with particular reference to the amounts payable on application, allotment and any calls. Note also the relevant date, dividend entitlement, etc.

The major stages of an issue of shares can be summarized as follows:

	STAGES				
	Application	Allotment	Calls	Forfeit	Reissue
Cash effects on company	Application money received	Allotment money received	Call money received	—	Reissue money received

The double entry to record all of these stages follows:

Stage	Transaction	Debit	Credit
1. Application	Money received	Cash	Application and allotment account
2. Allotment	Refund some application money	Application and allotment account	Cash

	Allotment money received	Cash	Application and allotment account
	Issue of shares partly paid	Application and allotment account	Share capital
	Share premium (if any)	Application and allotment account	Share premium
3. Call	Call made	Call account	Share capital
	Call money received	Cash	Call account
4. Forfeit	Called-up value of forfeited shares excluding share premium	Share capital	Forfeited shares account
	Premium included in amount called up (if any)	Share premium	Forfeited shares account
	Amount in the call account relating to arrears on forfeited shares	Forfeited shares account	Call account
5. Reissue	Nominal value of shares reissued called up	Reissues account	Share capital
	Money received	Cash	Reissues account
	Amount in forfeited shares account relating to reissue	Forfeited shares account	Reissues account
	Balance on reissues account	Reissues account	Share premium

An example can be used to show how these entries will be reflected in the various ledgers.

Example 28.1

The issued share capital of Stag plc was £100 million being 100 million ordinary shares of £1 each fully paid with no share premium account. Since the company wished to expand but had a bank balance of only £1 million it decided to issue more shares. On 2 January 19X1 the company offered 40 million shares to the public at £1.25 each, payable 40p on application, 30p on allotment and 55p on call at 30 June 19X1.

Applications closed on 31 January when applications had been received for 65 million shares. On 4 February, 15 million were rejected and money returned, and allotments were made pro rata to the remaining applicants.

Note that since 50 million share applications were not rejected, allotments were on the basis of four shares 50p paid (i.e. 50 million @ 40p ÷ 40 million) for every five shares applied for; a balance of only 30p − (50p − 40p) = 20p per share will be payable on allotment.

The amounts due on allotments were received in full by 28 February.

By 4 July, call money for 32 million shares had been received. The remaining shares (8 million) were forfeited. On 18 July 4 million forfeited shares were reissued at 75p each.

Workings
Application and allotment
Application money = 65 million @ 0.40 = £26 million
Refunded = 15 million @ £0.40 = £6 million
Allotment money = 40 million @ £0.20 = £8 million
Share premium per share = £1.25 − £1 = £0.25
Total share premium = 40 million @ £0.25 = £10 million
Nominal value of application and allotment = 40 million @ (£0.40 + £0.30 − £0.25) = £18 million.

Call
Nominal value of call = 40 million @ £0.55 = £22 million
Call money received = 32 million @ £0.55 = £17.6 million.

Forfeiture
Called-up value of forfeited shares excluding the share premium = 8 million @ £1 = £8 million
Premium included in the amount called up relating to forfeited shares = 8 million @ £0.25 = £2 million
Amount in call account relating to arrears on forfeited shares = 8 million @ £0.55 = £4.4 million.

Reissue
Reissue money received = 4 million @ £0.75 = £3 million
Nominal value of shares reissued called up = 4 million @ £1 = £4 million
Amount in forfeited shares account relating to reissue = 4 million @ (£0.40 + £0.30) = £2.8 million.

The entries to record the application and allotment will appear in the ledger as shown below (all amounts in £ millions):

Bank

2 Jan	Balance b/d	1	4 Feb	Appln. and Allotment	6
31 Jan	Appln. and Allotment	26		Balance c/d	29
28 Feb	Appln. and Allotment	8			
		35			35
	Balance b/d	29			

Application and allotment

4 Feb	Bank	6	31 Jan	Bank		26
4 Feb	Share capital	18	28 Feb	Bank		8
4 Feb	Share premium	10				
		34				34

Share capital

			2 Jan	Balance b/d	100
			4 Feb	Appln. and Allotment	18
					118

Share premium

			4 Feb	Appln. and Allotment	10

The call and forfeiture can then be entered in the ledger as follows:

Bank

	Balance b/d	29
4 July	Call	17.6
		46.6

Share capital

4 July	Forfeited shares	8		Balance b/d	118
	Balance c/d	132	30 June	Call	22
		140			140
				Balance b/d	132

Share premium

4 July	Forfeited shares	2		Balance b/d	10
	Balance c/d	8			
		10			10
				Balance b/d	8

Call

30 June	Share capital	22	4 July	Bank	17.6
			4 July	Forfeited shares	4.4
		22			22

Forfeited shares

4 July	Call	4.4	4 July	Share capital	8
	Balance c/d	5.6		Share premium	2
		10			10
				Balance b/d	5.6

Finally the amounts can be entered for the reissue of 4 million shares, thus:

Bank

	Balance b/d	46.6
18 July	Reissues	3
		49.6

Share capital

	Balance b/d	132
18 July	Reissues	4
		136

Share premium

	Balance b/d	8
18 July	Reissues	1.8
		9.8

Forfeited shares

18 July	Reissues	2.8	Balance b/d	5.6
	Balance c/d	2.8		
		5.6		5.6
			Balance b/d	2.8

Reissues

18 July	Share capital	4	18 July	Bank	3
	Share premium	1.8	18 July	Forfeited shares	2.8
		5.8			5.8

Note

1. The balances can be interpreted thus: the share capital represents the original shares of £100 million plus 36 million shares issued at £1 par value. The forfeited shares account balance of £2.8 million is the remaining 4 million shares not reissued at the 70p application and allotment amounts. The share premium comprises £9 million being the premium at 25p on the 36 million shares issued, plus the additional premium of £800,000 on the reissue–in the case of the 4 million reissued shares, 75p rather than just the call money of 55p was raised, giving 4 million $\times$ 20p = £800,000.

Rights issues

Offering shares for sale to the public is an expensive and potentially risky process. Costs can be saved by offering shares to existing shareholders at below the current market price. Failure to take up their rights to the issue would thus mean that shareholders lose the opportunity of making a gain. As a result, all shareholders can be expected either to take up the issue (providing it is priced sufficiently below the existing market price) or to sell their rights to someone who will. The success of the issue is thus much less risky.

If the full subscription price is payable upon issue, the accounting entries are simple. Recognition must be given to any premium included in the price. Thus, for a company with 15 million shares of £1 which decides to make a 1 for 5 rights issue at a price of £1.80 (when the market price is £2.50 say) the entries must reflect the 80p per share premium as shown below:

The Journal

	Debit £	Credit £
Bank (3 million × £1.80)	5,400,000	
Share capital		3,000,000
Share premium		2,400,000
	5,400,000	5,400,000

Bonus issues

Accounting for bonus issues is relatively straightforward. No cash is involved and the issue represents 'converting' capital or revenue reserves into shares and distributing these to existing shareholders. While some reserves may have a range of uses, shares are regarded as a particularly permanent form of capital. The effect of making a bonus issue is to adjust the capital structure portrayed in accounts. The increased permanence of capital this presents may be taken as an indicator of increased security.

The double entry may make use of a temporary bonus account so that credit amounts can be transferred from reserves to the bonus account and from this to share capital on the issue of the shares. For example, the capital structure of XS plc at 1 May 19X1 may be as follows:

	£'000
Share capital 10 million ordinary shares of £1 each	10,000
General reserves	1,800
Share premium	3,000
Shareholders interests	14,800

It has been decided to make a bonus issue of two ordinary shares for every five existing shares. Since general reserves represent revenue reserves, while share premium is a capital reserve for which the law permits only limited uses, it will probably be more attractive to the company to utilize the share premium first. The ledger entries (in £'000) will be as follows:

Share premium

Bonus shares	3,000	Balance b/d	3,000

General reserve

Bonus shares	1,000	Balance b/d	1,800
Balance c/d	800		
	1,800		1,800
		Balance b/d	800

Bonus shares account

Ordinary shares	4,000	Share premium	3,000
		General reserve	1,000
	4,000		4,000

Ordinary share capital

		Balance b/d	10,000
		Bonus shares	4,000
			14,000

Alternatively the bonus shares account may be omitted and the entries made between the reserve accounts and the share capital account directly.

The balance sheet would indicate a revised capital structure thus:

	£'000
Share capital 14 million ordinary shares of £1 each	14,000
General reserves	800
Shareholders interests	14,800

The same shareholders own the same assets but their ownership is represented by more shares. In theory, they should be in just the same financial position as before the issue.

Purchase and redemption of shares

By contrast to issuing new shares, we now turn to accounting for buying them back. The law identifies two types of buying back shares, purchase and redemption. Apart from the words that are used to describe the transactions and the change of name in account headings, the accounting procedures are identical for both types. The difference arises from the terms under which the shares are originally issued. Some shares are issued as 'redeemable shares'. This may be during a specifically defined period or merely at the discretion of the company or even the shareholder. Purchase takes place when shares which are not identifiable as 'redeemable' are purchased by the company.

In both cases, important legal restrictions are applicable. A company may only issue redeemable shares provided it has, in issue, some shares that are not redeemable. After any purchase of shares a company must have in issue shares such that at least two shareholders remain owning shares that are not redeemable. Only fully paid shares may be redeemed or purchased and all shares bought back by the company must be cancelled so they are not available for resale. The law does not restrict the classes of shares which may be redeemed, although most examples have tended to deal with preference shares. The illustrations tend to show redemption of preference shares, but purchase or redemption of ordinary shares could equally well be used.

A particular concern embodied in the law is to maintain the called-up capital (and capital reserves). This is intended as a protection for creditors. While shareholders may be entitled, under the Companies Acts, to receive dividends from distributable profits, called-up capital and (and capital reserves) cannot be freely distributed. If a company is wound up, creditors must be paid before shareholders get any capital repayment. The preferred position of the creditors would have been severely undermined if any earlier capital repayments had been made. The law restricts companies from using borrowing to make payments to shareholders beyond any profits made, since this may leave nothing for the creditors. The idea of maintenance of capital, introduced in accounting as a basis for measurement (see Chapter 2), is being utilized here, in restricting dividends to distributable profits, as a legal principle.

The legal considerations relating to the nominal value of shares are separated from those dealing with premiums, so initially this section will address redemption (or purchase) at nominal values first and then introduce the treatment of premiums.

Redemption (or purchase) at nominal value

The legal requirements for maintenance of capital when a redemption is made can be achieved by:

1. Setting aside distributable profits equal to the nominal value of capital redeemed by transferring that amount to a non-distributable reserve known as 'capital redemption reserve'. To enable this to be carried out, there must have been distributable profits sufficient to redeem the capital repaid and the transfer 'freezes' those profits in a capital form.
2. Issuing new shares explicitly for the purpose of providing funds for redemption with nominal value not less than that of the shares redeemed. This effectively replaces the capital redeemed by new capital.
3. A combination of new issues and transfers to capital redemption reserve which, in total, amount to the nominal value of capital redeemed.

Example 28.2 illustrates how these requirements are applied as follows:

Example 28.2
The following is the summarized balance sheet of J plc as at 30 June 19X1:

	£'000
Sundry assets	280
Bank	160
	440

Preference share capital	80
Ordinary share capital	200
Share premium	20
Unappropriated profit and loss	140
	440

If a company decided to redeem all the preference capital at par (i.e. the nominal value) without any new issue of shares, then the double entry would be thus:

The journal

	Debit £	Credit £
Preference share capital	80,000	
Bank		80,000

Being the repayment of shares

	Debit £	Credit £
Unappropriated profit and loss	80,000	
Capital redemption reserve		80,000

The last entry is the transfer of distributable profits to the capital redemption reserve to maintain non-distributable capital. The maintenance of capital can be readily identified by looking at an extract from the balance sheet before and after the redemption as shown below.

	Before £'000		After £'000
Preference share capital	80	Capital redemption reserve	80
Ordinary share capital	200		200
Share premium	20		20
Non distributable capital	300		300

Now suppose the company had only £60,000 bank and £380,000 sundry assets. It might wish to raise money to contribute to the redemption through the issue of shares. If a rights issue of £50,000 ordinary shares was made, at par, as part of the scheme of redemption the entries would be as follows:

The journal

	Debit £	Credit £
Bank	50,000	
Ordinary share capital		50,000
Preference share capital	80,000	
Bank		80,000
Unappropriated profit and loss	30,000	
Capital redemption reserve		30,000

The amount transferred to the capital redemption reserve is the excess of the shares redeemed over the nominal value of the capital issued (i.e. £80,000 − £50,000 = £30,000).

Again the maintenance of non-distributable capital can be demonstrated by looking at an extract from the balance sheet before and after the redemption shown below:

	Before £'000		After £'000
Preference share capital	80	Capital redemption reserve	30
Ordinary share capital	200		250
Share premium	20		20
Non-distributable capital	300		300

Redemption (or purchase) at a premium

Shares are often bought back at a price above the nominal value, the excess representing a premium. Unless the shares were originally issued at a premium, the premium paid must be transferred from distributable profits. Even where the shares were originally issued at a premium, there are limitations on the extent by which the transfer may be reduced. The amount is restricted to the smaller of:

1. the premium on the original issue of the shares;
2. the sum of the balance on the share premium account plus the premium on the new issue used to fund (in part) the redemption.

Example 28.3 illustrates how these rules are applied.

Example 28.3

The following is an extract from the balance sheet of K plc as at 31 December 19X0:

	£
Issued share capital	
100,000 ordinary A shares of £1 each fully paid	100,000
20,000 ordinary B shares of £1 each fully paid	20,000
Share premium on ordinary shares	3,000
Revenue reserves	50,000
Shareholders interests	173,000

The ordinary B shares were orignally issued at a premium of 25 per cent. On 1 January 19X1 the company purchased the 20,000 B shares for £29,000, issuing 12,000 A shares at £1.40 to contribute to the funding of the purchase. The relevant entries would be as follows:

Bank

Ordinary A shares	16,800	Ordinary B shares	29,000

Ordinary A shares

		Balance b/d	100,000
		Bank	12,000
			112,000

Share premium

Redemption premium	5,000	Balance b/d	3,000
Balance c/d	2,800	Bank	4,800
	7,800		7,800
		Balance b/d	2,800

Ordinary B shares

Bank	29,000	Balance b/d	20,000
		Redemption premium	9,000
	29,000		29,000

Redemption premium

Ordinary B shares	9,000	Share premium	5,000
		Revenue reserves	4,000
	9,000		9,000

Revenue reserves

Capital redemption reserve	8,000	Balance b/d	50,000
Redemption premium	4,000		
Balance c/d	38,000		
	50,000		50,000
		Balance b/d	38,000

Capital redemption reserve

	Revenue reserves	8,000

Balance sheet extract

	£
Issued share capital	
112,000 ordinary A shares	112,000
Share premium	2,800
Capital redemption reserve	8,000
Revenue reserves	38,000
Shareholders' interests	160,800

Notes

1. The amount transferred from revenue reserves to the capital redemption reserve is the excess of the nominal value of the shares redeemed over the nominal value of the new issue (i.e. £20,000 − £12,000 = £8,000).
2. The amount transferred from the redemption premium account of £5,000 to the share premium account is the maximum permissible amount. This is the lower of:
   (a) the original premium on the issue of 25 per cent of £20,000 = £5,000; or
   (b) the sum of the balance on the share premium account of £3,000 plus the premium on the new issue of £4,800 = £7,800.
3. The difference between the two sides of the redemption premium account of £4,000 after the transfer in note 2 of £5,000 must be set against the revenue reserves.

The next example brings together many of the matters considered in this chapter.

Example 28.4

The following items are extracted from the balance sheet of Weaver (Ropes) plc at 31 December 19X1:

	£
Issued share capital	
250,000 ordinary shares of £1 each fully paid	250,000
75,000 6 per cent redeemable preference shares	75,000
Share premium	5,000
Revenue reserves	70,000
Shareholders' interests	400,000

The preference shares were originally issued at a premium of 14 per cent.

On 1 January 19X2 the company made the following resolutions:

1. To issue 50,000 ordinary shares of £1 each at a premium of 10 per cent, payable 40 per cent on application and the balance on allotment; the issue is to be made to finance in part the redemption of preference shares.
2. To redeem the preference shares at a premium of 20 per cent.
3. To make a bonus issue of one ordinary share for every five ordinary shares.

These actions were duly taken by the company consecutively in the order shown. Applications were received for 54,000 ordinary shares, the application moneys for 4,000 shares being returned.

You are required to present the relevant ledger accounts to record the above transactions and to show how the items appear in Weaver's balance sheet after the transactions have been carried out.

The ledger accounts would appear as below:

Workings
Application and allotment
Application money = 54,000 @ 40 per cent (110 per cent × £1) = £23,760
Refunded = 4,000 @ £0.44 = £1,760
Allotment money = 50,000 @ 60 per cent (110 per cent × £1) = £33,000
Share premium per share = 10 per cent @ £1 = £0.10
Total share premium = 50,000 @ £0.10 = £5,000

Preference share redemption
Redemption payment = £75,000 @ 120 per cent = £90,000
Premium on redemption = £90,000 − £75,000 = £15,000

Bonus issue
One fifth of (250,000 + 50,000) = 60,000 @ £1

Application and allotment

Bank	1,760	Bank	23,760
Ordinary shares	50,000	Bank	33,000
Share premium	5,000		
	56,760		56,760

Ordinary shares

		Balance b/d	250,000
		Application and allotment	50,000
		CRR	25,000
		Revenue reserves	35,000
			360,000

Share premium

Premium on redemption	10,000	Balance b/d		5,000
		Application and allotment		5,000
	10,000			10,000

Preference shares

Bank	90,000	Balance b/d	75,000
		Redemption premium	15,000
	90,000		90,000

Premium on redemption

Preference shares	15,000	Share premium	10,000
		Revenue reserves	5,000
	15,000		15,000

Revenue reserves

Premium on redemption	5,000	Balance b/d	70,000
CRR	25,000		
Ordinary shares	35,000		
Balance c/d	5,000		
	70,000		70,000
		Balance b/d	5,000

Capital redemption reserve

Ordinary shares	25,000	Revenue reserves	25,000

Balance sheet extract

	£
Issued ordinary shares	360,000
Revenue reserves	5,000
Shareholders' interests	365,000

Notes

1. The amount transferred from revenue reserves to the capital redemption reserve (CRR) is the excess of the nominal value of the shares redeemed over the nominal value of the new issue (i.e. £75,000 − £50,000 = £25,000).

2. The amount transferred from the premium on redemption account of £10,000 to the share premium account is the lower of:
    (a) the original premium on the issue of 14 per cent of £75,000 = £10,500; or
    (b) the sum of the balance on the share premium account of £5,000, plus the premium on the new issue of £5,000 = £10,000.
3. The difference between the two sides of the premium on redemption account of £5,000 after the transfer in note 2 of £10,000 must be set against the revenue reserves.
4. Since the bonus share issue occurred after the redemption of the preference shares, the capital redemption reserve can be utilized to make this issue. As explained earlier in the chapter, because capital reserves have restricted uses, whereas revenue reserves can be distributed as dividends, it is usual to utilize the maximum possible amount of capital reserves to make a bonus issue. The remainder (i.e. £60,000 − £25,000 = £35,000) will have to be taken from the revenue reserves. Notice that the use of the capital redemption reserve to make a bonus issue does not reduce the non-distributable capital. This was £250,000 + £75,000 + £5,000 = £330,000, and is now £360,000.

Issue and redemption of debentures

Accounting for the issue and redemption of debentures follows the same principles as those for shares with one major difference that makes it considerably easier. There are no legal requirements for the maintenance of capital or restrictions on the treatment of any premium on redemption. Thus it is not necessary to either make a new issue of shares or debentures, or to transfer an equivalent amount of distributable profits to a capital reserve. Furthermore, any premium on redemption may be set against an existing balance on a share premium account or carried forward and set against any further share premium in the same year. Alternatively the premium may be charged to the profit & loss account. The same applies to any discount on the issue of debentures.

However, many academics argue that debenture discounts and premiums should pass through the profit & loss account because they represent a financing cost in the form of either a front or end-loaded interest rate adjustment. Also when debentures are not redeemed from a new issue of shares or debentures, some companies voluntarily create a capital redemption reserve either over the life of the debenture or at redemption. Thus students may encounter examination questions on the redemption of debentures which either allow the freedom of the law or contain specific requirements similar to the redemption of shares.

Summary

Changes in share capital occur when there is a public offer for sale of shares, a rights issue, bonus issue, redemption or purchase by a company of its own shares. When shares are offered for sale to the public, the price usually includes a premium, and is sometimes payable in instalments. These comprise amounts payable on application, allotment of the shares, and any number of later calls. If a shareholder fails to pay a call the shares may be forfeited and later reissued.

A rights issue is an issue of shares to existing shareholders based on the number of shares that they already hold. The price is usually below the current market price but frequently includes a premium. A bonus issue is also an issue of shares to existing shareholders based on the number of shares that they already hold. However, these are free of charge, and represent the conversion of reserves into shares. Companies normally prefer to convert capital reserves into bonus shares before utilizing revenue reserves for this purpose.

Some shares are issued as redeemable, such as redeemable preference shares. A company may also purchase and cancel non-redeemable shares. The law requires that before shares are redeemed or purchased, either (1) a new issue of shares must be made of an equivalent nominal value; or (2) distributable profits equal to the nominal value of the shares redeemed or purchased must be transferred to a capital redemption reserve (CRR); or (3) some combination of a new issue and transfer to a CRR equal to the nominal value of the shares redeemed or purchased. Shares may be redeemed or purchased either at par or at a premium. Any premium on redemption must be transferred from distributable profits, unless the shares were originally issued at a premium. In this case the transfer from distributable profits can be reduced by the lower of: (1) the premium on the original issue; or (2) the sum of the balance on the share premium account plus any premium on a new issue used to fund the redemption or purchase.

Key terms and concepts

Allotment, application, bonus issue, calls, forfeited shares, offer for sale, purchase of shares, redemption of shares, reissued shares, rights issue.

Exercises

An asterisk after the question number indicates that there is a suggested answer in the Appendix.

28.1. Describe the procedure relating to an issue of shares to the public where the price includes calls.

28.2. Explain the nature and purpose of: (a) a rights issue, and (b) a bonus issue of shares.

28.3. Describe the legal restrictions on the purchase and redemption of shares including the reasons for these restrictions.

28.4. The financial information below was extracted from the balance sheets of two companies as at 30 June 19X0.

	Postgate plc £'000	*Coalux plc* £'000
Authorized share capital		
£1 Ordinary shares	500	400
11 per cent £1 preference shares	250	—
Called-up share capital		
£1 Ordinary shares, fully paid	350	400
11 per cent £1 preference shares, fully paid	250	—
Reserves		
Share premium	150	200
Other capital reserves	250	100
Retained earnings	350	300
Loan capital		
9 per cent debenture stock (19X8)	200	—
10 per cent debenture stock (19X6)	—	50
Current liabilities	140	190

Additional information:

1. Both companies revalued their freehold land and buildings with effect from 1 July 19X0. The revaluations were as follows:

	Balance sheet value as at 30 June 19X0 £'000	*Balance sheet revaluation* £'000
Postgate plc	300	500
Coalux plc	150	200

2. The board of directors of Postgate plc had already approved a bonus issue of shares earlier in the year. The bonus issue is to be effected on 1 July 19X0 on the following terms: one bonus share for every ordinary share currently held. The issue is to be funded, one half from the capital reserves and one half from the retained earnings.

3. Coalux had approved a rights issue on the following terms: one new ordinary share for every two ordinary shares currently held. The issue price was fixed at £1.50 per share. The issue was fully subscribed and the funds received on 1 July 19X0.

You are required to show for each of the companies the effects on the balance sheet of items 1 to 3 above.   (AEB adapted)

28.5. The following is the summarized balance sheet of Shares Ltd as at 31 December 19X0:

	£'000		£'000
Authorized share capital			
500,000 Ordinary shares of £1 each	500	*Fixed assets*	695
Issued share capital			
250,000 Ordinary shares of £1 each fully paid	250	*Current assets*	865
Revenue reserves			
Unappropriated profit	125		
	375		
11 per cent debenture stock	50		
Current liabilities	1,135		
	1,560		1,560

In order to improve the company's liquidity and consolidate the capital position the following steps were taken:

1. A bonus issue of ordinary shares fully paid was made to the existing shareholders of two shares for every five shares held.
2. The authorized share capital was increased from 500,000 ordinary shares of £1 each to 1,000,000 ordinary shares of £1 each.
3. An issue of 250,000 ordinary shares was made at a premium of 10 per cent, 55p payable on application and 55p payable on allotment.
4. The debenture stock was redeemed in cash at a premium of 5 per cent.

The transactions took place as follows:

1 Jan 19X1	Debenture stock redeemed
	The authorized share capital increased
	The bonus issue of shares was made
	Applications were received for 400,000 shares.
21 Jan 19X1	The balance of cash due on allotment was received.

All applications for shares were reduced pro rata and the excess moneys received were retained on account of the amounts due on allotment.

You are required to:

(a) show by journal entries, including cash, the entries necessary to record the above transactions; and

(b) prepare a balance sheet to show the effect of the above proposals on the liquidity of the company.   (ACCA)

28.6. The authorized and issued share capital of Forward Ltd as at 31 May 19X1 was 150,000 ordinary shares of £1 each, fully paid. On 1 June 19X1, the authorized share capital was increased to £225,000 divided into ordinary shares of £1 each. On the same date 56,000 ordinary shares of £1 each were offered for sale at £1.25 per share payable as follows:

On application	60p
On allotment (including the premium of 25p per share)	40p
On first and final call on 1 September 19X1	25p

The lists were closed on 8 June 19X1 by which date application had been received for 94,000 shares and it was decided to deal with these as follows:

1. To refuse allotment to one applicant for 10,000 shares and return the cash paid in respect of these shares.

2. To reduce proportionately all the other applications and to utilize the surplus received on these applications in part payment of amounts due on allotment.

The amounts payable on allotment were received on 23 June 19X1 with the exceptional of £50 due from one allottee of 500 shares, and these shares were declared forfeited on 1 August 19X1. The forfeited shares were reissued on 29 September 19X1 as fully paid at £1.15. The first and final call due on 1 September 19X1 was duly paid by the remaining shareholders.

You are required to:

(a) record the above transactions in the appropriate ledger accounts; and

(b) show how the balances on such accounts would appear in the company's balance sheet as on 31 October 19X1.   (ACCA)

28.7.* The summarized balance sheet for Turner plc at 31 May 19X7 was as follows:

	£
Authorized capital	1,000,000
Issued share capital	
800,000 shares of 50p each fully paid	400,000
Revenue reserves	350,000
Shareholders interests	750,000

On 1 June 19X7, 200,000 shares were offered to the public at 60p, 20p payable on application, 20p on allotment and 20p on call at 31 December 19X7.

Applications were received for 300,000 shares. Those relating to 50,000 shares were returned, the balance of the excess application money being retained to reduce amounts due on allotment. All shares allotted were taken up, but call money on 10,000 shares remained unpaid at 31 January 19X8. These shares were forfeited and reissued as fully paid at 40p per share on 1 February 19X8.

On 29 February 19X8, Turner plc made a one for four bonus issue.

You are required to show the ledger accounts to record the above transactions, minimizing any reduction in revenue reserves.

28.8.* At 31 July 19X2, the balance sheet of Winder Engineering plc showed the following position:

	£
Issued share capital:	
80,000 10 per cent redeemable cumulative preference	
shares of £1 each	80,000
200,000 ordinary £1 shares	200,000
Share premium	20,000
Unappropriated profit and loss	140,000
Shareholders interests	440,000
Sundry assets	380,000
Cash	60,000
Net assets	440,000

The preference shares were originally issued at a premium of 10 per cent, and are redeemable at a premium of 5 per cent at any time during 19X2. The company decided it would redeem the preference shares as follows:

1 August: 40,000 preference shares redeemed for cash.

1 September: 25,000 ordinary £1 shares offered for sale at £1.20 per share, 70p on application, the balance on allotment, the issue being made to provide some of the funds for redeeming the remaining preference shares.

15 September: Application lists closed, applications for 30,000 shares having been received. Applications for 5,000 shares were unsuccessful and the cash received in respect of these applications was returned.

20 September: The balance due on allotment was received in full.

29 September: The remaining 40,000 preference shares were redeemed.

Required:
(a) Prepare the necessary journal entries to record the above transactions.
(b) Prepare a balance sheet at 30 September 19X2 which incorporates these changes. (Assume that no other transactions take place between 1 August and 30 September 19X2.)

29. The appraisal of company accounts using ratios

Learning objectives

After reading this chapter the student should be able to:

1. Explain the meaning of the key terms and concepts listed at the end of the chapter.
2. Explain the purposes of ratio analysis.
3. Compute various measures of return on investment and risk, explain what each is intended to measure, and evaluate the results.
4. Explain the nature of capital gearing, compute the gearing ratio, and describe the effect of gearing on the profit available for distribution as dividends and the earnings per share.
5. Compute various measures of a company's performance, explain what each is intended to measure, and evaluate the results.
6. Explain the nature of solvency and liquidity, and discuss the means by which insolvency may be predicted.
7. Compute various measures of liquidity and solvency, explain what each is intended to measure, and evaluate the results.
8. Compute various ratios used in the appraisal of working capital, explain what each is intended to measure, and evaluate the results.
9. Discuss the limitations of ratio analysis.

The purposes of ratio analysis

The main function of published company final accounts is to provide information that will enable shareholders and loan creditors to evaluate the performance and financial position of a company. However, the absolute amount of profit, or assets and liabilities, shown in the accounts is not usually a particularly meaningful criterion for evaluating the performance or financial position of a business. For example, if Company A has a profit of £200,000 and Company B has a profit of £1 million, one cannot conclude that B is more profitable than A. Company B may have used net assets of £10 million to generate this profit whereas Company A may have only used net assets of £0.5 million. Thus A is said to be more profitable than B because the profit is 40 per cent of the value of its net assets compared with only 10 per cent in the case of B. Similarly, if Company B had a profit of £900,000 last year, one cannot conclude that it is more profitable this year. The value of the net assets last year may only have been £8 million, which gives a return of 11.25 per cent compared with 10 per cent this year.

Indeed the terms *'profitability'* and *'return'* are taken as referring to the relationship between the profit and the value of the net assets/capital used to generate that profit. Thus in order to evaluate a company's performance and financial position over time, or in relation to other companies, it is necessary to compute various accounting ratios and percentages. These are primarily intended for the use of external groups of users such as shareholders, loan and trade creditors, etc., whose only source of accounting information is that contained in published accounts.

It is important to appreciate at the outset that accounting ratios and percentages have a number of limitations. One of these stems from the aggregate nature of information in published accounts. Companies are not required to disclose all the items which enter into the computation of profit or values of assets and liabilities in the balance sheet. As a result the information needed to compute some ratios may not be available. This necessitates the use of surrogate data in the calculation of some ratios. Furthermore, comparisons of ratios over time and between companies can be misleading when economic conditions change and/or where the companies concerned are operating in substantially different industries. Ratios must therefore always be interpreted in the light of the prevailing economic climate and the particular circumstances of the company or companies concerned. The limitations of ratio analysis will be discussed in the context of each ratio and are summarized at the end of the chapter.

There are a large number of ratios that can be calculated from the information contained in published accounts. These ratios may be grouped under four main headings, each heading reflecting what the ratios are intended to measure: (1) measures of return on investment and risk; (2) measures of a company's performance; (3) measures of solvency and liquidity; and (4) measures of the control of working capital. The most common ratios in each of these four classes are described on the following pages and illustrated using the information in Example 29.1.

Example 29.1
The following is an extract from the published accounts of A. Harry plc, for the year ending 31 January 19X8.

Profit and loss account

	£'000
Turnover	5,280
Cost of sales	(3,090)
Gross profit	2,190
Distribution costs	(560)
Administrative expenses	(230)
Interest payable on loan stock	(400)
Profit on ordinary activities before taxation	1,000
Tax on profit on ordinary activities	(250)
Profit on ordinary activities after taxation	750
Proposed dividend on ordinary shares	(400)
Retained profit for the financial year	350

Balance sheet

	£'000	£'000
Fixed assets at cost		9,470
Aggregate depreciation		(2,860)
Current assets		6,610
Stocks	850	
Trade debtors	1,070	
Bank and cash	1,130	
	3,050	
Creditors: amounts falling due within one year		
Trade creditors	(1,030)	
Proposed dividend	(400)	
Corporation tax	(250)	
	(1,680)	
Net current assets		1,370
Total assets less current liabilities		7,980
Creditors: amounts falling due after more than one year:		
10 per cent loan stock of £100 each		(4,000)
Net assets		3,980
Capital and reserves		
Called-up share capital: 2,000,000 ordinary shares of £1 each		2,000
Profit and loss account		1,980
Shareholders' interests		3,980

Further information
The ordinary shares and loan stock are currently quoted on the International Stock Exchange, London, at £4 and £90 respectively.

Measures of return on investment and risk

This group of ratios is primarily intended for the use of shareholders, although a company's management will probably monitor these ratios as a guide to how investors view the company. There are a number of investment ratios some of which are published in The Financial Times. These include the following:

The dividend yield

This is calculated as:

$$\frac{\text{annual ordinary dividend}}{\text{current market value of the ordinary shares}} \times 100$$

For Example 29.1 this will give:

$$\frac{£400,000 \div 2,000,000}{£4} \quad \text{or} \quad \frac{£400,000}{2,000,000 \times £4} \times 100 = 5 \text{ per cent}$$

The same principle can be used to calculate the dividend yield on preference shares and the interest yield on debentures and loan stock.

The dividend yield is said to measure the ordinary shareholders' annual return on investment, and may be compared with what could be obtained by investing in some other company. However, such comparisons can be misleading for two main reasons. Firstly, companies have different risk characteristics. A comparison of the dividend yields of, for example, a steel company and a bank would be misleading because the former is a riskier investment than the latter. Secondly, companies have different dividend policies, in that some distribute a greater proportion of their annual profit than others. Put slightly differently, the annual dividend is only part of an investor's total return, in that the investor will also expect to make a capital gain in the form of an increase in the market price of shares. This partly results from companies retaining a proportion of their annual profits.

The dividend yield is often between 2 and 5 per cent, but varies between companies for the reasons outlined above. Some investors regard the dividend yield as important because they are primarily interested in maximizing their annual income (e.g. retired person). However, for other investors the dividend yield may only be of limited importance because they are more interested in capital gains (e.g. for tax reasons) resulting from an increase in the share price. They are therefore often attracted to companies with a low dividend yield but high retained profits.

Dividend cover

This is calculated as:

$$\frac{\text{profit after corporation tax and preference dividends}}{\text{annual ordinary dividend}}$$

For Example 29.1 this will give:

$$\frac{£750,000}{£400,000} = 1.875$$

The profit after corporation tax and preference dividends is used in the calculation of this ratio because it represents the profit available for distribution as dividends to ordinary shareholders.

The dividend cover indicates how likely it is that the company will be able to maintain future dividends on ordinary shares at their current level if profits were to fall in future years. It is thus a measure of risk. The amount by which the dividend cover exceeds unity represents what might be called the margin of safety. Thus a company with a high dividend cover would be more likely to be able to maintain the current level of ordinary dividends than a company with a low dividend cover. The average dividend cover for companies whose shares are listed on the International Stock Exchange, London, is about 2 but clearly this depends on a company's dividend policy.

Earnings per share (EPS)

This is calculated as:

$$\frac{\text{profit after corporation tax and preference dividends}}{\text{number of ordinary shares in issue}}$$

For Example 29.1 this will give:

$$\frac{£750,000}{2,000,000} = £0.375$$

The profit after corporation tax and preference dividends is used in the calculation of this ratio because it represents the profit available for distribution as dividends to ordinary shareholders. This is referred to as the earnings. There are complex rules for ascertaining the number of ordinary shares but these are beyond the scope of this book. The rules are applied where the allotted share capital has changed during the year, because, for example, there has been an issue of shares during the year. The calculation involves determining an average number of shares for the year.[1]

EPS is not strictly a measure of return on investment. However, as will be discussed below, it is included in the calculation of another widely used accounting ratio. Furthermore, EPS is generally regarded as an important consideration in investment decisions; it was the subject of one of the first accounting standards (SSAP3) which requires that it be disclosed in published profit and loss accounts for all listed companies.

As explained earlier, the absolute amount of profit (in this context, available for distribution as dividends) is not usually a satisfactory measure of performance because it ignores the amount of net assets/capital which has been used to generate that profit. However, EPS takes this into consideration in the form of the number of ordinary shares and thus provides a useful means of evaluating performance (where performance is defined from the shareholders' point of view as relating to the profit available for distribution as dividends). The trend in EPS over time indicates growth or otherwise in the profit attributable to each ordinary share. Inter-firm comparisons of EPS are not advisable.

The price–earnings (P–E) ratio

This is calculated as

$$\frac{\text{current market price of each ordinary share}}{\text{earnings per share}}$$

For Example, 29.1 this will give:

$$\frac{£4}{£0.375} = 10.67$$

The P–E ratio is often between 10 and 25 but varies considerably between different industries and companies in the same industry. Many authors shy away from explaining the P–E ratio because its meaning is somewhat ambiguous, despite the fact that this is probably the most widely cited accounting ratio. The P–E ratio is a reflection of risk in that it represents the number of years' earnings that investors are prepared to buy at their current level. This is probably better explained in terms of what is essentially a payback period. The P–E ratio shows the number of years it will take to recoup the current price of the shares at the present level of EPS (the share price being recouped in the form of dividends and retained profits). Where an investment is risky, investors will want to get their money back relatively quickly, whereas if an investment is comparatively safe a longer payback period will be acceptable. Thus companies in risky industries such as mining and construction tend to have a low P–E ratio, whereas companies in relatively safe industries such as utilities, and those which are diversified, tend to have a high P–E ratio.

The P–E ratio also varies between companies in the same industry. If investors think that a company's earnings are going to decline, the P–E ratio will tend to be lower than the average for the industry. Conversely if profits are expected to rise, the P–E ratio will tend to be higher, both of which occur because of decreases and increases in the share price respectively. The P–E ratio is therefore also a reflection of the expected earnings growth potential of a company. This means that sometimes industries which one would expect to have a high P–E ratio, since they are relatively safe, in fact have a low P–E ratio because the earnings are expected to decline.

It appears that the P–E ratio is sometimes also used in practice to identify shares which are over- or under-priced. A share is said to be over-priced if its P–E ratio is higher than the norm for the industry or other similar companies, and under-priced if the P–E ratio is lower than the norm for the industry or other similar companies. However, as explained above, this is probably an over-simplification because the intrinsic/real value of a share will depend on the expected future earnings of the particular company.

Another way of looking at the P–E ratio is to invert the formula and express the result as a percentage. This is referred to as *the earnings yield*. For Example 29.1 this will give:

$$\frac{£0.375}{£4} \text{ or } \frac{£750,000}{2 \text{ million @ } £4} \times 100 = 9.375 \text{ per cent}$$

The earnings yield is not really a yield in the same sense as the dividend yield, since not all of the earnings are distributed as dividends. However, it is often referred to as a measure of return on investment. As in the case of EPS, the earnings yield is a useful means of evaluating performance (where performance is defined from the shareholders' point of view as relating to the profit available for distribution as dividends). The trend in the earnings yield over time indicates how efficiently and effectively a company has utilized the amount of money the shareholders have invested in the company in terms of the current share price. It can also be used to compare the performance of different companies.

Learning activity 29.1

Obtain two copies of The Financial Times, one for a Monday and one for any other day of the week. Turn to the last two pages but one of the section called 'companies and markets' headed 'London share service'. Look at the columns in the Tuesday to Saturday editions headed 'Yld Gr's' and 'P/E' which refer to the dividend yield (gross) and price-earnings ratio respectively. Similarly look at the column in the Monday edition headed 'div.cov.' which refers to the dividend cover. Examine the values of these three ratios for some large public limited companies in different industries. What do these ratios tell you above those companies?

The return on equity/shareholders' interests (ROE)

This is calculated as:

$$\frac{\text{profit after corporation tax and preference dividends}}{\text{shareholders' interests (excluding preference shares)}} \times 100$$

For Example 29.1 this will give:

$$\frac{£750,000}{£3,980,000} \times 100 = 18.8 \text{ per cent}$$

However, some people calculate this ratio using the profit before corporation tax (but after preference dividends) to avoid the distortions that can arise when comparing companies with different tax positions.

The return on equity is essentially the same as the earnings yield. The difference is that, instead of expressing the earnings as a percentage of the market price/value of the ordinary shares, this is expressed as a percentage of the book value of the ordinary shares in the form of the shareholders' interests. Since the latter is not the 'real' (i.e. market) value of the shareholders' investment this ratio can be said to be inferior to the earnings yield.

However, the return on equity, like the earnings yield, is a common measure of return on investment which is used to evaluate profitability (where profitability is defined from the shareholders' point of view as relating to the profit available for distribution as dividends). It is said to indicate how efficiently and effectively a company's management has utilized the shareholders' interests. The ratio may be used to compare the profitability of different companies and/or to examine trends over time.

The gearing ratio

Gearing, or leverage as it is called the USA, refers to the relationship between the amount of fixed interest capital (i.e. loan stock, debentures, preference shares, etc.) and the amount of equity capital (i.e. ordinary shares). In discussions of gearing the fixed interest capital is frequently referred to as the debt capital, which is taken to include preference shares. As a broad generalization, where the value of fixed interest capital is less than the value of equity, a company is said to have low gearing. Where the value or debt capital is more than the value of equity, a company is said to have high gearing.

There are two main ways of expressing the gearing ratio. The basis most commonly used in the financial press is to express the debt capital as a fraction (or percentage) of the equity capital thus:

$$\text{Debt/equity ratio} = \frac{\text{Debt capital}}{\text{Equity capital}} \ (\times 100)$$

However, in accounting it is more common to compute the gearing ratio by expressing the debt capital as a fraction (or percentage) of the total capital thus:

$$\text{Gearing ratio} = \frac{\text{Debt capital}}{\text{Debt capital} + \text{Equity capital}} \ (\times 100)$$

Using this basis, the next issue concerns how the debt and equity capital are to be measured/valued. There are three main methods as follows:

1. *Using the nominal values* of fixed interest capital and ordinary share capital thus:

$$\frac{\text{nominal value of debt capital}}{\text{nominal value of debt capital} + \text{nominal value of ordinary shares}} \times 100$$

The debt capital refers to the preference shares, loan stock, debentures, bank loans, mortgages and any other long-term borrowing, such as an overdraft for more than one year. An illustration of the calculation of the gearing ratio using this formula is given in Example 29.2. This also highlights the difference between low gearing and high gearing.

Example 29.2

	Company with low gearing £	Company with high gearing £
Ordinary shares of £1 each	400,000	100,000
10 per cent preference shares of £1 each	30,000	150,000
10 per cent debentures of £100 each	70,000	250,000
	500,000	500,000
Gearing ratio	20 per cent or 1 : 4	80 per cent or 4 : 1

2. *Including the reserves and retained profits as part of the equity capital* thus:

$$\frac{\text{nominal value of debt capital}}{\text{nominal value of debt capital} + (\text{nominal value of ordinary shares} + \text{reserves} + \text{retained profits})} \times 100$$

Returning to the data in Example 29.1 this would be calculated as follows:

$$\frac{£4,000,000}{£4,000,000 + (£2,000,000 + £1,980,000)} \times 100 = 50 \text{ per cent}$$

This method of expressing the gearing ratio is considered to be superior to the first because reserves and retained profits constitute part of the shareholders' interests and thus the capital which they provide. The logic behind this is perhaps more obvious when the gearing ratio is calculated in terms of the book value of the assets, thus:

$$\frac{\text{nominal value of debt capital}}{\text{total assets less current liabilities}} \times 100 = \frac{£4,000,000}{£7,980,000} \times 100 = 50 \text{ per cent}$$

This formula highlights that the gearing ratio shows the proportion of the assets which are financed by fixed interest capital.

3. *Using the current market prices* of a company's ordinary shares and debt capital, thus:

$$\frac{\text{market value of debt capital}}{\text{market value of debt capital} + \text{market value of ordinary share capital}} \times 100$$

Using the data in Example 29.1 this would be calculated as follows:

$$\frac{40{,}000 \text{ @ £90 (or £4{,}000{,}000} \times \text{£90/£100)}}{(40{,}000 \text{ @ £90}) + (2{,}000{,}000 \text{ @ £4})} \times 100 = 31 \text{ per cent}$$

This is generally regarded as being a more theoretically sound method of expressing the gearing ratio because market prices are said to represent the 'real' value of the debt capital and shareholders' interests as distinct from the nominal or book values.

There are a number of other ways of expressing gearing, which show the relationship between the annual amount of interest on debt capital and the profit for the year. However, these are not used very often.

The gearing ratio is a measure of the '*financial risk*' attaching to a company's ordinary shares which arises because of the prior claim that fixed interest capital has on the annual income and assets (in the event of liquidation). This financial risk is additional to the 'operating risk' that is associated with the particular industry(ies) in which a company is trading.

Companies are said to engage in gearing because it usually produces substantial benefits for the ordinary shareholders. In crude terms the money provided by loan creditors is used to generate income in excess of the loan interest. The tax deductibility of interest contributes to this benefit. In technical terms, gearing usually increases the profit available for distribution as dividends to ordinary shareholders and thus the earnings per share (EPS), although it does have an impact on the riskiness of the earnings. These effects are illustrated numerically in Example 29.3. The data are taken from Example 29.2. These two companies are assumed to be identical in all respects except their gearing. Both have a profit after tax (but before interest) of £50,000 and an EPS of 10 pence in year 1. Although this example is clearly unrealistic, it illustrates vividly the impact of gearing.

Now suppose the profit of both companies doubles in year 2 (as shown on page 397). In the case of the company with low gearing, a 100 per cent increase in the profit after tax (but before interest) in year 2 results in a 125 per cent increase (from £40,000 to £90,000) in the profit available for distribution as dividends to ordinary shareholders. By contrast, in the case of the highly geared company, a 100 per cent increase in the profit after tax in year 2 results in a 500 per cent increase (from £10,000 to £60,000) in the distributable profit. Similarly, a 100 per cent increase in the profit after tax results in a 125 per cent increase in the EPS of the low-geared company, compared with a 500 per cent increase for the company with high gearing. This can be summarized in the form of a general rule as follows: any increase in profit (before charging interest) will result in a *proportionately greater* increase in the profit available for distribution (and the EPS) of a highly geared company compared with an equivalent increase for a company with low gearing.

Example 29.3

	Company with low gearing		Company with high gearing	
Year 1				
	£	£	£	£
Profit before interest		50,000		50,000
Preference dividends	3,000		15,000	
Interest	7,000	10,000	25,000	40,000
Distributable profit		40,000		10,000
Earnings per share		10p		10p

Year 2

Profit before interest		100,000		100,000
Preference dividends	3,000		15,000	
Interest	7,000	10,000	25,000	40,000
Distributable profit		90,000		60,000
Earnings per share		22.5p		60p

However, gearing is a double-edged sword, in that the same occurs in reverse when there is a decrease in profit, as often happens when there is an economic recession. Imagine that the chronological sequence in Example 29.3 is reversed giving profit before interest of £100,000 in Year 1 and £50,000 in Year 2 representing a 50 per cent decrease in the profit after tax (but before interest). This results in a reduction in the distributable profit and EPS of 56 per cent in the case of the low-geared company, compared with 83 per cent for the company with high gearing. This can also be summarized in the form of a general rule as follows: any decrease in the profit (before charging interest) will result in a proportionately greater reduction in the profit available for distribution (and the EPS) of a highly geared company compared with an equivalent decrease for a company with low gearing.

Furthermore, the level of gearing affects a company's break-even point. A company with high gearing will have a larger break-even point than an equivalent company with low gearing. This is because the interest charges of a highly geared company are greater than for an equivalent company with low gearing. In Example 29.3 the break-even point of the highly geared company is £30,000 (i.e. £40,000 − £10,000) higher than that of the low-geared company. This means that a company with high gearing has to earn a greater profit (before interest) before it can declare a dividend compared with an equivalent company that has low gearing. Thus if the profit after tax of these companies fell to, say £20,000, the company with low gearing would still be able to declare an ordinary dividend from the current year's trading profit whereas the highly geared company could not.

To sum up, the ordinary shareholders in a highly geared company benefit from gearing when profits are relatively large. However, they run two risks. Firstly, when profits are small the dividends will be less than would be the case with low gearing. Secondly, if the company goes into liquidation they will not be repaid the value of their shares until after all the fixed interest capital has been repaid. Usually very little or nothing is left for the ordinary shareholders. Thus the tendency to assume that gearing is advantageous may be a misconception because while it frequently results in a proportionately greater increase in the distributable profit it also makes the ordinary shares riskier. To use an analogy, one should not bet on an outsider in a horse race merely because the winnings would be greater than betting on the favourite. One must weigh up the possible return in relation to the perceived risk.

Measures of a company's performance

The main function of published company final accounts is to provide information that will enable shareholders and loan creditors to evalute the performance and financial position of a company. Performance may relate to a number of things, such as productivity, energy conservation, pollution control, etc. From the ordinary shareholders' point of view, performance is usually equated with the profit available for distribution as dividends, or the earnings per share. However, the term 'performance' is normally associated with an entity view of business enterprises. This section therefore examines various measures of a company's performance from the point of view of it being an economic entity separate from the shareholders, and irrespective of the way in which its assets are financed (i.e. the proportion of debt to equity capital).

Return on capital employed (ROCE)

A number of accounting ratios are used to measure different aspects of performance. Many of these are derived from a single ratio known as the return on capital employed. This is ascertained as follows:

$$\frac{\text{profit before tax and interest on long-term loans}}{\text{net capital employed}} \times 100$$

Net capital employed refers to the shareholders' interests + long-term liabilities. Using the data in Example 29.1 this is calculated thus:

$$\frac{\text{£}1,000,000 + \text{£}400,000}{\text{£}3,980,000 + \text{£}4,000,000} \times 100 = 17.5 \text{ per cent}$$

The logic behind this ratio is perhaps more obvious when it is calculated as the return on assets as follows:

$$\frac{\text{profit before tax and interest on long-term loans}}{\text{total assets less current liabilities}} \times 100$$

$$\frac{\text{£}1,000,000 + \text{£}400,000}{\text{£}7,980,000} \times 100 = 17.5 \text{ per cent}$$

Some authors advocate expressing the return on capital employed in terms of the gross capital employed. This refers to the shareholders' interests + long-term liabilities + current liabilities. A somewhat easier way of calculating this is fixed assets + current assets. Clearly the return on gross capital employed/total assets will be different from the return on net capital employed/total assets less current liabilities. The latter is more common in practice.

Whatever method is used there is a problem concerning the point in time at which the capital employed should be measured. In the above computation this was taken as being the end of the accounting year, for simplicity. However, this is not really justifiable because the capital employed includes the retained profit for the year and any additional capital raised during the year. The retained profit for the year was not available to generate the profit throughout this year, and it is unlikely that any capital raised during the year provided a significant contribution to the profit for the year. Given the time lags between capital expenditure and assets becoming productive, it may be more appropriate to use the capital employed at the start of the accounting year. Alternatively, if the additional capital is known to have generated profit during the year, the average capital employed for the year would be used. The same considerations apply to the return on equity discussed earlier.

The return on capital employed is a measure of profitability that is used to indicate how efficiently and effectively a company has utilized its assets during a given accounting period. It is a common means of evaluating a company's profitability over time, and comparing the profitability of different companies. As a rough guide, the normal target ROCE of many large companies is about 15%.

However, the use of historical cost data in the calculation of this ratio can give a distorted view of the profitability for two reasons. Firstly, during times of rising prices the denominator in the formula comprises a mixture of assets acquired at various points in time when the prevailing levels of prices were different. In times of rising prices, the denominator is also understated because assets are not shown in the balance sheet at their current value. Secondly, the numerator tends to be overstated, since the historical cost profit is calculated by matching current selling prices with historical costs. Thus the effect of historical cost accounting in both the denominator and the numerator is to inflate the return on capital.

The profit margin and asset turnover ratios

The return on capital employed (ROCE) can be broken down into two further ratios, as follows:

$$\text{ROCE} = \text{profit margin} \times \text{asset turnover ratio}$$

The profit margin is computed thus:

$$\frac{\text{profit before tax and interest on long-term loans}}{\text{turnover}} \times 100$$

Using the data in Example 29.1 this will give:

$$\frac{£1,000,000 + £400,000}{£5,280,000} \times 100 = 26.5 \text{ per cent}$$

The profit margin is often described as a measure of profitability that shows what percentage of sales revenue is profit. Different products have different profit margins. Jewellery and greengrocery, for example, usually have a higher profit margin than electrical goods and clothing. Also, different sized businesses have different profit margins. Small shops, for example, usually have a higher profit margin than supermarkets. Inter-firm comparisons of profit margins should therefore only be made between companies in the same industry and of a comparable size.

The Companies Act requires the disclosure of an analysis of profit and turnover for each class of business. It is therefore possible to calculate the profit margin for each class of business. These could be used in inter-firm comparisons of performance. However, this can be misleading because the profit margin constitutes an average for all the products comprising one particular class of business, and few firms sell exactly the same combination of products (i.e. product mix). Time series analysis of profit margins is likely to be more meaningful. Variations in the profit margin over time can be due to a number of factors relating to changes in the product mix, selling prices and unit costs.

The second of the above ratios is referred to as *the asset turnover ratio* which is calculated as follows:

$$\frac{\text{turnover}}{\text{total assets less current liabilities}}$$

Using the data in Example 29.1 this will give:

$$\frac{£5,280,000}{£7,980,000} = 0.66$$

This shows the amount of sales revenue that has been generated per £ of capital employed. It is a measure of the level of activity and productivity. Different industries have different asset turnover ratios primarily because of differences in technology. Labour intensive industries usually have a high asset turnover ratio, whereas capital intensive industries tend to have a lower asset turnover ratio. Inter-firm comparisons of asset turnover ratios should therefore only be made between companies in the same industry. Time series analysis of asset turnover ratios is likely to be more meaningful. Changes in the asset turnover ratio over time can be due to a number of factors, such as producing at under capacity, labour inefficiency, overstocking, etc.

There is an important relationship between the asset turnover ratio and the profit margin. In order to achieve a satisfactory return on capital employed, a company with a low asset turnover ratio (e.g. capital intensive) will need a high profit margin on its products. Conversely a company with a high asset turnover ratio (e.g. labour intensive) will only require a low profit margin on its products in order to achieve a satisfactory return on capital employed. The former case of a capital intensive company can be illustrated arithmetically using the asset turnover ratio, profit margin and ROCE for Example 29.1, as follows:

$$0.66 \times 26.5 \text{ per cent} = 17.5 \text{ per cent}$$

The profit margin and asset turnover ratio may be broken down into a number of other ratios in order to pinpoint more precisely the reasons for changes in performance over time. These are as follows:

Profit margin:

$$\frac{\text{cost of sales}}{\text{turnover}} \times 100$$

$$\frac{\text{gross profit}}{\text{turnover}} \times 100$$

$$\frac{\text{distribution costs}}{\text{turnover}} \times 100$$

$$\frac{\text{administrative expenses}}{\text{turnover}} \times 100$$

Asset turnover ratio:

$$\frac{\text{turnover}}{\text{fixed assets}}$$

$$\frac{\text{turnover}}{\text{net current assets}}$$

The last ratio can be further subdivided into a number of other ratios relating to each constituent of net current assets. These are discussed in a later section on the appraisal of working capital.

Measures of solvency and liquidity

The main function of published accounts is to provide information that will enable shareholders and loan creditors to evaluate the performance and financial position of a company. The phrase 'financial position' is normally taken as including whether or not a company will be able to pay its debts as and when they become due. A business that is unable to do so is said to be *insolvent*, and will usually be forced into compulsory liquidation by its creditors. Sometimes profitable businesses face financial crisis, frequently because of overtrading. This broadly means that a company has invested too much in fixed assets and stock but too little in liquid assets and is thus short of cash.

Solvency does not mean that at any point in time a business must have enough money to pay its liabilities. These will fall due at various dates in the future. *Solvency* therefore refers to whether or not liabilities are covered by assets which will be realized as the liabilities fall due. Thus if the value of current assets is less than the amount of current liabilities a business may be insolvent.

However, even if current assets are equal to or greater than current liabilities this is no guarantee of solvency, since some current assets are less liquid than others. *Liquidity* refers to the ease with which an asset can be turned into cash without loss. Cash in hand and money in a bank current account are the most liquid types of asset, followed by listed investments, trade debtors and stock. Current assets are usually presented in published accounts in what is referred to as a reverse order of liquidity.

Two fairly crude but common ratios used to measure liquidity are explained below.

The working capital/current ratio

This is calculated thus:

$$\frac{\text{current assets}}{\text{current liabilities}}$$

Using the data in Example 29.1 this gives:

$$\frac{£3,050,000}{£1,680,000} = 1.8$$

This is a measure of the extent to which current liabilities are covered by current assets. As a generalization, the current ratio should be between 1.5 and 2 although this depends on the type of industry and the prevailing economic climate. A ratio of lower than 1.5 may indicate a poor liquidity position and thus future insolvency. At the other extreme a business can have too much working capital, which normally means that its assets are not being used as profitably as they otherwise might.

The working capital ratio has a serious limitation as a measure of liquidity, which is that some current assets are less liquid than others. In particular, stocks and work in progress are not easily realized without loss in the short term. A better criterion for measuring a company's ability to pay its debts as and when they become due is the liquidity ratio. In this ratio stocks and work in progress are excluded from current assets.

The liquidity/quick ratio or acid test

This is calculated thus:

$$\frac{\text{current assets} - \text{stocks and work in progress}}{\text{current liabilities}}$$

Using the data in Example 29.1 this gives:

$$\frac{£3,050,000 - £850,000}{£1,680,0000} = 1.3$$

Bank overdrafts are frequently excluded from the current liabilities in the calculation of this ratio because, although an overdraft is usually legally repayable at short notice, in practice it is often effectively a long-term liability.

The liquidity ratio indicates whether a company is likely to be able to pay creditors, current taxation, dividends and other current liabilities from its cash at bank, the proceeds of sale of listed investments, and the amounts collected from debtors, that is, without having to raise additional capital or sell fixed assets. As a generalization, the liquidity ratio should therefore be at least one. However, this criterion cannot be applied to all types of businesses. Large retailing companies, for example, often have a liquidity ratio of less than one. They buy goods on credit, sell them for cash, and turn over their stock rapidly. Thus stock is a relatively liquid asset. It is therefore only necessary for the working capital ratio to be at least one.

A poor liquidity position usually arises from continual losses, but can be the result of overtrading. At the other extreme a business can have too much liquidity. Where this is not temporary, the excess should be invested in fixed assets (assuming that there are profitable investment opportunities).

The prediction of insolvency

The working capital and liquidity ratios are, at best, crude conventional measures of liquidity. Most users of published accounts are interested in liquidity as an indicator of whether a company will be able to pay its debts, or alternatively if it is likely to go into liquidation in the near future. There is empirical research which demonstrates that the working capital and liquidity ratios are not particularly good predictors of insolvency. However, certain other ratios have been found to be useful in predicting corporate failure. The two most often cited studies of bankruptcy are by Altman[2] in the USA and Taffler[3] in the UK. They each identify a set of five accounting ratios which provide successful predictions of company failure. These are as follows:

Altman	*Taffler*
$\dfrac{\text{profit before interest and tax}}{\text{total assets}}$	$\dfrac{\text{profit before interest and tax}}{\text{opening total assets}}$
$\dfrac{\text{working capital}}{\text{total assets}}$	$\dfrac{\text{working capital}}{\text{net worth}}$
$\dfrac{\text{sales}}{\text{total assets}}$	$\dfrac{\text{sales}}{\text{average stock}}$
$\dfrac{\text{retained earnings}}{\text{total assets}}$	$\dfrac{\text{quick assets}}{\text{total assets}}$
$\dfrac{\text{market value of equity}}{\text{book value of total debt}}$	$\dfrac{\text{total liabilities}}{\text{net capital employed}}$

Both of these studies make use of a statistical technique known as multiple discriminant analysis. This involves taking several ratios together in a multiple regression model. The set of five ratios in Altman's model enabled him to correctly classify as bankrupt or non-bankrupt 95 per cent of the cases in a sample of failed and non-failed US companies. He further claims that these ratios can be used to predict bankruptcy up to two years prior to actual failure. Similarly, Taffler correctly classified all but one company in a sample of UK companies, and asserts that his model exhibits predictive ability for about three years prior to bankruptcy.

However, there are doubts about the validity of the results of studies such as these for a number of reasons. Firstly, the research is not based on a theory which explains why particular ratios should provide successful predictions of insolvency. Secondly, these studies make use of historical cost data, the deficiencies of which have already been explained. Finally, there are several problems involved in the use of statistical techniques such as discriminant analysis which make the results questionable.

The appraisal of working capital

The phrase working capital has two slightly different meanings. In computational terms it relates to the amount of the net current assets. However, it is also used in a general sense to refer to the current assets and current liabilities. In this section the phrase 'working capital' is intended to be interpreted in the latter sense.

One way of looking at the appraisal of working capital is in terms of the interrelationship between a company's performance and liquidity position. As regards performance, the analysis of working capital is an extension of the asset turnover ratio (or more precisely the ratio of turnover to net current assets) which shows how effective a company's management have been in utilizing the various constituents of working capital. This in turn affects a company's liquidity position.

If there has been a significant change in the working capital and/or liquidity ratios one would want to try to pinpoint the cause(s). In crude terms, the appraisal of working capital reveals whether too much or too little is invested in, for example, debtors and stock relative to a company's level of activity (i.e. turnover). In theory there is an optimal level of working capital. However, in practice all that users of published accounts can do is to identify changes in the relative level of current assets such as debtors and stock. These are taken as prima facie indicators of the effectiveness of credit control and stock control respectively.

There are a number of ratios that can be calculated relating to those items which make up the working capital. Each of these must be considered in the light of the particular circumstances of the company, the type of industry, and the prevailing economic climate. The most common ratios used in the appraisal of working capital are given below.

The average period of credit taken by trade debtors/debtors' ratio

This is calculated thus:

$$\frac{\text{trade debtors}}{\text{turnover}} \times \text{the number of days in a year}$$

Using the data in Example 29.1 this gives:

$$\frac{£1,070,000}{£5,280,000} \times 365 = 74 \text{ days}$$

Instead of using the debtors at the end of the accounting year in the numerator some authors compute the average trade debtors as follows:

$$\frac{\left(\begin{array}{c}\text{debtors at the end of} \\ \text{the previous year}\end{array}\right) + \left(\begin{array}{c}\text{debtors at the end of} \\ \text{the current year}\end{array}\right)}{2}$$

The argument for using this method of computation is that it gives a more representative figure for the 'normal' level of debtors. However, the important point is that the ratio should be computed on a consistent basis, otherwise comparisons will be misleading. Another method of expressing this ratio is referred to as the debtors' turnover ratio. It is calculated by inverting the fraction (and excluding the number of days in a year).

As the title above suggests, this ratio shows the average number of days' credit taken by trade debtors. The most common terms of credit in the UK is that an invoice is due for payment by the end of the calendar month following the calendar month in which the goods are delivered/invoiced. The minimum average period of credit is thus approximately 45 days (i.e. 1½ months). However, many debtors take a longer period than this if they can, since it is obviously beneficial for them to do so. An average period of credit of around 75 days (i.e. 2½ months) is therefore not uncommon.

However, when this ratio is calculated from the information in published accounts it may be nothing like any of these figures. This occurs if a company has both cash and credit sales. Since trade debtors arise because of credit sales, the denominator in the ratio should obviously comprise only the credit sales. However, these are not disclosed separately in published accounts. Consequently, the aggregate of cash and credit sales has to be used in the computation, which results in a lower debtors collection period than if the denominator comprises only the credit sales. This is therefore clearly not the 'real' average period of credit, and a change in the proportion of cash to credit sales can distort the ratio over time.

The debtors collection period can also be abnormally high or low because a business's sales are seasonal such as where these are heavily concentrated in either the summer (e.g. ice cream, soft drinks), winter, Easter or Christmas. This can result in an exceptionally high or low debtors figure depending on when the accounting year ends, and thus a correspondingly high or low debtors ratio.

The average period of credit taken by trade debtors varies between industries and according to the economic situation. Retailers, for example, usually grant little or no credit whereas wholesalers and manufacturers often allow a considerable period of credit. Comparisons should therefore really only be made between businesses in the same industry and for a particular company over time. Where the period of credit is high compared with other firms (or with the average for the industry), and/or increasing over time, this is normally taken as indicating inadequate credit control procedures.

The average period of credit received from trade creditors/creditors' ratio

The basic principle used in the calculation of the ratio for trade debtors can also be applied to trade creditors in order to ascertain the average period of credit taken by the reporting entity. This is calculated as follows:

$$\frac{\text{trade creditors}}{\text{purchases for the year}} \times 365$$

As in the case of debtors, the figure of trade creditors used in the computation of this ratio may be an average of those at the end of the previous year and the end of the current year. Another method of expressing this ratio is referred to as the creditors' turnover ratio. It is calculated by inverting the fraction (and excluding the number of days in a year).

The amount of purchases is not normally disclosed in published accounts. However, if the company is a non-manufacturing business these can be calculated by adjusting the cost of sales figure (given in the profit and loss account) by the change in stock (given in the balance sheet) over the year as follows:

Cost of sales
Add: stock at end of current year
Less: stock at end of previous year
= Purchases

Where the company is a manufacturing business, or the stock at the end of the previous year is not given as a comparative figure, instead of purchases a surrogate has to be used, such as the cost of sales.

Using the data in Example 29.1 this will give:

$$\frac{£1,030,000}{£3,090,000} \times 365 = 122 \text{ days}$$

It is obviously beneficial to delay paying creditors for as long as possible. However, this may adversely affect the company's credit rating, and creditors may refuse to supply further goods on credit. Also, where the period of credit is high compared with other firms (or with the average for the industry) and/or increasing over time, this may be an indication of financial weakness.

The stock turnover ratio

This is calculated thus:

$$\frac{\text{cost of sales}}{\text{stock of finished goods}}$$

Using the data in Example 29.1 this will give:

$$\frac{£3,090,000}{£850,000} = 3.64$$

As in the calculation of the average period of credit for debtors and creditors, there is an argument for using an average of the stock at the end of the previous year and the current year as the denominator in this ratio. Once again the important point is that a consistent basis of computation should be used to ensure meaningful comparisons. Another method of expressing this ratio is referred to as the number of days' sales from stock. It is calculated by inverting the fraction and multiplying the answer by 365.

The stock turnover ratio shows the number of times that a business 'turns over'/sells its average/normal level of stock during the accounting year. In very simple terms, a greengrocer who goes to market once a week and sells all of these goods during that week would have a stock turnover ratio of 52 (because there are 52 weeks in a year). Stock turnover ratios vary between industries. Food retailers, for example, have a relatively high stock turnover ratio whereas jewellery retailers normally have a much lower ratio. Comparisons should therefore really only be made between firms in the same industry and for a particular company over time. Where the stock turnover ratio is low compared with other firms (or with the average for the industry), and/or decreasing over time, this is normally taken as indicating a lack of adequate stock control.

Learning activity 29.2

Write to the head office of a large public limited company asking for a copy of their latest annual report and accounts. Using the information contained in this document, compute all the ratios discussed in this chapter for the current and previous year. List any apparent material changes in the value of these ratios, and outline their possible causes. To obtain the maximum benefit from this exercise, choose a company that is known to have recently had financial problems.

The limitations of ratio analysis

Example 29.1 was deliberately kept simple for the purpose of illustration. In particular, it contains no comparative figures for the previous year. Thus no time series analysis was possible. Also, in the calculation of some ratios (e.g. earnings per share, return on equity, return on capital employed) the amount at the end of the accounting year was used when it would have been more appropriate to take the figure at the beginning of the year or an average for the year. Companies are required by law to include comparative figures for the previous year in their published accounts. These would therefore usually be available and should be used where appropriate.

Ratio analysis has a number of limitations. Most of these have already been explained in the context of particular ratios but can be summarized as follows:

1. Comparisons between companies and for a particular company over time may be misleading if different accounting policies are used to calculate profits and value assets.
2. Ratios usually have to be calculated using historical cost data since few companies publish a current cost profit and loss account and balance sheet. These ratios will therefore be distorted because of the effects of inflation and thus comparisons may be misleading.
3. The data needed to compute some ratios is not disclosed in published accounts and thus surrogates have to be used (e.g. the aggregate cash and credit sales in the calculation of the average period of credit taken by trade debtors). This may also mean that comparisons are misleading.
4. The general yardsticks or performance criteria which may be applied to particular ratios (e.g. a liquidity ratio of at least one) are not appropriate for all types of industries.
5. Changes in a given ratio over time and differences between companies must be considered in the light of the particular circumstances of the reporting entity, the type of industry, and the general economic situation. They may also be due to deliberate

policy decisions by management such as a build-up of stocks prior to a sales promotion campaign.

6. A single ratio may not be very informative by itself, but a number of related ratios taken together should give a general picture of the company's performance or financial position (e.g. in the prediction of insolvency).

Summary

The main purpose of ratio analysis is to enable users of financial statements to evaluate a company's performance and financial position over time, and/or in relation to other companies. Ratios may be grouped under four main headings, each reflecting what the ratios are intended to measure, as follows:

1. Measures of return on investment and risk. These include the dividend yield, dividend cover, earnings per share, price-earnings ratio, earnings yield, return on equity, and capital gearing ratio.
2. Measures of a company's performance. These include the return on capital employed, profit margin and asset turnover ratio.
3. Measure of solvency and liquidity. Solvency refers to whether a company is able to pay its debts as they become due. Liquidity refers to the ease with which an asset can be turned into cash without loss. Measures include the current and liquidity ratios.
4. The appraisal of working capital. Measures include the debtors' ratio, creditors' ratio, and stock turnover ratio.

A single ratio may not be very informative, but a number of related ratios taken together can provide strong indications of a company's performance or financial position, such as in the prediction of insolvency. However, these must be interpreted in the light of the particular circumstances of the company, the type of industry, and the current economic climate. General yardsticks are not always appropriate. Furthermore, ratios must be interpreted with caution. The use of historical cost and surrogate data, as well as different accounting policies, can distort comparisons.

Key terms and concepts

Asset turnover ratio, creditors' ratio, debtors' ratio, dividend cover, dividend yield, earnings per share, earnings yield, financial risk, gearing, gearing ratio, insolvent, liquidity, liquidity ratio, price–earnings ratio, profitability, profit margin, ratio analysis, return, return on capital employed, return on equity, solvency, stock turnover ratio, working capital, working capital/current ratio.

References

1. Accounting Standards Steering Committee (1974). *SSAP3—Earnings per Share* (ICAEW).
2. Altman, E. A. (1968). Financial ratios, discriminant analysis and the prediction of corporate bankruptcy, *Journal of Finance* (September).
3. Taffler, R. J. (1982). Forecasting company failure in the UK using discriminant analysis and financial ratio data, *Journal of the Royal Statistical Society* **145**, Part 3.

Exercises

An asterisk after the question number indicates that there is a suggested answer in the Appendix.

29.1. Explain what each of the following is intended to measure: (a) dividend yield; (b) dividend cover; (c) earnings per share; (d) price-earnings ratio; and (e) return on equity.

29.2. (a) Explain what is meant by capital gearing/leverage.

      (b) Why might this influence a prospective investor's decision concerning whether or not to buy ordinary shares in a company?

29.3. Explain what each of the following is intended to measure:

  (a)   return on capital employed;
  (b)   profit margin;
  (c)   asset turnover ratio;
  (d)   working capital and liquidity ratios;
  (e)   average period of credit taken by debtors;
  (f)   stock turnover ratio.

29.4. Examine the empirical evidence relating to the predictive ability of accounting ratios with regard to insolvency.

29.5. Explain the limitations of using accounting ratios in time series analysis and interfirm comparisons, giving examples where appropriate.

29.6. Dale is in business as a sole trader. You are presented with the following summarized information relating to his business for the year to 31 October 19X8:

Trading, profit and loss account for the year to 31 October 19X8

	£'000	£'000
Sales: cash	200	
credit	600	800
Less: Cost of goods sold—		
opening stock	80	
purchases	530	
	610	
Less: Closing stock	70	540
Gross profit		260
Expenses		205
Net profit for the year		55

Balance sheet at 31 October 19X8

	£'000	£'000
Fixed assets		
Plant and machinery at cost	1,000	
Less: Accumulated depreciation	450	550

Current assets		
Stocks	70	
Trade debtors	120	
Cash	5	
	195	
Less: Current liabilities		
Trade creditors	130	65
		615
Capital		
As at 1 November 19X7		410
Net profit for the year	55	
Less: Drawings	50	5
		415
Loan		200
		615

Required:

(a) Based on the above information, calculate eight recognized accounting ratios; and

(b) list what additional information you would need in order to undertake a detailed ratio analysis of Dale's business for the year to 31 October 19X8.

Note that in answering part (a) of the question, each ratio must be distinct and separate. Marks will *not* be awarded for alternative forms of the same ratio. (AAT)

29.7.* White and Black are sole traders. Both are wholesalers dealing in a similar range of goods. Summaries of the profit calculations and balance sheets for the same year have been made available to you, as follows:

Profit and loss accounts for the year

	White		Black	
	£'000	£'000	£'000	£'000
Sales		600		800
Cost of goods sold		450		624
		150		176
Administrative expenses	64		63	
Selling and distribution expenses	28		40	
Depreciation—equipment and vehicles	10		20	
Depreciation—buildings	—	102	5	128
Net profit		48		48

Balance sheets as at end of year

	White		Black	
	£'000	£'000	£'000	£'000
Buildings		29		47
Equipment and vehicles		62		76

Stock		56		52
Debtors		75		67
Bank balance		8		—
		230		242
Creditors	38		78	
Bank balance	—	38	4	82
Capital		192		160

Required:
Compare the performance and financial position of the two businesses on the basis of the above figures, supporting your comments where appropriate with ratios and noting what further information you would need before reaching firmer conclusions.   (ACCA)

29.8* The following is an extract from the published accounts of Blue Light plc for the year ended 31 March 19X8.

Profit and loss account

	£'000	£'000
Turnover		4,230
Cost of sales		(2,560)
Gross profit		1,670
Distribution costs		(470)
Administrative expenses		(380)
Interest payable on debentures		(240)
Profit on ordinary activities before taxation		580
Tax on profit on ordinary activities		(270)
Profit on ordinary activities after taxation		310
Proposed dividend on ordinary shares		(200)
Retained profit for the financial year		110

Balance sheet

		£'000
Fixed assets at cost		7,240
Aggregate depreciation		(2,370)
		4,870

Current assets		
Stocks	480	
Trade debtors	270	
Bank and cash	320	
	1,070	

Creditors: amounts falling due within one year		
Trade creditors	(260)	
Proposed dividends	(200)	
Corporation tax	(270)	
	(730)	

Net current assets	340
Total assets less current liabilities	5,210
Creditors: amounts falling due after more than one year:	
8 per cent debentures of £100 each	(3,000)
Net assets	2,210

Capital and reserves	
Called up share capital: 500,000	
ordinary shares of £1 each	500
Profit and loss account	1,710
Shareholders' interests	2,210

Further information

The ordinary shares and debentures are currently quoted on the London Stock Exchange at £5 and £10 respectively.

You are required to calculate the ratios that you would include in a report to a prospective investor relating to measures of return on investment and risk, performance, liquidity, and the appraisal of working capital. Comment briefly on the results and the limitations of your analysis.

29.9.* The following is a summary of some of the accounting ratios of two companies in the same industry and of a comparable size for the year ended 30 June 19X5.

	Fish plc	*Chips plc*
Dividend yield	4 per cent	7 per cent
Dividend cover	3.6	2.1
Earnings per share	17p	23p
P–E ratio	14	8
Return on equity	22 per cent	27 per cent
Return on capital employed	18 per cent	15 per cent
Profit margin	20 per cent	25 per cent
Asset turnover ratio	0.9	0.6
Gearing ratio	28 per cent	76 per cent

You are required to write a report to a prospective investor on the comparative return on investment, risk and performance of these two companies.

29.10.* B. Beasley Ltd manufactures components for the motor vehicle industry. The following is a summary of some of its accounting ratios as at 30 April 19X3 and 30 April 19X4:

	19X3	*19X4*
Working capital ratio	1.5	1.7
Liquidity ratio	1.1	0.8
Stock turnover	6.3	5.9
Debtors' ratio	52 days	63 days
Creditors' ratio	71 days	78 days

You are required to write a report to one of the company's major shareholders on the change in its liquidity and working capital position over the year ended 30 April 19X4.

29.11. Two retailers show the following accounts for the year to 31 December 19X9.

Balance sheets as at 31 December 19X9

	A. Ltd £'000	£'000	B. Ltd £'000	£'000
Fixed assets				
Premises		5,000		8,000
Fixtures		500		1,000
		5,500		9,000
Current assets				
Stock	800		900	
Debtors	50		60	
Bank	330		720	
	1,180		1,680	
Current liabilities	850		980	
		330		700
		5,830		9,700
Long-term loans		800		5,000
		5,030		4,700
Share capital—				
ordinary shares of £1		3,000		2,000
Retained profits		2,030		2,700
		5,030		4,700

Profit and loss accounts for the year ended 31 December 19X9

	£'000	£'000	£'000	£'000
Turnover		13,360		16,020
Cost of sales		8,685		10,090
		4,675		5,930
Distribution	2,300		2,870	
Administration	1,375		1,670	
		3,675		4,540
Operating profit		1,000		1,390
Interest		65		400
Net profit		935		990
Dividend		300		400
Retained profit for year		635		590

You are required to:
(a) compute for each of the two companies:
   (i)   one ratio relevant to an assessment of liquidity;
   (ii) one ratio relevant to an assessment of gearing;
   (iii) three ratios relevant to an assessment of profitability and performance.
(b) summarize briefly the overall strengths and weaknesses of Company A, using each of the ratios you have computed.   (JMB)

29.12. The outline balance sheets of the Nantred Trading Co. Ltd were as shown below:

Balance sheets as at 30 September

	19X5 £	19X5 £	19X6 £	19X6 £
Fixed assets (at written down values)				
Premises	40,000		98,000	
Plant and equipment	65,000		162,000	
		105,000		260,000
Current assets				
Stock	31,200		95,300	
Trade debtors	19,700		30,700	
Bank and cash	15,600		26,500	
	66,500		152,500	
Current liabilities				
Trade creditors	23,900		55,800	
Corporation tax	11,400		13,100	
Proposed dividends	17,000		17,000	
	52,300		85,900	
Working capital		14,200		66,600
Net assets employed		119,200		326,600
Financed by				
Ordinary share capital	100,000		200,000	
Reserves	19,200		26,600	
Shareholders' funds		119,200		226,600
7 per cent debentures		—		100,000
		119,200		326,600

The only other information available is that the turnover for the years ended 30 September 19X5 and 19X6 was £202,900 and £490,700, respectively, and that on 30 September 19X4 reserves were £26,100.

Required:
(a)   Calculate, for each of the two years, six suitable ratios to highlight the financial stability, liquidity and profitability of the company.
(b)   Comment on the situation revealed by the figures you have calculated in your answer to (a) above.   (ACCA)

29.13. You are given below, in summarized form, the accounts of Algernon Ltd for 19X6 and 19X7.

Balance sheets

	19X6 Cost £	19X6 Depn. £	19X6 Net £	19X7 Cost £	19X7 Depn. £	19X7 Net £
Plant	10,000	4,000	6,000	11,000	5,000	6,000
Building	50,000	10,000	40,000	90,000	11,000	79,000
			46,000			85,000

Investments at cost	50,000	80,000
Land	43,000	63,000
Stock	55,000	65,000
Debtors	40,000	50,000
Bank	3,000	—
	237,000	343,000

Ordinary shares £1 each	40,000	50,000
Share premium	12,000	14,000
Revaluation reserve	—	20,000
Profit and loss account	25,000	25,000
10 per cent debentures	100,000	150,000
Creditors	40,000	60,000
Proposed dividend	20,000	20,000
Bank	—	4,000
	237,000	343,000

Profit and loss accounts	19X6	19X7
	£	£
Sales	200,000	200,000
Cost of sales	100,000	120,000
	100,000	80,000
Expenses	60,000	60,000
	40,000	20,000
Dividends	20,000	20,000
	20,000	—
Balance b/f	5,000	25,000
Balance c/f	25,000	25,000

(a)   Calculate for Algernon Ltd, for 19X6 and 19X7, the following ratios:
Return on capital employed
Return on owners' equity (return on shareholders' funds)
Debtors' turnover
Creditors' turnover
Current ratio
Quick assets (acid test) ratio
Gross profit percentage
Net profit percentage
Dividend cover
Gearing ratio.
(b)   Using the summarized accounts given, and the ratios you have just prepared, comment on the position, progress and direction of Algernon Ltd.   (ACCA)

29.14. Delta Limited is an old-established light engineering company. The key performance data for the company between 19X3 and 19X7 are given below.

	19X3	19X4	19X5	19X6	19X7
Profit before tax and interest/sales (per cent)	3.6	0.5	0.6	8.1	9.8
Sales/fixed assets (times)	4.6	3.4	3.3	3.5	3.7
Sales/net current assets (times)	2.2	2.5	2.9	3.7	5.1
Cost of sales/stock (times)	1.9	2.0	2.4	2.7	2.9
Debtors/ave. days sales (days)	80	77	75	67	64
Creditors/ave. days sales (days)	58	57	61	64	71
Cost of sales/sales (per cent)	71	73.7	75	71	69.5
Selling and distribution/sales (per cent)	19	18.7	18.5	16	15.6
Administrative/sales (per cent)	6.4	7.1	5.9	4.9	5.1
Current ratio	4.9	2.8	3.3	2.1	1.8

You are required to examine the above data and write a report to the directors of Delta Limited analysing the performance of the company between 19X3 and 19X7.   (JMB)

30. Cash and funds flow statements

Learning objectives

After reading this chapter the student should be able to:

1. Explain the meaning of the key terms and concepts listed at the end of the chapter.
2. Explain the nature of and difference between the cash funds and working capital funds, and between cash flow statements and funds flow statements.
3. Explain the purpose, uses, advantages and limitations of cash flow statements and funds flow statements.
4. Explain the relationship between cash and funds flow statements, and between these and the profit and loss account and balance sheet.
5. Prepare simple funds flow statements for both bodies sole and limited companies.
6. Prepare classified cash flow statements using the indirect method for both bodies sole and limited companies in accordance with FRS1 (including notes).
7. Explain the nature of the groups of items and sub-totals found in classified cash flow statements conforming with FRS1.
8. Outline the main differences between the direct and indirect methods of preparing cash flow statements.

The nature and purpose of cash flow statements

The term 'funds' can be interpreted in two ways. The first, and simpler, equates funds with cash and money in a bank current/cheque account. This interpretation may be referred to as *cash funds*, and forms the basis of cash flow statements.

In simple terms, the purpose of a cash flow statement is to show the reasons for the change in the cash and bank balance over the accounting year. Another common way of expressing this is that the purpose of a cash flow statement is to show the manner in which cash has been generated and used (or where it has gone). It might be thought that this is relatively straightforward, since it could be done in the form of a summarized cash book or receipts and payments account. Unfortunately, however, it is usually not done in this way but rather in the form of changes in the value of the items in the balance sheet between the end of the previous year and the end of the current year.

These changes are classified as either sources or applications of cash funds. Sources essentially relate to receipts and applications to payments. However, in terms of changes in the items in the balance sheet, *sources of cash funds* comprise the following:

1. The net profit for the year. Any loss for the year is an application of cash funds.
2. Capital introduction and money borrowed during the year in the form of loans received.

433

3. Proceeds from the sale of fixed assets and investments.
4. Increase in current liabilities and decrease in current assets.

Applications of cash funds comprise the following:

1. Drawings.
2. Any capital or loans repaid during the year.
3. Purchases of fixed assets and investments.
4. Increase in current assets and decreases in current liabilities.

The net profit is a source of cash funds because the amount by which sales exceed purchases and expenses, even though any or all of these may have been on credit, will eventually result in a net cash inflow.

Probably the most confusing aspect of cash flow statements is the changes in current assets and liabilities. Some simplified examples may thus be helpful. An increase in creditors is a source of funds because the money that would otherwise have been used to pay these creditors is available for other purposes. A decrease in debtors is also a source of funds since this results in an inflow of additional money. Similarly a decrease in stock is a source of funds because the proceeds of sale result in more money being available. Conversely an increase in stock is an application of funds since money will have been used to pay for it. Similarly an increase in debtors is an application of funds because allowing debtors additional credit is like giving them a loan. A decrease in creditors is also an application of funds since money will have been paid out to them. Frequently, certain sources of funds have corresponding applications. For example, an increase in stock may be 'financed' by an increase in creditors.

A simple cash flow statement might consist of the above list of sources and applications of cash funds including a breakdown of the changes in current assets and current liabilities between creditors, debtors and stock. This is illustrated in Example 30.1.

Example 30.1
The following are the balance sheets of A. Cash as at 30 September 19X4 and 30 September 19X5:

		30 Sept 19X4		*30 Sept 19X5*
	£	£	£	£
Fixed assets				
at cost		85,000		97,000
Current assets				
Stock	13,600		10,800	
Debtors	8,400		9,700	
Cash and bank	2,500		3,600	
	24,500		24,100	
Current liabilities				
Creditors	(7,300)		(6,100)	
Net current assets		17,200		18,000
Total assets less				
current liabilities		102,200		115,000

Long-term liabilities		
Bank loan	(20,000)	(15,000)
Net assets	(82,200)	100,000
Capital		
At start of year	77,700	82,200
Add: Capital		
introduced	2,800	4,300
Profit for the year	21,600	34,200
	102,100	120,700
Less: Drawings	(19,900)	(20,700)
At end of year	82,200	100,000

You are required to prepare a cash flow statement for the year ended 30 September 19X5.

A. Cash
Cash flow statement for the year ended 30 September 19X5

	£	£
Sources of cash funds:		
Profit for the year		34,200
Capital introduced		4,300
Decrease in stock (13,600 − 10,800)		2,800
		41,300
Applications of cash funds		
Drawings	(20,700)	
Repayment of bank loan (20,000 − 15,000)	(5,000)	
Purchase of fixed assets (97,000 − 85,000)	(12,000)	
Increase in debtors (9,700 − 8,400)	(1,300)	
Decrease in creditors (7,300 − 6,100)	(1,200)	
		(40,200)
Increase (decrease) in cash and bank balance		1,100
Cash and bank balance at 1 Oct 19X4		2,500
Cash and bank balance at 30 Sept 19X5		3,600

Advantages and limitations of cash flow statements

The advantages of cash flow statements are often presented in terms of the deficiencies of profit and loss accounts and balance sheets. This should not be interpreted to mean that cash flow statements are an alternative to profit and loss accounts. The profit and loss account and balance sheet have a number of limitations, and cash flow statements provide useful additional information for the following reasons:

1. Most readers and potential readers (e.g. private shareholders) appreciate the meaning and importance of cash and will therefore find cash flow statements easier to understand and more relevant. In contrast, the nature of profit and capital and the contents of the profit and loss account and balance sheet are more difficult to understand.

2. Cash flow statements are more objective in that cash received and paid are observable events. In contrast, the profit and loss account and balance sheet are based on the accruals, matching and prudence concepts which involve subjective allocations, valuations, etc.

3. Cash flow statements therefore permit more meaningful comparisons of performance over time, and between actual performance and forecasts.

4. Profit is only a symbol or measure of performance. The ultimate success and survival of an enterprise depend on its ability to generate and use cash in the most efficient manner. The cash flow statement provides information that facilitates an evaluation of the efficiency with which cash has been generated and used.

5. Future dividends, the repayment of loans and payments to trade creditors depend primarily on the availability of cash and not profits. Cash flow statements provide information which allows users of company published accounts to make more accurate predictions of future dividends, insolvency, etc.

Few accountants would quarrel with the assertion that cash (or funds) flow statements provide useful additional information. However, most would be opposed to the idea that they should replace the profit and loss account for the following reasons:

1. A statement which is easier to understand is not necessarily more relevant or useful.

2. The preparation of cash flow statements also involves subjective judgements.

3. The use of cash flow statements in making comparisons and the evaluation of performance can be misleading. The pattern of cash flows over time is often erratic and therefore not indicative of an enterprise's long-term performance.

4. Cash flow statements focus on the financing activities of an enterprise rather than the economic or trading activities. They therefore do not provide meaningful information on either past or future economic performance.

The nature and purpose of funds flow statements

There is a second, more common and more complex interpretation of the term 'funds' which is broader than simply equating funds with cash. In this case funds is taken as referring to the current assets and current liabilities. This interpretation may be labelled *working capital (WC) funds*, and forms the basis of funds flow statements, which until fairly recently have been presented in company published accounts as a *Statement of Source and Application of Funds* in accordance with SSAP10.[1]

This interpretation of the term funds usually causes great confusion in the minds of students. A simple analogy may therefore be helpful. A friend informs you that it is your turn to buy a round of drinks. You reply that you are short of funds. He interprets this to mean short of cash because you left your money at home and therefore offers to lend you some money. You decline because what you meant was that not only do you not have any cash but you do not anticipate receiving any money in the near future and will thus be unable to repay his loan. In short, your friend interpreted the term funds to mean cash whereas you used the term funds to mean working capital, in that not only do you not have any cash but you also have no current assets, such as debtors from which you anticipate receiving cash in the near future.

In simple terms, the purpose of a WC funds flow statement is to show the reasons for the change in working capital over the accounting year. In slightly different terms, the purpose of a statement of source and application of funds is said to be to 'show the manner in which the operations of a company have been financed and in which its financial resources have been used'.[1]

As in the case of cash flow statements, it is usual for the funds flow statement to be presented in the form of changes in the value of the items in the balance sheet between the end of the previous year and the end of the current year. These changes are normally classified as either: (1) sources of WC funds; (2) applications of WC funds; or (3) increases/decreases in working capital. The items that fall into each of these categories are shown in Figure 30.1 which also highlights the difference and relationship between cash funds and working capital funds. A numerical illustration is given in Example 30.2 which is based on the data in Example 30.1.

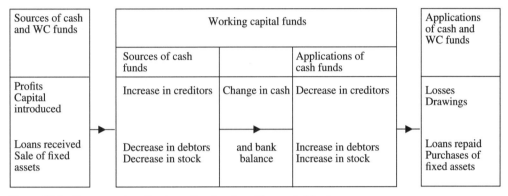

Figure 30.1 Sources and applications of cash and working capital funds.

Example 30.2
A. Cash
Statement of source and application of funds for the year ended 30 September 19X5

	£	£
Sources of funds:		
Profit for the year		34,200
Funds generated from operations		34,200
Funds from other sources:		
Capital introduced		4,300
		38,500
Applications of funds:		
Drawings	(20,700)	
Repayment of bank loan	(5,000)	
Purchase of fixed assets	(12,000)	
		(37,700)
		800
Increase (decrease) in working capital:		
Increase in debtors	1,300	
Increase in cash and bank	1,100	
Decrease in creditors	1,200	
Decrease in stock	(2,800)	
		800

Advantages and limitations of funds flow statements

The main reason for conceptualizing funds in terms of working capital, and the principal advantage of funds flow statements, is to focus attention on the change in the working capital. Any change in the cash and bank balance is regarded as of only secondary importance. Similarly changes in the composition of specific items such as stock, debtors and creditors are also of only secondary importance. The composition of working capital is usually continually changing, which is why these are sometimes referred to as circulating assets. A shift of funds between say, cash and stock, or a shortage of cash, is often only a temporary phenomenon and therefore of limited interest. However, a change in the total working capital is a significant, relatively permanent event since it will involve an increase or decrease in capital and/or a shift of funds between working capital and fixed assets. A funds flow statement is intended to highlight this event and show the sources of any increase in the working capital or the way in which any decrease has been applied.

The disadvantages or limitations of funds flow statements are usually presented in terms of the advantages of cash flow statements. These were explained earlier in this chapter.

Preparation of cash and funds flow statements of companies

The preparation of cash and funds flow statements of companies involves some additional considerations as follows:

Sources of funds include:

1. The profit for the year before taxation and dividends. This is because these two items are shown separately as applications of funds.
2. Capital introduced will comprise the amount received from any issues of shares and debentures during the year.

Applications of funds include:

1. Corporation tax paid during the year. For examination questions up to 1998 this will be the taxation on the previous year's profit since until that data corporation tax was payable nine months after the end of the accounting year. The examples and exercises in this edition of the book are all pre 1998. However, examination questions after 1998 will be based on the new rules which require most companies to pay corporation tax during the year in which the profits arise. The amount paid during the current year is thus likely to be either given as further information in the question, or may be calculated by adjusting the charge shown in the profit & loss account for the amount outstanding at the end of the current year.
2. Instead of drawings, the amounts paid during the year in respect of preference and ordinary share dividends. This will normally comprise the interim dividend plus the final dividend of the previous accounting year.
3. Capital repaid will consist of any shares and debentures redeemed during the year.

The preparation of cash and funds flow statements for both sole traders and companies involve some further complications with regard to the figure for profit (or loss) which is included in the statement. This should reflect the funds generated from a business's operating activities. However, the amount of profit shown in the profit and loss account is after deducting (and adding) certain items which do not involve the movement of cash or WC funds. These consist of:

1. Provisions for depreciation on fixed assets
2. Profits and losses on the sale of fixed assets
3. Increases and decreases in provisions for bad debts.

All of these items are purely accounting adjustments which arise from the preparation of the profit and loss account on an accruals basis. They do not represent movements of cash or WC funds. It is therefore necessary to adjust the figure of profit shown in the profit and loss account in respect of these items to arrive at the *funds generated from operations* that is entered in the cash or funds flow statement as follows:

Profit per profit and loss account
Add: Provisions for depreciation
        Losses on sale of fixed assets
        Increase in provision for bad debts
Less: Profits on sale of fixed assets
        Decrease in provisions for bad debts
=   Funds generated from operations

This is illustrated in Example 30.3.

Example 30.3
The following are the balance sheets of C. F. Flow Ltd as at 31 March 19X1 and 31 March 19X2:

	£	31 Mar 19X1 £	£	31 Mar 19X2 £
Fixed assets				
at cost		173,000		165,000
Less: Aggregate		(46,000)		(52,000)
depreciation		127,000		113,000
Current assets				
Stock	48,400		56,700	
Debtors	39,100		36,200	
Less: Provision	(1,700)		(1,400)	
for bad debts				
	37,400		34,800	
Cash and bank	8,600		17,300	
	94,400		108,800	
Creditors: amounts falling				
due within one year				
Creditors	(31,400)		(32,800)	
Corporation tax	(15,700)		(18,500)	
Proposed dividends	(26,200)		(29,600)	
	(73,300)		(80,900)	

Net current assets		21,100	27,900
Total assets less			
current liabilities		148,100	140,900
Creditors: amounts falling due			
after more than one year			
10 per cent			
debentures		(52,000)	(20,000)
Net assets		96,100	120,900
Allotted and called up share			
capital			
Ordinary shares of			
£1 each		50,000	60,000
Reserves			
Share premium	18,000		26,000
General reserve	6,400		9,600
Profit and loss account	21,700		25,300
		46,100	60,900
Shareholders' interests		96,100	120,900

Further information

1. Fixed assets which cost £8,000 and had a written down value of £4,200 were disposed of during the year ended 31 March 19X2 at a price of £3,500. There were no other acquisitions or disposal of fixed assets during the year.
2. The total depreciation on fixed assets for the year was £9,800.
3. The corporation tax outstanding at 31 March 19X1 of £15,700 was paid on 31 December 19X1.
4. The proposed ordinary dividend at 31 March 19X1 of £26,200 was paid on 1 May 19X1. In addition an interim ordinary dividend of £8,600 was paid on 1 October 19X1.
5. During the year 10,000 ordinary shares were issued at a price of £1.80 each.

You are required to prepare a cash flow statement for the year ended 31 March 19X2.

This example, like most examination questions, does not contain a profit and loss account. In order to ascertain the profit before tax and dividends, it will therefore be necessary to reconstruct the appropriation section of the profit and loss account. The corporation tax and final dividends must either be given as a note in the question or included under current liabilities on the balance sheet at the end of the current year. Any interim dividends must be given as further information in the question. Note that for examination questions after 1998, the corporation tax shown as a current liability will not be the same as the charge to the profit & loss account for that year. The latter is likely to be either given as further information in the questions, or may be calculated by adjusting the corporation tax paid during the current year for the amount outstanding at the end of the current year. Transfers to reserves and the retained profit of the current year are found by calculating the difference between the amounts shown on the balance sheet at the end of the current year and the end of the previous year for these items. This is shown below.

Computations of profit before taxation and dividends

	£	£
Increase in balance on profit and loss account—		3,600
(25,300 − 21,700)		
Transfer to reserve (9,600 − 6,400)		3,200
Ordinary dividends—		
Interim	8,600	
Proposed final	29,600	38,200
Corporation tax		18,500
Profit before taxation and dividends		63,500

C. F. Flow Ltd
Cash flow statement for the year ended 31 March 19X2

	£	£
Sources of cash funds		
Profit for the year before tax and dividends	63,500	
Add (Less): Adjustments for items not		
involving the movement of funds—		
Provision for depreciation	9,800	
Loss on sale of fixed assets		
(4,200 − 3,500)	700	
Decrease in provision for bad debts		
(1,700 − 1,400)	(300)	
Funds generated from operations		73,700
Issue of shares (10,000 × £1.80)		18,000
Proceeds of sale of fixed assets		3,500
Increase in creditors (32,800 − 31,400)		1,400
Decrease in debtors (39,100 − 36,200)		2,900
		99,500
Applications of cash funds		
Tax paid	(15,700)	
Dividends paid (26,200 + 8,600)	(34,800)	
Repayment of debentures		
(52,000 − 20,000)	(32,000)	
Increase in stock (56,700 − 48,400)	(8,300)	
		(90,800)
Increase (decrease) in cash and bank balance		8,700
Cash and bank balance at 1 April 19X1		8,600
Cash and bank balance at 31 March 19X2		17,300

Notes

1. The proceeds from the issue of shares of £18,000 (given in Further information above) should correspond with the increase in ordinary share capital (£60,000 − £50,000) and share premium account (£26,000 − £18,000) shown in the balance sheet (i.e. £10,000 + £8,000).

2. The details relating to the acquisition and disposal of fixed assets, and depreciation (given in Further information) should also correspond with the changes in fixed assets and aggregate depreciation shown in the balance sheet as follows:

Fixed assets

19X1			19X2		
1 Apr	Balance b/d	173,000	31 Mar	Bank	3,500
			31 Mar	Provision for depreciation (8,000 − 4,200)	3,800
			31 Mar	Loss on sale	700
			31 Mar	Balance c/d	165,000
		173,000			173,000

Provision for depreciation

19X1			19X1		
31 Mar	Fixed assets (8,000 − 4,200)	3,800	1 Apr	Balance b/d	46,000
			19X2		
31 Mar	Balance c/d	52,000	31 Mar	Depreciation expense	9,800
		55,800			55,800

The reason for understanding how the Further information in respect of issues of shares, fixed assets and depreciation corresponds with changes in the balance sheet is that sometimes not all the information required is given as further information (e.g. acquisitions of fixed assets, revaluations of assets). The student will then have to ascertain the missing information by examining the changes in the balance sheet. A useful way of doing this is in terms of the ledger accounts.

3. A funds flow statement in respect of this example is shown below.

C. F. Flow Ltd
Statement of source and application of funds for the year ended 31 March 19X2

	£	£
Sources of funds		
Funds generated from operations (show computation)		73,700
Funds from other sources:		
Issues of shares		18,000
Proceeds of sale of fixed assets		3,500
		95,200
Applications of funds		
Tax paid	(15,700)	
Dividends paid	(34,800)	
Repayment of debentures	(32,000)	
		(82,500)
		12,700

Increase (decrease) in working capital

Increase in stock	8,300
Increase in cash and bank	8,700
Decrease in debtors	(2,900)
Increase in creditors	(1,400)

12,700

4. In the preparation of either a cash or funds flow statement, investment held as a fixed asset are treated in the same way as other fixed assets. However, investments held as a current asset are treated in the same way as cash and bank. Any change in the amount of current asset investments is added to or subtracted from the change in the cash and bank balance and shown on cash flow statements as 'cash and cash equivalents' or on funds flow statements as 'movements in net liquid funds'. *Cash equivalents* have been defined as short term highly liquid investments which are readily convertible into known amounts of cash without notice and which were within three months of maturity when acquired; less advances from banks repayable within three months from the date of advance. *Net liquid funds* are defined as 'cash at bank and in hand and *cash equivalents* (e.g. investments held as current assets) less bank overdrafts and other borrowings repayable within one year of the accounting date'.[1]

5. The dividends used to compute the profit before tax and dividends include the proposed final dividend outstanding at the end of the current accounting year (£29,600) because this will have been deducted in arriving at the retained profit for the year of £3,600. It is often given as a note in examination questions, failing which the amount can be found as a current liability on the balance sheet at the end of the current year. In contrast, the dividends shown as an application of funds include the proposed final dividend at the end of the previous accounting year (£26,200) since this will have been paid during the current year. It is often given as a note in examination questions, failing which the amount can be found as a current liability on the balance sheet at the end of the previous accounting year.

6. The corporation tax used to compute the profit before tax and dividends is the amount outstanding at the end of the current accounting year (£18,500) because this will have been deducted in arriving at the retained profit for the year of £3,600. It is often given as a note in examination questions, failing which the amount can be found as a current liability on the balance sheet at the end of the current year. In contrast the corporation tax shown as an application of funds (£15,700) is that relating to the previous year since this will have been paid during the current year. It is often given as further information in examination questions, failing which the amount can be found as a current liability on the balance sheet at the end of the previous year. Note that the whole of this paragraph only applies to the pre-1998 examples and exercises in this edition of the book. Post-1998 examination questions will have to give either the charge to the profit & loss account and/or the amount paid during the year. If either of these is not given the missing figure can be computed by adjusting the other for the amount outstanding shown as a current liability for corporation tax at the end of the current year.

7. In arriving at the profit before tax and dividends it will also be necessary to add any transfer to reserves to the retained profit for the year. This usually has to be identified from the balance sheets at the end of the previous and current accounting years.

8. Any interim dividend paid would have to be given as a note in the examination question or could be ascertained from the profit and loss account in the unlikely event of it being shown in the question.

9. The current assets might have included prepaid expenses and the current liabilities may have included accrued expenses. These could be dealt with separately in the cash flow statement as sources or applications of cash, and in the funds flow statement as increases or decreases in working capital. However, another acceptable and more expedient treatment is simply to aggregate prepayments with debtors, and accruals with creditors.

Relationship between cash/funds flow statements, profit and loss accounts and balance sheets

Cash and funds flow statement are intended to complement the profit and loss account and balance sheet. The main difference between a cash/funds flow statement and a profit and loss account lies in the observation that profit is not the same as the increase in cash over a given accounting period, but rather is only one source of funds. The relationship between a cash/funds flow statement and a balance sheet is that the former 'identifies the movements in assets, liabilities and capital which have taken place during the year and the resultant effect on net liquid funds'[1] shown on the latter. It also provides a link between the balance sheet at the beginning of the period, the profit and loss account for the period, and the balance sheet at the end of the period.

Classified cash flow statements—FRS1

In 1991 the Accounting Standards Board (ASB) issued *Financial Reporting Standard 1— Cash Flow Statements* (FRS1). This replaced SSAP10 and thus most published company accounts are now required to include a cash flow statement and not a statement of source and application of funds (or funds flow statement). FRS1 was revised in 1996.

FRS1 defines *cash flow* as 'an increase or decrease in an amount of cash'. *Cash* is defined as 'cash in hand and deposits repayable on demand with any qualifying financial institution, less overdrafts repayable on demand. Deposits are repayable on demand if they can be withdrawn at any time without notice and without penalty or if a maturity or period of notice of not more than 24 hours or one working day has been agreed.[2]

FRS1 requires the items that are normally contained in a cash flow statement to be classified/grouped under seven headings in the following order:

1. *Net cash inflow (or outflow) from operating activities*
   This refers to the net increase (or decrease) in cash that results from a company's trading activities. It is discussed in depth in a later section of the chapter.

2. *Returns on investments and servicing of finance*
   This refers to receipts arising from the ownership of investments and payments to the providers of finance and non-equity shareholders. Cash inflows comprise interest and dividends received. Cash outflows comprise interest and dividends paid on preference shares.

3. *Taxation*
   This refers to cash received and paid to taxation authorities in respect of a reporting entity's revenue and capital profits. It usually only relates to the corporation tax paid

on a company's annual profit. It does not include value added tax (VAT) or property taxes.

4. *Capital expenditure*

   This refers to cash flows arising from the acquisition and disposal of fixed assets. The entries in the cash flow statement should distinguish between tangible fixed assets and intangible fixed assets. In each case the receipts from disposal must be shown separately from the payments in respect of acquisitions.

5. *Equity dividends paid*

   This refers to the dividends paid on ordinary shares during the year.

6. *Management of liquid resources*

   Liquid resources are defined in FRS1 as 'current asset investments held as readily disposable stores of value. A readily disposable investment is one that: (a) is disposable by the reporting entity without curtailing or disrupting its business; and is either: (b) (i) readily convertible into known amounts of cash at or close to its carrying amounts, or (b) (ii) traded in an active market'. In short, this refers to cash flows arising from the purchase and sale of current asset investments. Notice the similarity between liquid resources and cash equivalents, and in particular the separate treatment of liquid resources required by FRS1 which is inconsistent with the International Accounting Standard and most other countries accounting standards.

7. *Financing*

   This refers to cash received and paid to external providers of finance in respect of the principal amounts of finance. The most common external providers of finance are shareholders, loan stock and debenture holders. The term 'principal amounts' refers to the amount borrowed in the case of loans; the essential point being that interest and dividends are not included under this heading, but rather under point 2 above. Cash inflows include the proceeds from issuing shares, loan stock, debentures and other forms of borrowing. Cash outflows include the repayment of loan stock, debentures and other amounts borrowed, and payments to reacquire or redeem the entity's shares.

Notice that the first three groups of items (i.e. 1, net cash inflow from operating activities; 2, return on investments and servicing of finance; and 3, taxation) are principally revenue transactions, whereas the last four (i.e. 4, capital expenditure; 5, equity dividends paid; 6, management of liquid resources; and 7, financing) are mostly capital transactions.

In addition to presentation, the main differences between the cash flow statement as shown in the earlier sections of this chapter and that required by FRS1 are: (a) the latter necessitates investment income and interest paid to be disclosed under the heading 'returns on investments and servicing of finance'; (b) it also requires a separate disclosure of cash equivalents under the heading 'management of liquid resources'; and (c) the 'net cash inflow from operating activities' is fundamentally different from the 'funds generated from operations'. The latter is discussed in depth in a later section of this chapter.

The purpose, uses and advantages of classified cash flow statements

The purpose of cash flow statements is often expressed in a number of different ways. At the start of this chapter it was given in simple terms as being to show the reasons for the change in the cash and bank balance over the accounting year. However, the grouping of items in the classified cash flow statement permits a more precise definition, as follows. *The purpose of a classified cash flow statement is to show the effects on cash flows of an entity's operating, investing and financing activities for a period.* This definition may be expanded and expressed in slightly different terms to emphasize the potential uses of cash flow statements, as follows:

1. To enable management, investors, creditors and others to see how the various activities of the company have been financed (e.g. which activities have net cash outflows and which have net cash inflows).
2. Historical cash flow information may assist users of financial statements in making judgements on the amount, timing and degree of certainty of future cash flows. According to FRS1 it also gives an indication of the relationship between profitability and cash generating ability, and thus of the quality of the profit earned. Historical cash flow information could be useful to check the accuracy of past assessments and indicate the relationship between the entity's activities, and its receipts and payments.'[2]
3. According to FRS1 'a cash flow statement in conjunction with a profit & loss account and balance sheet provides information on financial position and performance as well as liquidity, solvency, and financial adaptability'.[2] The cash flow statement may therefore be useful to management, investors, creditors and others in assessing the enterprise's ability to:
    (a) pay its debts (i.e. loan repayment, trade creditors, etc.) as and when they become due;
    (b) pay loan interest, dividends, etc.
    (c) decide whether it will need to raise additional external finance (e.g. issue shares or debentures) in the near future.
4. To explain why an enterprise may have a net profit for the year but nevertheless has less cash at the end of that year (or vice versa), and thus, for example, is only able to pay a small dividend.
5. To allow users to see directly the reasons for the difference between the net profit and its associated cash receipts and payments (i.e. the net cash inflow from operating activities).

When answering examination questions it is often advisable to assume that the function/objective/purpose(s), uses and advantages of cash flow statements all require similar answers but the amount of detail increases with each, respectively. The reader may, therefore, find it useful at this point to refer back to the earlier section of this chapter which deals with the advantages of cash flow statements.

In addition, cash flow statements are said to have a number of advantages over statements of source and application of funds (or funds flow statements). Those highlighted by FRS1 are summarized below:

1. Cash flow statements are based on the concept of cash funds whereas funds flow statements focus on the concept of working capital funds. The cash funds concept is more widely understood than the working capital funds concept.
2. Changes in working capital shown in funds flow statements are not the most useful indicators of liquidity since, for example, stock is not easily converted into cash without loss. Furthermore, funds flow statements can obscure movements relevant to the liquidity and solvency of an entity. For example, a significant decrease in cash may be masked by an increase in stocks or debtors. Similarly, a decrease in working capital does not necessarily indicate a cash shortage and a danger of failure.

3. Funds flow statements comprise mainly a summary of the differences between the balance sheets at the end of two consecutive accounting years. Therefore, they essentially only reorganize data rather than provide new information. In contrast, cash flow statements *may* provide additional information.

Net cash inflow from operating activities

As the wording suggests, the net cash inflow from operating activities refers to the (net) amount of cash generated from a company's trading activities. According to FRS1 'cash flows from operating activities are in general the cash effects of transactions and other events relating to operating or trading activities normally shown in the profit and loss account in arriving at operating profit.'[2]

The net cash inflow from operating activities is sometimes crudely referred to as the cash profit, or more accurately the operating cash flows or profit computed on a cash basis. In contrast, the 'funds generated from operations' shown in the cash and funds flow statements earlier in this chapter refers to the funds profit, or more accurately the operating funds flow or profit computed on an accrual basis as adjusted for certain non-cash items (such as provision for depreciation and bad debts). It can therefore be argued that including the latter in a cash flow statement (as earlier in this chapter) is theoretically unsound. The funds generated from operations is based on the concept of working capital funds and thus more appropriate in a funds flow statement, not a cash flow statement. The complexity of the difference between these two concepts of operating cash flows and operating funds flows is the reason why they have not been discussed until this point. It is also the reason why the cash flow statements have been presented thus far in a theoretically inferior but expedient manner. This will now be remedied.

Under FRS1 the derivation of the net cash inflow from operating activities must be shown in the form of a reconciliation between the operating profit reported in the profit & loss account and the net cash flow from operating activities. This should be given either adjoining the cash flow statement or as a note. It must be compiled using what is known as the indirect method. However, there is another method, known as the direct method, which the ASB does not require but wishes to encourage companies to use. At present this would have to be in addition to the indirect method. Both the direct and indirect methods give the same figure of operating cash flows. Most companies use the indirect method. The reasons are probably because it does not require the disclosure of any new information and if they were to use the direct method this would have to be additional to the indirect method. All the examples and exercises in this book are based on the indirect method.

The direct method involves converting all the individual items in the profit and loss account from an accrual basis to a cash basis. It therefore shows the cash received from customers, cash paid to suppliers, and cash paid in wages and for operating expenses. This is all new information not shown elsewhere in the published accounts.

The indirect method involves adjusting the operating profit (before tax and dividends) for changes in the working capital and non-cash items such as provisions for depreciation and bad debts, and profits and losses on the disposal of fixed assets. Notice that the operating profit is not the same as the profit before taxation and dividends. The operating profit excludes investment income and is before deducting interest charges.

The indirect method also serves to demonstrate the difference between the net cash inflow from operating activities and the funds generated from operations discussed above. The former is simply the latter adjusted for changes in working capital (other than cash).

The requirements of FRS1 with regard to the application of the indirect method of deriving the net cash inflow from operating activities are illustrated in Example 30.4 below using the answer to Example 30.3 (shown on page 439). For the purpose of this illustration it is only necessary to make one change to the question. Let us assume that the net profit before taxation and dividends includes interest received of £5,400 and is after deducting debenture interest paid of £4,700. This means that the operating profit will be the net profit (before tax and dividends) less the interest received, plus the interest paid (i.e. £63,500 − £5,400 + £4,700 = £62,800).

Example 30.4
Notes to the cash flow statement

1. *Reconciliation of operating profit to net cash inflow from operating activities*:

	£
Operating profit	62,800
Depreciation charges	9,800
Loss on sale of tangible fixed assets	700
Provision for bad debts (decrease)	(300)
Increase in creditors	1,400
Decrease in debtors	2,900
Increase in stock	(8,300)
Net cash inflow from operating activities	69,000

Preparation of the classified cash flow statement

The specimen cash flow statement in FRS1 shows only the total of each of the seven groups of items described earlier. Most companies also follow this format. Students may therefore also wish to adopt this approach. However, it necessitates preparing notes to the cash flow statement that show a list of the items under each heading. Thus given the time constraint in examinations, a quicker and perfectly acceptable alternative adopted in this book is to include the items under each heading within the cash flow statement. This is permissible under FRS1 which states that 'individual categories of inflows and outflows under the standard headings should be disclosed separately either in the cash flow statement or in a note to it'. This is shown below as a continuation of Example 30.4 using the answer to Example 30.3.

Example 30.4 (continued)
C. F. Flow Ltd
Cash flow statement for the year ended 31 March 19X2

	£	£
Net cash inflow from operating activities		
(from note 1 above)		69,000
Returns on investments and servicing of finance:		
Interest received	5,400	
Interest paid	(4,700)	
		700

Taxation		(15,700)
Capital expenditure:		
Receipts from sale of tangible fixed assets	3,500	
Payments to acquire tangible fixed assets	—	
		3,500
		57,500
Equity dividends paid		(34,800)
		22,700
Management of liquid resources		—
Financing		
Issue of ordinary share capital	18,000	·
Repayment of debenture loan	(32,000)	
		(14,000)
Increase in cash		8,700

Any receipts from sales of intangible fixed assets and payments to acquire intangible fixed assets must each be shown separately under the heading of capital expenditure. Similarly any receipts and payments relating to current asset investments mush each be shown separately under the heading of management of liquid resources.

As mentioned above, Note 1—reconciliation of operating profit to net cash inflow from operating activities must be either adjoining the cash flow statement or as a note. That is, it should be shown immediately above or below the cash flow statement. Immediately above is the most common and most practical since it has to be prepared first. It is probably inadvisable to include it in the cash flow statement, even though this appears to be permissible under FRS1, since examiners seem to expect it to be shown separately as in the example in FRS1.

FRS1 also requires two further notes to the cash flow statement. These comprise a reconciliation of net cash flow to movement in net debt and an analysis of changes in net debt. The former must be given either adjoining the cash flow statement or in a note, and the latter should be shown as a note. Net debt is defined in FRS1 as 'the borrowing of the reporting entity less cash and liquid resources. Where cash and liquid resources exceed the borrowings of the entity reference should be made to "net funds" rather than to "net debt"'. Note that debt does not include non-equity/preference shares. According to FRS1 'the objective of the reconciliation of cash flows to the movement in net debt is to provide information that assists in the assessment of liquidity, solvency and financial adaptability'.

An illustration of these two further notes is given below as a continuation of Example 30.4 using the information in Example 30.3.

Example 30.4 (continued)
Notes to the cash flow statement (continued)

2. *Reconciliation of net cash flow to movement in net debt*

	£	£
Increase in cash in the period	8,700	
Cash to repurchase debenture	32,000	
Cash used to increase liquid resources	—	

Change in net debt		40,700
Net debt at 1 April 19X1	(52,000−8,600)	(43,400)
Net debt at 31 March 19X2	(20,000−17,300)	(2,700)

3. *Analysis of changes in net debt*

	At 1 April 19X1	Cash flows	At 31 Mar 19X2
	£	£	£
Cash in hand, at bank	8,600	8,700	17,300
Overdrafts	(—)	—	(—)
		8,700	
Debt due within 1 year	(—)	—	(—)
Debt due after 1 year	(52,000)	32,000	(20,000)
Current asset investments	—	—	—
Total	(43,400)	40,700	(2,700)

Notice that the following are all shown in brackets—net debt and overdrafts (i.e. credit balances), increase in borrowings, sales of current asset investments and decreases in cash; whereas the following are not shown in brackets—net funds, cash in hand and current asset investments (i.e. debit balances), repayment of debt, purchases of current asset investments and increases in cash.

Finally, to return to the purpose and uses of classified cash flow statements, the cash flow statement for C. F. Flow Ltd in Example 30.4 can be interpreted as showing the following. The cash generated from operating activities of £69,000 has been used to pay corporation tax of £15,700 and dividends of £34,800. There has been no expansion in the business's activities, indeed there has been a slight contraction as shown by the net cash inflow from investing activities of £3,500. The cash generated from operating activities together with the proceeds of issuing additional ordinary shares have been used to repay the debenture loan. In short, this cash flow statement paints a picture of a company well able to cover its financing charges and taxation by cash inflows from operating activities, and which is seeking to reduce its dependence on debt capital by partly replacing it with more permanent ordinary shares. This scenario is often associated with a process of consolidation likely to result in greater financial stability in times of increasing interest rates and falling profits which frequently occur during an economic recession such as that experienced in the UK in the early 1990s.

Learning activity 30.1

Write to the head office of a large public limited company asking for a copy of their latest annual report and accounts. Examine the contents of the cash flow statement and write a short report about the effects on cash flows of the company's operating, investing and financing activities during the year.

Summary

There are two basic concepts of funds—cash funds and working capital (WC) funds. Cash funds form the basis of cash flow statements, and WC funds form the basis of funds flow statements or statements of source and application of funds. The purpose of a cash flow statement is to show the reasons for the change in the cash and bank balance over an accounting year. Another common way of expressing this is that a cash flow statement shows the manner in which cash has been generated and used. The purpose of a funds flow statement is to show the reasons for the change in working capital over an accounting year. The reasons for the change in cash and WC funds are shown in these statements as either sources or applications of funds. Cash and funds flow statements are intended to complement the profit and loss account and balance sheet by providing additional information. They are often regarded as alternatives, each with its own advantages and limitations. However, cash and funds flow statements are intended to serve different purposes.

FRS1 requires most companies to include a classified cash flow statement in their annual accounts. The purpose of a classified cash flow statement is to show the effects on cash flows of an entity's operating, investing and financing activities for a given period. The items normally shown in a cash flow statement are classified into seven groups—net cash inflow (or outflow) from operating activities, returns on investments and servicing of finance, taxation, capital expenditure, equity dividends paid, management of liquid resources, and financing. FRS1 requires the net cash inflow (or outflow) from operating activities to be compiled in a note to the statement using the indirect method. However, there is another method, referred to as the direct method, which the ASB wishes to encourage because it may provide more useful information.

Key term and concepts

Applications of funds, capital expenditure, cash, cash equivalents, cash flows, cash flow statement, cash funds, direct method, financing activities, funds flow statement, funds generated from operations, indirect method, liquid resources, net cash inflow from operating activities, net liquid funds, returns on investments and servicing of finance, sources of funds, statement of source and application of funds, working capital funds.

References

1. Accounting Standards Steering Committee (1978). *Statement of Standard Accounting Practice 10—Statements of Source and Application of Funds* (ICAEW).
2. Accounting Standards Board (1996). *Financial Reporting Standard 1—Cash Flow Statements* (ASB).

Exercises

An asterisk after the question number indicates that there is a suggested answer in the Appendix.

30.1.   (a)   Explain the meaning of the term 'funds' in the context of cash flow statements.
   (b)   Explain the purpose(s) of a cash flow statement.

30.2.   Describe the advantages and limitations of cash flow statements.

30.3. (a) Explain the meaning of the term funds in the context of statements of source and application of funds.
(b) Explain the purpose(s) of a statement of source and application of funds.

30.4. Describe the advantages and limitations of funds flow statements.

30.5. Compare and contrast the nature of cash funds and working capital funds.

30.6. Explain how cash and funds flow statements differ from: (a) profit and loss accounts; and (b) balance sheets.

30.7. Explain the meaning of each of the following in the context of cash and funds flow statements:
(a) cash;
(b) cash equivalents;
(c) net liquid funds;
(d) liquid resources.

30.8. List and describe the contents of the seven headings/groups of items found in a cash flow statement prepared in accordance with FRS1.

30.9. Explain the purpose, uses and advantages of classified cash flow statements prepared in accordance with FRS1.

30.10. Discuss the advantages that a cash flow statement is said in FRS1 to have over a statement of source and application of funds.

30.11. Explain fully the difference between 'funds generated from operations' shown in a statement of source and application of funds, and 'net cash inflow from operating activities' shown in a cash flow statement.

30.12. J. White, a sole trader, has produced the following balance sheets for the years ended 31 March 19X6 and 31 March 19X7.

Balance sheet at 31 March 19X6

	£	£		£	£	£
Capital			*Fixed assets*:	*Cost*	*Depn.*	*Net*
J. White—capital			Freehold premises	10,000	—	10,000
account		15,000	Shop fittings	1,000	750	250
Current account	3,000		Motor vehicle	800	400	400
Profit for the year	5,400					
	8,400			11,800	1,150	10,650
Less: Drawings	3,200	5,200	*Current assets*			
Trade creditors		12,000	Stock	11,000		
			Debtors	1,000		
			Cash at bank	9,500		
			Cash in till	50		21,550
		£32,200				£32,200

Balance sheet at 31 March 19X7

Capital			*Fixed assets*:	*Cost*	*Depn.*	*Net*
J. White—Capital			Freehold premises	10,000	—	10,000
account		15,000	Shop fittings	1,200	870	330
Current account	5,200		Motor vehicle	800	600	200
Profit for the year	5,800					
	11,000			12,000	1,470	10,530
Less: drawings	4,500	6,500	*Current assets*:			
Trade creditors		8,000	Stock	15,400		
			Debtors	540		
			Cash at bank	3,000		
			Cash in till	30		18,970
		£29,500				£29,500

He is unable to understand why, after he has made a profit for the year ended 31 March 19X7 of £5,800, his bank balance has fallen by £6,500.

You are required to prepare a report explaining how this has occurred. (ACCA)

30.13. Prepare a cash flow statement in accordance with FRS1 using the information in Question 30.12. There was no investment income or interest paid during the year ended 31 March 19X7.

30.14. Prepare a statement of source and application of funds (or funds flow statement) using the information in Question 30.12.

30.15. The following are the balance sheets of A. Brooks as at 30 June 19X6 and 30 June 19X7:

	30 June 19X6		30 June 19X7	
	£	£	£	£
Fixed assets at cost		65,000		72,000
Aggregate depn.		(13,000)		(14,500)
		52,000		57,500
Current assets				
Stock	6,700		7,300	
Debtors	5,400		4,100	
Cash and bank	—		900	
	12,100		12,300	
Current liabilities				
Creditors	(4,800)		(6,200)	
Bank overdraft	(1,300)		(—)	
	(6,100)		(6,200)	
Net current assets		6,000		6,100
Total assets less current liabilities		58,000		63,600
Bank loan (5 years)		(15,000)		(10,000)
Net assets		43,000		53,600

Capital

At start of year	38,500	43,000
Capital introduced	2,700	20,000
Profit for the year	14,100	—
	55,300	63,000

Loss for the year	(—)		(1,800)	
Drawings	(12,300)		(7,600)	
		(12,300)		(9,400)
At end of year		43,000		53,600

There were no disposals of fixed assets during the year.

Brooks cannot understand how there can be a loss for the year 19X6/X7 when there has been an increase in the cash and bank balance. You are required to explain this by preparing a cash flow statement for the year ended 30 June 19X7.

30.16.* Prepare a cash flow statement in accordance with FRS1 using the information in Question 30.15. During the year ended 30 June 19X7 there was interest received of £900 and bank interest paid of £1,250.

30.17.* Prepare a statement of source and application of funds (or funds flow statement) using the information in Question 30.15.

30.18. The balance sheet of C.F. plc for the year ended 31 December 19X4, together with comparative figures for the previous year, is shown below (all figures in £'000s).

		19X4		*19X3*
Fixed assets		270		180
Less: Depreciation		(90)		(56)
		180		124
Current assets:				
Stock	50		42	
Debtors	40		33	
Cash	—		11	
		90		86
Current liabilities:				
Trade and operating creditors	(33)		(24)	
Taxation	(19)		(17)	
Dividend	(28)		(26)	
Bank overdraft	(10)		—	
		(90)		(67)
Net current assets:		—		19
Net assets		180		143

Represented by:

Ordinary share capital £1 shares	25	20
Share premium	10	8
Profit and loss account	65	55
Shareholders' funds	100	83
15% Debentures, repayable 19X8	80	60
Capital employed	180	143

You are informed that:

1. There were no sales of fixed assets during 19X4.
2. The company does not pay interim dividends.
3. New debentures and shares issued in 19X4 were issued on 1 January.

Required:
(a) Show your calculation of the operating profit of C.F. plc for the year ended 31 December 19X4.
(b) Prepare a cash flow statement for the year, in accordance with FRS1, Cash flow statements, including the reconciliation of operating profit to net cash inflow from operating activities.
(c) State the headings of the other notes which you would be required to include in practice under FRS1.
(d) Comment on the implications of the information given in the question plus the statements you have prepared, regarding the financial position of the company.
(e) FRS1 supports the use of the indirect method of arriving at the net cash inflow from operating activities, which is the method you have used to answer part (b) of this question. What is the direct method of arriving at the net cash inflow from operations? State, with reasons, whether you agree with the FRS1 acceptance of the indirect method. (ACCA)

30.19.* The directors of J. Kitchens Ltd were pleased when their accountants informed them that the company had made a profit of £24,000 during the year ended 31 December 19X3. However, their pleasure was turned into confusion when the cashier showed them a letter he had received from their banker. This indicated that he had reviewed Kitchens' account and was concerned to note the deterioration in their bank position. During 19X3 a small overdraft of £500 had reached £9,800 and was nearing the limit of their security. The directors would like to see an explanation of this increased overdraft, particularly as they had declared lower dividends than for the previous year. You are given the balance sheets at 31 December 19X2 and 31 December 19X3:

	19X2		19X3	
	£	£	£	£
Fixed assets				
Leasehold premises—cost	30,000		30,000	
—depn.	6,000	24,000	9,000	21,000
Plant—cost	41,000		48,000	
—depreciation	7,000	34,000	9,500	38,500
		58,000		59,500

Current assets

Stock	14,900		22,500	
Debtors	11,300	26,200	16,400	38,900
		84,200		98,400

Share capital and reserves

Share capital	20,000		20,000	
Reserves	35,000	55,000	51,000	71,000
Current liabilities				
Creditors	19,700		17,600	
Overdraft	500		9,800	
Dividends payable	9,000	29,200	—	27,400
		£84,200		£98,400

Notes

1. Dividends:

	19X2	*19X3*
Interim	3,000	8,000
Final	9,000	—
	£12,000	£8,000

2. During the year plant costing £10,000 with a net book value of £6,000 was sold for £6,400.
3. The amount included for debtors at 31 December 19X3 is after making a provision for bad debts of £600 (19X2: £400).

You are required to prepare a cash flow statement showing why the overdraft has increased.

30.20.* Prepare a cash flow statement in accordance with FRS1 using the information in Question 30.19. During the year ended 31 December 19X3 there was bank interest paid of £750.

30.21.* Prepare a statement of source and application of funds (or funds flow statement) using the information in Question 30.19.

30.22.* The following are the balance sheets of L. Tyler Ltd as at 31 May 19X8 and 31 May 19X9:

	31 May 19X8		31 May 19X9	
	£	£	£	£
Fixed assets at cost		143,000		131,000
Aggregate depreciation		(28,000)		(37,000)
		115,000		94,000
Current assets				
Stock		21,600		19,400
Debtors	11,800		14,200	
Less: provision for bad debts	500		700	

	11,300		13,500	
Investments	3,900		17,100	
Cash and bank	4,600		12,800	
	41,400		62,800	

Current liabilities				
Creditors	(8,400)		(6,700)	
Corporation tax	(5,800)		(7,200)	
Proposed dividends	(19,600)		(21,800)	
	(33,800)		(35,700)	

Net current assets		7,600		27,100
Total assets less current liabilities		122,600		121,100
Long-term liabilities				
8 per cent loan stock		(30,000)		(5,000)
		92,600		116,100

Allotted share capital				
Ordinary shares of 50p each		60,000		70,000
Reserves				
Share premium	25,000		34,000	
Revenue reserve	4,200		6,900	
Profit and loss account	3,400		5,200	
		32,600		46,100
Shareholders' interests		92,600		116,100

Notes

1. Fixed assets which cost £12,000 and had a book value of £7,500 were sold during the year ended 31 May 19X9 for £8,100. There were no other purchases or sales of fixed assets during that year.
2. The amounts of corporation tax and proposed dividends shown in the balance sheet as outstanding at 31 May 19X8 were paid during the year ended 31 May 19X9. In addition an interim dividend of £6,400 was paid on 1 January 19X9.

You are required to prepare a cash flow statement for the year ended 31 May 19X9.

30.23.* Prepare a cash flow statement in accordance with FRS1 using the information in Question 30.22. During the year ended 31 May 19X9 there was interest received of £1,800 and loan stock interest paid of £1,600.

30.24.* Prepare a statement of source and application of funds (or funds flow statement) using the information in Question 30.22.

30.25. The balance sheet of Euston Ltd as at 31 December 19X8, with corresponding amounts, showed the following:

	19X8		19X7	
	£'000	£'000	£'000	£'000
Freehold property at cost		2,000		2,000
Plant and machinery:				
Cost	3,500		3,000	
Depreciation	1,300		1,000	
		2,200		2,000
		4,200		4,000
Current assets:				
Stock	470		400	
Debtors	800		600	
Prepayments	60		50	
Bank	20		150	
	1,350		1,200	
Current liabilities:				
Creditors	230		200	
Taxation	100		80	
Dividends	50		30	
Accruals	70		90	
	450		400	
Net current assets		900		800
		5,100		4,800
12 per cent debentures		1,000		800
		4,100		4,000
Share capital		2,500		2,500
Retained profit		1,600		1,500
		4,100		4,000

Notes relevant to 19X8

1. An item of plant costing £100,000 with a written down value of £60,000, was sold at a profit of £15,000 during the year. This profit has been included in the profit and loss account for the year.
2. No interim dividend was paid during the year.
3. Tax paid during the year was £76,000.

You are required to prepare a cash flow statement for the year 31 December 19X8. (JMB adapted)

30.26. Prepare a cash flow statement in accordance with FRS1 using the information in Question 30.25. During the year ended 31 December 19X8 there was no interest received but there was debenture interest paid of £108,000. None of the debenture interest was accrued at the end of either 19X7 or 19X8.

30.27. The following are the balance sheets of Waterloo plc for the last two financial years ended on 30 September.

	19X8		19X7		Notes
	£'000	£'000	£'000	£'000	
Fixed assets					
Intangible					
Goodwill		200		200	1
Tangible					
Buildings	970		720		2
Plant and machinery	350	1,320	370	1,090	2
		1,520		1,290	
Current assets					
Stocks	420		300		
Trade debtors	220		120		
Balance at bank	—		20		
	640		440		
Creditors, less than one year					
Bank overdraft	120		—		
Trade creditors	190		200		
Proposed dividends	60		45		3
	(370)		(245)		
Net current assets		270		195	
		1,790		1,485	
Creditors, more than one year					
9 per cent debentures		(360)		(400)	
		1,430		1,085	
Capital and reserves:					
Ordinary shares, of 50p					
each, full paid		750		500	4
Share premium	100		350		4
Revaluation reserve	300		—		
Retained profit	280	680	235	585	
		1,430		1,085	

Explanatory notes to the balance sheets:

1. Goodwill arising from the purchase of a business on 1 November 19X6 was valued at £200,000. It is the policy of the company to hold purchased goodwill as a permanent asset in the books of account.

2. The movement during the year to 30 September 19X8 in fixed tangible assets was as follows:

	Buildings		Plant and machinery	
	£'000	£'000	£'000	£'000
Cost at 1 October 19X7	820		600	
Surplus on revaluation	300		—	
Additions	—		100	
Disposals	—		(50)*	
		1,120		650

Provision for depreciation				
at 1 October 19X7	100		230	
Depreciation on disposal	—		(40)*	
Depreciation for year	50	(150)	110	(300)
30 September 19X8		970		350

*The plant and machinery disposed of during the year was sold for £5,000.

3. Apart from the final proposed dividends shown in each balance sheet, interim dividends were paid in each of the years as follows:

19X8   *19X7*
£25,000   £15,000

4. There was a bonus issue during the year to 30 September 19X8 of one new ordinary share for every two held.

Prepare a source and application of funds statement for the year ended 30 September 19X8, together with a statement showing the movement in working capital.   (AEB)

30.28. Prepare a cash flow statement in accordance with FRS1 using the information in Question 30.27. There was no investment income for the year ended 30 September 19X8 but there was debenture interest paid of £35,000 during the year.

30.29. The summarized balance sheets as at 31 March 19X8 and 19X9 of Higher Limited are as follows:

	19X9		*19X8*		*Additional*
	£'000	£'000	£'000	£'000	*information*
Fixed assets; at net book value		175		150	1
Current assets	90		80		2
Creditors, less than one year	(70)		(50)		
		20		30	
		195		180	
Creditors, more than one year		(30)		(30)	
		165		150	
Capital and reserves					
Ordinary shares of £1 each		90		80	3
8 per cent redeemable preference					
shares of 50p each		—		30	3
Share premium account		25		20	3
Capital redemption reserve		15		—	
Profit and loss account		35		20	
		165		150	

Additional information:

1. Fixed assets

	Cost £'000	Depn. £'000	Net book value £'000
Balance at 31 March 19X8	200	50	150
Additions	60	—	60
Disposals	(40)	(25)	(15)
Depreciation for the year to 31 March 19X9	—	20	(20)
	220	45	175

Fixed assets disposed of during the year were sold for £22,000.

2. Current assets at 31 March for each of the two years comprise the following:

	19X9 £'000	19X8 £'000
Stocks	35	27
Debtors	22	28
Bank	24	22
Cash	9	3
	90	80

3. The preference shares were redeemed during the year ended 31 March 19X9. This redemption was funded by a new issue of ordinary shares at a premium.

4. A transfer of £15,000 from the profit and loss account was made to the capital redemption reserve.

Required:

(a) Prepare a source and application of funds statement for Higher Limited for the year ended 31 March 19X9, showing clearly the change in the working capital.

(b) Explain the purpose and uses of the source and application of funds statement. (AEB)

30.30. Prepare a cash flow statement in accordance with FRS1 using the information in Question 30.29. Assume that there was no investment income, interest paid or dividends paid during the year ended 31 March 19X9.

31. Value added tax, columnar books of prime entry and the payroll

Learning objectives

After reading this chapter the student should be able to:

1. Explain the meaning of the key terms and concepts listed at the end of the chapter.
2. Outline the system of value added tax (VAT) found in the UK.
3. Show the entries in the books of prime entry and ledger in respect of VAT.
4. Explain the purpose of columnar books of prime entry.
5. Show the entries in columnar day books and the cash book, and the posting of these entries to the ledger.
6. Outline the PAYE system found in the UK, prepare a simple payroll and explain its contents.
7. Show the journal and ledger entries relating to the items usually contained in a payroll.

Value added tax

Value added tax is a *sales tax* that is ultimately borne by the customer. Most businesses charge their customer with (output) VAT and buy goods and services which are subject to (input) VAT. However, these businesses do not usually suffer VAT as a cost of inputs, in that the input VAT is set off against the output VAT and periodically the difference is paid to HM Customs & Excise or a refund obtained. Consequently none of the items shown in the accounts normally includes VAT. The only exceptions to this are debtors and creditors. Furthermore, there may be a current liability for VAT at the end of an accounting year that represents the difference between output and input VAT which has not been paid to HM Customs & Excise at that date.

A number of rates of VAT have existed at various times. For some time the standard rate was 15 per cent but in 1991 this was raised to 17.5 per cent. Some products are zero rated, i.e. bear no VAT; some businesses are exempt so that they do not charge VAT on their outputs but do have to pay VAT on their inputs.

The accounting entries for VAT are relatively straightforward in principle. When goods which are subject to VAT are purchased for cash, the price including VAT is credited in the cash book. The corresponding debit consists of two entries—the cost excluding VAT is debited to the purchases account, and the amount of VAT is debited to a VAT account. Similarly when goods that are subject to VAT are purchased on credit, the price including

VAT is credited to the creditors' account. The corresponding debit consists of two entries—the cost excluding VAT is debited to the purchases account, and the amount of VAT is debited to a VAT or HM Customs & Excise account which is essentially a personal account. Conversely, when goods which are subject to VAT are sold on credit, the price including VAT is debited to the debtors' account. The corresponding credit consists of two entries—the price excluding VAT is credited to the sales account, and the amount of VAT is credited to the VAT account. A simple illustration is given in Example 31.1 below.

Example 31.1

A. Ltd buys goods on credit from B. Ltd at a price of £200 plus 17.5 per cent VAT. A. Ltd then sells these goods to C. Ltd for £320 plus 17.5 per cent VAT. Show the ledger entries in the book of A. Ltd.

		B. Ltd		
			Purchases + VAT	235
		Purchases		
B. Ltd		200		
		Value added tax		
B. Ltd		35	C. Ltd	56
		C. Ltd		
Sales + VAT		376		
		Sales		
			C. Ltd	320

Periodically the VAT account is balanced and the difference between the two sides paid to HM Customs & Excise where this is a credit balance, or a refund obtained where there is a debit balance.

A further complication with VAT is that some businesses are classed as either *zero rated* or *exempt*. This means that they do not have to charge their customers with VAT. In the case of zero rated businesses, they obtain a refund of the VAT that they have paid on goods and services purchased. Thus input VAT is debited to the VAT account, and the only credit entry in this account is a cheque received from HM Customs & Excise as a refund. However, businesses that are classed as exempt do not get a refund. In this case there is no VAT account in the ledger because the cost of goods and services purchased including VAT is simply debited to the relevant nominal account.

Columnar books of prime entry

A columnar book of prime entry is one which contains analysis columns. The use of analysis columns in a petty cash book was described in Chapter 8. In practice most of the other books of prime entry, namely the day books and cash book, also frequently contain analysis columns. Each is described below.

The simplest are the sales day book and sales returns day book. These often contain analysis columns relating to the different departments or types of products that the business sells. This makes it possible to compute the gross profit of each department in departmental trading accounts. The sales and returns day books also usually contain an analysis column in respect of value added tax.

The purchases day book and purchases returns day book also often contain analysis columns. These may relate to the different departments or types of products. However, a more common form of columnar purchases day book contains not just credit purchases of goods for resale, but also expenses incurred on credit (e.g. the purchase of stationery) and the purchase of fixed assets on credit. Indeed any invoice received in respect of good or services purchased on credit is often recorded in the columnar purchases day book. The purchases and returns day books usually contain an analysis column relating to value added tax.

Lastly, the cash book frequently also contain memorandum analysis columns on both the debit and credit sides. Those on the credit side are much the same as in the petty cash book. The columns on the debit side are used in the same way but obviously relate to different types of receipts. The cash book also usually contains an analysis column on each side relating to value added tax.

As explained in the context of columnar petty cash books, the purpose of having analysis columns in books of prime entry is to facilitate the posting of the ledger. Each column relates to a particular type of income or expenditure such as stationery, motor expenses, etc. Every transaction is entered in a total column and an appropriate analysis column. At the end of each calendar month the total of each column is posted to the relevant account in the ledger. Thus instead of posting each transaction to the ledger separately, income and expenditure of the same type is collected together in analysis columns and the total for the period posted to the relevant account.

Illustrations of the use of columnar day books and cash books are given in Examples 31.2 and 31.3 respectively.

Example 31.2

A. Singh is in business as a builders' merchant. The following credit transactions took place during August 19X5:

  2 Aug   Purchased goods for resale from AB Ltd for £560 plus 17.5 per cent VAT.
  5 Aug   Bought stationery from CD Ltd for £120 plus 17.5 per cent VAT.
 10 Aug   Purchased fixtures and fittings for the shop from EF Ltd for £2,000 plus 17.5 per cent VAT.
 18 Aug   Sold goods to YZ Ltd for £1,000 plus 17.5 per cent VAT.
 23 Aug   Sold some old loose tools previously used in the shop to WX Ltd for £1,600 plus 17.5 per cent VAT.
 25 Aug   Returned goods costing £200 + VAT to AB Ltd and received a credit note.
 29 Aug   Returned stationery costing £40 + VAT to CD Ltd and received a credit note.

You are required to make the necessary entries in the relevant columnar books of prime entry and the ledger.

Purchases day book (PDB)

Date	Name of creditor	Total	VAT	Purchases	Stationery	Misc.
2 Aug	AB Ltd	658	98	560		
5 Aug	CD Ltd	141	21		120	
10 Aug	EF Ltd	2,350	350			2,000
		3,149	469	560	120	2,000

Sales day book (SDB)

Date	Name of debtor	Total	VAT	Sales	Misc.
18 Aug	YZ Ltd	1,175	175	1,000	
23 Aug	WX Ltd	1,880	280		1,600
		3,055	455	1,000	1,600

Purchases returns day book (PRDB)

Date	Name of creditor	Total	VAT	Purchases	Stationery	Misc.
25 Aug	AB Ltd	235	35	200		
29 Aug	CD Ltd	47	7		40	
		282	42	200	40	—

The ledger

Purchases
31 Aug	Total per PDB	560			

Stationery
31 Aug	Total per PDB	120	31 Aug	Total per PRDB	40

Fixtures and fittings
10 Aug	EF Ltd	2,000			

VAT
31 Aug	Total per PDB	469	31 Aug	Total per SDB	455
			31 Aug	Total per PRDB	42

AB Ltd
25 Aug	Returns + VAT	235	2 Aug	Purchases + VAT	658

CD Ltd
29 Aug	Stationery + VAT	47	5 Aug	Stationery + VAT	141

EF Ltd
			10 Aug	Fixtures + VAT	2,350

Purchases returns
			31 Aug	Total per PRDB	200

Sales
			31 Aug	Total per SDB	1,000

Loose tools
			23 Aug	WX Ltd	1,600

YZ Ltd
18 Aug	Sales + VAT	1,175			

WX Ltd
23 Aug	Loose tools + VAT	1,880			

Note

1. The amount of each invoice (including VAT) shown in the total columns of the day books is posted individually to the debtors' and creditors' personal accounts in the normal way. The total of the VAT columns in each day book is posted to the VAT account. Similarly the total of each of the other analysis columns in the day books is posted to the relevant ledger account. The only exception to this is the miscellaneous column where each entry would have to be posted separately because they normally involve more than one ledger account.

Example 31.3 (continuation of Example 31.2)
A. Singh had the following cheque receipts and payments during September 19X5:

1 Sept	Balance at bank £8,000.
3 Sept	Introduced additional capital of £900.
7 Sept	Sold goods for £400 plus 17.5 per cent VAT.
12 Sept	Received a cheque from YZ Ltd for £1,140 after deducting £35 cash discount.
20 Sept	Drawings £250.
22 Sept	Purchased goods for resale costing £320 plus 17.5 per cent VAT.
23 Sept	Bought stationery costing £200 plus 17.5 per cent VAT.
25 Sept	Purchased a motor vehicle for £5,000 plus 17.5 per cent VAT.
27 Sept	Paid AB Ltd £398 after deducting £25 cash discount.
29 Sept	Paid HM Customs & Excise the VAT outstanding at the end of August 19X5 of £28.

You are required to make the necessary entries in a columnar cash book and the ledger.

The columnar cash book (debit side) (CB)

Date	Details	Total	VAT	Debtors	Discount allowed	Sales	Misc.
19X5							
1 Sept	Balance b/d	8,000					8,000
3 Sept	Capital	900					900
7 Sept	Sales	470	70			400	
12 Sept	YX Ltd	1,140		1,140	35		
		10,510	70	1,140	35	400	8,900

The columnar cash book (credit side) (CB)

Date	Details	Total	VAT	Creditors	Discount received	Purchases	Stationery	Misc.
19X5								
20 Sept	Drawings	250						250
22 Sept	Purchases	376	56			320		
23 Sept	Stationery	235	35				200	
25 Sept	Motor vehicles	5,875	875					5,000
27 Sept	AB Ltd	398		398	25			

29 Sept	HM Customs & Excise	28	28					
	Totals	7,162	994	398	25	320	200	5,250
30 Sept	Balance c/d	3,348						
		10,510						

The ledger

Capital

			19X5			
			3 Sept	Bank		900

Sales

			31 Aug	Total per SDB	1,000
			30 Sept	Total per CB	400

YZ Ltd

18 Aug	Sales + VAT	1,175	12 Sept	Bank	1,140
			12 Sept	Discount allowed	35
		1,175			1,175

Discount allowed

30 Sept	Total per CB	35

Drawings

20 Sept	Bank	250

Purchases

31 Aug	Total per PDB	560
30 Sept	Total per CB	320

Stationery

31 Aug	Total per PDB	120	31 Aug	Total per PRDB	40
30 Sept	Total per CB	200			

Motor vehicles

25 Sept	Bank	5,000

AB Ltd

25 Aug	Returns + VAT	235	2 Aug	Purchases + VAT	658
27 Sept	Bank	398			
27 Sept	Discount received	25			
		658			658

Discount received

| | | | 30 Sept | Total per CB | 25 |

VAT

31 Aug	Total per PDB	469	31 Aug	Total per SDB	455
31 Aug	Balance c/d	28	31 Aug	Total per PRDB	42
		497			497
30 Sept	Total per CB		1 Sept	Balance b/d	28
	(credit)	994	30 Sept	Total per CB	
				(debit)	70
			30 Sept	Balance c/d	896
		994			994
1 Oct	Balance b/d	896			

Notes

1. The total of all the analysis columns on the debit side of the cash book except the discount allowed columns should equal the total of the total column. Similarly the total of all the analysis columns on the credit side of the cash book except the discount received column should equal the total of the total column.
2. The total of each analysis column in the cash book is posted to the relevant ledger account. The exceptions to this are miscellaneous, debtors' and creditors' columns where each item has to be posted to the ledger individually.
3. Where cheques are received from debtors and paid to creditors, the VAT included in these amounts is not shown in the VAT column of the cash book. This would result in double counting because the VAT has already been entered in the VAT account in the ledger via the VAT columns of the day books when the goods were purchased/sold. The total amount of the cheque is therefore entered in the debtors' and creditors' columns and posted to the personal accounts.

Accounting for wages

The main purpose of this section is to explain the ledger entries relating to wages and salaries, including the source of the data.

The term wages is usually taken to refer to payments to employees that are made weekly and/or computed using an hourly rate. The term salaries is usually taken to refer to payments that are made monthly and/or computed by reference to an annual remuneration. However, the distinction is not critical in that both are often entered in a wages and salaries account.

What is referred to as an employees *gross pay* is usually computed in one of three ways:

1. The employees annual salary divided by 12 if paid monthly, or by 52 if paid weekly.
2. On an hourly basis comprising the basic pay plus any overtime. The basic pay is the number of hours worked by an employee in a given week (excluding any overtime) multiplied by his/her hourly rate (e.g. 40 hours @ £6 per hour = £240). The overtime pay is the number of hours worked by an employee in excess of the basic hours

multiplied by the hourly overtime rate which is often something like one and a half times the basic hourly rate (e.g. 5 hours @ [$1\frac{1}{2}$ × £6] = £45).

3. On a piecework basis whereby the number of units of output produced by an employee in a given week is multiplied by his/her piecework rate per unit of output (e.g. 200 units @ £1 per unit = £200).

The gross pay may also include any bonus based on some measure of performance. Bonus schemes vary considerably between businesses but a performance measure may take the form of time saved, cost reductions, profit increases, etc..

The amount of money that an employee actually receives is referred to as the *net pay*. This is the gross pay less various deductions which in the UK include the following:

1. Income tax under the Pay As You Earn (PAYE) system. The amount, which is said to be 'deducted at source', is determined from tax tables using the employees tax code number, both of which are supplied to the employer by the Inland Revenue.
2. National Insurance contributions (NIC). The amount of this is also determined from information supplied to the employer by the Inland Revenue, and usually takes the form of a given percentage of the employees gross pay.

There may be other deductions from an employees gross pay such as superannuation contributions to a pension fund set up by the employer.

In the UK the employer is also required to pay national insurance contributions in respect of each employee. Similarly an employer often makes superannuation contributions on behalf of each of its employees. Neither of these are deducted from the employees gross pay. From the employers point of view they represent wage costs that are additional to the gross pay.

Employees wages are computed using a document known as the *payroll*. An illustration of a payroll is given in Figure 31.1.

Some people regard the payroll as a book of prime entry rather than a basic document. Others argue that the ledger entries relating to wages and salaries should first be recorded in the journal.

Before examining the ledger entries it is important to first understand some basic principles. The wages and salaries account(s) is used to determine the total wage costs to the employer which will be charged to the profit & loss account. This consists of the total gross pay plus the employers national insurance contributions and any superannuation contributions it has to make. This is not immediately obvious from the ledger entries because the entries representing the gross pay take the form of the net pay and the various deductions from the employees gross pay.

Payroll No.	Employees name	Gross pay	Deductions			Net pay	Employers NIC
			PAYE tax	NIC	Total		
1002	J. Lennon	360	47	36	83	277	54
1003	R. Starr	240	29	24	53	187	36
1005	G. Harrison	320	38	32	70	250	48
1008	P. McCartney	380	55	38	93	287	57
		1,300	169	130	299	1,001	195

Figure 31.1 Payroll

The reason why the deductions are shown separately arises from the need for a double entry to a liability account representing the employers responsibility to pass on any deductions from the employees pay to the appropriate authority. In the case of the PAYE income tax and national insurance contributions this is the Inland Revenue.

An illustration of the ledger entries for wages and salaries is given in Example 31.4 which uses the data in Figure 31.1.

Example 31.4

Wages & salaries

Bank/cash—net pay	1,001	
Inland revenue—		
PAYE tax	169	
employees NIC	130	
Gross pay	1,300	
Employers NIC	195	

Bank/cash

Wages & salaries	1,001

Inland Revenue

Wages & salaries—	
PAYE tax	169
employees NIC	130
employers NIC	195

Summary

Most businesses charge their customers with (output) VAT and buy goods and services that are subject to (input) VAT. Periodically the input VAT is set off against the output VAT, and the difference paid to HM Customs & Excise. Most businesses therefore neither benefit from output VAT, nor suffer input VAT. Thus VAT is not included in any of the income, expense or asset accounts (other than debtors and cash) in the ledger or final accounts. VAT is only entered in the cash/bank accounts, and personal accounts of debtors and creditors, with a corresponding entry in a VAT account. However, the accounting treatment of VAT in businesses that are either zero rated or exempt is slightly different.

In practice it is common for all books of prime entry (other than the journal) to be kept in columnar form. The sales and sales return day books may have analysis columns that relate to departments or products. So may the purchases and purchases returns day books, although it is more common for these to include columns representing the different expenses incurred on credit, and purchases of fixed assets on credit. The cash book also usually has analysis columns on each side. Those on the debit side normally relate to sales and cheques received from debtors. Those on the credit side normally relate to cheques paid to creditors, purchases, and various expenses. The cash book and all the day books also usually have an analysis column for VAT. The purpose of columnar day books and cash books is to facilitate the periodic bulk posting of transactions of the same type to the ledger.

Employee wages are computed using a document known as a payroll. This shows each employees gross pay, deductions in respect of PAYE tax and national insurance contributions, and the resulting amount of net pay. It also shows that employers national insurance contributions. The net pay, PAYE tax and national insurance contributions of both the employee and employer are all debited to the wages and salaries account in the ledger. The PAYE tax and national insurance contributions are credited to a liability account since these have to be paid to the Inland Revenue.

Key terms and concepts

Columnar books of prime entry, exempt, gross pay, net pay, payroll, PAYE, sales tax, value added tax, zero rated.

Exercises

An asterisk after the question number indicates that there is a suggested answer in the Appendix.

31.1. (a) Briefly explain the nature of value added tax (VAT) and its associated cash flows.
   (b) Describe how this affects the items shown in the final accounts of businesses.
   (c) What does it mean when a business is classified as: (i) zero rated; and (ii) exempt for VAT purposes?

31.2. (a) Explain the main purpose of columnar day books.
   (b) Describe the possible format of: (i) a columnar purchases day book; and (ii) a columnar cash book. Your answer should include reference to value added tax.

31.3. (a) Briefly describe how each of the following are computed: (i) employees gross pay; (ii) employees net pay.
   (b) Outline the nature of those items that are required by UK law to be deducted from employees wages and salaries.

31.4.* The following are extracts from the payroll of J. Sutcliffe Ltd for the week ending 24 January 19X9.

	£
Gross wages	6,800
National insurance contributions—	
employees	680
employers	1,020
PAYE tax	950

There were no other deductions from the employees pay.

You are required to show the journal entries to record the relevant items in the weekly payroll (including any cash payments).

31.5. Mudgee Ltd issued the following invoices to customers in respect of credit sales made during the last week of May 19X7. The amounts stated are all net of value added tax. All sales made by Mudgee Ltd are subject to VAT at 15 per cent.

Invoice No.	Date	Customer	Amount £
3045	25 May	Laira Brand	1,060.00
3046	27 May	Brown Bros	2,200.00
3047	28 May	Penfold's	170.00
3048	29 May	T. Tyrell	460.00
3049	30 May	Laira Brand	1,450.00
			5,340.00

On 29 May Laira Brand returned half the goods (in value) purchased on 25 May. An allowance was made the same day to this customer for the appropriate amount.

On 1 May 19X7 Laira Brand owed Mudgee Ltd £2,100.47. Other than the purchases detailed above, Laira Brand made credit purchases of £680.23 from Mudgee Ltd on 15 May. On 21 May Mudgee Ltd received a cheque for £2,500 from Laira Brand.

Required:
(a) Show how the above transactions would be recorded in Mudgee Ltd's sales books for the week ended 30 May 19X7.
(b) Describe how the information in the sales book would be incorporated into Mudgee Ltd's double entry system.
(c) Reconstruct the personal account of Laira Brand as it would appear in Mudgee Ltd's ledger for May 19X7. (AAT)

31.6. Kwella Ltd received the following invoices from suppliers during the week commencing 23 November 19X7. All purchases made by Kwella Ltd are subject to value added tax at 15 per cent. The following list gives the *gross* value of each invoice received.

Date received	Invoice No.	Date of invoice	Supplier	Gross amount £
23 Nov	GL 788	19 Nov	Glixit plc	506.00
24 Nov	899330	19 Nov	Moblin Ltd	115.00
25 Nov	G 1101	17 Nov	S & G Gates	724.50
26 Nov	AX 1256	23 Nov	Goldrins Glues	1,115.50
27 Nov	CS 772	25 Nov	Wixit Wires Ltd	1,794.00

On 25 November Kwella Ltd rejected all the goods invoiced on 19 November by Moblin Ltd (invoice no. 899330) because they were not what had been ordered. The good were returned to Moblin Ltd along with Kwella Ltd's debit note (D 56) for the full invoice amount.

On 26 November Kwella Ltd had to return some of the goods purchased on 17 November from S & G Gates (invoice no. G1101) because there were sub-standard. A debit note (D 57) for a gross value of £241.50 was returned with the goods.

Required:
- (a) Write up Kwella Ltd's purchases book and purchases returns book for the week commencing 23 November 19X7 totalling the columns off as at 28 November 19X7.
- (b) Describe how the information in the purchases book and purchases returns book would be incorporated into Kwella Ltd's ledger.
- (c) The balance brought forward on S & G Gates' account at 1 November 19X7 was £920.00 which Kwella Ltd settled in full by cheque on 13 November after deducting 5 per cent discount. There were no other transactions with S & G Gates during the month of November other than those detailed above.

Reconstruct Kwella Ltd's ledger account for S & G Gates for the month of November 19X7 balancing off the accounts as at 30 November 19X7.   (AAT)

31.7. A business commenced trading for the week commencing 28 May 19X0 with £79 in cash and a bank overdraft of £515.

The following receipts and payments occurred during the week ending 3 June 19X0.

28 May   Paid travelling expenses of £37 in cash.

29 May   Paid a telephone bill of £115 (including £15 value added tax) by cheque.

29 May   Grant Degan, a credit customer, settled an invoice for £90 paying £81 in cash and receiving £9 discount for prompt settlement.

30 May   Made cash sales totalling £460 including £60 value added tax. The amount was received by cheque and was immediately banked.

31 May   Paid an invoice for £100 from Gaga Ltd by cheque for £92. £8 discount was received for prompt settlement.

1 June   Made cash purchases totalling £115 including value added tax of £15 paying by cheque.

1 June   Made cash sales of £230 inclusive of value added tax of £30.

2 June   Paid staff wages of £300. This was partly paid by cheques totalling £230, the balance being paid in cash.

2 June   Paid £200 from the till into the business bank account.

Required:
- (a) Draw up a cash book with separate columns for dates, narrations, folios, discount, VAT, bank and cash. Enter the opening balances and record the transactions for the week commencing 28 May 19X0. Balance the cash book as at 3 June 19X0.
- (b) Describe how the totals for the Discount and VAT columns will be entered into the ledger.   (AAT)

31.8.* After completing a training course at a technical college, Michael Faraday set up in business as a self-employed electrician on 1 January 19X5.

He was very competent at his job, but had no idea how to maintain proper accounting records. Sometimes during 19X5 one of his friends asked Michael how well his business was doing. He replied 'All right...I think...but I'm not quite sure'.

In the ensuing conversation his friend asked whether he had prepared accounts yet, covering his first quarter's trading, to which Michael replied that he had not. His friend then stressed that, for various reasons, it was vital for accounts of businesses to be prepared properly.

Shortly afterwards Michael came to see you to ask for your help in preparing accounts for his first quarter's trading. He brought with him, in a cardboard box, the only records he had, mainly scribbled on scraps of paper.

He explained that he started his business with a car worth £700, and £2,250 in cash of which £250 was his savings and £2,000 had been borrowed from a relative at an interest rate of 10 per cent per annum. It was his practice to pay his suppliers and expenses in cash, to require his customers to settle their accounts in cash and to bank any surplus in a business bank account. He maintained lists of cash receipts and cash payments, of supplies obtained on credit and of work carried out for customers and of appliances sold, on credit.

The list of credit suppliers comprised:

Date supplied 19X5	Supplier	Amount owed £	Date paid 19X5	Amount paid £	Remarks
January	Dee & Co.	337.74	March	330.00	Received discount £7.74
	AB Suppliers	528.20	March	528.20	
February	Simpson	141.34	March	138.00	Received discount £3.34
	Cotton Ltd	427.40	March	130.00	Payment on account
			April	297.40	Remainder
	Dee & Co.	146.82	March	140.00	Received discount £6.82
March	AB Supplies	643.43	April	643.43	
	Simpson	95.60			Not yet paid

The purchase in January from Dee & Co. was of tools and equipment to enable him to carry out electrical repair work. All the remaining purchases were of repair materials, except for the purchase in February from Cotton Ltd, which consisted entirely of electrical appliances for resale.

In addition to the above credit transactions, he had bought repair materials for cash, as follows:

19X5	£
January	195.29
February	161.03
March	22.06

Other cash payments comprised:

19X5		£
January	Rent of premises for January to June 19X5	400.00
	Rates of premises for January to March 19X5	150.00
	Stationery	32.70
	Car running expenses	92.26
February	Sundries	51.54
	Car running expenses	81.42
March	Sundries	24.61
	Car running expenses	104.52
	Transfer to bank	500.00

He had also withdrawn £160.00 in cash at the end of each month for living expenses.

The list of credit customers comprised:

Date of sale 19X5	Customer	Amount owed £	Date received 19X5	Amount received £	Remarks
January	D. Hopkins	362.80	February	357.00	Allowed discount £5.80
	P. Bolton	417.10	March	417.10	
February	G. Leivers	55.00	March	55.00	
	M. Whitehead	151.72	April	151.72	
	N. John Ltd	49.14	April	49.14	
	A. Linnekar	12.53	March	12.53	
March	E. Horton	462.21	April	462.21	
	S. Ward	431.08	March	426.00	Allowed discount £5.08
	W. Scothern & Co.	319.12			Not yet received
	N. Annable	85.41			Not yet received

The above amounts relate to charges for repair work which he had carried out, except that the amounts shown in February for G. Leivers, N. John Ltd and A. Linnekar are for sales of electrical appliances.

In addition to the above credit transactions, he had cash takings, as follows:

19X5		£
January	Repair work	69.44
February	Repair work	256.86
March	Repair work	182.90
	Appliances	112.81

He estimated that, at the end of March 19X5, his stock of electrical repair materials was £691.02 and of electrical appliances for resale was £320.58, his tools and equipment were worth £300.00 and his car, £600.00.

Apart from loan interest, the only accrual was for heating and lighting, £265.00.

Required:

(a) Prepare:

   (i) purchase day book with analysis columns for each type of purchase, and

   (ii) sales day book with analysis columns for each class of business undertaken.

(b) Open, post to 31 March 19X5 only, and balance a columnar cash book suitably analysed to facilitate ledger postings.

(c) Open, post to 31 March 19X5 only, and balance a creditors' ledger control account and a debtors' ledger control account. Use the closing balances in your answer to (g) below. (NB: Individual accounts for creditors and debtors are *not* required.)

(d) Open, post and balance sales and cost of sales accounts, each with separate columns for 'Repairs' and 'Appliances'.

(e) Prepare M. Faraday's trading account for the quarter ended 31 March 19X5, distinguishing between gross profit on repairs and on appliance sales.

(f) Prepare M. Faraday's general profit and loss account for the quarter ended 31 March 19X5.

(g) Prepare M. Faraday's balance sheet as at 31 March 19X5.   (ACCA)

31.9.* M. Essex is in business as a wholesale coal merchant. The following transactions took place during December 19X7:

1 Dec	Balance at bank £5,000.
3 Dec	Purchased goods on credit from English Coal for £400 plus VAT.
4 Dec	Received an invoice for £240 plus VAT from Solihull Garage in respect of vehicle repairs on credit.
5 Dec	Bought stationery costing £240 plus VAT and paid by cheque.
6 Dec	Sold goods on credit to Black for £600 plus VAT.
7 Dec	Bought goods on credit from Scottish Coal for £320 plus VAT.
8 Dec	Paid wages by cheque of £350.
10 Dec	Sold goods for £520 plus VAT and received a cheque for this amount.
11 Dec	Purchased goods costing £720 plus VAT and paid by cheque.
12 Dec	Sold goods on credit to White for £800 plus VAT.
13 Dec	Received an invoice for £360 plus VAT from Solihull Garage relating to motor expenses incurred on credit.
14 Dec	Bought goods for resale costing £480 plus VAT and paid by cheque.
15 Dec	Purchased a motor vehicle on credit from Solihull Garage costing £4,000 plus VAT.
16 Dec	Received telephone bill from English Telecom for £560 plus VAT.
17 Dec	Sold a motor vehicle on credit to Solihull Garage for £2,000 plus VAT.
18 Dec	Sold goods for £640 plus VAT and received a cheque.
19 Dec	Paid insurance premium on vehicles of £720 by cheque.
20 Dec	Purchased stationery for £160 plus VAT by cheque.
23 Dec	Sold on old motor vehicle for £3,000 plus VAT and received a cheque for this amount.
28 Dec	Received a cheque from Black for £680 after deducting £25 cash discount.

29 Dec   Received a cheque from White for £905 after deducting £35 cash discount.

30 Dec   Paid English Coal £450 by cheque after deducting cash discount of £20.

31 Dec   Paid Scottish Coal £346 by cheque after deducting cash discount of £30.

You are required to:

(a) Write up the sales and purchases day books and the cash book using appropriate analysis columns where there is more than one transaction of the same type.

(b) Make the necessary entries in the ledger.
Assume the rate of VAT to be 17.5 per cent.

32. The use of computers in accounting

Learning objectives

After reading this chapter the student should be able to:

1. Explain the meaning of the key terms and concepts listed at the end of the chapter.
2. Describe the nature of basic computer concepts.
3. Describe the main advantages of computerized accounting systems.
4. Discuss the expanding role of computerized accounting systems.
5. Explain the main factors which need to be taken into consideration in the design, operation and management of computerized accounting systems.
6. Discuss the limitations of computer systems.

Some basic computer concepts

Computer-based accounting systems were originally the preserve of big organizations, who could afford the substantial investment required to buy a large central computer, or *mainframe*. However, the years which followed saw a dramatic change in the range of computer equipment available for commercial users. The arrival of the *personal computer* (PC) small enough to sit on an office desk, has now made computing accessible to even the smallest business. The miniaturization of components and the development of flat-screen technologies has produced ever-smaller *portable PC's*, variously referred to as *laptops*, *notebooks*, *or palmtops*, depending on their size.

In between these two extremes, a variety of *mid-range* machines is available (sometimes referred to as *mini-computers*). These may be used by medium-sized companies who need more power than is available on a PC, or by larger companies who want to dedicate a machine to a specific purpose (such as controlling stock in a warehouse).

Computers can be linked together in various ways. Even small offices may find it advantageous to set up a *local area network* (LAN), linking together a number of PC's. This enables the users to have shared access to programs and files, and to share the use of other equipment, especially printers. In this case, control over the local network will be given to one of the PC's (usually a more powerful one) which adopts the role of the *server*.

Links over longer distances are provided by *wide area networks* (WAN), enabling accounting information to be exchanged more or less instantaneously between offices many miles apart. Some accounting systems work on a *client-server* principle: the *server* in this case is a powerful machine (perhaps at Head Office) which handles all the main accounts. The *clients* are PC's located in subsidiary offices which do a limited amount of local processing, in a way which is closely controlled by the server.

The diversification of computer processors has been matched by new and ingenious ways of entering and retrieving data, (the devices for doing this sometimes being referred to as computer *peripherals*). For input, the mainstay for most data is still the *keyboard*. However, data may also be read in directly from printed text, using *optical character recognition*, or converted from the spoken word, using *voice recognition*. Product information may be stored in *bar codes*, which can be read by scanners in check-outs or by scanner 'guns', some of which can operate several metres away from the bar code symbols. Newer *two-dimensional bar codes* extend the amount of information which can be stored in a single label, so that a lot of supplementary information can be included as well as the basic product code.

Perhaps the greatest revolution in computer use has resulted from the development of facilities which are used by moving and clicking the computer *mouse*. Such facilities depend on a *graphical user interface*, which enables users to make selections by using the mouse to point at small pictures (*icons*) or to activate *menus* which offer a range of choices. Some accounting packages now permit almost all routine activities to be carried out via the mouse, for example by providing a numeric keypad on the *screen/monitor* at appropriate points in the transaction (see Figure 32.1).

Technology has also advanced in respect of devices for data storage and output. PC's routinely store hundreds of millions of characters (or *bytes*) on a machine's *magnetic disk*, and *CD-ROM* technology, very similar to that used for audio and video recordings, offers even larger storage capacities. Output can be routed to *laser* or *inkjet printers*, which can reproduce images as well as text, and increasingly provide options for printing in colour.

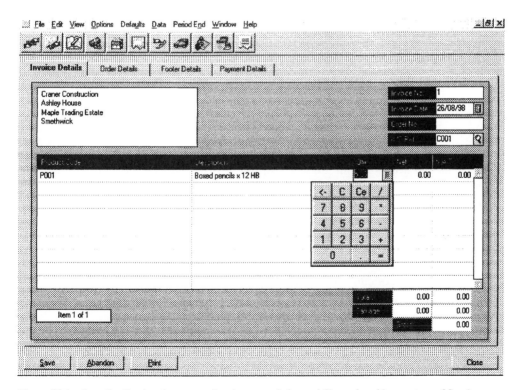

Figure 32.1   Sage Sterling invoice screen showing numeric keypad (Reproduced by courtesy of Sage).

Images can also be transferred from the computer to *microfiche* or *microfilm*, usually where there is a lot of information to be held over a long period in an archive.

From the accountant's point of view, the visible technology (*hardware*) is of only minor importance. Far more important are the *programs* which execute in the computer. This invisible *software* determines how the accounting information is actually processed and stored. Accounting software is commonly purchased in the form of an accounting *package*, which can be set up on the computer in a matter of minutes. Companies with specialized needs may decide to commission software to be written for them: this is sometimes known as *bespoke software*, and may take months to write and test. Three important points should be noted with respect to accounting software of all kinds:

- if there are any errors in the software, these can be extremely difficult to diagnose and correct. Since accountants are dedicated to making figures as accurate as possible, they must be sure that software is error-free. This aspect of the accountant's concern with accuracy is discussed further at a later point in the chapter.
- a considerable amount of effort is usually needed to ensure that the accounting codes and conventions used in the software are set up in ways which match the working practices of the business. It is unrealistic to expect to be able to install accounting software and then use it immediately, as might be done with software for *wordprocessing* or *spreadsheets*.
- appearances can be deceptive. Being able to bring up all kinds of impressive facilities at the click of an icon provides no guarantee that the system can carry out all the accounting functions which are actually needed by the business. It is important that the system can handle the kind of processes which really matter to the business, for example by tracking costs for particular items or activities, offering customer discounts, or handling payments made in instalments.

Advantages of computerized accounting systems

In the early days of commercial computing, most of the savings made by companies came from reductions in the numbers of clerks needed to process routine transactions. For example, a company with several hundred employees might use the computer to carry out the weekly payroll calculations: computers could usually work out the employees' entitlements and deductions in a fraction of the time required by the clerical teams they displaced. Accounting applications were a popular first choice to be implemented on the computer, because they necessarily involved many such repetitive activities. Often a set of identical tasks, such as calculating the pay for each employee, would be run through the computer in a *batch*, and this mode of operation became known as *batch processing*.

Batch processes saved labour, but the programs carrying out the processing tended to be very inflexible. The accounting data would be stored in a way which suited the accounting program, making it difficult to get at for any other kind of analysis. There was no way in which accounting reports could be created 'on demand'. Furthermore, since highly specialized skills were needed to program and operate the computer, departments wishing to use the accounting data had to explain their needs to systems analysts, who in turn specified how new programs should be coded and appropriate reports generated.

Many of these cumbersome procedures were swept away with the arrival of *on-line* or *interactive processing* in the late 1970's. This style of working is taken for granted today, since it is used by everything from a PC package (such as a spreadsheet) to mainframe-based services (for example, as used in telephone-based insurance or banking services). At the time, however, it was regarded as a tremendous innovation for users to be able to interact directly with the computer. As the new interactive techniques developed, so did most of the advantages which can be found in computer systems today. Two particular advantages can be summarized as follows:

Simultaneous access to data

Only a handful of people can study a set of conventional books simultaneously. Through interaction with a computer system, on the other hand, large numbers of users can all have access to the same information. Not only can they gain immediate access to ledger entries of customer X or supplier Y, they can do so without worrying about where the ledgers are held, or whether someone else might be using them at the same time. Similarly, if a change is made to the ledger (for example, customer X finally gets round to making an overdue payment), this information is instantly available to everyone else logged in to the accounting system.

Improved accuracy of data

If data is being entered interactively (perhaps with an operator filling in an 'electronic form' on the computer screen) the accounting program can carry out a certain amount of checking while the data entry is in progress. It cannot, of course, prevent the operator from making quite fundamental mistakes, such as typing in the wrong amount for a quantity ordered. However, it can do numerous other checks – for example, to prevent a key item of data from being omitted by mistake, or to ensure that the amount received in a payment matches the amount due.

Mistakes can also be avoided by reducing the need for data to be keyed in repeatedly. For example, a customer's address and other basic details can be typed in during an initial setting-up session: thereafter, the details can be stored in the computer's files, and altered only when there is a change in the customer's circumstances (such as a change of address or telephone number). In many systems, the operator merely has to initiate a search using the customer reference number or surname, and all the relevant details are brought up on the screen. The operator's task is then simply to check that the details being shown match up with those of the customer in question.

Some systems carry this approach further by providing *default values* for entries where the input is going to be predictable in the great majority of cases. Thus a default may be set for the price of an item, the size of a discount, or the number of days within which payment is due. In a small minority of cases, it may be necessary for the operator to change the default to another value. Most of the time, however, the operator merely has to confirm the default value, thus reducing the amount of typing required, and making it less likely that erroneous values will be entered. A screen illustrating ways of avoiding repeated data capture in this way is shown as Figure 32.2.

Apart from the benefits which result from interactive working, computerized accounting has brought benefits in two other main areas:

Improved detail

Storage in a computer system is not confined in the same way as the pages of a book. It can handle a more or less indefinite number of rows and columns. Records of transactions do not therefore have to be confined to basic information such as the date and amount: a variety of other details can easily be added, so that for example when a sale is made,

Order No. 10025			Thomas Tanks plc, 15, Railway Cuttings, Birmingham B15 2TT
Customer code	T009		
Date received	25 09 98		
Date required	9 10 98		Credit Limit 4000.00
Product code	Quantity	Description	Value
PR5544	20	A4 paper	216.20
PR5592	12	markers, black	15.24

Figure 32.2   A simplified screen layout for order entry. The operator only needs to enter the shaded values—the computer can generate a new order number, provide today's date, and retrieve details such as the customer's address and the price and description of each product.

codes can be recorded to show what category of customer this was, the identity of the salesperson, the product type, the sales district, and so on. When details on perhaps hundreds of customers are recorded in this way, they provided a rich source of data for the company to analyse.

Improved reporting

Having recorded accounting transactions in electronic form, the production of reports becomes a matter of running appropriate software to turn the data into summaries and tables (for management accounting) or standard balance sheet and profit and loss statements (for financial accounting). No longer do staff have to work from ledger entries, taking up large amounts of their time, and, almost inevitably, resulting in errors of calculations or transcription. There is, of course, an important proviso: the software used to generate the reports must be free of any errors in its logic. This raises important questions about the role of the accountant. Is he or she to take the computer figures at face value? If so, does this not hand over too much responsibility to the computer programmer? Of course, the accountant cannot check through every line of code appearing in the program, but at the same time he or she should be conscious that no programmer is infallible. In future, a growing proportion of accountants' expertise is likely to centre on checking the reasonableness and consistency of figures generated from computers.

Most accounting software (particularly off-the-shelf packages) provides facilities for generating period-end and year-end reports as described elsewhere in this book, and will produce a 'trial balance'. This trial balance does not have quite the same role as that described in Chapter 5. For example, most accounting software, while adhering to double-entry conventions in presenting ledger information, does not actually require the user to post the amount on both sides of the ledger—this is usually taken care of automatically by the system. If any errors are apparent in a trial balance the finger of suspicion should fall first and foremost on possible flaws in the software.

Most companies like to be able to analyse accounting data in other ways, besides the rather formalized summaries provided in the standard financial reports. Reports can generally be produced in one of three ways:

SALES LEDGER: ACCOUNT BALANCES (AGED)

Cust Code	Cust Name	Credit Limit	Balance	Current Period	30 Days	Over 30 Days
T009	T. Tanks	4000	1760.15	1203.45	556.70	0.00
T011	B. Timms	5000	4516.25	4020.15	324.10	172.00
T016	N. Todd	1500	1035.65	1035.65	0.00	0.00
T023	M. Tubbs	2500	519.23	380.12	98.56	40.55

Figure 32.3   Part of a typical computer-generated report. It enables customers with large or long-standing debts to be quickly identified.

(i)   the accounting software itself may allow users to select certain pre-programmed reports. For example, a commonly used report is an analysis of the sales ledger, to determine which customers are slow payers. An example of an Aged Debtors report of this kind is shown in Figure 32.3.

(ii)   the accounting software may contain a general purpose 'report generator'. This permits a more 'do-it-yourself' approach to report generation. The user can design a report from scratch, defining where fields are to appear, what should be shown in each field, and what titles and headings are to be used.

(iii)   the third option is to transfer data from the accounting system into an entirely separate piece of software. The most common choice for this is a spreadsheet. The accounting system will offer an *extract* or *export* feature, which allows selected data to be written out to a file in a rows-and-columns format.

The three ways in which reports can be generated are summarized in Figure 32.4:

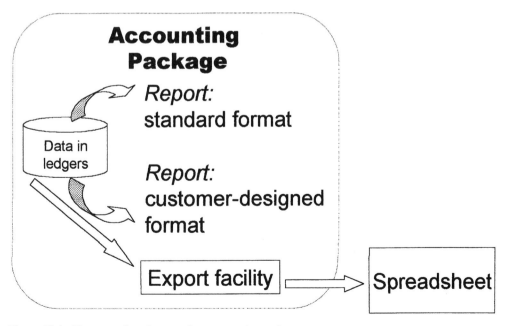

Figure 32.4   The generation of reports from accounting packages.

Once accounting software has become firmly established in the organization, a final benefit can be achieved from having data for successive years or periods held in electronic form. This makes it possible to look at how key financial indicators have changed with time, and to predict what will happen if particular trends continue. Once again, this can be done much more quickly and accurately than would be possible by staff working from paper records.

Expanding the role of the accounting system

All the facilities described thus far are those which would be used primarily within the accounting department. However, the interactive nature of the computer system can be exploited much more widely than this. With the advent of computer networks (of which the *Internet* is probably the best known example) new possibilities have opened up for inter-connecting accounting with other functions elsewhere in the firm, and even for accounting systems in different companies to communicate directly with each other.

Interconnection of this kind permits almost instant communication, but quite often time-saving is not the main object of the exercise. This can perhaps best be illustrated by reference to computer-to-computer links via *Electronic Data Interchange*. Businesses using *EDI* agree to exchange accounting documents (such as orders and invoices) in a standard electronic format. The EDI 'form' is generated from the accounting records of firm A and transmitted directly to the accounting system of firm B by way of an electronic message. At no stage does the form need to be printed out on paper, and nobody in firm B has to re-key any information from a paper document back into the computer. This saves staff time and expense, but perhaps more importantly it eliminates a possible source of errors (typing mistakes).

EDI messages can be sent across any kind of Wide Area Network—the type of technology to be used will depend on factors such as the volume of traffic being sent and the distance to be covered. Figure 32.5 shows how EDI might be used, with the messages being sent across a satellite link.

A similar approach to by-passing paperwork can be used inside the organization, in this case by creating links between the accounting software and other internal computer systems. For example, connections may be made with systems in a warehouse or on the production line, as shown in Figure 32.6.

The way in which the accounting function is integrated with other systems will vary in different organizations. In some cases, all the different software will be run on the same central computer. In others, the software will be run on local machines, with links being provided through a LAN or WAN.

This kind of integration opens up possibilities for working in entirely new ways. For example, an order entry clerk can check the availability of stock in the warehouse before taking the processing of an order any further. Similarly, information about the overall stock position can be fed routinely into the accounting system, making it much easier to make periodic valuations such as those discussed in Chapter 15. As more and more activities within an organization become computerized, and many of them generate information relevant to accounting, the opportunities for cross-linkages become more numerous. In some cases, companies have carried this integration a stage further. Rather than linking together a number of existing systems, they have completely re-invented their procedures for handling activities such as issuing purchase orders and processing accounts payable. This is known as *Business Process Reengineering*.

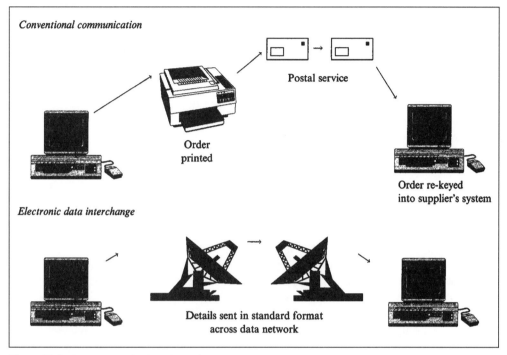

Figure 32.5 Intercommunication alternatives.

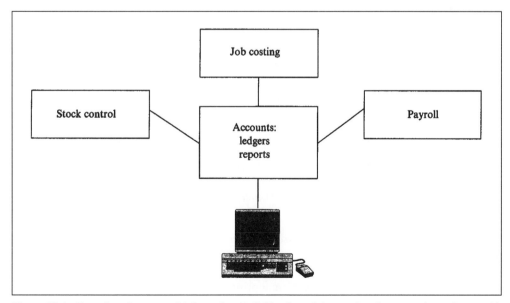

Figure 32.6 Extending the range of information available, through integrating the accounting software with software used in other parts of the company.

The design of computerized accounting systems

Even the creation of the most modest accounting package calls for some 're-engineering' of accounting processes as they are transferred to the new technology. Software designers, anxious to make the changeover as easy as possible for users who are familiar with traditional methods, usually retain many of the terms and conventions of book-keeping. This *user friendly* approach makes it easier to learn how to use the new system, and enables companies to make a more gradual transition, with paper-based functions running alongside computer-based at interim stages of the changeover.

However, the best systems go a good deal further than simply 'putting ledgers on a screen'. For example, traditional methods often centre around day books, which are a convenient place to gather together the records of a series of similar items, such as credit sales. Much of this information may need to be transcribed later into the ledger. Day books are one way of dividing up the process of data capture, so that manageable amounts of work are assigned to different members of the accounting team. As we have seen, the computer system designer does not have to worry about such constraints, as large numbers of people can all be given concurrent access to the same information. In the same way, there's no need to copy data out of one book and into another, since the computer can be programmed to do this kind of thing automatically.

The designer must also try to anticipate the kind of enquiries which the system users may want to make. For example, suppose that a customer rings up to complain about the non-delivery of goods. Something has clearly gone wrong, but where? The clerk may want to find out when the goods were originally ordered, whether despatch has been requested, what delivery address was specified, and so on. Paper-based methods would call for a lot of hunting through ledgers and filing cabinets at this point. However, a good computer system will allow the clerk to *navigate* easily through different screens of information while talking to the customer, so that everything can be resolved quickly—if possible, while he or she is still on the line.

The management and operation of computerized accounting systems

New methods of carrying out the accounting function call for new approaches to managing them. One of the most important roles is that of the system manager. To some extent, the systems manager makes decisions and carries responsibilities which would previously have belonged to the head or supervisor of a traditional accounts department. However, much of the work is more technical in nature, and has to be carried out using privileged access to the system (protected by a *password* or some other form of security). It requires above all a good understanding of the way the software operates. The system manager will be able to set, and modify, options such as the following:

- the dates and durations of accounting periods
- the codes to be used for accounts, discounts, sales areas, etc.
- the default settings to be used, e.g. for credit limits
- the format of standard reports
- the routeing of routine output to different printers
- the kind of access allowed to more junior users of the system
- the activation of audit and logging facilities

Because of the complexity of setting up some of these options, it is sometimes assumed that it is best left to technical staff. This is unwise. In assuming that it is 'just a technical matter', the system manager is handing over key areas of control to others, who may not understand the implications of what they are doing, or could use their privileged position to instigate fraud.

System security is one of the biggest challenges facing the system manager. Each user of the system must have access to the facilities needed for the job in hand—but no more. As is shown by the example of the clerk dealing with customers over the phone (described earlier), it can be difficult to anticipate exactly what access will be needed, since the clerk may need to search through a different set of screens each time, depending on the nature of the enquiry. Particular care has to be taken in assigning access rights which involve permission for key values to be altered—for example, it might be specified that only a supervisor can change standard prices, or over-ride pre-set credit limits. If the system is linked to other computers across networks, attention will also have to be given to risks arising from malicious intruders (or *hackers*) trying to gain access to the accounts or modifying the figures in EDI messages.

Back-up is another key responsibility. Particularly if the accounting is being done on a central machine, the entire set of accounting records may be held on a single magnetic disk. This is asking for trouble – if the disk malfunctions, all the records will be lost. It is a relatively simple matter to take back-up copies regularly. For a small system, it may be feasible to copy all the records on a daily basis. For larger systems, a different approach is sometimes used, where a complete copy is made to start with, but thereafter only the changes are backed up. In either case, the back-up copy needs to be moved to a separate, secure location for storage.

Finally, the system manager should ensure that provision is made for keeping proper *audit trails*. The trail should enable an auditor to check a transaction through every stage of its progress, including any steps handled by the computer. In smaller systems, this may be done by taking regular print-outs of key records or documents. More sophisticated systems keep a special log file on disk, which can be used to ascertain when activities were carried out and by whom. As more companies move towards the 'paperless office', and business is done over the Internet or through EDI rather than by post, computer-generated evidence will become an ever more important part of the audit trial.

Some limitations of computer systems

Thus far, it may seem that computers have brought unremitting benefits to accounting. However, they have also thrown up a number of recurring problems for users. The designers of accounting packages, for example, are constantly seeking to include every feature which they think a user might need. However, this can mean that the system manager is presented with a bewildering set of options, and has to devote a lot of time to deciding which features to activate and which to reject. Even then, it is quite likely that some desirable features will be missing, as each business tends to have its own unique requirements. The choice then is between adapting the business's methods to fit in with the way the software works, or seeking special modifications to the software—which is usually an expensive option.

Inflexibility can also appear in a quite different form if accounting operations need to be merged—for example, as a result of one company taking over another. Combining two different computerized systems is rarely straightforward, particularly if they have come from different suppliers. Because each accounting system stores data in its own individual way, moving from one system to another can be a lengthy and cumbersome process.

Finally, the speed and accessibility of computer systems, which make them so attractive to businesses, also make them particularly vulnerable. This is the main inhibiting factor in the development of *electronic commerce* using the Internet. The technology is already available to enable members of the public to transmit orders directly to vendors' systems, and to make payments electronically. However, making systems accessible to the public also makes them more open to attacks by hackers and fraudsters. The development of protective measures against ever more ingenious and sophisticated forms of electronic attack will be a preoccupation of the computer industry for many years to come.

Future directions for computerized accounting

Accounting systems are evolving rapidly. More 'user-friendly' methods are constantly being found of communicating with users, exploiting images and sounds in ways which are far removed from work with traditional ledgers. Greater use of 'intelligent' software will enable systems to offer more guidance to users who get into difficulties, and will also help in detecting and preventing fraud. Improved links between systems will cause some of the traditional barriers between accounting and other functions to disappear. All this will present new challenges for the accountant, in safeguarding the probity and accuracy of accounting information.

Summary

Computerized accounting can be carried out on many different types of hardware, ranging from mainframes to portable PC's. Many options are available for entering data into systems. Keyboards are widely used, while a mouse can be used to make selections via a Graphical User Interface. Other methods include bar code readers, optical character recognition, and voice recognition.

The most important element of an accounting system is the accounting software which runs on the computer. Early computer systems processed tasks in batches, but modern systems allow interaction directly with users. This gives rise to many of the advantages of computerized working—in particular, through allowing several users to see the same information at once, and in checking data as it is fed in. Computer-based systems can also provide more detail in the accounting records, and can generate a wide range of reports on demand.

Computerized systems have adopted much of the terminology and conventions of traditional book-keeping, but actually store and process accounting information in different ways. This in turn means that different approaches need to be taken to their management and control. A systems manager should ensure that staff can gain access only to the facilities they need in their work, and should also ensure that back-up copies of data are made and that audit trails are created.

Computerized accounting systems will continue to become more integrated with other systems, both within and outside the host organization, and this in turn will call for changes in emphasis in the work of the accountant. In particular, accountants will have to devise ways of checking the accuracy of output from the computer, without being able to refer to source documents, day books and ledgers.

Key terms and concepts

Audit trails, back-up copies, bar codes, batch processing, bespoke software, Business Process Reengineering, bytes, CD-ROM, default values, electronic commerce, electronic data interchange, graphical user interface, hacker, hardware, icons, interactive processing, Internet, keyboard, local area network (LAN), magnetic disk, mainframe computer, menu, microfiche, microfilm, mini-computer, monitor/display screen, mouse, on-line, optical character recognition, package, password, peripherals, personal computer (PC), printer, program, server, software, spreadsheet, system security, user-friendly, wide area network (WAN), wordprocessing.

Exercises

An asterisk after the question number indicates that there is a suggested answer in the Appendix.

32.1. Explain the difference between: (a) hardware and software; (b) 'batch' and 'interactive' processing; and (c) a LAN and a WAN.

32.2. A new computerized accounting system is to be introduced into an accounts department which has hitherto used only traditional bookkeeping. Six people work in the department. What advantages might they hope to see from the new system?

32.3. Give an example of *one* way in which a computerized accounting system might:
(a) reduce errors;
(b) improve customer service:
(c) improve the quality of accounting reports.

32.4.* 'Good accounting software has the look and feel of traditional bookkeeping methods'. Explain the benefits that might follow from such an approach. Identify *one* accounting function where this approach might not be the best one, and describe how a different approach might be implemented, taking advantage of some of the new possibilities of computing technology.

32.5. A 'system manager' will normally be appointed to take charge of a computerized accounting system. Draw up a brief job description, outlining the duties of such an appointment.

32.6. Explain the main limitations of computer systems.

32.7. Information technology and computerized systems are rapidly increasing in importance in data recording. Do you consider that this trend will eventually remove the need for control accounts to be incorporated in the design of accounting systems? Explain your answer briefly.   (ACCA adapted)

32.8. Over the past few decades, routine bookkeeping and accountancy work has been transformed by the extensive use of computers to perform that work.

Required:
(a) List and briefly explain *two* types of error which could occur in a manual sales ledger system which *could not* occur in a computerized system.
(b) List and briefly explain *two* types of error which could occur in a manual sales ledger system which *could also* occur in a computerized system.
(c) Explain the main advantages and disadvantages of computerized accounting systems compared with manual systems.   (ACCA)

33. Accounting for changing price levels

Learning objectives

After reading this chapter the student should be able to:

1. Explain the meaning of the key terms and concepts listed at the end of the chapter.
2. Discuss the limitations of historical cost accounting in times of rising prices including their impact on the profit and loss account and balance sheet.
3. Explain the nature of and difference between forms of price level changes including how they can be measured.
4. Describe different concepts of capital maintenance.
5. Explain how assets are valued using historical cost, current cost and current purchasing power accounting.
6. Describe the main conceptual differences between current cost accounting and current purchasing power accounting.
7. Prepare simple profit and loss accounts and balance sheet using current cost accounting and current purchasing power accounting.

Recording transactions at historical cost in the measurement of income

The fundamental ideas of profit introduced in Chapter 2 were based on the accounting definition that profit was the maximum amount that could be withdrawn from a business while leaving the capital intact. This approach as a measure of performance has considerable appeal. As residual beneficiaries the owners' benefits from the business are entirely dependent on the success of the business. Such success can be readily assessed in terms of what can be taken out of the business while leaving it no worse off than it was at the start of the period. When this is also seen in the more dynamic terms of being the amount by which the revenue earned exceeds the cost of producing those revenues, it is also seen as a measure of operating efficiency—increasing the value of outputs as represented by revenues, while achieving a relative decrease in the inputs measured by the costs matched against that revenue.

It was again in Chapter 2 that the measurement approach utilized by historical cost accounting was described in terms of recording transactions. Subsequent chapters have illustrated this time and again. As an approach to measurement, the transaction basis contributes well to the objectivity and verifiability attributes. In the historical cost balance sheet, assets are represented by the capitalized expenditures which have not yet been matched against revenue through depreciation for example. In the profit and loss account, revenues and costs have all been quantified on the basis of transactions.

However, it would be wrong to deduce that the historical cost basis is entirely objective and verifiable. Subjectivity has entered in deciding whether an expenditure should be capitalized or not, i.e. whether or not it represented an asset. Choice of methods of depreciation and the determination of provisions both involve substantial judgment. Similar scope exists in the allocation of indirect costs to stock values.

When considered in relation to other measurement attributes, historical cost may stand up less well, particularly when price changes are prevalent either in general, due to inflation, or for specific items arising as a result of changes in technology, tastes or other factors. The asset values will be dependent upon timing so that the same asset may have a different value depending only upon when it is purchased. This promotes neither consistency nor comparability and we are likely to get varying mixtures of ages of expenditures both between businesses and between periods for the same business. If prices are generally rising then, although asset values may be regarded as prudent, matching older expenses based on correspondingly lower prices may understate costs relative to revenues and thus overstate profit. Understating asset values and overstating profit cannot be considered free from bias let alone prudent.

The historical cost convention has adopted particular approaches to the three basic dimensions. The unit of measurement is the currency unit, i.e. the pound sterling in the UK. Even if the purchasing power of the pound changes, there is no response in this dimension by the historical cost convention. As implied above, the valuation model used measures asset values at the original transaction price modified by provisions and write downs due to depreciation, etc. The capital maintained is the money value of the shareholders' contributed capital plus accumulated profits.

Price change considerations and inflation accounting

Current purchasing power accounting

Price change has two broad impacts on the accounting approaches which have been described. First *general price change* through *inflation* undermines the stability of the value of the currency unit. Reducing the *purchasing power* of the pound through inflation means that comparison of amounts measured in pounds at different times is distorted.

One response to the problems of price change is to restate the accounts produced on a historical cost basis by adjusting for change in purchasing power. The procedure is to restate opening and closing balance sheets by indexing all items in the opening balance sheet and all non-monetary items including owners' capital in the closing balance sheet using *general price level indices*. Monetary items in the closing balance sheet would require no adjustments as they are already stated in current terms. The capital increase shown between the restated balance sheets would be the current purchasing power profit. This approach involves only limited adjustment from historical cost and, since these can be based on publicly available indices such as the *retail price index*, properties of objectivity and verifiability are not substantially reduced.

The unit of measurement that would then be employed would be the pound of current purchasing power at the year end. The purchasing power of the owners' capital would be maintained since it is restated in these terms. However the valuation model which adjusts asset values for general changes in prices may result in asset values that are considered to be an entire fiction. Assets do not all change price in line with inflation. In addition the increase that is being reported would be a combination of realized and unrealized gains, since the upward revaluation of assets by indexing them would be, increasingly, a value without the external evidence that would meet the needs of prudence and realization. A version of this approach known as *current purchasing power accounting* (CPPA) was put forward in the UK but, given the limitations identified and others, it has been largely rejected.

Current cost accounting

The second major aspect of price change is the *specific price changes* in asset values. The historical cost approach, which recognizes revenues only when they are realized, will produce periodic profits which represent both the results of the current year's operations and gains made in previous periods which are only realized in the current period (although gains which are unrealized in the current period are excluded).

A response which can be made to this problem is to recognize unrealized gains in the period to which they relate but to treat these not as part of operating profit. Instead they can be regarded as *holding gains*, i.e. gains from continuing to own assets during price rises. Measuring profit in relation to opening and closing capital restated to include holding gains of the period produces a *physical concept of capital maintenance*, i.e. identifying the gains that can be withdrawn while permitting a business to own the same physical assets. Profit would be restated by eliminating holding gains. This is aptly described as operating profit, showing the ability of a business to produce revenues over and above the current cost of producing them through operating activities. Any adjustments necessary to eliminate holding gains from profit would be those necessary to restate historical costs, included in the profit and loss account, to current costs.

A version of this approach known as *current cost accounting* (CCA) includes such adjustments in three components. These are a *depreciation adjustment*, modifying depreciation to one based on the current cost of assets rather than the historical cost; a *cost of sales adjustment*, adjusting stock values and purchases to current costs; a *monetary working capital adjustment*, adjusting for the price change of purchases during the creditor period and sales during the debt collection period. There has been much debate about whether there should also be a fourth adjustment, known as a *gearing adjustment*. This is intended to reflect the benefits of having debt capital during periods of increasing prices, similar in principle to the monetary working capital adjustment with respect to trade creditors. These two adjustments are relatively complicated, and generally regarded as beyond the introductory level. Considerable subjectivity is involved in identifying suitable *specific price level indices* for each of the possible specific price changes. The resulting reduction in objectivity and verifiability together with the costs of implementing the approach with all its complexities are considered to outweigh the advantages, particularly where the period of holding assets is relatively short and hence the impact of the adjustments was small. Current cost accounting has been widely abandoned as a result.

Realistic examples of accounting for changing price levels are usually very complex and beyond the scope of this book and accounting examinations at this level. However, a relatively simple numerical illustration of current cost accounting (CCA) and current purchasing power accounting (CPPA) is shown in Example 33.1.

Example 33.1

A. Solent commenced trading on 1 January 19X5 as a ships' chandler. The capital in cash was £15,000. On that date A. Solent purchased a boathouse for £10,000 and a boat for resale at a price of £5,000. The boathouse is leasehold over a period of 50 years and depreciated using the straight line/fixed instalment method. The replacement cost of the boathouse on 31 December 19X5 was estimated to be £13,000.

The boat was sold on 1 July 19X5 for £8,000 and on the same day an identical boat was purchased for £6,000. This was unsold at 31 December 19X5 and is estimated to have a replacement cost of £7,000.

The retail price index (RPI) at 1 January 19X5 stood at 100, at 1 July 19X5 was 105, and at 31 December 19X5 was 110.

You are required to prepare a profit and loss account for the year and balance sheet at 31 December 19X5 using:

(a)   historical cost accounting;
(b)   current cost accounting (using replacement cost);
(c)   current purchasing power accounting;
(d)   historical cost accounting with adjustments for current costs.

A. Solent
Profit and loss account for the year ended 31 December 19X5

	HCA	CCA	CPPA
	£	£	£
Sales	8,000	8,000	8,381
Cost of sales	(5,000)	(6,000)	(5,500)
Gross profit	3,000	2,000	2,881
Depreciation	(200)	(260)	(220)
Operating profit	2,800	1,740	2,661
Loss on holding monetary assets	—	—	(95)
Net profit	2,800	1,740	2,566

Workings

$$\text{HCA depreciation} = \frac{£10,000}{50 \text{ years}} = £200$$

$$\text{CCA depreciation} = \frac{£13,000}{50 \text{ years}} = £260$$

$$\text{CPPA sales} = £8,000 \times \frac{110}{105} = £8,381$$

$$\text{CPPA cost of sales} = £5,000 \times \frac{110}{100} = £5,500$$

$$\text{CPPA depreciation} = \left(£10,000 \times \frac{110}{100}\right) \div 50 \text{ years} = £220$$

CPPA loss on holding monetary assets: cash of £8,000 − £6,000 = £2,000 from 1 July 19X5 to 31 December 19X5:

$$\frac{110 - 105}{105} \times £2,000 = £95$$

A. Solent
Balance sheet as at 31 December 19X5

	HCA £	CCA £	CPPA £
Boathouse	10,000	13,000	11,000
Depreciation	(200)	(260)	(220)
	9,800	12,740	10,780
Stock	6,000	7,500	6,286
Cash	2,000	2,000	2,000
	17,800	22,240	19,066
Capital	15,000	15,000	15,000
Capital maintenance reserve	—	5,500	1,500
Profit	2,800	1,740	2,566
	17,800	22,240	19,066

Workings
CCA capital maintenance:

Boathouse   Stock
$(£13,000 - £10,000) + (£7,500 - £5,000) = £5,500$

CPPA stock $= £6,000 \times \dfrac{110}{105} = £6,286$

CPPA capital maintenance $= £15,000 \times \dfrac{110 - 100}{100} = £1,500$

A. Solent
Profit and loss account (HC adjusted for CC) for the year ended 31 December 19X5

	£
Sales	8,000
Cost of sales	(5,000)
Historical cost gross profit	3,000
Depreciation	(200)
Historical cost net profit	2,800
Cost of sales adjustment (£6,000 − £5,000)	(1,000)
Depreciation adjustment (£260 − £200)	(60)
Current cost net profit	1,740

The HC balance sheet adjusted for CC will be as shown for CCA.

Summary

The use of historical cost accounting in times of rising prices is said to overstate the profit because older lower costs are matched against more recent higher sales prices. It is also said to distort the values of assets and liabilities in the balance sheet. The assets will have been bought at various points in time when the prevailing levels of prices were different. Also the assets are not shown in their current values.

Profit can be conceptualized as the amount that could be withdrawn from a business while leaving the capital intact. This highlights the need for capital maintenance. There are three main concepts of capital maintenance—the maintenance of historical cost, physical/operating capital maintenance, and the maintenance of purchasing power.

Changes in price levels take two forms: general price changes associated with inflation which reduce the purchasing power of money, and are measured in the UK by the retail price index (RPI); and specific price changes which refer to the change in price of a specific category of good or asset (e.g. vehicles).

Assets can be valued at either their historical cost, current/replacement cost, or purchasing power of the money invested in the asset. Current/replacement cost is commonly measured using a specific price index, and purchasing power is measured by means of a general price index such as the RPI. These three methods of asset valuation give rise to three corresponding methods of accounting known as historical cost accounting (HCA), current cost accounting (CCA), and current purchasing power accounting (CPPA), respectively.

In HCA assets are valued at their historical cost, and profit is measured while ensuring the maintenance of historical cost capital. It is argued that in times of changing price levels, CCA or CPPA is more appropriate. In CCA assets are usually valued at replacement cost, and profit is measured while ensuring the maintenance of physical capital or the operating capability of a business. In CPPA assets are valued in terms of current purchasing power, and profit is measured while ensuring the maintenance of the purchasing power of capital.

A variation of CCA involves adjusting the profit computed on a historical cost basis to give the current cost profit. This necessitates a cost of sales adjustment, depreciation adjustment, and monetary working capital adjustment. There has been much debate about whether there should also be a gearing adjustment.

Key terms and concepts

Cost of sales adjustment, current cost accounting, current purchasing power accounting, depreciation adjustment, gearing adjustment, general price change, general price level indices, holding gains, inflation, monetary working capital adjustment, physical capital maintenance, purchasing power, retail price index, specific price change, specific price indices.

Exercises

An asterisk after the question number indicates that there is a suggested answer in the Appendix.

33.1. Explain the limitations of historical cost accounting in times of rising prices.

33.2. Explain fully why there is said to be a need to account for changing prices in published company accounts.

33.3. Explain the differences and/or interrelationship between: (a) changes in specific price levels; (b) changes in general price levels; (c) inflation; and (d) the retail price index (RPI).

33.4. (a) Outline the concept of economic income as defined by Hicks (1946) and explain its relevance in the measurement of profit (see Chapter 2).
(b) Describe three different concepts of capital maintenance.

33.5. Explain how assets are valued using each of the following measurement methods: (a) historical cost; (b) current cost; and (c) current purchasing power.

33.6. Describe the main conceptual differences between current cost accounting and current purchasing power accounting.

33.7. Explain why the profit computed using historical cost accounting usually differs from that when calculated using replacement cost accounting and current purchasing power accounting.

33.8.* Sally Johnson, while holidaying on a remote island, decides to supplement her holiday money by selling slices of water melon on the beach. She purchases 50 melons for a total of 500 francs and during the week sells them all by slicing each melon into four and selling each slice for 5 francs. At the end of the week she returns to the fruit market and discovers that the price of 50 melons has risen to 650 francs. On her way to the market she had purchased a newspaper in which the headline read 'Island inflation rate now 5 per cent per week'.

(a) You are required to compute Sally's income for the first week on:
  (i)   an historical cost basis;
  (ii) a replacement cost basis;
  (iii) a current purchasing power basis.
(b) Comment upon the usefulness of the three income figures you have calculated.

(JMB)

33.9. A. Daley commenced trading on 1 January 19X8 as a second-hand car dealer. His capital in cash was £20,000. On that date Daley acquired a 5 year lease on a lock-up garage at a cost of £5,000.
The following transactions took place during the year, all in cash:

		£
31 Mar 19X8	Purchased a car for resale	10,000
30 June 19X8	Sold the car	13,000
30 Sept 19X8	Bought another car for resale	14,000

The relevant indices during the year were:

	RPI	Garage	Vehicles
1 January 19X8	100	100	100
31 March 19X8	106	108	105
30 June 19X8	112	117	110
30 September 19X8	118	125	115
31 December 19X8	124	130	120

You are required to prepare a profit & loss account for the year and a balance sheet at 31 December 19X8 using:

(a) historical cost accounting
(b) current cost accounting
(c) current purchasing power accounting
(d) historical cost accounting with adjustments for current costs

Make all computations to the nearest £.

34. The conceptual framework of accounting

Learning objectives

After reading this chapter the student should be able to:

1. Explain the meaning of the key terms and concepts listed at the end of the chapter.
2. Explain the nature of a qualitative characteristic of financial information and how it differs from an accounting concept.
3. Discuss the qualitative characteristics of financial information contained in the ASB *Statement of Principles for Financial Reporting* (1995).
4. Explain the nature, purpose and scope of the conceptual framework of accounting including the main contents of the ASB *Statement of Principles for Financial Reporting* (1995).
5. Describe the conceptual framework and standardization debates and discuss related issues.
6. Describe the main types of accounting theories and their implications for a conceptual framework of accounting.

Theoretical review of basic accounting procedures

The foundations of financial accounting were introduced in Chapters 1 and 2 and were extended in Chapter 10 to consider the fundamental accounting concepts, bases and policies. Having looked at how these are used in a range of accounting applications, it is now possible to review the accounting processes from a theoretical perspective. It may be helpful, at this stage, to re-read the material in Chapters 2 and 10 and to consider how they have contributed to the various accounting procedures that have been covered in this book.

The major considerations can be briefly restated as follows:

1. Definition of the accounting entity is used to determine the boundaries of the organizational unit to be reported upon. The accounting entity is created as an artificial construct, and as such cannot own itself. The external owner's interest is identified as capital in the accounting equation.
2. The life of a business is divided into accounting periods usually of a year, each seen as a separate entity. Accounts are produced to show the results relating to a particular period. Division into periods is reflected by the emphasis given to periodic reporting.
3. Profit can be defined in terms of changes in capital represented in the balance sheets at the start and end of the period. A parallel approach is transaction based or net production. Here, revenues are recognized in the period when they are realized and the matching principle identifies the costs to be traced to the appropriate period.

Critical in this process is the classification of expenditure as either capital or revenue. Costs which are capitalized are carried forward from period to period as balance sheet items. Assets in the balance sheet are carried forward in anticipation of providing benefits to future periods and this may then lead to matching in those periods.

4. In measuring the values to be included in accounting reports four concepts have been set down in accounting standards and in particular SSAP2—*Disclosure of Accounting Policies*. In addition to the accruals concept and matching principle this stresses the concepts of prudence, going concern and consistency.

5. Other measurement properties were also considered in Chapter 10 including objectivity, verifiability and freedom from bias and materiality.

6. Any system of accounting for profit has to define either explicitly or implicitly three basic dimensions. These are the units of measurements, the valuation model and the concept of capital maintenance.

Accounting concepts and qualitative characteristics

Chapter 10 explained in some depth the four fundamental accounting concepts in SSAP2 and two others which are common in examination questions. SSAP2 is currently the only mandatory SSAP or FRS on accounting concepts that has been published by the ASC or ASB. However, in 1995 the Accounting Standards Board (ASB) published a *Statement of Principles for Financial Reporting*[1] which at the current time has the status of an Exposure Draft. This follows very closely the text of another document published in 1989 by the International Accounting Standards Committee (IASC) known as *Framework for the Preparation and Presentation of Financial Statements*.[2]

Chapter 2 of the ASB *Statement of Principles for Financial Reporting* describes what are referred to as the 'qualitative characteristics of financial information'. Chapter 10 of this book, like SSAP2, dealt with some of these under the umbrella label of accounting concepts. However, the *Statement of Principles for Financial Reporting* makes a distinction between accounting concepts, or underlying assumptions, and qualitative characteristics.

According to the *Statement of Principles for Financial Reporting* 'qualitative characteristics are the characteristics that make the information provided in financial statements useful to users for assessing the financial position, performance and financial adaptability of an enterprise'.[1] In contrast the underlying assumptions, specifically the going concern concept and the accruals basis, are measurement conventions which arise from the application of the qualitative characteristics in accomplishing the objective of financial reporting.

The current situation therefore appears to be that the 'official definitions' of the going concern and accruals concepts are as per SSAP2. However, the two other concepts in SSAP2, namely consistency and prudence, together with the other accounting concepts of objectivity and materiality discussed in Chapter 10 of this book will in time be redefined or replaced by the qualitative characteristics in the ASB *Statement of Principles for Financial Reporting*.

The qualitative characteristics of financial information

The ASB has developed a chart showing the qualitative characteristics of financial information and how these characteristics are related to each other. This is shown in Figure 34.1.

THE QUALITATIVE CHARACTERISTICS OF FINANCIAL INFORMATION

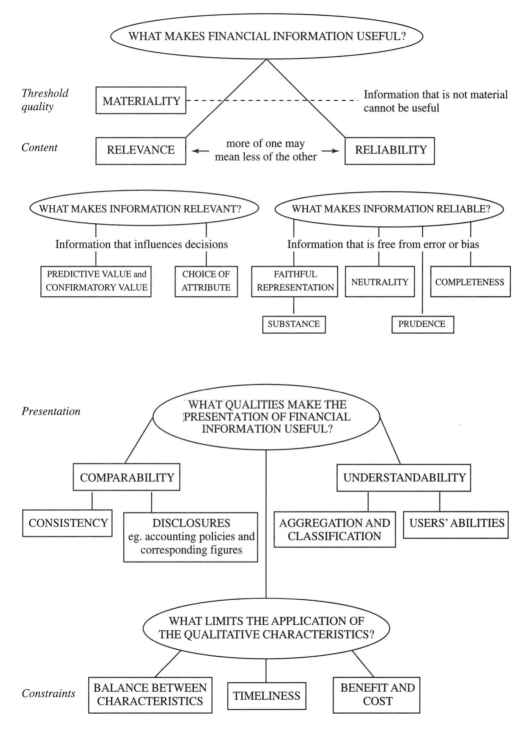

Figure 34.1   The qualitative characteristics of financial information (ASB, 1995).

According to the ASB *Statement of Principles for Financial Reporting*, as shown by the chart, there is a threshold quality (of materiality), two qualitative characteristics relating to the content of the information contained in financial statements, two others that relate to how that information is presented, and three constraints. These are summarized below:

Qualitative characteristics relating to content
1. Relevance comprising: (a) predictive value and confirmatory value; and (b) choice of attribute.
2. Reliability comprising: (a) faithful representation; (b) substance; (c) neutrality; (d) prudence; and (e) completeness.

Qualitative characteristics relating to presentation
1. Comparatively comprising: (a) consistency; and (b) disclosures.
2. Understandability comprising: (a) aggregation and classification; and (b) users' abilities.

Constraints
1. Balance between qualitative characteristics.
2. Timeliness.
3. Benefit and cost.

Each of these is explained below.

Threshold quality: materiality

A threshold quality is one that needs to be considered before the other qualities of information. If any information does not pass the test of the threshold quality, it does not need to be considered further.

The only threshold quality identified is that of materiality. This was explained in depth in Chapter 10. The definition in the ASB *Statement of Principles for Financial Reporting* is reproduced below:

> Information is material if it could influence users' decisions taken on the basis of the financial statements. If that information is misstated or if certain information is omitted the materiality of the misstatement or omission depends on the size and nature of the item in question judged in the particular circumstances of the case.

Characteristics relating to content

1. **Relevance**

   According to the ASB *Statement of Principles for Financial Reporting*, 'to be useful, information must be relevant to the decision-making needs of users. Information has the quality of relevance when it has the ability to influence the decisions of users by helping them evaluate past, present or future events or confirming, or correcting their past evaluations'.[1]

   To be relevant, information should have the following characteristics:
   (a) *Predictive value and confirmatory value*
       According to the ASB *Statement of Principles for Financial Reporting,* 'relevant information has either predictive value or confirmatory value'[1]. This is explained as follows:

       > The predictive and confirmatory roles of information are interrelated. For example, information about the current level and structure of asset holdings has value to users when they endeavour to predict the enterprise's ability to exploit opportunities and react to adverse situations. The same

information plays a confirmatory role in respect of past predictions about, for example, the structure of the enterprise and the outcome of operations.

Information about financial position and past performance is frequently used in making predictions of future financial position and performance and other matters in which users are directly interested, such as dividend and wage payments, security price movements and the ability of the enterprise to meet its commitments as they fall due. To have predictive value, information need not be in the form of an explicit forecast. The ability to make predictions from financial statements is enhanced, however, by the way in which information about past transactions and events is displayed. For example, the predictive value of the statements of financial performance is enhanced if unusual, abnormal and infrequent items of income or expense are separately disclosed.

(b) *Choice of attribute*

According to the ASB *Statement of Principles for Financial Reporting*, 'the choice of the attribute to be reported in financial statements should be based on its relevance to the economic decisions of users'[1]. This is explained as follows:

The financial statements themselves can represent only attributes that can be expressed in monetary terms. There are several monetary attributes that could be represented in financial statements, for example historical cost, replacement cost or net realizable value.... Information on alternative attributes, including some that cannot be expressed in monetary terms (such as quantities and maturity dates) may be conveyed by the description of the items in the financial statements or given by way of note.

2. Reliability

According to the ASB *Statement of Principles for Financial Reporting*, 'to be useful information must also be reliable. Information has the quality of reliability when it is free from material error and bias and can be depended upon by users to represent faithfully what it either purports to represent or could reasonably to be expected to represent'.[1]

It should be noted that reliability includes faithful representation and neutrality both of which are a more contemporary replacement of the objectivity concept described in Chapter 10.

To be reliable, information should have the following characteristics.

(a) *Faithful representation*

According to the ASB *Statement of Principles for Financial Reporting*, 'information must represent faithfully the effect of the transactions and other events it either purports to represent or could reasonably be expected to represent'. This is explained as follows:

Most financial information is subject to some risk of being less than a faithful representation of what it purports to portray. This is due to inherent difficulties either in identifying the transactions and other events to be measured or in devising and applying measurement and presentation techniques that can convey messages that correspond with those transactions and events. In certain cases, the measurement of the financial effects of items could be so uncertain that enterprises generally would not recognize them in the financial statements. In other cases, however, it may be relevant to recognize items and to disclose the risk of error surrounding their recognition and measurement.[1]

The observant reader may notice a similarity between the description of a faithful representation in the middle two sentences of the last paragraph and that aspect of the objectivity concept explained in Chapter 10 in terms of verifiability. The above two sentences are essentially a description of lack of verifiability. Faithful representation may thus be said to be a more contemporary replacement of the verifiability concept.

(b) *Substance*

According to the ASB *Statement of Principles for Financial Reporting* 'if information is to represent faithfully the transactions and other events that it purports to represent, it is necessary that they are accounted for and presented in accordance with their substance and commercial effect and not merely their legal form'.[1]

This is explained as follows:

> The substance of transactions and events is not always consistent with that which is suggested by their legal form: although the effects of the legal characteristics of a transaction are themselves a part of its substance and commercial effect, they have to be construed in the context of the transaction as a whole (including any related transactions). For example, an enterprise may pass legal ownership of a property to another party; yet, when the circumstances are looked at as a whole, it may be found that arrangements exist that ensure that the enterprise continues to have access to the future economic benefits embodied in the property. In such circumstances, the reporting of a sale would not represent the transaction faithfully for financial reporting purposes.

The classic example is certain types of leases, such as where a company has contracted to lease a motor vehicle at a given monthly rental for a period of, say, three years, at the end of which it has the option to purchase the vehicle for a nominal/small amount. The legal form of this transaction is a rental agreement. If the legal form were to dictate the accounting entries, the rental payments would appear as an expense in the profit and loss account and the vehicle would not be included in the fixed assets on the balance sheet. This is why such transactions are referred to as a form of *off-balance sheet finance*. However, the economic substance of this transaction is the purchase of a vehicle payable by instalments, very similar to a hire purchase transaction (the accounting entries for which are explained in Chapter 21). Thus the substance characteristic dictates that the rental payments are not treated as an expense; instead they are capitalized. This means that the vehicle is recorded as the purchase of a fixed asset and the total rental payments for the three years are shown as a creditor.

(c) *Neutrality*

Neutrality was explained in some depth in Chapter 10. According to the ASB *Statement of Principles for Financial Reporting*, 'the information contained in financial statements must be neutral, i.e., free from bias. Financial statements are not neutral if they include information that has been selected or presented in such a way as to influence the making of a decision or judgement in order to achieve a predetermined result or outcome'.[1]

(d) *Prudence*

Prudence was also explained in depth in Chapter 10. The description in the ASB *Statement of Principles for Financial Reporting* is reproduced below:

> The preparers of financial statements have to contend with the uncertainties that inevitably surround many events and circumstances, such as the collectability of debts, the probable useful life of plant and equipment and the number and magnitude of warranty claims that may occur. Such uncertainties are recognized by the disclosure of their nature and extent and by the exercise of prudence in the preparation of the financial statements. *Prudence is the inclusion of a degree of caution in the exercise of the judgements needed in making the estimates required under conditions of uncertainty, such that income or assets are not overstated and expenses or liabilities are not understated.* However, the exercise of prudence does not allow, for example, the creation of hidden reserves or excessive provisions, the deliberate understatement of assets or income, or the deliberate overstatement of liabilities or expenses, because the financial statements would not be neutral and, therefore, not have the quality of reliability.

(e) *Completeness*

According to the ASB *Statement of Principles for Financial Reporting*, 'the information in financial statements must be complete within the bounds of materiality and cost. An omission can cause information to be false or misleading and thus unreliable and deficient in terms of its relevance'.[1]

Characteristics relating to presentation

1. **Comparability**

According to the ASB *Statement of Principles for Financial Reporting*, 'users must be able to compare the financial statements of an enterprise over time to identify trends in its financial position and performance. Users must also be able to compare the financial statements of different enterprises to evaluate their relative financial position, performance and financial adaptability. It is therefore necessary for similar events and states of affairs to be represented in a similar manner'.[1]

To be comparable, information should have the following characteristics:

(a) *Consistency*

According to the *Statement of Principles for Financial Reporting*, 'comparability requires the measurement and display of the financial effect of like transactions and other events to be carried out in a consistent way within each accounting period and from one period to the next, and also in a consistent way by different entities. Although consistency is necessary to attain comparability, it is not in itself always sufficient'[1]. This is explained as follows:

> For example, if assets are consistently measured on a historical cost basis during a period of inflation, two entities with precisely similar economic conditions and performance will report different results if they acquired their assets at different times.

(b) *Disclosures*

According to the *Statement of Principles for Financial Reporting*, 'a prerequisite of comparability is disclosure of the accounting policies employed in the preparation of the financial statements and also any changes in those policies and the effects of such changes. Users need to be able to identify differences between the accounting policies for like transactions and other events used by the same enterprise from period to period and by different enterprises. Because users wish to compare the financial position, performance and changes in financial position of an enterprise over time, it is important that the financial statements show corresponding information for one or more preceding periods'[1].

Many academics regard disclosure as a fundamental qualitative characteristic of financial statements. In crude terms, it is argued that if companies use different accounting policies and/or these change over time (i.e. there is a lack of consistency), and/or if companies do not comply with accounting standards, this is not critical; provided there is full disclosure of how the figures are derived, users can make the necessary adjustments in order to achieve comparability.

2. **Understandability**

According to the *Statement of Principles for Financial Reporting*, 'an essential quality of the information provided in financial statements is that it should be readily understandable by users'.

To be understandable, information should have the following characteristics:

(a) *Aggregation and classification*

According to the *Statement of Principles for Financial Reporting*, 'an important factor in the understandability of financial information is the manner in which the information is presented. An understandable presentation requires that items are aggregated and classified in an appropriate way'[1].

(b) *Users abilities*

According to the *Statement of Principles for Financial Reporting*, 'general purpose financial statements are prepared to meet the needs of a variety of users who have different degrees of knowledge of business and economic activities and accounting. However, financial information is generally prepared on the assumption that users have a reasonable knowledge of business and economic activities and accounting and a willingness to study the information with reasonable diligence. Information about complex matters that should be included in the financial statements because of its relevance to the economic decision-making needs of users should not be excluded merely on the grounds that it may be too difficult for some users to understand'.[1]

Constraints on the qualitative characteristics

According to the *Statement of Principles for Financial Reporting*, 'it is seldom possible to prepare financial information that is completely reliable, relevant, comparable and understandable'. This is because of the existence of three constraints which comprise: (1) balance between qualitative characteristics; (2) timeliness; and (3) benefit and cost, each of which is explained below.

1. ***Balance between qualitative characteristics***

   The ASB *Statement of Principles for Financial Reporting* extends the description of this balance given in the IASC 'framework' to include the possible conflict between neutrality and prudence as follows:

   One constraint is that a balancing, or trade-off, between qualitative characteristics is often necessary. For example, information that is more reliable is frequently less relevant and vice versa. Generally the aim is to achieve an appropriate balance among the characteristics in order to meet the objective of financial statements. The relative importance of the characteristics in different cases is a matter of judgement. Another example of the potential conflict between qualitative characteristics is that between neutrality and prudence, both characteristics of reliability. Neutrality is freedom from bias. However, the application of excessive prudence will result in the understatement of assets and profits and the overstatement of liabilities, losses and expenses. (As a result, in subsequent accounting periods profits are overstated or losses are understated). To avoid this risk to neutrality, prudence should not be understood as a systematic measurement bias. Rather prudence should be understood as an attitude of mind that demands a careful assessment of uncertainties and a vigilance to possible risks. Ideally, the degree of scepticism resulting from a prudent approach exactly counteracts any tendency to undue optimism.

2. ***Timeliness***

   The timeliness constraint is explained in the ASB *Statement of Principles for Financial Reporting* as follows:

   If there is undue delay in reporting information it may lose its relevance. Management may need to balance the relative merits of timely reporting and the provision of reliable information. To provide information on a timely basis it may often be necessary to report before all aspects of a transaction or other event are known, thus impairing reliability. Conversely, if reporting is delayed until all aspects are known, the information may be highly reliable but of little use to users who have had to make decisions in the interim. In achieving a balance between relevance and reliability, the overriding consideration, subject to any legal requirements on timing, is how best to satisfy the economic decision-making needs of users.

3. *Benefit and cost*

The benefit and cost constraint is explained in the ASB *Statement of Principles for Financial Reporting* as follows:

The balance between benefit and cost is a pervasive constraint rather than a qualitative characteristic. The benefits derived from information should exceed the cost of providing it. The evaluation of benefits and costs is, however, substantially a judgemental process. Furthermore, the costs do not necessarily fall on those users who enjoy the benefits. Benefits may also be enjoyed by users other than those for whom the information is prepared. For these reasons, it is often difficult to apply a cost-benefit test in a particular case. Nevertheless, the Board in setting standards, as well as the preparers and users of financial statements, should be aware of this constraint.

Most of the costs of providing accounting information are borne by the preparer, that is, the business entity. They include materials (e.g. paper ink, etc.), labour (the accounting staff time), expenses (e.g. printing), valuation fees, etc. Such costs are potentially measurable although there can be a high degree of subjectivity involved in their selection. Furthermore, many companies claim that the disclosure of certain information can give their competitors an advantage. In theory, this is a cost. In practice, it would be extremely difficult both to conceptualize and to measure.

Most of the benefits of accounting information are thought to accrue to the users of financial statements such as existing and potential shareholders, loan creditors, analysts and advisers (e.g. stockbrokers), trade unions, trade creditors, customers, government, the public, etc. These benefits comprise both economic and social gains arising from better decision making. Economic gains include higher dividends, increases in share prices and a more efficient allocation of society's resources. Social gains might take the form of less damage to the environment, improvements in the treatment of minority groups, etc. It can therefore be seen that the benefits are extremely difficult both to conceptualize and to measure.

In sum, many of the costs of providing information in financial statements are potentially measurable. Others are highly subjective. Most of the benefits of providing information in financial statements are difficult both to conceptualize and to measure. The decision whether the benefits exceed the cost, and thus whether information should be included in financial statements is, therefore, a matter of professional judgment. However, such judgments are not usually made by accountants on a day-to-day basis, since the latter are primarily concerned with ensuring that financial statements comply with the law, stock exchange regulations and accounting standards. Judgments about the costs and benefits are most commonly made by the ASB in its deliberations about the requirements of Financial Reporting Standards that it is considering issuing.

The conceptual framework of accounting

The nature of a conceptual framework—an analogy

At about this point in their studies students can feel rather confused and frustrated by accounting theory. It is a hurdle that has to be overcome. On the one hand students frequently have a perception of accounting as being definitive, because much of it is based on the law, and they have been taught a simplified set of rules about double entry bookkeeping which is very systematic. On the other hand they frequently think that accountants tend to bend the rules (or 'cook the books'), also known as *creative accounting*. Many of the later chapters of this book may reinforce this view because they often suggest that some transactions can be treated in different ways, thus giving possible alternative figures of profit.

It is important to appreciate the difference between 'cooking the books' and the professional judgment involved in decisions between alternative methods of accounting. An analogy may prove useful. Imagine you went to a private consultant because you had backache. In order to maximize his or her fee, the consultant might decide to operate on you. If this was the sole consideration, it would be unethical of the surgeon. Similarly, an accountant who chose a particular form of accounting treatment with the sole intention of reducing the net profit would be acting unethically. However, an ethical physician or accountant is still faced with a number of possible forms of treatment. The physician might prescribe a number of different drugs, but needs to ascertain which is likely to be most appropriate for you. Similarly, the accountant has to choose which accounting treatment of, say, development costs, is the most appropriate in the circumstances.

This analogy can be extended further to illustrate another very important relevant idea. The physician's judgment about your treatment for backache is guided by a body of expert knowledge and research, loosely known as medical science. This includes such disciplines as anatomy, chemistry, etc., which are based on generally accepted theories and concepts similar, in principle, to those discussed in this chapter relating to accounting. Similarly, the accountant's judgment about the most appropriate treatment of certain types of transactions is guided by a body of expert knowledge and research, which is loosely referred to as the theoretical or conceptual framework of accounting.

However, unlike medical science, the conceptual framework of accounting is not well developed and thus, as explained earlier in the chapter, may contain apparently inconsistent concepts, such as matching and prudence. Also, it is unlikely that a conceptual framework of accounting could be as definitive as, say, medical science in the foreseeable future since accounting theory, like other social sciences, is fundamentally different from natural sciences, such as medical science.

This tension between the need for a set of concepts/principles to guide the practice of accounting, and the awareness that these are unlikely to be conclusive/definitive, has given rise to an extensive debate over the last two decades about the development of a conceptual framework of accounting or what are sometimes called '*generally accepted accounting principles* ' (GAAP). Note, however, that the abbreviation GAAP is more commonly taken as referring to generally accepted accounting practice, i.e. accounting standards.

The conceptual framework of accounting—a brief history

In order to appreciate fully the sources of authoritative pronouncements about the nature, purpose and scope of a conceptual framework of accounting, it is necessary to start with a brief history of the accountancy profession's attempts to develop a conceptual framework

The earliest comprehensive conceptual framework project started in the middle 1970s in the USA by the Financial Accounting Standards Board (FASB), which is the US equivalent of the ASB. This is still the most advanced and comprehensive treatment of the subject in the world. It has also probably been a major influence on subsequent conceptual framework projects by the IASC and ASB discussed below.

In 1989 the International Accounting Standards Committee (IASC) published what might be described as an abbreviated conceptual framework entitled *Framework for the Preparation and Presentation of Financial Statements*.[2]

Then in 1995 the ASB published a *Statement of Principles for Financial Reporting*[1] as part of its work in developing a statement on the principles that underlie accounting and financial reporting, which is generally interpreted as being a conceptual framework of accounting. This document closely follows the structure of the IASC framework. Indeed the ASB stated explicitly that 'it proposes to use wherever possible the IASC text'.

The conceptual framework of accounting—nature, purpose, scope and contents

Probably one of the most concise definitions of a conceptual framework of accounting is contained in the ASC, *Setting Accounting Standards: a consultative document*: 'a set of broad, internally consistent fundamentals and definitions of key terms'.[3]

Another slightly more informative definition is provided by the FASB in its *Scope and Implications of the Conceptual Framework Project*: 'a constitution, a coherent system of interrelated objectives and fundamentals that can lead to consistent standards and that prescribe the nature, function and limits of financial accounting and financial statements'.[4]

Leaving aside a detailed description of the nature and scope of a conceptual framework for a moment, the FASB definition highlights one of the main purposes of a conceptual framework. That is, to provide standard-setting bodies with a set of internally consistent definitions of accounting principles which can be used as a basis for setting accounting standards that are not contradictory or in conflict with each other. The other main purpose of a conceptual framework, explained earlier using the analogy with medicine, is to provide guidance to accountants in their day-to-day work to choosing appropriate forms of accounting treatments for various transactions and items. These two main purposes and a number of others are contained in an earlier version of the ASB *Statement of Principles for Financial Reporting* issued in 1991 which is reproduced below:

1. Assist the Board in the development of future accounting standards and in its review of existing accounting standards.
2. Assist the Board by providing a basis for reducing the number of alternative accounting treatments permitted by law and accounting standards.
3. Assist preparers of financial statements in applying accounting standards and in dealing with topics that do not form the subject of an accounting standard.
4. Assist auditors in forming an opinion whether financial statements conform with accounting standards.
5. Assist users of financial statements in interpreting the information contained in financial statements prepared in conformity with accounting standards.
6. Provide those who are interested in the work of the Board with information about its approach to the formulation of accounting standards.

The IASC framework[2] has an almost identical list of purposes except that these are expressed in terms of developing international accounting standards and promoting international harmonization.

Returning to the nature and scope of a conceptual framework, various authors and bodies have described this in simple terms as an agreed set of answers to the following sorts of question. For whom are accounts to be prepared? For what purposes do they want to use them? What kind of accounting reports do they want? How far are present accounts suitable for these purposes, and how could we improve accounting practice to make them more suitable?[3]

Probably the most informative way of examining the nature of a conceptual framework in more detail is by reviewing the contents of the frameworks that have been developed to date. The shortest of these is the IASC framework, the scope of which is reproduced below.

Scope

The framework deals with:

1. The objective of financial statements.
2. The qualitative characteristics that determine the usefulness of information in financial statements.
3. The definition, recognition and measurement of the elements from which financial statements are constructed.
4. Concepts of capital and capital maintenance.[2]

The ASB framework is set out in its *Statement of Principles for Financial Reporting* (1995)[1], the contents of which are similar to those of the IASC, but with some significant differences. This is shown below.

Chapter 1   The objective of financial statements
Chapter 2   The qualitative characteristics of financial information
Chapter 3   The elements of financial statements
Chapter 4   Recognition in financial statements
Chapter 5   Measurement in financial statements
Chapter 6   Presentation of financial information
Chapter 7   The reporting entity

The contents of Chapter 1 of the *Statement of Principles for Financial Reporting* have been summarized in Chapter 1 of this book, and the contents of Chapter 2 have been summarized earlier in this chapter. It is beyond the introductory nature of this book to deal with the other chapters of the *Statement of Principles for Financial Reporting* in depth but these may be compared with the FASB conceptual framework shown in diagrammatic form in Figure 34.2. Notice in particular its hierarchical nature.

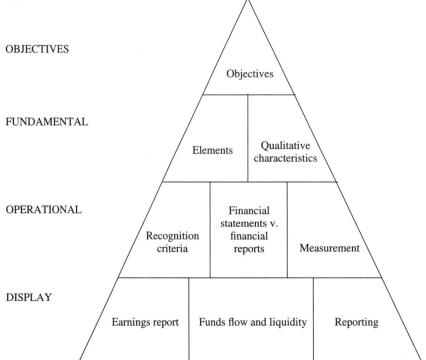

Figure 34.2   The FASB conceptual framework for financial accounting and reporting.

Having identified the scope or structure of the conceptual frameworks produced to date, the contents of these may be briefly explained as essentially comprising the following:

1. *The objective of financial reporting* including the users of financial statements and their information needs.
2. *The attributes or qualitative characteristics* of accounting information that enable financial statements to fulfil their objective, determine what is useful information, and provide criteria for choosing among alternative accounting methods.
3. Definitions of the *elements* of financial statements such as the nature of assets, liabilities and ownership interest. According to the ASB *Statement of Principles for Financial Reporting* 'assets are rights or other access to future economic benefits controlled by an entity as a result of past transactions or events. Liabilities are obligations of an entity to transfer economic benefits as a result of past transactions or events. Ownership interest is the residual amount found by deducting all of the entity's liabilities from all of the entity's assets' (ASB, 1995).[1]
4. A set of criteria for deciding when the elements are to be *recognized* in financial statements. According to the ASB *Statement of Principles for Financial Reporting*, 'recognition involves depiction of the element both in words and by a monetary amount, and the inclusion of that amount in the statement totals. An element should be recognized if: (a) there is sufficient evidence that the change in assets or liabilities inherent in the element has occurred (including, where appropriate, evidence that a future inflow or outflow of benefit will occur); and (b) it can be measured at a monetary amount with sufficient reliability' (ASB, 1995).[1]
5. A set of *measurement* rules for determining the monetary amounts at which the elements of financial statements are to be recognized and carried in the accounts. For example, these might comprise historical cost, replacement cost, net realizable value or present value.
6. Guidelines for the *presentation and disclosure* of the elements in financial statements. These currently take the form of statements of financial performance, (i.e. a profit and loss account and a statement of total recognized gains and losses) a balance sheet and cash flow statement. Alternatives include a funds flow statement.

The conceptual framework debate, standardization and choice

Much controversy has surrounded the idea of developing a conceptual framework of accounting, particularly in the UK where the self-regulatory standard setting institutions have limited resources. There are two main related issues. The first is whether the cost of preparing a conceptual framework is justified in terms of its benefits, including whether it is possible to develop a set of consistent fundamentals and if these will lead to improvements in accounting standard setting. The second issue concerns whether accounting standards just make published accounts more consistent rather than comparable, or alternatively whether more meaningful comparisons would result from allowing companies to choose those accounting policies which are appropriate to their individual circumstances. This has always been an issue in standard setting, but the development of a conceptual framework accentuates the debate because it will presumably lead to greater standardization.

There are a wide variety of schools of thought on the conceptual framework debate but for the sake of structuring and simplifying the discussion these can be grouped into two extremes comprising the normative/deductive approach and the positive/empiricist approach.

The normative/deductive approach regards a conceptual framework as absolutely essential. *Normative theories* view accounting as a technical process which is capable of measuring the 'true income' of a business given a set of theories which specify how this should be done (e.g. Hicks, 1946). They often use the analogy that financial statements are like maps which have the potential to provide a faithful representation of reality given a set of underlying consistent rules (i.e. a conceptual framework). Similarly, *deductive theories* view accounting as a technical process but advocates a user needs approach based on identifying the objectives of financial statements similar to that taken in all the conceptual framework projects to date.

In contrast to positive/empiricist approach regards a conceptual framework as at best unnecessary, and at worst positively dysfunctional. *Empirical theories* view accounting as an economic process, and the objective of financial statements to facilitate predictions (e.g. of dividends, insolvency, etc.). Thus accounting methods should be selected on the basis of which gives the best predictions, that is, not according to some conceptual framework. Many *positive theories* view accounting, and particularly standard setting, as a political process which may exploit class interests. They often describe standard setting as quasi-legislation, and use the analogy that company law is determined by Parliament which is a political process. The setting of standards therefore demand consensus and not dictatorial pronouncements based on a conceptual framework which itself is the product of a particular set of class interests (e.g. shareholders interests).

Advocates of a pragmatic deductive approach appear to have won the debate in the UK. However, it remains to be see whether the monetary costs of preparing a conceptual framework by the ASB will be justified in terms of the benefits in the form of improvements in standard setting.

Furthermore, the development of a conceptual framework is unlikely to quieten those who argue that accounting standards may promote more consistency of accounting policies between companies but this does not necessarily result in greater comparability. This is the second issue referred to at the start of this section. The reasoning behind the assertion that a conceptual framework of accounting may lead to accounting standard which do not provide comparability between companies is similar to the old argument against accounting standards. There are said to be 'circumstantial variables' or 'differences in circumstances' between companies which necessitate the exercise of managerial discretion in the choice of accounting methods. It is argued that standardization forces companies to use the same accounting policies, it does not necessarily mean that they are the most appropriate accounting policies for each company and thus comparisons may be misleading. The existence of a conceptual framework is likely to lead to greater standardization and, it is said, more rigidity, a lack of flexibility, and thus less innovation. It is easy to be cynical about innovations when it takes the form of creative accounting but it must be recognized that standardization taken to the extreme (as uniformity) would probably reduce innovation, which is said to be the case in some countries with uniform national accounting systems specified solely by law.

Summary

All professions need a body of either theological, empirical and/or theoretical knowledge to guide the actions of their practitioners. In accounting this is not as well developed as in some other professions such as medicine, nor is it likely to be in the foreseeable future. The tension between this need for a set of rules to guide practice, and the awareness that these are unlikely to be definitive, has given rise to an extensive debate about the current development of a conceptual framework of accounting, also known as generally accepted accounting principles (GAAP).

The FASB, IASC and ASB have all published conceptual frameworks of accounting. The main purpose of a conceptual framework of accounting are to provide a basis for the development and review of accounting standards, and to assist preparers, users and auditors of financial statements. This takes the form of an internally consistent set of interrelated objectives and fundamentals that prescribe the nature, function and limits of financial statements.

The ASB conceptual framework is contained in its *Statement of Principles for Financial Reporting* (1995). This sets out the objective of financial statements, the qualitative characteristics of financial information, the elements of financial statements, recognition criteria, measurement rule, and guidelines for the presentation of items in financial statements.

This chapter examined in depth the qualitative characteristics of financial information. Qualitative characteristics are the attributes that make the information provided in financial statements useful to users. These differ from the underlying assumptions such as going concern and the accruals basis, which are measurement conventions. The qualitative characteristics of accounting information comprise the threshold quality of materiality, characteristics relating to contents, and those relating to presentation. The characteristics relating to content are composed of relevance and reliability. Relevance includes predictive and confirmatory value, and choice of attribute. Reliability includes faithful representation, substance, neutrality, prudence and completeness. The characteristics relating to presentation are composed of comparability and understandability. Comparability includes consistency and disclosures. Understandability includes aggregation and classification, and users' abilities. There are also certain constraints that limit the application of the qualitative characteristics. These are composed of balance between characteristics, timeliness, and benefit and cost.

Key terms and concepts

Aggregation and classification, balance between qualitative characteristics, benefit and cost, choice of attribute, comparability, completeness, conceptual framework of accounting, confirmatory value, consistency, creative accounting, deductive theory, disclosures, empirical theory, faithful representation, generally accepted accounting practices (GAAP), materiality, neutrality, normative theory, off-balance-sheet finance, positive theory, predictive value, prudence, qualitative characteristics, relevance, reliability, substance, threshold quality, timeliness, understandability, users' abilities.

References

1. Accounting Standards Board (1995). *Statement of Principles for Financial Reporting* (ASB).
2. International Accounting Standards Committee (1989). *Framework for the Preparation and Presentation of Financial Statements* (IASC).

3. Accounting Standards Committee (1978). *Setting Accounting Standards: a consultative document* (ICAEW).

4. Financial Accounting Standards Board (1976). *Scope and Implications of the Conceptual Framework Project* (FASB).

Exercises

An asterisk after the question number indicates that there is a suggested answer in the Appendix.

34.1. (a) Briefly explain the nature of a qualitative characteristic of financial information.

(b) Prepare a chart showing the qualitative characteristics of financial information identified in the ASB *Statement of Principles for Financial Reporting* (1995) and the relationship between each.

34.2. Define and explain the qualitative characteristic of relevance including its predictive and confirmatory value, and choice of attribute.

34.3. Define and explain the qualitative characteristic of reliability including the attributes of faithful representation, substance, neutrality, prudence and completeness.

34.4. Define and explain the qualitative characteristics of comparability and understandability.

34.5. Define and explain the threshold quality of materiality.

34.6. Define and explain the constraints that limit the application of qualitative characteristics in financial statements.

34.7. 'There is a potential conflict between the qualities of neutrality and prudence' (ASB, 1995). Explain and discuss.

34.8.* Describe the purposes of a conceptual framework of accounting.

34.9.* Describe the nature and contents of a conceptual framework of accounting.

34.10. 'It is unrealistic to expect a conceptual framework of accounting to provide a basis for definitive or even generally accepted accounting standards in the foreseeable future because of inherent conflicts and inconsistencies between, for example, the qualitative characteristics of accounting information as well as the differing information needs and abilities of users'. Discuss.

34.11. 'A conceptual framework of accounting is likely to lead to greater standardization, less choice, less innovation and thus reduced comparability because of the existence of fundamental differences between companies in the way they conduct their activities'. Discuss.

Appendix

Solutions to exercises

Contents

Preface to appendix

This appendix contains suggested answers to those exercises with an asterisk after the question number. These comprise most of the numerical exercises that were written by the author, and some of those of the examining bodies. All the short written questions at the start of each exercise are designed so that they can be answered directly from the relevant section of the chapter. There is thus little point in reprinting these sections as suggested solutions. However, the Appendix includes suggested answers to the other written questions designed by the author, where they are sufficiently demanding to constitute a possible examination question.

This appendix is intended to enable the student to monitor the progress of his/her learning. It will be most effective if you first attempt each question without referring to the answer. When you have finished, or done as much as you are able, then check your answer against the suggested solution. Students are also strongly advised to record the time it takes them to answer each question. Most questions carry around 20 to 25 marks, which means that the time allowed to answer them in a 3 hour examination is about 36 to 45 minutes. If you take considerably longer than this, attempt the question again at a later date (eg for revision) to see whether you can do it quicker. When you can answer most of the questions in the allocated time, you should be sufficiently prepared for the examination!

1.   The nature and objectives of financial accounting

1.7   (a)   There are three sources of rules and regulations that govern the content and format of company final accounts as follows:

1.   The Companies Acts (the most recent being the 1985 Act as modified by the 1989 Act) with which all companies are required to comply.
2.   The International Stock Exchange, London Admission of Securities to Listing (commonly known as the Yellow Book) regulations with which all companies whose shares are listed on the London Stock Exchange are expected to comply.
3.   Statements of Standard Accounting Practice (SSAP) issued by the Accounting Standards Committee (ASC), and Financial Reporting Standards (FRS) issued by the Accounting Standards Board (ASB) with which most (but not all) companies are expected to comply.

(b)   The institutional framework by which the accountancy profession has influenced the content and format of company final accounts during the last two decades primarily comprises the Accounting Standards Committee (ASC) and the Accounting Standards Board (ASB). From 1975 to 1990 the ASC issued accounting standards known as Statements of Standard Accounting Practice (SSAP). The ASB was formed in 1990, and since then has issued accounting standards known as Financial Reporting Standards.

The ASB is a subsidiary of the Financial Reporting Council (FRC) which has overall responsibility for standard setting in the UK. The FRC has another subsidiary, the Financial Reporting Review Panel (FRRP), which investigates complaints about any company's final accounts that do not comply with the Companies Acts and/or accounting standards.

The ASB also has a committee, the Urgent Issues Task Force (UITF), which publishes Abstracts. These are intended to clarify the accounting treatment that should be adopted where an accounting standard or Companies Act provision exists, but the interpretation is ambiguous.

2.   The accounting equation and its components

2.7   *J. Frank*
Balance sheet as at 1 January 19X9

Assets	£	Liabilities	£
Land & buildings	7,500	Mortgage	4,000
Fixtures	560	Capital	5,800
Bank	1,740		
	9,800		9,800

J. Frank
Balance sheet as at 31 December 19X9

Assets	£	Liabilities	£
Land & building	7,500	Mortgage	5,000
Fixtures	560	Sundry creditors	800
Delivery van	650	Capital	5,450
Sundry debtors	470		
Stock	940		
Bank	1,050		
Cash	80		
	11,250		11,250

Note

In both of the above balance sheets the capital is the difference between the two sides after entering all the assets and liabilities.

J. Frank
Statement of profit or loss for the year ended 31 December 19X9

	£
Capital at 31 December	5,450
Less: Capital at 1 January	5,800
Apparent loss	(350)
Add: Drawings	500
Net profit for the year	150

3.   Basic documentation and books of account

3.5   (i)   The sales day book is used to record the sale on credit of those goods bought specifically for resale. It is written up from copies of the sales invoices and debit notes retained by the seller.

(ii)   The sales returns day book is used to record goods sold on credit that are returned by customers. It is written up from copies of the credit notes retained by the seller.

(iii)   The purchases day book is used to record the purchase on credit of goods intended for resale. It is written up from the purchase invoices and debit notes received from suppliers.

(iv)   The purchases day book is used to record goods purchased on credit that are returned to suppliers. It is written up from the credit notes received from suppliers.

(v)   The cash book is used to record cheques received and cash paid into the bank and payments by cheque. It is written up from the bank paying-in book and cheque book stubs.

(vi)   The petty cash book is used to record cash received and cash paid. It is written up from receipts and petty cash vouchers.

(vii)   The journal is used to record transactions and items not appropriate to any of the other books of prime entry such as the purchase and sale of fixed assets on credit, correction of errors, etc. It is written up from copies of the invoices.

(viii)   The bills receivable book is used to record bills of exchange received by the business. It is written up from copies of the bills of exchange receivable.

(ix)   The bills payable book is used to record bills of exchange given to creditors as a means of payment. It is written up from copies of the bill of exchange payable.

4.   The general ledger

4.1

Cash

19X6				19X6		
Oct 1	Capital	5,000		Oct 1	Rent	200
Oct 6	S. Ring	3,500		Oct 2	Purchases	970
Oct 12	Sales	1,810		Oct 4	Fixtures & fittings	1,250
Oct 24	Sales	1,320		Oct 9	Motor vehicles	2,650
				Oct 15	Wages	150
				Oct 18	Purchases	630
				Oct 19	Drawings	350
				Oct 21	Motor expenses	25
				Oct 22	Printing	65
				Oct 25	Motor expenses	45
				Oct 27	Wages	250
				Oct 28	Stationery	35
				Oct 30	Rates	400
				Oct 31	Drawings	175
				Oct 31	Balance c/d	4,435
		11,630				11,630
Nov 1	Balance b/d	4,435				

Capital

				Oct 1	Cash	5,000

Loan-S. Ring

Oct 6	Cash	3,500

Sales

Oct 12	Cash	1,810
Oct 24	Cash	1,320

Rent & rates

Oct 1	Cash	200
Oct 30	Cash	400

Purchases

Oct 2	Cash	970
Oct 18	Cash	630

Fixtures & fittings

Oct 4	Cash	1,250

Motor vehicles

Oct 9	Cash	2,650

Wages

Oct 15	Cash	150
Oct 27	Cash	250

Drawings

Oct 19	Cash	350
Oct 31	Cash	175

Motor expenses

Oct 21	Cash	25
Oct 25	Cash	45

Printing & stationery

Oct 22	Cash	65
Oct 28	Cash	35

4.2

Bank

19X8				19X8			
Mar 1	Capital	10,000		Mar 1	Leasehold		
Mar 18	Sales	540			premises	5,000	
Mar 28	G. Lion	280		Mar 2	Office equipment	1,400	
				Mar 6	Postage	35	
				Mar 9	Purchases	420	
				Mar 13	Drawings	250	
				Mar 20	Telephone	120	
				Mar 24	Light & heat	65	
				Mar 26	E. Lamb	230	
				Mar 30	Light & heat	85	
				Mar 31	Bank charges	45	
				Mar 31	Balance c/d	3,170	
		10,820				10,820	
Apl 1	Balance b/d	3,170					

Capital

Mar 1	Bank	10,000

Sales

Mar 11	G. Lion	880
Mar 18	Bank	540

G. Lion

Mar 11	Sales	880	Mar 22	Sales returns	310
			Mar 28	Bank	280

Sales returns

Mar 22	G. Lion	310

Leasehold premises

Mar 1	Bank	5,000

Office equipment

Mar 2	Bank	1,400

Postage & telephone

Mar 6	Bank	35
Mar 20	Bank	120

Purchases

Mar 4	E. Lamb	630
Mar 9	Bank	420

E. Lamb

Mar 16	Purchases returns	180	Mar 4	Purchases	630
Mar 26	Bank	230			

Purchases returns

	Mar 16	E. Lamb	180

Drawings

Mar 13	Bank	250

Light & heat

Mar 24	Bank	65
Mar 30	Bank	85

Bank charges

Mar 31	Bank	45

5. The balancing of accounts and the trial balance

5.2 *S. Baker*
Trial balance as at 31 January 19X0

	Debit £	Credit £
Cash	875	
Capital		1,000
Loan—London Bank		500
Sales		600
Rent	100	
Fixtures & fittings	300	
Purchases	400	
Carriage inwards	25	
Stationery	50	
Wages	200	
Drawings	150	
	2,100	2,100

5.3 *H. George*
Trial balance as at 31 October 19X6

	Debit £	Credit £
Cash	4,435	
Capital		5,000
Loan—S. Ring		3,500
Sales		3,130
Rent & rates	600	
Purchases	1,600	
Fixtures & fittings	1,250	
Motor vehicles	2,650	
Wages	400	
Drawings	525	
Motor expenses	70	
Printing & stationery	100	
	11,630	11,630

5.4 *L. Johnson*
Trial balance as at 31 March 19X9

	Debit £	Credit £
Bank	3,170	
Capital		10,000
Sales		1,420
G. Lion	290	
Sales returns	310	
Leasehold premises	5,000	
Office equipment	1,400	
Postage & telephone	155	
Purchases	1,050	
E. Lamb		220
Purchases returns		180
Drawings	250	
Light & heat	150	
Bank charges	45	
	11,820	11,820

5.6 *C. Rick*
Trial balance as at 31 May 19X3

	Debit £	Credit £
Bank	2,368	
Purchases	12,389	
Sales		18,922
Wages & salaries	3,862	
Rent & rates	504	
Insurance	78	
Motor expenses	664	
Printing & stationery	216	
Light & heat	166	
General expenses	314	
Premises	10,000	
Motor vehicles	3,800	
Fixtures & fittings	1,350	
Debtors	3,896	
Creditors		1,731
Cash	482	
Drawings	1,200	
Capital		12,636
Bank loan		8,000
	41,289	41,289

5.7   *R. Keith*
       Trial balance as at 30 June 19X2

	Debit £	Credit £
Capital		39,980
Drawings	14,760	
Loan—Bromsgrove Bank		20,000
Leasehold premises	52,500	
Motor vehicles	13,650	
Investments	4,980	
Trade debtors	2,630	
Trade creditors		1,910
Cash	460	
Bank overdraft		3,620
Sales		81,640
Purchases	49,870	
Returns outwards		960
Returns inwards	840	
Carriage	390	
Wages & salaries	5,610	
Rent & rates	1,420	
Light & heat	710	
Telephone & postage	540	
Printing & stationery	230	
Bank interest	140	
Interest received		620
	148,730	148,730

5.9   (a) Debit wages account with £250
       (b) Credit sales account with £100
       (c) Credit creditors account with £9 (ie. £198 – £189)
       (d) Change the amount shown in the trial balance in respect of drawings to £300
       (e) Debit the bank account with £172 (ie. £86 × 2)

6.   Day books and the journal

6.4   *Purchases day book*

Date	Name of creditor	Amount
19X7		£
Aug 1	Desks Ltd	750
Aug 3	Chairs Ltd	350
Aug 18	Cabinets Ltd	720
		1,820

Purchases returns day book

Date	Name of creditor	Amount
19X7		£
Aug 10	Desks Ltd	225
Aug 21	Chairs Ltd	140
		365

Sales day book

Date	Name of debtor	Amount
19X7		£
Aug 6	British Cars Ltd	630
Aug 13	London Beds Ltd	680
Aug 23	English Carpets Ltd	1,170
		2,480

Sales returns day book

Date	Name of debtor	Amount
19X7		£
Aug 16	British Cars Ltd	270
Aug 25	London Beds Ltd	85
		355

The ledger

Purchases

19X7		
Aug 31	Per PDB	1,820

Purchases returns

		19X7		
		Aug 31	Per PRDB	365

Desks Ltd

Aug 10	Returns	225	Aug 1	Purchases	750
Aug 31	Balance c/d	525			
		750			750
			Sept 1	Balance b/d	525

Chairs Ltd

Aug 21	Returns	140	Aug 3	Purchases	350
Aug 31	Balance c/d	210			
		350			350
			Sept 1	Balance b/d	210

Cabinets Ltd

			Aug 18	Purchases	720

Sales

			Aug 31	Per SDB	2,480

Sales returns

Aug 31	Per SRDB	355

British Cars

Aug 6	Sales	630	Aug 16	Returns	270
			Aug 31	Balance c/d	360
		630			630
Sept 1	Balance b/d	360			

London Beds

Aug 13	Sales	680	Aug 25	Returns	85
			Aug 31	Balance c/d	595
		680			680
Sept 1	Balance b/d	595			

English Carpets

Aug 23	Sales	1,170

6.5   *The journal*

Date	Details/account		Debit	Credit
19X5			£	£
April 20	Plant &machinery	Dr	5,300	
	To Black Ltd			5,300
	Being purchase of machine on credit			
April 23	White Ltd	Dr	3,600	
	To Motor vehicles			3,600
	Being sale of delivery vehicle on credit			
April 26	Fixtures & fittings	Dr	480	
	To Grey Ltd			480
	Being purchase of shop fittings on credit			
April 28	Yellow Ltd	Dr	270	
	To Office equipment			270
	Being sale of typewriter on credit			

The ledger

Plant & machinery

19X5
Apl 20   Black Ltd   5,300

Black Ltd

                                     19X5
                                     Apl 20   Plant & machinery   5,300

White Ltd

Apl 23   Motor vehicles   3,600

Motor vehicles

                                     Apl 23   White Ltd   3,600

Fixtures & fittings

Apl 26   Grey Ltd   480

Grey Ltd

                                     Apl 26   Fixtures & fittings   480

Yellow Ltd

Apl 28   Office equipment   270

Office equipment

                                     Apl 28   Yellow Ltd   270

6.6   *The journal*

Date	Details/account		Debit	Credit
19X8			£	£
Aug 1	Premises	Dr	55,000	
	Plant & machinery	Dr	23,000	
	Stock	Dr	14,600	
	Trade debtors	Dr	6,300	
	To Trade creditors			2,900
	To Capital			96,000
			98,900	98,900
	Being assets and liabilities introduced into business by owner from takeover of L. House			

The ledger

Premises

19X8 Aug 1	Capital	55,000

Plant & machinery

Aug 1	Capital	23,000

Stock

Aug 1	Capital	14,600

Trade debtors

Aug 1	Capital	6,300

Trade creditors

		19X8 Aug 1	Capital	2,900

Capital

		Aug 1	Assets & liabilities	96,000

Note

1. The trade debtors and creditors would be entered in their individual personal accounts.

7.   The cash book

7.5   *The cash book*

Date	Details	Memo discount allowed	Bank	Cash	Date	Details	Memo discount received	Bank	Cash
19X7		£	£	£	19X7		£	£	£
Sept 1	Balance b/d		1,950	860	Sept 4	Purchases			230
Sept 3	Sales		470		Sept 6	Light & heat		510	
Sept 9	Sales		380		Sept 10	Wages		250	
Sept 12	Sales			290	Sept 15	Travelling expenses			40
Sept 22	Cash		350		Sept 16	Rates		410	
Sept 24	Capital		500		Sept 19	Drawings			150
Sept 26	B. Jones–loan		1,000		Sept 20	Purchases		320	
Sept 27	Purchases returns			170	Sept 21	Postage & telephone			30
Sept 29	Bank			180	Sept 22	Bank			350
Sept 30	British Cars	10	350		Sept 25	Vehicles		2,500	
Sept 30	London Beds	15	580		Sept 28	Motor expenses			280
Sept 30	English Carpets		1,100		Sept 29	Cash		180	
					Sept 30	Desks Ltd	25	500	
					Sept 30	Chairs Ltd	20	190	
					Sept 30	Cabinets Ltd		500	
					Sept 30	Balance c/d		1,320	420
		25	6,680	1,500			45	6,680	1,500
Oct 1	Balance b/d		1,320	420					

7.6   *The ledger*

Capital

		19X7		
		Sept 1	Balance b/d	2,810
		Sept 24	Bank	500
				3,310

Loan—B. Jones

		Sept 26	Bank	1,000

Sales

		Aug 31	Per SDB	2,480
		Sept 3	Bank	470
		Sept 9	Bank	380
		Sept 12	Cash	290
				3,620

Sales returns

19X7		
Aug 31	Per SRDB	355

British Cars

Sept 1	Balance b/d	360	Sept 30	Bank	350
			Sept 30	Discount allowed	10
		360			360

London Beds

Sept 1	Balance b/d	595	Sept 30	Bank	580
			Sept 30	Discount allowed	15
		595			595

Discount allowed

Sept 30	Total per Cash Book	25

English Carpets

Aug 23	Sales	1,170	Sept 30	Bank	1,100
			Sept 30	Balance c/d	70
		1,170			1,170
Oct 1	Balance b/d	70			

Purchases

Aug 31	Per PDB	1,820
Sept 4	Cash	230
Sept 20	Bank	320
		2,370

Purchases returns

			Aug 31	Per PRDB	365
			Sept 27	Cash	170
					535

Desks Ltd

Sept 30	Bank	500	Sept 1	Balance b/d	525
Sept 30	Discount received	25			
		525			525

Chairs Ltd

Sept 30	Bank	190	Sept 1	Balance b/d	210
Sept 30	Discount received	20			
		210			210

Discount received

			Sept 30	Total per Cash Book	45

Cabinets Ltd

Sept 30	Bank	500	Aug 18	Purchases		720
Sept 30	Balance c/d	220				
		720				720
			Oct 1	Balance b/d		220

Light & heat

Sept 6	Bank	510

Wages

Sept 10	Bank	250

Travelling expenses

Sept 15	Cash	40

Rates

Sept 16	Bank	410

Drawings

Sept 19	Cash	150

Postage & telephone

Sept 21	Cash	30

Motor vehicles

Sept 25	Bank	2,500

Motor expenses

Sept 28	Cash	280

B. Player
Trial balance as at 30 September 19X7

	Debit £	Credit £
Cash	420	
Bank	1,320	
Capital		3,310
Loan—B. Jones		1,000
Sales		3,620
Sales returns	355	
Discount allowed	25	
English Carpets	70	
Purchases	2,370	
Purchases returns		535
Discount received		45
Cabinets Ltd		220
Light & heat	510	
Wages	250	
Travelling expenses	40	
Rates	410	
Drawings	150	
Postage & telephone	30	
Motor vehicles	2,500	
Motor expenses	280	
	8,730	8,730

Note

1. Discount taken by debtors such as English Carpets which is not allowed is usually simply not entered in the discount allowed column of the cash book since the business whose books we are preparing have disallowed the discount.

8. The petty cash book

8.3

Petty cash book

Debit amount	Date	Details	Credit amount	Purchases	Wages	Motor expenses	Travelling expenses	Printing & stationery	Postage & telephone	Misc.
£	19X2		£	£	£	£	£	£	£	£
400	Feb 1	Balance b/d								
	Feb 1	Purchases	31	31						
	Feb 3	Wages	28		28					
	Feb 6	Petrol	9			9				
	Feb 8	Bus fares	3				3			
	Feb 11	Pens & pencils	8					8		
	Feb 12	Casual labour	25		25					
	Feb 14	Repairs	17			17				
	Feb 16	Paper	15					15		
	Feb 19	Purchases	22	22						
	Feb 20	Train fares	12				12			
	Feb 21	Repairs to premises	35							35
	Feb 22	Postage	6						6	
	Feb 23	Drawings	20							20
	Feb 24	Taxi fares	7				7			
	Feb 25	Envelopes	4					4		
	Feb 26	Purchases	18	18						
	Feb 27	Wages	30		30					
	Feb 28	Petrol	14			14				
304	Feb 28	Bank	304	71	83	40	22	27	6	55
	Feb 28	Balance c/d	400							
704			704							
400	Mar 1	Balance b/d								

The ledger

Purchases

19X2			
Feb 28	Per PCB	71	

Wages

Feb 28	Per PCB	83	

Motor expenses

Feb 28	Per PCB	40	

Travelling expenses

Feb 28	Per PCB	22	

Printing & stationery

Feb 28	Per PCB	27	

Postage & telephone

Feb 28	Per PCB	6	

Repairs to premises

Feb 21	Cash	35	

Drawings

Feb 23	Cash	20	

Bank

	19X2		
	Feb 28	Cash	304

9.   The final accounts of sole traders

9.4   *R. Woods*
Trading and profit & loss accounts
For the year ended 30 September 19X6

	£	£
Sales		18,922
Less: Cost of sales		
Stock at 1 Oct 19X5	2,368	
Add: purchases	12,389	
	14,757	
Less: stock at 30 Sept 19X6	2,946	
		11,811
Gross profit		7,111
Less: Expenditure		
Salaries & wages	3,862	
Rent & rates	504	
Insurance	78	
Motor expenses	664	
Printing & stationery	216	
Light & heat	166	
General expenses	314	
		5,804
Net profit for year		1,307

R. Woods
Balance sheet as at 30 September 19X6

	£	£
Fixed assets		
Premises		5,000
Motor vehicles		1,800
Fixtures & fittings		350
		7,150
Current assets		
Stock	2,946	
Debtors	3,896	
Bank	482	
	7,324	
Less: Current liabilities		
Creditors	1,731	
Net current assets		5,593
Net assets		12,743
Capital		
Balance at 1 Oct 19X5		12,636
Add: profit for the year		1,307
		13,943
Less: drawings		1,200
Balance at 30 Sept 19X6		12,743

9.5   *Joytoys*
Trading and profit and loss accounts
For the year ended 31 December 19X3

	£	£	£
Sales			167,000
Less: returns inwards			1,000
Net sales			166,000
Less: Cost of sales			
Stock at 1 Jan 19X3		12,000	
Add: purchases	108,000		
Less: returns outwards	4,000	104,000	
		116,000	
Less: stock at 31 Dec 19X3		19,500	
			96,500
Gross profit			69,500
Add: discount received			3,000
			72,500
Less: Expenditure			
Rent, rates & insurance		15,000	
Discount allowed		1,600	
Bank interest		400	
Wages & salaries		13,000	
Light & heat		9,000	
			39,000
Net profit for the year			33,500

Joytoys
Balance sheet as at 31 December 19X3

	£	£
Fixed assets		
Plant & machinery		70,000
Office furniture & fittings		24,000
		94,000
Current assets		
Stock	19,500	
Debtors	22,500	
Bank	500	
	42,500	
Less: Current liabilities		
Creditors	16,000	
Net current assets		26,500
Total assets less current liabilities		120,500
Less: Long term liabilities		
Bank loan		22,000
Net assets		98,500
Capital		
Balance at 1 Jan 19X3		75,000
Add: profit for the year		33,500
		108,500
Less: drawings		10,000
Balance at 31 Dec 19X3		98,500

9.6   *A. Evans*
Trading and profit & loss accounts
For the year ended 30 June 19X2

	£	£	£
Sales			81,640
Less: returns inwards			840
Net sales			80,800

	£	£	£
Less: Cost of sales			
Stock at 1 July 19X1		5,610	
Add: purchases	49,870		
Less: returns outwards	960	48,910	
		54,520	
Less: stock at 30 June 19X2		4,920	
			49,600
Gross profit			31,200
Add: interest received			620
			31,820
Less: Expenditure			
Carriage outwards		390	
Rent & rates		1,420	
Light & heat		710	
Telephone & postage		540	
Printing & stationery		230	
Bank interest		140	
			3,430
Net profit for the year			28,390

A. Evans
Balance sheet as at 30 June 19X2

	£	£	£
Fixed assets			
Leasehold premises			52,500
Motor vehicles			13,650
			66,150
Current assets			
Stock		4,920	
Debtors		2,630	
Investments		4,980	
Cash		460	
		12,990	
Less: Current liabilities			
Creditors	1,910		
Bank overdraft	3,620	5,530	
Net current assets			7,460
Total assets less current liabilities			73,610
Less: Long term liabilities			
Loan—Solihull Bank			20,000
Net assets			53,610
Capital			
Balance at 1 July 19X1			39,980
Add: profit for the year			28,390
			68,370
Less: drawings			14,760
Balance at 30 June 19X2			53,610

Note

1. The student should state that she or he is assuming that the investments are intended to be held for less than one year from the date of the balance sheet and are thus a current asset. Alternatively it may be assumed that the investments are to be held for more than one accounting year and are therefore a fixed asset.

10. Accounting concepts, principles and conventions

10.10 The answer to this question should start with an outline of the prudence and objectivity concepts, and then the following discussion.

A beef herd would be classed as work in progress (WIP). The prudence concepts as applied in SSAP9 dictates that WIP should be valued at the lower of cost or net realizable value (NRV). The NRV of WIP is the estimated proceeds of sale at the date of completion less the costs of completion.

Your client is therefore justified in arguing that her beef herd should be valued at NRV, and that this ought to be based on the price she expects to receive at a date in the future when the cattle reach maturity (ie. completion).

However, the estimate of the NRV must be based on verifiable evidence, such as a valuer's certificate, or alternatively reasonable assumptions, such as expert opinion or generally accepted beliefs. This would mean that the valuation at NRV does not contravene the objectivity concept since this refers to the existence of verifiable evidence.

10.11 The answer to this question should start with an outline of the objectivity concept, and then the following discussion.

This item and a number of intangible fixed assets such as goodwill and brand names are controversial issues in accounting and there is no definitive answer to the debate. The ASC and ASB take the view that where there is not an arm's length transaction or a well developed readily available market for such assets, they should not be included in the accounts because it contravenes the objectivity concept. However, some companies and academics argue that these are intangible fixed assets which can be valued, are thus verifiable and do not contravene the objectivity concept.

However, if the asset is included in the accounts to boost the value of assets in order to obtain a loan this clearly breaches the neutrality criterion and thus the objectivity concept.

10.12 The answer to this question should start with an explanation of the materiality concept and then discuss whether it contradicts the consistency concept and the matching principle. The inconsistency in the treatment of office equipment is generally accepted accounting practice on the grounds of materiality.

10.13 The answer to this question should start with an explanation of the materiality and consistency concepts, and then explain their relevance to the items in the question. The separate disclosure of plant hire charges is generally accepted accounting practice on the grounds of materiality, and required by the Companies Acts in the case of company accounts.

11. Depreciation and fixed assets

11.14 *Workings*

Cost of machines purchased on 1 October 1990 should include all transportation and installation expenditure:
$$£3,100 + £130 + £590 + £180 = £4,000$$
$$\text{Cost per machine} = £4,000 \div 2 = £2,000$$

Disposal
Aggregate depreciation from the date brought into use (1 April 1991) until the date of disposal (31 March 1999):

$10\% \times £2,000 \times 8$ years $= £1,600$
Book value at 31 March 1999 $= £2,000 - £1,600 = £400$
Proceeds of sale $= £800 - £100 = £700$
Profit on sale $= £700 - £400 = £300$

(b) *Provision for depreciation* for year ended 30 September 1999:

Machine owned all year: $10\% \times £2,000 = £200$
Machine sold: $10\% \times £2,000 \times 6$ months $= £100$
Machine acquired—depreciation from the date brought into use (1 July 1999) to the end of the accounting year:
$10\% \times £2,800 \times 3$ months $= £70$
Total depreciation expense for year:
$£200 + £100 + £70 = £370$

(a) *The journal*

				Debit £	Credit £
1999					
31 March	Machinery disposals	Dr		2,000	
	Machinery account				2,000
	Being the transfer of the cost of the machine sold to the disposals account				
31 March	Depreciation expense	Dr		100	
	Provision for depreciation				100
	Being depreciation for the current year on the machine sold				
31 March	Provision for depreciation	Dr		1,600	
	Machinery disposals				1,600
	Being the aggregate depreciation on the disposal				
31 March	H Johnson/bank	Dr		800	
	Machinery disposals				800
	Being proceeds of sale of machinery sold				
31 March	Machinery disposals	Dr		100	
	Wages				100
	Being the labour cost of dismantling the machine sold				
31 March	Machinery disposals	Dr		300	
	Profit and loss account				300
	Being profit on sale of machine				
1 May	Machinery account	Dr		2,800	
	R Adams/bank				2,800
	Being purchase of new machine				

Notes

1. It is likely that in practice the entries relating to depreciation and the profit on sale would be done at the end of the accounting year. However, examination questions like this often expect students to do them on the date of disposal.
2. Although not required by the question, students may find it useful to start by constructing the machinery disposals account in rough form as follows:

Machinery disposals

Machinery—cost	2,000	Provision for depreciation		
Wages—dismantling		—aggregate depreciation	1,600	
costs	100	H Johnson—proceeds of		
P & L—profit on sale	300	sale	800	
	2,400		2,400	

11.16 Workings

Plant
Cost at 31 December 1993 = 96,920 + 33,080 − 40,000 = £90,000
Depreciation for 1993 = 10% × 90,000 = £9,000

Disposal:
Aggregate depreciation = 10% × 40,000 × 6 years = £24,000
book value at disposal = 40,000 − 24,000 = £16,000
loss on sale = 16,000 − 15,000 = £1,000

Vehicles
Disposal 1:
Aggregate depreciation—
$1990 = 25\% \times 3,200 = 800$
$1991 = 25\% \times (3,200 - 800) = 600$
$1992 = 25\% \times (3,200 - [800 + 600]) = 450$
total $= 800 + 600 + 450 = £\underline{1,850}$
book value at disposal $= 3,200 - 1,850 = £\underline{1,350}$
loss on sale $= 1,350 - 1,300 = £\underline{50}$

Disposal 2:
Aggregate depreciation—
$1991 = 25\% \times 4,800 = 1,200$
$1992 = 25\% \times (4,800 - 1,200) = 900$
total $= 1,200 + 900 = £\underline{2,100}$
book value at disposal $= 4,800 - 2,100 = £\underline{2,700}$
profit on sale $= 2,960 - 2,700 = £\underline{260}$

Remainder:
Cost at 31 December 1993
$= 25,060 + 4,750 - 3,200 - 4,800 = £21,810$
Aggregate depreciation at 31 December 1993
$= 14,560 - 1,850 - 2,100 = £\underline{10,610}$
Depreciation for 1993 $= 25\% ((21,810 - 10,610) = £\underline{2,800}$

(a) *The ledger*

Plant

1993			1993		
Jan 1	Balance b/d	96,920	Dec 31	Bank	15,000
Dec 31	Bank	33,080	Dec 31	Provision for dep'n	24,000
			Dec 31	P & L—loss	1,000
			Dec 31	Balance c/d	90,000
		130,000			130,000
1994					
Jan 1	Balance b/d	90,000			

Provision for depreciation on plant

1993			1993		
Dec 31	Plant	24,000	Jan 1	Balance b/d	50,120
Dec 31	Balance c/d	35,120	Dec 31	P & L	9,000
		59,120			59,120
			1994		
			Jan 1	Balance b/d	35,120

Vehicles

1993			1993		
Jan 1	Balance b/d	25,060	Dec 31	Bank—Vehicle 1	1,300
Dec 31	Bank	4,750	Dec 31	Provision for dep'n	1,850
			Dec 31	P & L—loss	50
			Dec 31	Bank—Vehicle 2	2,960
Dec 31	P & L—profit	260	Dec 31	Provision for dep'n	2,100
			Dec 31	Balance c/d	21,810
		30,070			30,070
1994					
Jan 1	Balance b/d	21,810			

Provision for depreciation on vehicles

1993			1993		
Dec 31	Vehicles	1,850	Jan 1	Balance b/d	14,560
Dec 31	Vehicles	2,100	Dec 31	P & L	2,800
Dec 31	Balance c/d	13,410			
		17,360			17,360
			1994		
			Jan 1	Balance b/d	13,410

Profit & loss account

Dep'n on plant	9,000	Profit on sale vehicle		260
Dep'n on vehicles	2,800			
Loss on sale plant	1,000			
Loss on sale vehicle	50			

(b) *The journal*

				Debit	Credit
1993				£	£
Dec 31	Profit & loss account		Dr	9,000	
	Provision for dep'n—plant				9,000
	Being depreciation on plant for 1993				
Dec 31	Profit & loss account		Dr	2,800	
	Provision for dep'n—vehicles				2,800
	Being depreciation on vehicles for 1993				

Alternative method—disposals account

Plant

1993			1993		
Jan 1	Balance b/d	96,920	Dec 31	Disposals	40,000
Dec 31	Bank	33,080	Dec 31	Balance c/d	90,000
		130,000			130,000
1994					
Jan 1	Balance b/d	90,000			

Plant disposals

1993			1993		
Dec 31	Plant	40,000	Dec 31	Bank	15,000
			Dec 31	Provision for dep'n	24,000
			Dec 31	P & L—loss	1,000
		40,000			40,000

Vehicles

1993			1993		
Jan 1	Balance b/d	25,060	Dec 31	Disposal 1	3,200
Dec 31	Bank	4,750	Dec 31	Disposal 2	4,800
			Dec 31	Balance c/d	21,810
		29,810			29,810
1994					
Jan 1	Balance b/d	21,810			

Vehicle disposals

1993			1993		
Dec 31	Vehicles 1	3,200	Dec 31	Bank— Vehicle 1	1,300
Dec 31	Vehicles 2	4,800	Dec 31	Provision for dep'n	1,850
			Dec 31	P & L—loss	50
			Dec 31	Bank— Vehicle 2	2,960
Dec 31	P & L—profit	260	Dec 31	Provision for dep'n	2,100
		8,260			8,260

12.   Bad debts and provisions for bad debts

12.5   *Workings*

	£
Debtors at 31 July 19X1	15,680
Less: bad debts (410 + 270)	680
Revised debtors at 31 July 19X1	15,000

Provision for bad debts = 4% × £15,000 = £600

The ledger

A. Wall

19X1			19X1		
July 31	Balance b/d	410	July 31	Bad debts	410

B. Wood

July 31	Balance b/d	270	July 31	Bad debts	270

Bad debts

July 31	A. Wall	410	July 31	Profit & loss	680
July 31	B. Wood	270			
		680			680

Provision for bad debts

			July 31	Profit & loss	600

Profit & loss account

Bad debts	680			
Provision for bad debts	600			

12.6   *Workings*

	£
Debtors at 30 April 19X5	19,500
Less: bad debts (620 + 880)	1,500
Revised debtors at 30 April 19X5	18,000
Provision for bad debts at 30 April 19X5	
(3% ×18,000)	540
Less: provision for bad debts at 30 April 19X4	750
Reduction in provision for bad debts	210

The ledger

A. Winters

19X5			19X5		
Apl 30	Balance b/d	620	Apl 30	Bad debts	620

D. Spring

Apl 30	Balance b/d	880	Apl 30	Bad debts	880

Bad debts

Apl 30	A. Winters	620	Apl 30	Profit & loss	1,500
Apl 30	D. Spring	880			
		1,500			1,500

Provisions for bad debts

19X5			19X4		
Apl 30	Profit & loss	210	Apl 30	Balance b/d	750
Apl 30	Balance c/d	540			
		750			750
			19X5		
			Apl 30	Balance b/d	540

Profit & loss account

Bad debts	1,500	Provision for bad debts	210

12.11 *Workings*

	£	£	£
Provision for bad debts			
Specific provision (320 − 70)			250
General provision—			
debtors at 31 Dec 19X7		12,610	
Less: bad debts (210 + [260 − 110])	360		
specific provision	250	610	
Revised debtors at 31 Dec 19X7		12,000	
Provision at 31 Dec 19X7			
(5% × 12,000)			600
Total provision for bad debts at 31 Dec 19X7			850
Less: provision for bad debts at 31 Dec 19X6			1,260
Reduction in provision for bad debts			410

Provision for depreciation

Date of purchase or sale	Details	Depreciation on disposals	Depreciation for year ended 31 Dec 19X7
		£	£
	Depreciation on disposal		
1 July 19X5	For year ending 31.12.X5—		
	25% × 8,000 × $^6/_{12}$	1,000	
	For year ending 31.12.X6—		
	25% × (8,000 − 1,000)	1,750	
31 Mar 19X7	For year ending 31.12.X7—		
	25% × (8,000 − [1,000 +		
	1,750]) × $^3/_{12}$	328	328
		3,078	
	Book value at 31.12.X7:		
	8,000 − 3,078 = £4,922		
	Loss on sale:		
	4,922 − 4,000 = £922		
	Depreciation on acquisition		
31 Mar 19X7	25% × (4,000 + 1,000) × $^9/_{12}$		938
	Depreciation on remainder		
	Cost = 30,000 − 8,000 = £22,000		
	Aggregate depreciation:		
	12,500 − (1,000 + 1,750) = £9,750		
	WDV = 22,000 − 9,750 = £12,250		
	Depreciation = 25% × 12,250		3,063
			4,329

(a) *The ledger*

A. Bee

19X7				19X7		
Jan 1	Balance b/d	320		Apl 30	Bank	70
				Apl 30	Balance c/d	250
		320				320
May 1	Balance b/d	250				

J. Kay

Jan 1	Balance b/d	210		June 15	Bad debts	210

C. Dee

Jan 1	Balance b/d	180		Aug 3	Bank	180

F. Gee

Jan 1	Balance b/d	260	Oct 7	Bank	110
			Oct 7	Bad debts	150
		260			260

Bad debts

June 15	J. Kay	210	Dec 31	Profit & loss	360
Oct 7	F. Gee	150			
		360			360

Provision for bad debts

Dec 31	Profit & loss	410	Jan 1	Balance b/d	1,260
Dec 31	Balance c/d	850			
		1,260			1,260
			19X8		
			Jan 1	Balance b/d	850

Plant & machinery

Jan 1	Balance b/d	30,000	Mar 31	Part exchange	4,000
Mar 31	Bank	1,000	Dec 31	Provision for	
Mar 31	Part exchange	4,000		depreciation	3,078
			Dec 31	Profit & loss-	
				loss on sale	922
			Dec 31	Balance c/d	27,000
		35,000			35,000
19X8					
Jan 1	Balance b/d	27,000			

Provision for depreciation

Dec 31	Plant &		Jan 1	Balance b/d	12,500
	machinery	3,078	Dec 31	Profit & loss	4,329
Dec 31	Balance c/d	13,751			
		16,829			16,829
			19X8		
			Jan 1	Balance b/d	13,751

Profit & loss account

Bad debts	360	Provision for bad debts	410
Provision for depreciation	4,329		
Loss on sale of plant	922		

(b)   Provisions for bad debts and depreciation are both provisions. A provision is the setting aside of income to meet a known future liability or loss, the amount of which cannot be ascertained exactly, and thus an estimate has to be made. Provisions for bad debts and depreciation are both intended to provide for a future loss. A provision for bad debts provides for the loss which occurs when debtors fail to pay their debts. Depreciation is the loss in value of a fixed asset, and a provision for depreciation is intended to provide for the loss when fixed assets are sold at a price below their cost.

Provisions for bad debts and depreciation are both applications of the prudence concept. This dictates that 'provision is made for all known liabilities (expenses and losses) whether the amount of these is known with certainty or is a best estimate in the light of the information available' (ASC, SSAP2, 1971).

13.   Accruals and prepayments

13.2   *The ledger*

Rent

19X2			19X2		
Jan 1	Prepayment b/d	300	Dec 31	Profit & loss	3,730
Jan 29	Bank	930	Dec 31	Prepayment c/d	320
May 2	Bank	930			
July 30	Bank	930			
Nov 5	Bank	960			
		4,050			4,050
19X3					
Jan 1	Prepayment b/d	320			

Light & heat

19X2			19X2		
Mar 6	Bank	420	Jan 1	Accrual b/d	140
June 4	Bank	360	Dec 31	Profit & loss	1,450
Sept 3	Bank	270			
Dec 7	Bank	390			
Dec 31	Accrual c/d	150			
		1,590			1,590
			19X3	Accrual b/d	150

Workings

Rent prepaid at 1 Jan 19X2 = $\frac{1}{3} \times 900 = £300$
Rent prepaid at 31 Dec 19X2 = $\frac{1}{3} \times 960 = £320$
Light & heat accrued at 1 Jan 19X2 = $\frac{1}{3} \times 420 = £140$
Light & heat accrued at 31 Dec 19X2 = $\frac{1}{3} \times 450 = £150$

13.5   The entries in a rent receivable account are on the opposite side to those in a rent payable account. The credit to the profit and loss account is the difference between the two sides of the ledger account after entering all the prepayments (or accruals).

The derivation of the purchases on credit will be unfamiliar to students at this point in their studies. It is discussed in depth in Chapter 19. However, the principle is very similar to expense accounts containing accruals. A total creditors (control) account is used in place of the individual personal accounts of the creditors. The creditors at the start and end of the year are entered on the same sides as accruals in an expense account, as are the payments. The credit purchases for the year is then the difference between the two sides of the creditors account.

The ledger

Rents receivable

19X5			19X4		
May 31	P & L	4,004	June 1	Prepayment b/d	463
May 31	Prepayment c/d	517	19X5		
			May 31	Bank	4,058
		4,521			4,521
			1 June	Prepayment b/d	517

Rent & rates payable

19X4			19X4		
June 1	Prepayment b/d	1,246	June 1	Accrual b/d	315
19X5			19X5		
May 31	Bank-rent	7,491	May 31	P & L	10,100
May 31	Bank-rates	2,805	May 31	Prepayment c/d	1,509
May 31	Accrual c/d	382			
		11,924			11,924
June 1	Prepayment b/d	1,509	June 1	Accrual b/d	382

Total creditors

19X5			19X4		
May 31	Bank	75,181	June 1	Balance b/d	5,258
May 31	Discount rec'd	1,043	19X5		
May 31	Balance c/d	4,720	May 31	P & L—purchases	75,686
		80,944			80,944
			June 1	Balance b/d	4,720

14.   The preparation of final accounts from the trial balance

14.1   *C. Jones, Extended trial balance as at 31 December 19X9*

	Trial balance		Adjustments		Profit & loss a/c		Balance sheet	
	Dr	Cr	Dr	Cr	Dr	Cr	Dr	Cr
Capital		45,214	9,502					35,712
Drawings	9,502			9,502				
Purchases	389,072				389,072			
Sales		527,350				527,350		
Wages & salaries	33,440		3,012	3,012	36,452			3,012
Rent & rates	9,860		1,972	1,972	7,888		1,972	
Light & heat	4,142				4,142			
Bad debts	1,884		1,420		3,304			
Provision doubtful debts		3,702	158			158		3,544
Debtors	72,300			1,420			70,880	
Creditors		34,308						34,308
Bank	2,816						2,816	
Cash	334						334	
Stock	82,124		99,356	82,124	82,124	99,356	99,356	
Motor car-cost	7,200						7,200	
Motor car-depreciation		2,100		1,440	1,440			3,540
Profit					102,442			102,442
	612,674	612,674			626,864	626,864	182,558	182,558

C. Jones
Trading and profit & loss accounts
For the year ended 31 December 19X9

	£	£
Sales		527,350
Less: cost of sales		
Stock at 1 Jan 19X9	82,124	
Add: purchases	389,072	
	471,196	
Less: stock at 31 Dec 19X9	99,356	371,840
Gross profit		155,510
Add: reduction in provision for doubtful debts		158
		155,668
Less: Expenditure		
Wages & salaries	36,452	
Rent & rates	7,888	
Light & heat	4,142	
Bad debts	3,304	
Provision for depreciation	1,440	
		53,226
Net profit		102,442

C. Jones
Balance sheet as at 31st December 19X9

	£	£	£
Fixed assets			
Motor car at cost			7,200
Less: provision for depreciation			3,540
			3,660
Current assets			
Stock		99,356	
Prepayments		1,972	
Debtors	70,880		
Less: provision for doubtful debts	3,544	67,336	

	£	£	£
Bank		2,816	
Cash		334	
		171,814	
Less: Current liabilities			
Creditors	34,308		
Accruals	3,012	37,320	
Net current assets			134,494
Net assets			138,154
Capital			
Balance at 1 Jan 19X9			45,214
Add: net profit for the year			102,442
			147,656
Less: drawings			9,502
Balance at 31 Dec 19X9			138,154

14.2   J. Clark

Trading and profit and loss accounts
For the year ended 31 March 19X6

	£	£	£
Sales (58,640 – 400)			58,240
Less: Returns inwards			3,260
Net sales			54,980
Less: Cost of sales—			
Opening stock		4,670	
Add: Purchases (34,260 – 350)	33,910		
Less: Returns outwards	2,140		
	31,770		
Add: Carriage inwards	730	32,500	
		37,170	
Less: Closing stock (3,690 + 300)		3,990	33,180
Gross profit			21,800
Add: Discount received			1,970
Investment income			460
			24,230
Less: Expenditure			
Carriage outward		420	
Discount allowed		1,480	
Depreciation on plant			
(25% × [11,350−4,150])		1,800	
Depreciation on vehicles		1,986	
Loss on sale of vehicle		264	
Interest payable		1,000	
Wages		7,180	
Rent & rates (4,300 – 210)		4,090	
Provision for bad debts			
([10% × (8,070−370−400)]−530)		200	
Bad debts		370	
Light & heat (2,640 + 130)		2,770	
Stationery (450−230)		220	21,780
Net profit			2,450

J. Clark

Balance sheet as at 31ˢᵗ March 19X6

	£	£	£
	Cost	*Aggreg. depn.*	*W.D.V.*
Fixed assets			
Freehold premises	32,000	—	32,000
Plant & machinery (4,150 + 1,800)	11,350	5,950	5,400

	£	£	£
Motor vehicles (13,290 − 1,000)	12,290	4,498	7,792
	55,640	10,448	45,192
Goodwill			5,000
			50,192

Current assets

Stationery stock		230	
Stock (3,690 + 300)		3,990	
Prepayments		210	
Trade debtors (8,070−370−400)	7,300		
Less: Provision for bad debts	730	6,570	
Sundry debtor		458	
Quoted investments		6,470	
Bank & cash		2,850	
		20,778	

Less: Current liabilities

Accruals	130		
Creditors	4,340	4,470	
Net current assets			16,308
Total assets less current liabilities			66,500
Less: Long term liabilities			
Mortgage on premises			10,000
Net assets			56,500

Capital

Balance at 1 April 19X5	60,000
Add: Net profit for year	2,450
	62,450
Less: Drawings (5600 + 350)	5,950
Balance at 31 March 19X6	56,500

Workings: Depreciation on vehicles

	Previous years £	This year £
Disposal		
19X3/X4 20% × £1,000 × 3/12	50	
19X4/X5 20% × (£1,000 − £50)	190	
	240	
19X5/X6 20% × [£1,000 − (£50 + £190)] × 3/12	38	38
	278	

Book value at sale = £1,000 − £278 = £722
Loss on sale = £722 − £458 = £264
Depreciation on remaining

20% × [(£13,290 − £1,000) − (£2,790 − £240)]		1,948
		1,986

Aggregate depreciation at 31 March 19X6
£2,790 + £1,986 − £278 = £4,498

Note

1.   It is assumed that the quoted investments are to be held for less than one accounting year.

15.   Manufacturing accounts and the valuation of stocks

15.11 *Upton Upholstery*
Manufacturing, trading and profit & loss accounts
For the year ended 30 April 19X4

	£		£
Direct materials			
Stock at 1 May 19X3	4,000	*Cost of completed*	
Add: purchases	84,000	*production* c/d	114,900
carriage inwards	1,200		
	89,200		
Less: stock at 30 Apl 19X4	5,400		
	83,800		
Direct wages (19,900 + 600)	20,500		
Prime costs	104,300		
Factory overheads			
Depreciation: machinery			
(28,000 ÷ 7)	4,000		
Light & heat (3,000 × ⁴/₅)	2,400		
Rent & rates			
(6,600 − [¹/₃ × 600]) × ³/₄	4,800		
Manufacturing costs	115,500		
Add: WIP at 1 May 19X3	16,400		
	131,900		
Less: WIP at 30 Apl 19X4	17,000		
	114,900		114,900
Finished goods		Sales	140,000
Stock at 1 May 19X3	9,000		
Add: cost of completed			
production b/d	114,900		
	123,900		
Less: stock at 30 Apl 19X4	8,000		
Cost of sales	115,900		
Gross profit c/d	24,100		
	140,000		140,000
Selling & distribution costs:		*Gross profit* b/d	24,100
Carriage outwards	700		
Sales commission	1,400		
Provision for doubtful debts	1,000		
Administrative costs:			
Depreciation: equipment			
25% × (2,000 − 800)	300		
Light & heat (3,000 × ¹/₅)	600		
Rent & rates			
(6,600 − [¹/₃ × 600]) × ¹/₄	1,600		
Office wages (5,200 + 100)	5,300		
	10,900		
Net profit	13,200		
	24,100		24,100

Upton Upholstery
Balance sheet as at 30 April 19X4

	£	£	£
Fixed assets	Cost	Aggreg. depn.	WDV
Factory machinery			
(5,000 + 4,000)	28,000	9,000	19,000
Office equipment			
(800 + 300)	2,000	1,100	900
	30,000	10,100	19,900

	£	£	£
Current assets			
Stocks			
(5,400 + 17,000 + 8,000)		30,400	
Prepaid rent		200	
Trade debtors	15,000		
Less: provision for bad debts	1,000	14,000	
Cash & bank		2,300	
		46,900	
Less: Current liabilities			
Trade creditors	16,000		
Accrued costs (600 + 100)	700	16,700	
Net current assets			30,200
Total assets less current liabilities			50,100
Less: long term liabilities			
Bank loan			11,000
Net assets			39,100
Capital			
Balance at 1 May 19X3			35,000
Add: profit for the year			13,200
			48,200
Less: drawings			9,100
Balance at 30 April 19X4			39,100

Note

1. The manufacturing, trading and profit & loss accounts have been shown in account form for the purpose of emphasizing that these are accounts in the ledger. However, students are advised to use vertical form in answering other questions in this exercise.

15.12 *Manufacturing account for the year ended 31 December 19X9*

	£	£
Raw materials:		
Stock at 1 Jan 19X9		2,453
Add: purchases (47,693 – 2,093)	45,600	
Less: returns outward	4,921	
		40,679
		43,132
Less: stock at 31 Dec 19X9		3,987
		39,145
Direct wages (23,649 – 549)		23,100
Direct expenses:		
Carriage inwards	683	
Royalties	7,500	8,183
Prime cost		70,428
Factory overheads:		
Supervisors wages	5,617	
Electricity—factory	2,334	
Depreciation on plant	13,400	
Rent and rates—factory	3,600	
Insurance on plant	1,750	
Repairs to plant	917	27,618
Factory costs		98,046
Add: WIP at 1 Jan 19X9		1,617
		99,663
Less: WIP at 31 Dec 19X9		2,700
		96,963
Less: proceeds from the sale of scrap		199
Factory cost of completed production		96,764

Trading and profit and loss account
For the year ended 31 December 19X9

	£	£
Sales		145,433
Less: cost of sales:		
Stock of finished goods at 1 Jan 19X 9	3,968	
Add: factory cost of production	96,764	
Purchases of finished goods	367	
	101,099	
Less: stock of finished goods at		
31 Dec 19X9	5,666	
Cost of sales		95,433
Gross profit		50,000
Add: discount received		2,310
		52,310
Administrative overheads:		
Salaries	10,889	
Light and heat	998	
Depreciation—fixtures & furniture	1,900	
Rent and rates	1,200	
Postage and telephone	714	
Printing and stationery	363	
	16,064	
Selling and distribution overheads:		
Carriage outwards	487	
Salaries and commission	8,600	
Bad debts	726	
Discount allowed	1,515	
Depreciation—vehicles	3,700	
Delivery expenses	593	
Advertising	625	
	16,246	
Financial charges:		
Loan interest	3,000	
Bank charges	100	
	3,100	
		35,410
Net profit		16,900

Notes

1. The carriage inwards could have been added to the cost of purchases of raw materials.
2. The proceeds from the sale of scrap metal could have been deducted from the cost of raw materials.

15.18 (a) *Cost of sales*

FIFO

Purchases			Cost of sales			Stock		
Quantity	Price	Value	Quantity	Price	Value	Quantity	Price	Value
	£	£		£	£		£	£
1,200	1.00	1,200				1,200	1.00	1,200
1,000	1.05	1,050				2,200		2,250
			800	1.00	800	400	1.00	400
						1,000	1.05	1,050
						1,400		1,450
600	1.10	660				2,000		2,110
			400	1.00	400			
			200	1.05	210	800	1.05	840
			600		610	600	1.10	660
						1,400		1,500

Purchases			Cost of sales			Stock		
Quantity	Price	Value	Quantity	Price	Value	Quantity	Price	Value
900	1.20	1,080				2,300		2,580
			800	1.05	840			
			300	1.10	330	300	1.10	330
			1,100		1,170	900	1.20	1,080
						1,200		1,410
800	1.25	1,000				2,000		2,410
			300	1.10	330			
			900	1.20	1,080			
			100	1.25	125	700	1.25	875
			1,300		1,535			
700	1.30	910				1,400		1,785
			400	1.25	500	300	1.25	375
						700	1.30	910
5,200		5,900	4,200		4,615	1,000		1,285

LIFO

Purchases			Cost of sales			Stock		
Quantity	Price	Value	Quantity	Price	Value	Quantity	Price	Value
	£	£		£	£		£	£
1,200	1.00	1,200				1,200	1.00	1,200
1,000	1.05	1,050				2,200		2,250
			800	1.05	840	200	1.05	210
						1,200	1.00	1,200
						1,400		1,410
600	1.10	660				2,000		2,070
			600	1.10	660	1,400		1,410
900	1.20	1,080				2,300		2,490
			900	1.20	1,080			
			200	1.05	210			
			1,100		1,290	1,200	1.00	1,200
800	1.25	1,000				2,000		2,200
			800	1.25	1,000			
			500	1.00	500	700	1.00	700
			1,300		1,500			
700	1.30	910				1,400		1,610
			400	1.30	520	300	1.30	390
						700	1.00	700
5,200		5,900	4,200		4,810	1,000		1,090

Weighted average

	£
Purchases	5,900
Less: stock 1,000 @ (5,900 ÷ 5,200)	1,135
Cost of sales	4,765

(b) **Workings**

Sales

Quantity Units	Price £	Value £
800	1.70	1,360
600	1.90	1,140
1,100	2.00	2,200
1,300	2.00	2,600
400	2.05	820
4,200		8,120

Bank

Capital	6,000	Purchases	5,900
Sales	8,120	Expenses	
		(1,740 − 570)	1,170
		Balance c/d	7,050
	14,120		14,120
Balance b/d	7,050		

	FIFO	LIFO	WA
Profit & loss account	£	£	£
Sales	8,120	8,120	8,120
Less: cost of sales	4,615	4,810	4,765
Gross profit	3,505	3,310	3,355
Less: expenses	1,740	1,740	1,740
Net profit	1,765	1,570	1,615
Balance sheet			
Stock	1,285	1,090	1,135
Bank	7,050	7,050	7,050
Total assets	8,335	8,140	8,185
Less: accrued expenses	570	570	570
Net assets	7,765	7,570	7,615
Capital at start of period	6,000	6,000	6,000
Add: profit for year	1,765	1,570	1,615
Capital at end of period	7,765	7,570	7,615

16.   The bank reconciliation statement

16.4   *The ledger*

Cash book

Balance b/d	2,880	Bank charges	105
Dividends	189	Refer to drawer	54
		Error (£141 x 2)	282
		Balance c/d	2,628
	3,069		3,069

Grow Ltd
Bank reconciliation statement at 31 March 19X9

	£	£
Balance per cash book		2,628
Add: Cheques not yet presented (642 + 1,200)		1,842
		4,470
Less: Amounts not yet credited	1,904	
Cheque debited in error by bank	216	
		2,120
Balance per bank statement		2,350

16.5   (a) *Mrs Lake*
Bank reconciliation statement as at 30 April 19X8

	£	£
Balance per bank account		1,310.40
Add: Error cheque no.236130 (£87.77 − £77.87)	9.90	
Receipts not entered in bank account	21.47	
Cheques not yet presented (£30 + £52.27)	82.27	113.64
		1,424.04

Less: Payments not entered in bank account			
(£12.80 + £32.52)		45.32	
Amounts not yet credited		192.80	238.12
			1,185.92
Less: Undetected error			19.47
Balance per bank statement			1,166.45

(b) The undetected error would require further investigation. The amount is the same as cheque number 427519 on 10 April. This cheque number is different from the sequence of the others which suggests that it may have been debited to Mrs Lake's account in error.

Note:

1. Students should have realized that cheques numbered 236126 and 236127 shown on the bank statement are in the cash book for March and were unpresented at 31 March (Reconciliation at 31 March 19X8: £1,053.29 − £15.21 − £210.70 = £827.38). No entries are required in the bank reconciliation at 30 April 19X8 since these are on the bank statement for April.

17.   Control accounts

17.2 *The ledger*

Sales ledger control

19X6				19X7		
July 1	Balance b/d	40,000		June 30	Returns inwards	15,750
19X7				June 30	Discount allow.	5,443
June 30	Sales	386,829		June 30	Bad debts	3,400
				June 30	Bank	230,040
				June 30	Balance c/d	172,196
		426,829				426,829
July 1	Balance b/d	172,196				

Purchases ledger control

19X7				19X6		
June 30	Returns outwards	8,660		July 1	Balance b/d	31,200
June 30	Discount received	3,187		19X7		
June 30	Bank	108,999		June 30	Purchases	222,954
June 30	Balance c/d	133,308				
		254,154				254,154
				July 1	Balance b/d	133,308

17.4 *The ledger*

Debtors control account

19X1				19X1		
Jan 1	Balance b/d	4,200		Jan 1	Balance b/d	300
Jan 31	Sales	23,000		Jan 31	Returns inward	750
Jan 31	Dishonoured cheques	1,850		Jan 31	Bank	16,250
				Jan 31	Discount allow.	525
Jan 31	Bad debts recovered	230		Jan 31	Bad debts	670
				Jan 31	Bills receivable	5,300
Jan 31	Interest on overdue accts	120		Jan 31	Creditors contra	930
				Jan 31	Allowances	340
Jan 31	Balance c/d	240		Jan 31	Balance c/d	4,575
		29,640				29,640
Feb 1	Balance b/d	4,575		Feb 1	Balance b/d	240

Creditors control account

Jan 1	Balance b/d	250	Jan 1	Balance b/d	6,150
Jan 31	Returns		Jan 31	Purchases	21,500
	outward	450	Jan 31	Balance c/d	420
Jan 31	Bank	19,800			
Jan 31	Discount rec'd	325			
Jan 31	Bills payable	4,500			
Jan 31	Debtors contra	930			
Jan 31	Allowances rec'd	280			
Jan 31	Balance c/d	1,535			
		28,070			28,070
Feb 1	Balance b/d	420	Feb 1	Balance b/d	1,535

Notes:

1. The following items do not appear in control accounts: carriage inwards, carriage outwards; provision for bad debts; cash received from bills receivable; cash paid on bills payable.
2. The debit balance on the debtors control account is calculated by subtracting the total of the credit side from the debit side. The credit balance on the creditors control account is calculated in a similar way.
3. The credit balances on the debtors control account are probably the result of debtors overpaying, possibly in instances where they have been sent a credit note for goods and also paid for them. Similarly the debit balances on the creditors control account may be due to this business overpaying some of its creditors.
4. Although credit balances on the debtors control account and debit balances on the creditors control account are frequently encountered in examinations, in practice each control account can only throw up one balance which would naturally be the difference between the two sides of the control account. This balance should then agree with the difference between the total of the debit and credit balances of the personal accounts in the personal ledger.
5. Sometimes goods are bought from a business to whom goods were also sold. In these circumstances the amounts owed may be set off against each other and a cheque paid/received for the difference. The amount set off is referred to as a personal ledger contra and in the above example is £930.
6. It is assumed that the actual money received that relates to debts that were previously written off as bad (£230) is included in cheques received from debtors. Thus the item 'bad debts recovered' is treated as an instruction to reverse the entry by which they were originally written off.

17.5   (a) *The ledger*

Debtors control

Balance b/d	14,364	Cheques	118,258	
Sales	138,208	Discount allowed	3,692	
Bad debts recovered	84	Returns inwards	1,966	
Cash	132	Bills receivable	6,486	
Interest on overdue accts	20	Bad debts	1,186	
		Creditors ledger	606	
		Balance c/d	20,614	
	152,808		152,808	
Balance b/d	20,614			

	£
(b) *Debtors ledger control account*	
Original balance	20,614
Add: Sales day book under-cast	1,000
	21,614
Less: Discount allowed omitted	50
Amended balance	21,564
Debtors ledger	
Original balances	20,914
Add: Amount of cheque transposed (£4,300 − £3,400)	900
	21,814
Less: Returns posted incorrectly (£125 × 2)	250
Amended balance	21,564

17.6   (a) *The ledger*

Debtors control

Balance b/d	17,220	Cheques	45,280
Sales	98,730	Returns inwards	18,520
		Bills of exchange	29,160
		Discount allowed	6,940
		Bad debts	4,920
		Transfer to creditors	2,850
		Balance c/d	8,280
	115,950		115,950
Balance b/d	8,280		

Creditors control

Cheques	38,020	Balance b/d	20,490
Returns outwards	16,010	Purchases	85,860
Bills of exchange	21,390	Cash	2,430
Discount received	7,680		
Transfer to debtors	2,850		
Balance c/d	22,830		
	108,780		108,780
		Balance b/d	22,830

	£
(b) *Creditors ledger*	
Original balances	20,700
Add: cheque posted wrongly (£3,400 − £340)	3,060
	23,760
Less: returns outward error (£180 × 2)	360
Amended balance	23,400
Creditor ledger control	
Original balance	22,830
Add: discount received (£210 − £120)	90
	22,920
Less: purchases day book overcast	500
Amended balance	22,420

Undetected error = £23,400 − £22,420 = £980

18.   Errors and suspense accounts

18.4   *Journal*

			Debit £	Credit £
1.	Light & heat	Dr	32	
	Suspense			32
	Being correction of posting error			
2.	Suspense	Dr	28	
	Wages			28
	Being correction of arithmetic error			
3.	Rent	Dr	720	
	Suspense			720
	Being correction of transposed figures			
4.	Motor vehicles	Dr	300	
	Purchases			300
	Being correction of error of principle			

5.	A. Watson	Dr	80	
	A. Watt			80

Being correction of an error of commission

6.	Sales	Dr	100	
	Loose tools			100

Being correction of error of principle

7.	Postage & telephone	Dr	17	
	Carriage outwards			17

Being correction of error of commission

8.	Bank charges	Dr	41	
	Cash book			41

Being correction of error of omission

9.	Stationery	Dr	9	
	Sales			9

Being correction of a compensating error

10.	J. Bloggs/Debtors control	Dr	108	
	Sales			108

Being correction of error of prime entry

11.	Suspense	Dr	124	
	Trial balance			124

Being correction of extraction error

The ledger

Suspense

Difference per trial balance	600	Light & heat	32
Wages	28	Rent	720
Extraction error	124		
	752		752

18.8 (a) ***Journal***

			Debit £	Credit £
19X9				
March 31	Cash book	Dr	10,000	
	Suspense account			10,000

Being correction of under-cast on debit side of cash book

	Freehold premises	Dr	5,000	
	Suspense account			5,000

Being correction of purchase of building in cash book not posted to ledger

	Suspense account	Dr	900	
	Purchases			900

Being correction of purchases of £100 entered in PDB summary as £1,000

	Carriage	Dr	405	
	Suspense account			405

Being correction of transport charge of £450 entered in PDB summary as £45

Rent receivable	Dr	45		
Suspense account			45	

Being correction of rent received of
£45 posted twice to the ledger

Debtors control	Dr	100		
Suspense account			100	

Being correction of under-cast on
debit side of debtors control
account

Notes

1. Item 3 relates to errors in a PDB summary which is used to post the nominal ledger. It is assumed that the creditors personal ledger is posted from the PDB and not the summary, and thus the individual creditors personal account and control account are correct.
2. Item 5 assumes that the debtors control account is part of the double entry in the ledger and thus the balance is included in the balance sheet.
3. Items 6 to 9 do not necessitate entries in the suspense account but will require journal entries for their correction.
4. Check that the balance on the suspense account has been eliminated as follows:

Suspense

Per trial balance	14,650	Cash book	10,000
Purchases	900	Freehold premises	5,000
		Carriage	405
		Rent receivable	45
		Debtors control	100
	15,550		15,550

(b) Workings

For examination purposes these are probably best done by simple horizontal calculations. However, the ledger accounts are shown below to aid the students understanding of the double entry involved.

Bank account

Correction of undercast	10,000	Balance b/d	1,230
		Bank charges	3,250
		Balance c/d	5,520
	10,000		10,000
Balance b/d	5,520		

Freehold premises

Balance b/d	60,000	
Correction of posting error	5,000	
	65,000	

Debtors control

Balance b/d	37,140	
Correction of undercast	100	
	37,240	

Provision for depreciation on vehicles

		Balance b/d	11,935
		P & L a/c	500
			12,435

Stock

Balance b/d	75,410	
Undervaluation	1,250	
	76,660	

Creditors control

	Balance b/d	41,360
	Purchases	2,110
		43,470

Profit and loss account

Carriage	405	Balance b/d		33,500
Rent receivable	45	Purchases		900
Bank charges	3,250	Stock		1,250
Depreciation on vehicles	500			
Purchases	2,110			
Revised profit	29,340			
	35,650			35,650

Miscup
Balance sheet as at 31 March 19X9

	£	£	£
Fixed assets	Cost	Acc.dep'n	WDV
Freehold premises	65,000	—	65,000
Motor vehicles	25,000	12,435	12,565
Fixtures and fittings	1,500	750	750
	91,500	13,185	78,315
Current assets			
Stock		76,660	
Debtors		37,240	
Bank		5,520	
Cash		75	
		119,495	
Less: Current liabilities			
Trade creditors and			
accrued charges		43,470	
Net current assets			76,025
Net assets			154,340
Capital			125,000
Add: profit for the year			29,340
			154,340

19.   Single entry and incomplete records

19.2   *Workings for plant*

	£	£
Cost at 30 June 19X4		50,000
Add: additions		20,000
		70,000
Less: disposals		10,000
Cost at 30 June 19X5		60,000
Aggregate depreciation		
Depreciation at 30 June 19X4		
(£50,000 – £31,000)		19,000
Add: depreciation for the year		
on addition (10% × £20,000 × 3 mths)	500	
on disposal (10% × £10,000 × 3 mths)	250	
on rest (10% × [£50,000 − £10,000])	4,000	
		4,750
		23,750
Less: aggregate depreciation on disposal		
10% × £10,000 × 2 years 9 mths		2,750
Depreciation at 30 June 19X5		21,000

Round Music
Balance sheet as at 30 June 19X5

	£	£	£
Fixed assets			
Plant at cost			60,000
Less: aggregate depreciation			21,000
			39,000
Current assets			
Stock (8,630 – 1,120)		7,510	
Prepayments		80	
Debtors	6,120		
Less: provision for doubtful debts	310	5,810	
		13,400	
Less: current liabilities			
Creditors	3,480		
Accruals	130		
Bank overdraft	1,430	5,040	
Net current assets			8,360
Total assets less current liabilities			47,360
Less: long term loan			7,000
Capital at 30 June 19X5			40,360

Round Music
Statement of profit for the year ended 30 June 19X5

	£
Capital at 30 June 19X5	40,360
Less: Capital at 30 June 19X4	42,770
	(2,410)
Add: drawings (18,500 + 750)	19,250
	16,840
Less: capital introduced	5,000
Profit for the year	11,840

19.4   *Workings*

Credit purchases = £5,720 + 33,360 − 5,220 = £33,860
Total purchases = £33,860 + 1,120 + 4,500 = £39,480
Credit sales = 5,840 + 31,860 − 6,540 = £31,160
Cash sales = £18,920 + 4,000 + 1,120 + 980 + 170 = £25,190
Total sales = £25,190 + 31,160 = £56,350
Telephone = £120 + 280 − 140 = £260
Light & heat = £370 + 290 − 60 = £600
Motor expenses = £1,810 + 980 = £2,790
Depreciation on fixtures and fittings =
    20% × £5,800 = £1,160
Accumulated depreciation on fixtures and fittings =
    (£10,000 − £5,800) + £1,160 = £5,360

A. Fox
Trading and profit & loss accounts
For the year ended 31 July 19X9

	£	£
Sales		56,350
Less: cost of sales—		
Stock at 1 Aug 19X8	3,300	
Add: purchases (39,480 − 530)	38,950	
	42,250	
Less: stock at 31 July 19X9	3,920	
		38,330
Gross profit		18,020
Less: expenditure		
Wages	5,640	

Telephone (120 + 280 – 140)	260		
Light & heat (370 + 290 – 60)	600		
Motor expenses (1,810 + 980)	2,790		
Printing	560		
Cleaning	170		
Depreciation (20% × 5,800)	1,160		
		11,180	
Net profit		6,840	

A   Fox
Balance sheet as at 31 July 19X9

	£	£	£
Fixed assets	*Cost*	*Agg.depn.*	*WDV*
Freehold land & buildings	35,000	—	35,000
Fixtures & fittings	10,000	5,360	4,640
	45,000	5,360	39,640
Current assets			
Stock		3,920	
Debtors		5,840	
Prepayments		140	
Bank		8,260	
		18,160	
Less: current liabilities			
Creditors	5,720		
Accruals	290	6,010	
Net current assets			12,150
Net assets			51,790
Capital			
Balance at 1 Aug 19X8			48,480
Add: capital introduced			1,000
Profit for year			6,840
			56,320
Less: drawings (4,000 + 530)			4,530
Balance at 31 July 19X9			51,790

20.   The final accounts of clubs

20.8   The ACCA suggested answer to this question is presented in horizontal/account form which is therefore obviously acceptable. However, to improve understandability, and for consistency with the answer to the example in the textbook the author has adopted a vertical presentation.

(a) Elite Bowling & Social Club
Statement of affairs as at 31 October 19X7

	£	£	£
Fixed assets	*Cost*	*Agg.depn.*	*WDV*
Furniture, fixtures & fittings	440	44	396
Mower	120	100	20
	560	144	416
Current assets			
Subscriptions in arrear		30	
Bar stock		209	
Bank—deposit account		585	
—current account		263	
Cash		10	
		1,097	
Less: current liabilities			
Bar creditors	186		
Accrued rent & rates	12		
Accrued light & heat	9	207	
Net current assets			890
General fund at 31 Oct 19X7			1,306

Workings

1. Net credit bar purchases

Creditors control

19X8				19X7		
Oct 31	Bank	1,885		Oct 31	Balance b/d	186
Oct 31	Balance c/d	248		19X8		
				Oct 31	Net purchases	1,947
		2,133				2,133

2. Subscriptions

Subscriptions

19X7				19X8		
Oct 31	Subs in arrear b/d	30		Oct 31	Bank	648
19X8				Oct 31	Subs in arrear c/d	50
Oct 31	Subs for year	624				
Oct 31	Subs in advance c/d	44				
		698				698

3. Fixed assets
(a) Depreciation on furniture, fixtures & fittings =
    10% × (£440 + £460) = £90
(b) Accumulated depreciation on furniture, fixtures and fittings =
    (£440 − £396) + £90 = £134
(c) Profit on disposal of mower = £40 − £20 = £20
(d) Cost of new mower = £120 + £40 = £160

Elite Bowling & Social Club
Bar trading account for the year ended 31 October 19X8

	£	£
Bar takings		2,285
Less: cost of sales—		
Bar stock at 1 Nov 19X7	209	
Add: purchases	1,947	
	2,156	
Less: bar stock at 31 Oct 19X8	178	
		1,978
Gross profit		307

(b) Elite Bowling & Social Club
Income & expenditure account for the year ended 31 October 19X8

	£	£
Income		
Subscriptions		624
Profit on bar		307
Spectators entrance fees		54
Deposit account interest		26
Catering receipts	120	
Less: catering purchases	80	
Profit on catering		40
Profit on disposal of mower		20
		1,071
Less: expenditure		
Wages	306	
Stewards bonus (40% × £40)	16	
Rent & rates (184 − 12 + 26)	198	
Light & heat (143 − 9 + 11)	145	
General expenses	132	
Depreciation on furniture	90	
		887
Excess of income over expenditure		184

(c) Elite Bowling & Social Club
Balance sheet as at 31 October 19X8

	£	£	£
Fixed assets	*Cost*	*Agg.depn.*	*WDV*
Furniture, fixtures & fittings	900	134	766
Mower	160	—	160
	1,060	134	926
Current assets			
Subs in arrear		50	
Bar stock		178	
Bank—deposit account		497	
current account		176	
Cash		8	
		909	
Less: current liabilities			
Bar creditors	248		
Accrued rent & rates	26		
Accrued light & heat	11		
Stewards bonus	16		
Subs in advance	44	345	
Net current assets			564
Net assets			1,490
General fund			
Balance at 31 Oct 19X7			1,306
Add: excess of income over expenditure			184
Balance at 31 Oct 19X8			1,490

Notes

1. If it had been known that the wages were paid to bar staff, these would have been put in the bar trading account.
2. All the items relating to the catering, including the stewards bonus, could have been put in the bar trading account.

20.9 The ACCA suggested answer to this question is presented in horizontal/account form which is therefore obviously acceptable. However, to improve understandability, and for consistency with the answer to the example in the textbook, the author has adopted a vertical presentation.

Assumption
In order to answer this question it is necessary to make an assumption about the cost of the defence bonds. The £1,500 given in the question is their face value. They could have been purchased at any price. However, the most reasonable assumption is that they were purchased at their face value of £1,500.

Workings

1. Accumulated/General fund
Statement of affairs at 30 June 19X7

	£	£	£
Fixed assets	*Cost*	*Agg.depn.*	*WDV*
Freehold building	6,000	—	6,000
Billiard tables (see workings 3.)	1,200	500	700
	7,200	500	6,700
Prize fund investments			1,500
			8,200
Current assets			
Subs in arrear		20	
Bar stock		150	
Bank		390	
		560	

Less: *current liabilities*

Accrued interest on mortgage (5% × £4,000)	200		
Net current assets		360	
Total assets less current liabilities		8,560	
Less: *long term liabilities*			
5% mortgage		4,000	
Net assets		4,560	
Accumulated fund (balancing figure)		2,585	
Life members fund (see workings 2.)		400	
Prize fund (see workings 4.)		1,575	
		4,560	

Note: The ACCA suggested answer has another treatment for the prize fund. The prize fund and prize fund investment accounts are ignored, and the interest is removed from the bank balance. This is essentially a short cut method for the purpose of calculating the accumulated fund.

2. Subscriptions

Subscriptions

19X7			19X8		
June 30	Subs in arrear b/d	20	June 30	Bank	340
19X8			June 30	Subs in arrear c/d	10
June 30	Subs for year	330			
		350			350

Life members fund

19X8			19X7		
June 30	Accum.fund		June 30	Balance b/d	
	(3 @ £16)	48		(25 @ £16)	400
June 30	Balance c/d		19X8		
	(25 + 5−3) @ £16	432	June 30	Bank	80
		480			480

3. Fixed assets: billiard tables

Aggregate depreciation at 30 June 10X7 =
5 years × (£1,200 ÷ 12) = £500
Depreciation for year = (£1,200 + £300) ÷ 12 = £125
Aggregate depreciation at 30 June 19X8 = £500 + £125 = £625

4. Prize fund

Prize fund

19X8			19X7		
June 30	Bank—prizes	75	June 30	Balance b/d	
June 30	Balance c/d	1,575		(1,500 + 75)	1,575
			19X8		
			June 30	Bank—income	75
		1,650			1,650

There are no entries in the prize fund investment account.

Bar trading account
For the year ended 30 June 19X8

	£	£
Bar receipts		4,590
Less: cost of sales		
Stock at 1 July 19X7	150	
Add: purchases	3,680	
	3,830	
Less: stock at 30 June 19X8	180	
	3,650	
Stewards wages & expenses	400	4,050
Gross profit on bar		540

Income & expenditure account
For the year ended 30 June 19X8

	£	£	£
Income			
Annual subscriptions			330
Profit on bar			540
Sundry lettings			180
Receipts for billiards		275	
Less: repairs to tables	50		
depreciation of tables	125	175	
Surplus from billiards			100
			1,150
Less: expenditure			
Rates		140	
Light & heat		72	
Cleaning & laundry		138	
Sundry expenses		80	
Mortgage interest (5% × £4,000)		200	630
Excess of income over expenditure			520

Balance sheet as at 30 June 19X8

	£	£	£
Fixed assets	*Cost*	*Agg.depn.*	*WDV*
Freehold building	6,000	—	6,000
Billiard tables	1,500	625	875
	7,500	625	6,875
Prize fund investments			1,500
			8,375
Current assets			
Subs in arrear		10	
Bar stock		180	
Bank		95	
		285	
Less: current liabilities		—	
Net current assets			285
Net assets			8,660
Accumulated fund			
Balance at 1 July 19X7			2,585
Add: excess of income over expenditure			520
transfer from life members fund			48
gifts from members			3,500
Balance at 30 June 19X8			6,653
Life members fund			
Balance at 1 July 19X7		400	
Add: subscriptions received		80	
		480	
Less: transfer to accumulated fund		48	
Balance at 30 June 19X8			432
Prize fund			
Balance at 1 July 19X7		1,575	
Less: prizes awarded for previous year		75	
		1,500	
Add: income		75	
Balance at 30 June 19X8			1,575
			8,660

Notes

1. The ACCA suggested answer has another treatment for the prize fund investment account. The £75 included in the bank balance at 30 June 19X8 relating to the income from the defence bonds is added to the

prize fund investment account and removed from the bank balance as shown on the balance sheet. This highlights that it is an asset of the prize fund even though it is held in a general bank account, and is probably a better method for the purpose of presenting an informative balance sheet. The method adopted by the author above reflects the balances on the relevant ledger accounts.

2. Notice that the gifts from members are not included in the income & expenditure account because the amount is so large and presumably non-recurring.

3. The mortgage is computed as follows:

$$(5\% \times 2 \text{ years}) \times m = \pounds 4,400 - m$$

$$\frac{10m}{100} = \pounds 4,400 - m$$

$$\frac{110m}{100} = \pounds 4,400$$

$$m = \pounds 4,000$$

21.   Accounting for hire purchase transactions

21.3   *(a) Annuity method*

	Year 1 £	Year 2 £	Year 3 £
Outstanding	4,000	2,400	1,688
Capital repayments	1,600	712	797
Balance	2,400	1,688	891
Interest @ 12%	288	203	109
Capital repayments	712	797	891
Instalments	1,000	1,000	1,000

The journal

			Debit £	Credit £
19X1				
Jan 3	Plant & machinery	Dr	4,000	
	Lawrence Ltd			4,000
	Being purchase of machine from Lawrence Ltd on HP			
Jan 3	Lawrence Ltd	Dr	1,600	
	Bank			1,600
	Being payment of initial deposit under HP agreement			
Dec 31	Lawrence Ltd	Dr	712	
	HP interest expense	Dr	288	
	Bank			1,000
	Being apportionment of annual instalment between capital repayment and interest			
19X2				
Dec 31	Lawrence Ltd	Dr	797	
	HP interest expense	Dr	203	
	Bank			1,000
	Being apportionment of annual instalment between capital repayment and interest			

19X3					
Dec 31	Lawrence Ltd	Dr	891		
	HP interest expense	Dr	109		
	Bank				1,000
	Being apportionment of annual instalment between capital repayment and interest				

(b) Rule of '78 method

Total payments = £1,600 + 1,000 + 1,000 + 1,000 = £4,600
Total interest = £4,600−£4,000 = £600

Sum of the years' digits = 3 + 2 + 1 = 6
Interest allocation:
19X1 = 3/6 × £600 = £300
19X2 = 2/6 × £600 = £200
19X3 = 1/6 × £600 = £100

The journal

			Debit £	Credit £
19X1				
Jan 3	Plant & machinery	Dr	4,000	
	Lawrence Ltd			4,000
	Being purchase of machine from Lawrence Ltd on HP			
Jan 3	Lawrence Ltd	Dr	1,600	
	Bank			1,600
	Being payment of initial deposit under HP agreement			
Dec 31	Lawrence Ltd	Dr	700	
	HP interest expense	Dr	300	
	Bank			1,000
	Being apportionment of annual instalment between capital repayment and interest			
19X2				
Dec 31	Lawrence Ltd	Dr	800	
	HP interest expense	Dr	200	
	Bank			1,000
	Being apportionment of annual instalment between capital repayment and interest			
19X3				
Dec 31	Lawrence Ltd	Dr	900	
	HP interest expense	Dr	100	
	Bank			1,000
	Being apportionment of annual instalment between capital repayment and interest			

22. Investment accounts

22.1

		Nominal	Income	Capital			Nominal	Income	Capital
				6% Government Stock					
19X0					19X0				
May 1	Cash—				July 1	Cash—			
	Purchase	34,000	680	25,840		interest		1,020	
Sept 30	Profit & loss—				Sept 30	Balance c/d	34,000	510	25,840
	Interest		850						
		34,000	1,530	25,840			34,000	1,530	25,840
19X0					19X0				
Oct 1	Balance b/d	34,000	510	25,840	Dec 1	Cash—sale	33,000	(165)	25,575
Dec 1	Profit & loss—				19X1				
	profit on sale			495	Jan 1	Cash—			
19X1						interest		1,020	
Sept 30	Profit & loss—				July 1	Cash—			
	Interest		390			interest		30	
					Sept 30	Balance c/d	1,000	15	760
		34,000	900	26,335			34,000	900	26,335
Oct 1	Balance b/d	1,000	15	760					

Workings

Purchase 1 May 19X0
Price = £34,000 @ 78 = £26,520
Interest = 4 mths @ 6% pa × £34,000 = £680
Capital = £26,520−£680 = £25,840

Interest received 1 July 19X0
6 mths@ 6% pa × £34,000 = £1,020

Interest accrued 30 September 19X0
3 mths @ 6% pa × £34,000 = £510

Sale 1 December 19X0
Price = £33,000 @ 77 = £25,410
Interest = 1 mth @ 6% × £33,000 = £165
Capital = £25,410 + £165 = £25,575
Cost of sale = £33,000/£34,000 × £25,840 = £25,080
Profit on sale = £25,575−£25,080 = £495

Interest received 19X0/X1
1 January 19X1—
6 mths @ 6% × £34,000 = £1,020
1 July 19X1—
6 mths @ 6% × £1,000 = £30

Interest accrued 30 September 19X1
3 mths @ 6% × £1,000 = £15

23. Departmental and branch accounts

23.4

		Memo				Memo	
				Branch stock account			
Stock b/d		9,360	8,320	Returned by			
Goods to branch		100,080	88,960	branch	1,008	896	
P & L—gross profit		—	9,836	Debtors—sales	54,000	54,000	
				Bank—cash sales	43,200	43,200	
				Branch expenses	1,944	1,944	
				Reduction in selling prices	1,098	—	
				Balances c/d: stock	7,380	6,560	
				goods in transit	540	480	
				cash at branch	36	36	
				Stock loss	234	—	
		109,440	107,116		109,440	107,116	

Balances b/d:

stock	7,380	6,560
goods in transit	540	480
cash at branch	36	36

Branch debtors

Balance b/d	10,000	Bank	48,000
Branch stock	54,000	Balance c/d	16,000
	64,000		64,000
Balance b/d	16,000		

Goods sent to branch

Branch stock— returns	896	Branch stock— goods sent	88,960
HO trading account (or purchases)	88,064		
	88,960		88,960

Branch expenses

Branch stock	1,944	Branch P & L	1,944

Cash book

Branch stock	43,200
Branch debtors	48,000

Branch profit & loss account

Local expenses	1,944	Branch stock— gross profit	9,836
Net profit c/d	7,892		
	9,836		9,836
Capital account	7,892	Net profit b/d	7,892

Note

1. The arithmetic accuracy of the gross profit can be checked as follows:

$$\left(\frac{12^{1}/_{2}}{100 + 12^{1}/_{2}} \times [54,000 + 43,200 + 1,944 + 1,098 + 36] \right) - \left(\left[\frac{100}{100 + 12^{1}/_{2}} \times 234 \right] + 1,098 \right)$$

$$= 11,142 - 1,306 = 9,836$$

23.5

Branch stock account

Stock b/d	9,360	Returned by branch	1,008
Goods to branch	100,080	Debtors—sales	54,000
		Bank—cash sales	43,200
		Branch expenses	1,944
		Stock mark-up— reduction in prices	1,098
		Balances c/d:	
		stock	7,380
		goods in transit	540
		cash at branch	36
		Stock mark-up— stock loss	234
	109,440		109,440
Balances b/d:			
stock	7,380		
goods in transit	540		
cash at branch	36		

Branch stock mark-up

	£		£
Returned by branch	112	Unrealized profit b/d	1,040
Branch stock:		Goods to branch	11,120
reduction in prices	1,098		
stock loss	234		
Unrealized profit c/d:			
stock	820		
goods in transit	60		
P & L—gross profit	9,836		
	12,160		12,160

Unrealized profit b/d:		
stock		820
goods in transit		60

Note

1. All the other accounts will be the same as those in the answer to Question 23.4.

23.6

Branch stock

	£000 Memo	£000		£000 Memo	£000
Goods to branch	120	80	Cash received	56	56
Gross profit	—	26	Branch expenses	5	5
			Balances c/d:		
			stock	18	12
			debtors	12	12
			cash at branch	2	2
			cash in transit	9	9
			goods in transit	15	10
			Stock loss	3	—
	120	106		120	106

Total branch sales = 56 + 5 + 12 + 2 + 9 = £84

The Hat Shop
Profit & loss accounts
For the year ended 30 April 19X7

	Head Office £000	£000	Branch £000	£000	Combined £000	£000
Sales		114		84		198
Less: cost of sales						
Stock at 1 May 19X6	13		—		13	
Purchases (147−80)/transfers	67		80		147	
	80		80		160	
Less: stock at 30 Apl 19X7	4		22		26	
(12 + 10)		76		58		134
Gross profit		38		26		64
Less: expenditure						
Expenses (10 + 5)	16		15		31	
Depreciation	1		2		3	
		17		17		34
Net profit for year		21		9		30

The Hat Shop
Balance sheet as at 30 April 19X7

	£000 Cost	£000 Agg.depn.	£000 WDV
Fixed assets			
Premises (9 + 1)	25	10	15
Fixtures and fittings	8	2	6
	33	12	21

Current assets

Stocks (4 + 12 + 10)	26	
Debtors	12	
Bank	6	
Cash (9 +2)	11	55
Net assets		76

Capital

Balance at 1 May 19X6	46
Add: profit for the year	30
Balance at 30 April 19X7	76

23.7

Branch stock account

	£000		£000
Goods to branch	120	Cash received	56
		Branch expenses	5
		Balances c/d:	
		stock	18
		debtors	12
		cash at branch	2
		cash in transit	9
		goods in transit	15
		Stock mark-up a/c—	
		stock loss	3
	120		120
Balances b/d:			
stock	18		
debtors	12		
cash at branch	2		
cash in transit	9		
goods in transit	15		

Branch stock mark-up

	£000		£000
Unrealised profit c/d:		Goods to branch	40
stock	6		
goods in transit	5		
Branch stock—			
stock loss	3		
P & L—gross profit	26		
	40		40
		Unrealized profit b/d:	
		stock	6
		goods in transit	5

Note

1. The profit and loss accounts and balance sheet will be the same as in the answer to Question 23.6

23.9 *Workings*

Branch current account

Balance b/d	46,000	Goods to branch—	
		goods in transit	12,000
		Cash in transit	10,000
		Balance c/d	24,000
	46,000		46,000
Balance b/d	24,000		

Goods sent to branch

Branch current—		Balance b/d	166,000
goods in transit	12,000		
P & L account	154,000		
	166,000		166,000

Goods in transit

P & L account—   10,000
(100/120 × £12,000)

Cash in transit

Branch current   10,000

Stocks
At 1 July 19X7 at branch at cost
= 100/120 × £9,000 = £7,500
At 1 July 19X7 combined = £15,000 + £7,500 = £22,500
At 30 June 19X8 at branch at cost
= 100/120 × £24,000 = £20,000
At 30 June 19X8 at head office at cost
= £20,000 + (100/120 × £12,000) = £30,000
At 30 June 19X8 combined
= £30,000 + £20,000 = £50,000

Provision for unrealised profit
At 30 June 19X8
= 20/120 × £24,000 = £4,000
Increase in provision
= £4,000−£1,500 = £2,500

(a) Mapp
Profit & loss accounts
For the year ended 30 June 19X8

	Head office £000	Head office £000	Branch £000	Branch £000	Combined £000	Combined £000
Sales-external		350		215		565
—internal		154		—		—
		504				
Less: cost of sales						
Stock at 1 July 19X7	15		9		22.5	
Add: purchases	225		154		225	
	240		163		247.5	
Less: stock at 30 June 19X8	30		24		50	
		210		139		197.5
Gross profit		294		76		367.5
Less: expenditure						
Administrative expenses	135		9		144	
Distribution costs	30		12		42	
		165		21		186
		129		55		181.5
Less: increase in provision for unrealised profit		2.5		—		—
Net profit		126.5		55		181.5

(b) Mapp
Balance sheets as at 30 June 19X8

	Head office £000	Head office £000	Branch £000	Branch £000	Combined £000	Combined £000
Fixed assets						
Plant & machinery		383		38		421
Current assets						
Stocks	30		24		50	
Debtors	15		20		35	
Bank & cash (19 + 10)	29		2		31	
	74		46		116	

Less: current liabilities					
Creditors	22.5		5	27.5	
Net current assets		51.5	41		88.5
		434.5	79		509.5
Branch current account					
(24 + 55)	79		—	—	
Less: provision for					
unrealised profit	4	75	—	—	—
Net assets		509.5	79		509.5
Capital/HO current account					
Balance b/f		328	24		328
Add: net profit		181.5	55		181.5
Balance c/f		509.5	79		509.5

24. The final accounts of partnerships

24.7 *Workings*

Interest on loan:
  Hammond—5% × £20,000 × 3/12 = £250

Interest on capital:
  Clayton—(8% × £90,000) + (8% × £10,000 × 8/12) = £7,733
  Hammond—8% × £60,000 = £4,800

Interest on drawings:
  Clayton—
  4% × £3,000 × 9/12 = £ 90
  4% × £5,000 × 4/12 = £ 67
  £157

  Hammond—
  4% × £2,000 × 9/12 = £ 60
  4% × £1,000 × 4/12 = £ 13
  £ 73

Clayton and Hammond
Profit & loss appropriation account 30 June 19X6

	£	£		£	£
Interest on loan:			Net profit b/d		67,500
Hammond		250			
			Interest on		
Salaries:			drawings:		
Clayton	17,000				
Hammond	13,000	30,000	Clayton	157	
			Hammond	73	230
Interest on capital:					
Clayton	7,733				
Hammond	4,800	12,533			
Shares of residual					
profit:					
Clayton	12,474				
Hammond	12,473	24,947			
		67,730			67,730

Current account

	Clayton £	Hammond £		Clayton £	Hammond £
Drawings	8,000	3,000	Balance b/d	16,850	9,470
Interest on drawings	157	73	Interest on		
Balance c/d	45,900	36,920	loan	—	250
			Salaries	17,000	13,000
			Interest on		
			capital	7,733	4,800
			Shares of		
			residual		
			profit	12,474	12,473
	54,057	39,993		54,057	39,993
			Balance b/d	45,900	36,920

Capital

	Clayton	Hammond		Clayton	Hammond
			Balance b/d	90,000	60,000
			Bank	10,000	—
				100,000	60,000

Loan—Hammond

Bank	20,000

24.10 Workings

Interest on loan:
  Peace—5% × £2,000 × 3/12 = £25

Interest on capital:
  Peace-
  10% × (£10,000−£1,000−£2,000) = £700
  10% × £1,000 × 9/12   = £ 75
                                £775

Quiet—10% × £5,000 = £500

Interest on drawings:
  Peace—8% × £2,200 × 8/12 = £117
  Quiet—8% × £1,800 × 4/12 = £48

Peace & Quiet
Trading and profit and loss account
For the year ended 31 December 19X8

	£	£
Sales		69,830
Less: cost of sales		
Stock at 1 Jan 19X8	6,630	
Add: purchases	45,620	
	52,250	
Less: stock at 31 Dec 19X8	5,970	
		46,280
Gross profit		23,550
Less: expenditure		
Shop assistants salaries	5,320	
Light & heat (1,850 + 60)	1,910	
Stationery (320−50)	270	
Bank interest and charges	45	
Depreciation on equipment		
10% × (8,500−1,200)	730	
		8,275
Net profit		15,275

Profit & loss appropriation account 31 December 19X8

	£	£	£
Net profit			15,275
Add: Interest on drawings—			
Peace		117	
Quiet		48	165
			15,440
Less: Interest on loan—Peace		25	
Interest on capital—			
Peace	775		
Quiet	500	1,275	
Salaries—			
Peace	6,200		
Quiet	4,800	11,000	
			12,300
			3,140
Shares of residual profit—			
Peace			1,570
Quiet			1,570
			3,140

Current accounts

	Peace	Quiet		Peace	Quiet
Drawings	2,200	1,800	Balance	1,280	3,640
Interest on drawings	117	48	Interest on		
Balance c/d	7,533	8,662	loan	25	—
			Interest on		
			capital	775	500
			Salaries	6,200	4,800
			Shares of		
			residual		
			profit	1,570	1,570
	9,850	10,510		9,850	10,510
			Balance b/d	7,533	8,662

Capital accounts

	Peace	Quiet		Peace	Quiet
Loan account	2,000		Balance b/d	10,000	5,000
Balance c/d	8,000	5,000			
	10,000	5,000		10,000	5,000
			Balance b/d	8,000	5,000

Peace & Quiet
Balance sheet as at 31 December 19X8

	£	£	£
Fixed assets	*Cost*	*Agg.depn.*	*WDV*
Leasehold shop	18,000	—	18,000
Equipment (1,200 + 730)	8,500	1,930	6,570
	26,500	1,930	24,570
Current assets			
Stock		5,970	
Stationery		50	
Debtors		1,210	
Bank		3,815	
		11,045	

Less: current liabilities			
Creditors	4,360		
Accrued expenses	60	4,420	
Net current assets			6,625
Net assets			31,195
Capital	*Peace*	*Quiet*	
Capital accounts	8,000	5,000	13,000
Current accounts	7,533	8,662	16,195
	15,533	13,662	29,195
Loan—Peace			2,000
			31,195

24.11 *Workings*

Interest on loan:
  Peter—5% × £12,000 = £600

Interest on capital:
  Peter—10% × £100,000 = £10,000
  Paul—10% × £80,000 = £8,000

Interest on drawings:
  Peter—5% × £6,000 × 4/12 = £100
  Paul—5% × £8,000 × 9/12 = £300

Peter & Paul
Trading and profit & loss accounts
For the year ended 30 June 19X8

	£	£
Sales (56,332−200)		56,132
Less: cost of sales		
Stock at 1 July 10X7	6,734	
Add: purchases	19,868	
	26,602	
Less: stock at 30 June 19X8	8,424	
		18,178
Gross profit		37,954
Add: decrease in provision for bad debts		
(216−180)		36
		37,990
Less: expenditure		
Light & heat (3,428−58 + 82)	3,452	
Warehouses wages (23,500−6,000−8,000)	9,500	
Rates (5,169−34)	5,135	
Postage & telephone	4,257	
Printing & stationery	2,134	
Selling expenses	1,098	
Bad debts	240	
Depreciation—plant & machinery		
(10% × 77,000)	7,700	
Depreciation—vehicles		
(20% × 36,500)	7,300	
Depreciation—loose tools		
(1,253 −927)	326	
		41,142
Net loss		3,152

Profit & loss appropriation account 30 June 19X8

	£	£
Net loss for year		3,152
Add: Interest on loan—Peter		600
Interest on capital—		
Peter	10,000	
Paul	8,000	18,000
Salaries—		
Peter	20,000	
Paul	18,000	38,000
		59,752
Less: Interest on drawings—		
Peter	100	
Paul	300	400
		59,352
Shares of residual loss—		
Peter		29,676
Paul		29,676
		59,352

The ledger

Current accounts

	Peter	Paul		Peter	Paul
Balance b/d	804	—	Balance b/d	—	21,080
Drawings	6,000	8,000	Interest on		
Interest on			loan	600	—
drawings	100	300	Interest on		
Shares of			capital	10,000	8,000
residual loss	29,676	29,676	Salaries	20,000	18,000
Balance c/d	—	9,104	Balance c/d	5,980	—
	36,580	47,080		36,580	47,080
Balance b/d	5,980	—	Balance b/d	—	9,104

Peter & Paul
Balance sheet as at 30 June 19X5

	£	£	£
Fixed assets	Cost or	Agg.	WDV
	valuation	depn.	
Freehold premises	115,000	—	115,000
Plant & machinery (22,800 + 7,700)	77,000	30,500	46,500
Motor vehicles (12,480 + 7,300)	36,500	19,780	16,720
Loose tools	1,253	326	927
	229,753	50,606	179,147
Current assets			
Prepayments		34	
Stock (8,264 + 160)		8,424	
Debtors (4,478−200−240)	4,038		
Less: provision for band debts	180	3,858	
Bank		7,697	
		20,013	
Less: current liabilities			
Creditors	3,954		
Accruals	82	4,036	
Net current assets			15,977
Net assets			195,124
Capital	Peter	Paul	
Capital accounts	100,000	80,000	180,000
Current accounts	(5,980)	9,104	3,124
	94,020	89,104	183,124
Loan—Peter			12,000
			195,124

24.12

	Depreciation on sale £	Depreciation this year £
Workings—vehicles		
Depreciation on disposal:		
19X7—10% × £2,400 × 9/12	180	
19X8—10% × £2,400	240	
19X9—10% × £2,400 × 10/12	200	200
Aggregate depreciation	620	
Book value = £2,400−£620 = £1,780		
Profit on sale = £1,900−£1,780 = £120		
Depreciation on remainder:		
10% × (£30,000−£2,400)		2,760
		2,960

Aggregate depreciation at 31 December 19X9:
£18,000 + £2,960−£620 = £20,340

Simon, Wilson & Dillon
Trading and profit & loss accounts
For the year ended 31 December 19X9

	£	£	£
Sales			130,000
Less: returns			400
			129,600
Less: cost of sales			
Stock at 1 Jan 19X9		34,900	
Add: purchases	64,000		
Less: returns	600	63,400	
		98,300	
Less: stock at 31 Dec 19X9		31,000	67,300
Gross profit			62,300
Add: investment income			
(800 + 320)			1,120
profit on sale of vehicle			120
			63,540
Less: expenditure			
Salesmen's salaries		19,480	
Rates (12,100−160)		11,940	
Motor expenses (2,800 + 240)		3,040	
Mortgage interest (8% × 40,000)		3,200	
Printing and stationery (1,100−170)		930	
Bad debts		2,000	
Provision for bad debts—			
2% × (28,000 − 2,000)−400		120	
Provision for depreciation—			
Vehicles		2,960	
Tools (1,200−960)		240	
Bank charges		130	44,040
Net profit c/d			19,500

Profit & loss appropriation account 31 December 19X9

	£	£	£
Net profit b/d			19,500
Less: salaries—			
Simon	15,000		
Dillon	10,000		
		25,000	
Interest on capital—			
Simon (10% × 35,000)	3,500		
Wilson (10% × 25,000)	2,500		
Dillon (10% × 10,000)	1,000		
		7,000	

	£	£	£
			32,000
			(12,500)
Shares of residual loss—			
Simon			5,000
Wilson			5,000
Dillon			2,500
			12,500

The ledger

Current accounts

	S	W	D		S	W	D
Balance b/d	—	—	1,800	Balance b/d	5,600	4,800	—
Shares of				Salaries	15,000	—	10,000
residual loss	5,000	5,000	2,500	Interest	3,500	2,500	1,000
Balance c/d	19,100	2,300	6,700				
	24,100	7,300	11,000		24,100	7,300	11,000
				Balance b/d	19,100	2,300	6,700

Simon, Wilson & Dillon
Balance sheet as at 31 December 19X9

	£	£	£
	Cost	Agg.depn.	WDV
Fixed assets			
Freehold land & buildings			
(65,000 + 5,000)	70,000	—	70,000
Delivery vehicles (30,000−2,400)	27,600	20,340	7,260
Loose tools	1,200	240	960
	98,800	20,580	78,220
Goodwill			11,000
Unquoted investments			6,720
			95,940
Current assets			
Prepayments		160	
Stocks (31,000 + 170)		31,170	
Sundry debtor		1,900	
Debtors (28,000−2,000)	26,000		
Less: provision for bad debts	520	25,480	
Bank (10,100−130)		9,970	
Income accrued		320	
		69,000	
Less: current liabilities			
Accruals (240 + 1,600)	1,840		
Creditors	25,000	26,840	
Net current assets			42,160
Total assets less current liabilities			138,100
Less: long term liabilities			
8% mortgage on premises			40,000
Net assets			98,100
Capital accounts—			
Simon			35,000
Wilson			25,000
Dillon			10,000
			70,000
Current accounts			
Simon		19,100	
Wilson		2,300	
Dillon		6,700	28,100
			98,100

Notes

1. It is assumed that the unquoted investments are intended to be kept for more than one accounting year.
2. The capital and current accounts could have been presented in the balance sheet in columnar form.

25.   Changes in partnerships

25.7   Workings

				£
	Shares of goodwill:			
	Brown $^1/_2$ × £90,000			45,000
	Jones $^1/_2$ × £90,000			45,000
				90,000
	Jones $^3/_5$ × £90,000			54,000
	Smith $^2/_5$ × £90,000			36,000
				90,000

The ledger

Revaluation account

Stock		4,000	Premises	35,000
Provision for bad debts		3,000	Fixtures	8,000
Profit—				
Brown	18,000			
Jones	18,000	36,000		
		43,000		43,000

Capital

	Brown	Jones	Smith		Brown	Jones	Smith
Goodwill	—	54,000	36,000	Balance b/d	110,000	87,000	—
Cash	173,000	—	—	Cash	—	—	100,000
Balance c/d		96,000	64,000	Profit on revaluation	18,000	18,000	—
				Goodwill	45,000	45,000	—
	173,000	150,000	100,000		173,000	150,000	100,000
				Balance b/d	—	96,000	64,000

25.8   Workings

	£
Valuation of goodwill:	
Net asset value before revaluation (£30,100−£2,500)	27,600
Less: loss on revaluation (see below)	600
Net asset value after revaluation	27,000
Estimated profit for 19X9	48,750
Less: partners salaries (3 @ £15,000)	45,000
Earnings/super profit	3,750

$$\text{P–E ratio} = \frac{\text{price}}{\text{earnings}}$$

∴ Price = earnings × P–E ratio

Capitalised value of estimated super profits = £3,750 × 8 = £30,000

Goodwill = £30,000 − £27,000 = £3,000

The ledger

Vehicles

Balance b/d	7,000	
Revaluation	1,500	
	8,500	

Stock

Balance b/d	9,200	Revaluation	1,200
		Balance c/d	8,000
	9,200		9,200
Balance b/d	8,000		

Provision for bad debts

	Revaluation	900

Revaluation account

Stock	1,200	Vehicles		1,500
Provision for bad debts	900	Loss on revaluation—		
		Capital B	200	
		Capital P	200	
		Capital N	200	
				600
	2,100			2,100

Capital

	B	P	N	L		B	P	N	L
Revaluation	200	200	200	—	Balance b/d	10,000	8,000	5,000	—
Loan					Bank	—	—	—	6,000
account	—	—	5,800	—	Goodwill	1,000	1,000	1,000	—
Balance c/d	10,800	8,800	—	6,000					
	11,000	9,000	6,000	6,000		11,000	9,000	6,000	6,000
					Balance b/d	10,800	8,800	—	6,000

Goodwill

Capital—Blackburn	1,000
Capital—Percy	1,000
Capital—Nelson	1,000
	3,000

Current account—Nelson

Loan account	1,400	Balance b/d	1,400

Loan—Nelson

	Capital account	5,800
	Current account	1,400
		7,200

26. The nature of limited companies and their capital

26.5

Ordinary/equity shares	*Preference shares*	*Loan stock/debentures*
1. Owners of the company who are normally entitled to vote at general meetings of the company's shareholders (eg. To elect directors)	1. No voting rights	1. No voting rights
2. Receive a dividend the rate of which is decided annually by the company's directors. It varies each year depending on the profit and is an appropriation of profit	2. Receive a fixed rate of dividend each year which constitutes an appropriation of profit. Have priority over ordinary dividends	2. Receive a fixed rate of interest which constitutes a charge against income in computing the profit. Have priority over preference dividends
3. Last to be repaid the value of their shares in the event of the company going into liquidation	3. Repaid before the ordinary shareholders in the event of liquidation	3. Repaid before the ordinary and preference shareholders in the event of liquidation
4. Non-repayable except on the liquidation of the company	4. All but one particular type are non-repayable except on liquidation	4. Normally repayable after a fixed period of time
5. Rights in Articles of Association	5. Rights in Articles of Association	5. Rights specified in the terms of of issue
6. Dividends non-deductible for tax purposes	6. Dividens non-deductible for tax purposes	6. Interest deductible for tax purposes

27.   The final accounts of limited companies

27.19 *D. Cooper Ltd*
Profit and loss account
For the year ended 30 September 19X9

	£	£
Sales		135,250
Less: Cost of sales		
Stock at 1 October 19X8	9,400	
Add: purchases	49,700	
	59,100	
Less: stock at 30 September 19X9	13,480	
		45,620
Gross profit		89,630
Add: Investment income		650
		90,280
Less: Expenditure		
Director's salaries	22,000	
Rates (4,650−1,150)	3,500	
Light and heat	3,830	
Plant hire	6,600	
Interest on debentures (10% × 24,000)	2,400	
Preliminary expenses	1,270	
Provision for bad debts		
(10% × 11,200)−910	210	
Audit fees	1,750	
Bad debts	700	
Depreciation on plant (15% × 80,000)	12,000	
Depreciation on tools (9,100−7,800)	1,300	
		55,560
Profit on ordinary activities before taxation		34,720
Less: tax on profit on ordinary activities		6,370
Profit on ordinary activities after taxation		28,350
Less: Dividends—		
preference (7% × 25,000)	1,750	
ordinary (3,250 + 13,000)	16,250	18,000
Retained profit for the financial year		10,350
Less: Transfer to reserve		2,500
		7,850

D Cooper Ltd
Balance sheet as at 30 September 19X9

	£	£	£
Fixed assets	*Cost or Valuation*	*Agg. depn.*	*WDV*
Leasehold premises	140,000	—	140,000
Plant and machinery	80,000	25,100	54,900
Loose tools	13,000	5,200	7,800
	233,000	30,300	202,700
Goodwill			20,000
			222,700
Current assets			
Stock		13,480	
Prepayments		1,150	
Debtors	11,200		
Less: provision for bad debts	1,120	10,080	
Listed investments		8,000	
		32,710	
Less: creditors: amounts falling due within one year			
Creditors	8,300		
Bank overdraft	7,800		
Corporation tax	6,370		

Debenture interest (2,400−1,200)	1,200		
Preference dividends	1,750		
Ordinary dividends	13,000	38,420	
Net current liabilities			(5,710)
Total assets less current liabilities			216,990
Less: creditors: amounts falling due after more than one year			
10% debentures			24,000
Net assets			192,990
Authorised, allotted and called-up share capital			
100,000 Ordinary shares of £1 each			100,000
50,000 7% Preference shares of 50p each			25,000
			125,000
Reserves			
Share premium		35,000	
Revaluation reserve		9,860	
Revenue reserve (10,200 + 2,500)		12,700	
Profit and loss account (2,580 + 7,850)		10,430	
			67,990
Shareholders interests			192,990

Notes

1. Preliminary expenses could have been written off against the balance on the share premium account instead of being charged to the profit and loss account.
2. It is assumed that listed investments will be held for less than one accounting year.
3. Aggregate depreciation on plant and machinery = £80,000−£66,900 + £12,000 = £25,100.
4. Aggregate depreciation on loose tools = £13,000−£7,800 = £5,200.

27.20 *L Johnson Ltd*
Profit and loss account
For the year ended 31 December 19X8

	£	£	£
Turnover			130,846
Less: returns inwards			1,629
Net sales			129,217
Less: cost of sales—			
Stock at 1 January 19X8		9,436	
Add: purchases	78,493		
Less: returns outwards	1,834	76,659	
		86,095	
Less: stock at 31 December 19X8		12,456	73,639
Gross profit			55,578
Add: Other income			
Reduction in provision for bad debts			
(860−[5% × 11,600])			280
Discount received			270
Dividends received			310
Share transfer fees			126
			56,564
Less: Expenditure			
Wages and salaries		5,948	
Bad debts		656	
Discount allowed		492	
Directors' emoluments		13,000	
Rates (596−100)		496	
Light and heat (1,028 + 220)		1,248	
Audit fee		764	
Depreciation on:			
vehicles (25% × 29,400)	7,350		
plant (20% × 32,950)	6,590		
development costs (10% × 6,600)	660	14,600	
Debenture interest (10% × 30,000)		3,000	40,204

Profit on ordinary activities before taxation		16,360
Less: tax on profit on ordinary activities		2,544
Profit on ordinary activities after taxation		13,816
Less; dividends—		
preference shares (5% × 50,000)	2,500	
ordinary shares (6.25 × 80,000)	5,000	7,500
Retained profit for the financial year		6,316
Less: transfer to revenue reserve		4,000
		2,316

L Johnson Ltd
Balance sheet as at 31 December 19X8

	£	£	£
Fixed assets	*Cost or*	*Agg.*	*WDV*
	Valuation	*depn.*	
Freehold buildings	137,000	—	137,000
Motor vehicles	35,000	12,950	22,950
Plant & machinery	40,000	13,640	26,360
Development costs	10,000	4,060	5,940
	222,000	30,650	191,350
Goodwill			10,000
			201,350
Current assets			
Prepayments		100	
Stock		12,456	
Debtors	11,600		
Less: provision for bad debts	580	11,020	
Listed investments		4,873	
		28,449	
Less: creditors: amounts falling due within one year			
Accruals	220		
Creditors	8,450		
Bank overdraft	3,643		
Debenture interest	3,000		
Corporation tax	2,544		
Preference dividend (2,500−1,250)	1,250		
Ordinary dividend	5,000	24,107	
Net current assets			4,342
Total assets less current liabilities			205,692
Less: creditors: amounts falling due after more than one year			
10% debentures			30,000
Net assets			175,692
Authorised capital			
200,000 ordinary shares of £1 each			200,000
90,000 5% preference shares of £1 each			90,000
			290,000
Allotted and called-up share capital			
80,000 ordinary shares of £1 each			80,000
50,000 5% preference shares of £1 each			50,000
			130,000
Reserves			
Share premium (5,600−250)		5,350	
Revaluation reserve		13,500	
Capital redemption reserve		9,000	
Revenue reserve (8,400 + 4,000)		12,400	
Profit & loss account (3,126 + 2,316)		5,442	45,692
Shareholders interests			175,692

Notes

1. It is assumed that the listed investments are to be held for less than one accounting year.

2. Aggregate depreciation on:
    motor vehicles = £35,000−£29,400 + £7,350 = £12,950
    plant & machinery = £40,000−£32,950 + £6,590 = £13,640
    development costs = £10,000−£6,600 + £660 = £4,060

27.21 *Oakwood Ltd*
Profit & loss account
For the year ended 30 June 19X5

	£	£	£
Sales (120,640−1,000)			119,640
Less: returns inwards			230
Net sales			119,410
Less: cost of sales			
Stock at 1 July 19X4		8,760	
Add: purchases	81,230		
Less: returns outwards	640		
	80,590		
Add: carriage inwards	310	80,900	
		89,660	
Less: stock at 30 June 19X5		12,180	
(11,680 + 500)			77,480
Gross profit			41,930
Add: other income			
Discount received		300	
Interest received		410	
Share transfer fees		140	
Provision for bad debts		260	
(5% × [10,400−1,000])−730			1,110
			43,040
Less: expenditure			
Administrative salaries		6,370	
Bad debts		740	
Discount allowed		290	
Audit fee		390	
Directors remuneration		14,100	
Rates (600−150)		450	
Light & heat (940 + 270)		1,210	
Postage & telephone		870	
Consumable tools		300	
Debenture interest (10% × 20,000)		2,000	
Depreciation on—			
development costs (25% × 5,400)		1,350	
vehicles (10% × 18,700)		1,870	
plant (20% × [31,900−300])		6,320	
			36,260
Profit on ordinary activities before taxation			6,780
Less: tax on profit on ordinary activities			1,080
Profit on ordinary activities after taxation			5,700
Add: retained profit of previous years			7,700
			13,400
Less: dividends—			
preference (5% × 60,000)		3,000	
ordinary (2,000 + [3.2 × 125,000])		6,000	9,000
Undistributed profits			4,400
Less: transfer to reserve			3,000
Retained profit at end of financial year			1,400

Oakwood Ltd
Balance sheet as at 30 June 19X5

	£	£	£
Fixed assets	Cost	Agg. depn.	WDV
Freehold buildings	165,000	—	165,000
Development costs	12,000	7,950	4,050
Delivery vehicles	28,000	11,170	16,830
Plant & machinery (34,000−300)	33,700	8,420	25,280
	238,700	27,540	211,160
Goodwill			8,000
			219,160
Current assets			
Prepayments		150	
Stock (11,680 + 500)		12,180	
Debtors (10,400−1,000)	9,400		
Less: provision for bad debts	470	8,930	
Listed investments		3,250	
		24,510	
Less: creditors: amounts falling due within one year			
Accruals	270		
Creditors	7,890		
Bank overdraft	2,630		
Corporation tax	1,080		
Debenture interest	2,000		
Preference dividends (3,000−1,500)	1,500		
Proposed ordinary dividend	4,000	19,370	
Net current assets			5,140
Total assets less current liabilities			224,300
Less: creditors: amounts falling due after more than one year			
10% Debentures			20,000
Net assets			204,300
		Authorised	Called-up
Share capital			
Ordinary shares of £1 each		150,000	125,000
5% Preference shares of £1 each		70,000	60,000
		220,000	185,000
Reserves			
Share premium (9,000−200)		8,800	
Revenue reserve (6,100 + 3,000)		9,100	
Profit & loss account		1,400	19,300
Shareholders interests			204,300

Notes

1. It is assumed that the investments are to be held for less than one accounting year.
2. Aggregate depreciation on:
    development costs = £12,000−£5,400 + £1,350 = £7,950
    delivery vehicles = £28,000−£18,700 + £1,870 = £11,170
    plant & machinery = £34,000−£34,900 + £6,320 = £8,420

27.25 (a) (i) *Topaz Ltd*
Profit & loss account for the year ended 31 December 19X6

	£000	£000
Turnover:		
Continuing operations		68,000
Discontinued operations		13,000
		81,000
Cost of sales (41 + 8)m		(49,000)
Gross profit		32,000
Net operating expenses (6 + 1 + 4 + 2)m		(13,000)

Operating profit

Continuing operations (68−41−6−4)m	17,000	
Discontinued operations (13−8−1−2)m	2,000	
		19,000
Profit on disposal of discontinued operations		2,500
Reorganization costs of continuing operations		(1,800)
Profit on ordinary activities before interest		19,700
Interest payable		(1,000)
Profit on ordinary activities before taxation		18,700
Tax on profit on ordinary activities		(4,800)
Profit on ordinary activities after taxation		13,900
Dividends (2 + 4)m		(6,000)
Retained profit for the financial year		7,900

Notes

1. *Analysis of cost of sales and net operating expenses*

	Continuing £'000	Discontinued £'000
Cost of sales	41,000	8,000
Net operating expenses:		
Distribution costs	6,000	1,000
Administrative expenses	4,000	2,000
	10,000	3,000

2. *Distribution costs* for continuing operations include a bad debt of £1.9m that is regarded as an exceptional item under FRS3.

(ii) **Statement of total recognized gains and losses**

	£'000
Profit for the financial year	13,900
Unrealized surplus on revaluation of properties	4,000
Total gains (and losses) relating to the year and recognized since last annual report	17,900

(b) The reasons why the changes to the profit and loss account introduced by FRS3 improve the quality of information available to users of the financial statements are because they facilitate more meaningful comparisons over time, with other companies and/or forecasts. They also facilitate more accurate predictions of future profits, cash flows, dividends, etc. This is achieved because FRS3 requires an analysis of turnover and operating profit between continuing operations, acquisitions and discontinued operations. It also demands the disclosure of various exceptional items, extraordinary items, and prior period adjustments. For example, exceptional items, include profits or losses on the disposal of discontinued operations. This is a classic example of an item that users would need to exclude in making predictions of future profits based on the current years results because it is of a non-recurring nature.

28.   Changes in share capital

28.7   *Workings*

Application and allotment
Application money = 300K @ £0.20 = £60K
Refunded = 50K @ £0.20 = £10K
Allotment money = (200K @ £20)−(50K @ £0.20) = £30K
Share premium per share = £0.60−£0.50 = £0.10
Total share premium = 200K @ £0.10 = £20K
Nominal value of application and allotment =
    200K @ (£0.20 + £0.20−£0.10) = £60K

Call
Nominal value of call = 200K @ £0.20 = £40K
Call money received = 190K @ £0.20 = £38K

Forfeiture
Called up value of forfeited shares excluding the share premium =
    10K @ £0.50 = £5K
Premium included in the amount called up relating to forfeited shares =
    10K @ £0.10 = £1K
Amount in call account relating to arrears on forfeited shares =
    10K @ £0.20 = £2K

Reissue
Reissue money received = 10K @ £0.40 = £4K
Nominal value of shares reissued =
    10K @ £0.50 = £5K

Bonus issue
(800K + 200K) ÷ 4 = 250K @ £0.50 = £125K

The ledger

Cash

Application	60,000	Application-refund	10,000
Allotment	30,000	Balance c/d	122,000
Call	38,000		
Reissue	4,000		
	132,000		132,000
Balance b/d	122,000		

Application and allotment

Cash—refund	10,000	Cash—application	60,000
Share capital	60,000	Cash—allotment	30,000
Share premium	20,000		
	90,000		90,000

Share capital

Forfeited shares	5,000	Balance b/d	400,000
Balance c/d	625,000	Appl. & allot.	60,000
		Call	40,000
		Reissue	5,000
		Bonus issue	125,000
	630,000		630,000
		Balance b/d	625,000

Share premium

Forfeited shares	1,000	Appl. & allot.	20,000
Share capital—		Reissue	3,000
Bonus issue	22,000		
	23,000		23,000

Call

Share capital	40,000	Cash	38,000
		Forfeited shares	2,000
	40,000		40,000

Forfeited shares

Call	2,000	Share capital	5,000
Reissue	4,000	Share premium	1,000
	6,000		6,000

Shares reissued

Share capital	5,000	Cash	4,000
Share premium	3,000	Forfeited shares	4,000
	8,000		8,000

Revenue reserves

Share capital—		Balance b/d	350,000
bonus issue	103,000		
(125,000−22,000)			
Balance c/d	247,000		
	350,000		350,000
		Balance b/d	247,000

Check: *Balance sheet*	£
Share capital	625,000
Revenue reserves	247,000
	872,000
Sundry assets	750,000
Cash	122,000
	872,000

28.8 *(a)* **Journal**

				Debit £	Credit £
19X2					
Aug 1	Preference shares	Dr		40,000	
	Share premium	Dr		2,000	
	Cash				42,000
				42,000	42,000
	Being redemption of 40,000 preference shares				
Aug 1	Profit & loss account	Dr		40,000	
	Capital redemption reserve				40,000
	Being transfer of distributable profits to capital reserve due to redemption of shares				
Sept 15	Cash	Dr		21,000	
	Application & allotment				21,000
	Being application money on issue of ordinary shares				
Sept 15	Application & allotment	Dr		3,500	
	Cash				3,500
	Being refund of application money for 5,000 shares				
Sept 20	Cash	Dr		12,500	
	Application & allotment				12,500
	Being balance of allotment money received				
Sept 20	Application & allotment	Dr		30,000	
	Ordinary share capital				25,000
	Share premium				5,000
				30,000	30,000
	Being allotment of 25,000 ordinary shares				
Sept 29	Preference shares	Dr		40,000	
	Share premium	Dr		2,000	
	Cash				42,000
				42,000	42,000
	Being redemption of remaining preference shares				
Sept 29	Profit & loss account	Dr		15,000	
	Capital redemption reserve				15,000
	Being transfer of distributable profits to capital reserve due to redemption of shares				

(a) *Winder Engineering plc*
  Balance sheet as at 30 September 19X2

	£	£
Sundry assets		380,000
Cash (60−42 + 21−3.5 + 12.5−42)		6,000
		386,000
Issued share capital		
225,000 ordinary shares of £1 each		225,000
Reserves		
Share premium (20−2 + 5−2)	21,000	
Capital redemption reserve (40 + 15)	55,000	
Profit & loss (140−40 −15)	85,000	161,000
Shareholders interests		386,000

29. The appraisal of company accounts using ratios

29.7 When answering questions such as this with apparently open ended requirements that do not specify which ratios to calculate, it is very important to consider the data carefully in order to decide what ratios should be computed. First, not that these are sole traders not companies. Second, a related point, as in the case of companies where no share price is given, it is not possible to compute the return on investment ratios. Third, there are no long term liabilities and thus no gearing ratio. Fourth, search the requirements carefully for key words and phrases such as in this question, performance and financial position. The latter is often taken to include solvency, liquidity and the appraisal of working capital. Fifth, the number of ratios you are expected to compute may be influenced by the marks/time allocated to the question.

The ACCA suggested answer contains references to the following accounting ratios:

	White	*Black*
Return on capital employed	$\frac{£48}{£192} \times 100 = 25\%$	$\frac{£48}{£160} \times 100 = 30\%$
Gross profit to sales	$\frac{£150}{£600} \times 100 = 25\%$	$\frac{£176}{£800} \times 100 = 22\%$
Net profit to sales	$\frac{£48}{£600} \times 100 = 8\%$	$\frac{£48}{£800} \times 100 = 6\%$
Turnover of capital employed	$\frac{£600}{£192} = 3.125$	$\frac{£800}{£160} = 5$
Stock turnover	$\frac{£450}{£56} = 8$	$\frac{£624}{£52} = 12$
Debtors collection period	$\frac{£75}{£600} \times 52 = 6.5$ weeks	$\frac{£67}{£800} \times 52 = 4.4$ weeks
Creditors period of credit	$\frac{£38}{£450} \times 52 = 4.4$ weeks	$\frac{£78}{£624} \times 52 = 6.5$ weeks
Liquidity ratio	$\frac{£75 + £8}{£38} = 2.2$	$\frac{£67}{£78 + £4} = 0.82$

Comparison of ratios

1. Black has a higher ROCE than White which shows that it is more profitable.
2   Black has a lower GP and NP to sales (profit margin) than White which suggests either higher unit costs and/or lower selling prices.
3. Black has a higher turnover of capital employed (asset turnover) than White. The lower profit margin and higher asset turnover ratio may be the result of selling large quantities at a lower price. This strategy appears to be resulting in a higher ROCE.
4. Black has a higher stock turnover ratio and longer period of credit from creditors than White, and a lower debtors collection period. This suggests that Black is more effective and efficient at controlling its working capital.
5. Black has a considerably lower liquidity ratio than White which shows that it is stretching itself financially and may encounter liquidity problems.

Overall impressions

Blacks performance is superior to Whites. It is more profitable, has a higher level of activity and better control of working capital. However, Black appears to have a weak liquidity position. This may be the result of overtrading.

Further information needed

1. Do either of Black or White work in their businesses? If one does and the other does not the profit is not strictly comparable without a notional salary for the one who does work in the business.
2. There is a difference in accounting policy for the depreciation of buildings. Black has a charge of £5,000 whereas White has no depreciation. This distorts comparisons. Are there any other differences in accounting policies?
3. Are there differences between the two businesses in the ages of their fixed assets such as equipment and vehicles? These will also make comparisons misleading.
4. What differences are there between the two businesses with regard to their trading policies? For example, Blacks lower margin (and presumably selling prices) may be offset by higher selling and distribution expenses.

29.8

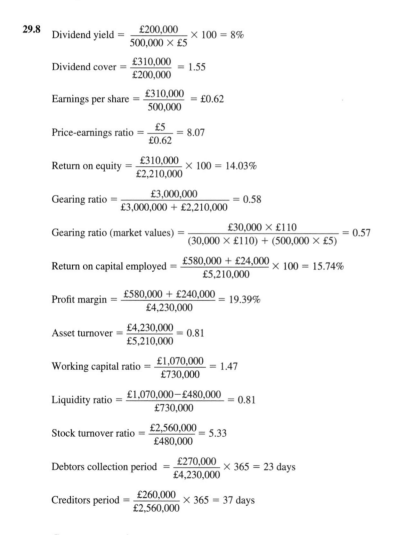

$$\text{Dividend yield} = \frac{£200,000}{500,000 \times £5} \times 100 = 8\%$$

$$\text{Dividend cover} = \frac{£310,000}{£200,000} = 1.55$$

$$\text{Earnings per share} = \frac{£310,000}{500,000} = £0.62$$

$$\text{Price-earnings ratio} = \frac{£5}{£0.62} = 8.07$$

$$\text{Return on equity} = \frac{£310,000}{£2,210,000} \times 100 = 14.03\%$$

$$\text{Gearing ratio} = \frac{£3,000,000}{£3,000,000 + £2,210,000} = 0.58$$

$$\text{Gearing ratio (market values)} = \frac{£30,000 \times £110}{(30,000 \times £110) + (500,000 \times £5)} = 0.57$$

$$\text{Return on capital employed} = \frac{£580,000 + £24,000}{£5,210,000} \times 100 = 15.74\%$$

$$\text{Profit margin} = \frac{£580,000 + £240,000}{£4,230,000} = 19.39\%$$

$$\text{Asset turnover} = \frac{£4,230,000}{£5,210,000} = 0.81$$

$$\text{Working capital ratio} = \frac{£1,070,000}{£730,000} = 1.47$$

$$\text{Liquidity ratio} = \frac{£1,070,000 - £480,000}{£730,000} = 0.81$$

$$\text{Stock turnover ratio} = \frac{£2,560,000}{£480,000} = 5.33$$

$$\text{Debtors collection period} = \frac{£270,000}{£4,230,000} \times 365 = 23 \text{ days}$$

$$\text{Creditors period} = \frac{£260,000}{£2,560,000} \times 365 = 37 \text{ days}$$

Comments on ratios

(1) The dividend cover is somewhat low and the gearing ratio is rather high. These make the ordinary shares a risky investment.

(2) The working capital and liquidity ratios are weak in indicating a poor liquidity position and possible insolvency.
(3) The asset turnover ratio appears low (but may be because company is capital intensive).
(4) The return on equity and return on capital employed are reasonable indicating satisfactory profitability.
(5) The dividend yield is high which means an above average return on investment.
(6) The debtors and creditors ratios are very low. See below.
(7) The P–E ratio, profit margin and stock turnover ratio are probably about normal.

Limitations include:

(1) The lack of comparative figures for previous years and other companies means generalisations about the results can only be tentative.
(2) It is not possible to make judgements about the acceptability of these ratios without knowing the type of industry and the current economic climate.
(3) The ratios may be distorted since they are calculated using historic cost data.
(4) The calculation of some ratios necessitates the use of surrogate data which may give misleading results. For example, the debtors (and creditors) collection period appears to be extremely low which may be because the turnover (cost of sales) includes cash sales (purchases).

29.9   The following are points that should be included in a report.

Comparison of ratios

1. The dividend yield of Chips plc is relatively high.
2. The dividend cover of Fish plc is relatively high.
3. The EPS are not really comparable.
4. The PE ratio of Fish plc is above average; earnings growth may be expected. The PE ratio of Chips plc is slightly below average; little growth in earnings may be expected.
5. The ROCE suggests Fish plc has made more profitable use of its assets.
6. The profit margin indicates Chips plc has higher selling prices and/or lower unit costs.
7. The asset turnover suggests both companies are capital intensive but Fish plc has higher level but Fish plc has higher level of activity.
8. The gearing of Chips plc is high suggesting greater financial risk.
9. The high gearing ratio of Chips plc has probably resulted in a larger return on equity.

Overall impressions

Fish plc may be a better investment because it has a lower financial risk (ie. low gearing and high dividend cover), is more profitable (ie. greater ROCE), and has a higher level of activity (ie. asset turnover). Also, although Fish plc has a lower dividend yield, it probably offers growth in earnings (and thus dividends) resulting from retained profits (as shown by the high dividend cover and PE ratio). It appears to be pursuing a policy of low selling prices, high turnover, and expansion by internal financing from retained profits.

In contrast Chips plc provides a higher dividend yield but with greater risk.

29.10   The following are points that should be included in a report.

Comparison of ratios

1. The working capital ratio has improved but the liquidity ratio has got worse. This suggests a possible build up of stocks.
2. The stock turnover has slowed which also points to either an increase in stocks and/or a decrease in sales.
3. The debtors ratio shows that debtors are being allowed to take a considerably longer period of credit.
4. The creditors ratio shows that this company is taking longer to pay its debts.

Overall impressions

A deterioration in liquidity and control of working capital. It appears that there is overstocking, poor stock control, and a relaxation of credit control procedures.

30.   Cash and funds flow statements

30.15 *A Brooks*
Cash flow statement
For the year ended 30 June 19X7

	£	£
Sources of cash funds		
Capital introduced		20,000
Decrease in debtors (5,400−4,100)		1,300
Increase in creditors (6,200−4,800)		1,400
		22,700
Applications of cash funds		
Net loss for the year	(1,800)	
Less: provision for depreciation		
(14,500−13,000)	1,500	
Funds applied in operations	(300)	
Drawings	(7,600)	
Repayment of bank loan (15,000−10,000)	(5,000)	
Purchase of fixed assets (72,000−65,000)	(7,000)	
Increase in stock (7,300−6,700)	(600)	
		(20,500)
Increase in cash and bank balance		2,200
Bank balance at 30 June 19X6 (overdraft)		(1,300)
Cash & bank balance at 30 June 19X7		900

30.16 *A Brooks*
Notes to the cash flow statement
1. *Reconciliation of operating loss to net cash inflow from operating activities*

	£
Operating loss (1,800 + 900−1,250)	(1,450)
Depreciation charges	1,500
Increase in stock (7,300−6,700)	(600)
Decrease in debtors (5,400−4,100)	1,300
Increase in creditors (6,200−4,800)	1,400
Net cash inflow from operating activities	2,150

A   Brooks
Cash flow statement
For the year ended 30 June 19X7

	£	£
Net cash inflow from operating activities		2,150
Returns on investments and servicing of finance		
Interest received	900	
Interest paid	(1,250)	(350)
Taxation		—
Capital expenditure		
Payments to acquired tangible fixed assest (72,000−65,000)		(7,000)
		(5,200)
Equity dividends paid		—
		(5,200)
Management of liquid resources		
Financing		—
Capital introduced	20,000	
Drawings	(7,600)	
Repayment of bank loan (15,000−10,000)	(5,000)	7,400
Increase in cash		2,200

Notes to the cash flow statement (continued)
2. *Reconciliation of net cash flow to movement in net debt*

	£
Increase in cash in period	2,200
Cash to repay bank loan	5,000
Change in net debt	7,200
Net debt at 1 July 19X6 (15,000 + 1,300)	(16,300)
Net debt at 30 June 19X7 (10,000−900)	(9,100)

3. *Analyis of changes in net debt*

	At 1 July 19X6 £	Cash flows £	At 30 June 19X7 £
Cash in hand, at bank	—	900	900
Overdrafts	(1,300)	1,300	—
		2,200	
Debt due after 1 year	(15,000)	5,000	(10,000)
Total	(16,300)	7,200	(9,100)

30.17 *A Brooks*
Statement of source and application of funds
For the year ended 30 June 19X7

	£	£
Source of funds		
Capital introduced		20,000
Application of funds		
Net loss for the year	(1,800)	
Less: provision for depreciation		
(14,500−13,000)	1,500	
Funds applied in operations	(300)	
Drawings	(7,600)	
Repayment of bank loan (15,000−10,000)	(5,000)	
Purchase of fixed assets (72,000−65,000)	(7,000)	
		(19,900)
		100
Increase (decrease) *in working capital*		
Increase in creditors (6,200−4,800)	(1,400)	
Decrease in debtors (5,400−4,100)	(1,300)	
Increase in stock (7,300−6,700)	600	
Increase in cash and bank (900 + 1,300)	2,200	
		100

30.19 *Workings*

Provision for depreciation plant

19X3				19X3			
Dec 31	Plant—			Jan 1	Balance b/d		7,000
	depn. on disposal			Dec 31	Profit & loss		6,500
	(10,000−6,000)	4,000					
Dec 31	Balance c/d	9,500					
		13,500					13,500

The charge to the profit & loss account in respect of depreciation on plant for the year of £6,500 is the difference between the two sides of the above account.

Plant

19X3				19X3			
Jan 1	Balance b/d		41,000	Dec 31	Bank—disposal		6,400
Dec 31	Profit & loss—			Dec 31	Depn. On disposal		
	profit on sale		400		(10,000−6,000)		4,000
Dec 31	Bank—			Dec 31	Balance c/d		48,000
	acquisitions		17,000				
			58,400				58,400

The cost of plant acquired of £17,000 is the difference between the two sides of the above account.

J Kitchens Ltd
Cash flow statement
For the year ended 31 December 19X3

	£	£
Sources of cash funds		
Profit for the year	24,000	
Add (*less*): Adjustments for items not involving		
the movement of funds—		
Depreciation on plant (workings above)	6,500	
Depreciation on premises (9,000−6,000)	3,000	
Profit on sale of plant (6,400−6,000)	(400)	
Increase in provision for bad debts		
(600−400)	200	
Funds generated from operations		33,300
Proceeds of sale of plant		6,400
		39,700
Applications of cash funds		
Dividends paid (9,000 + 8,000)	(17,000)	
Purchases of plant (workings above)	(17,000)	
Increase in stock (22,500−14,900)	(7,600)	
Increase in debtors		
(16,400 + 600)−(11,300 + 400)	(5,300)	
Decrease in creditors (19,700−17,600)	(2,100)	
		(49,000)
Decrease in cash & cash equivalents		(9,300)
Cash & cash equivalents at 31 Dec 19X2		(500)
Cash & cash equivalents at 31 Dec 19X3		(9,800)

30.20 *Workings*
See answer to Question 19.

J. Kitchens Ltd
Notes to the cash flow statement

1. *Reconciliation of operating profit to net cash inflow from operating activities*

	£	£
Operating profit (24,000 + 750)		24,750
Depreciation charges—		
plant (see workings)	6,500	
premises (9,000−6,000)	3,000	9,500
Profit on sale of tangible fixed assests		
(6,400−6,000)		(400)
Provision for bad debts (600−400)		200
Increase in stock (22,500−14,900)		(7,600)
Increase in debtors		
(16,400 + 600)−(11,300 + 400)		(5,300)
Decrease in creditors (19,700−17,600)		(2,100)
Net cash inflow from operating activities		19,050

J. Kitchens Ltd
Cash flow statement
For the year ended 31 December 19X3

	£	£
Net cash inflow from operating activities		19,050
Returns on investments and servicing of finance		
Interest paid		(750)
Taxation		—
Capital expenditure		
Payments to acquire tangible fixed assets		
(see workings)	(17,000)	
Receipts from sales of tangible fixed assets	6,400	(10,600)

	7,700
Equity dividends paid (9,000 + 8,000)	(17,000)
	(9,300)
Management of liquid resources	—
Financing	—
Decrease in cash	(9,300)

Notes to the cash flow statement (continued)

2. *Reconciliation of net cash flow to movement in net debt*

	£
Decrease in cash in the period	(9,300)
Change in net debt	(9,300)
Net debt at 1 Jan 19X3	(500)
Net debt at 31 Dec 19X3	(9,800)

3. *Analysis of changes in net debt*

	At 1 Jan 19X3 £	Cash flow £	At 31 Dec 19X3 £
Overdrafts	(500)	(9,300)	(9,800)

30.21 Workings
See answer to Question 19

J. Kitchens Ltd
Statement of source and application of funds
For the year ended 31 December 19X3

	£	£
Source of funds		
Profit for the year	24,000	
Add (less): Adjustments for items not involving the movement of funds—		
Depreciation on plant (see workings)	6,500	
Depreciation on premises (9,000−6,000)	3,000	
Profit on sale of plant (6,400−6,000)	(400)	
Increase in provision for bad debts (600−400)	200	
Funds generated from operations		33,300
Funds from other sources—		
Proceeds of sale of plant		6,400
		39,700
Application of funds		
Dividends paid (9,000 + 8,000)	(17,000)	
Purchases of plant (see workings)	(17,000)	
		(34,000)
		5,700
Increase (decrease) in working capital		
Increase in stock (22,500−14,900)	7,600	
Increase in debtors		
(16,400 + 600)−(11,300 + 400)	5,300	
Decrease in creditors (19,700−17,600)	2,100	
Decrease in cash & cash equivalents		
(9,800−500)	(9,300)	
		5,700

30.22 *Workings*

Provision for depreciation

19X9			19X8		
May 31	Fixed assets—		May 31	Balance b/d	28,000
	depn. On		19X9		
	disposal		May 31	Profit & loss	13,500
	(12,000−7,500)	4,500			
May 31	Balance c/d	37,000			
		41,500			41,500

The charge to the profit and loss account in respect of depreciation for the year of £13,500 is the difference between the two sides of the above account.

Computation of profit before taxation and dividends

	£	£
Increase in balance on P & L account		
(5,200−3,400)		1,800
Transfer to reserve (6,900−4,200)		2,700
Ordinary dividends—		
interim	6,400	
proposed final	21,800	
		28,200
Corporation tax		7,200
		39,900

L. Tyler Ltd
Cash flow statement
For the year ended 31 May 19X9

	£	£
Sources of cash funds		
Profit for the year before tax & dividends	39,900	
Add: (*less*): Adjustments for items not		
involving the movement of funds—		
Provision for depreciation (see workings)	13,500	
Profit on sale of fixed assets (8,100−7,500)	(600)	
Increase in provision for bad debts (700−500)	200	
Funds generated from operations		53,000
Issue of shares		
(70,000−60,000) + (34,000−25,000)		19,000
Proceeds of sale of fixed assets		8,100
Decrease in stock (21,600−19,400)		2,200
		82,300
Application of cash funds		
Tax paid	(5,800)	
Dividends paid (19,600 + 6,400)	(26,000)	
Repayment of loan stock (30,000−5,000)	(25,000)	
Increase in debtors (14,200−11,800)	(2,400)	
Decrease in creditors (8,400−6,700)	(1,700)	
		(60,900)
Increase in cash & cash equivalents		21,400
Cash & cash equivalents at 31 May 19X8		
(3,900 + 4,600)		8,500
Cash & cash equivalents at 31 May 19X9		
(17,100 + 12,800)		29,900

30.23 *Workings*

See answer to Question 22.

L. Tyler Ltd
Notes to the cash flow statement
1. *Reconciliation of operating profit to net cash inflow from operating activities*

	£
Operating profit (39,900 + 1,600−1,800)	39,700
Depreciation charges (see workings)	13,500
Profit on sale of tangible fixed assets (8,100−7,500)	(600)
Provision for bad debts (700−500)	200
Decrease in stock (21,600−19,400)	2,200
Increase in debtors (14,200−11,800)	(2,400)
Decrease in creditors (8,400−6,700)	(1,700)
Net cash inflow from operating activities	50,900

L. Tyler Ltd
Cash flow statement
For the year ended 31 May 19X9

	£	£
Net cash inflow from operating activities		50,900
Returns on investments and servicing of finance		
Interest received	1,800	
Interest paid	(1,600)	200
Taxation		(5,800)
Capital expenditure		
Receipts from sales of fixed assets		8,100
		53,400
Equity dividends paid (19,600 + 6,400)		(26,000)
		27,400
Management of liquid resources		
Purchase of investments (17,100−3,900)		(13,200)
Financing		
Issuing of ordinary share capital		
(70,000−60,000) + (34,000−25,000)	19,000	
Repayment of loan stock (30,000−5,000)	(25,000)	(6,000)
Increase in cash		8,200

Notes to the cash flow statement (continued)

2. *Reconciliation of net cash flow to movement in net debt*

	£
Increase in cash in the period	8,200
Cash to repay loan stock	25,000
Cash used to increase liquid resources (17,100−3,900)	13,200
Change in net debt	46,400
Net debt at 1 June 19X8 (30,000−[3,900+ 4,600])	(21,500)
Net funds at 31 May 19X9 (5,000−[17,100 + 12,800])	24,900

3. *Analysis of changes in net debt*

	At 1 June 19X8	Cash flows	At 31 May 19X9
	£	£	£
Cash in hand, at bank	4,600	8,200	12,800
Debt due after 1 year	(30,000)	25,000	(5,000)
Current asset investments	3,900	13,200	17,100
Total	(21,500)	46,400	24,900

30.24 *Workings*
See answer to Question 22

L. Tyler Ltd
Statement of source and application of funds
For the year ended 31 May 19X9

	£	£
Source of funds		
Profit for the year before tax & dividends	39,900	
Add (*Less*): Adjustments for items not		
involving the movement of funds—		
Provision for depreciation (see workings)	13,500	
Profit on sale of fixed assets (8,100−7,500)	(600)	
Increase in provision for bad debts (700−500)	200	
Funds generated from operations		53,000
Funds from other sources—		
Issue of shares		19,000
(70,000−60,000) + (34,000−25,000)		
Proceeds of sale of fixed assets		8,100
		80,100
Application of funds		
Tax paid	(5,800)	
Dividends paid (19,600 + 6,400)	(26,000)	
Repayment of loan stock (30,000−5,000)	(25,000)	
		(56,800)
		23,300
Increase (*decrease*) *in working capital*		
Decrease in stock (21,600−19,400)	(2,200)	
Increase in debtors (14,200−11,800)	2,400	
Decrease in creditors (8,400−6,700)	1,700	
Increase in cash & cash equivalents	21,400	
(17,100 + 12,800)−(3,900 + 4,600)		23,300

31.   Value added tax, columnar books of prime entry and the payroll

31.4 *The journal*

		Debit £	Credit £
Wages & salaries	Dr.	7,820	
Bank/cash			5,170
Inland revenue			2,650
		7,820	7,820

Being record of payroll for w/e 24 Jan. 19X9

Workings
Net wages = £6,800−(£950 + £680) = £5,170
Inland Revenue = £950 + £680 + £1,020 = £2,650

31.8 (*a*) (*i*) *Purchases day book*

Date		Total	Repair materials	Tools and equipment	Appliances for resale
19X5		£	£	£	£
Jan	Dee & Co.	337.74		337.74	
	AB Supplies	528.20	528.20		
Feb	Simpson	141.34	141.34		
	Cotton Ltd.	427.40			427.40
	Dee & Co.	146.82	146.82		
March	AB Supplies	643.43	643.43		
	Simpson	95.60	95.60		
		2,320.53	1,555.39	337.74	427.40

(ii) Sales day book

Date		Total	Repair work	Appliance sales
19X5		£	£	£
Jan	D. Hopkins	362.80	362.80	
	P. Bolton	417.10	417.10	
Feb	G. Leivers	55.00		55.00
	M. Whitehead	151.72	151.72	
	N. John Ltd	49.14		49.14
	A. Linnekar	12.53		12.53
March	E. Horton	462.21	462.21	
	S. Ward	431.08	431.08	
	W. Scothern	319.12	319.12	
	N. Annable	85.41	85.41	
		2,346.11	2,229.44	116.67

(b) Cash book (debit side)

Date	Item	Discount allowed	Total	Debtors	Repair work	Appliance sales	Sundries
19X5		£	£	£	£	£	£
Jan	Capital		250.00				250.00
	Loan		2,000.00				2,000.00
	Repairs		69.44		69.44		
Feb	D. Hopkins	5.80	357.00	357.00			
	Repairs		256.86		256.86		
Mar	P. Bolton		417.10	417.10			
	G. Leivers		55.00	55.00			
	A. Linnekar		12.53	12.53			
	S. Ward	5.08	426.00	426.00			
	Repairs		182.90		182.90		
	Appliances		112.81			112.81	
		10.88	4,139,64	1,267.63	509.20	112.81	2,250.00
						Capital	250.00
						Loan	2,000.00
							2,250.00

Cash book (credit side)

Date	Item	Discount received	Total	Creditors	Repair materials	Drawings and bank	Expenses
19X5		£	£	£	£	£	£
Jan	Repair materials		195.29		195.29		
	Rent		400.00				400.00
	Rates		150.00				150.00
	Stationery		32.70				32.70
	Car expenses		92.26				92.26
	Drawings		160.00			160.00	
Feb	Repair materials		161.03		161.03		
	Sundries		51.54				51.54
	Car expenses		81.41				81.42
	Drawings		160.00			160.00	
Mar	Dee & Co.	7.74	330.00	330.00			
	AB Supplies		528.20	528.20			
	Simpson	3.34	138.00	138.00			
	Cotton Ltd		130.00	130.00			
	Dee & Co	6.82	140.00	140.00			

Repair materials		22.06		22.06		
Sundries		24.61				24.61
Car expenses		104.52				104.52
Drawings		160.00			160.00	
Bank		500.00			500.00	
	17.90	3,561.63	1,266.20	378.38	980.00	937.05
Balance c/d		578.01				
		4,139.64				

Drawings	480.00	
Bank	500.00	
	980.00	

Rent	400.00
Rates	150.00
Stationery	32.70
Car expenses	278.20
Sundries	76.15
	937.05

(c)

Creditors ledger control

19X5		£	19X5		£
March	Cash paid	1,266.20	March	Purchases	2,320.53
	Discount received	17.90			
	Balance c/d	1,036.43			
		2,320.53			2,320.53
			April	Balance b/d	1,036.43

Debtors ledger control

		£			£
March	Sales	2,346.11	March	Cash received	1,267.63
				Discount allowed	10.88
				Balance c/d	1,067.60
		2,346.11			2,346.11
April	Balance b/d	1,067.60			

(d)

Sales

		Repairs £	Appliances £			Repairs £	Appliances £
March	Trading account	2,738.64	229.48	March	Debtors ledger control	2,229.44	116.67
					Cash received	509.20	112.81
		2,738.64	229.48			2,738.64	229.48

Cost of sales

		Repairs £	Appliances £			Repairs £	Appliances £
March	Creditors ledger control	1,555.39	427.40	March	Stock c/d	691.02	320.58
					Trading a/c	1,242.75	106.82
	Cash paid	378.38					
		1,933.77	427.40			1,933.77	427.40

(e)
M. Faraday
Trading and profit and loss account
For the quarter ended 31 March 19X5

	Repairs £	Appliances £	Total £
Sales	2,738.64	229.48	2,968.12
Cost of sales	1,242.75	106.82	1,349.57
Gross profit	2,495.89	122.66	1,618.55

(f)	*Add*: Discount received		17.90
			1,636.45
	Less:		
	Discount allowed	10.88	
	Rent (400.00−200.00 prepaid)	200.00	
	Rates	150.00	
	Stationery	32.70	
	Car expenses	278.20	
	Sundry expenses	76.15	
	Heating and lighting	265.00	
	Loan interest (10% × £2,000 × $^3/_{12}$)	50.00	
	Depreciation:		
	car (700.00−600.00)	100.00	
	tools and equipment		
	(337.74−300.00)	37.74	
			1,200.67
	Net profit		435.78

(g)
M. Faraday
Balance sheet as at 31 March 19X5

	Cost £	Depn. £	Net £
Fixed assets			
Tools and equipment	337.74	37.74	300.00
Car	700.00	100.00	600.00
	1,037.74	137.74	900.00
Current assets			
Stocks: repair materials	691.02		
: appliances	320.58		
		1,011.60	
Debtors		1,067.60	
Prepayments		200.00	
Bank		500.00	
Cash		578.01	
		3,357.21	
Less current liabilities			
Creditors	1,036.43		
Accruals (£50 interest plus			
£265 heating)	315.00		
		1,351.43	
Net current assets			2,005.78
Total assets less current liabilities			2,905.78
Less: *long term liabilities*			
10% loan			2,000.00
Net assets			905.78
Capital: opening (700 + 250)		950.00	
Add: net profit for quarter		435.78	
		1,385.78	
Less: drawings		480.00	
Capital: closing			905.78

31.9 *Purchases day book*

Date	Name of creditor	Total	VAT	Purchases	Motor expenses	Misc.
19X7		£	£	£	£	£
Dec 3	English Coal	470	70	400		
Dec 4	Solihull Garage	282	42		240	
Dec 7	Scottish Coal	376	56	320		
Dec 13	Solihull Garage	423	63		360	
Dec 15	Solihull Garage	4,700	700			4,000
Dec 16	English Telecom	658	98			560
		6,909	1,029	720	600	4,560

Sales day book

Date	Name of debtor	Total	VAT	Sales	Misc.
19X7		£	£	£	£
Dec 6	Black	705	105	600	
Dec 12	White	940	140	800	
Dec 17	Solihull Garage	2,350	350		2,000
		3,995	595	1,400	2,000

*Cash book (**debit side**)*

Date	Details	Total	VAT	Debtors	Disc. allow.	Sales	Misc
19X7		£	£	£	£	£	£
Dec 1	Balance b/d	5,000					5,000
Dec 10	Sales	611	91			520	
Dec 18	Sales	752	112			640	
Dec 23	Motor vehicle	3,525	525				3,000
Dec 28	Black	680		680	25		
Dec 29	White	905		905	35		
		11,473	728	1,585	60	1,160	8,000
19X8							
Jan 1	Balance b/d	7,727					

*Cash book (**credit side**)*

Date	Details	Total	VAT	Creditors	Disc. rec'd	Purchases	Stationery	Misc
19X7		£	£	£	£	£	£	£
Dec 5	Stationery	282	42				240	
Dec 8	Wages	350						350
Dec 11	Purchases	846	126			720		
Dec 14	Purchases	564	84			480		
Dec 19	Motor expenses	720						720
Dec 20	Stationery	188	28				160	
Dec 30	English Coal	450		450	20			
Dec 31	Scottish Coal	346		346	30			
		3,746	280	796	50	1,200	400	1,070
Dec 31	Balance c/d	7,727						
		11,473						

The ledger

Sales

	£	19X7		£
		Dec 31	Total per SDB	1,400
		Dec 31	Total per CB	1,160
				2,560

Black

19X7						
Dec 6	Sales + VAT	705	Dec 28	Bank		680
			Dec 28	Discount allowed		25
		705				705

White

Dec 12	Sales + VAT	940	Dec 29	Bank	905
			Dec 29	Discount allowed	35
		940			940

Purchases

Dec 31	Total per PDB	720
Dec 31	Total per CB	1,200
		1,920

English Coal

Dec 30	Bank	450	Dec 3	Purchases + VAT	470
Dec 30	Discount received	20			
		470			470

Scottish Coal

Dec 31	Bank	346	Dec 7	Purchases + VAT	376
Dec 31	Discount received	30			
		376			376

Motor expenses

Dec 19	Bank	720
Dec 31	Total per PDB	600
		1,320

Motor vehicles

Dec 15	Solihull Garage	4,000	Dec 17	Solihull Garage	2,000
			Dec 23	Bank	3,000

Solihull Garage

Dec 17	Vehicles + VAT	2,350	Dec 4	Motor expenses + VAT	282
Dec 31	Balance c/d	3,055	Dec 13	Motor expenses + VAT	423
			Dec 15	Vehicles + VAT	4,700
		5,405			5,405
			Jan 1	Balance b/d	3,055

Telephone & postage

Dec 16	English Telecom	560

English Telecom

		Dec 16	Telephone + VAT	658

Printing & stationery

Dec 31	Total per CB	400

Wages

Dec 8	Bank	350

Discount allowed

Dec 31	Total per CB	60

Discount received

		Dec 31	Total per CB	50

VAT

Dec 31	Total per PDB	1,029	Dec 31	Total per SDB	595
Dec 31	Total per CB	280	Dec 31	Total per CB	728
Dec 31	Balance c/d	14			
		1,323			1,323
			Jan 1	Balance b/d	14

32.   The use of computers in accounting

32.4   If the 'look and feel' of software resembles that of traditional book-keeping this is likely to have several advantages for the staff who are using it. Many of them will have had training in book-keeping, or will have previous experience of book-keeping using paper records. If they find that the headings and terminology are familiar, they will feel comfortable with the software, which should mean that they will have fewer problems learning how to use it. This should reduce the costs of training staff, and make it easier to recruit clerks to look after the entering of data and other routine activities on the system.

Staff will also be less likely to make mistakes, particularly if they have responsibility for activities such as entering corrections via journals or setting up new account codes on the ledgers, since they should find that all the nomenclature is clear and unambiguous.

If the software presents its output and reports in the format used for conventional financial reports, these will be readily understood by a wide range of people. As far as they are concerned, the fact that a computer system has been used in the preparation of the report will be irrelevant.

Finally, the ability of external auditors to check the accounts should be improved, since the entries adhere to all the normal conventions, and the auditors will know exactly where to look for the entries which they expect to find.

An example of a function which might present accounting information in a new and different way is in order tracking. In a conventional accounting system, the information about any particular order will be fairly limited and difficult to get at. The individual events in the life of the order (the order receipt, despatch, invoice, payment, etc) will be recorded as a series of separate entries in books or on forms.

The computerised system, on the other hand, can link all these events together and present them in a combined report on the screen. It can also tap into records held as part of the stock control or manufacturing systems in the company, enabling an account clerk to find out whether the goods ordered have left the warehouse or are still being manufactured. The computer software should also be better at presenting more complex situations, such as those where orders have been part-filled or substitutions have been made.

Thus by focusing on the progress of the order over time (which is the way the customer sees it) rather than the entries in the accounting books (which represent the way accountants see things) the clerk should be able to respond quickly to enquiries from customer and thereby encourage them to feel that the company is efficient and concerned about their well-being.

33.   Accounting for changing price levels

33.8   *(a)   Workings*

HCA sales = (50 × 4) @ F5 = F1,000

CPPA sales = $F1,000 \times \dfrac{105}{102.5}$ = F1,024

CPPA cost of sales = $F500 \times \dfrac{105}{100}$ = F525

CPPA loss from holding monetary assets—cash of F1,000: $\dfrac{105 - 102.5}{102.5} \times F1,000$ = F24

Sally Johnson
Profit & loss account
For the week ended

	HCA	RCA	CPPA
	F	F	F
Sales	1,000	1,000	1,024
Less: cost of sales	500	650	525
Operating profit	500	350	499
Less: loss from holding			
monetary assets	—	—	24
Net profit	500	350	475

Sally Johnson
Balance sheet as at

	HCA	RCA	CPPA
	F	F	F
Assets			
Cash	1,000	1,000	1,000
Capital			
Introduced	500	500	500
Capital maintenance reserve	—	150	25
Net profit	500	350	475
	1,000	1,000	1,000

(b)

The HCA profit of F500 may be useful if Sally returns home after a week's holiday and thus does not intend to replace the melons or make further purchases in Francs (although this ignores the effect of inflation on the exchange rate). Generally HCA is of limited usefulness where the replacement cost of assets or inflation is rising.

However, the question implies that Sally intends to replace the melons. Since the cost has risen by F150, she needs to provide for the increased replacement cost, which means that her profit on a RCA basis is only F350. RCA is useful because it takes into account the increased replacement cost of the goods sold.

The purchasing power of Sally's capital of F500 has reduced by 5% of F500 = F25 which means that her profit on a CPPA basis is only F475. CPPA is useful because it takes into account the reduction in the purchasing power of a currency. It is also said to make accounts more comparable over time since they are computed on a uniform basis.

In this case, because the replacement cost of melons is greater than the historical cost and the inflation adjusted cost, it may be argued that RCA is more useful than either HCA or CPPA.

34.   The conceptual framework of accounting

34.8   According to the Accounting Standards Board (ASB), *Statement of Principles for Financial Reporting* (1991), the purposes of a conceptual framework of accounting are to:

1. assist the Board in the development of future accounting standards and in its review of existing accounting standards;
2. assist the Board by providing a basis for reducing the number of alternative accounting treatments permitted by law and accounting standards;
3. assist preparers of financial statements in applying accounting standards and in dealing with topics that do not form the subject of an accounting standard;
4. assist auditors in forming an opinion whether financial statements conform with accounting standards;
5. assist users of financial statements in interpreting the information contained in financial statements prepared in conformity with accounting standards; and
6. provide those who are interested in the work of the Board with information about its approach to the formulation of accounting standards.

34.9   Various authors and bodies have described the nature and contents of a conceptual framework of accounting in simple terms as an agreed set of answers to the following sorts of question: For whom are accounts to be prepared? For what purposes do they want to use them? What kind of accounting reports do they want? How far are present accounts suitable for these purposes, and how could we improve accounting practice to make them more suitable? (ASC, 1978).

Probably one of the most concise definitions of a conceptual framework of accounting is contained in the Accounting Standards Committee, *Setting Accounting Standards: a consultative document* (1978), as follows:

'a set of broad, internally consistent fundamentals and definitions of key terms' (ASC, 1978).

Another slightly more informative definition is provided by the Financial Accounting Standards Board in its *Scope and Implications of the Conceptual Framework Project* (1976), as follows:

'a constitution, a coherent system of interrelated objectives and fundamentals that can lead to consistent standards and that prescribe the nature, function and limits of financial accounting and financial statements' (FASB, 1976).

The contents of a conceptual framework of accounting are set out in the Accounting Standards Board, *Statement of Principles for Financial Reporting* (1995) as follows:

1. *The objective of financial reporting* including the users of financial statements and their information needs.
2. *The attributes or qualitative characteristics* of accounting information that enable financial statements to fulfil their objective, determine what is useful information, and provide criteria for choosing among alternative accounting methods.
3. Definitions of the *elements* of financial statements such as the nature of assets, liabilities, and ownership interest.
4. A set of criteria for deciding when the elements are to be *recognized* in financial statements.
5. A set of *measurement* rules for determining the monetary amounts at which the elements of financial statements are to be recognized and carried in the accounts.
6. Guidelines for the *presentation and disclosure* of the elements in financial statements.

Index